D1448005

Information Sources of Political Science

INFORMATION
SOURCES

OF **POLITICAL SCIENCE**

Fourth Edition

Frederick L. Holler

JA
71
.H 644x
1986
WEST

ABC-CLIO
Santa Barbara, California
Oxford, England

ASU WEST LIBRARY

 CIRCULATING

Copyright © 1986 by Frederick L. Holler

All rights reserved. No part of this publication may be reproduced, stored in a retrieval system, or transmitted, in any form or
by any means, electronic, mechanical, photocopying, recording, or otherwise, except for the inclusion of brief quotations in a
review, without prior permission in writing from the publisher.

Library of Congress Cataloging-in-Publication Data

Holler, Frederick L.
    Information sources of political science.

    Includes indexes.
    1. Political science—Bibliography.   I. Title.
Z7161.H64 1985 [JA71] 016.32   85-11279
ISBN 0-87436-375-6

ABC-Clio, Inc.
2040 Alameda Padre Serra, Box 4397
Santa Barbara, California 93103

Clio Press Ltd.
55 St. Thomas Street
Oxford, OX1 1JG, England

Design by Tom Reeg

Manufactured in the United States of America

Knowledge carries with it both a tremendous joy and a great despair — a joy of being at one with the whole area of living human activity, and a great despair in recognizing how little this oneness really is compared to what it might be.

C. West Churchman

The Design of Inquiring Systems: Basic Concepts of Systems and Organization. New York: Basic Books, 1971. p. 11.

An educated person is one who has learned that information always turns out to be at best incomplete and very often false.

Russell Baker

"Terminal Education." In *The New York Times Magazine,* 9 November 1980, p. 29.

Contents

Chapter 2
Social Sciences

Chapter 3
American Government, Politics, and Public Law

CONTENTS

Chapter 4
International Relations and Organizations

Chapter 5
Comparative and Area Studies of Politics and Government

CONTENTS

Preface to the Fourth Edition

Despite advances in electronic telecommunications technology, the task of learning about political life is getting more and more difficult. The huge quantity of information scattered through the electronic and printed media, the enormous but often confusing holdings of library and other repository collections, and the ever-present time pressure combine to make it now significantly harder for most persons to inform themselves adequately. This guidebook, like its earlier editions, is devoted to the removal of political ignorance from the halls of academia and elsewhere. It provides a detailed, descriptive inventory of reference sources that can lead the reader to unknown political information. The fourth edition differs significantly from all previous editions by offering the reader the following important innovations designed to make political information retrieval more efficient.

REVISED AND EXPANDED POLITICAL REFERENCE THEORY

The new edition offers a revised and expanded political reference theory that advances an alternative, unique conception of political inquiry. Supplementing the essentially disjointed and amorphous approach presented by traditional indexing techniques, the political reference theory provides a cohesive set of conceptual, hypothetical, and pragmatic propositions for identifying and accessing systematically the stored information about the political world. Detailed in Part I of the three-part guidebook, the political reference theory consists of 19 conceptual components, 9 of which identify, at a very high level of abstraction, the essential elements of the political world about which information is retrievable. The other 10 components describe the means by which political phenomena are made known and accessible. The entire reference theory not only affords the researcher a bird's eye view of the political information retrieval mechanism but also offers quick and cohesive access to the most appropriate reference sources described in Part II of the guidebook.

UPDATED AND EXPANDED DATABASE

The retrieval mechanism for stored political information has undergone many changes and continues to exhibit extensive growth and increased complexity since the third edition of this guidebook was published barely three years ago. The new edition takes account of this development by providing—in Part II of the guidebook—2,423 citations for printed and computerized reference works, many of which have only recently come into existence. In fact, more than half of the entries in this edition relate to reference works that are either completely new, have significantly altered their coverage, or have assumed increased importance for the political researcher, such as economic data and tax law sources. Revised and expanded annotations, headnotes, and introductions throughout seven major chapters of Part II offer new and more incisive information about the utility of the listed reference sources.

IMPROVED FINDING AIDS

Apart from the political reference theory, the fourth edition also offers five other extensive finding aids for identifying desired reference sources listed in the guidebook. Each of these finding aids is based on a different approach to the reference literature, namely,

1. A general table of contents and seven specialized tables of contents for identifying reference sources by field, topic, and form
2. An alphabetical author index for identifying reference sources if only the author's name is known
3. A subject index for the major topics covered by the reference instruments
4. A title index for identifying reference sources if only the title is known
5. A typology index for identifying reference sources if only the generic reference form category and a subject field are known

With the exception of the general table of contents and the specialized tables of contents, all finding aids are grouped together in Part III of the guidebook. A summary table, entitled "How To Use This Book" appears immediately after the Preface pages and lists all appropriate page numbers for the finding aids.

More than ever before, the new edition will serve a triple purpose. It should be viewed, first of all, as an educational instrument essential for systematic course work in political science, library science, and other academic disciplines. Second, the guidebook will be useful as a ready reference tool in libraries, offices, or at home. Its organization and detailed finding aids will allow students, professors, librarians, and other professional users to identify quickly the desired reference works under several different approaches. Because of its broad and up-to-date database, the book will complement, within the limits of its scope, such standard guidebooks as Sheehy's *Guide to Reference Books* or Walford's *Guide to Reference Material*. Last, but not least, the fourth edition is offered as a contribution to the efforts of political scientists, librarians, publishers, and other information managers interested in improving reference control of political information. A careful study of the guidebook will reveal gaps and imperfections that can serve as clues to further refinements of the political reference mechanism.

Entries in the fourth edition reflect imprint dates up to December 1983, although a few 1984 titles were also included if sufficient information was available about them. As in any endeavor of this kind, some important titles may have been omitted as a result of the time and organizational constraints under which the project labored. Like many other libraries, the California State University, Northridge, Library was negatively affected by severe budget cuts and loss of positions during a time of higher enrollment and greatly increased patron usage. Due to internal university restrictions, an institutional grant was also unavailable for the project since under penalty of disqualification it was not possible to reveal in a grant proposal the identity of the author and the title of this standard reference work.

While final responsibility for this edition rests with the author, many students, social scientists, librarians, journalists, and other persons have provided helpful hints in the preparation of this manuscript. Their valuable contributions are gratefully acknowledged. The author is particularly grateful to Henry Brompton of the Department of Political Science and various members of the Library Reference Department, notably Barry Elcano, Charlotte Oyer, and Don Read for valuable input in the final stages of the manuscript. Lastly, a special word of appreciation must go to Eric H. Boehm, Gail Schlachter, and Barbara Pope of the American Bibliographical Center, whose continued encouragement and assistance contributed immeasurably to the quality of this guidebook.

Frederick L. Holler

California State University,
Northridge

How To Use This Book

This guidebook can be used by reading it cover to cover or by focusing on one or more of its six finding aids to

1. locate introductory text sections as well as general or specific reference sources in major disciplines and subfields as listed in the *Contents* on pages vii–xiii
2. identify reference sources by author names as listed in the *Author Index* on pages 371–379
3. identify reference sources by their titles as listed in the *Title Index* on pages 381–404
4. identify reference sources by key subject terms as listed in the *Subject Index* on pages 405–411
5. identify reference sources by form categories (i.e., bibliographies, dictionaries, encyclopedias, handbooks, online databases, yearbooks, etc.) as listed in the *Typology Index* on pages 413–417

6. find an explanation of the basic mechanism of political information retrieval and identify the major reference sources in nine substantive areas of political inquiry as outlined in the *Political Reference Theory* section on pages 1–31, and by taking careful note of the annotations accompanying each bibliographic entry in chapters 1–7 of the guidebook, for the purpose of improving library collections, the design of new or the improvement of existing reference works, the preparation of academic term or other research papers, or the analysis of political situations.

PART I
THE POLITICAL REFERENCE THEORY

PART I
THE POLITICAL REFERENCE THEORY

A PROBLEM OF DEFINITION

Anyone reading the first sentence in the introductory chapter of the *International Handbook of Political Science*[1] published in 1982 will be struck by the fact that it is identical with the first sentence of the first issue of the first professional political science journal — the *Political Science Quarterly*, published in 1886. Both publications begin with the statement, *"the term 'political science' is greatly in need of definition."*

While the first use of this statement in 1886 may indicate the birth pangs of a new academic discipline, the continued use of the quote nearly 100 years later in a reference work about the international development of the discipline clearly suggests that the initial problem of definition — namely, What is political science? — has not been answered. In fact, as the individual country chapters of the *International Handbook of Political Science* amply demonstrate, the perplexity over the identity of political science continues unabated. Throughout these chapters of the handbook names like *politology, state science, theory of state and law, science of constitutional law, public law, political studies, government studies*, and others are used in addition to the designation *political science* itself. One author even comments that we are not a discipline but a problem area parasitic upon other disciplines. Many other authors see the distinguishing feature of political science in its focus on power and on governmental institutions or personnel that wield that power. Nearly all authors acknowledge the existence of an identity crisis for political science by commenting on it in one way or another without necessarily offering a widely acceptable solution.

As perplexing as the problem of definition may appear to political scientists, it should not be a source of confusion for the users of this reference book. Although this book employs the term *political science* in its title, the scope of the book is not bound by any definition of what political scientists do or ought to do. This book is a guide to political information sources or, more precisely, to selected information sources for a substantial body of political knowledge. As the following pages will demon-strate, our initial concern is therefore to find out what is meant by the terms knowledge and political information.

THE TWO KINDS OF KNOWLEDGE

Some 200 years ago Dr. Samuel Johnson observed that there are two kinds of human knowledge. He said, "We know a subject ourselves or we know where we can find information upon it." Since Dr. Johnson's time, enormous advances have been made in the first kind of knowledge, but a comparable improvement in the second kind of knowledge has regrettably not yet been achieved. As knowledge on all subjects increased, it became increasingly difficult to find information about what was already known. A law of inverse knowledge relationship was born. Stated in its simplest terms the law means that the more knowledge becomes available to mankind the less the individual knows how to retrieve it. Indeed the deficiency in the second knowledge is so great that knowledge of the first kind is constantly recreated and frequently lost.

This paradoxical situation is the result as well as the cause of specialization in research, which is a fundamental feature of modern educational systems and modern civilizations. Unable to master human knowledge as a whole, the individual tends to concentrate on smaller and smaller segments of it, and thus the existing boundaries of the individual's knowledge may reach unprecedented depths rather than breadths. Educational progress is gauged by how well individuals know a particular subject, regardless of their ability to *find* information in or outside their field of specialization. Our elaborate educational systems teach individuals what they must know about a subject, and the complex division of labor in society ensures that gaps in knowledge are filled or compensated by subject specialists whenever necessary.

While this emphasis on the acquisition of subject knowledge has worked reasonably well in most fields, there are indications that the neglect of adequate retrieval knowledge may be disastrous in the political area. Because of the peculiar nature of politics and political research, an adequate body of political knowledge is tantamount to the ability to find information of political significance in the published literature, computerized databases, and other repositories.

THE NEED FOR RETRIEVAL COMPETENCE

The need for a special competence in political information retrieval arises from many different causes but is inextricably linked to the work performed and *not performed* by political scientists. There is, as we have seen, no single universally accepted definition of political science, but it is probably fair to say that political scientists investigate or study the facts of politics and subsequently report, decide, or lecture on them. The difficulty facing political scientists is therefore one of defining politics and determining what political facts are. Some confusion begins to emerge at this point because the English-language words *politics* and *facts* have lost the precise denotations of their Greek and Latin origins. The word *politics* derives from the Greek root word *politeia*, which means community of citizens. All activities directed toward or from the community of citizens are therefore political. But in English the noun *politics* is applied only to the tussle over the formation of a course of action. The course of action finally adopted or pursued is called policy. No such distinction exists in the German, Italian, and French languages, where *Politik*, *politica*, or *politique* denotes the struggle preceding the adoption of a line of action as well as the course of action adopted and pursued. The result of this linguistic distinction in the United States and other English-language countries has been that policy studies in political science have been comparatively neglected and at best delegated to other social sciences.

Similar loss of meaning is also noticeable when the word *fact* is compared with the Latin *facere* or *factum* or with its German equivalent *Tatsache*. The German word provides a clue, for it really consists of two separate words: *Tat*, which means act or deed, and *Sache*, which is translated as thing or matter. Political science, therefore, should be concerned with political action, acts, or activities as well as political things and their relationships. Regrettably, however, the word *fact* has often been deceptively interpreted in political studies with the result that one or the other but not both factual components were duly studied. Political studies either emphasized the activity or behavioral aspects of political facts, such as voting, campaigning, decision making, etc., or misinterpreted the material components, notably the political object, the state or other institutionalized bodies. This, of course, should come as no surprise, because neither the political things — objects, structures, or institutions — nor political acts and processes are directly observable. Political

science is thus fundamentally different from such disciplines as astronomy and physiology, for instance, where objects of study (e.g., celestial bodies or body organs) can be viewed directly by any observer. Unlike the astronomer, physician, physicist, psychologist, or most other natural scientists, political scientists can observe only indirectly, and they must rely heavily on reported information about political matters and activities. Even where political scientists appear to observe directly, as for example in field studies and interviews, their view is distorted by the inter-position of the cultural or ideological perspectives of the observer.

Since the number of political activities and political matters to be reported is of almost infinite magnitude and since the reporting must reflect any number of impressions, methods, or values, political reporting cannot be undertaken by the members of a single occupational group or a single academic discipline, such as political science. Apart from political scientists there are therefore at least eight other academic disciplines engaged in work on political phenomena, namely anthropology, economics, education, geography, history, legal science, psychology, and sociology. In addition, professionals other than academicians, notably government and other political officials, military officers, journalists, as well as laymen produce vital political information as a result of their occupational role or other special exposure to political phenomena.

In view of the innumerable, inseparable links and ramifications of political phenomena across ill-defined boundaries of these academic disciplines and their applied fields, almost any systematic inquiry sooner or later leads the academic researchers and occupational practitioners out of their field of subject competence, thereby requiring them to *find* or *retrieve* information. Furthermore, even if it were possible to acquire and retain an all-encompassing or sufficiently broad subject knowledge, it would be of limited value. Unlike the phenomena observed in most other academic disciplines, the institutions, processes, and conditions encountered by political actors, including social scientists, are highly unstable and subject to constant, often rapid change. In order to understand the various aspects and details of an unstable, constantly changing political life, scholars and practitioners cannot depend on a one-time acquisition of subject knowledge — they must rely on a continual flow of data from a comprehensive information exchange and reference system that has been developed to a high degree of perfection over the last several decades.

Unfortunately, this information exchange and reference system — utilizing as it does several different transfer channels and a multitude of individual reference works — is exceedingly complex. History as well as common observation shows that most people, while bombarded daily with fragmentary information through the mass media, have great difficulty in unearthing vital and comprehensive political information that is available in ever increasing quantities in libraries, computerized databases, and other repositories. A large amount of activity and interest has consequently been focused on the task of carrying the inquirer back to the information deposited in these repositories. To a massive extent this carry-back or reference activity is undertaken by specially trained librarians. But it has become painfully obvious that the inability of users to find information without assistance is not thereby eliminated. The primary reason for this undesirable situation is that librarian assistance is essentially a service activity rather than an educational endeavor. In spite of the recommendations in the Weinberg[2] and SATCOM[3] reports decades ago that the technique of handling information be more widely taught, the majority of the high schools, colleges, and universities in the United States and other countries still do not offer sufficient instruction in political information retrieval. The details of the elaborate mechanism for transferring to a user vital political information stored in repositories are therefore unknown not only to most students in these educational institutions but also to most members of the general public, including many political actors themselves. Since political facts, as stated before, are not directly observable in any corporeal sense and have to be gleaned from documentation stored in libraries and other repositories, this ignorance of the political information retrieval mechanism is therefore a form of functional illiteracy that is often costly not only to the individual but also to society as a whole. Political history reveals many instances where political decision-makers and important population groups have failed to make correct political decisions because they were unable to find or utilize vital new information beyond their existing subject knowledge.

THE NEED FOR A POLITICAL REFERENCE THEORY

One of the most insidious results in which the lack of adequate retrieval competence can express itself is the illusion gained by many library or database users that they have collected sufficient information for a particular line of reasoning or action if they have found a lot of information. Due to the mass of available information it is frequently quite easy to find what seems to be more than enough information on a particular topic of inquiry. The mistaken belief that one is adequately informed as a result of being exposed to prodigious amounts of information is a very common error in academic institutions — one that occurs occasionally also in the highest echelons of government. An example in the latter category is the unex-

pected truck bombing of the U.S. Marine Headquarters Building in Beirut on October 23, 1983. This truck bombing with the loss of 241 lives could not have succeeded the way it did had the U.S. Marine Command properly dissected — by the tenets of analytical theory — the massive amounts of publicly available information about the political situation in Lebanon and then acted accordingly. Analytical dissection of the available information would have yielded sufficient historical evidence for the likelihood of precisely such truck bomb attacks from the violent political behavior reported about no less than 25 different clandestine or terrorist organizations operating in Lebanon.

The following pages are therefore devoted to the exposition of a theory of political reference that can be of assistance to all persons or organizations desiring to find adequate, rather than merely plentiful political information.

A prevalent fallacy, usually not regarded as such, is the opinion that theory and practice are two opposing approaches to solving a particular problem. Theory, in this line of thinking, is regarded as a somewhat impractical or ineffective method of problem solving because it is essentially fictional. The truth of the matter, of course, is that theory is an eminently practical way to attack a complex task. By virtue of its structure of concise, leading sentences and keywords, theory is a superb device for reducing the complexity of a problem to simple proportions, thus making the solution to the problem comparatively easier.

The political reference theory simplifies the enormously complex study of political phenomena by offering a cohesive set of conceptual, hypothetical, and pragmatic propositions for identifying political information stored in library collections, computerized databases, and other repositories.

THE 19 ELEMENTS OF THE THEORY

In order to find all relevant political information, a researcher will find it useful to know two separate sets of conceptual categories that express procedural and substantive propositions of the reference theory. The procedural propositions describe the means by which political phenomena are made known. The substantive propositions identify, at a very high level of abstraction, the essential elements of the political world about which information is available for retrieval. The political reference theory consists of ten procedural and nine substantive categories, as follows:

PROCEDURAL REFERENCE CATEGORIES

1. Information
2. Documentation
3. Sources
4. Users (Recipients)
5. Information Channels
6. Scientific Methods
7. Classification
8. Retrieval Tools (Reference Works)
9. Access Points and Entry Symbols
10. Time

SUBSTANTIVE REFERENCE CATEGORIES

11. Laws and Other Legal Directives
12. Political Actors
13. Political Entities
14. Political Events
15. Political Languages
16. Political Objects, Policies, and Programs
17. Political Processes
18. Political Thought
19. Societal Factors

Each of these categories functions as a hub for several hypothetical and pragmatic propositions by which political facts can be ascertained. For greater clarity, exposition of each of the nine substantive reference categories is divided into three sections that contain (1) a general definition, (2) a list of the appropriate reference sources, and (3) an explanation of what needs to be done. All 19 reference categories and their propositions form a cohesive set, however, so that disregarding one or the other reference category may result in incomplete or misleading information retrieval.

Information

Information is a process as well as a product of the human brain and senses that has the potential to reduce uncertainty within a specific parameter or limit. This assumption does not imply that information must necessarily be correct or complete, for in fact much information is false and fragmentary. Inherent in the definition, however, is the implication that information is relative to a specific source or recipient. Information cannot be assumed to be a reduction of uncertainty per se, as some authors have suggested, because information may create new uncertainty outside its parameter or may fail to reduce uncertainty in recipients who are either certain or doubtful of a solution to a problem.

As an intellectual product, information is expressed in words, numbers, and other audiovisual forms. While ordinarily fleeting and elusive, information can also be stored for wider dissemination and later retrieval. Information is thus an indispensable prerequisite not only for individual action but also for group and mass behavior, most notably political behavior. Information should be regarded as political if it refers to forms of reality that relate to an institutionalized system of imperative control[4] or authoritative direction requiring obedience or acceptance of its prescripts or directives by all members of its entity. There are many different institutions in society that exercise varying degrees of control over human beings, most notably governments, political parties, labor unions, business corporations, professional associations, military organizations, churches, crime syndicates, and others. Information about phenomena connected with the authority or control patterns of these organizations must all be considered political.[5] Information about phenomena related to governmental control will, however, occupy the bulk of the reference mechanism for political information retrieval, because a government, acting like a flywheel in maintaining the balance of power in society for its optimum performance, is the only institution whose primary purpose is the exercise of control.

Apart from its uncertainty-reducing properties, political information has the capacity to form aggregates of support or opposition in the political processes occurring among political actors. Because of its uncertainty-reducing and aggregate-forming properties, political information is often subject to suppression (i.e., censorship, access classification, etc.), either at its source or at the user's end, by groups of political actors aiming for temporary advantage. Even in the United States, where more information is produced and disseminated than in other countries, political directives limit the freedom of information[6] on the basis of security classification or other reasons. The resulting suppression of information is, however, by no means confined to governmental actors since many political interest groups may use their vast economic power to curtail the dissemination of information inimical to their interests.

Documentation

Information retrieval is greatly facilitated by the existence of media serving as information vehicles or carriers that document (package), store, and disseminate information for increased, widespread, or delayed usage. The following types of media may be distinguished:

Handwritten or typewritten documents (scripts).
Information may be recorded in handwritten or typewritten documents, such as letters, notes, reports, or diaries, for storage and limited dissemination. These documents are collected mainly in special libraries or archives.

Printed documents. Handwritten or typed documents may be changed into printed media for greatly increased storage, dissemination, or retrieval. Printed media or publications fall into several categories of form and function, notably, newspapers, periodicals and other serials, books, pamphlets, and prints. The latter two categories are heavily used in political documentation for legal or legislative items.

Audiovisual media. Voiced or visualized information may be recorded in audio, visual, and audiovisual media, such as discs, tapes, films, and slides.

Microforms. Scripts and printed documents may be reduced in size for increased storage capacity. Several different microforms exist, such as microfilms, microfiche, and microcards.

Machine-readable media. Information may be recorded on punched cards, magnetic or optical disks, or tapes for retrieval and dissemination by computers and telecommunication tools (terminals).

Copied documents. Any of the scripts and printed documents may also exist in copied form as a result of xerography or other duplicating processes. Microform documents can also be converted into copied documents legible without enlargement.

For each of the first five named documentation categories one or more reference sources exist that provide an inventory, description, or locating information for the individual items available in each medium. The following reference works will be most useful for the identification of

1. Manuscript collections:	*National Inventory of Documentary Sources in the United States* (555), *National Union Catalog of Manuscript Collections* (556)
2. Printed Documents:	
a. books in print:	*Books in Print* (39, 40, 41, 42, 43)
b. newspapers published:	*Editor and Publisher* (131), *N.W. Ayer* (132)
c. periodicals published:	*Standard Periodical Directory* (205), *Ulrich's International Periodicals Directory* (206– 210)
d. serials published:	*Irregular Serials and Annuals* (207)
3. Audiovisual media:	*NICEM* (495, 496), *NUC AV* (62)
4. Microforms:	*Guide to Microforms in Print* (124)
5. Machine-readable databases:	*Directory of Online Databases* (6), *Directory of Online Information Resources* (7)

Sources

Information originates from people and organizations that will be designated as sources. Three different source categories may be distinguished for political information: (1) scientific sources, (2) official sources, and (3) nonscientific, unofficial sources.

The findings of research scholars are recorded in scientific documents, such as research papers, reports of scientific institutions and conferences, dissertations, and scholarly books and articles. The evidentiary power of these documents derives primarily from the soundness of scientific principles and methods employed and from the degree of acceptance and verification by scientists. A fundamental weakness of the scientific political documentation is the frequent lack of universal acceptance of scientific findings because of questions as to the objective validity of the values that scientists inevitably employ in the analysis of political objects and societal factors. A completely value-free political documentation, however, appears to be neither possible nor desirable.

Governmental and other official bodies are responsible for the authoritative documentation of laws, decrees, orders, court and administrative decisions, and other official outputs. Official documentation derives its power essentially from the legitimacy myth. This myth is an effective set of memories, beliefs, and presumptions that accords official information preferential treatment, attention, compliance, and support. The myth may be rebutted, however, in specific instances by competent evidence from scientific and nonscientific sources. Official documentation is frequently segregated physically in library collections as well as in the reference instruments.

Nonscientific sources generate political documents not included in the preceding categories. Books, articles in periodicals and newspapers, and other published or unpublished papers written by laymen and other persons under nonscientific methods in an unofficial capacity constitute the bulk of political documentation. Its evidentiary power is often problematical but rests mostly on quality factors of observation and knowledge, such as immediacy, directness, involvement, victimization, and so on. The true evidentiary power of the nonscientific, unofficial documentation is often overestimated as a result of extraneous factors, such as mass circulation or other effective channelling, popularity, dramatization, linguistic impact, or quasi-scientific presentation. On the other hand many important nonscientific sources, for lack of proper documentation, fail to achieve a sufficiently large audience. This is particularly true where self-observations, reactions, or needs are recorded solely in diaries and other unpublished papers that do not receive adequate dissemination and reference treatment.

Many specific items of political documentation derive from all three source categories. A newspaper, for instance, may contain the text of an official statement, a scientific article, and several feature stories written by desk writers. This situation obviously poses problems of identification and evaluation for the user. While there are many bibliographic instruments that separate documentation into scientific, official, and nonscientific categories, better and more precise tools are needed to avoid presently existing ambiguities.

Users (Recipients)

Political information and documentation is essentially user-oriented. Depending on the nature of the political process for which information and documentation is generated, the following major user categories may be distinguished:

- students
- political and other scientists
- government and other officials
- interest group actors
- lawyers
- business executives
- journalists
- general public

Significant differences exist between the information used by students and academicians, and that used by politicians. The former use information that is predominantly discipline-, field-, or subject-oriented. Couched in scientific terms, academic information is often limited to specific models or narrow topics, usually somewhat removed from practical day-to-day realities. The information exchanged among politicians is essentially interdisciplinary, issue-based, or mission-oriented. Political actors in the governmental and interest structure rely heavily on face-to-face communication, whereas the academic user extracts desired information mostly from documents. Where personal information exchange occurs among scientists, notably at professional conferences and meetings, it regrettably does not always lead to political documentation, thus generating information gaps of varying dimensions. Information generated for lawyers and judicial process officials is heavily law-oriented, while journalistic information reflects fragmentary observations of current factual situations. Information for business executives and interest group actors tends to be action-oriented, usually within narrow topics and without broad overall perspective.

Despite these diversities, users of all categories will ultimately depend on broad-based information retrieval from libraries and computerized data systems for an optimal reduction of their political uncertainties.[7] This information retrieval can be successful only to the extent that users desire to use documented information and have sufficient knowledge of the rather complex retrieval methodology from prior education, experience, or reference assistance. The desire for documented information is deemed to be the result of the user's external and internal situation of uncertainty, stemming from role and prior knowledge, and the user's learned behavioral response pattern in uncertainty situations.

Information Channels

Information retrieval requires the existence of one or more channels that permit the flow of information from a source to its destination. Channels are physical or organizational arrangements, such as telephone and other telecommunication networks, postal services, line organizations, and — most important in the context of information storage and retrieval — archives, computerized database systems, and libraries.

Each of these information channels has a distinct carrying capacity that puts a limit on the availability (flow) of information. For this reason, two or more information channels need to be utilized by persons or organizations dependent on the optimum flow of information. Political information is now made available to the public through the following channels:

- political party channels
- commercial subscription services for books, periodicals, newspapers, radio and television programs
- holdings in individual archives and libraries
- interlibrary loan facilities
- interactive computerized information retrieval through arrangement with time-sharing companies

While the political party channel is still most heavily used in many political systems for the political education of large population groups, libraries are the best channels for the reduction of political ignorance. Although the political party channel allows a more concentrated directionality of the information flow for narrow ideological or action-oriented purposes, libraries are able to offer a combination of all other existing channels for the broadest, individually tailored retrieval of all essential or desired information.

A recent development in political communication technology, however, is the emergence of the "fleet" concept for the optimal operation of the various information channels in a particular country. According to this concept, one information channel will serve as the flagship for political information dissemination while all other channels — to the extent that they disseminate political information—tend to be merely supporting units. The flagship is either an independent, subscription financed radio and television network or a highly developed national library system.

Scientific Methods

Scientific methods are a variety of systematic techniques, rules, or procedures applied by political and other scientists in the inquiry or explanation of some class of phenomena, including those of the political world. The application of scientific methods is designed to result in more accurate, exact, or definite information but often leads to controversial, disputed information because of disagreement among the scientists about the appropriateness of the methods actually used. Thus, there is considerable methodological pluralism among social scientists, and no one method is exclusively appropriate for the investigation or interpretation of political reality in all its aspects.

Among the methods employed by political and other social scientists are ideological constructs, conceptual, disciplinary, or field approaches, mathematical or statistical procedures, interviews, questionnaires, sample surveys, tests and scales, models, general theories, temporal analyses, in addition to direct observation.

The reference literature provides, with the help of several

1. bibliographic instruments, indirect access to the vast methodological literature itself, or individual documents that reflect a particular method applied, and
2. handbooks and other fact retrieval books, direct access to concise, explanatory information about the individual scientific methods and techniques.

Notable examples in these categories are:

BIBLIOGRAPHIES FOR THE METHODOLOGICAL LITERATURE

Anthropology, 357
Economics, 383, 398, 399, 404, 410, 421
Education, 485, 490–492, 498
Geography, 516, 518, 519, 520
History, 587, 593, 599
Interdisciplinary, 320
International Relations, 1577
Philosophy, 2259–2262
Political Science, 670, 671, 680
Psychology, 750, 751, 753, 755–757, 796
Public Administration, 2364, 2367, 2373, 2387, 2388, 2390
Sociology, 800, 810, 818–820, 830, 836

BIBLIOGRAPHIES IDENTIFYING INDIVIDUAL STUDIES REFLECTING A SCIENTIFIC METHOD

415, 676, 821, 1286, 1326, 1572, 1895, 1897, 1898, 2382

HANDBOOKS AND OTHER FACT RETRIEVAL TOOLS

Economics, 479, 480
Education, 509, 513
Political Science, 724, 725, 726
Psychology, 781, 785, 786, 787–792, 795
Social Sciences, 339
Sociology, 859, 860, 863, 864, 866

Classification

Classification is a common method for reducing an amorphous mass of information or documentation to structured and manageable proportions. Information or documentation is arranged according to its degree of likeness and separated according to degrees of difference. Classification is usually made by source names or titles, but most often by subject or knowledge areas of information.

Bibliographic control of political information and documentation has been insufficiently achieved by several classification schemes, none of which has gained universal acceptance. Library collections and some bibliographies are arranged according to the Library of Congress subject classification system, the Dewey decimal classification system, and the UNESCO classification schedule, as well as several others. The three major classification schemes, which are illustrated in abridged versions here, arrange documentation material according to knowledge areas defined by academic disciplines. While each of these classification schemes contains a separate class for political science, considerable political information is allocated to other classes, where it is often submerged in nonpolitical information categories. Furthermore, the principal conceptual categories within the political science class itself are not ideally representative of the major elements by which a political system manifests itself. Thus, there is no single, cohesive, and hierarchically arranged classification scheme for all political information, as Tables 1–3 illustrate:

TABLE 1

LIBRARY OF CONGRESS SUBJECT CLASSIFICATION

(Abridged Version)

Class J Political Science
  J Official Documents
    1–9 United States Documents
      (for congressional hearings, reports, etc., see class K)
    100–981 Other Countries
  JA Collections and General Works
  JC Political Theory, Theory of the State
    311–323 Nationalism, Minorities, Geopolitics
    325–341 Nature, Entity, Concept of the State
    345–347 Symbolism, Emblems of the State
    348–497 Forms of the State (including imperialism, the
      world state, monarchy, aristocracy, democracy, etc.)
    501–628 Purpose, Functions, and Relations of the State
    571–628 The State and the Individual
  JF Constitutional History and Administration
    201–723 Organs and Function of Government
    800–1191 Political Rights and Guarantees
    1321–2112 Government, Administration, Civil Service,
      Political Parties
  JK United States
  JL British America, Latin America
  JN Europe
  JQ Asia, Africa, Australia, Oceania
  JS Local Government
  JV 1–5299 Colonies and Colonization
    6001–9500 Emigration and Immigration
  JX International Law
    63–1195 Collections, Documents, Treaties, Cases
    1305–1598 International Relations, Foreign Relations
      (for history of events, diplomatic history, see classes
      D–F)
    1625–1896 Diplomacy, The Diplomatic Service
    1901–1995 International Arbitration, World Peace,
      International Organization
    2001–5800 International Law
    6001–6650 Private International Law

For full details of the classification table shown in outline in Table 1, see U.S. Library of Congress, Subject Cataloging Division, *Classification: Class J. Political Science* (Washington, DC: 1924, reprinted 1966). This book presents the current arrangement of the literature of political science in the Library of Congress and all other libraries that have adopted the LC classification system. An alphabetical index for locating subject matter in the classification tables is also included.

TABLE 2

DEWEY DECIMAL CLASSIFICATION (Simplified Version)

Class 320 Political Science
    The State
    Comparative Government
    Political Theories and Ideologies
    Political Situations and Conditions

321 Types and Forms of State
322 Relation of State to Organized Groups
323 Relations of State to Individuals and Groups
324 Suffrage
    Qualifications for Voting
    Elections
    Corruptions and Irregularities in Elections
325 International Migration
    Immigration
    Emigration
    Colonization
326 Slavery and Emancipation
327 International Relations
    International Politics
    Diplomacy
    Foreign Policies of Specific Nations
328 Legislation
329 Practical politics
    Political Propaganda
    Political Parties
    Pressure and Other Interest Groups
    Study of Public Opinion

For complete details of the classification system shown in Table 2, see Melvil Dewey, *Dewey Decimal Classification and Relative Index* (New York: Forest Press, Inc., of Lake Placid Club Education Foundation, 1965, or later edition).

TABLE 3

UNESCO CLASSIFICATION SCHEME (Abridged Version)

A. Political Science
B. Political Thought
  1. History of Ideas
  2. Ideological Foundations of Political Systems
C. Government and Public Administration
  1. The State
  2. Political Systems
  3. The Powers (Organs)
  4. Freedom and Civil Rights
  5. Economic and Social Functions of Government
  6. Instruments of Government
  7. Local Government
  8. Government of Non-Autonomous Territories
D. Governmental Process
  1. Political Influences and Trends
  2. Political Parties
  3. Political Behavior
E. International Relations
  1. International Organization
  2. International Politics
F. Area Studies
  1. Africa
  2. America
  3. Asia
  4. Europe
  5. Middle East
  6. Pacific
  7. Union of Socialist Republics

TABLE 3 (Continued)

UNESCO CLASSIFICATION SCHEME (Abridged Version)

Details of the classification scheme shown in Table 3 are printed in all editions of the *International Bibliography of Political Science* (Paris: UNESCO, 1954–1961; Chicago: Aldine Publishing Co., 1962–).

The two most widely accepted classification schemes, the Library of Congress subject classification system and the Dewey decimal system, are essentially book-shelving systems for libraries and ignore the classification of periodical articles, unpublished research papers, and similar material. The UNESCO classification schedule, which includes the classification of periodical articles, has failed to gain wide acceptance and consequently covers only a small portion of the total information material. Library book classification faces an insurmountable shelving problem because the content of the book may suggest several classification categories, of which only one can be used for the shelving position.

In spite of these limitations, the Library of Congress classification system, the Dewey decimal classification system, and the UNESCO classification system constitute a useful method for aggregating political documentation of identical or closely related content.

Retrieval Tools (Reference Works)

The mass, complexity, and continuous growth of political documentation requires retrieval tools with specific structural and functional properties. These retrieval tools are known collectively as the political reference literature, which comprises the collective method and results of transforming or processing politically significant information in a concise and systematic manner. The main function of the reference literature is to organize data for research and action.

The relationship between political reference literature and the study of political phenomena is comparable to the role that accounting plays for business activities. Economics, management science, and business administration are entirely dependent on accounting as a formalized survey and control system for economic activities. Similarly, political reference literature collects, lists, and describes a wealth of essentially historical data in conformity with widely accepted rules and assumptions of political reference theory.

A very important characteristic of the political reference literature—regardless of its existence in printed or electronic format—is its typological structure, which is comparable to the set of accounts used in an accounting system. Present information transfer technology relies predominantly on ten different types of retrieval tools that fulfill three categories of reference functions, namely:

1. Document retrieval
2. Fact or knowledge retrieval
3. Mixed fact and document retrieval

According to this functional differentiation, the following types of reference works may be distinguished:

DOCUMENT RETRIEVAL TOOLS

1. *Bibliography.* This is essentially an author/title listing of published or unpublished information material. The listings are usually arranged by author or by subject and author, and may vary according to the purpose of the bibliography. Bibliographies purport to announce and identify documentation and information material within the following variations:

Accession list. A supplementary list of publications acquired by a specific library or group of libraries.

Annotated bibliography. A publication list with descriptive notes for each listed title. Annotations are valuable because pure author/title listings insufficiently convey the nature of the informational content or the utility of the listed publications.

Announcement bibliography. A list of new publications available from a publisher or other institution.

Citator. An inventory of citations for ideas or legal points contained in scholarly publications, statute books, casebooks, etc.

Classified bibliography. A list of publications arranged under a definite, usually subject- or form-oriented organization plan.

Comprehensive bibliography. A list of most of the publications or unpublished information items relevant to a specific topic.

Critical bibliography. A publication with evaluative annotations or an evaluative arrangement.

Current bibliography. A bibliography that is kept up to date by regularly or frequently issued supplements. In view of the instability of political information matter and the continued growth of political documentation, most bibliographies should be current or serialized, but for a variety of reasons this is not presently possible.

Exhaustive bibliography. A list of all the published or unpublished information material on a given topic.

Guidebook. A special type of bibliography that is not simply an annotated list but presents a systematic introduction to the literature of a particular field of inquiry. Many bibliographies entitled guides or guidebooks are mislabeled and are no more than ordinary bibliographies.

9

Index publication. A bibliography of periodical articles, newspaper articles, or book sections arranged by subject, author, or keyword. Keyword indexes are title listings arranged by each significant word in the title of the listed publications, either in context (KWIC) or out of context (KWOC). Keyword indexes are usually computer-produced and often constitute an improvement over regular indexes.

Library catalog. A bibliography of publications or other information material available in a particular library or group of libraries. Catalogs are issued in card or book form.

National bibliography. A list of publications published or available in a particular country.

Retrospective bibliography. A bibliography that has a definite closing date and is not kept current. Ideally, retrospective bibliographies should cover a conclusively researched subject only, but this is rarely the case.

Selective or selected bibliography. A list of certain publications or unpublished information material recommended for study or further reading.

Trade bibliography. A list of books and other publications available from publishers or the book trade.

Union list. A bibliography that identifies the location of periodicals, newspapers, or other publications in a group of libraries.

FACT OR KNOWLEDGE RETRIEVAL TOOLS

2. *Casebook.* A reference book containing a record or description of cases that are typical, appropriate, or illustrative for general principles or significant situations and developments. Casebooks feature prominently as retrieval tools for court decisions.

3. *Dictionary.* A reference work that records and defines the meanings of words. Specific dictionaries exist for the vocabulary of an entire academic discipline, or subfield of a discipline or other closed language system. A special form of dictionaries are thesauri, which list the retrieval words of specific manual or computerized reference instruments.

4. *Directory.* An alphabetical or classified list of names of persons or organizations connected with a particular locality, profession, or service. Politically useful directories may vary from simple listings of addresses to detailed descriptions of the background and activities of political actors.

5. *Document collection.* A reference work that provides a systematic assembly of the texts of significant records created by governments, private individuals, or organizations. Document collections are essential reference tools for the study of international relations.

6. *Encyclopedia.* A reference work that presents a comprehensive summary of existing knowledge in one or more fields of inquiry. Usually written in alphabetically arranged topical articles with bibliographic references to the most important literature on the topic.

7. *Handbook, manual, or compendium.* This category of reference works offers a concise treatment or survey of a particular subject or field of knowledge. Although individual reference works of this type vary considerably in arrangement and format, they bear a certain resemblance to encyclopedias. Compendia are heavily used for convenient collections of statistical data, and may exist in printed or computerized format.

8. *Yearbook or almanac.* An annually published reference work usually containing a description of factual or other developments during the preceding 12 months. These reference works focus on information that is subject to change or requires frequent updating, such as statistical data.

MIXED FACT AND DOCUMENT RETRIEVAL TOOLS

9. *Abstracts, digests, and full text retrievers.* Abstracts services are bibliographies that offer, in addition to bibliographic citations, a summary of the informational content of each periodical article or book cited. Digests provide identification, summation, or condensed accounts of events, legal rules, or court decisions together with bibliographic references to the original source documents. Full text retrievers are computerized reference tools that can find, display, and print out online the full text of previously published information as well as offer citations to the published source document.

10. *Book reviewing media.* Book reviews are written by scholars or other experts and provide critical or evaluative examinations of books. The reviews are published either in full-length reviewing journals or as part of periodicals and newspapers, but are indexed and excerpted in separate reference instruments.

From the foregoing description it is apparent that the various types of retrieval tools derive their identity not only from the kind of data that are fed into them but also from the particular form in which the data are processed. Occasionally reference instruments do not fit into any one of the basic categories because they may be hybrids or combinations of two or more basic types.

Each retrieval tool type comprises numerous individual reference works identified by a distinct title. The reference works may exist in printed format or increasingly also as computerized tools. Bibliographies, directories, legal and statistical compilations are presently the reference works most frequently available in computerized versions in addition to the regular printed editions.

As a result of functional specialization each reference work has a clearly articulated subject and media coverage so that the entire political reference literature exhibits certain structural properties. At the present stage of its development political reference literature is structured mainly along

- documentation categories,
- source categories, and
- entity categories,

which serve as the primary building blocks for the organization of information. Several other, mostly substantive reference categories such as legal directives, language, political actors, political processes, societal factors, etc., may be used as secondary building blocks. The details of these structural elements are made explicit by

- the Typology Index (pp. 413–417)
- the Inventory of Citations (p. 12)
- the seven chapters of Part II of this guidebook.

In spite of some recent, significant improvements the political reference literature, as it presently exists in printed and electronic format, is still beset by a number of minor and major problems. It is irritating to note, for instance, that reference publications are frequently mistitled by authors and publishers. Thus one may find handbooks that are really bibliographies, encyclopedias that are directories, directories that are bibliographies, or dictionaries that are directories. No agreement exists as yet among scholars and publishers concerning the proper usage of titles for reference publications.

A more serious weakness is the unequal and frequently unsatisfying quality of the access mechanism provided by the bibliographic instruments. In far too many instances only one subject term or descriptor is used for accessing several separate categories of information contained in a document. The practice of using a string of subject terms in a subject profile index or assigning as many as 20 or more needed descriptors to a single book, article, or other publication is rare. The result is that a user retrieves far too many unwanted documents because the retrieval mechanism is not discriminating enough.

There are also far too many gaps in reference coverage. Each distinct body of information should receive appropriate reference treatment, but this is frequently not the case. An example is the surprising lack of adequate reference treatment for political speech material outside the legislative or congressional process. Supporting, rejecting, or modifying statements made by political actors in the articulation of demands or positions, notably in controversial social or policy issues, cannot easily be tracked down. While some informational aspects are covered better than others, the reference system is still mostly a patchwork of individual efforts rather than an interlocking system of full reference control.

Another astonishing weakness of the political reference mechanism is the continuing lack of integration between the citation and document retrieval in other than costly full text retrieval databases. The technical possibilities for automating information retrieval from microformed documents in cassettes, for instance, have not yet been fully utilized, and users already in possession of the necessary bibliographic citations face the time-consuming task of tracking down manually the cited printed or microform documents that are distributed over many different locations.*

In contrast to these deficiencies, much political reference literature duplicates existing coverage. Many reference tools could be eliminated or consolidated because of partial coverage by other instruments. The uncoordinated duplication of reference instruments that is now extending also to the computerized databases causes unnecessary confusion and delays in research and is itself a waste of skilled manpower and financial resources.

While the necessary consolidation of reference instruments does not occur, considerable instability of the reference mechanism is caused by unwanted discontinuation of titles and reference services. In a deplorable number of instances, valuable reference publications in serial format are suddenly terminated or important monographic publications are not updated. The flow of information is thereby interrupted and at best redirected into other publications after intolerable periods of delay.

Perhaps the most troublesome aspect of the political reference system lies in the quantity of existing reference instruments. Because of the ubiquitous character of political phenomena, any delimitation of the number of reference works is difficult. There is in fact no other major area of human interest where a user is confronted by so many different reference instruments in order to get to necessary or desired information. Even a selective inventory such as that attempted in this guidebook includes nearly 2,450 titles. Other selective inventories have identified several thousand reference sources in one or two of the political subfields alone. It is self-evident as well as empirically demonstrable that the sheer quantity of the reference instruments effectively prevents a prospective user from being thoroughly familiar with all available instruments. Predictably, there will be further substantial increases in the quantity of printed and computerized reference instruments offered to the public in coming years. This unchecked proliferation of reference instruments will ultimately destroy the first and foremost function of the

* For an exception, see annotation under items 248 and 249.

reference mechanism itself, namely, to be of such clearly limited dimension so as to be comprehensible to a user inundated by an explosive flood of information.

INVENTORY OF CITATIONS

Since a majority of the reference sources available to the user are discipline- or field-oriented, this taxonomic structure of the reference literature in its various form categories has been used as the guiding principle for the arrangement of the 2,423 citations listed in seven major chapters of Part 2 of the guidebook, as follows:

Chapter 1 General Reference Sources (273 citations)

Chapter 2 Social Sciences (Multidisciplinary Reference Sources, Anthropology, Economics, Education, Geography, History, Political Science, Psychology, and Sociology) (593 citations)

Chapter 3 American Government, Politics, and Public Law (695 citations)

Chapter 4 International Relations and Organizations (330 citations)

Chapter 5 Comparative and Area Studies of Politics and Government (363 citations)

Chapter 6 Political Theory (109 citations)

Chapter 7 Public Administration (60 citations)

Suitable subdivisions in these seven chapters aggregate listings by functional categories of information and the form classes of the reference instruments that cover the various information categories. The result is the classification of the political reference literature into a limited number of discipline- or field-oriented segments and form clusters for easy access and study. This arrangement complements the classification of the reference literature according to the nine substantive elements of the political reference theory offered in Part 1 of the guidebook.

Entries in each of the seven chapters contain three bibliographic elements: author(s), title, and facts of publication. A fourth element in each entry is an annotation that describes the content and utility of the listed reference item. In many instances, two or more entries are combined for a single annotation. This is done in all instances where

1. a reference instrument is available in dual mode, namely as a computerized database and in a fully equivalent printed edition. The database entry is always accompanied—for proper identification—by the appropriate vendor information. Computerized databases that have either more than one equivalent printed edition or no printed equivalent are listed separately, however.

2. several printed reference works cover an identical or closely related subject matter.

3. the reference work has undergone significant title changes while maintaining a continuing flow of data.

The author and/or title citations provided for each reference work are considered sufficient for locating each item in the card or online catalog of the local library in order to obtain the necessary call number for the shelving position. Readers are cautioned, however, to expect occasional minor variations in bibliographic style or punctuation when comparing the entries in this guidebook with those listed in local library catalogs.

Access Points and Entry Symbols

Reference tools use a variety of entry symbols to lead the user to desired information or documentation from one or more specific intellectual access points already known to the user. The entry symbols can be a single letter, a combination of letters, numerals, alphanumeric characters, and punctuation marks. The access points may be an entire subject collection of documents or the topic of a single document, the source or form of a document, or the specific date relating to the information or documentation. Table 4 offers a typology of the most widely used entry sumbols and access points by which desired information or documentation can be retrieved.

TABLE 4

TYPOLOGY OF ACCESS POINTS AND ENTRY SYMBOLS

Entry Symbols	Access Points
1. Single Letters	A range of information, such as an entire subject class in the Library of Congress classification (J—Political Science), or a corporate author class in the U.S. Superintendent of Documents classification system[8] (A—Agriculture Department)
2. Combination of Letters	
a. two letters	A body of information, such as a subdivision of a major subject class in the Library of Congress classification (JS—Local Government), or a corporate author class in the U.S. Superintendent of Documents classification system (PR—president of the United States)
b. names	*Source Identification:* personal or corporate authors, editors,

TABLE 4 (Continued)

TYPOLOGY OF ACCESS POINTS AND ENTRY SYMBOLS

Entry Symbols	Access Points
	translators, illustrators, compilers, publishers, printers, etc.
	Geographical Identification: place of publication, place of documentation source, place of information, validity, scope, or subject content (country or other entity)
	Symbolic Identification: language of information or documentation (i.e., English, French, etc.)
	Subject Identification: persons as subjects, legal cases (litigants)
c. titles	*Form Identification:* books or monographs, periodicals, newspapers, serials, articles, or other written, spoken, filmed, or recorded production items
d. subject terms (subject headings, keywords, descriptors, etc.)	*Content Identification:* subject matter of information or documentation
e. cross-reference words	*Access Identification:* directional words such as *see* or *see also* references to access points from other, nonaccess subject terms
3. Numerals	*Activity Identification:* contract number, meeting number, project number, task number
	Chronological Identification: date of documentation, period of information validity, date of event, date of process action, date of subject coverage, etc.
	Cost Identification: prices, charges
	Form Identification: abstract number, accession number, bill number, book number, column number, deck number, edition number, entry number, issue number, page number, part number, patent number, public law number, report number, section number, size or dimension, serial number, treaty number, volume number, etc.

Entry Symbols	Access Points
4. Alphanumeric Characters	Access to information and documentation may be provided by symbols that combine letters and numerals, such as Library of Congress call numbers, classification numbers, United Nations document symbols, U.S. Superintendent of Documents (SuDoc) symbols, legal citation symbols, etc.
5. Punctuation or Other Marks	Various marks such as asterisk, comma, dash, point, slash, or blank space may be used as a delimiter separating subelements of main access points or otherwise indicating a specific aspect of information or documentation

Table 4 indicates that a user has to choose an entry symbol for a known access point to progress with the help of a reference work via referenced entry symbols to additional, previously unknown access points where the desired documentation or information can be found. The following example illustrates this procedure:

Desired Information:	Statistical data on personal income of the American population, by state or census division, during the 1970s
Chosen Access Point:	Subject Matter (content identification)
Chosen Reference Work:	*American Statistics Index*
Chosen Entry Symbols:	
1. Name	United States, Census Division
2. Subject Terms	Population, Personal Income
Referenced Entry Symbols:	
1. Accession Number	2702—1.724
2. Title	*Survey of Current Business*
3. Volume Number	58
4. Issue Number	6
5. Part Number	1
6. Date Number	6—1978
7. S/N Number	003-010-80001-1
8. SuDoc Number	C 59.11
9. LC Number	21-26819
10. Monthly Catalog (MC) Number	78-2896
11. Name of Author	Robert L. Brown
12. Title (of article)	Revised Quarterly State Personal Income, 1969—77
Choose appropriate reference work for access to physical location	Local library catalog or serials list
Select best entry symbol Title of Serial	*Survey of Current Business*

cont. —

Find referenced entry
symbol
    LC Call Number   HC 101 A 13

Which of the above-listed entry symbols for physical location access (Title, SuDoc number, MC number, or LC call number) will have to be used to obtain the desired document will depend ultimately on the holdings and shelf arrangements of the local library. If the chosen reference work, the *American Statistics Index*, could not have been selected by the user on the basis of prior knowledge, this guidebook—through its subject index and referenced entry symbols—would have led to the identification of the *American Statistics Index* as the appropriate reference tool for this or similar inquiries.

Among the various entry symbols, the selection of the correct subject heading or descriptor presents the greatest problem to the user of bibliographic reference instruments. Correct subject terms can be often identified with the help of the *LC Subject Headings List* (57), the *Sears List of Subject Headings* (58), and the various thesauri listed in the Typology Index.

Time

Information is retrievable only in segments of time relating to the chronological validity of the information itself, the dates of issuance of the documentation, the scope and availability of the retrieval instruments, the accessibility of the channels, and the uncertainty and behavioral response situation under which the user labors at any one time. Disregarding the time element in information retrieval will result in errors that may mislead the user in thought or action.

While all reference instruments specify the issue date of documentation, identifying the chronological validity of the information may often present a serious challenge to the user. Only the legal information and the events information is adequately referenced for chronological validity, and much process information is sufficiently identified by time elements. Most other substantive political information categories exhibit, however, chronological validity problems to a varying degree as a result of insufficient updating frequency through appropriate reference instruments.

Laws and Other Legal Directives

WHAT THEY ARE

A political system is based on the expectation that officially issued prescriptions or directives, backed by sanctions positive or negative if disregarded, will be complied with by all members of the political entity affected.

The motives of compliance usually rest on a wide range of considerations varying from simple habituation, tradition, devotion, or apathy to purely rational calculation[9] of advantage or fearful submission to coercive force. It is the purpose of legal directives to define the rights and corresponding obligations of individuals and organizations within the political entity, and to serve as a guide to action that compels particular choices among alternatives.[10] In the United States and other countries too the most binding authoritative directives or imperatives are expressed in the following forms or categories of law:

1. *Constitution*. A fundamental law that identifies the proper locus of political authority and spells out basic rights and obligations.
2. *Statute*. A specific act or law passed by the legislature defining, commanding, or prohibiting something.
3. *Administrative regulation (rule)*. A law by an administrative agency designed to carry out or explain specific statutes or executive orders under which the agency operates.
4. *Executive order*. A law issued by the president or other chief executive to direct the operation of governmental agencies.
5. *Administrative decisions (ruling)*. A decision of an administrative agency resolving a specific controversy through the application of administrative regulations and their governing statutes.
6. *Judicial decision (opinion)*. A court decision and explanation of the application of constitutional, statutory, and other law in a specific dispute (case).
7. *Treaty (international agreement)*. A law created by international agreement between two or more countries.
8. *Charter*. A fundamental law of an international organization, municipality or other local unit of government by which designated political functions are authorized.
9. *Ordinance*. A law passed by a local legislative unit of government, i.e., city or county.

WHERE YOU FIND THEM

Law in the above-mentioned categories is retrievable at various access points, namely, by issuing authority, keyword, proximity words in the legal text, number, popular name, subject heading or title within limits of political entity (jurisdictional area) and time. Table 5 identifies the most appropriate reference sources, described in this guidebook, for the most typical inquiries relating to three jurisdictional areas of law, namely, (A) Comparative Law (the law of countries other than the United States), (B) International Law, and (C) United States Law.

TABLE 5

REFERENCE SOURCES FOR THREE JURISDICTIONAL AREAS OF LAW

Law Category	Type of Information Desired	Appropriate Reference Source and Access Number
A. COMPARATIVE LAW		
All Categories	Author, country, and subject identification of books or articles dealing with the law in specific countries	*Bibliographic Guide* (1313), *Foreign & Comp. Law Subject* (2123), *Index to Foreign Legal Periodicals* (2121), *Register* (2124), Szladits (2122), also *Law Information* (1322), *LC Catalog* (85), *MARC* (60), *National Union Catalog* (62), *REMARC* (61), PAIS (292, 291)
	Tax law summaries:	
	a. Africa	a. *African Tax System* (2131)
	b. Asia & Pacific	b. *Taxes and Investment in Asia and the Pacific* (2135)
	c. Europe	c. *Guides to European Taxation* (2133), *Supplementary Service* (2134)
	d. Middle East	d. *Taxes and Investment in the Middle East* (2136)
	e. Latin America	e. *Corporate Taxation in Latin America* (2132)
Constitutions	Text of constitutions	Blaustein (2127, 2128), Peaslee (2130)
Statutes	Summaries or full texts of:	
	a. commercial laws	a. *Commercial, Business and Trade Laws of the World* (2137), *Investment Laws of the World* (2147), Simmonds (2149)
	b. human rights legislation	b. *Yearbook on Human Rights* (2150)
	c. Press laws	c. *World Press Encyclopedia* (128)
	d. Latin American legislation	d. *LOCIS—Scorpio* (1002), *Mining and Petroleum Legislation* (2148), Szekely (2144)
	e. territorial sea law	e. Durante (2140), Henderson (2145), Nordquist (2141), Sebek (2142)
B. INTERNATIONAL LAW		
Charters and Other Constitutional Documents	Text of charter or other constitutional documents of international organizations	Brownlie (1559), Peaslee (1823), *Treaties and Alliances* (1530)
Judicial Decisions	Text of national court decisions	*International Law Reports* (1542), *American International Law Cases* (1554), *British International Law Cases* (1556)
	Text of judgment by Permanent Court of International Justice or International Court of Justice	*PCIJ Collection of Judgements* (1543), *ICJ Reports of Judgements* (1544)
	Text of decision by arbitration court	*Reports of International Arbitral Awards* (1553)
Treaties and Other International Agreements	Text of United States treaties	TIAS (1517), UST (1518), Bevans' set (1520) or other U.S. treaty collection
	Text of treaties concluded by countries other than the United States	*League of Nations Treaty Series* (1528), *U.N. Treaty Series* (1524), *Consolidated Treaty Series* (1525)
	Current validity of treaties concluded by United States with foreign countries	*Shepard's United States Citations* (1507), *Treaties in Force* (1513)
	Index to treaty texts—U.S. only	*Treaties in Force* (1513), *UST Cumulative Indexes* (1508-1511)
	Index to treaty texts—all countries	*Index to Multilateral Treaties* (1514), *World Treaty Index* (1516)

TABLE 5 (Continued)

REFERENCE SOURCES FOR THREE JURISDICTIONAL AREAS OF LAW

Law Category	Type of Information Desired	Appropriate Reference Source and Access Number
	Text of international conventions:	
	a. armed conflict	*The Laws of Armed Conflicts* (1529)
	b. human rights	*Human Rights* (1561)
	c. international relations, law of treaties, sea law	Brownlie (1559)
	d. terrorism	*Transnational terrorism* (1523)
All Categories	Topical summary of international law practice	
	a. United States	*Digest of International Law* (1531–1533), *Digest of United States Practice in International Law* (1534)
	b. France, Great Britain, Italy, Switzerland only	Kiss (1537), Parry (1538), Ago (1535), Guggenheim (1536)
	c. Worldwide	Sen (1501)
	Articles on principles, cases, or problems in international law	*Annuaire Français* (1502), *British Yearbook of International Law* (1503)
	Books on topics in international law:	
	a. general	*Bibliographic Guide to Law* (1313), Delupis (1486), *Harvard University Catalog* (1484), *Law Books, 1876–1981* (1320), *Law Information 1982* (1321), *Law Information Update* (1322), *Peace Palace Library Catalog* (1483)
	b. air law	b. Heere (1490)
	c. criminal law	c. Schutter (1493), also Lewis (1491)
	d. sea law	d. Papadakis (1492)
	Guide to major reference and other works in international law	Robinson (1482), Schwarzenberger (1500)
	Indexes to periodical articles	*Current Law Index* (1314), *Index to Legal Periodicals* (1316), *Legal Resource Index* (1307, 1315), *Peace Palace Library Catalogue* (1483), *Public International Law* (1485)
	Text of current treaties, court cases, and other documents	*International Legal Materials* (1558), *The Law of War* (1560)

C. UNITED STATES LAW

Law Category	Type of Information Desired	Appropriate Reference Source and Access Number
1. Federal Law Administrative Decisions	Text of agency decision	*Decisions on Federal Administrative Agencies* (1421), or individual agency sets, like *CAB* (1422), *FCC* (1423), *FPC* (1424), *FTC* (1425), *INS* (1426), *ICC* (1427), *NLRB* (1428), *SEC* (1429), or *BNA, CCH,* or *P-H* reporter sets (1452 to 1480)
	Locator aids for administrative decisions:	
	a. NLRB — labor law	a. *Classified Index* (1432), *Laborlaw* (1306), *Lexis* (1308), *Shepard's Federal Labor Law Citations* (1439), *Westlaw/System II* (1312)
	b. FPC, FERC — energy law	b. *Federal Energy Law Citations* (1438)
	c. tax law	c. *P-H Federal Taxes Citator* (1384), *PhiNet* (1311), *Lexis* (1308), *Shepard's Federal Tax Locator* (1440)

TABLE 5 (Continued)

REFERENCE SOURCES FOR THREE JURISDICTIONAL AREAS OF LAW

Law Category	Type of Information Desired	Appropriate Reference Source and Access Number
	d. other	d. *Shepard's U.S. Administrative Citations* (1443)
Administrative Regulations	Text of federal administrative regulations:	
	a. all agencies	a. *CFR* (1414), *Federal Register* (1416), *Lexis* (1308), *Westlaw/System II* (1312)
	b. tax regulations only	b. *Federal Tax Regulations* (1417), Mertens set (1418)
	c. IRS revenue rulings and procedures	c. *Internal Revenue Bulletin* (1419), Mertens set (1420)
	d. specific subject areas	d. *BNA, CCH,* or *P-H* reporter sets (1452 to 1480)
	Notice of new regulations, proposed rules, hearings, etc.	*Federal Register Abstracts* (1434, 1435), *Federal Register* (1416)
	Finding aids (indexes, etc.) for administrative regulations	*CIS Federal Register Index* (1430), *Index to CFR* (1436), or the *CFR's* and *FR's* own indexes
Constitution	Text or interpretation of U.S. Constitution	*Constitution of the US* (1363), USCA (1362), or casebooks (1353 to 1361)
	Index to U.S. Constitution Books and periodical articles about U.S. Constitution	Mitchell's *Index* (1352), Hall (1349), McCarrick (1350), Millett (1351)
Executive Orders	Text of executive order	*Federal Register* (1416), *CFR* (1414), *Codification* (1415), *Lexis* (1308), *Westlaw/System II* (1312)
	Finding aids for executive orders	see finding aids for administrative regulations or use *Public Papers* (1125)
Judicial Decisions or Opinions	Text of principal court decisions regardless of jurisdiction	*American Law Reports* (1387), *National Reporter System* (1388), *Lexis* (1308), *Westlaw/System II* (1312)
	Text of U.S. Supreme Court decisions	*Supreme Court Reporter* (1397), *United States Reports* (1398), *United States Supreme Court Reports, L.Ed.* (1401), *U.S. Law Week* (1396), *U.S. Supreme Court Bulletin* (1402)
	Oral arguments before U.S. Supreme Court	*Complete Oral Arguments* (1393)
	Briefs submitted to U.S. Supreme Court	*Records and Briefs* (1394, 1395)
	Summaries of U.S. Supreme Court decisions	*Decisions of the U.S. Supreme Court* (1389)
	Text of lower federal court decisions	*National Reporter System* (1388)
	Text of tax cases	*American Federal Tax Reports* (1403, 1404), *U.S. Tax Cases* (1405), *Tax Court Reporter* (1409), *U.S. Tax Court Reports* (1410, 1411)
	Locator aids for decisions of federal courts:	
	a. U.S. Supreme Court	a. *American Digest* (1378), Blandford (1379), *Digest of U.S. Supreme Court Reports* (1381), Guenther (1380), *Lexis* (1308), *Modern Federal Practice Digest* (1383), *Shepard's U.S. Citations* (1386), *U.S. Supreme Court Digest* (1382), *Westlaw/II* (1312)

TABLE 5 (Continued)

REFERENCE SOURCES FOR THREE JURISDICTIONAL AREAS OF LAW

Law Category	Type of Information Desired	Appropriate Reference Source and Access Number
	b. U.S. Courts of Appeal, U.S. Courts of Claims, U.S. Court of Customs and Patent Appeals, U.S. District Courts	b. *American Digest* (1378), *Lexis* (1308), *Modern Federal Practice Digest* (1383), *Westlaw/II* (1312)
	c. tax cases only	c. *PhiNet* (1311), *Prentice-Hall Federal Taxes Citator* (1384), *Shepard's Federal Tax Locator* (1440), also *Lexis* (1308) and *Westlaw/II* (1312)
Statutes	Text of public law	*Slip Laws* (1369), *U.S. Law Week* (1373), *U.S. Statutes at Large* (1374)
	Subject codification of federal statutes	*U.S. Code* (1370), *U.S. Code Annotated* (1371), *U.S. Code Service* (1372)
	Explanation of tax laws, notably Internal Revenue Code	*CCH Standard Federal Tax Reporter* (1447), *P-H Federal Taxes* (1445), Rabkin & Johnson (1446)
	Locator aids for federal statutory law	*Lexis* (1308), *Monthly Catalog* (892, 893), Index volumes of *U.S. Code* (1370), and *U.S. Code Annotated* (1371), *Shepard's Acts and Cases* (1367), *Shepard's U.S. Citations* (1368), Indexes in *U.S. Statutes at Large* (1374), *Westlaw/II* (1312)
All Categories	Explanation of legal abbreviations	*Black's Law Dictionary* (1330), Price's *Effective Legal Research* (1303), *Radin Law Dictionary* (1336)
	Guides to legal research and reference sources	Coco (1299), Cohen (1300), Henke (1301), Jacobstein (1302), Statsky (1305)
	Indexes to periodical literature	*Current Law Index* (1314), *Index to Legal Periodicals* (1316), *Legal Contents* (1325), *Legal Resource Index* (1307, 1315), PAIS (291, 292)
	Identification of recent law books	*Bibliographic Guide to Law* (1313), *Law Information Update* (1322)
	Summary of the law by topic	*American Jurisprudence* (1339), *American Law Reports* (1387), *Corpus Juris Secundum* (1340), *Guide to American Law* (1344b)
2. State Law Constitutions	Indexes to state constitutions	*Index Digest* (1365)
	Text of state constitutions	Constitutions (1364)
Judicial Decisions	Locator aids for state court decisions:	
	a. Atlantic region	a. *American Digest System* (1378), *Atlantic Digest* (1378), individual state digests, *Lexis* (1308), *Shepard's Atlantic Reporter Citations* (1386), *Westlaw/II* (1312)
	b. northeastern region	b. *American Digest System* (1378), individual state digests, *Lexis* (1308), *Shepard's Northeastern Reporter Citations* (1386), *Westlaw/II* (1312)
	c. northwestern region	c. *American Digest System* (1378), *North Western Digest* (1378), also individual state digests, and *Shepard's Citations*, *Lexis* (1308), *Westlaw/II* (1312)
	d. Pacific region	d. *American Digest System* (1378), individual state digests, *Lexis* (1308), *Pacific Digest*,

TABLE 5 (Continued)

REFERENCE SOURCES FOR THREE JURISDICTIONAL AREAS OF LAW

Law Category	Type of Information Desired	Appropriate Reference Source and Access Number
		Shepard's Pacific Reporter Citations (1386), *Westlaw/II* (1312)
	e. southeastern region	e. *American Digest System* (1378), individual state digests, *Lexis* (1308), *Shepard's Southeastern Reporter Citations* (1386), *Westlaw/II* (1312)
	f. southern region	f. *American Digest System* (1378), individual state digests, *Lexis* (1308), *Shepard's Citations, Southern Digest, Westlaw/II* (1312)
	g. southwestern region	g. *American Digest System* (1378), individual state digests, *Lexis* (1308), *Shepard's Southwestern Reporter Citations* (1386), *Westlaw/II* (1312)
	Text of state court decisions	*National Reporter System* (1388)
Statutes	Bibliographic guide to state law compilations	Foster (1375)
	Summary of state law	*Martindale-Hubbell*, v. 5 (1376), Robinson (1377), also state encyclopedias (1341–1344)
3. Local Law	Text of state statutes or codified state law	Individual state code and statutes sets
Charters and Ordinances	Finding aids and texts	*Index to Current Urban Documents* and its microfiche set (1228)

WHAT YOU NEED TO DO

- Familiarize yourself with the techniques of legal research and the form of legal abbreviations by using the listed guidebooks and dictionaries.
- To find out what law applies to a specific factual situation, determine first the appropriate category of law and the type of legal information you need. Select and use the listed reference tools according to that determination, and make use of all suitable finding aids supplied with the reference works.
- Make sure that you have accurately established the current validity of the law by checking the current supplements of the appropriate legal reference source(s).

Political Actors

WHAT THEY ARE

Political actors are individuals and organizations that participate in the political system by their role in the governmental, interest, or communication structure. The following categories of political actors may be distinguished:

a. *Officials and Official Organizations.* This category includes intergovernmental organizations (IGOs), governments, legislatures, courts, administrative agencies, and their members, whose primary function is the authoritative control of society by the issuance and/or implementation of binding directives.

b. *Political Parties and Interest Organizations, their Organs and Members.* A political system also comprises a variety of nongovernmental or nonofficial organizations and associations who function politically by influencing the official decisions and activities — in the process or policy stage — in accordance with the interests of their members. Differences in the political systems of the world are the result of variations in the form, number, and membership of such organizations existing in the individual political entities, but two fundamentally different categories of party or interest organizations may be distinguished:

1. Legitimately operating political parties or movements, labor unions, business and professional organizations, churches, and other interest or pressure groups.

2. Illegal or clandestine organizations, such as outlawed political parties, terrorist organizations, and guerilla groups. These organizations operate in

19

violation of existing national or international law, and may or may not have the support from or an affiliation with official organizations, either in the same political entity or in another.

c. Producers or Purveyors of Meaning.[11] Official decisions and directives are also shaped by a large number of individuals and organizations who function politically by providing description, rational interpretation, advisory opinion, or meaning of societal, politically relevant phenomena. The welfare of modern political systems or the formation of public opinion—the most striking political phenomenon of this century—is largely determined by economists, historians, political scientists, sociologists, and other scientists, educators, lawyers, librarians, journalists, and commentators as well as their support organizations (universities, publishing companies, television and broadcasting companies, etc.) who control, produce, or purvey a most valuable and scarce human resource, namely, the political meaning of societal factors.

WHERE YOU FIND OUT ABOUT THEM

Political actors appear as authors as well as subjects in the reference system. They are identifiable for each political entity by name, organizational unit, or functional responsibility mainly through directories that offer contact, biographical and/or background information, and occasionally some activity information.

Role and activity information about political actors is retrievable mainly with the help of indexes and other bibliographic instruments that will also provide leads to biographical information.

Summarized assessment information about political actors is provided mainly by encyclopedias.

The following reference works are most useful:

DIRECTORIES

a. Regional: Africa, 1981, 1982; Asia, 2029, 2033, 2034; Europe, 2061; Latin America, 2094
b. United States, federal: 939–993, 1078, 1087–1093, 1695; state: 1217–1223; local: 1240–1242
c. Worldwide: 628, 629, 2103–2120, 1698–1704
d. Purveyors of meaning only: 330–335, 367–369, 475–478, 548, 549, 705–711, 779, 780, 854, 855
e. International organizations, Europe: 1843; UN: 1887, 1889

ENCYCLOPEDIAS

a. Producers of meaning: 321, 336, 337, 339
b. U.S. political actors: 509, 633, 637, 1682
c. Worldwide: 635, 1679–1681, 1927, 1931

INDEXES

a. Newspapers: 140–187
b. Periodicals: 244–253
c. U.S. executive processes: 1094–1124
d. U.S. legislative processes: 1000, 1004–1014, 1017
e. U.S. judicial processes: 1079–1086
f. Worldwide biographical publications: 2098–2102

See also historical bibliographies, notably 594–605, 1246–1260.

WHAT YOU NEED TO DO

Use the listed reference tools to determine

- the identity, location, political orientation, or academic discipline of the political actors involved in the pursuit of the political object under your investigation.
- what information or documentation has been published by and about the political actor who is the subject of your interest.
- what implications for the political process or policy stage of a particular issue or conflict the existence of specific political actors, their behavioral characteristics, and activities has or has not had.

Political Entities

WHAT THEY ARE

Political phenomena exhibit their distinctive properties primarily within specific frameworks known as entities or polities. Entities exist either as geographical or legal bodies, and have an identity of their own apart from the identity of their members.

Geographical entities are the world, the continents, regions, and areas, such as the Middle East, Africa South of the Sahara, Southeast Asia, and others. Legal entities include federal and individual states, provinces, cities, counties, districts, and corporations, as well as associations or groupings of states based on common law, conventions, treaties, or international declarations, such as the Commonwealth, the French Community, the European Communities, the Third World, and many others.

WHERE YOU FIND OUT ABOUT THEM

The reference system uses legal or geographical entities in several ways, notably,

1. to indicate in bibliographic instruments
   a. the corporate source of official documentation in appropriate bibliographic entries, such as "California. Legislature. Senate," or "Great Britain. Foreign Office," or "United States. Department of State."

b. the subject access to information and documentation by suitable arrangements and index entries in the reference instruments. Names of legal entities show up either as direct entries in catalogs, indexes, or other bibliographic instruments (example: "Great Britain — Politics and Government"), or as subdivisions of other subject terms, such as "Education — Great Britain."

c. the scope of specific reference works by appropriate titles, such as *Monthly Catalog of U.S. Government Publications*, *Shepard's Federal Tax Locator*, *World Treaty Index*, *Asian Recorder*, and others.

or

2. to assemble or summarize a variety of descriptive, statistical, or terminological information about specific countries, regions, or other entities in fact retrieval tools, such as

a. area handbooks, like *Africa South of the Sahara* (1981), *Middle East Contemporary Survey* (2031), and others;

b. dictionaries, like the *African Political Dictionary* (1976), *Political Dictionary of the Middle East in the 20th Century* (2021), and others;

c. encyclopedias, like the *Encyclopedia of the Third World* (1920), *World Encyclopedia of Political Systems* (1918), *Worldmark Encyclopedia of Nations* (1921), and others;

d. yearbooks, like the *Statesman's Yearbook* (2236), *Statistical Yearbook* (2239), *Yearbook of National Accounts Statistics* (2242), and others.

WHAT YOU NEED TO DO

Determine

- whether the "entity" information you need is of a kind most likely to be found in one of the fact retrieval books or would have to be searched for in bibliographic instruments.

- whether the information you need to search for in bibliographic instruments is essentially journalistic or scientific, since this will dictate the choice of reference works. Journalistic information is published in newspapers or general periodicals for which separate indexes exist.

Political Events

WHAT THEY ARE

Political events are noteworthy natural or manmade occurrences that may influence — often with sudden or dramatic impact — the direction of governmental policies or the action in the political processes. No complete inventory of political events can be drawn up here, but such occurrences as natural disasters, i.e., earthquakes, floods, fires, hurricanes, etc., or manmade disasters, like airplane crashes or industrial accidents, etc., or spectacular acts of violence, notably insurrections, revolutions, coups d'etat, assassinations, bombings, shooting incidents, wars, etc., or impressive nonviolent mass behavior, such as civil disobedience, demonstrations, strikes, or government resignations are prime examples of politically significant events. Major breakthroughs in science and technology, like the invention of nuclear bombs, computers, birth control pills, etc., are also events of frequently lasting, but often misunderstood political importance.

WHERE YOU FIND OUT ABOUT THEM

Reports of new events or "news" are disseminated mainly in news agency wires, newspapers, and news weeklies, for which indexes and digests in printed and electronic format exist. Older events are described in historical yearbooks, dictionaries, and encyclopedias.

Events information is thus retrievable for various time intervals, i.e., daily, weekly, quarterly, annually, or longer periods. Access is provided by specific keywords under which the event has become known, by name of country where the event occurred, by names of persons, organizations, or areas involved, by priority assessment (i.e., urgent, regular) or by news category.

The following reference works are most useful for the retrieval of events information:

1. Full text retrievers: 13, 20, 22, 181–187
2. Indexes: 140–181, 257–270
3. News digests: 640–664
4. Dictionaries and encyclopedias: 622–626, 632–639

WHAT YOU NEED TO DO

Determine

- the incidence, duration, and major characteristics of the political event by date, location, or name with the help of the most suitable reference works, as listed above.

- who or what caused the event, noting — where applicable — the demonstrated political behavior of the responsible actors. Use additional reference works to gain access to this information in newspapers, periodicals, books, or other documentation items.

- the exact relationship between a specific event or series of events and the political response to it, notably in terms of initiation, escalation, postponement, success or failure, etc., of governmental action. Use retrieval tools in other substantive reference categories, mainly legal, policy, or process tools whenever necessary.

Political Languages

WHAT ARE THEY

The political languages consist of a series of more or less distinctive but interrelated vocabularies created and employed by the various political actors. Most noteworthy are the rigorous legal terminology and the precise social-scientific vocabularies used by the academic or professional producers of meaning to effect rational understanding and methodological control of the societal infrastructure of the political system and its performance.

A second distinct kind of political terminology is the somewhat technical language of the government institutions and bureaucracies by which their structures, processes, and rules are expressed.

A third kind of political language consists of the catch-words and phrases of the politicians and campaigners that have led and misled millions, held out promises and false hopes, or stereotyped and oversimplified ideas for widespread mass appeal.

Finally, a fourth kind of political language encompasses the jargon and the metaphors of the news media intent upon capturing the essence of the political scene with vivid word pictures.

WHERE YOU FIND OUT ABOUT THEM

The reference system uses a large number of dictionaries and encyclopedias to offer an interpretative record of and quick access to the available terminological and conceptual wealth of the political languages. The dictionaries are frequently organized along disciplinary lines, into specific subfields, or by occupational usage. No single dictionary or encyclopedia offers, however, an exhaustive inventory of the existing terminology, even within its defined scope.

The following dictionaries are considered most useful for

1. Legal terminology: 1330, 1332 – 1334, 1336 – 1345
2. Process and government vocabularies:
   a. American: 1197 – 1206, 2419
   b. International: 1673 – 1678
   c. Regional: Africa, 1976; Asia, 2021 – 2023; Europe, 1841, 1842, 2055, 2056; Latin America, 2091
3. Political thought: 2325 – 2328
4. Social scientific vocabularies:
   a. Anthropology: 365, 366
   b. Economics: 437 – 459, 461
   c. Education: 499 – 505
   d. Geography: 540, 543, 545 – 547
   e. Political Science: 698, 700 – 704
   f. Psychology: 764 – 777
   g. Sociology: 845 – 850, 853
   h. Social sciences together: 325, 326, 328, 329

In addition, most of the encyclopedias identified in the Typology Index of this guidebook will provide valuable information about politically significant terms and phrases.

WHAT YOU NEED TO DO

- Determine the particular vocabulary category of the word or phrase for which you are seeking a definition. Use one or more dictionaries in this vocabulary category to locate the desired definition.
- For scientific communication avoid, if at all possible, the use of words for which the dictionaries provide several different meanings, or add precise qualifiers if usage of the term is unavoidable.

Political Objects, Policies, and Programs

WHAT THEY ARE

Political objects are the targets of political processes and policies. Having emerged from the mass of societal factors through the political processes, the political objects are a set of specific conditions desired or opposed by the prevailing will of the political actors. For their realization political objects require implementation through policies — a series of authoritative official actions based on agreed-upon decisions. Policies are usually supported by programmed resource flows from taxes, dues, fees, and other governmental revenues, but their costs are also often borne by deficits and loans.

For maximum effectiveness political objects, policies, and their fiscal programs need to be coherent, well balanced and noncontradictory. It is misleading, however, to assume that all political entities have fixed political objects and coherent policies to realize them. Political objects and policies are subject to constantly shifting priorities among them, due to adjustments that need to be made to the political realities of events, changing societal factors, available resources, and obtainable political consensus. The inevitably occurring adjustment failures eventually cause the emergence of special political objects or new policies following changes in the official organizations or their membership (government reorganization, electoral changes, resignations, special appointments, etc.) brought about through political processes.

The individual policies are differentiated according to the political object to which they are directed. The following list identifies some of the more important policies and their political objects:

Policy Name	Political Object	Policy Name	Political Object
Agricultural Policy	A stable, prosperous farming sector, adequate supply of food at reasonable prices, efficient marketing or distribution	Incomes Policy	Reduction of the growth of nominal income, such as wages and profits, to restrain inflation
Antitrust Policy	Prevention of private monopoly	Industrial Policy	Improved growth and structure of industry, using less energy and achieving higher value added through investment incentives, labor market stabilization, research promotion
Civil Rights Policy	Promotion and protection of civil rights		
Commercial Policy	International economic order		
Communications Policy	Access to information		
Cultural Policy	Promotion of cultural activities	Labor Policy	Adequate labor supply for all production and service needs, harmonious labor-management relations
Defense or Military Policy	National security		
Development Policy	Basic improvement of the infrastructure, human and natural resources		
Disarmament Policy	Reduction of armaments	Law Enforcement Policy	Protection from crime and criminals
Economic Policy	A healthy political economy exhibiting rapid growth, stable prices, and a sustainable balance of payments	Monetary Policy	Matching money supply with money demand consistent with economic growth, control of inflation
Educational Policy	Economic efficiency, social mobility, maximum self-realization, improvement of human relations, reduction of ignorance	Nuclear Policy	Prevention of or defense in nuclear war
		Population Policy	Control of excessive population growth
Energy Policy	Adequate supply of energy at reasonable cost	Social Policy	Promotion of social security, health care, education, employment, and training
Environmental Policy	Minimizing environmental pollution		
Ethnic or Racial Policy	Minimizing conflict between different ethnic or racial groups in society	Transportation Policy	Alleviation of national and urban transportation problems
		Urban Policy	Revitalization of urban areas
Federal Reserve Policy (U.S. version of monetary policy)	Control of prices, output and exchange rates through reserve rate requirements, discount rate, and open market operations	Wage Policy	Control of minimum and/or maximum rates of payment for work performed
Fiscal Policy	Macroeconomic benefits through judicious government spending and taxation	Wage-Price Policy	Control of wages and prices
Foreign Exchange Policy	Currency stability and income stability; "virtuous circle"[12]		
Foreign Policy	Promotion of national interests in the international community; national security		
Full Employment Policy	Low unemployment		
Immigration Policy	Control of immigration, alleviation of international refugee problem		

WHERE YOU FIND OUT ABOUT THEM

Reference treatment of object- and policy-oriented information is not as advanced as in some of the other substantive areas of political knowledge, notably the legal field. Subject access to desired information is hampered by inconsistent usage of subject headings or descriptors (see annotation under item 57) and inadequate bibliographic and fact retrieval tools.

In spite of these shortcomings, considerable amounts of useful information can be retrieved from the reference instruments identified in Table 6.

TABLE 6

REFERENCE SOURCES FOR OBJECT- AND POLICY-ORIENTED INFORMATION

Political Object or Policy	Type of Information Desired	Appropriate Reference Source
All or Most Governmental Policies and Political Objects	Bibliographic citations to:	
	a. all documentation categories	a. Birch (910), *BRS after Dark* (12), *Cato Institute Catalog* (912), Goehlert (913a), *Knowledge Index* (19), *Nexis* (20), Murin (906), *Pais* (292), *Pais International* (291), *Robey* (917)
	b. books only	b. *AEI Publications* (909), *Books in Print* (40), *LC Catalog* (85), *Libcon* (59), *Marc* (60), *National Union Catalog* (62), *Remarc* (61), *UN Monthly Bibliography* (318)
	c. newspapers only	c. *Christian Science Monitor Index* (143), *Editorials on File* (166), *Information Bank* (172), *London Times Index* (154), *National Newspaper Index* (175, 176), *N.Y. Times Index* (150), *Newsearch* (178), *NYTOL* (183), and others
	d. periodicals only	d. *ABC Pol Sci* (669), *Information Bank* (246), *International Political Science Abstracts* (671), *Magazine Index* (248, 249), *Readers Guide* (253), *SSCI* (309, 311), *Social Scisearch* (311), *Social Sciences Index* (312), *UN Monthly Bibl.* (318), *US Political Science Documents* (674), *USPSD* (675)
	e. official U.S. publications only	e. *CIS/Index* (1000), *CIS Hearings Index* (1035), *Monthly Catalog* (892), 893), and others
	Summaries of U.S. policies	*Congress and the Nation* (1042–1046), *Public Policy* (1052)
Defense Objects and Policies	Bibliographic citations	*Abstracts of Military Bibliography* (1628), *Air University Library Index* (1630), *Arkin* (1632), Greenwood (1637), Lane (1666), Larson (1638), *Naval Abstracts* (1629), *Peace Research Abstracts Journal* (1642), *Quarterly Strategic Bibliography* (1631), see also Higham (589, 590)
	Principal documents of U.S. defense policy	*Documents of the NSC* (1731, 1732), *Public Statements* (1739), *U.S.-Vietnam Relations* (1743), *The War in Vietnam* (1754)
	Summaries of international defense policies, national security problems, etc.	*Military Balance* (1717), *Strategic Survey* (1718)
Development Policies	Bibliographic citations	Colleta (1906), *Developing Areas* (1909), *JDA Bibliography* (1894), Powelson (1914), Requa (1904), Spitz (1905)
Disarmament Policies	Bibliographic citations	Arkin (1632), Burns (1619), Clemens (1620), *Disarmament* (1622), *Peace Research Abstracts Journal* (1642), *Repertory* (1621), Swarthmore College *Catalog* (1643)
	Digest or summary information	*Arms Control Reporter* (1684), *SIPRI Yearbooks* (1722)

TABLE 6 (Continued)

REFERENCE SOURCES FOR OBJECT- AND POLICY-ORIENTED INFORMATION

Political Object or Policy	Type of Information Desired	Appropriate Reference Source
Economic Object-Oriented Policies	Bibliographic citations for: a. books only	a. *Economic Books* (398), *Economics Selections* (399), *Journal of Economic Literature* (404), *NYPL Bibliographic Guide* (414)
	b. periodicals only	b. *ABI/Inform* (386), *Business Index* (390), *Business Periodicals Index* (391), *Business Publications Index* (392), *Economic Abstracts International* (395), *Economic Literature Index* (400), *International Bibliography of Economics* (410), *IMF List* (417), *Journal of Economic Literature* (404), *Key to Economic Science* (397)
	Principal documents for U.S. policies	*Papers of the Fed* (1076), *U.S. National Economy* (1077)
Educational Policies	Bibliographic citations	*CIJE* (490), *Education Index* (494), *ERIC* (492), *RIE* (491)
Energy Policies	Bibliographic citations	*DOE Energy* (1072), *Energy Abstracts for Policy Analysis* (1073), *Energy Information Abstracts* (296), *Energyline* (297), *Rycroft* (918)
Environmental Policy	Bibliographic citations	*Environmental Abstracts* (523), *Environline* (522), *Environmental (Periodicals) Bibliography* (525, 526), *Pollution Abstracts* (528, 529)
Federal Reserve Policy	Principal documents	*Papers of the Fed* (1076)
Foreign Exchange Policy	Summaries	*Price-Waterhouse* (1940), *Yeager* (1723)
Foreign Policy	Bibliographic citations	see various bibliographies (1562 to 1671) in Chapter 4
	Principal documents	see various document collections (1725 to 1808) in Chapter 4
	Principal features of U.S. foreign policy	*Encyclopedia of American Foreign Policy* (1682)
Immigration Policy	Background documents for U.S. policy	*Papers of the Select Commission* (1059)
Labor Policy	Bibliographic citations	*International Labour Documentation* (411), *Labordoc* (412)
Law Enforcement Policy and Programs	Bibliographic citations	*Felkenes* (2391), *Hewitt* (2393), *NCJRS* (1309), *Police Science Abstracts* (2378), *Prostano* (2394); see also *Abstracts on Criminology* (802), *Criminal Justice Abstracts* (803), *Criminal Justice Periodical Index* (805)
Population Policy	Bibliographic citations	*Population Bibliography* (813), *Population Index* (814), *Population Index Bibliography* (815), *World Population Policy* (1908)
Social Policy	Bibliographic citations	*Human Resources Abstracts* (409), *Kotz* (915), *Sociological Abstract* (819, 820). *Social Work Research and Abstracts* (818)
Transportation Policy	Outline of U.S. policies	*National Transportation Policies* (1064)
Urban Policy	Bibliographic citations	*Index to Current Urban Documents* (1228), *Palumbo* (1227), *Sage Urban Studies Abstracts* (1229)

TABLE 6 (Continued)

REFERENCE SOURCES FOR OBJECT- AND POLICY-ORIENTED INFORMATION

Political Object or Policy	Type of Information Desired	Appropriate Reference Source
U.S. Government Programs	Descriptive inventory including funding information	*Budget of the United States Government* (1127–1130), *Catalog of Federal Domestic Assistance* (1131), *FAPRS* (1132), *Government Programs and Project Directory* (949), Raffa (916)

WHAT YOU NEED TO DO

• Select a political object in the United States or other political entity and determine what specific governmental policy or program is directed toward it.
• Determine the nature and other details of this policy from what is published about it by social scientists, the mass media, and official sources, thereby using both general and specific policy-oriented reference tools.
• Determine whether the policy under your investigation is basically successful, essentially misdirected, or ineffective in the estimation of the various political actors, and what policy alternatives are offered. Since the existing reference mechanism is not that sophisticated, use available title clues in the reference instruments to narrow your search.

Political Processes

WHAT THEY ARE

As a general concept, political process[13] is often synonymous with "politics," meaning the activities of political actors as they struggle for—or use—power to achieve or maintain political objects. Based on the structure or arena in which the struggle occurs, it has been customary to distinguish between at least six major processes, namely,

1. communication processes
2. electoral processes
3. executive-administrative processes
4. international relations processes
5. judicial processes
6. legislative processes

each of which may in turn be subdivided into subprocesses, such as budgetary, appropriation, nominating, planning, voting, and other activities. All political processes are essentially decision-making processes characterized not only by the struggle about conflicting demands or goals, but also by frequent debates, speeches, and other oral argumentation, massive amounts of documentation, and ultimate outcomes.

WHERE YOU FIND OUT ABOUT THEM

Process-related information is published in virtually all documentation categories, but the reference treatment for the six processes is of varying dimension and quality. It is the primary purpose of the reference instruments to disclose the final result of the political process and to identify the political actors and objects involved. The text of debates, speeches, oral argumentation, and printed documentation is fully retrievable—in the United States—for the legislative and judicial processes only and much less so for the other processes. In particular, the reference coverage for the international relations and executive-administrative processes labors under various disclosure restrictions. Surprisingly, a computerized comparative reference system for political rhetoric, while already in use in some European countries, is still nonexistent in the United States or on a worldwide basis.

Table 7 identifies the most useful reference sources for the various political processes.

TABLE 7

REFERENCE SOURCES FOR POLITICAL PROCESSES

Political Process	Appropriate Reference Sources
Communication Process	
1. All political actor categories, worldwide (addresses, speeches, statements, etc.)	1. Bibliographic citations for: a. books of speeches, 39–43, 54, 55, 59–62, 83–85 b. broadcast material, 259, 261, 263–270 c. newspaper material, 150, 154, 161, 167, 168, 171, 172, 179, 180 d. periodical material, 244–256, 290–293, 1571, and regional indexes listed in Chapter 5 e. translated material, 271, 272, 196 f. full text retrieval: *Current World Leaders* (2103), *NEXIS* (20), *NYTOL* (183), *UPI news* (187), *Source* (22), *Vu/Text* (185, 186), *What They Said* (1943)

TABLE 7 (Continued)
REFERENCE SOURCES FOR POLITICAL PROCESSES

Political Process	Appropriate Reference Sources
2. U.S. political actors:	
a. interest groups (public statements, speeches, press releases, etc.)	a. *Vital Speeches of the Day* (1265), *UPI News* (187), also all newspaper indexes (140 to 186)
b. mass media (editorials, commentaries, letters to the editor, etc.)	b. *Editorials on File* (166), also all newspaper indexes (140 to 186)
c. political parties (convention proceedings, platforms, party statements, etc.)	c. Bain (1266), Chester (1261), Johnson (1262, 1263), *National Party Conventions* (1267)
d. presidency (inaugural addresses, debates, messages, press conferences, state of the union addresses, etc.)	d. *A Compilation of the Messages and Papers* (1134), *Inaugural Addresses* (1137), *Presidential Campaign 1976* (1139), *Presidential Press Conferences* (1138), *Public Papers* (1125), Roosevelt, F. D. (1140, 1141), *State of the Union Messages* (1142), *Weekly Compilation* (1132, 1133)
e. secretaries of state and defense	e. 1736–1739, 1747, 1749, 1752
f. scholarly purveyors	f. *Communications Abstracts* (1273), *Communication Information* (1274), Gitter (1276), Gordon (1277), Kaid (1251), Lasswell (1280, 1281), Nimmo (1269), Mowlana (1278), Shearer (1285), Smith (1282, 1283)
Election Processes, U.S.	a. compendia and guidebooks (1183–1196)
	b. newspaper indexes (140–157, 159, 160, 166, 169, 170, 172–178, 183)
	c. popular periodical indexes (244–253)
	d. retrospective bibliographies: Bain (1266), Garrison (1247, 1248), Schlachter (1249)
	e. Scientific periodical indexes (290–293, 596, 597, 669, 674, 675, 680, 685)
Election Processes, Other Countries	Cook (1927, 2061), Mackie (2251), Rokkan (2211), Rose (1930), also newspaper and periodical indexes (140–187, 244–253, 290–293)

Political Process	Appropriate Reference Sources
Executive-Administrative Processes:	
a. U.S. federal agencies	a. see information sources listed for each agency in *Federal Regulatory Directory* (948) and in O'Hara (1069), also BNA, CCH, GFS, and P-H loose-leaf services (1452–1480), *GAO Docs* (1057), *Requirements* (1067), and listings under administrative law
b. U.S. presidency	b. *Presidential Documents Series* (1135)
c. scientific references	c. Gellhorn (932, 933), guidebooks (2364–2371), bibliographies, catalogs, and indexes (2372–2407), casebooks (2408–2418), dictionaries (2419), directories (2420, 2421), document collections (2422, 2423)
International Relations Processes	see Chapter 4, International Relations (1562–1808)
Judicial Processes, U.S.	*Complete Oral Arguments* (1393), *Landmark Briefs and Arguments* (1390), *U.S. Law Week* (1396), *U.S. Supreme Court Records and Briefs* (1395); see also Laws and Other Legal Directives in this section
Legislative Processes, U.S.	see Chapter 3, Congressional Information, especially 1000, 1002–1014, 1017–1019, 1039, 1040, etc.
Summaries of Process Issues, U.S.	*Congressional Digest* (1047), Isaacson (935), Rosenbaum (936), *Scorpio/issue files* (1002)

WHAT YOU NEED TO DO

Determine

- which of the six principal processes is currently or was historically involved in the achievement of a political object under your investigation.
- what was the outcome of the historical process or what is the current status in the contemporary process.
- what information and documentation about the underlying societal factors and their conversion or resolution into a political object, policy, or legal directive has become available through the political process stage.
- who are or were the principal political actors involved in the political process.

- what particular action did the political actors take in the political process and what specific process avenues have yet to be pursued by the political actors to obtain the desired political object.

Select and use the most promising reference tools listed in Table 7 for the six major political processes. Whenever necessary read the annotations for the listed reference works to avoid false starts and dead ends in your search for information.

Political Thought

WHAT IT IS

While a precise determination of its scope is difficult to achieve, political thought primarily refers to

1. a variety of organized belief, creed, or value systems that serve as guidance for political action, notably the public selection and pursuit of political objects. Although differing greatly in their individual political orientation, the various thought systems all share the common characteristics of being explicitly formulated, closed to novel ideas, insistent on conduct compliance and consensus, and closely associated with a specific corporate body intended to realize the pattern of belief. Notable examples in this category of political thought are
   a. ideologies, such as communism, democracy, imperialism, marxism, nationalism, socialism, Zionism, and others
   b. religions, such as Buddhism, Christianity, Hinduism, Islam, Judaism, and others.
2. a variety of politically significant ideas that regardless of their chronological, cultural, or disciplinary origin continue to be of pivotal importance in the constitution or performance of political systems throughout the world. Notable examples are authority, autonomy, environmental protection, equality, freedom, free trade, integration, justice, loyalty, nationalization (denationalization), peace, power, property, self-determination, separation, utility, value, war (militarism), and many others.

Since political thought, like law, serves as a guidance mechanism for political action, its basic values need to be fully reflected in law, as they ordinarily are, to avoid conflict. Inevitably, however, conflicts do arise because political thought, unlike law, frequently travels across international boundaries, thereby challenging the jurisdictional monopoly of another political entity.

WHERE YOU FIND OUT ABOUT IT

Due to the ubiquity of political thought, information may be found about it in practically all documentation and reference instrument categories, but the following types of reference works will facilitate access to the details of political thought:

1. Specific bibliographic instruments, such as guidebooks, bibliographies, or indexes that serve as finding aids for pertinent books or articles: 28– 38, 40– 43, 54, 55, 59– 62, 83– 85, 118, 119, 121, 122, 140– 180, 182– 199, 244– 256, 259, 261– 270, 306, 596– 601, 605, 666, 668– 676, 678– 682, 685– 688, 755– 757, 761, 1577, 2255– 2319, 2321
2. Fact retrieval tools, such as dictionaries, encyclopedias, and historiographies that offer summaries of essential information: 336, 339, 2320, 2322– 2359

Access in these reference works is provided by topical subject headings, keywords, and/or names of political philosophers.

WHAT YOU NEED TO DO

- With the help of suitable fact retrieval tools familiarize yourself with the essential elements of the principal thought systems and ideas for the contemporary or any historical period.
- Use suitable bibliographic instruments to find information for the purpose of determining which ideas or thought systems present a challenge or assistance to
   a. the officially constituted organizations (governments, legislatures, courts, etc.) or their specific membership,
   b. the articulation of societal needs,
   c. the political processes and policies
   d. the legal system (law and order) in a particular political entity and why.

Societal Factors

WHAT THEY ARE

A political system derives its justification from its capacity to deal effectively with a multitude of constantly changing societal factors that have become pressing problems requiring authoritative intervention. The societal factors are people, their activities, feelings, and—most notably—their needs, subjected to biological, economic, geographic/environmental, and group dynamic forces, as well as historical experiences and continuities, inter-societal rivalries, and repeated doses of ignorance. Many, but not all, of these societal factors will emerge as problems, challenges, or issues due to demand, interest, or meaning articulation by political actors.

In view of their great complexity and variety, societal factors are systematically studied and monitored by several academic disciplines, notably anthropology, economics, psychology, sociology, and others that act as auxiliary sciences to political science itself and its various subfields. Many societal factors transcend, however, the individual boundaries of these academic disciplines. The most important and consistently problematical societal factors have led to governmental institutionalization, i.e., the creation of official agencies whose prime function is the control or regulation of specific societal factors, such as educational needs, health and welfare needs, defense needs, agricultural and commerce needs, environmental needs, etc., and the interest conflicts they create.

WHERE YOU FIND OUT ABOUT THEM

A considerable part of the political reference literature is devoted to information available in descriptive, analytical, or statistical form about the societal factors requiring political intervention. This information may be of scientific, official, or nonscientific origin disseminated in books, articles, and other documentation categories. Much of the scientific information is made accessible by reference works that are organized mainly along disciplinary lines. Both document and fact retrieval tools are available. The nonscientific information about societal factors is referenced mainly by indexes to newspapers and popular periodicals. A third category of information about societal factors is published officially and is made accessible through bibliographies and statistical compendia organized mainly for retrieval by political entity.

Subject access to societal factor information is not as good as would be desirable and is provided most often by topical keywords expressing broad concepts, like aging, alienation, commerce, consumer protection, crime and criminals, education, employment, environment, health care, housing, immigration, monopoly, population, poverty, transportation, unemployment, violence, etc. Several social science thesauri exist, however, that offer an inventory of narrower terms as used in specific bibliographic instruments.

Table 8 delineates the most appropriate reference instruments for the various categories of information available about societal factors.

TABLE 8

REFERENCE SOURCES FOR SOCIETAL FACTORS

Reference Type	Available Information	Appropriate Reference Source
Bibliographic Citations with or without Abstracts	All source categories, books only	*Books in Print* (40, 42), *CBI* (55), *Libcon* (59), *Library of Congress Catalog* (85), *Marc* (60), *National Union Catalog* (62), *Remarc* (61)
	Comparative or area studies	see bibliographies listed in Chapter 4
	Nonscientific information, newspapers only	indexes (140 to 186)
	Nonscientific information, periodicals only	indexes (244 to 256)
	Official information	*CIS/Index* (1000), *Index to U.S. Government Periodicals* (885), *Monthly Catalog* (892, 893, 896, 897), Parish (899), *NYPL Bibliographic Guide* (886)
	Social-scientific information, books and/or periodicals	see listings for bibliographic instruments in Chapter 2
Computerized Full Text Retrieval	Nonscientific information:	
	a. newspapers only	a. *Infoglobe* (182), *NYTOL* (183)
	b. newsletters, newspapers, periodicals, radio broadcasts	b. *NEXIS* (20)
Statistical Compendia	U.S. data only	general compendia (1161 to 1167), demographic compendia (1168 to 1170), socioeconomic compendia (1171–1182)
	Worldwide or area data	gazetteers (541, 542, 544), handbooks (1981–1985, 2029, 2031, 2036, 2095), international compendia, current (2212 to 2247), international compendia, retrospective (2248 to 2253)
	National data	national compendia (2254)

TABLE 8 (Continued)

REFERENCE SOURCES FOR SOCIETAL FACTORS

Reference Type	Available Information	Appropriate Reference Source
Statistical Indexes	U.S. data	ASI (1154, 1155), *Datamap* (1159), SRI (1160)
	Worldwide data	ASI (1154, 1155), Cyriax (2205), Dicks (2206), *Index to International Statistics* (2209)

WHAT YOU NEED TO DO

Use bibliographic tools and statistical compendia to

- familiarize yourself with the major categories of American societal factors for which statistical data are published monthly, annually, or at other intervals.
- identify scholarly works (books, periodical articles, etc.) written about American societal factors, either generally or specifically.
- determine which American societal factors currently occupy the attention of the mass media.
- determine which societal factors have been the target of recent attention in a particular American political process (i.e., administrative-executive, legislative, judicial, election, or communication process) and which have not, although clearly related to the political phenomenon under investigation.
- determine the statistical size and historical trend of specific societal factors targeted by an American political process.
- determine which societal factors remain pressing problems despite process and policy action in the United States and why.
- conduct a similar analysis for societal factors in other countries.

SUMMARY OF POLITICAL REFERENCE THEORY

The political reference theory, detailed on the preceding pages, advances an alternative conception of political inquiry that rejects the traditional disjointed atomism of specialized scientific investigation as frequently inadequate or misleading. Political reference theory is based on the realization that individual political phenomena often make sense only if looked upon in the totality of their parts.

Although political phenomena are usually not recognizable as visual experience, they behave nevertheless like visual phenomena, such as trees, houses, animals, or persons. Just as trees, houses, animals, and persons group themselves in particular ways to form a specific visual landscape, the political world consists of countless particles that separate themselves from the surrounding universe to form nine more or less distinct and coherent units. These nine units, namely

1. entities
2. laws
3. political actors
4. policies, programs, and their objects
5. events
6. processes
7. political thought
8. political language
9. societal factors

are made visible by ten procedural elements that must be present for the proper recognition of the political landscape. To illustrate this assertion, let us take the example of gun control as an American political phenomenon.

The subject of gun control separates itself from the surrounding political universe to emerge as a distinct political phenomenon within the *entity* of the United States and its individual states, counties, and cities. More than 20,000 federal, state, and local *laws*, most notably the second amendment to the United States Constitution and the Gun Control Act of 1968 *(82 Stat 1213)*, already exist for the regulation of guns, but numerous groups of *political actors* strive for additional legal directives that are either more restrictive or less so. The specific *objects* of the political actors may enhance or jeopardize existing law enforcement programs or specific economic and social *policies* aimed at broader but related objects.

Gun control derives considerable justification from noteworthy *events*, such as the successful and unsuccessful attempts to assassinate U.S. presidents Lincoln, Roosevelt, Kennedy, and Reagan, among others, and the existence of an unusually complex array of *societal factors*. These include the occurrence of some 30,000 deaths from guns annually, the availability of some 120 million guns in the country, the presence of an extensive criminal subculture, the continued manufacture and sale of guns and ammunition, a dismal record of public opinion, and many others.

Several American political *processes*, most notably the legislative and judicial processes, continue to be involved in gun control with the introduction of bills, the scheduling of hearings, or the formulation of judicial opinions. Gun control is heavily influenced by the prevalence of cherished *political thoughts*, such as freedom, right to bear arms, free enterprise, and others. It is also complicated by certain expressions of the *political language*, exemplified by such slogans as "guns don't kill, people do" or "when guns are criminal, only criminals will have guns."

These and other more exact details that shape the phenomenon of gun control would not be visible without *information* disseminated in numerous books, periodicals, newspapers, and other *documentation* categories. This information originates from three distinct *sources*, but much of it is generated by *scientific methods*, such as statistical procedures, surveys, and other approaches. Due to the explosive dimension of the total information flow through the various *information channels*, neither an adequate quantity of information nor even individual items of information about gun control could be retrieved by a *user* without the use of *reference tools*, *entry symbols*, and documentation *classification* identified in this part of the guidebook.

Only after considerable amounts of information in all nine substantive reference categories have been retrieved for a sufficiently large *time* frame in accordance with the instructions supplied by the reference theory, will it become apparent where past political efforts have failed and where precisely the focus of future political activities must lie if the problem of guns is to be brought under control.

Notes

1. William G. Andrews, *International Handbook of Political Science* (Westport, CT: Greenwood Press, 1982), p. 1.
2. U.S. President's Science Advisory Committee, *Science, Government and Information* (Washington, DC: U.S. Government Printing Office, 1963), p. 28.
3. National Academy of Sciences, Committee on Scientific and Technical Communication, *Scientific and Technical Communication* (Washington, DC, 1969), p. 62.
4. This term is a somewhat inadequate translation of the German word *Herrschaft* as analyzed in Max Weber, *The Theory of Social and Economic Organization*, translated by A. M. Henderson and Talcott Parsons (New York: The Free Press, 1947), pp. 152 and 324. *Herrschaft* is considered the most useful term for describing the scope of the political reference system. Varying in meaning from domination or rule to mere situational existence, *Herrschaft* (literally "lordship") encompasses domination by people or classes, rule by law or words, or the reign of conditions and circumstances. The latter meaning acquires special significance when domination or rule breaks down and gives way to chaotic conditions. The political reference system thus retrieves information about all situations in which people are dominated by other people, ruled by law or words, or subjected to conditions of anarchy and chaos.
5. See, for instance, Harry Eckstein, "Authority Patterns: A Structural Basis for Political Inquiry," *American Political Science Review*, 67: 4 (December 1973).
6. See the Freedom of Information Act, *81 Stat 54* and *88 Stat 1561*, and Executive Order 12356 *(3 CFR Chapter IV)*, dated 2 April 1982.
7. Not all scholars agree with this conclusion, maintaining in fact that the user is already overloaded with information to such an extent that the personal experience values—that is, the undocumented and nonreferenced experience values of individuals—do not find adequate expression in political decision making. See, for instance, Karl Steinbuch, *Masslos Informiert—Die Enteignung unseres Denkens (Informed without Moderation: The Expropriation of our Thinking)* (Munich: Herbig Verlag, 1978).
8. A complete listing of the letter symbols in the Superintendent of Documents (SuDoc) classification system can be found in John L. Andriot, *Guide to U.S. Government Publications* (McLean, VA: Documents Index, 1981–).
9. Note that "we cannot explain the validity claim of norms without recourse to rationally motivated agreement or at least to the conviction that consensus on a recommended norm could be brought about *with reasons*. In that case the model of contracting parties who need know only what an imperative means is inadequate. The appropriate model is rather the communication community of those affected, who as participants in a practical discourse test the validity claims of norms and, to the extent that they accept them with reasons, arrive at the conviction that in the given circumstances the proposed norms are right." See Jürgen Habermas, *Legitimation Crisis* (Boston: Beacon Press, 1973), p. 105.
10. Eckstein, p. 1152.
11. For a detailed but highly critical analysis of this group of political actors, see, for instance, Helmut Schelsky, *Die Arbeit tun die Anderen: Klassenkampf und Priesterherrschaft der Intellektuellen* (Opladen: Westdeutscher Verlag, 1975).
12. The virtuous circle is a set of mutually reinforcing economic developments, aimed for by the exchange rate policy in conjunction with appropriate monetary and fiscal policy, by which the economy is stabilized at low levels of inflation and unemployment. The alternative is the vicious circle, in which high levels of domestic inflation usually fed by low levels of interest rates from excessive money supply devalue the currency—thereby importing more foreign inflation that in turn causes additional devaluation of the currency and still higher domestic inflation through excessive wage increases, etc. For further details about this phenomenon, see, for instance, William A. Allen, *Exchange Rates and Balance of Payments Adjustment: General Principles and Some Recent Experiences*, Bank for International Settlements Working Papers, July 1980.
13. For a summary description of this concept, see Bertram M. Gross, "The Political Process," in *International Encyclopedia of the Social Sciences* (New York: Macmillan, 1968), vol. 12, pp. 265–273.

PART II
THE REFERENCE SOURCES

Chapter 1

General Reference Sources

INTRODUCTION

Chapter 1 of this guidebook is devoted to an evaluative description of selected general reference instruments for the principal information carriers in all fields of human knowledge. At the present stage of communication technology, political and other information is brought to the user by information carriers distinguishable according to the following categories:

1. Automated carriers
2. Books
3. Dissertations and theses
4. Micropublications
5. Newspapers and news retrieval tools
6. Periodicals
7. Radio and television broadcasts
8. Translated books, periodicals, or newspapers

Automated information carriers are utilized mainly in service arrangements contracted by libraries or individual users with time-sharing companies. Large collections of machine-readable data under the control of a central computer are accessible by remote control on a concurrent or time-sharing basis. Books, micropublications, newspapers, and periodicals are available to users mainly by purchase from publishers and their distributors or on loan in or from libraries. Information originally disseminated to large audiences in radio or television broadcasts is retrievable in libraries from regular print or microform versions. Considerable amounts of foreign-language material are translated into English and likewise made retrievable from print or microform documents. Information retrieval in each of these carrier categories is facilitated by separate reference instruments specially created according to form or usage characteristics.

AUTOMATED CARRIERS AND CHANNELS

Introduction

For more than a generation now the application of new technologies for storing and processing information by means of punched cards, magnetic tapes, disks, computers, and telecommunication tools has made it possible to automate the retrieval, manipulation, and dissemination of information. Although it is now technically feasible to store the entire body of human knowledge in machine-readable form and carry it with telecommunication tools automatically to the user on request, there is as yet no generally or partially accepted concept for automated retrieval and dissemination of all human knowl-edge in existence. What exists at present is a large and growing number of uncoordinated and frequently duplicated efforts to create and maintain automated retrieval systems for specific, limited categories of information and specific user purposes. We can distinguish three different kinds of automated retrieval systems that use machine-readable information carriers:

1. systems that merely produce new or improved bibliographic instruments in printed form for printed information
2. systems that provide an alternative but not necessarily superior retrieval mechanism for machine-readable information that is also accessible in regular printed form by printed retrieval tools
3. systems that provide an exclusive retrieval mechanism for machine-readable information that is not otherwise available in regular printed form.

Many of the printed bibliographic instruments listed in this guidebook are produced as a result of computerized processes. The annotations occasionally mention this fact, but it was not considered useful to list all or most of these bibliographies in a special category since the user is not involved in the automation process.

Computer-readable bibliographic instruments, such as *Books in Print, GPO Monthly Catalog, Sociological Abstracts*, and others that offer the researcher an alternative retrieval method with online entry and inquiry are normally listed and described in connection with the equivalent printed reference tool in the appropriate sections of this guidebook. In many instances, the online reference instrument bears the same name or title as the printed version so that only the vendor information and the annotation for the title identify the dual retrieval capability.

There are also several databases or database systems in existence, such as LEXIS or NEXIS, that have a retrieval capability equivalent or superior to several printed versions. These databases are listed separately throughout the book in order to bring out the special character of the retrieval mechanism.

Systems that permit the automated retrieval, manipulation, or dissemination of bibliographical, political, or socioeconomic information not otherwise available in conventional printed carriers are also of great importance to readers of this guidebook. An example is the *OCLC* system, for which no printed union catalog exists. Other examples are the several hundred machine-readable data collections of the Inter-University Consortium for Political and Social Research (ICPSR), for which an appropriate guidebook has been listed and described under item 341.

In recent years there has been a sharp increase in the

number of online reference instruments available in American libraries. Online reference work is now possible in a wide range of subject areas, including all of the social sciences, law, congressional processes, and library holdings. Online reference work is most efficient or productive in situations where there are several variables or retrieval needs from a massive supply of information. On the other hand, there are still many problems associated with computerized reference instruments. While online databases exhibit generally less time lag than their printed counterparts, computerized information retrieval may not necessarily be faster than manual reference work. Looking up a single item in a printed dictionary or encyclopedia, for instance, is usually quicker than a computer search.

Another shortcoming of computerized databases is their limited chronological coverage, often extending back only a few years, and their often limited relevance. Frequently, items listed or displayed may not relate at all to the subject inquiry even though the words match. Repetitive listings are another disquieting aspect of computer searches.

The most serious disadvantage of computerized information retrieval, however, may be the cost to the individual user. Due to conservative American political philosophy that favors limitation of social costs, computerized information retrieval, unlike manual reference work, is not generally adequately tax-supported. To the extent that libraries offer computerized information retrieval, search costs are usually passed on to the end user. This is most unfortunate in political inquiries that produce no immediate pecuniary use value, since political education with a cultivated humanitarian outlook, always in short supply even under the best of circumstances, becomes thereby further restricted for millions of people who are perhaps most in need of it.

A further characteristic of online reference tools is that they are rarely bought or leased directly from the producer or publisher but are made available to library and other institutional or personal subscribers by commercial distributors or vendors. The following companies are major suppliers of online databases for political reference purposes:

- ADP Network Services, Inc., 175 Jackson Place, Ann Arbor, MI 48106
- BRS/Bibliographic Retrieval Services, 1200 Route 7, Latham, NY 12110
- Chase Econometrics/Interactive Data, 150 Monument Rd., Bala Cynwyd, PA 19004
- CompuServe, Inc., 5000 Arlington Centre Blvd., Columbus, OH 43220
- Data Resources, 1750 K Street, NW, Washington, DC 20006
- Dialog Information Services, Inc., 3460 Hillview Ave., Palo Alto, CA 94304

- Dow Jones News/Retrieval, Box 300, Princeton, NJ 08540
- Mead Data Central, 200 Park Ave., New York, NY 10017
- QL Systems Ltd., 1018 Place de Ville, Tower B, 112 Kent Street, Ottawa, Ontario K1P 5P2
- SDC Search Service, 2500 Colorado Ave., Santa Monica, CA 90406
- I.P. Sharp Associates, Ltd., Box 148, Exchange Tower, 2 First Canadian Place, Toronto, Ontario M5H 1J8
- Source Telecomputing Corporation, 1616 Anderson Road, McLean, VA 22101
- West Publishing Company, P.O. Box 3526, St. Paul, MN 55165

Each of these companies issues a frequently revised catalog or other descriptive literature identifying the available databases, service hours, special search features, and terminal compatibility. Potential users of online reference instruments are advised to inquire at the reference desk of the local library about access possibilities, search costs, and available assistance in connection with computerized information retrieval. To assist users in these inquiries the name of the service vendor is included in the bibliographic entry for each computerized reference instrument listed in this guidebook. In addition, a list of the political online reference instruments offered by each vendor is provided under the heading Online databases in the Typology Index. The reader is also alerted to the possibility that many of these computer-readable reference instruments may be usable outside of libraries in homes and offices.

Guidebooks

1   Chen, Ching-chih, and Susanna Schweizer. *Online Bibliographic Searching: A Learning Manual*. New York: Neal-Schuhman, 1981.

2   Fenichel, Carol H., and Thomas H. Hogan. *Online Searching: A Primer*. Marlton, NJ: Learned Information, 1981.

3   Hartner, Elizabeth P. *An Introduction to Automatic Literature Searching*. New York: Marcel Dekker, 1981.

4   Meadow, Charles T., and Pauline Atherton Cochrane. *Basics of Online Searching*. New York: John Wiley, 1981.

In view of the rapid changes and lack of standardization in the online industry, sufficient guidance for the acquisition of required skills in automated literature searching is not readily available. The four guidebooks cited above attempt to introduce the reader to the vocabulary, techniques, and practices of online searching. Unfortunately, the search examples and instructions given in the texts may often be less than adequate for the novice.

Directories

5   *DataPro Directory of Online Services*. Delran, NJ: Datapro Research Corporation, 1982–.

Currently issued in loose-leaf format with monthly updates, the two-volume directory lists and describes about 500 online databases. There are 15 physically separated and tabbed sections, entitled: User's Guide, Inquiry Service, General Index, Applications Index, Company Index, Database Index, Online Services, Company Profiles, Online Databases, Vendor Office Locations, User Ratings, Feature Reports, Vendor Listing Forms, Glossary, and Newsletter. The descriptive online database section is located in Volume 2, divided into alphabetically arranged subsections. Subject listings are found in the applications index, with a separate listing for government information.

6   *Directory of Online Databases*. Santa Monica, CA: Cuadra Associates, 1979–.

The directory provides a quarterly updated inventory of machine-readable databases that are composed of bibliographic, numeric, or other types of information and are commercially or publicly available for online searching. The description of the more than 1,000 databases currently listed includes information on the producer, vendor, subject content, geographical and chronological coverage, and updating frequency. Five indexes offer listings by subject, producer, online service (with names of databases serviced), telecommunication networks by online service, and name of database. Source (numeric or full text) databases are listed in boldface type to differentiate them from bibliographic instruments.

7   *Directory of Online Information Resources*. Kensington, MD: CSG Press, 1983.

Issued in revised editions at irregular intervals, the directory lists online databases with descriptions of their subject and chronological coverage, file size, and access costs. The name of the producer and vendor is also listed. Separate subject, vendor, and producer indexes provide a key to the listed databases. Addresses and telephone numbers of the vendors and producers are listed separately at the end of the book.

8   Hall, James L., and Marjorie J. Brown. *Online Bibliographic Databases: An International Directory*. London: Aslib, 1983.

Considerably smaller than the two previously listed directories, this volume identifies and describes only 200 bibliographic databases. Entries are arranged in alphabetical order by the name of the database and include descriptive information about the subject field covered, printed versions, updating frequency, and other basic details.

9   Schmittroth, John, Jr. *Encyclopedia of Information Systems and Services*. Detroit: Gale Research Company, 1982.

10   *New Information Systems and Services*. Detroit: Gale Research Company, 1982–.

This frequently revised and periodically updated reference work identifies organizations, systems, and services using computer and related new technologies to produce access to bibliographic, full text, directory, numeric, and other types of information in all subject areas. Each of the more than 2,500 entries includes descriptive information items, such as name, address, telephone number, founding date, head of unit, function, scope or subject matter, input sources, holdings, publications, computer-based products and services, availability, etc. Twenty-three separate indexes offer access to the entries for computer-readable databases, publications, library and information networks, software products, abstracting and indexing services, professional organizations, computerized searching, consulting and planning services, database producers and publishers, data collection and analysis, information on demand, library management systems, micrographic applications, online vendors, research projects, current awareness, videotext/teletext, community information and referral systems, document delivery systems, personal name, geographic location, and subject. An all-inclusive master index is also provided. Supplementary entries can be found in the *New Information and Services*, issued periodically by the publisher.

11   Williams, Martha E., Laurence Lannom, and Carolyn G. Robins. *Computer-Readable Databases. A Directory and Data Sourcebook*. White Plains, NY: Knowledge Industry Publications, Inc., for American Society for Information Science, 1982–.

Initially published as a loose-leaf subscription service, this directory is now issued in revised editions at irregular intervals. This edition identifies 773 bibliographic, bibliographic-related, or other natural-language databases. Following an introductory description of the data entries within specific databases, the directory lists databases in alphabetical sequence and describes them under eight categories of information. These include information on the producer and vendor, availability and cost, subject matter and scope, data elements present, data services offered, and user aids available. Four separate indexes by subject, producer, processor, and name are included.

The directory is kept up to date by a monthly periodical, entitled *Database Alert*, that reports on new databases, discontinuation of databases, cost, scope, or coverage changes of the databases. Each issue of the periodical is indexed by distributor and database.

General, Multidocumentary Databases

12   *BRS after Dark*. Latham, NY: Bibliographic Retrieval Services, varying dates. (Vendor: BRS)

BRS after Dark is a low-cost bibliographic retrieval service that allows owners of home computers during evening hours from 6 P.M. to midnight local time to search online for desired information disseminated in books, periodicals, and other documentation media. Users have a choice of several computerized databases, of which the following may contain political information:

- *ABI/Inform*, 1971 – .
- *Books in Print*, Current
- *DOE Energy Database*, 1974 – .
- *ERIC*, 1966 – .
- *Management Contents*, 1974 – .
- *PAIS International*, 1976 – .
- *Psycinfo*, 1967 – .

These databases, more fully described in the appropriate sections of this guidebook, offer bibliographic citations and — with the exception of the *Books in Print* and *PAIS International* databases — abstracts of the literature fitting the search term.

13   *CompuServe*. Columbus, OH: CompuServe Consumer Information Service, current. (Vendor: CompuServe)

As presently constituted, this computerized information service is not a major source for political information, but is likely to become so in the future. It allows the owners of personal computers in homes and offices access to several databases that contain a variety of general, business, and financial information. Political information is limited to Washington, United States, and world news as provided by the *Washington Post*, the *St. Louis Post-Dispatch*, and the *Associated Press Viewdata Wire*. *CompuServe* also includes the *Citibase* and *Site II* databases, which offer statistical data on such items as money supply, interest rates, industrial production, economic indicators, and population characteristics for various geographic and political areas in the United States.

14   *Cross*.

15   *File*.

16   *Term*.
Latham, NY: BRS-Bibliographic Retrieval Services, 1983 – . (Vendor: BRS)

These master indexes, available online from Bibliographic Retrieval Services, serve as selection aids for all the publicly offered BRS databases. *Cross* identifies the number of postings for a search term in the various databases. *File* offers descriptive information about each database, such as subject coverage, type of materials, special features, etc. *Term* provides the searcher with controlled vocabulary or natural-language synonyms for thousands of concepts in the social and behavioral sciences. The synonyms are those terms that occur in the databases and permit proper access to the stored information.

17   *Data Base Index (DBI)*. Santa Monica, CA: Systems Development Corporation, to date. (Vendor: SDC)

Available with the SDC Search Service, this database is the master index to all SDC databases. For each search term entered, a ranked list of the databases in which the term appears is shown. Political terms may appear in social science, business, economics, or multidisciplinary databases.

18   *Dialogindex*. Palo Alto, CA: Dialog Information Services, to date. (Vendor: Dialog — File 411)

This online database is the computerized master index to all Dialog databases. It provides the number of postings for each search term in each of the Dialog databases, thus permitting the user to narrow or broaden the search.

19   *Knowledge Index*. Palo Alto, CA: Dialog Information Services, 1972 – . (Vendor: Dialog)

This index is a service of Dialog Information Services, Inc., that provides, at reduced cost, personal computer users in homes and offices with password access to over ten million citations or summaries of articles, reports, and books stored in several computerized databases, including:

Books in Print
ABI/INFORM
Standard & Poor's News
ERIC
GPO Publications Reference File
NTIS
Magazine Index
Newsearch
National Newspaper Index
Psycinfo

These databases, more fully described in the appropriate sections of this guidebook, cover a considerable amount of political information, published in a variety of formats and drawn from many occupational groups, sources, and subject areas. The chronological coverage varies with each database. Access hours to this index are limited from 6 P.M. to 5 A.M. (the next morning) Mondays through Thursdays, 6 P.M. to midnight on Fridays, 8 A.M. to midnight on Saturdays, and 3 P.M. to 5 A.M. on Sundays. The *Knowledge Index* also allows the user to purchase the full text of documents cited while online. In 1983 document ordering charges were $4.50 plus 20 cents per page photocopied. To initiate service for the *Knowledge Index*, a customer agreement form has to be completed and signed that will allow the vendor to bill charges for the use of this index to the customer's credit cards.

20   *NEXIS.* Dayton, OH: Mead Data Central, 1975–. (Vendor: MDC)

Available directly from the producer, this computerized database system offers the online user full text retrieval of general, political, and economic news and other information from several:

Wire services — AP, Reuters, UPI, Xinhua, and others
Digests — *Facts on File*
Newspapers — *Washington Post, New York Times, Christian Science Monitor, Manchester Guardian Weekly,* and others
Periodicals — *Business Week, Congressional Quarterly Weekly Report, Dun's Review,* the *Economist, Industry Week, National Journal, Newsweek, Oil and Gas Journal, U.S. News and World Report,* and others
Government publications — *Federal Register, Code of Federal Regulations, Federal Reserve Bulletin, Weekly Compilation of Presidential Documents*
Radio Broadcasts — *BBC Summary of World Broadcasts*
Newsletters — *Defense and Foreign Affairs Daily, Defense and Foreign Affairs Weekly, East Asian Executive Reports, Latin America Regional Reports, Latin America Weekly Reports, Middle East Executive Reports, Morgan Guaranty Survey, World Financial Markets,* and others
Encyclopedias — *Encyclopedia Britannica,* including *Britannica Book of the Year*

Updating varies according to the source material used, and occurs typically within 12 hours for wire services, daily for newspapers, and weekly for weekly magazines. Apart from full text retrieval, the user can also search for bibliographic citations and keywords in context (KWIC) formats.

21   *The Search Helper.* Menlo Park, CA: Information Access Corporation, varying dates. (Vendor: IAC)

The computerized *Search Helper* is a low-cost bibliographic retrieval tool that can print out online up to 20 of the most recent citations for articles in newspapers and periodicals on any

- person, including political actors
- place, including political entities
- subject, including legal, social factor, and other political topics, or
- brand name product

Users have a choice of six databases only, namely:

1. The *Magazine Index,* 1977 to 30 days ago
2. The *National Newspaper Index,* 1979 to 30 days ago
3. The *Legal Resource Index,* 1980 to 30 days ago
4. The *Trade and Industry Index,* 1981 to 30 days ago
5. *Management Contents,* 1974 to 30 days ago
6. *Newsearch,* last 30 days

The contents of these six databases, completely retrievable under the Dialog system, are more fully described under their appropriate sections in this guidebook. While selecting only 20 recent citations from these databases, the *Search Helper* does indicate the total number of available references on the desired search item in each chosen database. To facilitate subject inquiries, the producer also issued a printed *Subject Guide to IAC Databases* (Menlo Park, CA: Information Access Corporation, 1982) that lists more than 40,000 topical subject terms used in IAC's databases.

22   *The Source.* McLean, VA: Source Telecomputing Corporation, varying dates. (Vendor: STC)

Accessible from virtually any home or office equipped with a telephone, a modem and a terminal, microcomputer, or communicating word processor, the *Source* may be used to retrieve a variety of political information. Consisting of several computerized databases and electronic communication services, representing nearly 800 specific services, the *Source* permits

1. the monitoring of the schedules of congressional committees, U.S. regulatory agencies, and the president
2. the retrieval of current UPI news stories from around the world
3. the retrieval of political speeches, press conference material, and political commentaries
4. obtaining abstracts from articles in leading business and management periodicals
5. access to corporate income, balance sheet, and stock market data for up to 3,800 companies, as well as economic forecasts, reports, etc.

Chronological coverage varies from file to file, but emphasis is on current information. Further details about the *Source* and its information services can be found in a user's manual supplied with the subscription contract.

23   *Wilsonline*. New York: H. W. Wilson, 1984– . (Vendor: H. W. Wilson)

For many years the H. W. Wilson Company has been the publisher of several printed indexes for important segments of the scholarly as well as the popular nonscientific literature. These indexes, most of which are more fully described in the appropriate sections of this guidebook, include the *Cumulative Book Index*, the *Business Periodicals Index*, *The Reader's Guide to Periodical Literature*, *Book Review Digest*, *Index to Legal Periodicals*, *Applied Science and Technology Index*, and the *Biological and Agricultural Index*.

Wilsonline now offers online access by subject descriptors, title words, and author names to bibliographic citations that continue to be also distributed over the various printed Wilson indexes. While each of the above-named indexes can be searched separately, two, more, or all of the equivalent computerized files can be combined for efficient online searching of all indexed publications relating to a specific topic.

Review Media

24   *Database. The Magazine of Database Reference and Review*. Weston, CT: Online, Inc., 1978– .

25   *Online*. Weston, CT: Online, Inc., 1977– .

26   *Online Review*. Oxford: Learned Information Ltd., 1977– .

27   *Online Chronicle*. Weston, CT: Online, Inc., 1981– .

Among the many periodicals published in the field of computer application, the first three items listed above are specialized publications most useful to online searchers. The three periodicals, issued quarterly and bimonthly, respectively, offer reviews and comparisons of new databases, specific hints of search techniques, and other news of interest to the researcher. *Online Chronicle* is a computerized database that is available with the Dialog system and is updated biweekly. It offers online full text retrieval of the latest news about new databases and other developments in the online industry. Each textual record in the database is derived from the news sections in the *Online* and *Database* magazines and is made accessible by keyword indexing from a controlled vocabulary.

BOOKS

Introduction

Since the invention of the printing press, books have been one of the most efficient carriers for the widespread dissemination of information. They have retained their leading position in academic information systems in spite of the challenges posed by other information carriers, notably the computerized databases, radio and television broadcasts, periodicals, etc. The book has the advantage of being mobile and easy to use. It is flexible in size and arrangement of information. Its production costs, while steadily rising, are still comparatively low. On the other hand, books are the slowest information carriers since they take months or even years to prepare, produce, and distribute. Books are therefore most suitable for carrying information of a static, durable, or historical nature. Books continue to play an important role even in political science, where the proportion of unstable information is relatively high, since they contain a body of knowledge of immense historical and analytical value.

Books are available to the student and researcher in all subject fields and in most major languages, either for purchase from publishers and distributors or for loan use in libraries. The following pages contain listings and descriptions of those printed or computerized reference tools that will identify books by author, title, subject, or location under a variety of usage conditions.

Books For Sale

TRADE BIBLIOGRAPHIES

Trade bibliographies are esssential research tools in all situations where a local library for financial, organizational, or other reasons does not or not yet have a desired book in its collection, or where the purchase of a personal copy of a book is contemplated. Trade bibliographies identify books that are currently in print or in advanced stages of production. Separate series of trade bibliographies exist for books sold by commercial publishers or distributors in the United States, and publishers located in other countries. At present, the general trade bibliographies for United States publishers are not exhaustive since the publications of legal publishers and some research institutions are usually not included. In some instances, a political researcher will therefore be compelled to consult a separate trade bibliography for legal books (i.e., *Law Books Published*, item 1319) and other special lists for books not included in the standard general trade bibliographies.

28   *African Books in Print.* Salem, N.H.: Mansell, 1975 — .

29   *Australian Books in Print.* Melbourne: D. W. Thorpe, 1911 — .

30   *British Books in Print.* London: J. Whitaker, 1874 — .

31   *Canadian Books in Print.* Toronto: University of Toronto Press, 1967 — .

32   *French Books in Print.* Detroit: Gale Research Company, 1972 — .

33   *German Books in Print.* New York: R. R. Bowker, 1972 — .

34   *Italian Books in Print.* New York: R. R. Bowker, 1972 — .

35   *Libros en venta en Hispano-America y Espana.* New York: R. R. Bowker, 1964 — .

These are some of the major trade bibliographies for books published outside the United States in the principal European languages. Books can be identified by author, title, and subject. Additional trade bibliographies are listed in Sheehy's *Guide to Reference Books* and its supplements.

36   *American Book Publishing Record Cumulative 1876 – 1949.* New York: R. R. Bowker, 1980.

37   *American Book Publishing Record Cumulative 1950 – 1977.* New York: R. R. Bowker, 1979.

38   *American Book Publishing Record.* New York: R. R. Bowker, 1960 — .

Currently published monthly with annual cumulations, this reference work lists newly published or reprinted works in a subject arrangement according to the Dewey decimal system. The entries, except those marked otherwise, represent Library of Congress cataloging for books published in the United States or offered for sale by a sole American distributor or agent. Not included are official publications of the federal government and the state governments, dissertations, and serial publications. Access to the subject listings is facilitated by separate author and title indexes, and a list of subject headings with corresponding Dewey decimal and Library of Congress classification numbers.

Two cumulative editions list more than 700,000 works under Dewey decimal classes with separate author and title indexes and a subject guide.

39   *Books in Print: An Author-Title-Series Index to Publishers' Trade List Annual.* New York: R. R. Bowker, 1948 — .

40   *Books in Print: Subject Guide. An Index to the Publishers' Trade List Annual.* New York: R. R. Bowker, 1957 — .

41   *Books in Print Supplement.* New York: R. R. Bowker, 1972/1973 — .

42   *Books in Print Data Base.* New York: R. R. Bowker, 1900 — . (Vendor: BRS; Dialog — File 470)

43   *Booksinfo.* Williamsport, PA: Brodart, Inc. (Vendor: BRS)

These are the printed and computerized reference sources for identifying, by different approaches, books published and currently in print in the United States. Separate printed volumes are issued annually for author/title, title/author, and subject listings of the more than 600,000 books currently available from nearly 14,000 American publishers or distributors. Entries include the date of publication, the name of the publisher, price information, LC card number, and ISBN number. The subject headings are based on Library of Congress subject headings, but almost 60,000 cross-references are also provided. A directory of United States publishers and their addresses is available in the title volumes of the printed reference set. BIP supplements are issued between the annual revisions.

The computerized BIP database, available with the Dialog system, is updated monthly and includes also a record of the paperbound books and forthcoming books. Bibliographic, subject, price details, LC and Dewey decimal numbers are included in *Booksinfo.*

44   *Books in Series 1876 – 1949.* New York: R. R. Bowker, 1982.

45   *Books in Series.* New York: R. R. Bowker, 1984.

Availability of these reference works has rendered one of the most difficult research problems in information retrieval more manageable. Identification of original, reprinted, in-print, and out-of-print books issued in series in the United States since 1876 is now possible by series heading, subject heading, author, and title. More than 3,500 Library of Congress subject headings and over 10,500 cross-references are used to lead the researcher to appropriate series headings. Full bibliographic data are provided on each title in each series. Separate volumes are issued for series, author, and title entries. Indexes by series heading, author/title, subject headings are part of the access mechanism of these trade bibliographies, which also offer price information on currently available books in series.

46   *Books on Demand. Author Guide. Title Guide. Subject Guide.* Ann Arbor, MI: University Microfilms International, 1977—.

Many valuable books originally published from the 1450s through the present time are currently no longer in stock. Through agreement with more than 300 cooperating publishers, however, University Microfilms International makes available more than 84,000 selected out-of-stock books as on-demand reprints. These reprints are full-sized bound books reproduced by a xerographic printing process and made available upon special order on 30-day delivery. Identification of these on-demand reprints is made possible by separate author, title, and subject listings. As thousands of titles are added to the reprint program each year, supplementary listings are issued at appropriate intervals.

47   *Forthcoming Books.* New York: R. R. Bowker, 1966—.

48   *Subject Guide to Forthcoming Books.* New York: R. R. Bowker, to date.

American books just published or scheduled to be published within the next five months are identifiable with the help of these reference works, which update the annual editions of *Books in Print*. Issued bimonthly, these forecasts offer separate author, title, and subject listings. The latter use the main heading Government and Political Science with numerous suitable subdivisions for books of political subject matter.

49   *Guide to Reprints.* Washington, DC: NCR Microcard Editions, 1967—.

Books, journals, and other materials currently out of print but available in reprint form are listed by author in this annual, cumulative trade bibliography. The entries provide the title and date of publication with identification of the reprint publisher. A separate listing, entitled *Announced Reprints*, is published quarterly and lists forthcoming reprints that have been announced by publishers but not yet produced.

50   *Paperbound Books in Print, an Index to Actively Available Inexpensive Reprints and Originals with Selective Subject Guide.* New York: R. R. Bowker, 1955—.

Separate author, title, and subject listings are provided for currently available paperbound books. Entries include price information for these generally inexpensive editions. The subject listings use less than 150 rather broad headings, which include political science, international relations, study aids, history, etc.

51   *The Publishers' Trade List Annual.* New York: R. R. Bowker, 1873—.

The multivolume set, issued annually, is used to identify American books if only the publisher is known. The set is a collection of order lists from several thousand publishers in the United States. The lists are arranged alphabetically by the name of the publisher and offer author, title, and imprint information for books currently available for sale. Beginning with the 1978 issue PTLA also contains a separate section that lists publishers under subject headings that identify their publishing programs. Government, political science, history, law, business, economics, social science, scholarly, reference, bibliography are some of the subject headings used in this section. PTLA is not a complete record of all American books offered for sale since many publishers and many series publications of university presses are omitted.

52   *Publishers' Weekly, the American Book Trade Journal.* New York: R. R. Bowker, 1872—.

53   *Publishers' Weekly. International Edition.* New York: R. R. Bowker, 1970—.

New and forthcoming books are listed and evaluated in this reference publication of the American book trade. A special feature is a weekly listing of current American book production as cataloged by the Library of Congress and arranged alphabetically by author (Weekly Record). The international edition is published at irregular intervals and contains information about new books published outside the United States.

54   *The United States Catalog: Books in Print.* New York: H. W. Wilson, 1928.

55   *Supplement Cumulative Book Index: A World List of Books in the English Language.* New York: H. W. Wilson, 1928—.

This monthly bibliography provides an author, title, and subject listing of books published in the English language anywhere in the world. Government publications, most pamphlets, cheap paperbound books, editions limited to 500 copies, local directories, and ephemeral material are not included. The annual cumulation of CBI constitutes a permanent record of English-language books published in the preceding year.

Books in Libraries

Libraries exist to the number of thousands, and books in libraries exist to the number of millions. These massive book collections would be valueless unless it were possible to locate any desired book by author or by subject.

At least four different patterns of control have emerged to facilitate access to the book literature in libraries, namely, reference instruments dealing with (1) subject headings, (2) library holdings (catalogs), (3) reference books, and (4) scholarly books. The following sections identify the principal general reference works within these control patterns.

SUBJECT HEADING LISTS

Every day students leave libraries convinced that there is no book in the collection on their topic of study. In most instances, however, there is a great deal of book information available in the library, but it is not accessible to the researcher under every word describing the subject of inquiry. Neither all the nouns of the English language nor even all the appropriate scholarly terms of each academic discipline are used as headings in card catalogs. The identification of the proper subject heading under which books are listed in the library catalogs is facilitated by subject heading lists available in nearly all libraries. The following printed subject heading lists exist.

56   Atkins, Thomas V. *Cross-reference Index, a Subject Heading Guide*. New York: R. R. Bowker, 1947.

Since there is no standard set of subject headings used in common by all libraries for all documentation, a cross-reference guide to the appropriate headings employed in some of the most widely used reference tools is of great practical value to the researcher. This reference book presents an alphabetical listing of subject headings in six widely used reference sources for books, periodicals, and newspaper articles, namely, (1) the Library of Congress subject heading list, (2) the Sears list of subject headings, (3) the *Reader's Guide to Periodical Literature*, (4) the *New York Times Index*, (5) the *PAIS Bulletin*, and (6) the *Business Periodical Index*. Usage of this reference tool permits a more consistent identification of the literature pertinent to the subject of inquiry.

57   U.S. Library of Congress. Subject Cataloging Division. *Library of Congress Subject Heading*. 9th ed. Washington, DC: 1980.

————. *Supplements*. 1980– .

Subject headings established by the Library of Congress and currently applied in the catalogs of most academic libraries as well as in several periodical indexes are listed in the ninth edition of *Library of Congress Subject Headings* and its quarterly and annually cumulated supplements. Subject terms used in the library catalogs are printed in boldface type, and synonymous or alternative words not used are printed in lightface roman with a "see" reference directing the user to the appropriate subject term used. Below the subject heading is a record of additional subject headings (sa: see also; xx: see also from)

under which material of a related nature is listed in the catalogs. The subject terms are listed in alphabetical sequence together with the LC (subject) class numbers wherever possible. Four kinds of subdivisions may be used under the subject headings, provided appropriate publications are in the library collection:

1. Topical subdivisions, e.g., economic conditions, foreign relations, history, politics and government, and others
2. Form subdivisions, e.g., bibliography, dictionaries and encyclopedias, directories, maps, and others
3. Period subdivisions, e.g., 1850–1950, 1941– , or other time frames either closed or open-ended
4. Local subdivisions, e.g., by name of political entity

A complete list of all subdivisions that may be used under directly entered place names, such as countries, regions, states or provinces, cities, etc., appears in the supplements. Policy-related information is, however, represented by only seven subdivisional headings, namely, commercial policy, cultural policy, economic policy, full-employment policies, military policy, population policy, and social policy. Several other policies, such as fiscal policy, energy policy, labor policy, monetary policy, as well as population policy show up as separate headings. A few policies, notably foreign exchange policy, foreign policy, industrial policy, immigration policy, law enforcement policy, and transportation policy are not listed under these headings and are at best subsumed under a broader, object-related term. In recent years, the phrase, Government Policy, has frequently been used as a topical subdivision under the subject headings referring to groups of people (i.e., Aged-Government Policy).

58   Westby, Barbara M. *Sears List of Subject Headings*. New York: H. W. Wilson, 1982.

Many catalogs of small college and public libraries are based on this list of subject headings compiled from suggestions by catalogers, teachers of cataloging, and the staff of the H. W. Wilson Company. A majority of the headings, however, are identical with the Library of Congress subject headings. Each subject heading listed includes the classification number of the Dewey decimal classification system suggested for this subject matter. Dewey decimal numbers are also used in many bibliographies for the subject arrangement of the listed items. The current edition of this reference work is the twelfth since its inception and reflects recent ideas, events, or developments.

LIBRARY CATALOGS

A search for book information will ordinarily begin with consultation of the local library catalog that identifies the library's holdings by author, series, subject, and title entries and offers a distinct call number for locating the desired item on the library shelves. In many instances, however, the holdings of the local library will be far too limited to permit an in-depth study of complex problem areas. As a result of budgetary constraints, even the large university libraries in the major metropolitan areas of the United States have frequently less than ideal holdings for many specialized topics of inquiry. While most United States manufacturers are probably able to account for every item produced, a student of politics will often be hard put to extract from the local library catalog a complete publications record of the scholars and other information purveyors in the field of inquiry.

Whether they are concerned with improving their insufficient collections, facilitating access to them, or expediting the delivery of interlibrary loan materials to the user, all libraries must consequently rely on external catalogs that identify book material on a nationwide basis. The titles listed and described on the following pages refer to those computerized and printed catalogs whose scope transcends the holdings of any one library and includes book listings for all or nearly all fields of inquiry.

For ease of retrieval identification, the presently available catalogs are listed according to four categories of access points, namely, (1) multiple access, (2) author or main entry only, (3) subject access only, and (4) title access only.

Multiple Access

59   *Libcon*. Reading, MA: Information Dynamics Corporation, 1965–. (Vendor: SDC)

This computerized database, updated weekly, contains all the MARC records of the Library of Congress in addition to a wide range of foreign-language, audiovisual, and other book material cataloged by the Library of Congress but ordinarily not available in the standard MARC files. There are 23 different categories of bibliographic information accessible for online searching. Cataloged items can be identified through various print commands when only the author, title, series note, subject heading, LC call number, Dewey number, ISBN number, LC card number, publication date, or imprint information of the desired monographs is known. Any combination of these and other bibliographic data, including single words (keywords) from the title of the publication, will suffice for the search statement.

60   *Marc*. Washington, DC: Library of Congress, 1968–. (Vendor: Dialog — File 426)

61   *Remarc*. Arlington, VA: Carrollton Press, 1897–1967. (Vendor: Dialog — Files 421, 422, 423, 424, 425)

Online identification of all books cataloged by the Library of Congress from 1897 to the present is possible by

author, title, subject, series, publication date, and other access points with these two databases available with the Dialog system.

The computerized *Marc* database, updated monthly, contains complete bibliographic records for all books in English since 1968, with added coverage of books in other languages from 1970 to the present.

The computerized *Marc* database contains a record of all English-language works prior to 1968 and other language books up to the date when they entered the *Marc* database. Chronological coverage of the various Dialog files is as follows: File 421, pre-1900 and undated; File 422, 1900–1939; File 423, 1940–1959; File 424, 1960–1969; and File 425, 1970–1980.

62   *The National Union Catalog*. Washington, DC: Library of Congress, 1983–.

Issued in computer output microform (COM), the new microfiche *National Union Catalog* consists of four parts: *NUC Books*, *NUC U.S. Books*, *NUC AV*, and *NUC Cartographic Materials*. Each of these four parts appears as a register with indexes. Entries in the register are numbered in sequence as they are added and contain all the bibliographic information traditionally found on LC printed cards. Four separate indexes by author, title, subject, and series offer access by register number to the complete entries in the register. Each entry in the register also shows the location symbol for the library that did the cataloging. If additional locations of the cataloged item are desired, the cumulative microform edition of the *Register of Additional Locations* must be consulted.

63   *OCLC Catalog*. Columbus, OH: OCLC, Inc., 1967–. (Vendor: OCLC)

64   *RLIN Catalog*. Stanford, CA: Research Libraries Group, 1972–. (Vendor: RLG)

OCLC and *RLIN* are interactive automated systems for cataloging as well as online files of machine-readable bibliographic records for books and other library materials. The *OCLC* database is most useful as a tool for identifying the location of books, serials, manuscripts, maps, music scores, and sound recordings in any of the more than 2,500 participating libraries throughout the United States. Libraries linked to the database can determine the existence and library location of a publication by one or more of ten search keys. The most frequently used search keys are four-character strings derived and truncated from names of authors and titles of publications, but searches by ISBN, LC card number, ISSN, and government document number are also possible. In spite of earlier projections, the retrieval capability of the OCLC system by subject or classification number was still not operational during the early 1980s.

The *RLIN* database contains all MARC records

since 1968 as well as the records of the currently 26 RLG member libraries. Access to the more than 6.5 million records for books and more than 1 million records for serials and other library materials is provided by 18 general indexes and 10 local indexes that apply only to the individual library. The indexes allow online searches by both phrases and free-text words, including subject phrases, title phrase and title word, corporate/conference name phrase and word, author/title combinations, etc. The subject phrase searches act on LC subject headings, but not as yet on LC subdivisions.

Author or Main Entry Access Only

65   *A Catalog of Books Represented by Library of Congress Printed Cards Issued from August 1898 to July 31, 1942.* 167 vols. Ann Arbor, MI: Edwards Bros., 1942–1946 (Reprint ed.: New York: Rowman and Littlefield).

_____ . *Supplement: Cards Issued August 1, 1942–December 31, 1947.* 42 vols. Ann Arbor, MI: J. W. Edwards, 1948 (Reprint ed.: New York: Rowman and Littlefield).

66   U.S. Library of Congress. *Library of Congress Author Catalog: A Cumulative List of Works Represented by Library of Congress Printed Cards, 1948–1952.* 24 vols. Ann Arbor, MI: J. W. Edwards, 1953 (Reprint ed.: New York: Rowman and Littlefield).

67   *The National Union Catalog, 1952–1955; An Author List Representing Library of Congress Printed Cards and Titles Reported by Other American Libraries.* 10 vols. Ann Arbor, MI: J. W. Edwards, 1961.

68   *The National Union Catalog: A Cumulative Author List, 1953–1957; Representing Library of Congress Printed Cards and Titles Reported by Other American Libraries.* 2 vols. Ann Arbor, MI: J. W. Edwards, 1958 (Reprint ed.: New York: Rowman and Littlefield).

69   *The National Union Catalog, Pre-1956 Imprints: A Cumulative List by Author . . . Compiled and Edited with the Cooperation of the L. of C. and the N.U.C. Subcommittee of the Resources Committee of the Resources and Technical Services Div. A.L.A.* 610 vols. London: Mansell, 1968.

70   *The Library of Congress and National Union Catalog. Author Lists 1942–1962. A Master Cumulation.* 300 vols. Detroit: Gale Research Company, 1970.

71   *The National Union Catalog: A Cumulative Author List, 1958–1962.* 54 vols. New York: Rowman and Littlefield, 1963.

72   *The National Union Catalog: A Cumulative Author List, 1963–1967.* Ann Arbor, MI: J. W. Edwards, 1969.

73   *The National Union Catalog, 1956 through 1967.* Totowa, NJ: Rowman and Littlefield, 1970.

74   *The National Union Catalog: A Cumulative Author List, 1968–1972.* Washington, DC: Library of Congress, 1973.

75   *The National Union Catalog: A Cumulative Author List, 1973–1977.* Washington, DC: Library of Congress, 1978 (New York: Rowman and Littlefield).

76   *The National Union Catalog.* Washington, DC: Library of Congress, 1978–1982.

77   *Register of Additional Locations, 1963–1967, 1968–1972, 1973–1979.* Washington, DC: Library of Congress, 1967–1979.

78   *Register of Additional Locations, Cumulative Microform Edition, 1968– .* Washington, DC: Library of Congress, 1980– .

The preceding entries refer to various editions in book form of the author and main entry catalog of books in the Library of Congress, United States government department libraries, and more than 1,100 major libraries in the United States. In view of the cooperative efforts of these libraries to acquire at least one copy of all books of some importance published anywhere in the world, the *National Union Catalog* is of primary importance to the researcher or bibliographer. It provides a retrospective, cumulative inventory by author of the library resources in the United States up to 1982 and permits the authoritative verification of bibliographic information as well as the locating of books in the cooperating libraries.

No printed editions of the *National Union Catalog* were published after December 1982, as it is superceded by the new microfiche *National Union Catalog*, published since January 1983 in register/index format. The *Register of Additional Locations*, issued in various cumulated editions in book form until 1979 and in a cumulative microform edition since 1968, identifies additional locations of books in sequence of LC card numbers.

79   *British Library Automated Information Service (Blaise).* London: British Library, 1950– . (Vendor: Blaise-Line)

80   British Library. *The British Library General Catalogue of Printed Books to 1975.* London: Clive Bingley, 1979–1984.

81   British Library. Reference Division. *General Catalogue of Printed Books, 1976–1982*. London: British Library, 1982.

82   British Museum. Department of Printed Books. *General Catalogue of Printed Books*. London: Trustees of the British Museum, 1931–1966.

————— . *Ten Year Supplement, 1956–1965*. London: Trustees of the British Museum, 1968.

————— . *Five Year Supplement, 1966–1970*. London: Trustees of the British Museum, 1972.

————— . *Five Year Supplement, 1971–1975*. London: British Museum Publications, 1978.

The British Museum, founded by act of Parliament in 1753, contains not only departments concerned with antiquities but also three library departments that together constitute the National Library of Great Britain, now called the British Library. The Department of Printed Books is the largest of the library departments. Its collection of early printed books, early English books, and books in all European languages offers unique research possibilities.

Two printed catalogs exist that provide a complete record of the printed books acquired by the British Museum with imprint dates from the fifteenth century through 1975. The entries in both catalogs are arranged by author, but the great advantage of the new catalog set in 360 volumes is its cumulative aspect that obviates the need to consult supplements.

A general catalog, published in 1982 on microfiche only, records all publications dated 1976 or later, and publications dated 1971–1975 cataloged more recently.

All current monographs and nonmonograph booklets published in the United Kingdom can be identified from the computerized *UK MARC* files offered by the *British Library Automated Information Service*. The current file records UK imprints from 1977 onwards and two retrospective files contain bibliographic data from 1950 through 1976.

Subject Access Only

83   *Subject Index of the Modern Works Added to the Library of the British Museum in the Years 1881–1900*. London: Trustees of the British Museum, 1902, 1903.

84   British Museum. Department of Printed Books. *Subject Index of the Modern Works Added to the British Museum Library*. London: British Museum, 1901– .

Several subject index sets have been published that offer access by subject and country headings to the book collection acquired by the British Museum since 1881.

Under each country, subheadings will be found for books dealing with the following subjects: Army, Colonies, Constitution and Government, History, Law (general systems and codes), Navy, Politics, Social Life, Trade, and Finance. There also exists a separate heading Law with subheadings for commercial law, criminal law, ecclesiastical law, international law, military law, naval and maritime law, etc.

85   U.S. Library of Congress. *Library of Congress Catalog – Books: Subjects; A Cumulative List of Works Represented by Library of Congress Printed Cards*. Washington, DC: Library of Congress, 1950–1982.

Subject identification of books cataloged in the United States with imprint dates from 1945 to 1982 is possible with this printed catalog set available with several quinquennial and annual cumulations. The subject headings under which the catalog entries are arranged are based on the fifth and later editions of the *Library of Congress Subject Headings* and its supplements. No editions of this subject catalog exist after 1982, since subject access to books with imprint dates of 1983 or later is provided by the microfiche *National Union Catalog*, issued in register/index format.

Title Access Only

86   *Cumulative Title Index to the Classified Collections of the Library of Congress: 1978*. Arlington, VA: Carrollton Press, 1980.

Title access to all books catalogued by the Library of Congress from 1897 to 1978 is provided by this reference set in 132 volumes. Entries are arranged in alphabetical sequence by title and include the name of the author or other main entry, date of publication, LC card number, and LC classification number.

GUIDES TO REFERENCE BOOKS

The enormous expansion of printed information in all fields of human knowledge has made the use of special retrieval tools — reference books — absolutely essential. Unfortunately for the user, the reference literature itself, which ideally should be limited in quantity, has proliferated to the point where even moderate-sized libraries have to have thousands of reference books in their collection. In many research situations the retrieval of stored information therefore has to begin with the identification of a suitable reference work with the help of guidebooks for reference books. The titles listed in the following section represent general guides to the reference literature. Apart from these general guides there are, however, numerous other, more specialized guidebooks available that are listed and described according to their scope in the appropriate sections of other chapters in this book.

87   Brewer, Annie M. *Indexes, Abstracts, and Digests*. Detroit: Gale Research Company, 1982.

Apart from directories, bibliographic reference sources, such as indexes, abstracts, and digests are the most heavily needed finding tools in research inquiries. Individual reference works in this category can be quickly identified by academic discipline (political science, law, social sciences, etc.), LC class letters, or keywords with the help of this classified bibliography. It reproduces the pertinent LC cards with full bibliographic information, including call numbers. A table of contents based on the LC classification scheme and a keyword index are included to facilitate access to desired entries.

88   Ethbridge, James H., and Cecilia Ann Marlow. *The Directory of Directories 1983*. Detroit: Gale Research Company, 1982.

Identification and description of the voluminous reference literature in directory format is offered by this guidebook, now in its second edition. Nearly 6,800 directories available in 16 fields of activity are listed as follows: (1) general business directories, (2) specific industries and lines of business, (3) banking, finance, insurance, and real estate, (4) agriculture, forestry, mining, and fishing, (5) law and government, (6) science and engineering, (7) education, (8) social sciences and humanities, (9) biographical directories, (10) arts and entertainment, (11) public affairs and social concerns (12) health and medicine, (13) religious, ethnic, and fraternal affairs, (14) genealogical, veteran, and patriotic affairs, (15) hobbies, travel and leisure, and (16) sports and outdoor recreation. Each entry includes the number of listings and coverage of the directory, its arrangement, size, frequency of publication, and price. Separate title and subject indexes offer additional access to the listings, which are updated by periodic supplements, entitled *Directory Information Service*.

89   Mark, Linda. *Reference Sources*. Ann Arbor, MI: Pierian Press, 1977–.

90   *Reference Services Review*. Ann Arbor, MI: Pierian Press, 1973–.

Keeping up to date with the ever increasing number of new reference works in all fields of knowledge is facilitated by the *Reference Services Review*. The quarterly publication offers reviews of current reference material, an index to the location of additional reviews in the trade or professional literature, and a descriptive inventory of other reference publications received but not yet reviewed. Author and title indexes to all the material reviewed or described are also provided. *Reference Sources* is an annually published guidebook to reference material.

91   Sheehy, Eugene P. *Guide to Reference Books*. 9th ed. Chicago: American Library Association, 1976.

————. *First Supplement*, 1980.

————. *Second Supplement*, 1982.

More than 15,500 reference books in all fields of knowledge are listed and described in the ninth edition of this standard guidebook and its supplements. Listings are classified by academic discipline or major field of knowledge. Entries are categorized by form in the following order: (1) guides and manuals, (2) bibliographies, (3) indexes and abstract journals, (4) encyclopedias, (5) dictionaries of special terms, (6) handbooks, (7) annuals and directories, (8) histories, (9) biographical works, (10) atlases, and (11) serial publications. Because of present inadequacies in the reference literature, these categories do not appear in all subject fields. In order to facilitate the finding of titles, each entry has been given a code number that can be looked up in the index. The guidebook also contains some brief suggestions on the use and study of reference works.

No attempt has been made to provide an exhaustive listing of reference works available in each field. U.S. government and foreign reference works are particularly underrepresented. The guidebook is kept up to date by supplements and new editions.

92   Walford, Albert John. *Guide to Reference Material*. Volume 1, *Science and Technology*; Volume 2, *Social and Historical Sciences, Philosophy and Religion*; Volume 3, *Generalities, Languages, the Arts and Literature*. Phoenix: Oryx Press, 1977–1982.

First published in 1959, this standard British guidebook to reference works issued throughout the world currently appears in three volumes, updated serially. Volume 2, published in 1982, contains 5,000 main entries for reference works in the area of statistics, population, political science, economics, law, public administration, education, commerce, customs and tradition, folklore, Christianity, non-Christian religions, area studies, geography, biography, history, and genealogy. The entries offer more content analysis of the listed titles than Sheehy's guidebook. Suitable subdivisions under the main subject headings identify bibliographies, encyclopedias, dictionaries, annuals, biographies, document collections, and other types of reference works. Each volume in the set contains a comprehensive index by author, title, and subject.

93   Wynar, Bohdan S. *American Reference Books Annual*. Littleton, CO: Libraries Unlimited, Inc., 1970–.

New general reference works as well as specialized

reference books in the social sciences, political science, law, and other fields of knowledge are listed and evaluated in this annual guidebook. The evaluations are often very critical and show the deficiencies of the existing reference literature. For a further evaluation of the listed reference works, citations are provided to reviews in three major reviewing journals, namely, *Choice, Library Journal*, and *Wilson Library Bulletin*.

GUIDES TO SCHOLARLY BOOKS

94   *Choice*. Chicago: Association of College and Research Libraries, American Library Association, 1964 – .

95   Gardner, Richard K., and Phyllis Grumm. *Choice — A Classified Cumulation*. Totowa, NJ: Rowman and Littlefield, 1976.

New scholarly books in each academic discipline are listed and evaluated in this monthly publication of the American Library Association. Each evaluation contains a recommendation concerning possible rejection or purchase by college and university libraries, as well as citations to other books in the same subject area. The evaluations are written by subject experts whose names appear at the end of each periodical issue. A nine-volume set, including one index volume, offers a cumulated subject arrangement of reviews published in the first ten volumes of *Choice* during 1964 – 1974.

96   Voight, Melvin J., and Joseph H. Treyz. *Books for College Libraries*. Chicago, American Library Association, 1975.

The guidebook offers a selective inventory of approximately 38,650 scholarly books considered essential as a core collection for undergraduates in any college or university. All fields of knowledge are covered, including political science. The arrangement of the titles is classified according to the major subdivisions of the Library of Congress classification system. The bibliography is particularly valuable for all students and professors of political science and related disciplines who need to construct basic reading lists as part of course requirements or otherwise need to identify the fundamental literature of a subject field.

Books in Bibliographies

Problems or events of a political nature often generate a substantial literature before they are solved or fully understood. Significant parts of the available literature will frequently be listed in bibliographies prepared by scholars, libraries, or other institutions. Due to the large number of such bibliographies or their form of publica-

tion, bibliographic access to the public leaves much to be desired. The identification and retrieval of bibliographies remains one of the irritating problems faced by researchers in their quest for available information. The following titles are considered most useful for the identification of bibliographies that are published either in book form or as parts of books and periodical articles.

CURRENT BIBLIOGRAPHIES OF BIBLIOGRAPHIES

97   *Bibliographic Index: A Cumulative Bibliography of Bibliographies*. New York: H. W. Wilson, 1937 – .

The index lists by subject those bibliographies that are published as parts of books, periodicals, and pamphlets or appear as separately published items. Comprehensive bibliographies are starred and listed first under the subject heading. The index is published semiannually with bound cumulations each December.

98   *Bibliographische Berichte/Bibliographical Bulletin*. Berlin: Staatsbibliothek Preussischer Kulturbesitz, 1959 – .

A semiannual record of bibliographies in all fields of human knowledge published throughout the world. "Hidden" as well as separately published bibliographies are listed. Several cumulative indexes have been issued by the publisher.

99   Cohan, Leonard. *Readers Advisory Service. Selected Topical Booklists*. New York: Science Associates/International, 1973 – .

A quarterly issued collection of topical subject bibliographies and literature guides prepared by libraries, professional organizations, and government agencies. Subjects covered include a wide range of topics in all fields of human knowledge. Topics of interest to students of politics are frequently included. A cumulative subject, title, and name index provides access to the various bibliographies.

100   Council of Planning Librarians. *Index to Council of Planning Librarians Exchange Bibliographies*. Monticello, IL: Council of Planning Librarians, 1958 – .

More than 1,500 bibliographies have been issued by the council with subject matter covering a wide range of human knowledge. A significant number of these bibliographies is devoted to political or social problems. The listed material includes books as well as periodical articles, dissertations, pamphlets, government publications, etc. The index provides author, keyword in title, and number listings of the bibliographies, which may be either annotated or unannotated.

RETROSPECTIVE BIBLIOGRAPHIES OF BIBLIOGRAPHIES

101   Besterman, Theodor. *A World Bibliography of Bibliographies and of Bibliographical Catalogues, Calendars, Abstracts, Digests, Indexes and the Like.* Lausanne: Societas Bibliographica, 1965–1966.

102   Toomey, Alice F. *A World Bibliography of Bibliographies, 1964–1974.* Totowa, NJ: Rowman and Littlefield, 1977.

The Besterman set is an international bibliography of bibliographies arranged by subject with subdivisions per country. About 16,000 subject headings and subdivisions are used for the more than 117,000 bibliographic volumes listed. Volume 5 in the reference set provides a separate index to authors, serial titles, anonymous works, library catalogs, etc. More recently published bibliographies can be identified in the two-volume set by Toomey, which lists 18,000 bibliographies under 600 subject headings. Only items cataloged by the Library of Congress are included.

103   *Bibliographical Services throughout the World, 1960–1964.* Paris: UNESCO, 1969.

104   *Bibliographical Services throughout the World, 1965–1969.* Paris: UNESCO, 1973.

105   *Bibliographical Services throughout the World, 1970–1974.* Paris: UNESCO, 1978.

These reference books, published in new editions within five-year intervals, identify the bibliographical instruments produced by individual countries throughout the world for books, periodicals, government publications, university theses or dissertations, and maps and atlases.

Books in Reviews

Critical and evaluative reviews of books constitute an effective and much-needed control mechanism for the mass of publications. Since book reviews are scattered throughout thousands of periodicals, newspapers, and other publications, it would be difficult and time-consuming to identify the reviews without a proper reference system. A variety of indexes exists, however, which offer access by author, title, or subject to the massive review literature.

BIBLIOGRAPHIES OF BOOK REVIEW INDEXES

106   Gray, Richard A. *A Guide to Book Review Citations. A Bibliography of Sources.* Columbus, OH: Ohio State University Press, 1968.

Although somewhat out of date, the guidebook will be useful for the identification of older book review indexes and similar reference works. Titles are listed and briefly described under broad subject headings, including sociology, political science, business and economics, law, geography and history, etc. A separate subject index, personal name index, title index, chronology index, and exclusive country of origin index are included.

BOOK REVIEW INDEXES FOR NEWSPAPERS

Book reviews published in newspapers are usually identifiable with the help of indexes that may exist for a particular newspaper or group of newspapers. A lengthy list of such newspaper indexes may be found in a separate section of this guidebook devoted to the reference instruments for newspapers. The indexes ordinarily employ the headings Books Reviewed or Book Reviews for the review listings. Reviews may also be located in the following reference works for the *New York Times*.

107   *The New York Times Book Review, Oct. 1896–.* New York: Arno Press, 1968–.

108   *The New York Times Book Review Index, 1896–1970.* New York: New York Times Corporation, 1973.

109   *The New York Times Index.* New York: New York Times Corporation, 1913–.

Book reviews originally published in the *New York Times* may be located and read in a multivolume set presently issued semiannually under the title *The New York Times Book Review*. The set contains its own indexes, which list the reviews by author, byline, subject, and literary category. The subject listings include the names of persons who have been the subject of biographical books. Political books are usually listed under country names with the subheading politics and government or foreign relations. Regrettably, the subject headings are sometimes not detailed enough or sufficient to provide adequate access to the review material under many research conditions.

There also exists a cumulative index that covers 75 years of book reviewing in the *New York Times*. Indexing to book reviews is also provided under this heading by author in the semimonthly and annual cumulations of *The New York Times Index*, which will identify the date and page number of the newspaper where the review was printed.

BOOK REVIEW INDEXES FOR PERIODICALS

110   *Book Review Digest.* New York: H. W. Wilson, 1905–.

Published monthly (except February and July) with annual cumulations, *Book Review Digest* offers excerpts from book reviews in addition to bibliographic citations to all the reviews used. Currently some 83 periodicals from various subject fields are used as sources of book reviews, but only very few political science journals are covered. Separate subject and title indexes offer additional access to the author-listed entries.

For computerized retrieval of book review citations, see *Wilsonline*, described previously in this guidebooks, as well as the following entry.

111 *Book Review Index*. Detroit: Gale Research Company, 1965 – .

112 *Book Review Index Database*. Detroit: Gale Research Company, 1969 – . (Vendor: Dialog — File 137)

All reviews of books and periodical titles published in over 380 periodicals are identifiable with this index, available in printed form and as a computerized database accessible for online searching in the Dialog system. The printed index, issued bimonthly with annual and decennial cumulations, is arranged by author names, but a title index to the author names is also provided. The computerized *BRI* record includes author, book or periodical title reviewed, document type code (e.g., reference work), source, and publication data of the review, and is searchable in any combination of these.

113 *Current Book Review Citations*. New York: H. W. Wilson, 1976 – .

Book reviews published in more than 1,200 periodicals in all fields of knowledge are cited by author and by title. The index is published monthly with the exception of August, and is also cumulated annually. Foreign-language books and new editions of older books, if reviewed, are included. No subject listings are provided. Many of the review citations also appear in other Wilson indexes, notably the *Social Sciences Index* and the *Humanities Index*.

114 *Index to Book Reviews in the Humanities*. Williamstown, MI: Phillip Thomson, 1960 – .

For the purpose of this index, the humanities include biography, personal narratives, memoirs, philosophy, and history up to 1970, when coverage was dropped. Reviews are taken from about 375 periodicals and newspapers and indexed by author only.

115 *International Bibliography of Book Reviews of Scholarly Literature*. Osnabruck, West Germany: Felix Dietrich, 1971 – .

Reviews from about 550 periodicals published throughout the world are indexed by German, English, and French keywords, by authors reviewed, and by authors of reviews. The reference work is published semiannually.

116 *National Library Service Cumulative Book Review Index, 1905–1974*. Princeton, NJ: National Library Service Corporation, 1975.

This multivolume set is a cumulative index to book reviews cited in *Book Review Digest* from 1905 through 1974, and all reviews from *Library Journal*, 1907 through 1974, *Saturday Review*, 1924 through 1974, and *Choice*, 1964 through 1974. The reference work offers over 560,000 citations with a capability of locating more than one million reviews of books.

DISSERTATIONS AND THESES

Introduction

Dissertations and theses are of major interest to students of political science and other academic disciplines, but these scholarly works are ordinarily not published and available in libraries. This is particularly true for American, British, and Canadian dissertations, which are not normally printed and are often microfilmed or xerographed. Most European dissertations are printed and thus receive more regular distribution through the book trade or library acquisition. American and Canadian dissertations are accessible to the researcher either on interlibrary loan from the university where the dissertation was accepted or by purchase from University Microfilms International (UMI) in Ann Arbor, Michigan, if the dissertation was microfilmed.

The printed and computerized reference sources listed and described below provide information about the existence, content, and availability of American and foreign dissertations in political science and other fields. American dissertations in political science which are either in preparation or recently completed can be identified best through lists published annually in issues of *P.S.*, a quarterly periodical of the American Political Science Association.

Master's theses are not quite so accessible as dissertations but are identifiable to a limited degree in a separate reference work also listed in the section below.

Indexes and/or Abstracts

117 *American Doctoral Dissertations*. Ann Arbor, MI: Xerox University Microfilms, 1955/1956 – .

118 *Comprehensive Dissertation Index 1861–1972*. Ann Arbor, MI: Xerox University Microfilms, 1973.

_____ . *Supplements*. Ann Arbor, MI: Xerox University Microfilms, 1973 – .

119   *Dissertations Abstracts Online.* Ann Arbor, MI: Xerox University Microfilms, 1861–. (Vendor: BRS; Dialog—File 35)

120   *Dissertations Abstracts International.* Section A (The Humanities); Section B (The Sciences and Engineering); Section C (European Abstracts). Ann Arbor, MI: Xerox University Microfilms, 1938–.

The titles cited above comprise a comprehensive reference system for most American and Canadian dissertations accepted at an accredited institution since 1861, when academic doctoral degrees were first granted in the United States. Since 1976 reference coverage also includes an increasing number of European dissertations.

Issued annually, *American Doctoral Dissertations* is designed to list by subject categories and institutions as well as by author all doctoral dissertations accepted by American universities. While the entries contain full author and title information under the name of the degree-granting institution, no references are provided to abstract or order numbers for these documents.

Complete subject category, keyword, and author indexing together with references to order numbers as well as volume, issue, and page numbers for abstracts contained in the *Dissertations Abstracts International* set is provided by the *Comprehensive Dissertation Index* for all American dissertations since 1861 and some foreign dissertations accepted during more recent years. This index set is supplemented by annual and quinquennial cumulations.

Abstracts of doctoral dissertations submitted for microfilming by more than 450 educational institutions in the United States and some foreign countries can be found in a monthly compilation, entitled *Dissertations Abstracts International*, issued since 1938 and in an online display of the computerized database records since July 1980. *Dissertations Abstracts Online* also offers subject, title, and author access to bibliographic citations for virtually every American dissertation accepted at an accredited institution since 1861 and thousands of foreign dissertations included in the files during more recent years. In addition, citations for master's theses have been selectively indexed for online display since 1962. Copies of the complete text of all microfilmed dissertations and theses may be ordered online, by telephone or mail, from University Microfilms International in Ann Arbor, Michigan.

121   Bilboul, Roger R. *Retrospective Index to Theses of Great Britain and Ireland, 1716–1950.* Oxford: European Bibliographical Centre—Clio Press, 1975.

122   *Index to Theses Accepted for Higher Degrees by the Universities of Great Britain and Ireland and the Council*

for National Academic Awards. London: Aslib, 1950/1951–.

Some 50,000 theses accepted for higher degrees in the universities of Great Britain and Ireland between the early eighteenth century and 1950 are indexed separately by author and subject in a five-volume retrospective index set. Volume 1, *Social Sciences, Arts and Humanities*, indexes 13,000 theses in politics, economics, business, history, sociology, law, education, religion and theology, psychology, philosophy, anthropology, art, language and literature. Theses written after 1950 are identifiable in the annual Aslib index. Suitable symbols indicate the availability of the thesis for interlibrary loan, photocopying, or consultation.

123   *Master Abstracts.* Ann Arbor, MI: University Microfilms International, 1962–.

A small number of American colleges and universities cooperate in this quarterly reference service for master's theses. Abstracts of the master's theses are arranged by discipline, including political science, economics, history, and sociology. The full text of the listed and abstracted theses is available on microfilm or xerography at reasonable rates from the publisher.

MICROPUBLICATIONS

Introduction

Microfilms, microcards, microfiches, and other microforms are slow but otherwise efficient carriers of scientific, official, and unscientific information in all fields of human knowledge. Most micropublications are simply duplicates in microprint of previously published documentation and are produced many months or years after the publication dates of the original documents. As a general characteristic, micropublications therefore offer information that is of historical value or of a durable quality. Micropublications are more efficient information carriers than books, periodicals, or newspapers since considerably more information can be carried on a given amount of space as a result of print reduction. For that reason microforms are becoming available in ever increasing numbers in academic libraries of the United States and other countries.

For purposes of bibliographic control and information access, it is useful to distinguish between two different categories of micropublications:

1. Micropublications that are merely duplicates of individual books, long runs of back issues of a single periodical or newspaper, or single, previously unpublished documentation items

2. Micropublications that constitute a special collection of information material taken from a variety of previously published or unpublished source documents

Access to microform material of the first category presents no special problem and is facilitated by the same bibliographic instruments that exist for the original documentation. Library catalogs, periodical and newspaper indexes, for instance, will provide access to the information regardless of whether it is carried in books, periodicals, newspapers, or microforms of them. Access to the informational content of microform collections, however, often poses difficulties because of inadequate bibliographic control. As a general rule libraries do not prepare analytic cards for each information item in a microform collection, and not all microform collections possess external retrieval aids. On the other hand, there are many microform collections, such as the *Human Relations Area Files* or the *Library of American Civilization*, for which excellent printed bibliographic tools have been specially produced. Many of these special bibliographic instruments for microform collections are listed and described in this guidebook under sections that are most appropriate to the scope of the microform sets. The following titles, however, are useful as general reference tools for all categories of micropublications since they offer access by author, title, and main subject field.

Bibliographies

124   *Guide to Microforms in Print*. Washington, DC: Microcard Editions, 1961 – .

Books, periodicals, newspapers, government publications, and other documentation available on microfilm or other microforms are identifiable in this annually revised trade bibliography. Only micropublications from American publishers are listed, but the information content of the microforms may originate in the United States as well as in other countries and may be in English or other languages. Separate volumes are issued for author/title and subject entries. The subject listings are arranged under broad LC based headings, including Political Science — Official Documents; Political Science — General Works; Political Science — Theory of the State; International Law, etc. A list of microform publishers and their addresses is included.

125   *Microform Review*. Westport, CT: Microform Review, 1972 – .

126   *Microlist*. Westport, CT: Microform Review, 1977 – .

These quarterly reference aids offer annotated listings of new microform collections or other micropublications. *Microform Review* contains evaluative, critical reviews for microform collections and identifies the external or internal retrieval aids supplied with the collections. *Microlist* provides an international record of new micropublications.

Union Lists

127   Zlendich, Janice. *Union List of Microform Sets in the Libraries of the California State University and Colleges*. Fullerton, CA: California State University, Fullerton, 1976.

This is one of many union lists that identify library holdings of microform collections on a regional or institutional basis. For the identification of other union lists, readers are advised to consult the reference desk at the local library.

NEWSPAPERS AND NEWS RETRIEVAL TOOLS

Introduction

Much political information is disseminated by newspapers, either exclusively or ahead of subsequent publication in periodicals or books. As important sources of political information, newspapers exhibit, however, distinct characteristics in terms of content coverage while posing special problems of identity, evaluation, and accessibility. Although not as fast as radio or television transmissions, newspapers are an excellent daily as well as historical source of information about

- events, i.e., natural or man-made occurrences that may influence political processes or policies
- political actors, i.e., political personalities and organizations, their lives and actions
- speeches, statements, and commentaries (editorials) on policy, social, election campaign, or other issues
- attitudes and opinions as revealed by the results of public opinion polls
- social conditions, trends, or developments affecting all or specific societal groups in distinct areas or political entities

These categories of information are reported on the local, state, national, and international level, but the resulting portrayal of political reality is generally somewhat distorted. Nearly all newspapers report only what is considered unusual, illegal, or negative and do not regard ordinary, socially adapted human behavior or routine political activities as newsworthy. Frequently, not even all newsworthy items of information are reported because of restrictive editorial or business considerations by the newspaper.

Unlike books and periodicals, newspapers are not easily separable into scientific, official and nonofficial publications. It is true, of course, that some newspapers — usually in Europe or in Communist countries — are official publications, while other newspapers — usually in the United States — are entirely nonscientific publications. A great many newspapers, however, contain a varying mixture of scientific, official, and nonscientific information of a political nature. Many papers are organs of political parties or spokesmen for specific interest groups, making them specialized instruments of political indoctrination or political socialization. Only a selected number of newspapers are distinguished by their overall excellence and these often reflect the thinking of elite groups in society. Many other papers, although not of distinguished quality, may be important because of their geographic setting.

Recent developments in the technology of information dissemination have also affected the newspaper industry, and news or feature information is now carried by news agency wire as well as by printed and electronic newspapers. This information is, of course, only as useful as it is accessible to the researcher. Accessibility and retrievability of political news and feature items originally disseminated by news agencies and newspapers is facilitated by five kinds of reference instruments, namely:

1. *Guidebooks and bibliographies*. These instruments usually identify newspapers by country or city of publication and list circulation figures, editors, editorial bias, and other important details. Guidebooks often offer evaluative and critical comments about individual newspapers and survey the general press situation in the country of publication.
2. *Union Lists*. These reference works identify the location of individual newspapers in libraries or in the vaults of producers of newspapers in microform. Union lists are compiled on a regional, institutional, or countrywide basis. These lists are indispensable locator tools in the event that the local library does not hold a copy of the desired newspaper.
3. *Indexes*. Available in printed and/or computerized format, indexes identify by name or key term the subject content of individual articles in newspapers. They offer citations for the date, page, and column numbers of the newspaper where the desired article is printed. While printed indexes are issued only on the basis of monthly or longer time intervals, some computerized indexes are updated daily. A large number of newspaper indexes are prepared for a single

newspaper only, but several indexes for multiple coverage of newspapers also exist.
4. *Full text retrievers*. These are computerized databases that offer the user full text retrieval of news and feature items originally carried by news agency wire, a single newspaper, or several newspapers. All material is retrievable by using index terms and/or free-text searching. The search results may be viewable on terminals only or printed either online or offline.
5. *Press digests*. These reference works present a survey of the opinions and news stories published by the newspapers of a particular country. Important articles from various newspapers are selected for inclusion in the digests in abridged, excerpted, or unabridged form. Several digests exist to provide English-language translations from foreign-language newspapers. Many of these digests are prepared by American embassies abroad but are available for limited distribution only. Digests are usually issued on a daily or weekly basis.

The following titles represent the most useful reference aids for American, European, and other newspapers within the five categories enumerated above.

Guidebooks

128   Kurian, George Thomas. *World Press Encyclopedia*. New York: Facts on File, 1982.

The two-volume set offers a survey of the state of the press in 180 countries of the world. Information is arranged under four sections, namely, (1) The International Press, (2) The World's Developed Press Systems, (3) Smaller & Developing Press Systems, and (4) Minimal and Underdeveloped Press Systems. The elite newspapers, international information politics, press laws, and press councils are covered in the first section. The remaining three sections follow a country arrangement, and offer a survey of the press on the economic, political, professional and philosophical level. State-press relations are well described. Circulation figures and other basic data are provided. Bibliographies and listings of news agencies, media multinationals, press-related associations, unions, and organizations, as well as an index are included.

129   Merrill, John Calhoun, and Harold A. Fisher. *The World's Great Dailies: Profiles of Fifty Elite Newspapers*. New York: Hastings House, 1979.

In the midst of a vast desert of global mediocrity, there are only a handful of newspapers that offer reliable news, reasoned commentaries, and other high-quality reporting. This reference work provides a detailed profile of 50 leading newspapers regarded as the "elite" press because the papers are read by the elites and represent the very best in political news reporting and public opinion making. Selected bibliographic listings and an index are included.

130   Wynar, Lubomyr R., and Anna T. Wynar. *Encyclopedia Directory of Ethnic Newspapers and Periodicals in the United States*. Littleton, CO: Libraries Unlimited, 1976.

This reference book identifies 977 newspapers or periodicals issued by or for 63 ethnic groups in the United States. The arrangement of the entries is by individual ethnic group, but some presses are listed on the basis of language only, such as the Arabic press or the Spanish press. Entries offer information about the publisher, editor, sponsor, language, circulation, frequency, subscription rate, and editorial emphasis. Introductory sections in the reference volume provide useful statistical data and a description of the role and present status of the ethnic press. A title index to the listed publications is also included. The reference work does not cover the black American press, which can be identified in the *Editor and Publisher International Yearbook* or *Ayer Directory of Newspapers and Periodicals*. Similarly, the Indian press is not listed, for which Arnold Marquise's A *Guide to American Indians* (Norman: University of Oklahoma Press, 1974) should be consulted in addition to the above-listed directories.

Current Bibliographies

131   *Editor and Publisher International Yearbook*. New York: Editor and Publisher Company, 1920 – .

The annual reference book lists United States newspapers by state and city, and foreign newspapers by continent, country, and city. Apart from the title, the addresses, names of key personnel, political orientation, circulation figures, etc., are given. Separately listed are weekly newspapers of the United States, Negro (black) newspapers, and the principal foreign-language newspapers of the United States. Listings are also provided for the foreign press correspondents in the United States, and the feature news and picture syndicates.

132   *N. W. Ayer and Son's Directory of Newspapers and Periodicals*. Philadelphia: N. W. Ayer and Son, 1880 – .

The reference work, issued annually, lists the newspapers and daily periodicals of the United States, Canada, Bermuda, Panama, and the Philippines only. Entries are arranged by state and city and indicate political preference and circulation figures. Brief additional information is also given about the population, agricultural and industrial production, etc., of each city where the newspaper is published. Separate listings are included for weekly newspapers, newspaper syndicates, college publications,

foreign-language newspapers, Negro (black) newspapers, etc.

133   *Political Handbook and Atlas of the World*. New York: Harper & Row, 1927 – .

The political or party affiliation of the newspapers published in the various countries of the world can be identified in this regularly revised reference work. Since only prominent newspapers most likely to be quoted abroad are listed, many papers of large circulation or strong local influence may be omitted. Additional information is provided for political parties, the composition of the legislature, and the degree to which the press of the country is state-controlled.

134   *Underground Press Directory*. Stevens Point, WI: Counterpoint, 1967 – .

A relatively new phenomenon on the American press scene is the appearance of newspapers that express radically different viewpoints and report about repressed or social behavior. These papers are in a constant state of flux, with new newspapers appearing or others disappearing. The revised editions of this bibliographic volume list all new publications in addition to existing newspapers of this category.

135   *The Working Press of the Nation*. Vol. 1, *Newspapers and Allied Serials Directory*. Burlington, IA: National Research Bureau, 1974 – .

The annually revised volumes of this reference set contain listings of newspapers, news services, newsreels, and photo services arranged under 13 sections. Separate sections exist for daily newspapers, weekly newspapers, special interest newspapers, black newspapers, religious weekly newspapers, foreign-language newspapers published in the United States, Sunday magazine newspaper supplements, daily newspapers with weekend television sections. The political orientation and size of circulation are indicated. The names of the executive and editorial staff are listed, together with the full address of the newspaper publisher. The entries are arranged by state and city, but no index to the listings is included.

Union Lists

136   *The Center for Research Libraries Catalogue — Newspapers*. Chicago: Center for Research Libraries, 1978.

The Center for Research Libraries is a nonprofit organization operated and maintained by nearly 200 American and foreign universities for the purpose of increasing the library materials available to their readers for research. The catalog lists a majority of the approximately 3,000 foreign and domestic newspapers housed at and available from the center. Entries are arranged by title in alphabetical sequence and show place and frequency of publication, extent of holdings, and variations in title, if any. The catalog is updated by the center's *Handbook*, which is frequently revised and contains listings of the center's more recent acquisitions. In principle, any newspaper file, U.S. or foreign, needed for research is available from the center. If a newspaper is not already in the collection, the center will try to acquire it as quickly as possible.

137   Milner, Anita C. *Newspaper Indexes: A Location and Subject Guide for Researchers*. Metuchen, NJ: Scarecrow Press, 1977, 1979, 1982.

Several hundred indexes available for newspapers throughout the United States can be identified with the help of this reference book issued in several revised editions. Entries are arranged by state and county and include the name of the indexed newspaper, the years of index coverage, and an alphabetical code for the index repositories. The codes are listed alphabetically in the second half of the book, where the full name and address of the library or person offering in-house or commercial indexing of the newspaper is provided. Fees for checking the index or making a photocopy of a specific article are indicated. Interlibrary loan services, if available, are also mentioned. American foreign-language newspapers as well as church publications are separately listed.

138   U.S. Library of Congress. Catalog Publication Division. *Newspapers in Microform: United States, 1948–1972*. Washington, DC: Library of Congress, 1973.

_____ . *Newspapers in Microform: United States, 1973–1977*. Washington, DC: Library of Congress, 1978.

_____ . *Newspapers in Microform: Foreign Countries, 1948–1972*. Washington, DC: Library of Congress, 1973.

_____ . *Newspapers in Microform: Foreign Countries, 1973–1977*. Washington, DC: Library of Congress, 1978.

_____ . *Newspapers in Microform, 1978–*. Washington, DC: Library of Congress, 1979–.

These reference works constitute a continuing, partially cumulative series that brings under bibliographic control American and foreign newspapers that have been reduced to microform and are housed permanently in United States, Canadian, and other libraries as well as in the vaults of domestic and foreign commercial producers of microforms. Separate cumulative volumes are issued

for United States newspapers and the newspapers of foreign countries, but the annual supplements issued since 1978 contain combined listings. The bibliographic entries contain information about the location of the microforms and the publication dates of the holdings. Listings are arranged alphabetically by geographical headings (i.e., by country, state or province, and city) but title indexes are also included. More than 60,000 United States newspapers and over 20,000 foreign newspapers have so far been listed, together with their locations. Between the annual supplements the *Newspaper and Gazette Report*, issued three times annually, provides updated listings.

139   Wilcox, Dennis L. *English-language Dailies Abroad: A Guide to Daily Newspapers in Non-English Speaking Countries*. Detroit: Gale Research Company, 1967.

The existence of English-language newspapers in many non–English-speaking countries assumes great importance for students of political science in search of journalistic information originating in foreign countries. This reference work contains a union list of foreign English-language newspapers available in United States libraries, citing 202 newspapers from 56 foreign countries or regions. Entries include information about editorial policy, content, socioeconomic class of readership, news agencies used, etc.

Indexes

SINGLE NEWSPAPERS

140   *The Chicago Sun-Times, Bell & Howell's Newspaper Index to*. Wooster, OH: Bell & Howell, 1979–.

141   *The Chicago Tribune, Index to*. New York: New York Times Company, 1982–.

142   *The Chicago Tribune, Bell & Howell's Newspaper Index to*. Wooster, OH: Bell & Howell, 1971–.

143   *The Christian Science Monitor, Bell & Howell's Newspaper Index to*. Wooster, OH: Bell & Howell, 1951–.

144   *The Denver Post, Bell & Howell's Newspaper Index to*. Wooster, OH: Bell & Howell, 1979–.

145   *The Detroit News, Bell & Howell's Newspaper Index to*. Wooster, OH: Bell & Howell, 1976–.

146   *The Houston Post, Bell & Howell's Newspaper Index to*. Wooster, OH: Bell & Howell, 1976–.

147   *The Los Angeles Times, Bell & Howell's Newspaper Index to.* Wooster, OH: Bell & Howell, 1972—.

148   *The Milwaukee Journal, Bell & Howell's Newspaper Index to.* Wooster, OH: Bell & Howell, 1976—.

149   *The New Orleans Times-Picayune, Bell & Howell's Newspaper Index to.* Wooster, OH: Bell & Howell, 1972—.

150   *The New York Times Index.* New York: New York Times Company, 1851—.

151   *Palmer's Index to the Times Newspaper, 1790—1941.* London: Samuel Palmer, 1869—1943. Reprint ed. New York: Kraus Reprint Company, 1965.

152   *The San Francisco Chronicle, Bell & Howell's Newspaper Index to.* Wooster, OH: Bell & Howell, 1976—.

153   *The St. Louis Post-Dispatch, Bell & Howell's Newspaper Index to.* Wooster, OH: Bell & Howell, 1980—.

154   *The Times: Index to the Times.* London: Times Publishing Co., 1906—.

155   *The Wall Street Journal Index.* Wooster, OH: Bell & Howell, 1955—1957. Princeton, NJ: Dow Jones Books, 1958—.

156   *The Washington Post, Bell & Howell's Newspaper Index to.* Wooster, OH: Bell & Howell, 1971—.

157   *USA Today, Bell & Howell's Newspaper Index to.* Wooster, OH: Bell & Howell, 1983—.

All Bell & Howell's newspaper indexes are issued monthly in printed form with annual cumulations. They contain separate listings for personal names and subjects. Foreign events are usually listed in the subject index sections by name of country. Some policy information is listed by name of policy, e.g., economic policy, foreign policy, or military policy. Names of political organizations show up inconsistently as subject headings.

The *New York Times Index* is issued semimonthly in printed form with annual bound cumulations. It also contains brief abstracts of each news story.

The *Index to the [London] Times* is printed in monthly editions and annual cumulations. The newspaper suspended publication in 1978 but resumed publication in late 1979.

158   *Newsbase.* London: Fintel Ltd., 1981—. (Vendor: BRS)

Bibliographic references and abstracts for company and business information published in the London and Frankfurt editions of the *Financial Times* can be retrieved online from this computerized database available from Bibliographic Retrieval Services. The database is updated weekly.

159   *The Official Washington Post Index.* Woodbridge, CT: Research Publications, 1979—.

160   *Washington Post Index.* Woodbridge, CT: Research Publications, 1979—. (Vendor: Dialog — File 184)

News and feature stories on topics and people published in the *Washington Post* since 1979 can be identified with this index, available in monthly and annually cumulated printed editions as well as in online format. Editorials, letters to the editor, special commentaries, and book reviews are also indexed. All index citations refer to the microfilm edition of the *Washington Post*, which is widely available in libraries.

MULTIPLE COVERAGE

161   *The African Newspaper Index.* Langley Park, MD: Current Documents and Information, 1981—.

Published semiannually, the index selectively indexes articles in the *Daily Graphic* (Ghana), the *Daily Nation* (Kenya), the *Gambia News Bulletin* (Gambia), the *Herald* (Zimbabwe), and the *Zambia Daily Mail* (Zambia). Entries are arranged under geographical headings subdivided by topics. Domestic as well as international African political material is covered. Separate geographical and personal name indexes are included. The considerable time lag and omission of regionally important newspapers from Nigeria, Tanzania, and other countries impair the usefulness of this index for current events coverage.

162   *Alternative Press Index.* Baltimore: Alternative Press Center, 1969—.

More than 30 newspapers that publish unconventional, radical, or alternative viewpoints in the United States and Canada are indexed in this quarterly reference publication.

163   *California News Index.* Claremont: Center for California Public Affairs, 1970—1976.

The index was published twice a month with quarterly cumulative issues. It offers access to information about California published in 13 newspapers and periodicals during the early 1970s. The indexed newspapers include the *Los Angeles Times, Sacramento Bee, San Diego Union,* and *San Francisco Chronicle.* Indexing is selective and covers only government and politics, social and environmental issues, business and economics, education and cultural affairs, historical and biographical material relating to California.

164   *Canadian News Index.* Toronto: Information Access, 1977—.

165   *CNI. Canadian News Index.* Toronto: Micromedia Ltd., 1977—. (Vendor: BRS, QL Systems Ltd., SDC)

Events and people making the news in Canada and around the world are identifiable with this index, available in monthly and annually cumulated printed editions as well as a monthly updated computerized database. The printed edition contains separate sections for biographical and subject entries. References are provided to seven Canadian newspapers, namely, the *Calgary Herald, Chronicle Herald, Montreal Gazette, Toronto Globe and Mail, Toronto Star, Vancouver Sun,* and *Winnipeg Free Press.*

166   *Editorials on File.* New York: Facts on File Publications, 1970—.

Newspaper editorials express important public reactions to public policies, political events and personalities. Published twice monthly, this reference work indexes and reprints editorials from some 125 American and Canadian newspapers that represent more than 40 percent of the total newspaper circulation in the United States and Canada. Each issue reprints about 200 editorials covering various opinions on 8 to 12 selected topics. Each topic is introduced by a brief summary of the factual background of the editorial. Monthly, quarterly, and annual cumulative indexes provide a key to the chronologically filed editorials.

167   *France-Actualité; Index de la Presse Ecrite Française.* Quebec: Microfor Inc., 1978—.

168   *France Actualité.* Quebec: Microfor, Inc., 1978—. (Vendor: European Space Agency)

Selective bibliographic citations and abstracts for information published in the French daily newspapers *Le Monde, Le Figaro,* and *L'humanité,* as well as complete indexing for the French weeklies *Le Nouvel Observateur* and *Le Point* are provided by this index, available in monthly and annually cumulated printed editions and as a monthly updated computerized database. The printed index is issued in two parts, containing an alphabetically arranged subject section and a chronological section with abstracts of the indexed articles. All information is in French only, but a French-English glossary of the subject descriptors is issued quarterly.

169   *Index to Black Newspapers.* Wooster, OH: Bell & Howell, 1977—.

170   *Index to Black Newspapers.* Wooster, OH: Bell & Howell, 1979—. (Vendor: SDC)

Bibliographic citations for articles published in ten prominent black newspapers in the United States can be obtained from this index, available in printed as well as computerized format. Indexing covers the *Amsterdam New York News, Atlanta Daily World, Baltimore Afro-American, Bilalian News, Chicago Defender, Cleveland Call and Post, Norfolk Journal and Guide, Los Angeles Sentinel, Michigan Chronicle, New Pittsburgh Courier.* Updating frequency for both reference formats is quarterly.

171   *Indian News Index.* Ludhiana, India: Panjab University, Extension Library, 1965—.

Up to 25 English-language newspapers published in India are indexed in this quarterly reference publication. The index contains subject, name, and geographical entries. The *Times of India, Hindustan Times, Free Press Journal* are among the papers indexed.

172   *The Information Bank.* New York: New York Times Company, 1969—. (Vendor: Mead Data Central)

Abstracts from and bibliographic citations to articles published about current events, political actors, and economic, social and political affairs in American newspapers can be retrieved online from this daily updated, computerized database. The following newspapers are selectively covered: *Atlanta Constitution, Chicago Tribune, Christian Science Monitor, Houston Chronicle, Los Angeles Times, Miami Herald, New York Times, San Francisco Chronicle, Seattle Times, Wall Street Journal,* and the *Washington Post.* Two different software packages are available for searching, using either a locked step, controlled vocabulary or a free-text search language. It is possible to focus on the desired news item by publication date, newspaper source, type of material (editorial, letter to the editor, news analysis, biographical sketch, obituary) or graphics (photos, charts, maps, etc.). Items are added to the database 24 hours after publication in the *New York Times* and on a priority schedule for other newspapers.

The controlled vocabulary for searching the *Information Bank* is listed in a printed *Information Bank Thesaurus* (New York: New York Times Company, 1981) that identifies terms for subjects, organizations, geographic and political entities in alphabetical sequence. A separate categories guide in the thesaurus lists terms from 70 major subject areas under ten broad categories, notably business and finance, politics and government, law, military, social conditions and trends, etc. It is noteworthy that the thesaurus does not offer a complete listing of all institutional political actors under each country and contains almost no terms for specific governmental policies.

173   *Monitor*. Wooster, OH: Bell & Howell, 1979—. (Vendor: SDC)

174   *Newspaper Index (NDEX)*. Wooster, OH: Bell & Howell, 1976—. (Vendor: SDC)

These two databases, available with SDC's Orbit system, offer online access to bibliographic citations for articles published in several American newspapers. While the *Monitor* corresponds to the printed index for the *Christian Science Monitor*, albeit with reduced retrospective coverage, the *Newspaper Index* is the equivalent of several, separately printed indexes. Indexed are the *Chicago Sun-Times, Chicago Tribune, Denver Post, Detroit News, Houston Post, Los Angeles Times, New Orleans Times-Picayune, San Francisco Chronicle, St. Louis Post-Dispatch*, the *Washington Post*, and ten black newspapers. Bibliographic records include author, title, and terms describing the content or form (photo, editorial, letter, etc.) of each news item. Since the database is updated on a monthly basis, it cannot be used for very current news events.

175   *National Newspaper Index*. Menlo Park, CA: Information Access Corporation, 1979—.

176   *National Newspaper Index*. Menlo Park, CA: Information Access Corporation, 1979—. (Vendor: Dialog—File 111; IAC)

Information published in three American elite newspapers, the *Christian Science Monitor*, the *New York Times* and the *Wall Street Journal* is identifiable by subject, name, or country with this monthly index, available in a COM (computer output microfilm) edition and as a computerized database. All articles, editorials, letters to the editor, obituaries, biographical pieces, cartoons, illustrations, and reviews are included, but stock market tables and weather reports are omitted. Both the COM edition and the online database yield all necessary bibliographic citations for locating the desired information in the three newspapers.

177   *The Newsbank*. New Canaan, CT: Newsbank, Inc., 1970—.

News reports about events and developments in more than 100 American cities are selected from some 200 United States newspapers. A monthly printed index lists the news reports under three main categories: (1) political development, (2) government structure, and (3) law and order, with numerous subheadings, such as blacks in politics, Chicanos in politics, clergymen in politics, labor in politics, mass media politics, budgets, government operations, lobbying groups, metropolitan governments, taxation, civil liberties, judicial administration, police, prisons, trials, violence, etc. Articles listed are available on microfiche together with the printed indexes. The

producer also offers an on-demand search service of its computerized database.

178   *Newsearch*. Menlo Park, CA: Information Access Corporation, current month only. (Vendor: Dialog—File 211; IAS)

Very current news stories, information articles, and book reviews published in over 1,400 newspapers or periodicals can be identified with the help of this computerized database, available with the Dialog system and as part of IAC's own *Search Helper*. Every working day the previous day's news stories from the *Washington Post* and the *Los Angeles Times* as well as other periodical and newspaper articles are indexed and the bibliographic citations added to the database. They are retrievable online from this database until purged on the Friday following the thirteenth of every month. Purging occurs after all citations from the previous month have been added to IAC's other databases, namely, the *Magazine Index*, the *National Newspaper Index*, the *Trade and Industry Index* and the *Legal Resource Index*. While there is a brief overlap period of a maximum of four days with these other databases, *Newsearch* is one of the most current bibliographic retrieval tools for events and other news stories published in American newspapers.

179   *Svenska Tidnings Artiklar*. Stockholm: 1953—. Lund, Sweden: Berlingska Boktryckeriet.

Articles published in Swedish newspapers are made accessible by subject or name with the help of this printed index.

180   *Zeitungsindex*. Pullach bei Munchen, West Germany: Verlag Dokumentation, 1974—.

German-language newspapers published in three European countries — the Federal Republic of Germany, Austria, and Switzerland — are indexed by subject term and geographical and personal names in this quarterly reference work. The index covers the *Neue Züricher Zeitung* and *Die Weltwoche*, published in Switzerland, *Frankfurter Allgemeine Zeitung, Stuttgarter Zeitung, Die Welt, Die Zeit, Süddeutsche Zeitung*, and several other West German newspapers as well as Austria's *Die Presse*. The news periodical *Der Spiegel* is also included in the index.

Full Text Retrievers

181   *Dow Jones News/Retrieval Service*. New York: Dow Jones and Company, 1974—. (Vendor: BRS; Dow Jones)

Current news and other data from the *Wall Street Journal, Barron's*, and the Dow Jones newswire, as well as selected stories from the *New York Times* can be retrieved online from this continually updated computerized database. In addition, quotes, 10-K extracts, and company profiles on all corporations listed on the New York and American stock exchanges can be retrieved from the *Disclosure Outline* files that are now part of the database. Information is retrieved by the use of category symbols that identify data by issuing agency (e.g., Congress, Justice Department, U.S. Supreme Court, FCC, FTC, etc.), by subject (e.g., economic news, federal government news, labor news, monetary news, etc.), industrial category (e.g., airlines, autos, banks, petroleum, etc.) or by market quotes requests for bonds, U.S. Treasury notes, preferred stocks, etc.

182   *Info Globe*. Toronto: Info Globe, 1977–. (Vendor: Info Globe)

The full text of all articles appearing in *The Globe and Mail,* Canada's national newspaper, can be searched and retrieved with this computerized database. The current day's paper is available by 8 A.M. each morning. A printed *Info Globe User's Manual* is available.

183   *The New York Times On Line (NYTOL)*. New York: New York Times Information Service, 1980–. (Vendor: Mead Data Central)

Full text retrieval of all articles appearing in the *New York Times* since June 1, 1980, is possible with this daily updated database. All material is retrievable both by free-text searching or by using index terms. The search results are viewable on terminals or printed online or offline. The most current articles can be retrieved 24 to 48 hours after the printed version of the newspaper has been published.

184   *Newstex.* Toronto: Canadian Press, 1974–. (Vendor: Q/L Systems)

All stories filed with the Canadian Press Wire Service since January 1974 are retrievable online in full text from this computerized database offered by Q/L Systems. While the database is the largest source of information on Canadian events, a significant amount of international news is also included. The database is updated daily.

185   *Philadelphia Daily News*. Philadelphia: Philadelphia Newspapers, 1980–. (Vendor: Vu/Text Information Services)

186   *Philadelphia Inquirer*. Philadelphia: Philadelphia Newspapers, 1981–. (Vendor: Vu/Text Information Services)

Virtually every article published in the two newspapers since 1980 and 1981, respectively, is stored in the Vu/Text database that offers full text retrieval online. In addition to full text searching, the database also includes supplementary keywords that clarify the news text. These keywords can also be used for searching. Online display of article texts is available within 24 hours after their appearance in print.

In 1983 the Vu/Text database was expanded to include the *Washington Post*, the *Lexington Herald-Leader*, and the *Wall Street Transcript*.

187   *UPI News*. New York: United Press International, 1983–. (Vendor: Dialog—Files 260 and 261; Mead Data Central)

Full text retrieval of news stories of current events, political speeches, and statements is possible online with this computerized database containing two separate files. All items carried by the United Press International wire in the area of United States news, international news, Washington, DC news, financial news, commentaries, and features can be retrieved. Each news item contains a priority assessment (e.g., urgent, flash, regular) indicating the importance of the event. The time and cycle (e.g., A.M. or P.M.) during which the item is transmitted over the UPI wire is included. Two days after the transmission, each news item is added to file 261, containing up to three months of records. The oldest month of records from file 261 is transferred monthly to file 260.

Both files can be searched by names of people, organizations, countries, and keywords across the three basic index fields of the lead paragraph, story identification line, and story text, as well as by reporting author, cycle, dateline, publication date, priority, news category, transmission time, and update fields.

Press Digests

AUSTRALIA

188   Australia. Department of Foreign Affairs. *Australia and Foreign Affairs; Digest of Press Opinions*. Canberra, 1973–.

The digest is issued weekly and summarizes comments from various Australian newspapers.

CHINA

189   U.S. Consulate, Hong Kong. *Survey of China Mainland Press*. Hong Kong, 1950–.

Issued daily or several times a week, this publication provides full translations or summaries of the contents of newspapers published in mainland China. A microfilm edition of this digest is available, albeit with some delay.

GERMANY

190   *German Press Review*. Washington, DC: Press Office of the Embassy of the Federal Republic of Germany, to date.

191   *The German Tribune*. Hamburg: Friedrich Reinecke Verlag, 1962–.

192   *Relay from Bonn*. New York: German Information Center, to date.

Abridged and unabridged translations of editorials, feature articles, and other material published in various West German newspapers are available in two daily and one weekly digest (*German Tribune*).

GREAT BRITAIN

193   *Today's British Papers*. New York: British Information Services, to date.

The daily digest provides excerpts from opinions or comments published in several British newspapers.

SOUTH AFRICA

194   *South African Digest*. Pretoria: Department of Information, to date.

A weekly digest of news stories and opinions published in the English and Afrikaans newspapers of South Africa.

SOVIET UNION

195   *Current Digest of the Soviet Press*. Columbus, OH: American Association for Advancement of Slavic Studies, 1949–.

Each week this digest presents a selection of the contents of the Soviet press either translated in full or objectively condensed. The contents of the two most important newspapers, *Pravda* and *Izvestia*, appear approximately one month after publication in Moscow. The contents of other newspapers appear after a considerably longer time lag. The CDSP provides its own indexing, by subject and personal name, on a quarterly basis, but separate annual indexes to the contents of *Pravda* are also available. At irregular intervals the publisher also issues separate spin-off publications, entitled *The USSR Today* and *Soviet Foreign Policy Today*, that contain a selection of the most important articles previously published in the digest.

196   *Reprints from the Soviet Press*. New York: Compass Publications, 1965–.

This biweekly publication offers unabridged translations of speeches, communiques, documents, and reports originally published in various Soviet newspapers. Annual indexes are included.

WORLDWIDE

197   *World Affairs Report* . Stanford, CA: California Institute of International Affairs, 1970–.

198   *World Affairs Report Database*. Stanford, CA: California Institute of International Affairs, 1970–. (Vendor: Dialog — File 167)

As a digest of worldwide news as seen from Moscow this reference source permits a continuing analysis of the Soviet attitude toward developments in all parts of the world. The excerpted information material is taken from Soviet news agency and newspaper reports with supplementary items provided from Western sources.

World Affairs Report is available as a quarterly publication and as a computerized database in the Dialog system offering access to the translated and excerpted news stories by subject and country. Bibliographical references to the original sources of the articles are provided.

199   *World Press Review*. New York: World Press Company, 1961 –.

This monthly digest offers translations of selected foreign newspapers and periodical articles. Although political material predominates, articles from the arts and related fields are also included. *World Press Review* has its own index for locating its articles, but it is also indexed in the *Magazine Index*, the *Information Bank*, and the *Reader's Guide to Periodical Literature*.

PERIODICALS AND SERIALS

Introduction

Periodical and serial publications enjoy at least two advantages over books (monographs) as information carriers. Because they are published weekly, monthly, quarterly, or at other frequent intervals, periodicals and serials disseminate their informational content faster than books and on a more regular and recurrent basis. The usefulness of periodicals as important and productive information carriers is, however, inextricably linked with the problem of accessibility to the researcher. Three different kinds of reference instruments have been designed to improve or facilitate the accessibility of periodical information to the researcher:

1. *Guidebooks and general bibliographies*. These instruments identify the existence of periodicals and serials by subject area, country of publication, political orientation, regional coverage, or other characteristics. Guidebooks additionally offer evaluative or critical comments about individual periodicals or serials.
2. *Union lists*. These reference publications specify the location of individual periodicals or serials in libraries on a regional or countrywide basis. Union lists are indispensable locator tools in the event that the local library does not hold a particular periodical or serial desired by the researcher.
3. *Indexes*. These instruments are available in printed and/or electronic format, and identify the subject content and authorship of individual articles in

periodicals. They offer bibliographic citations to issue, volume, and page numbers.

In spite of the valuable assistance offered by these bibliographic instruments, further improvements in the quality, coverage and frequency of the reference tools for periodicals need to be made. There is presently no bibliography available that lists all unindexed periodicals by subject or geographic area. There are at least 2,500 periodicals with political subject content, but their exact index coverage, availability of abstracts or translations, and their content or reference value are insufficiently known. Union lists do not always reflect the very latest library holdings or acquisitions, nor are all presently existing union lists adequately listed in current bibliographic tools.

The following titles are considered the most useful general reference instruments for the periodical and serial literature. Additional reference aids are listed in appropriate sections dealing with the literature of the social sciences, political science, and various related fields.

Guidebooks

200   Farber, Evan Ira, et al. *Classified List of Periodicals for the College Library*. Westwood, MA: F. W. Faxon Company, 1972.

A descriptive and evaluative inventory of important periodical publications in the major academic disciplines, including political science, area studies, economics, history, psychology, sociology, anthropology, etc. If a periodical is indexed in a separate periodical index, the title of that reference tool is indicated.

201   Katz, Bill, and Linda Sternberg Katz. *Magazines for Libraries*. New York: R. R. Bowker, 1982.

Out of some 65,000 possibilities, the editors and consultants of this frequently revised guidebook have selected approximately 6,500 periodicals and newspapers considered essential for a basic library collection. For the most part, only publications issued in the United States, Canada, and Great Britain are listed, and only very few foreign-language periodicals are included. Entries are arranged by major subject field, and periodicals with political subject content are listed under civil liberties, political science, law, geographic areas (Asia, Africa, Middle East, USSR and Eastern Europe, etc.), news and opinion, peace, and other headings. There is a separate heading for newspapers. The annotations for each title offer critical and evaluative comments as well as ratings according to the type of intended audience of the periodicals. External index coverage in several basic indexes is indicated wherever available. The guidebook is updated by a magazine

column edited by Bill Katz and published in each issue of *Library Journal*.

202   Marshall, Joan K. *Serials for Libraries*. Santa Barbara, CA: ABC-Clio Press, 1979.

Approximately 2,000 annuals, almanacs, directories, indexes, and other serials usually on hand as a standard reference collection in most libraries are identified and described in this guidebook. Entries are arranged by title according to academic disciplines or major subject areas, including Civil Rights and Human Rights, Government and Public Administration, Law, Management, Political Science, Public Finance and Taxation, Religion, Sociology, and others. Separate author/title and subject indexes are also included.

Current General Bibliographies

203   *Article and Issue Reprint Catalog*. Ann Arbor, MI: University Microfilms International, 1976– .

Due to budgetary constraints, libraries frequently do not possess specific periodicals desired by a user. Libraries respond to user needs in this respect with interlibrary loan facilities, but due to various restrictions and implementation difficulties the desired material may still be unobtainable in libraries. This reference work, updated irregularly, identifies nearly 10,000 periodicals for which copies of an article or even a complete issue can be obtained from University Microfilms International in Ann Arbor, Michigan, or London, England. The vendor has obtained copying permission from the publisher for each of the listed periodicals and offers a fast article-copying service for a fee. Article reprints must be prepaid by cash or by a patron's credit card (Master Charge or Bank-Americard) or deposit account. The catalog identifies UMI's holdings with beginning and closing dates, if any, and also lists for each periodical a separate order number that must be used when ordering a reprint.

204   Chicorel, Marietta. *Chicorel Index to Abstracting and Indexing Services: Periodicals in Humanities and the Social Sciences*. New York: Chicorel Library Publishing Corporation, 1974– .

The index provides a useful but not exhaustive inventory of the indexing or abstract coverage of the periodical literature. Entries are arranged by title of the periodicals. One or more of approximately 130 indexing or abstract publications are identified if they provide a key to the individual articles of a particular periodical. Years of indexing coverage for each periodical are not indicated, however.

205   *The Standard Periodical Directory*. New York: Oxbridge Communications, Inc., 1964/1965– .

More than 68,000 periodicals published in the United States and Canada are currently listed in this biannually revised reference work. Entries are arranged under 230 subject categories based on academic disciplines or major topics of inquiry. In addition to the title and imprint information, each entry contains a brief description of the editorial content, identification of the pertinent indexing or abstracting service, frequency and circulation size of the periodical, subscription rate, average number of pages per issue, and similar useful information. Periodicals issued by governmental agencies are included. A cross-reference guide to the appropriate subject heading used and a title index are also provided. The publisher also operates a computerized search service in response to written or telephone requests. Outputs are available in printouts or on index cards.

206   *Ulrich's International Periodicals Directory*. New York: R. R. Bowker, 1932 – .

207   *Irregular Serials and Annuals*. New York: R. R. Bowker, 1967 – .

208   *Ulrich's Quarterly*. New York: R. R. Bowker, 1977 – .

209   *Sources of Serials*. New York: R. R. Bowker, 1977 – .

210   *Ulrich's International Periodicals Directory Database*. New York: R. R. Bowker, to date. (Vendor: BRS; Dialog — File 235)

More than 100,000 regularly and irregularly issued periodicals and serials from 65,000 publishers in 181 countries are identifiable by subject area, title, any word in the title or former title, publisher, and country of publication in the reference sources listed above, which also offer other valuable information.

The biannually revised editions of the printed *Ulrich's International Periodicals Directory* list and describe more than 65,000 periodicals currently published throughout the world. Entries are arranged in some 250 subject areas and provide the title, frequency of publication, publisher's name and address, subscription price, Dewey decimal classification number, beginning date of publication, language of text, special features (bibliographies, reviews, etc.), internal indexes, coverage by external indexing and abstracting services, circulation figures, and other useful information for each periodical. If the periodical is also available in microform, such information is included in the entry. Separate sections contain a list of ceased titles, an index to publications of international organizations, and a title index.

Some 35,000 serials, annuals, continuations, conference proceedings, transactions, progress reports, and similar publications issued irregularly or less frequently than twice a year are currently listed and described in the biannually revised editions of *Irregular Serials and Annuals*. Entries follow the arrangement and format as provided in the periodicals directory. Separate sections permit easy identification of ceased titles, publications issued by the United Nations and other international organizations, the International Standard Serial Number (ISSN) of each listed publication, and the existence of currently available indexing and abstracting services. A separate title index is also included.

Since periodicals and serials undergo frequent changes, a separate publication, *Ulrich's Quarterly*, provides up-to-date information on changes and additions. Access to all listed periodicals and serials is also facilitated by a separate printed reference work, *Sources of Serials*, which lists the publications first by country and then by publisher. Governmental publishers are included.

The online *Ulrich's International Periodicals Directory Database* contains the contents of the four R. R. Bowker printed publications listed above it but is updated monthly. It permits access to any word of the title or any word of alternate or former titles of periodicals and serials.

211   *The Working Press of the Nation*. Vol. 2, *Magazine and Editorial Directory*. Burlington, IA: National Research Bureau, Inc., 1974 – .

This annually revised volume contains listings for over 4,500 periodicals published in the United States and Canada. There are three separate group indexes that establish interest categories for (1) service, trade, professional, or industrial publications; (2) farm and agricultural publications; and (3) consumer publications. These interest categories serve as the basis for the alphabetical arrangement of the periodicals in the book. Detailed information given for each publication includes name, address, editors, executives, deadlines, circulation, subscription rates, editorial content, and intended audience. Index coverage of the periodical contents, however, is not indicated. There is also an alphabetical index in the reference book that lists the title of the publication, address, and name of the editor with a cross-reference to the group number under which the more detailed information for each periodical can be found.

Retrospective General Bibliographies

212   California State University, Sacramento. Library. *Currents on the Left*. Sacramento: 1974.

213   ———. *Facing Right*. Sacramento: 1970.

214   ———. *Journals of Dissent and Social Change*. Sacramento: 1975.

Three useful, although partially out of date, bibliographies that aim to identify the periodicals issued by radical or extremist organizations. Brief annotations are provided with the listed titles.

215   Murphy, Dennis D. *Directory of Conservative and Libertarian Serials, Publishers, and Freelance Markets.* Tucson: Dennis D. Murphy, 1979.

Periodicals and other serials as well as publishers, book stores, book clubs, and other organizations involved in the dissemination of conservative or libertarian information can be identified in this bibliographic directory. Entries include brief annotations about the scope of the information activities provided by each publication or organization.

216   Marconi, Joseph V. *Indexed Periodicals.* Ann Arbor, MI: Pierian Press, 1976.

Since *Ulrich's International Periodicals Directory* identifies only the current indexing coverage of periodicals, the chief value of this bibliography lies in the historical description of the indexing coverage. Entries identify the dates of indexing coverage for the periodical literature during any period from 1802 into 1973. Approximately 11,000 periodical and serials titles, title changes and cross-references, and 33 American, British, and Canadian indexes are listed. Entries are arranged alphabetically by the title of the periodical or serial.

217   *The Oxbridge Directory of Ethnic Periodicals.* New York: Oxbridge Communications, Inc., 1979.

The bibliography lists some 3,500 ethnic periodicals, newsletters, newspapers, yearbooks, and other serial publications aimed at some 70 ethnic groups in the United States and Canada. Apart from a general section, entries are listed by ethnic group and include descriptive information, such as full bibliographic data, frequency of issue, subscription rate, circulation, editorial content, etc. A title index is also provided.

218   *Radical Periodicals in the United States, 1890–1960, Catalog.* Westport, CT: Greenwood Publishing Company, 1971.

The annotated bibliography serves as an external retrieval aid for a microform collection of radical periodicals published in the United States during a 70-year period. The collection includes radical labor publications as well as Communist, anarchist, and other political periodicals that have expressed radical viewpoints. Distinguished historians and commentators have provided useful introductions for each of the periodicals.

219   Shaffer, Harry G. *Periodicals on the Socialist Countries and on Marxism. A New Annotated Index of English-language Publications.* New York: Praeger Publishers, 1977.

Scientific, semischolarly and popular periodicals published in the United States, Great Britain, and other countries about Marxism and conditions in 16 Communist party states are listed alphabetically by title. The annotations provide a description of the contents and declared focus, special features, frequency, subscription rate, etc. Indexing coverage, if any, of the periodicals is not indicated. Each periodical is identified as Marxist (M), non-Marxist (N/M) or unclassified (U) depending on its political orientation. A geographical index is also included.

220   Spahn, Thordor J., and Janet P. Spahn. *From Radical Left to Extreme Right.* Metuchen, NJ: Scarecrow Press, 1976.

More up-to-date and detailed information than is available in the preceding three bibliographies is offered in this reference book. The bibliography provides details of the editorial policy, sample viewpoints, and content summaries for all periodicals that advocate radical or extremist viewpoints. The periodicals included reflect the following political orientations, among others: radical left, Marxist-socialist left, underground, anarchist, libertarian, utopian, liberal, civil rights, racial and ethnic pride, peace, conservative, anti-Communist, race supremacist, atheist, etc. Three separate indexes provide access to the listings by geographical location, editor and publisher, and opinions.

221   *World List of Social Science Periodicals.* Paris: UNESCO, 1953–.

The irregularly updated bibliography identifies the periodical literature of the social sciences by country. Each entry contains the title, name and address of publisher, frequency of publication, and the subject content of the periodical. There is also a separate index by subject, by institution, and by title.

Regional Bibliographies

AFRICA

222   Birkos, Alexander S., and Lewis A. Tambs. *African and Black American Studies.* Littleton, CO: Libraries Unlimited, 1975.

Periodicals and monographs series devoted to African and black American studies are listed and described. The description includes information about the editorial policy, area of interest, frequency, index coverage. Chronological, geographical, and topical indexes to the listings in the main sections of the book are included.

223   U.S. Library of Congress. General Reference and Bibliography Division. *Subsaharan Africa; A Guide to Serials*. Washington, DC: 1970

An alphabetical and partly annotated list of serial publications dealing with Africa south of the Sahara. Included are periodicals, monograph series, annual reports of institutions, yearbooks, and directories, but periodicals published by African governments or provincial, territorial, or municipal administrations are omitted. Most of the titles listed are held by the Library of Congress and large American university libraries. The locations of the various serials are indicated either by the LC call number or the appropriate symbol as used in the National Union Catalog. The guide also indicates index coverage, if any, of the serial. A separate subject index and index to organizations are included.

ASIA

224   Aman, Mohammed M. *Arab Periodicals and Serials: A Subject Bibliography*. New York: Garland, 1979.

About 2,700 periodicals and serials in Arabic, English, French, and other European languages are listed alphabetically in a broad subject arrangement. Subject categories include General, Economics, Middle East Studies, Public Administration, and others. No indexes are included.

225   U.S. Library of Congress. *South East Asia: Western Language Periodicals in the Library of Congress*. Washington DC: Library of Congress, 1979.

Nearly 2,300 periodicals containing information on Southeast Asian countries are listed. An index by geographical area is included.

EUROPE

226   Birkos, Alexander S., and Lewis A. Tambs. *Academic Writer's Guide to Periodicals: East European and Slavic Studies*. Kent, OH: Kent State University Press, 1973.

Periodicals and monograph series devoted to East European and Slavic studies are listed and described. The description provided about each title includes frequency of publication, editorial interest and policies, index coverage, and notes for authors. Chronological, geographical, and topical indexes are included.

227   *The USSR and Eastern Europe. Periodicals in Western Languages*. Washington, DC: U.S. Government Printing Office, 1967.

A useful, although somewhat out of date, inventory of periodicals in English, French, and German published in or dealing with the following countries: Albania, Estonia, Latvia, Lithuania, Bulgaria, Czechoslovakia, Hungary, Poland, Romania, Soviet Russia, and Yugoslavia. Entries are arranged by countries and include a brief description of content. A subject index and alphabetical list of titles are included.

LATIN AMERICA

228   Birkos, Alexander S., and Lewis A. Tambs. *Academic Writer's Guide to Periodicals: Latin America*. Kent, OH: Kent State University Press, 1971.

Periodicals and monograph series that have a primary or occasional interest in studies of Mexico, Central America, South America, and the West Indies are listed and described. The description includes information about the editorial policy, area of interest, frequency, index coverage, etc. Only periodicals that publish at least a portion of their articles in English are included.

229   Committee on Latin America. *Latin American Economic and Social Serials*. Hamden, CT: Archon Books, 1969.

The directory offers an inventory of Latin American serial publications with social or economic content, arranged by region or country. The publisher, beginning date, and holdings in British libraries are identified.

230   Mesa, Rosa Quintero. *Latin American Serial Documents*. Ann Arbor, MI: R. R. Bowker, 1971.

The multivolume set provides bibliographic information for serial publications issued in Latin American countries. A separate volume is published for each country with entries arranged alphabetically by title.

Disciplinary Bibliographies

HISTORY

231   Boehm, Eric H., Barbara H. Pope, and Marie S. Ensign. *Historical Periodicals Directory*. Vol. 1, *USA and Canada*; Vol. 2, *Europe: West, North, Central & South*; Vol. 3, *Europe: East & Southeast, USSR*; Vol. 4, *Africa, Asia & Pacific Area, Latin America & West Indies*; Vol. 5, *International Organizations, Addenda, Indexes*. Santa Barbara, CA: ABC-Clio, 1981–1984.

The five-volume set offers a descriptive inventory of the historical periodicals published throughout the world. Entries are arranged alphabetically by title within country of publication. The entries include the name of the publisher, subscription address, sponsoring institution, subject content, cumulative indexes, language of articles, index/abstract coverage, former titles, and notes. Each volume also contains a separate title index.

232   Steiner, Dale R. *Historical Journals*. Santa Barbara, CA: ABC-Clio, 1981.

Intended for prospective authors and reviewers, this guidebook presents a variety of useful facts about more than 350 major journals in history. Information is provided about each journal's editorial address, subject focus, primary readership, institutional affiliation, total circulation, and the specific requirements for submitted manuscripts or book reviews. A separate subject index is also included.

LAW

233   Mersky, Roy M., Robert C. Berring, and James K. McCue. *Author's Guide to Journals in Law, Criminal Justice, and Criminology*. New York: Haworth Press, 1979.

Primarily designed to assist prospective authors in their efforts to find an appropriate journal for the publication of their manuscripts, this guidebook provides useful information about a wide variety of legal publications and their editorial policies. Apart from index coverage and circulation data, information is presented on the type of articles likely to be accepted or the journal's area of specialization, publication lag time, style requirements, preprint policy, acceptance rate, manuscript review period, etc. The manuscript or subscription address and the journal's affiliation with a university or other organization is indicated. An introductory essay describes the basic characteristics of the legal periodical literature. A subject title, and keyword index is included.

POLITICAL SCIENCE

234   *Political and Social Science Journals*. Santa Barbara, CA: ABC-Clio, 1983.

Offering advice and assistance to prospective authors, this guidebook presents specific, easy-to-use facts about more than 440 journals in political science and related fields. For each journal information is presented concerning the editorial address, subject focus, primary readership, publication periodicity, index/abstract coverage, total circulation, and specific requirements for submitted manuscripts and book reviews. A separate subject index to the listed journal titles is also included.

PSYCHOLOGY

235   Markle, Allan, and Roger C. Rinn. *Author's Guide to Journals in Psychology, Psychiatry and Social Work*. New York: Haworth Press, 1977.

Primarily intended to assist prospective authors in the process of article submission, this guidebook provides useful information about the major journals in psychology and related fields. For each journal information is presented on the preferred topics, publication lag time, manuscript review period, style requirements, index/abstract coverage, total circulation, and other details. A subject, title, and keyword index is included.

SOCIOLOGY

236   Sussman, Marvin B. *Author's Guide to Journals in Sociology and Related Fields*. New York: Haworth Press, 1978.

Over 350 profiles of scholarly journals in sociology and related fields are presented by this guidebook. Each profile includes the manuscript or subscription address for the journal as well as information about the journal's subject area or preferred topics, publication lag time, style requirements, publication frequency, index coverage, total circulation, and other characteristics. A subject, title, and keyword index is included.

Union Lists

A large number of union lists have been compiled that identify library holdings of serials on a regional or constitutional basis in the United States and other countries. Regrettably no up-to-date bibliography exists that would provide a comprehensive inventory of these union lists. The reader is therefore advised to inquire about the availability of a suitable union list at the reference desk of the local library or consult the following union lists for the entire United States and Canada.

237   *New Serial Titles: A Union List of Serials Held by Libraries in the United States and Canada*. Washington, DC: Library of Congress, 1953–.

238   *New Serial Titles: 1950–1970 Cumulative*. New York: R. R. Bowker, 1972.

239   *New Serial Titles, 1971–1975 Cumulative*. Washington, DC: Library of Congress, 1976.

240   *New Serial Titles, 1976–1980 Cumulative*. Washington, DC: Library of Congress, 1981.

241   *New Serial Titles, Classed Subject Arrangement*. Washington, DC: Library of Congress, 1955–.

242   *Subject Index to New Serial Titles, 1950–1970*. Ann Arbor, MI: Pierian Press, 1975.

243   *Union List of Serials in Libraries of the United States and Canada*. 3rd ed. New York: H. W. Wilson, 1965.

The preceding titles comprise a comprehensive reference system for the identification and location of serials in academic and public libraries throughout the United States and Canada by title, subject category, Dewey decimal number, and library location. Apart from the 20-year and 5-year cumulations, *New Serial Titles* is published in eight monthly issues, three quarterly issues, and annual cumulations. Each entry contains full bibliographic information, including imprint data, beginning date, library location, as well as subject classification numbers according to the Dewey decimal and Library of Congress classification systems. New reports of additional library locations are published in each cumulative volume. The classed subject listings are available in 12 monthly issues and a 20-year subject index. The latter indexes the cumulative sets of *New Serial Titles* by Dewey decimal classification numbers. It provides parallel tables of sequential Dewey numbers and the corresponding page and column citations to the entries in *New Serial Titles*. Three separate indexes are offered: (1) a single subject index, (2) a comparative subject index, containing two parallel lists of Dewey numbers with their corresponding location numbers, and (3) a form index, containing alphabetically arranged subject headings and their corresponding Dewey numbers. Over 150,000 older serial titles can be found in the third edition of the *Union List of Serials*. Appropriate symbols indicate library locations, the lending policy of libraries, and the availability of photocopying or microfilm services.

Indexes

There are at present several printed and computerized indexes available that attempt to provide access to information published in mass circulation periodicals. Apart from their general utility, these indexes will be useful for identifying — by appropriate name or subject term — important information on

- political actors, i.e., individuals and organizations in all countries, their lives and actions during current and historical time periods
- individual countries notably
    their political processes, such as elections, government formations, partisan politics, reform movements, conflict resolutions, protests, demonstrations, insurrection and guerilla activities, etc.
    their public policies, notably economic policy, environmental policy, foreign relations policy, military policy, monetary policy, etc.
    their social conditions, notably trade and business situations, unemployment, poverty, crime, etc.
- major belief systems, such as Christianity, conservatism, Islam, Judaism, liberalism, Protestantism, socialism, Zionism, and others
- major political events, such as assassinations, coups d'etat, acts of violence, wars, summit meetings, conferences, etc.

In addition to these retrieval purposes, the indexes will also be useful bibliometrically for identifying political issues or ascertaining public awareness of or preoccupation with existing or nonexisting political problems and their possible solutions. The existence or absence of many references in these indexes on a particular topic may indicate widespread public consciousness or ignorance of a political problem or the necessary solution to a political problem. A current example is the mass preoccupation with atomic war, a political process or event that does not really exist now. A historical example is the delayed emergence of public awareness of the principle of self-determination applied to Indochina. Following the peace conference of 1919, the *Reader's Guide to Periodical Literature*, the only popular periodical index then available, contained index entries for self-determination, but none referring to the application of this principle in Indochina. The only entries referring to Indochina concerned hunting stories or description and travel stories. By the 1930s the *Reader's Guide to Periodical Literature* listed periodical articles depicting French problems in Indochina. Some ten years later the first articles appeared under the entry Self-determination for Asia. During the 1960s numerous index entries appeared under Vietnam and later Vietnamese War, but without an indication of a political solution. Finally, numerous subheadings under the main entry Vietnamese War showed that the public preferred a withdrawal of the United States and a negotiated settlement of the conflict that the political elite — President Wilson, Ho Chi Minh, and others — had created more than 40 years earlier by embracing the principle of self-determination.*

Similar analyses can be made bibliometrically for such current problems as the need for tax increases in the United States, the education and transportation crisis in the United States, the continuing worldwide energy crisis, the Third World debt crisis, and many others. For maximum utility, the *Reader's Guide to Periodical Literature*, the *Magazine Index*, and other popular periodical indexes listed below should be used in juxtaposition to the statistical reference works (indexes and compendia) and the scholarly indexes available in the various social sciences, area studies, or American government studies.

244   *Access: The Supplementary Index to Periodicals.* Evanston, IL: John Gordon Burke, 1975– .

Separate author and subject indexing is provided to the contents of more than 300 periodicals not covered by the *Reader's Guide to Periodical Literature*. Political subject matter is well represented in this index, which is

---

*In 1919 Ho Chi Minh sent a petition in pamphlet form — list of claims of the Vietnamese people — to President Wilson at the Versailles peace conference. For details, see Joseph Buttinger, *Vietnam: A Dragon Embattled* (New York: Praeger Publishers, 1967), p. 1250.

published three times a year, including an annual cumulated edition.

245   *Alternative Press Index*. Baltimore: Alternative Press Center, 1969—.

Approximately 200 periodicals and newspapers espousing alternative or radical viewpoints are indexed by subject and name in this quarterly index publication. The name entries include government agencies, organizations, countries, and individuals. The indexed publications are issued weekly or with some other periodicity. A complete list of them together with their publisher addresses is included in each issue of the index. No indication is provided about the availability of the cited articles, however.

246   *The Information Bank*. New York: New York Times Company, 1969—. (Vendor: Mead Data Central)

Abstracts from and bibliographic citations to articles published in some 40 periodicals can be retrieved online with this computerized database. Articles can be searched for by index terms as well as in free-text format. Items included in the daily updated database cover current events, economic, political, and social information published in the *Atlantic, Barron's, Business Week, California Journal, Economist, Forbes, Foreign Affairs, Foreign Policy, Fortune, Latin American Weekly, Middle East, National Journal, National Review, New Yorker, Saturday Review, Time, U.S. News and World Report, Washington Monthly,* and *World Press Review* as well as other periodicals and newspapers.

247   *The Left Index*. Santa Cruz, CA: The Left Index, 1983—.

The contents of more than 55 periodicals published in the United States and Europe with a Marxist, radical, or left perspective are indexed by author, subject, and journal title in this quarterly index. The indexed articles cover a variety of political and other topics that often refer to specific countries. The index is composed of six sections, namely: (1) author listings, (2) subject index, (3) book review citations, (4) journal index, (5) documents section, and (6) list of recent periodicals. The documents section contains references by country to speeches, communiques, statements, or special reports by leftist organizations.

248   *The Magazine Index*. Menlo Park, CA: Information Access Corporation, 1976—.

249   *The Magazine Index*. Menlo Park, CA: Information Access Corporation, 1959—. (Vendor: Dialog—File 47)

Articles appearing in some 370 popular periodicals published in the United States are indexed by author and

Library of Congress subject headings in this reference tool available on computer output microfilm (COM) and as an online database. The producer issues a single reel of 16 mm computer output microfilm every month to be used with a special catalog viewer. Each microfilm issue is totally cumulated for a five-year period. Printed volumes are issued for archival material no longer listed in the microfilm issues.

The computerized database, also updated monthly, permits online searching for periodical citations by author, title, subject term, periodical, and date of publication.

Current events and commentaries on political actors, processes, and policies in the United States and other countries are well covered in this index, which includes all magazines indexed in the *Reader's Guide to Periodical Literature*.

The full text of articles cited in the *Magazine Index* can now be retrieved quickly with the help of IAC's *Magazine Collection* in microfilm cartridge format. Since December 1983 a seven-character code appears at the end of the *Magazine Index* citations. This code indicates the number of, and the individual frame in, the *Magazine Collection* cartridges containing the full text of the cited articles. The user simply inserts the appropriate cartridge in a viewer/printer that automatically focuses on the indicated frame and its text. After pressing a button on the viewer/printer, the user can also obtain a copy of the cited article.

250   *Monthly Periodical Index*. Princeton, NJ: National Library Service, 1978—.

The continuously cumulated, monthly, semiannual, and annual index provides subject access to approximately 70 popular periodicals. More than 48 of these periodicals are also covered by other indexes.

251   *New Periodicals Index*. Boulder, CO: Mediaworks Ltd., 1977—.

Some 70 popular periodicals devoted to alternative viewpoints or cultures are indexed by subject-author entries. The index is issued semiannually.

252   *Popular Periodical Index*. Camden, NJ: Rutgers University, 1973—.

The index provides subject and name access to articles published in about 33 popular American periodicals not covered by the *Reader's Guide to Periodical Literature*. It is issued semiannually in March and September.

253   *Reader's Guide to Periodical Literature*. New York: H. H. Wilson, 1905—.

Due to its long existence, this reference is particularly useful for tracing the emergence of public perceptions of political problems or their solutions. It is a semimonthly, monthly, and annual index to approximately 180 popular periodicals published in the United States. Indexing is provided by author, title, and subject in dictionary format.

254   *Bibliographie der fremdsprachigen Zeitschriftenliteratur.* Leipzig: Dietrich, 1911–1964.

255   *Internationale Bibliographie der Zeitschriftenliteratur (International Bibliography of Periodical Literature Covering All Fields of Knowledge).* Osnabruck, West Germany: Dietrich, 1965– .

256   *French Periodical Index.* Westwood, MA: F. W. Faxon, 1973– .

In terms of periodical coverage the *International Bibliography of Periodical Literature,* published semiannually, provides the widest possible subject access to articles in all fields of knowledge. Truly international in scope, the bibliography offers an added dimension to the amount and content of information available from United States sources. Listings of English- and other-language articles published in scholarly and nonscholarly periodicals are arranged under German subject headings. Non-German readers are provided throughout the bibliography with English as well as French subject headings. There is also a separate author index.

Nine major French language periodicals are subject indexed to an annual reference work published in the United States. Entries are under 26 subject categories, including business, the world, nation, environment, etc.

RADIO AND TELEVISION BROADCASTS

Introduction

Broadcasts emanating from domestic and foreign radio and television stations are the fastest information disseminators for large population groups. Studies have shown that within one or two hours 80 percent of the national population can be reached with broadcast information. In some instances, even the president of the United States first learned of a new development in another country from news broadcast over foreign radio stations. In several European countries political mass communication by radio and television broadcasts has been built up to a high level of perfection with comparative neglect of libraries and other communication channels. Broadcast information suffers, however, from the rule of ephemeral impression, which means that informational content is quickly forgotten or displaced unless recorded or printed. For this reason, the preservation of information broadcast by radio and television stations

about political developments, events, and propaganda in many parts of the world is of particular importance to political scientists. Indexes, abstracts, and digests are the preferred reference tools for the preservation and control of the massive amounts of broadcast information. Separate instruments exist for the reference treatment of information broadcast in the United States and other countries.

United States Indexes and Abstracts

257   Columbia Broadcasting System, Inc. *CBS News Index.* Glen Rock, NJ: Microfilming Corporation of America, 1976– .

CBS newscasts and special programs like "60 Minutes," "Magazine," and "CBS Reports" that are broadcast or televised in the United States are available in complete verbatim transcripts on microfiche. A hard copy index provides access to the material.

258   Columbia Broadcasting System, Inc. *CBS News—Face the Nation.* Metuchen, NJ: Scarecrow, 1972– .

Complete transcripts of this CBS television program in which leading politicians face the nation are available. Subject and name indexes provide access to the material.

259   *Television News Index and Abstracts.* Nashville, TN: Vanderbilt Television News Archive, Joint University Libraries, 1968– .

The Vanderbilt Television News Archive consists of a videotape collection of the evening newscasts by three major commercial television networks in the United States—ABC, CBS, and NBC.* The collection, begun in 1968, is available for use at the archive and on loan basis for use elsewhere. A printed reference set, issued monthly with annual cumulations, offers access to the taped newscasts by personal and geographical names and by subject terms. The index entries refer to abstracts of the newscasts, which contain a brief summary of the televised news item in addition to identification of the network, reporter, date and time of the broadcast.

Worldwide Document Collections and Indexes

260   British Broadcasting Corporation. *Radio News.* Teaneck, NJ: Somerset House, 1978– .

Typescripts of the 6 P.M. radio news on the BBC radio

---

*For an excellent analysis of television network news, see, for instance, Herbert J. Gans, *Deciding What's News. A Study of CBS Evening News, NBC Nightly News, Newsweek and Time.* (New York: Pantheon Books, 1979).

and television service are reproduced on microfiche and indexed quarterly in a separate printed index. The material is made available within six weeks after the actual newscast.

261   British Broadcasting Corporation. Monitoring Service. *Digest of World Broadcasts 1939–1947.*

_____ . *Summary of World Broadcasts, 1947–1959.*

_____ . *Summary of World Broadcasts, 1972– .*
       Tylers Green, England: University Microfilms Ltd.
       Although Great Britain cooperates with the United States in the monitoring of radio broadcasts from areas of political unrest and Communist party rule, the transcripts from the BBC Monitoring Service are not completely identical with the *FBIS Daily Reports*. The present series is offered in various parts containing translations of broadcast information from the Soviet Union, Eastern Europe, the Far East, the Middle East, and Africa. Paper and microform editions exist but no indexes.

262   U.S. Foreign Broadcast Information Service. *Daily Report.* Washington, DC: 1941– .

263   *Index to Daily Report: Asia & Pacific.* Greenwich, CN: Newsbank, 1978– .

264   *Index to Daily Report: Eastern Europe.* Greenwich, CN: Newsbank, 1978– .

265   *Index to Daily Report: Latin America.* Greenwich, CN: Newsbank, 1978– .

266   *Index to Daily Report: Middle East & Africa.* Greenwich, CN: Newsbank, 1978– .

267   *Index to Daily Report: People's Republic of China.* Greenwich, CN: Newsbank, 1975– .

268   *Index to Daily Report: Soviet Union.* Greenwich, CN: Newsbank, 1977– .

269   *Index to Daily Report: Western Europe.* Greenwich, CN: Newsbank, 1980– .

270   *Index to Daily Report: South Asia.* Greenwich, CN: Newsbank, 1980– .
       The *Daily Report* contains translations of radio broadcasts, television broadcasts, news agency transmissions, and selected newspaper and periodical articles originating in countries other than the United States. The information is presented either in full text, excerpted, summarized, or abstracted. All translations are now issued on microfiche and are available in depository librar-

ies in the United States. The individual reports are grouped into series based on geographical area as indicated above.
       Separate indexing by subject and name to the voluminous material is issued in printed form by a commercial publisher. Very current information material cannot be retrieved from these reference sources since both the *FBIS Daily Reports* and the quarterly indexes are issued with a time lag of up to several months.

TRANSLATED BOOKS, NEWSPAPERS, AND PERIODICALS

Introduction

The existence of translations for the content of foreign-language books and other forms of documentation assumes great importance in view of the foreign-language barrier confronting many users of political information. Considerable amounts of valuable information material originally disseminated in foreign-language media are made available, after greater or lesser periods of delay, in English-language editions of books or English-language summaries or excerpts of selected newspapers, periodicals, or other documentation. Their identification is facilitated by the regular trade bibliographies, catalogs, and other reference instruments previously listed.
       A separate international bibliography of translations offers additional convenient access points for translated material published throughout the world. Massive amounts of English-language translations are also produced as a result of centralized acquisition and translation programs by the United States Joint Publications Research Service. This valuable material is made available in depository libraries or through subscription plans, and is bibliographically controlled by a detailed index as described below.

Indexes

271   *Bibliography Index to Current U.S. JPRS Translations.* Vols. 1–8, 1962–1970. New York: Research and Microfilm, Inc.

272   *Transdex Index.* Wooster, OH: Bell & Howell, 1970– .
       Foreign-language books, periodicals and newspaper articles published in more than 145 countries other than the United States are translated into English by the United States Joint Publications Research Service (JPRS) and made available as series or ad hoc documents in deposi-

tory libraries. The translations are also obtainable individually or as part of subscription plans from the National Technical Information Center and the Microphoto Division of the Bell & Howell Company. The various series and ad hoc documents are available in microfiche only and usually bear the name of a particular region or country, such as *Latin America Report, Sub-Saharan Africa Report, China Report, USSR Report, Worldwide Report,* etc. The translations cover all subject areas but are especially rich in political material.

All JPRS documents can be identified with the help of the *Transdex Index*, issued monthly in paper form and cumulated annually in microform. There are four divisions in the *Transdex Index*, namely, (1) a series and ad hoc title section, (2) a bibliographic section, (3) a keyword index section, and (4) a personal name section. The bibliographic section is arranged in numerical sequence of the JPRS numbers and lists all bibliographic data. The keyword index section uses keywords out of context (KWOC) and identifies all appropriate JPRS and page numbers. The personal name section lists not only names of authors but also all individuals who are indicated in article titles as interviewees or key subjects, to-

gether with all appropriate JPRS and page numbers. A separate terms/stop word list contains all keyword terms together with the frequency in the files. Prior to the appearance of the *Transdex Index*, access to the JPRS translations was provided by the *Bibliography Index* issued in four sections: (1) China and Asia, (2) Soviet Union, (3) East Europe, and (4) International Developments. Each monthly section of that index contained separate listings for social science subjects.

The JPRS translation program does not include all foreign-language publications since translations are undertaken only at the request of at least one United States government agency.

273   *Index Translationum: International Bibliography of Translations*. Paris: UNESCO, 1949– .

The annual bibliography offers multiple access to translations published throughout the world. Translations are listed by country of publication as well as under ten major subject headings. Separate indexes by author, publisher, and translator are also provided. Entries include full bibliographic information, including original language, title, publisher, and date.

Chapter 2

Social Sciences

INTRODUCTION

The second chapter of this guidebook contains a taxonomic and descriptive inventory of the principal reference instruments for the social sciences that are likely to yield significant information for the understanding of political phenomena. Appropriate subdivisions separate the listed material into those reference tools that cover all of the social sciences and those that limit themselves to a single discipline, i.e., anthropology, economics, education, geography, history, political science, psychology, and sociology.

The combination of the various listings into a separate chapter gives recognition to the fact that the study of political phenomena must utilize information coming from all the social sciences. Political actors, processes, and policies are greatly influenced by economic, educational, historical, and other societal factors as seen and articulated by scientists in eight different social disciplines. The relationship between the social sciences and politics remains, however, highly problematical. Much information generated within the framework of any one social discipline is contradictory, and considerable information fully accepted in any one social discipline stands in contradiction to scholarly findings in one or more of the other social disciplines. Political actors within the gov-

ernmental and interest structure seem unable to understand the contradictory character of the social sciences and in practice either favor certain tenets of one or the other discipline or ignore the scholarly findings altogether. *

It is the regrettable result of this misunderstanding of the social sciences that the political convulsions manifesting themselves as endless series of economic pathologies (unemployment, recessions, depressions, monetary devaluations, etc.), social pathologies (crime, terrorism, civil and international war, etc.) or mental pathologies (alienation, loss of national identity, racism, etc.) cannot be sufficiently contained by scientific findings and are, in fact, often aggravated by them. This unhappy state of affairs will continue to a much greater extent than is really necessary as long as social scientists as well as political actors fail to utilize *in a more balanced way* the information coming from the various avenues of inquiry into the human condition.

The reference sources listed in this part of the guidebook should, therefore, be considered as interdependent and mutually supportive elements of a retrieval

*An extensive description of this problem can be found in Gene M. Lyons, *The Uneasy Partnership, Social Science and the Federal Government in the Twentieth Century* (New York: Russell Sage Foundation, 1969).

system for essential information that provides new means of lessening the calamity inherent in our political options.

MULTIDISCIPLINARY REFERENCE SOURCES

Bibliographic Instruments

GUIDEBOOKS

274   Gray, Richard A. *Serial Bibliographies in the Humanities and Social Sciences*. Ann Arbor, MI: Pierian Press, 1969.

The purpose of this guidebook is to identify the existence and characteristics of current bibliographies that are issued either separately or as parts of periodicals in an effort to provide organized access to the massive literature published in all forms of documentation in the social sciences and the humanities. Entries are arranged according to the Dewey Decimal Classification System and include codes that indicate the characteristics of each bibliography, such as language, degree of selectivity, frequency, form or bibliographic arrangement. Due to its publication date this guidebook has to be used in conjunction with other, more recently issued guidebooks that offer updated information in some respects.

275   Harzfeld, Lois A. *Periodical Indexes in the Social Sciences and Humanities: A Subject Guide*. Metuchen, NJ: Scarecrow Press, 1978.

This guidebook offers a well-annotated inventory of indexes for the periodical literature in African studies, anthropology, archeology, architecture, art, Asian studies, criminology, economics, education, ethnic studies, film, folklore, geography, history, history of science, humanities, Jewish studies, journalism, linguistics, Latin American studies, law, library and information science, literature, medieval studies, music, Neareastern studies, philosophy, political science, popular culture, psychology, public administration, religion, reviews of books and records, Slavic and East European studies, social sciences, sociology, special education, theater arts, and women's studies. A small number of discontinued or retrospective bibliographies is also cited.

276   Hoselitz, Bert F. *A Reader's Guide to the Social Sciences*. New York: Free Press, 1970.

The aim of this guidebook is to provide an introduction to the important publications in the literary output of the various social sciences. In separate chapters devoted to anthropology, economics, geography, political science, psychology, and sociology, the more important "classics" in each discipline are cited and their contribution to the advancement of knowledge described. The chapter on

political science was written by Heinz Eulau, who surveys the political literature in all its aspects and approaches.

277   Li, Tze-chung. *Social Science Reference Sources. A Practical Guide*. Westport, CT: Greenwood Press, 1980.

Divided into three parts and nineteen chapters, the guidebook offers a description of the nature of the social sciences and their reference or other information sources. Ten chapters in part 1 are devoted to general bibliographic instruments, encyclopedias, dictionaries, directories, biographies, handbooks, yearbooks, statistical sources, periodicals, government publications, unpublished materials, and computerized databases relating to all of the social sciences. Eight chapters in part 2 focus on the reference sources and periodicals in the subdisciplines of anthropology, economics and business, education, history, law, political science, psychology, and sociology. A final chapter deals with bibliographical services in the social sciences. The titles of the individual reference works are interwoven into the narrative text. Separate name and title indexes are included, but the omission of a subject index is a serious handicap. Approximately 800 social science reference sources are listed and evaluated in this guidebook, but many of them are, by definition or content, not scientific.

278   McInnes, Raymond G., and James W. Scott. *Social Science Research Handbook*. New York: Barnes & Noble, 1974.

A narrative survey of the reference literature in the social sciences and area studies is offered by this guidebook. Approximately 1,500 reference sources are included in the text, which is arranged in seventeen parts for the various disciplines and geographical areas of study. Textual comments provide evaluative details for each cited reference work. Full bibliographic information for the cited titles is, however, given only in a separate bibliography at the end of the book. This bibliography follows the same arrangement as the textual parts of the guidebook, which makes it difficult for the novice to locate a desired item in the book. There are no author and subject indexes in the guidebook.

279   Vesenyi, Paul E. *European Periodical Literature in the Social Sciences and the Humanities*. Metuchen, NJ: Scarecrow Press, 1969.

The guidebook lists and describes indexes, abstracts, union lists, and other bibliographies and directories published in Europe in the social sciences and humanities. The reference instruments are listed by country of publication and described by date of origin, frequency, coverage, language of publication, and other useful information. A separate rate subject index lists all reference works by academic discipline. A separate title index is also included. No updated edition of this European reference inventory is available.

280   White, Carl Milton. *Sources of Information in the Social Sciences*. Chicago: American Library Association, 1973.

Surpassing in its scope all other guidebooks listed in this section, this reference work offers a wide-ranging survey of the literary output of the various social sciences with the help of descriptive essays and bibliographic listings. Separate chapters are organized for anthropology, education, geography, economics, history, political science, psychology, and sociology. Reference works are arranged by type or content, but major scholarly works in each discipline are also identified.

LIBRARY CATALOGS

281   Kiel. Institute for World Economics. Library.

Bibliographical and Biographical Catalog of Persons (Personenkatalog).

Catalog of Administrative Authorities (Behorderkatalog).

Catalog of Corporations (Korperschaftenkatalog).

Regional Catalog (Regionenkatalog).

Subject Catalog (Sachkatalog).

Shelf List of Periodical Holdings (Standortskartei der Periodika).

Title Catalog (Titelkatalog).
    Boston: G. K. Hall, 1969.
    The Institute for World Economics Library is the central library for the economic sciences in the Federal Republic of Germany. Since economic phenomena can only be understood in their interrelationship with time, space, and society, the library also includes publications on history, politics, law and administration, culture and sociology, geography, area studies, etc., thus making it a major research library for the entire social sciences. The library's acquisition program is worldwide in scope, with 73 percent of the collection originating outside of Germany. Approximately 30 percent of the titles refer to English-language publications. Special efforts have been made to collect official and semiofficial documentation as well as literature published in Oriental and Slavic languages or material originating in countries with inadequate bibliographic control.
    There are 207 volumes altogether in seven sections containing 3,381,200 cards for 900,000 volumes and

19,000 periodicals. The listed material for the United States is voluminous and extends over 1,153 pages in volumes 9 and 10 of the *Catalog of Administrative Authorities*, beginning on page 308. Nearly 6,000 pages of material are listed in the *Regional Catalog*, starting with page 528 of volume 46. Subject headings in the *Subject Catalog* are in German, but a separate index volume (Registerband) includes an extensive list of German equivalents for English subject terms. A complete list of all German subject headings and their subdivisions is also given.

The catalog is kept up to date since 1977 by the *ECONIS Bibliographie*, a computer-produced list of the library's recent acquisitions. Entries offer access by title, keyword, subject, region, names of individuals and institutions, including conferences.

282   Stanford University. The Hoover Institution on War, Revolution and Peace.

Catalog of the Western Language Collection.

─────── . *1st Supplement, 1972; 2nd Supplement, 1977*.

Catalogs of the Western Language Serials and Newspaper Collections.

Catalog of the Chinese Collection.

─────── . *1st Supplement, 1972; 2nd Supplement, 1977*.

Catalog of the Japanese Collection.

─────── . *1st Supplement, 1972; 2nd Supplement, 1977*.

Catalog of the Arabic Collection.

Catalog of the Turkish and Persian Collections.
    Boston: G. K. Hall, 1970.
    The rich resources of the Hoover Institution's collections are of unique research value for the study of twentieth-century politics, notably in Europe and Asia. Many of the documents collected are the only ones in existence in the United States. The catalogs, consisting of more than 100 volumes, therefore constitute an indispensable research tool for reference and interlibrary loan purposes. The *Catalog of the Western Language Collection* together with its supplements contains approximately 1,263,900 cards for printed and archival material in 36 languages. It includes special catalogs for government documents, society publications, rare manuscript material, personal papers of politicians and other prominent people, and archival files. The catalogs for the various Asian collections, together with their supplements, in-

clude nearly 400,000 cards and represent unique holdings in various forms of documentation for the study of political and social developments in Asia.

CURRENT BIBLIOGRAPHIES

283   *Australian Public Affairs Information Service.* Canberra: National Library of Australia, 1945—.

284   *Canadian Periodicals Index.* Ottawa: Canadian Library Association, 1928—.

285   *Guide to Indian Periodical Literature.* Gurgaon, India: Indian Documentation Service, 1964—.

286   *Index to New Zealand Periodicals.* Wellington: National Library of New Zealand, 1940—.

287   *Index to South African Periodicals.* Johannesburg: City of Johannesburg Public Library, 1940—.

The English-language periodical literature published in Australia, Canada, India, New Zealand, and South Africa is separately indexed by subject and author in the five index instruments listed above. Professional journals in the social sciences are well covered, but a number of popular magazines is also included. The Australian and Canadian indexes are issued monthly, the Indian index is published quarterly, while the remaining two indexes are annual publications. Reviews of scholarly books are also listed in most indexes. The Canadian and South African indexes also cover periodical articles published in French and Afrikaans, respectively.

288   *Bibliographie der Sozialwissenschaften.* Göttingen: Vandenhoeck & Ruprecht, 1905—1967.

289   *Bibliographie der Wirtschaftswissenschaften.* Göttingen: Vandenhoeck & Ruprecht, 1968—.

Multiple access to books and periodicals published in English and other European languages is provided by this bibliographic instrument, currently issued twice a year. The entries are arranged under a detailed classification plan with separate sections for the politics and policies in various subject areas, such as economic policy, public finance policy, money and credit policy, social policy, price control, international economic relations, etc. Annual author, subject, regional, and journal indexes offer additional access avenues to the listed material. The title change of the reference work reflects current predominance of the economic sciences in political matters.

290   *Cumulative Subject Index to the Public Affairs Information Service Bulletins 1915—1974.* Arlington, VA: Carrollton Press, 1977.

291   *PAIS International.* New York: Public Affairs Information Service, 1972—. (Vendor: BRS; Dialog— File 49)

292   *Public Affairs Information Service Bulletin.* New York: Public Affairs Information Service, 1915—.

293   *Public Affairs Information Service Foreign Language Index.* New York: Public Affairs Information Service, 1972—.

The computerized *PAIS International* database and its two printed equivalents, the *PAIS Bulletin* and the *PAIS Foreign Language Index*, are among the most heavily used bibliographic tools for identifying published information relating to social, economic, or political issues and governmental policies throughout the world. Articles from over 800 English-language periodicals in the social sciences and related areas are indexed in the *PAIS Bulletin*, while more than 400 foreign-language periodicals are covered in the *PAIS Foreign Language Index*. In addition, both indexes list all types of monographs: trade books, yearbooks, directories, U.S. and foreign government publications.

The *PAIS Bulletin* is published twice monthly with annual cumulations. A separate 60-year index is also available. The *PAIS Foreign Language Index* is issued quarterly and in annual bound volumes. The computerized database is updated monthly for the *PAIS Bulletin*, covered since 1976, and quarterly for the *PAIS Foreign Language Index*, covered since 1972.

294   *Current Contents—Social and Behavioral Sciences.* Philadelphia: Institute for Scientific Information, 1969—.

As a current awareness tool for the periodical literature in the social and behavioral sciences, this pocket-sized reference work provides the table of contents pages from more than 1,300 periodicals, published throughout the world. There is no subject index, but a separate author index with address directory is included. The publisher also offers an article-copying service for the listed material as well as an automatic subject citation alert (ASCA), which notifies subscribers of new materials within a personally programmed interest profile.

295   *Energy Index.* New York: Environment Information Center, 1971—.

296   *Energy Information Abstracts.* New York: Environment Information Center, 1976—.

297   *Energyline.* New York: Environment Information Center, 1976—. (Vendor: BRS; Dialog—File 69; SDC)

Information on energy is multidisciplinary in origin since activities relating to the production and usage of energy have technical, economic, environmental, political, sociological, and other aspects. Past failure to integrate, for purposes of study and action, the access possibilities and usage of energy information arising from several academic disciplines contributed to the serious crisis that affected the well-being of the United States and many other countries during the early 1970s. Available in printed or computerized format, the three reference instruments cited above attempt to provide a more integrated approach to the bulk of information produced about the energy situation.

The annually published *Energy Index* identifies by subject terms, SIC (Standard Industrial Classification) code numbers, geographic terms, source documents, and author names newspaper and periodical articles as well as books published during the preceding year about all aspects of energy planning, production, and consumption. Apart from the bibliographic citations to the source documents, the index entries also contain an accession number by which abstracts of the indexed material can be found in the *Energy Information Abstracts*. In addition, a review of major energy-related events, important energy statistics, a summary and status board of legislation acted upon in the United States Congress, a list of major energy conferences, and a listing of new books and films can also be found in the *Energy Index*.

The monthly issued *Energy Information Abstracts* offer detailed abstracts of the energy literature arranged under 21 major categories that reflect the multidisciplinary character of the information, as follows: U.S. economics, U.S. policy and planning, international, research and development, general, resources and reserves, petroleum and natural gas resources, coal resources, unconventional resources, solar energy, fuel processing, fuel transport and storage, electric power generation, electric power storage and transmission, nuclear resources and power, thermonuclear power, consumption and conservation, industrial consumption, transportation consumption, residential consumption, and environmental impact. Each issue also includes indexes by subject, corporate source, and author.

Online access to bibliographic citations and abstracts of the energy literature is offered by the computerized *Energyline* database. A separate printed user's manual lists more than 7,000 search terms in alphabetical order and by major subject category to facilitate online searching. The publisher also operates a document delivery system that makes cited documents available in microfiche or hard copy on demand, as a full collection or by major subject categories.

298   *Energy Review*. Santa Barbara, CA: Environmental Studies Institute, 1974 – .

Abstracts of energy-related information published in journal articles, books, corporate newsletters, government reports, and various other documentation can also be found in this bibliographic publication issued six times a year. While all abstracts are arranged alphabetically under subject headings, there is also a separate subject index included in each issue. Cumulated subject and author indexes are additionally provided once a year.

299   Fondation Nationale des Sciences Politiques. *Bibliographie Courante sur Fiches d'Articles de Periodiques*. Paris: Service des Publications de la Fondation Nationale des Sciences Politiques, 1955 – .

300   *Index to Post-1944 Periodical Articles on Political, Economic and Social Problems*. Boston: G. K. Hall, 1968.

_____ . *Supplements*. Boston: G. K. Hall, 1969 – .

301   *Bulletin Analytique de Documentation Politique, Economique et Social Contemporaine*. Paris: Presses Universitaires de France, 1946 – .

Since its creation in 1945 the Fondation Nationale des Sciences Politiques in Paris has pursued the development of documentation and reference services, the organization of research centers, and the publication of scientific work. Its Center for Contemporary Documentation maintains a card index on political, economic, and social problems, *Bibliographie Courante sur Fiches d'Articles de Periodiques*, with approximately 20,000 cards covering 1,500 periodicals issued annually. For each periodical article selected, a card is prepared containing all bibliographic information and a brief content analysis. About one-third of the periodicals covered are in French, with the rest originating from all over the world. To meet the requirements of libraries and other documentation centers, the Center for Contemporary Documentation undertook in 1955 to reproduce these cards and send them on a continuing basis to the interested organizations.

The *Index* is a multivolume set that provides a reproduction of the cards arranged by country or geographic area. The base set of 17 volumes includes over 400,000 card entries, and annual supplements have so far offered well over 270,000 additional entries.

The *Bulletin* is a monthly bibliography containing selected, annotated listings from the card index of the Documentation Center. Entries are classified in two parts, namely, (1) national problems and (2) international problems and relations and comparative studies. The arrangement in the first part is alphabetical by country with suitable subdivisions. Listings in the second part are divided into political studies, social studies, economic studies, development and foreign aid, and regional problems.

302 *Index to Social Sciences and Humanities Proceedings*. Philadelphia: Institute for Scientific Information, 1979 – .

303 *Interdok. Directory of Published Proceedings. Series SSH – Social Sciences/Humanities*. White Plains, NY: Interdok Corporation, 1968 – .

304 New York (City). Public Library. Research Libraries. *Bibliographic Guide to Conference Publications*. Boston: G. K. Hall, 1974 – .

The meetings of professional organizations play an important role in the production and exchange of information in the social sciences. The three printed reference instruments listed above provide various, although partially overlapping access avenues to the scientific conference literature. The quarterly reference tool *Interdok* lists conferences, meetings, seminars, symposia, and congresses with parallel citations to the published results of such meetings. Entries are arranged chronologically based on the original meeting dates. Indexing is provided by means of an editor index, location index, and subject index. All citations reflect meetings held after January 1964 anywhere in the world.

The *Index to Social Sciences and Humanities Proceedings* is a quarterly reference tool with annual cumulations that provides bibliographic details of approximately 1,000 proceedings in the social sciences and humanities each year. Proceedings are listed in a table of contents format. The conference name, date, and location are shown together with sponsors, editors, book title or journal information. Bibliographic identification of the conference papers is made possible by means of six indexes. There are separate indexes for author's names, sponsors, meeting location, title words, subject categories, and organizational affiliation of the authors.

The *Bibliographic Guide to Conference Publications* is published annually and lists without annotations conference publications in all languages and all subject fields. Listings are based on catalog entries of the Research Libraries of the New York Public Library and the MARC tapes of the Library of Congress. Entries are arranged in alphabetical sequence in an integrated format for all access points, namely, author, editor, title, series title, and subject heading. The entries include the call numbers of the cataloged conference publications.

305 *International Bibliography of the Social Sciences*. Paris: International Committee for Social Science Information and Documentation, 1979 – . (Vendor: QL Systems)

The computerized database offers online access to bibliographic citations for scholarly books and periodical articles published throughout the world on economic, sociological, and related social science subjects. The con-

tent of the database corresponds to the printed *International Bibliography of Economics* and the *International Bibliography of Sociology* with chronological coverage from 1979 and 1980, respectively. As time progresses, the publications of political science and anthropology will be added to the database. For a more detailed description of the subject categories covered in this rigorously selective database, see the annotations offered under items 410 and 810 in this guidebook.

306 *London Bibliography of the Social Sciences*. London: School of Economics, 1931 – 1932.

————. *Supplements*, London: School of Economics, 1934 – .

The multivolume bibliographic set offers subject access to books, pamphlets, and some government documents published throughout the world. Based on the holdings of the British Library of Political and Economic Science, the Edward Fry Library of International Law, and other libraries in London, the entries are arranged in chronological order under subject headings with subdivisions for countries wherever possible. The subject headings are mostly identical with Library of Congress subject headings, and a list of the used headings is printed in the final volume of each supplementary set. No annotations are provided, but the presence of a bibliography in the listed works is indicated. Beyond the supplementary volumes the bibliography is kept up to date by the *Monthly List of Additions* issued by the British Library of Political and Economic Science at the School of Economics.

307 Rand Corporation. *Index of Selected Publications, 1946 – 1962*. Santa Monica, CA: Rand Corporation, 1962.

308 Rand Corporation. *Selected Rand Abstracts*. Santa Monica, CA: Rand Corporation, 1963 – .

The Rand Corporation is an independent nonprofit organization engaged in research activities in the social, physical, and biological sciences. The research findings are reported chiefly in monographs published by the corporation and issued in various series, namely, reports (R series), Rand memoranda (RM series), papers (P series), and books. The RM series was discontinued in 1971. Single copies of Rand Corporation publications are available directly from the publisher or as part of subscription collections in some 250 libraries in the United States.

Selected Rand Abstracts is issued quarterly and contains separate subject and author indexes as well as serially arranged abstracts of the publications issued by the Rand Corporation. The subject indexes employ broad headings, such as political science, policy making, urban problems, minority groups, or names of countries. While a cumulative index is available for publications issued before 1963, the most recent Rand publications can be identified in a monthly *Rand Checklist* available free upon request. The Rand Corporation also maintains over 50 special subject bibliographies containing abstracts of Rand publications. These bibliographies cover specific regions of the world (Middle East, Europe, Asia, Africa, etc.), specific policy problems (i.e., arms control, civil defense, criminal justice, etc.) or societal factors, such as human resources, population, housing, and many others.

309   *Social Sciences Citation Index (SSCI)*, Philadelphia: Institute for Scientific Information, 1973 – .

310   *Arts and Humanities Citation Index (AHCI)*. Philadelphia: Institute for Scientific Information, 1978 – .

311   *Social Scisearch*. Philadelphia: Institute for Scientific Information, 1972 – . (Vendor: BRS; Dialog — File 7)

Multiple access to the works of scholars in the social sciences and humanities cited in footnotes or bibliographies is offered by these citation indexes available in printed and computerized format. The cited works may be books, periodical articles, theses, reports, proceedings of meetings and congresses, personal correspondence or other unpublished papers. Letter codes are used to identify the nature of the citing work, such as book reviews, corrections, letters, editorials, meeting abstracts, or notes, but a blank code appears for the usual type of article, report, or paper.

The printed citation sets consist of four separate indexes, namely, a source index, the citation index, the Permuterm subject index, and the corporate index. The source index is an author index to every item listed in the reference sets and provides the essential bibliographic description of all works cited in footnotes or bibliographies. The citation index is an alphabetical listing of all the references found for each author in the citing footnotes and bibliographies. The Permuterm subject index lists every significant word found in the title of the listed publications together with other qualifying words appearing in the title. Opposite each co-term is the name of the author of the journal article whose title includes the primary term and the co-term. The corporate index makes it possible to identify authors by their organizational affiliation, thus providing access to publications if only the university, department, or research organization is known. The SSCI and AHCI citation indexes utilize nearly 2,000 periodicals in the social sciences, theology, and other fields in the humanities as a database. The printed sets are issued three times a year, including an annual cumulated issue.

Social Scisearch is the online version of the printed citation indexes but utilizes an extended base by including more than 2,000 additional journals in the natural, physi-

cal, and biomedical sciences. Searches are possible by title words, source authors, journal names, corporate source, and cited references. The computerized database is updated monthly.

312   *Social Sciences Index*. New York: H. W. Wilson, 1975 – .

313   *Social Sciences and Humanities Index*. New York: H. W. Wilson, April 1965 – 1974.

314   *International Index to Periodicals: A Quarterly Guide to Periodical Literature in the Social Sciences and Humanities*. New York: H. W. Wilson, 1916 – March 1965.

This reference work has undergone title changes over the years. It is currently issued as a quarterly and annually cumulated author and subject index to periodical articles in the social sciences. Approximately 150 scholarly journals published in the United States are used as a database. The subject headings used in the index usually follow those of the Library of Congress. A separate book review index is also included.

315   *SSIE (Current Research)*. Washington, DC: Smithsonian Science Information Exchange, 1977 – . (Vendor: BRS, 1977 to present; Dialog — File 65, last two fiscal years; SDC, 1978 to present)

316   *Science and Technology Research in Progress*. Vol. 12: *Social Sciences*. Orange, NJ: Academic Media, 1973 – .

Available for online searching the *SSIE (Current Research)* is a computerized database offering citations and abstracts about reports of scientific research projects, either currently in progress or initiated and completed within the most recent two years. The research projects encompass all fields of the social sciences, natural and engineering sciences. The projects are either government or privately funded and must be registered with the Smithsonian Science Exchange (SSIE).

Identification of research projects in the social sciences is also possible by subject, funding organization, principal investigator, and research organization with the help of a printed reference set issued in updated editions by a commercial publisher.

317   United Nations. Dag Hammarskjold Library. *Current Bibliographical Information*. New York: United Nations, 1970 – .

318   United Nations. Library. Geneva. *Monthly Bibliography. Part 1 – Books, Official Documents, Serials; Part 2 – Selected Articles*. Geneva, 1928 – .

Many intrasocietal factors, political objects, and

policies are considered by the United Nations system because their implications transcend national boundaries. Two separate reference instruments offer a subject compilation of books, publications of governments and international organizations, and selected periodical articles that deal with topics considered by UN organs. The entries are arranged under major subject categories, such as political and security questions, economic questions, legal questions, social and cultural questions, public administration and management questions, science and technology, United Nations and other international organizations, etc. General reference works are listed in a separate category. The periodicals utilized in the reference works comprise nearly 3,500 publications issued throughout the world.

RETROSPECTIVE BIBLIOGRAPHIES

319   Maier, Mark, and Dan Gilroy. *Reading Lists in Radical Social Science*. New York: Monthly Review Press/Union for Radical Political Economics, 1982.

The Union for Radical Political Economics is an interdisciplinary educational association founded in 1968 by a group of socialist intellectuals and activists. Its primary work is oriented toward the development and application of political-economic analysis to social problems. The present title, cited above, is the fourth bibliographic volume in a series previously published since 1971 under the title *Reading Lists in Radical Political Economics*. The bibliography consists of a number of separate reading lists for such topics as Marxism and methodology, the state, development and regional studies, revolution, history, women, labor, the corporation, racism, law and crime, class, education, government regulation, energy, health, and hunger. The entries in each reading list refer to books and articles, but not to reference works. Entries are unannotated but frequently preceded by introductory headnotes.

320   Wilcox, Leslie D., Ralph M. Brooks, George M. Beal, and Gerald E. Klonglan. *Social Indicators and Societal Monitoring*. San Francisco: Jossey-Bass, 1972.

The monitoring of societal factors for purposes of policy formulation at various levels of government is a challenging task undertaken by scientists in several social science disciplines. An enormous amount of research is devoted to the development and improvement of a societal monitoring system based on social indicators. The bibliography offers an introductory survey of the various research trends and methodologies as well as a listing of over 1,000 selectively annotated entries for books, periodical articles, and research papers. Entries are arranged under nine categories, entitled (1) definition, (2) conceptual, (3) general theory, (4) methodology, (5) policy and planning, (6) application, (7) criticism and state of the art, (8) bibliography, and (9) related. Author,

keyword subject, and address indexes are also included. The address listings identify institutes, agencies, and individuals currently involved in social indicator research.

Book Reviewing Media

321   Bryfonski, Dedria, and Robert L. Brubaker. *Contemporary Issues Criticism*. Detroit: Gale Research Company, 1982–.

As producers of meaning social critics are an important and influential group of political actors. This reference work identifies authors of recent significant books and social criticism and offers excerpts from their books together with excerpts from others' criticism of these works. Entries are arranged by author and include the author's picture and a brief biographical introduction in addition to the excerpts. The length of the excerpts varies and may run up to two double-column pages or more. Complete citations to sources follow all excerpted material. An index to critics and subjects is also provided. The entire book series, once completed, will cover more than 550 social critics.

322   *Combined Retrospective Index to Book Reviews in Scholarly Journals, 1886–1974*. Arlington, VA: Carrollton Press, 1978.

More than 1.2 million book reviews published in 472 journals in history, political science, and sociology during a period of nearly 90 years can be identified by author/ title in this 15-volume set.

323   *Social Sciences Index*. New York: H. W. Wilson, 1975–.

Book reviews published in more than 150 American journals in the various social sciences can be identified with the help of this quarterly index. It contains a separate section for book reviews with listings arranged by author of the reviewed books.

Dictionaries and Thesauri

Language serves as the major production tool in the efforts of social scientists to express the meaning of societal phenomena. Carefully defined words and concepts expressed in well-chosen words make it possible to discern reality in more clearly delineated forms and to impose a meaningful order on human thought and action. Unlike the natural sciences the social sciences suffer, however, from a serious lack of precision in terminology and conceptualization. Several different terms are frequently applied to a single phenomenon. On the other hand, several different phenomena often share a single common term. This linguistic confusion hampers the communication process not only across the various fields of the social sciences but also between social scientists and other groups in society. It is therefore obvious that the clarification of terms and concepts as well as their usage is of the utmost importance in the social sciences. To the extent that they are used as reference tools, dictionaries help preserve whatever terminological and conceptual clarification presently exists or pave the way for even greater linguistic precision.

Subject access to computerized information is facilitated by thesauri that offer an inventory of the stored vocabulary by which bibliographic citations to pertinent documentation can be retrieved.

324   Aitchison, J. *UNESCO Thesaurus*. Paris: UNESCO, 1977.

The two-volume thesaurus offers a controlled inventory of subject descriptors for improved information processing and retrieval in the social sciences and related areas. Volume 1 contains a classified word listing, a permuted index, and a hierarchical display. Volume 2 provides an alphabetical listing of the descriptors.

325   *Diccionario de Ciencias Sociales*. Madrid: Instituto de Estudios Politicos, 1975.

Prepared by an international group of scholars from Spain and Latin American countries, this two-volume Spanish-language reference work contains detailed explanations for some 1,400 basic concepts in the social sciences. Sociological material occupies a central place, but concepts in the economic, political, anthropological, and psychological sciences as well as legal and criminological concepts have been well covered. Entries usually begin with the etymological origin of the term and proceed to detail currently accepted usages of the concepts.

326   Gould, Julius, and W. K. Kolb. *A Dictionary of the Social Sciences*. New York: Free Press of Glencoe, 1964.

The dictionary is the result of a UNESCO-sponsored effort by 270 social scientists from Great Britain and the United States to find synthetic scientific definitions that constitute a common denominator to the different usages of social science terminology. The reference work defines everyday usage as well as the most widely accepted scientific usage of approximately 1,000 key terms, adding a historical and analytical discussion of the meanings. Bibliographic citations provide etymologies for each term.

327   *The PAIS Subject Headings List*. New York: Public Affairs Information Service, 1983.

This thesaurus contains over 8,000 subject headings for social and political information covered in the printed and computerized PAIS databases. Many subject head-

ings contain scope notes for additional clarification. See and see also references are also included.

328   Reading, Hugh F. *A Dictionary of the Social Sciences*. London: Routledge and Kegan Paul, 1977.

329   Zadrozny, John T. *Dictionary of Social Sciences*. Washington: DC: Public Affairs Press, 1959.

These dictionaries are useful for students who desire only brief definitions of terms used in the social sciences. Many important political and economic terms are omitted, however.

Directories

The following, highly selective listings of directories are mainly offered for the identification of American scientists, their institutional affiliations, research specialization, etc. Where the need for additional directories, notably for the identification of scientists in other countries, arises, consult the previously listed general guidebooks to the reference literature.

330   *American Men and Women of Science*. New York: R. R. Bowker, 1906— .

331   *American Men and Women of Science*. New York: R. R. Bowker, updated every three years. (Vendor: Dialog — File 236)

This directory is available as a computerized database and as a printed reference set, composed of two sections: (1) physical and biological sciences and (2) social and behavioral sciences. It lists American men and women who by reason of experience, training, or position have achieved stature in scientific work. Information provided in each entry includes basic biographical and career data, research specialization, awards and honors, and address. Separate index volumes list scientists by discipline and geographical location.

332   Duffy, James, John Hevelin, and Suzanne Osterreicher. *International Directory of Scholars and Specialists in Third World Studies*. Los Angeles: Crossroads Press, 1981.

Biographical information on approximately 3,300 individuals specializing in Third World studies can be found in this directory. Coverage is international and includes information on the date and place of birth; country of nationality; degrees; current position; field of specialization; geographic area of specialization; research, residence and travel in Third World countries, current research activities, publications, society membership, honors, and permanent address.

333   *Directory of American Scholars.* New York: R. R. Bowker, 1942–.

This reference work is issued in four parts: (1) History, (2) English, Speech, and Drama, (3) Foreign Languages, Linguistics, and Philology, and (4) Philosophy, Religion and Law. Entries are arranged alphabetically by name of the scholar and include biographical and career information, research specialization, publications, address, etc.

334   *The National Faculty Directory.* Detroit: Gale Research Company, 1970–.

The frequently revised directory presently lists in alphabetical sequence more than 450,000 faculty members at some 3,000 junior colleges, colleges, and universities in the United States and Canada. Departmental affiliation and address are given with each name, but no biographical information is included.

335   *World Directory of Social Science Institutions.* Paris: UNESCO, 1979.

The UNESCO Social Science Documentation Centre systematically collects data relating to five files, namely, (1) social science research, documentation, institutions and professional bodies; (2) social scientists; (3) research projects; (4) research publications; (5) social science periodicals.

The directory is an outgrowth of the UNESCO/ DARE information system and lists social science institutions existing throughout the world. Apart from a separate section for international institutions, the entries are arranged by country in alphabetical sequence of institutional names. Information provided about each institution includes address, date of establishment, present head, size of staff, intellectual and geographical fields of interest, type of organization (private, public, profit, etc.), activity, finance, research facilities, method of data processing, publications, and explanatory annotations. A list of acronyms and titles is included.

Encyclopedias

336   *Encyclopedia of the Social Sciences.* New York: Macmillan, 1930–1935.

This is the first comprehensive encyclopedia for all fields of the social sciences. Prepared by eminent scholars, it contains lengthy articles on the development of social thought and institutions, the social sciences as disciplines in various countries, and all important topics of economics, law, political science, sociology, and related fields. The encyclopedia is also an excellent source for bibliographical and biographical information.

337   *Handwörterbuch der Sozialwissenschaften.* Stuttgart: Gustav Fischer, 1959–1968.

The multivolume German encyclopedia of the social sciences was prepared by university professors and qualified government officials. Articles of varying length summarize the major political, economic, and social characteristics of individual countries, describe and define terms and concepts, and present biographical material about the major personalities in the social sciences. The articles on various nations — a feature missing in the other two encyclopedic sets listed in this section — provide an analysis of geographic, demographic, political, and other societal foundations of each country and describe the character of the economic system and its achievements up to the sixth decade of this century. All articles include a bibliography of additional information sources. A separate index volume lists the articles in the encyclopedia by contributors, personal names, and subjects.

338   *Handwörterbuch der Wirtschaftswissenschaften.* Stuttgart: Gustav Fischer, 1977.

The new edition of the preceding reference work has a somewhat narrower scope, which is reflected in the title change. It omits sociological articles but includes political and other social science material if required for an understanding of economic cause-and-effect relationships. The articles present a detailed summary of current knowledge together with listings of additional information sources in book form or periodical format. A noteworthy strength of this reference work is the fact that policy problems in the economic and social area are well covered.

339   *International Encyclopedia of the Social Sciences.* New York: Macmillan, 1968.

_____. *Biographical Supplement.* New York: Free Press, 1979.

The encyclopedia is not a revision of the *Encyclopedia of the Social Sciences* but a completely new work by 1,500 scholars from 30 countries. It provides an authoritative and comprehensive account of current knowledge in the social sciences. The lengthy articles on each topic deal with the principal concepts, theories, historical development, and empirical findings. Each article concludes with a bibliography of important works that provide further information. There are also 600 biographical articles in the main set and an additional 215 biographies in the supplement for eminent social scientists born before 1908 whose research and writings have made an impact on the social sciences. Approximately 350 articles relate directly to political science. A separate index volume contains an alphabetical list of articles, a list of articles classified by discipline or field, and a subject index to the articles and their contents.

Unpublished Data Sources

ACCESSION LISTS AND GUIDEBOOKS

A considerable amount of information material in the social sciences is produced exclusively in machine-readable form and not otherwise retrievable by online reference instruments. The machine-readable data sets are collected in separate data archives or special repositories. This situation creates a problem for the researcher, who must first learn of the existence of the data set and then learn about the access conditions before usage of the machine-readable material is possible. The following reference instruments have been produced to serve the information needs of researchers in this respect.

340   Data Clearing House for the Social Sciences. *Social Sciences Data Inventory 1977*. Ottawa: Data Clearing House, 1978.

The reference book contains 900 entries for machine-readable data files in the social sciences. The entries provide a summary of the research project and information on the location and use of the data. Three indexes offer access to the listed material by investigator, report title, and topic.

341   Inter-University Consortium for Political and Social Research. *A Guide to Resources and Services*. Ann Arbor, MI: Institute for Social Research, University of Michigan, 1971 – .

The ICPSR is a partnership between the Center of Political Studies at the Institute for Social Research of the University of Michigan and over 260 member universities, colleges, and nonprofit research organizations located in the United States and 15 other countries. Its purpose is the creation and maintenance of one of the largest social science data archives in machine-readable form. The archival holdings presently comprise 17 categories of information, as follows: (1) census enumerations: historical and contemporary population characteristics; (2) community and urban studies; (3) conflict, aggression, violence and wars; (4) economic behavior and attitudes; (5) education; (6) elites and leadership; (7) environment and natural resources; (8) governmental structures, policies and capabilities; (9) health care and health facilities; (10) instructional packages and computer programs; (11) international systems: linkages, relationships, and events; (12) legal systems; (13) legislative and deliberative bodies; (14) mass political behavior and attitudes; (15) organizational behavior; (16) social indicators; and (17) social institutions and behavior. The data collections include information material from and about the United States and 130 other countries.

The annually revised guidebook is the official catalog of the ICPSR data holdings. It has six sections, entitled (1) Data Classes, (2) Archival Holdings, (3) Study No./Documentation Index, (4) Title/Documentation Index, (5) Principal Investigator Index, and (6) Subject Index. The subject index includes the names of the countries covered by the studies. The guidebook also provides information about the service policy, training programs, and computing assistance available from this organization. Access to the ICPSR resources is available, free of charge, to individuals at member institutions. Documentation in the form of codebooks and other reference materials is routinely supplied with the dissemination of the machine-readable data resources. A list of the available codebooks and their prices is published in the guidebook together with instructions for orders.

342   Sessions, Vivian S. *Directory of Data Bases in the Social and Behavioral Sciences*. New York: Science Associates International, 1973.

Some 1,500 groups of machine-readable data files from over 650 governmental, academic, and commercial organizations throughout the world can be identified with the help of this reference book. It provides information about the file title, time frame of data, geographic scope of data, data collection agency, storage medium, output medium, etc. Access conditions and services offered are indicated. Indexing is provided by keyword and subject, names of senior staff, and geographical location.

343   *SS Data. Newsletter of Social Science Archival Acquisitions*. Iowa City: Laboratory for Political Research, University of Iowa, 1971 – .

Published with the help of the National Science Foundation, the newsletter aims to communicate information on data sets acquired by the various data archives. It offers descriptive listings and abstracts of data sets grouped according to the academic discipline of the principal investigator. Most of the data sets relate to election statistics, census records, economic statistics, public opinion surveys, international conflict studies, etc. Brief articles about the various archives as well as a list of them are included. A cumulative index based on keywords and authors facilitates access to the listed material.

ANTHROPOLOGY

Introduction

Anthropology appears to be the most comprehensive discipline in the social sciences, with close links to the natural and biological sciences. The comprehensiveness characteristic of anthropology stems from its focus on man as a topic of study and research. The result has been a wide-ranging concern for human existence and development under all historical, geographical, socioeconomic, and biological conditions as well as the application of a multitude of methodological approaches. Anthropology is thus all-inclusive in principle, and the breadth of its topical interests has led to its fragmentation into several subfields, notably ethnology and social and cultural anthropology, all of which often share their subject matter with other established fields in the social sciences. Inevitably, this topical overlap has prompted rather widespread interdisciplinary collaboration plus the utilization of theoretical concepts and information carriers developed in other social sciences. In spite of these factors, the dissemination of anthropological information occurs within a distinct communication structure that includes a fair number of general, specific, and regional anthropological reference publications. These reference instruments are of great value in political research since they invariably add to the quantity of available information. Many scientific findings of crucial importance in understanding political phenomena are rooted in the biological, ethnic, and cultural foundations of society.

The following pages offer a selective inventory and description of those principal anthropological reference publications that provide worldwide coverage in all or most fields of anthropology. Not listed are bibliographies, handbooks, and other reference instruments with purely regional or specific field coverage. Many of these regional reference works can, however, be identified under the listings of Comparative and Area Studies in Chapter 5, as well as in the *Student Anthropologist's Handbook* cited below.

Bibliographic Instruments

GUIDEBOOKS

344   Frantz, Charles. *The Student Anthropologist's Handbook.* Cambridge, MA: Schenkman Publishing Company, 1971.

The guidebook provides a brief introduction to the subject matter of anthropology and its principal information sources. Individual chapters and sections are devoted to listings of reference instruments in general anthropology, social anthropology and ethnology, archeology and prehistory, biological anthropology, linguistics, and folklore. Reference tools that cover specific culture areas, regions, or societies are separately listed. All bibliographic entries are unannotated but preceded by brief introductory notes.

LIBRARY CATALOGS

345   Harvard University. Peabody Museum of Archeology and Ethnology.

Library. *Catalogue.* Boston: G. K. Hall, 1963.

_____ . *First Supplement.* Boston: G. K. Hall, 1967.

_____ . *Second Supplement.* Boston: G. K. Hall, 1971.

_____ . *Third Supplement.* Boston: G. K. Hall, 1975.

_____ . *Fourth Supplement.* Boston: G. K. Hall, 1979.

The Peabody Museum of Archeology and Ethnology is the oldest museum of anthropology in the United States and now holds the largest anthropological collection of library materials in the world. The library catalogs are issued in separate parts for author and subject entries, covering books, pamphlets, conference proceedings, periodical articles, and Festschriften in all fields of anthropology. All subject headings used in the catalogs are listed in a separate index.

CURRENT BIBLIOGRAPHIES

346   *Abstracts in Anthropology.* Farmingdale, NY: Baywood Publishing Company, 1970– .

The quarterly reference publication is a source for some 3,000 abstracts annually of periodical articles published throughout the world in four anthropological subfields: ethnology, archeology, linguistics, and physical anthropology. Separate author and subject indexes are included in each issue.

347   *Anthropological Literature. An Index.* Pleasantville, NY: Redgrave Publishing Company, 1979– .

Over 1,000 serial publications as well as symposia, Festschriften, and collective works published in English and other major European languages are indexed on a quarterly and annual basis. The entries are arranged in alphabetical order by author within five classified sections, namely, (1) General, Method and Theory; (2) Archeology; (3) Biological Anthropology; (4) Cultural Anthropology; and (5) Linguistics. All entries are indexed by archeological site, ethnic groups, and geographic area, but not by subject.

348   *HABS (HRAF Automated Bibliographic System).* New Haven, CT: HRAF, 1949– .

349   *Human Relations Area Files.* New Haven, CT: HRAF, 1949– .

350   *Index to the HRAF Files.* New Haven, CT: HRAF, 1972. *Supplement I,* 1979.

351   *Nature and Use of the HRAF Files: A Research and Teaching Guide.* New Haven, CT: HRAF, 1974.

352   *Outline of Cultural Materials (OCM).* New Haven, CT: HRAF, 1983.

353   *Outline of World Cultures (OWC).* New Haven, CT: HRAF, 1983.

354 *Sixty Cultures: A Guide to the HRAF Probability Sample Files.* New Haven, CT: HRAF, 1977.

355 *Source Bibliography: Cumulative.* New Haven, CT: HRAF, 1969—.

356 *THINCS (Theoretical Information Control System).* New Haven, CT: HRAF, current.

For more than 30 years the Human Relations Area Files, Inc. (HRAF), a nonprofit research corporation sponsored and controlled by major universities and research institutions, has been developing programs and services to facilitate the worldwide comparative study of human behavior. These programs and services have resulted in a comprehensive cultural information system containing the reference components cited above.

The basic activity at HRAF is the preparation and dissemination of indexed data files, in paper or microfiche format, for several hundred different cultures in all parts of the world. The files contain over 700 subject categories of descriptive data obtained from field observation. The basic arrangement of the files is by ethnic or other sociopolitical grouping in accordance with a code system listed and described in the *Outline of World Cultures (OWC).* Within each cultural unit file pages or cards are filed by subject content according to the classification system described in the *Outline of Cultural Materials (OCM).* Subject Classification numbers are assigned to all paragraphs or significant sentences in the original source document. The source documents utilized are listed in the annually updated *Source Bibliography: Cumulative* by alphanumerical sequence of the classification codes for the cultural units listed in the *Outline of World Cultures (OWC).* The bibliography also contains an alphabetical culture unit index and an author index. Subject indexing to the HRAF material is provided by the *Index to the HRAF Files.* For each subject heading listed in the *Outline of Cultural Materials (OCM),* citations are given to the pages of the HRAF material. *HABS* is a computerized bibliographic system enabling the user to retrieve bibliographic entries by subject, unit focus, time, area, culture, and data quality control factors, i.e., information about the author of a document and the research methods employed. *THINCS* is a special kind of computerized research tool for compiling theoretical propositions on almost any topic, from alcoholism to cultural evolution. It includes detailed descriptive or analytical information about each theory and the research used to test it. Separate manuals are available for guidance to the HRAF files and the HRAF Probability Sample files. The latter contain descriptive information on 60 cultural units from all over the world for testing social science hypotheses by means of statistical comparisons.

357 *International Bibliography of Social and Cultural Anthropology.* Paris: UNESCO, 1958—1961. Chicago: Aldine, 1962—.

The bibliography is prepared by the International Committee for Social Sciences Documentation and published annually as one of the four parts of the *International Bibliography of the Social Sciences.* It selectively lists the scientific literature of anthropology as it is published in books and periodicals throughout the world. Entries are arranged in an elaborate classification scheme containing the following major classes: (A) anthropology: general studies; (B) material and methods of anthropology; (C) morphological foundations; (D) ethnographic studies of peoples and communities; (E) social organization and relationships; (F) religion, magic, and witchcraft; (G) problems of knowledge, arts and science, folk traditions; (H) studies of culture and personality, national character; (I) problems of acculturation and social change, contact situations; and (J) applied anthropology. Numerous subdivisions of the main classes provide separate listings of the literature by major subjects or geographic regions. The annual volumes are also indexed by author and subject. The publication lag is approximately two years. Regrettably, not all subfields of anthropology are covered in the bibliography.

358 Royal Anthropological Institute of Great Britain and Ireland. Library. *Index to Current Periodicals in the Library of the Royal Anthropological Institute.* London: 1963—.

New periodical articles in anthropology are listed four times annually under six geographic headings: (1) general, (2) Africa, (3) America, (4) Asia, (5) Australasia, Pacific, and (6) Europe. The area headings are further subdivided by regions and subfields, namely, general anthropology, physical anthropology, archeology, cultural anthropology, ethnology, and linguistics.

RETROSPECTIVE BIBLIOGRAPHIES

359 Smith, Margo L., and Yvonne M. Damien. *Anthropological Bibliographies. A Selected Guide.* South Salem, NY: Redgrave Publishing Company, 1981.

Anthropological bibliographies as well as other bibliographies dealing with anthropological topics, published separately or as parts of books or periodicals, are identified in this bibliographic volume. The mostly unannotated entries are arranged on a geographic basis by continents, regions, and individual countries. Nongeographically based bibliographies are listed in ten broad topical categories. The index can be used to track down politically significant publications.

Book Reviewing Media

360   *American Anthropologist.* Washington, DC: American Anthropological Association, 1888– .

361   *Anthropos.* Fribourg, Switzerland: Editions St. Paul, 1906.

362   *Current Anthropology.* Chicago: University of Chicago, 1960– .

363   *Man.* London: Royal Anthropological Institute, 1966– .

364   *Reviews in Anthropology.* Pleasantville, NY: Redgrave Publishing Company, 1974– .

Scholarly reviews of anthropological books are published in a limited number of periodicals or sponsored by anthropological organizations. An attractive feature of the book review section in *Current Anthropology* is that reviews written by several scholars about a single title are published with the author's reply to the reviews.

Dictionaries

365   Davies, David. *A Dictionary of Anthropology.* New York: Crane Russak & Company, 1972.

366   Winnick, Charles. *Dictionary of Anthropology.* New York: Philosophical Library, 1956.

Anthropological dictionaries are not yet fully developed and usually contain numerous errors of omission and commission. These two dictionaries are moderately successful attempts to define the vocabulary of anthropology. Both dictionaries also include entries for important anthropologists.

Directories

367   *Fifth International Directory of Anthropologists.* Chicago, University of Chicago Press, 1975.

368   *Guide to Departments of Anthropology.* Washington, DC: American Anthropological Association, annual.

The first cited directory lists approximately 4,300 anthropologists throughout the world and identifies their current position, institutional affiliation, areas of interest, and major publications. The identification of names is facilitated by three indexes: (1) geographical index, (2) chronological index, and (3) subject and methodological index.

The second directory lists about 450 departments of anthropology in American universities, museums, and research associations. Entries include degrees offered, number and names of faculty, degree requirements, special programs, facilities, etc. A personal name index is also provided.

369   *Seminal and Contemporary Leaders in Anthropology. Their Theories and Methods.* Mt. Pleasant, IA: Social Science and Sociological Resources, 1972.

The directory provides biographical and bibliographical information about anthropologists who are considered to have made seminal contributions to their discipline. Listings are arranged by field of specialization, such a cultural anthropology, social anthropology, physical anthropology, linguistics, etc.

Encyclopedias

370   Hunter, David E., and Phillip Whitten. *Encyclopedia of Anthropology.* New York: Harper & Row, 1976.

The encyclopedia is the work of almost 100 anthropologists and other scientists affiliated with American universities. It contains approximately 1,400 articles in an alphabetical arrangement. The articles, varying in length from 25 to 3,000 words, deal not only with the concepts and terminology of anthropology but also with its theories and leading figures. There are also several hundred articles devoted to related fields. Photos, diagrams, and bibliographic citations accompany many of the articles.

371   Kroeber, Alfred L. *Anthropology Today.* Chicago: University of Chicago, 1953.

The reference work consists of 50 articles prepared by specialists who summarized existing knowledge in anthropology. The material is not arranged alphabetically but is divided into three main sections, namely, (1) problems of the historical approach, (2) problems of process, and (3) problems of application. Together, the 50 articles constitute 50 individual chapters, each a resume of thinking and inquiry on an important topic or problem. Bibliographic references complete each article. The volume includes a subject index and may be updated by articles published in *Current Anthropology*, issued five times a year by the same publisher.

Handbooks

372   Coult, Allan D., and Robert W. Habenstein. *Cross Tabulations of Murdock's World Ethnographic Sample.* Columbia: University of Missouri, 1965.

The book contains a complete set of all possible two-dimensional cross tabulations of Murdock's world ethnographic sample presented in 528 numerical tables accompanied by paired tables showing the level of significance and coefficient of association for the relationship between each pair of variables.

373   Honigman, John J. *Handbook of Social and Cultural Anthropology.* Chicago: Rand McNally & Co., 1973.

The handbook summarizes the current state of knowledge in 28 areas of social and cultural anthropology. Articles that may be useful for a better understanding of political phenomena cover such areas as cross-cultural studies, belief systems, economic anthropology, political anthropology, ethnography of law, the anthropology of war, pluralism, urban anthropology, psychological anthropology, anthropology of education, identity, culture and behavior, and others. Each article in the handbook closes with a bibliography of cited sources in the text. Name and subject indexes are included.

374   Textor, Robert B. A *Cross-Cultural Summary.* New Haven, CT: Human Relations Area Files, 1967.

This reference volume provides English-language statements of some 20,000 statistically significant correlations that tell us what classes of cultures co-occur or overlap with other classes. The classes of cultures are arranged in opposite dichotomy and selectively utilize all available sources of coded cross-cultural data for the 400 culture samples developed by George Murdock in the *Ethnographic Atlas.* The chief value of the handbook lies in the fact that it permits easy scientific verification of hypotheses or nonscientific statements concerning the association (or lack of it) between a large number of geographic, behavioral, or institutional variables in the cultures of the world.

ECONOMICS

Introduction

The discipline of economics is concerned with the scientific study of the production, distribution, and consumption of material goods and services intended to fulfill the needs of individuals and groups in society. The single most important assumption of economists is that material goods and services are scarce and insufficient to meet the needs of a growing world population. This factor necessitates fateful and frequently agonizing decisions of a political nature. Most notable are the decisions of political actors within the governmental structure in each country, which will occur within four major categories, namely decisions affecting

1. Structural principles of the economy. These decisions determine the basic character of the economic system and the degree of freedom individuals enjoy in the economic process.
2. Socioeconomic objects or objectives. These decisions are an outgrowth of the structural principles and are intended to fulfill a level of economic performance commensurate with the structural principles. Many decisions are required to correct or offset functional errors of the economic system.
3. Application of fiscal, monetary, and similar instruments. Taxation, subsidies, credit policies, deficit spending are some of the instruments by which governments try to influence the achievement of socioeconomic objects.
4. Control of economic behavior. If governmental decisions within the preceding three categories are to have their intended effect, deviations from the expected economic behavior of individuals and groups need to be minimized by control decisions of administrative or judicial bodies.

Much scientific writing in economics is therefore concerned with economic phenomena that serve as causes or consequences of political decisions. For centuries the political economic literature predominated to such an extent that economics was usually called political economy. Today the link between economic and political writing is as strong as ever because it is recognized that political institutions and processes derive their existence and justification essentially from the economic struggles of man.

The scientific documentation in economic subject matters has reached levels of unprecedented dimension and complexity. Not unexpectedly, the reference literature of economics is also voluminous, even though its organizing principles do not always sufficiently segregate the information material without political significance. The listings on the following pages are an attempt to select only those works of reference most suitable for opening up the vast literature of economics. Reference sources dealing with legislative, judicial, and administrative decisions in economic matters are listed, as far as the United States is concerned, in separate sections under American Government and Politics and United States Public Law. This applies also to statistical reference sources. Where additional reference sources in economics need to be identified, the reader is referred to the excellent guidebooks listed in the following section.

Bibliographic Instruments

GUIDEBOOKS

375   Azevedo, Ross E. *Labor Economics. A Guide to Information Sources.* Detroit: Gale Research Company, 1978.

As a subfield of economic science, labor economics is concerned with the way in which human resources are utilized for the production of goods and services needed in society. Its subject matter is of great political significance due to the government's role in controlling the dysfunctional aspects of the economic system, which are felt most strongly by the laboring classes in society. Unemployment, poverty, inflation, and proper income distribution are some of the persistent problems facing political actors in the governmental and interest structure.

The guidebook lists informative books and periodicals published in the United States about various aspects of labor economics. The unannotated entries are arranged under 53 sections reflecting the above-mentioned problems and other major topics of inquiry, including automation, discrimination, employment, hours of work, income, minimum wage, pensions, productivity, strikes, technological change, wage determination, etc. Separate author, title, and subject indexes offer additional access to the listed material.

376   Daniels, Lorna M. *Business Information Sources.* Berkeley: University of California Press, 1976.

The guidebook identifies reference and other information sources in business and economics under 20 chapters as follows: (1) methods of locating facts, (2) basic time-saving sources, (3) locating information on companies, organizations, and individuals, (4) basic U.S. statistical sources, (5) industry statistics, (6) foreign statistics and economic trends, (7) investment sources, (8) U.S. business and economic trends, (9) business in American society, (10) management, (11) management of public and nonprofit organizations, (12) accounting control and taxation, (13) computers and management information systems, (14) corporate finance and banking, (15) insurance and real estate, (16) international management, (17) management science and statistical methods, (18) marketing, (19) personnel management and industrial relations, (20) production and operations management. Introductory notes and annotations accompany the cited works.

377   Figueroa, Oscar, and Charles Winkler. *A Business Information Guidebook.* New York: Amacom, 1980.

This guidebook will be useful for the quick identification of officially or commercially published reference sources in a variety of business subject areas, such as accounting, advertising, banking, chambers of commerce, collective bargaining, commodities, corporations, exporting and importing, financial ratios, housing, industrial sites, insurance, market research, minority business, personnel policy, procurement by federal agencies, product liability, projections and trends, selling costs, standard industrial classification codes, trade names, and many others. Informative annotations accompany the entries.

378   Fletcher, John. *The Use of Economics Literature.* Hamden, CT: Archon Books, Shoe String Press, 1971.

A narrative description of the information sources in economics is offered by this guidebook. The titles of publications are interwoven in the text, which is arranged in 24 chapters. Separate chapters are devoted to general reference and bibliographic tools; periodicals; unpublished material; official publications of Great Britain, the United States, and international organizations; economic statistics; history of economic thought; economic development; business cycles; labor economics; industrial economics; agricultural economics; monetary economics; international economics; etc. The index is predominantly by subject only, which makes it difficult to locate specific titles listed in the book.

379   Mayros, Van, and D. Michael Werner. *Business Information. Applications and Sources.* Radnor, PA: Chilton Book Company, 1983.

The titles of information sources in six different form categories applicable in ten major areas of business inquiries are identified and described in this guidebook. It is organized into two major sections, entitled (1) Applications and (2) Sources. The applications section lists ten areas of business concern, namely, (1) banking, economics, and finance; (2) marketing planning; (3) sales planning; (4) marketing and sales promotion; (5) legal and legislative affairs; (6) environmental, social, and political affairs; (7) industrial and manufacturing planning; (8) research and development; (9) general management issues: domestic and international; and (10) long-range planning. Numerous subdivisions within these ten areas focus on more specific information needs for which the most useful information sources in the following six categories are listed: (1) general reference sources, (2) periodicals, (3) databases, (4) information services, (5) U.S. government agencies, and (6) U.S. government publications sources. A detailed description of the listed information sources can be found in section 2 of the guidebook, arranged by title within the six source categories. A directory of database vendors, an index to government publications by issuing agency, and a subject index are also included.

380   Melnyk, Peter. *Economics: Bibliographic Guide to Reference Books and Information Sources.* Littleton, CO: Libraries Unlimited, 1971.

Guidebooks, bibliographies, dictionaries, encyclopedias, directories, handbooks, and other reference publications are identified in annotated listings for the following fields of inquiry: (1) economic theory, (2) economic conditions in various countries, (3) private and public finance, (4) commerce and marketing, (5) international economics, (6) agricultural and land economics, economic geography, (7) industry and transportation, (8) labor economics, and (9) population and statistics. The guidebook also includes a selected list of periodicals and serials that have research value in the various areas of economics.

381   Ostrander, Judy Tarlton. *Investment Information Sources: Los Angeles Public Library's Investment Collection.* Los Angeles: Los Angeles Public Library, 1980.

A healthy investment climate is an essential precondition for the success of the political economy in the non-Communist countries of the world. This annotated bibliography identifies over 200 serialized information sources that contain corporate and/or industry financial data and/or economic, financial, business, or regulatory news useful for gauging investment opportunities in the United States and other parts of the world. Entries are arranged under 14 sections, entitled: (1) Stocks and Bonds, (2) Corporate Changes: Mergers, Acquisitions, Liquidations, Bankruptcies, (3) Mutual Funds, (4) Securities and Investment Company Regulation, (5) Stock Exchange Publications, (6) Magazines, (7) Foreign Stocks and Bonds — General, (8) Africa, (9) Asia and the Pacific, (10) Canada, (11) Europe, (12) Mexico and South America, (13) Middle East, (14) Foreign Exchange and Money Market. Author/title and subject indexes are included. For the most part, the listed sources will be available not only in the Los Angeles Public Library but also in all major university libraries in the United States and Canada. Note, however, that several private investment letters and political risk reference sources are not included in the listings.

382   Ryans, Cynthia C. *International Business Reference Sources.* Lexington, MA: D. C. Heath and Company, 1983.

Unlike European aand Japanese companies, the bulk of American business corporations have shown insufficient interest in and received inadequate governmental policy support for developing foreign markets for their products. This guidebook presents a representative list of the more essential sources of information useful for companies interested in doing business overseas. Listings are arranged in four chapters, entitled: (1) Government Publications, (2) Subscriptions and Continuations (journals, annuals, loose-leaf services), (3) International Business

Data Sources (directories, almanacs, handbooks), and (4) International Business Books. An appendix contains additional names and addresses of organizations where country or product data may be obtained, such as world trade centers, state industrial development agencies, U.S. state offices in Europe, U.S. export-promotion facilities abroad, U.S./foreign commercial service overseas posts, Department of Commerce programs, foreign embassies in the U.S., etc. Most of the printed sources are cited with LC call numbers and LC subject headings, together with brief subject content annotations. An index is also included, but fails to identify many policy-related publications listed in the guidebook.

383   Zaremba, Joseph. *Mathematical Economics and Operations Research: A Guide to Information Sources.* Detroit: Gale Research Company, 1978.

More than 1,600 books dealing with mathematical applications in economic, social, and political analysis can be identified with this guidebook. The annotated entries are arranged under 16 chapters grouped in three main parts, entitled Mathematics, Economics, and Operations Research. Separate chapters aggregate book listings relating to macroeconomics, microeconomics, input-output analysis, models, game theory, simulation, and similar topics. An appendix lists books describing mathematical models useful for economic policy. Author, title, and subject indexes are included.

LIBRARY CATALOGS

384   Harvard University. Graduate School of Business Administration. *Author-Title Catalog of the Baker Library. Subject Catalog of the Baker Library.* Boston: G. K. Hall, 1971.

————— . *First Supplement.* Boston: G. K. Hall, 1974.

The Baker Library of Harvard University is a major research library for information material in business and economics. The multivolume catalog contains nearly 700,000 cards that offer identification of the library holdings by author/title and subject entries.

385   World Bank and International Monetary Fund. *The Developing Areas: A Classed Bibliography of the Joint Bank-Fund Library.* Boston: G. K. Hall, 1976.

A major problem in international politics is the redistribution of economic wealth between the industrialized nations and the developing countries of the world. The multivolume catalog contains nearly 40,000 cards for books and serial publications dealing with economic and social conditions, trade and finance, money and banking in the developing areas.

CURRENT BIBLIOGRAPHIES

386   *ABI/INFORM*. Louisville, KY: Data Courier, 1971–. (Vendor: BRS; Dialog—File 15; SDC)

This computerized database offers online access to citations and abstracts for articles appearing in 550 periodicals. It covers all aspects of business management, public administration, and economics with special emphasis on decision making, finance, taxation, and policy-related topics. Each citation is typically assigned eight to twelve index terms from a controlled vocabulary listed in the *Search INFORM User Guide*. Access points include names of companies, organizations, geographic locations, or political entities as well as subject terms. All records are updated monthly. Online users can order full text copies of cited articles for mail delivery by Data Courier.

387   *Accountants Index*. New York: American Institute of Certified Public Accountants, 1921–.

388   *Accountants Index*. New York: American Institute of Certified Public Accountants, 1974–. (Vendor: SDC)

389   *Accounting Articles*. Chicago: Commerce Clearing House, 1967–.

Accounting is an information and measuring system designed to provide quantitative and monetary data about organizations engaged in economic activities. These data are used by governments to extract money from people and organizations in the form of legally prescribed taxation to pay for the costs of governmental programs. The principles and methods of accounting are therefore of fundamental importance for the evaluation of fiscal policies.

The three reference tools offer author, title, and subject access to books, periodical articles, pamphlets, and government publications dealing with all aspects of accounting and taxation. The *Accountants Index* is available in computerized form for online searching as well as in printed form with three quarterly issues and an annual cumulation. *Accounting Articles* is published in loose-leaf format only with monthly supplements.

390   *The Business Index*. Menlo Park, CA: Information Access Corporation, 1979–.

Published monthly in a COM (computer output microform) edition, the *Business Index* offers comprehensive indexing, by Library of Congress subject headings and personal, organizational, and country names, of 460 business periodicals, 1,100 general and legal periodicals, the *Wall Street Journal*, and the financial sections of the *New York Times*. All business-related information is covered, including information on economic, energy, en-vironmental, fiscal, monetary, and other business-oriented policies and politics. Coverage is worldwide with suitable headings and subdivisions by regions and countries. Biographical material and book review citations are also included. All reviews are graded according to the response of the reviewer, ranging from A (excellent) to F (terrible). The monthly editions contain cumulated index entries for five-year periods. Information originally published outside the five-year coverage is made accessible with annual printed indexes.

391   *Business Periodicals Index*. New York: H. W. Wilson, 1958–.

Articles published in 300 English-language business periodicals in the United States and other countries can be identified by subject with the help of this monthly (except August) index. It covers all business-related policies, but will also be productive for inquiries relating to accounting, advertising, banking and finance, insurance, labor and management, public administration, or general business affairs. Quarterly and annual cumulations of the index are also available.

392   *Business Publications Index and Abstracts*. Detroit: Gale Research Company, 1983–.

393   *Management Contents*. Northbrook, IL: Management Contents, Inc., 1974–. (Vendor: BRS; Dialog—File 75; SDC)

Subject and author citations to and abstracts from over 730 business, business law, and taxation periodicals are provided by this bibliographic instrument available in printed and computerized versions. Monthly subject and author citations are issued in printed format and merged into annually published cumulations. Likewise, monthly and annually cumulated abstracts are available in separately printed editions.

The computerized database allows online searches by subject descriptors, as well as by words and phrases occurring in the titles and abstracts.

Both versions of the reference work also cover important business books and conference proceedings, in addition to significant speeches published in *Vital Speeches of the Day* or other periodicals.

394   *Documentation Economique*. Paris: INSEE, 1934–.

Issued bimonthly, this French-language reference instrument indexes and abstracts periodical articles and other works published in French, English, German, and several other European languages. The entries are arranged under a detailed classification scheme with separate categories for reference works, political economy, economic activities, money and public finance, international economic relations, communication, and social questions. Separate indexes provide additional access by author, subject, and country.

395   *Economic Abstracts International*. London: Learned Information, Ltd., 1974 – . (Vendor: Dialog — File 90)

396   *Economic Titles/Abstracts*. The Hague: Martinus Nijhoff, 1973 – .

397   *Key to Economic Science and Managerial Science*. The Hague: Martinus Nijhoff, 1973 – .

Available in printed and COM-fiche editions as well as in a computerized database, these reference tools offer access to worldwide information concerning agricultural, development, monetary, fiscal, and other economic policies, economic trends, and key topics in economic science. The second and third titles listed above are published semimonthly and provide citations to books, periodical articles, and reports arranged by UDC (Universal Decimal Classification) numbers. Separate annual indexes by subject and country are also available. *Key to Economic Science and Managerial Science* offers a selection of abstracts published in *Economic Titles/Abstracts*. The electronic database contains additional material added by Learned Information, Ltd., and is updated monthly. Abstracts and bibliographic citations are retrievable by author, subject descriptor, geographic code, periodical title, publisher, and other file elements.

398   *Economic Books. Current Selections*. Fairfield, NJ: Augustus M. Kelley Publishers, 1974 – .

399   *Economics Selections: An International Bibliography*. New York: Gordon and Breach Science Publishers, 1954 – .

These partially overlapping annotated bibliographies list and describe new English-language books in economics, business, and finance. Sometimes selected titles in other languages are also included. Issued quarterly, the bibliographies list books under ten classes, as follows: 00 — general economics, theory, history, systems; 01 — economic growth, development, planning, fluctuations; 02 — economic statistics, computer methodology, and information systems; 03 — domestic monetary theory and fiscal theory and institutions; 04 — international economics; 05 — administration, business finance, marketing, accounting; 06 — industrial organization, technological change, industry studies; 07 — agriculture, natural resources; 08 — manpower, labor, population; 09 — welfare programs, consumer economics, urban and regional economics. There are also separate listings for bibliographies, reference works, and new journals. All entries provide full

bibliographic citations, price information, and description of contents. A system of letter codes (A to E) is employed for rating the usefulness of the listed books for various levels of collection building. An author index is also included. Editorial supervision for the listed material is exercised by the economics departments of several American universities.

400   *Economic Literature Index*. Pittsburgh: American Economic Association, 1969 – . (Vendor: Dialog — File 139)

401   *Index of Economic Journals, 1886 – 1965*. Homewood, IL: Richard D. Irwin, 1961 – 1967.

402   *Index of Economic Articles in Collective Volumes*. Homewood, IL: Richard D. Irwin, 1969 – 1972.

403   *Index of Economic Articles in Journals and Collective Volumes*. Homewood, IL: Richard D. Irwin, 1966 – .

404   *Journal of Economic Literature*. Nashville, TN: American Economic Association, 1963 – .

Articles published in major economic journals and in collective works since 1969 are identifiable by author and subject in online searches of the computerized *Economic Literature Index* database. It is updated quarterly and corresponds to the index sections of two printed bibliographic sets, the quarterly *Journal of Economic Literature* and the annual *Index of Economic Articles in Journals and Collective Volumes*, prepared under the auspices of the American Economic Association. Retrospective indexing for articles published in journals since 1886 and in collective works since 1960 is available in two other printed index sets, cited above.

Indexing in the annual and multiannual index sets is based on an elaborate classification system that contains 23 main classes and about 700 subclasses. The classification schedule and a topical index to it is printed in each volume. Policy-related information is identifiable under the main index term government economic policies, which offers references for the various economically oriented policies.

Book reviews and annotated listings for new books as well as indexing and abstracts of the current periodical literature are provided in the quarterly *Journal of Economic Literature*, which uses a classification system of 10 classes for its entries, as follows: 000 — general economics; 100 — economic growth; 200 — quantitative economic methods; 300 — domestic monetary and fiscal theory, institutions, and policies; 400 — international economics; 500 — administration, accounting; 600 — industrial organization; 700 — agriculture; 800 — manpower, labor, population; 900 — welfare programs, consumer economics, urban and regional economics. A separate author index is also included.

405   *F & S Index Europe.* Cleveland: Predicasts, 1978 – .

406   *F & S Index International.* Cleveland: Predicasts, 1968 – .

407   *F & S Index of Corporations and Industries.* Cleveland: Predicasts, 1960 – .

408   *Predicasts F & S Indexes.* Cleveland: Predicasts, 1972 – . (Vendor: BRS; Dialog — Files 18 and 98)

Sociopolitical, economic, industry, product, and company information published in over 2,500 periodicals, business-oriented newspapers, trade magazines, government publications, and special reports issued in the United States and other countries is made accessible by these indexes available in printed and electronic formats. The first two titles cited above cover information on European and other foreign corporations and industries, while the third title offers the same kind of information for U.S. companies and industries.

Material in the U.S. set, published weekly with monthly, quarterly, and annual cumulations, is arranged in two sections, namely, (1) Industries and Products, listed in sequence of SIC numbers for major industry groups; and (2) Companies, listed alphabetically by name. Subdivisions are made for economic information (population characteristics, labor force, employment, national income and expenditure, financial transactions, balance of payments, exchange rates, regional and local data, etc.) and governmental information relating to actions and statements by executive, legislative, and judicial bodies on the federal, state, and local level. The set is an excellent source for information on trends in business and finance, corporate management and labor relations, governmental regulation of business and the economy, product demand, industrial capacity, consumer spending, business investment, government spending, etc.

The same subject area of economic information is covered in the two foreign sets, which are issued monthly with quarterly and annual cumulations.

Domestic and international company, industry, product, and economics information can also be identified online with the computerized database, which offers citations and abstracts. Dialog's File 98 covers the period 1972 – 1978, and File 18 displays information from 1979 to the present.

409   *Human Resources Abstracts.* Beverly Hills, CA: Sage Publications, 1966 – .

Scholarly books and periodical articles, conference proceedings, and government publications dealing with the labor market, labor force characteristics, manpower policy, employment and unemployment, earnings and benefits, worklife, income distribution, income maintenance, equal employment opportunities, industrial and labor relations, and similar topics are listed under broad subject headings as well as author and subject indexed in this quarterly and annually cumulated reference publication.

410   *International Bibliography of Economics.* Paris: UNESCO, 1952 – 1959; Chicago: Aldine, 1960 – .

Like the companion sets in political science, sociology, and anthropology, this annual bibliography lists scientifically written books, periodical articles, and other publications within the framework of an elaborate classification scheme. The principal categories of the classification scheme are reference books, methods, general and basic works, history of economic thought, economic history, economic activity, organization of production, production (goods and services), price and markets, money and finance, income and income distribution, demand, social economics and policy, public economy, international economics. Listings are unannotated and are accessible not only by classification but also by separate author and subject indexes. The publication lag is two or more years. Coverage of the bibliography is international in all major languages.

411   International Labour Office. Central Library. *International Labour Documentation.* Geneva: ILO, 1957 – .

———— . *Subject Index, 1957 – 1964.* Boston: G. K. Hall, 1968.

———— . *Cumulative Edition, 1965 – 1969.* Boston: G. K. Hall, 1970.

———— . *Cumulative Edition, 1970 – 1971.* Boston: G. K. Hall, 1972.

———— . *Cumulative Edition, 1972 – 1976.* Boston: G. K. Hall, 1978.

412   *Labordoc.* Geneva: International Labour Office, 1965 – . (Vendor: SDC)

Much of the massive scientific, official, and other literature issued in book, periodical, report, or other format throughout the world about labor-related aspects of the economy, industrial technology, and the political and social system can be identified and read in abstracted form with the help of the above-cited reference sources, available in printed, microfilmed, and computerized format. *International Labour Documentation* is a current awareness bulletin containing abstracts and indexing by author, subject, and geographic term for all material cataloged by the Central Library of the International Labour Office. The cumulated editions are particularly useful for their detailed subject indexes that display at a glance everything that has been referenced concerning a particular country's labor situation. All subject entries are based on a controlled vocabulary listed in the *ILO Thesaurus* and include the first two lines of the abstract.

Online searches of the computerized database are possible under a variety of approaches and yield bibliographic citations as well as abstracts for the referenced literature.

413   *Medical Socioeconomic Research Sources.* Chicago: American Medical Association, 1971–1979.

While medical science has made significant advances during the twentieth century, the cost and quality of health care in the United States and several other industrialized countries continues to generate socioeconomic problems that require more satisfactory solutions. This quarterly reference publication provides some 4,000 citations annually to books, newspaper and periodical articles, dissertations, and unpublished material as well as government publications dealing with the socioeconomic factors underlying the provision of health services. Specifically covered are health insurance, medical care facilities, medical legislation, attitudes of physicians and patients, abortion, family planning, etc. The arrangement of the entries is alphabetically by subject and by author. The fourth issue each year is an annual cumulated issue. Currently suspended.

414   New York (City). Public Library. Research Libraries. *Bibliographic Guide to Business and Economics.* Boston: G. K. Hall, 1976–.

This series of annual, comprehensive bibliographies reproduces catalog entries in one alphabetical sequence by main entry, added entry, title, series title, and subject heading for books and series published throughout the world in all languages. The subject coverage includes LC classifications HA through HJ, containing material on economic history, theory and policy, labor, transportation, communication, monetary and fiscal policy, foreign exchange, business administration, taxation, industry, commerce, statistics, etc. Subject access is provided by LC subject headings and subdivisions. The lack of annotations and the limitations inherent in the LC subject headings curtail the usefulness of this bibliographic series.

415   Universal Reference System. *Economic Regulation, Business and Government.* Princeton, NJ: Princeton Research Publishing Company, 1968–.

The eighth volume of the Universal Reference System contains an annotated list of nearly 3,000 books and periodical articles to which access is provided by 33,200 index entries according to the Grazian system of topical and methodological descriptors. More than 300 bibliographies can also be identified with this indexing system. The most frequent listings concern economic tactics and measures, finance, economic systems in developing countries, diplomacy and economics, international trade, foreign aid, capitalism, group relations, etc. Annual supplementary volumes update the entries in the base volume.

416   Washington, DC. Joint Library of the International Monetary Fund and the International Bank for Reconstruction and Development. *List of Recent Additions.* Washington, DC: 1947–.

417   _____ . *List of Recent Periodical Articles.* Washington, DC: 1947–.

The two bibliographic lists are useful for identifying publications dealing with financial and monetary matters. New books, pamphlets, reports, and working papers, acquired by the library, are listed in the monthly *List of Recent Additions.* Entries are arranged under names of continents with reference publications listed in a separate category. Periodical articles can be identified in a separate list, which is organized in two sections. Part 1 lists nongeographic materials under specific subjects, such as agriculture, capital market, economic development, international economics, international monetary economics, investment, power resources, public finance, and others. Part 2 lists geographically oriented materials by regions and countries.

418   *Work Related Abstracts.* Detroit: Information Coordinators, 1950–.

Nowhere is the exercise of political power more decisively felt than in the working life of the population. The conditions under which the working population participates in the economic process are the result of a complex decision-making process in which several competing groups, notably entrepreneurs, managers, organized laborers, government administrators, and judges, are involved by virtue of specific power relationships.

Previously published under various titles, this monthly reference service in loose-leaf format indexes and briefly abstracts the most significant or informative articles about work-related developments in some 250 management, labor, government, professional, and university periodicals. The material is arranged under 20 broad subject categories: human behavior at work, labor-management relations, personnel management, employee representation, negotiation process and dispute settlement, current contracts, compensation and fringe benefits, safety and health, education and training, industrial engineering, socioeconomic and political issues, economics, labor force and labor market, occupations, government policies and actions, laws and legislation, litigation, management science, labor history, labor unions, and employee organizations. Individual entries may also be located with the help of a detailed subject and name index found at the back of each volume. All entries provide full bibliographic citations and a brief description of the contents. Most of the material relates to conditions in the United States, but some articles about the work situation in other countries are also included. A separately issued list of subject headings with many see and see also references facilitates the usage of this valuable reference work.

RETROSPECTIVE BIBLIOGRAPHIES

419   Cohen, Jacob. *Special Bibliography in Monetary Economics and Finance.* New York: Gordon and Breach Science Publishers, 1976.

Economic growth, high-level employment, reasonably stable prices, and equilibrium in the international balance of payments have generally been accepted as dominant goals in the economic systems of most countries. History has shown that achievement of these goals is dependent on sound monetary and fiscal policies by governmental authorities. The supply of money and credit, controlled spending, and taxation are the major instruments at the disposal of governmental decision-makers. Regrettably, many governments have been less than successful in the use of these instruments.

The bibliography lists important English-language books dealing with monetary and fiscal policy, expenditure decisions, and international financial problems, notably balance-of-payments deficits and foreign exchange instability. Entries follow a classified arrangement with separate listings of books relating to conditions in the United States and foreign countries. Well-written annotations describe content and significance of the listed works. Conflicting schools of thought, such as the quantity theory adherents and the Keynesian camp, are identified by representative works. An author index is included.

420   *Corporate America. A Historical Bibliography.* Santa Barbara, CA: ABC-Clio Information Services, 1984.

More than 1,350 abstracts of scholarly periodical articles dealing with American business, its social effects, environmental impacts, and its regulation by governmental agencies are reproduced in this reference work. The articles are drawn from American and foreign journals published during 1973–1982, but may cover any historical period up to the present. Entries are arranged under ten topical categories and are indexed by subject and author.

421   Fundaburk, Emma Lila. *The History of Economic Thought and Analysis: A Selective International Bibliography.* Vol. 1, *Development of Economic Thought and Analysis;* Vol. 2, *Specialization of Economic Thought and Analysis: Principles, Problems, and Policies of the Late 19th and 20th Centuries;* Vol. 3, *Comparative Economic Systems: Conditions and Policies;* Vol. 4, *Interdisciplinary Relationships of Economics;* Vol. 5, *Economic History: The Background of Economic Thought and Analysis;* Vol. 6, *Bibliographies of the Works of Selected Economists.* Metuchen, NJ: Scarecrow Press, 1973–.

422   Fundaburk, Emma Lila. *Reference Materials and Periodicals in Economics: An International List in Five Volumes.* Vol. 1, *Agriculture;* Vol. 2, *General Economics;* Vol. 3, *General Business, Industry and Commerce;* Vol. 4, *Specific Industries (Automotive, Chemical, Iron & Steel, Petroleum & Gas);* Vol. 5, *Specific Service Industries.* Metuchen, NJ: Scarecrow Press, 1971–.

Covering tens of thousands of publications in all major languages, the monumental bibliography cited first above is a not-yet-completed attempt to identify within the framework of one multivolume set the contemporary and retrospective writings relating to economic thought and the analysis of economic conditions, problems, and policies throughout the world. Summary works as well as specific works by country, methodology, period, or economic school are listed. Introductory essays precede the unannotated entries.

The second set identifies by form categories (i.e., bibliographies, indexes, dictionaries, etc.) the reference sources as well as the principal periodicals in general economics and specific activity areas. Both sets have author, subject, and title indexes.

423   Gagala, Kenneth L. *The Economics of Minorities.* Detroit: Gale Research Company, 1976.

The economic system of the United States, like that of many other countries, has been maximized for the benefit of a population majority with disadvantages accruing to specific minority groups. This annotated bibliography identifies relevant books and periodical articles dealing with the economic conditions of ethnic, racial, or linguistic minorities in the United States. The entries are arranged by author under twelve chapters that focus on an individual minority — black people, American Indians, Mexican-Americans, Puerto Ricans — or its specific problems in education, housing, employment, etc. Author, title, and subject indexes are included.

424   *The Great Depression.* Santa Barbara, CA: ABC-Clio Press, 1983.

The most spectacular failure of American economic policy occurred during the 1930s and early 1940s, resulting in the emergence and perpetuation of the most dire economic conditions, known as the Great Depression. This reference work offers more than 900 abstracts and annotations for scholarly articles published from 1973 to 1982 about the causes and manifestations of this phenomenon. A detailed multiterm subject index is also included.

425   Heggestad, Arnold A. *Public Regulation of Financial Services: Costs and Benefits to Consumers. A Bibliography.* Boulder, CO: Westview Press, 1977.

This bibliography is part of a study by Abt Associates Inc. for the National Science Foundation to evaluate the costs and benefits of public regulation of consumer financial services. Entries are arranged in two parts, entitled (1) Bibliography and (2) Abstracts. The bibliographic section offers unannotated listings for books, periodical articles, working papers, government publications, and dissertations relating to domestic monetary and financial theory and policy, commercial banking, and nonbank financial intermediaries. Numerous subdivisions aggregate listings by a narrower focus. Entries in the abstracts section are arranged by author. Apart from the table of contents, there is no other finding aid included in the book.

426   Hoskins, Linus A. *The New International Economic Order: A Bibliographic Handbook.* Lanham, MD: University Press of America, 1983.

427   Nawaz, Tawfique. *The New International Economic Order, a Bibliography.* Westport, CT: Greenwood Press, 1980.

428   *The New International Economic Order: A Selective Bibliography.* New York: United Nations, 1980.

While some 40 percent of the world's growing population exists under conditions of deprivation, undernourishment, substandard housing, insufficient employment opportunities, and inadequate health and social services, the establishment of a new international economic order (NIEO), envisioned by its proponents as a cure for these conditions, is a most intensely debated and researched topic before the international community.

The three bibliographies offer selective listings for books, periodical articles, and official documents that focus on the economic, legal, political, and social aspects of the current and envisioned new international economic order, its instrumentalities and key issues, notably the international monetary system, commodity trade agreements, transnational corporations, technology transfer, sovereignty over natural resources, development assistance, international cooperation, and others.

429   Neufeld, Maurice F., Daniel J. Leab, and Dorothy Swanson. *American Working Class History. A Representative Bibliography.* New York: R. R. Bowker, 1983.

The role of labor unions in the American economy and industrial relations from colonial times to the present is documented in a large number of publications and nonprint media. This unannotated bibliography contains over 7,000 entries for popular and scholarly books, periodical articles, union reports, management documents, dissertations, government publications, films and other nonprint items. Entries are arranged under 75 subject headings that permit access to the listings chronologically, geographically, by union, by industry or special interest. The conditions of labor before and after unionization, the role of the union leadership, and the emergence of labor legislation are well covered. A name index is also included.

430   O'Relley, Z. Edward. *Soviet-Type Economic Systems.* Detroit: Gale Research Company, 1978.

Soviet-type economic systems generate academic interest because their assumptions of economic justice, efficiency, and stability are fundamentally different from those of Western capitalist systems. The purpose of this unannotated bibliography is to aggregate English language publications of diverse origin and format relating to the theory, practice, and accomplishments of the Soviet economic system. Entries for books, periodical articles, and United States government publications are arranged under fourteen chapters as follows: (1) Overview, (2) Economic Organization and Structure, (3) Western Theories of Socialism, (4) Growth and Development, (5) Planning Theory, Practices and Methods, (6) Prices and Inflation, (7) Capital and Investment, (8) Population and Labor Force, (9) Wages and Consumer Welfare, (10) Efficiency and Productivity, (11) Sectoral Problems and Accomplishments, (12) Monetary and Fiscal Theory, Practices and Institutions, (13) Foreign Trade, and (14) Economic Reforms. Separate author, title, and subject indexes offer additional access to the listed material. Appropriate entries and subdivisions in the subject index identify material relating to a particular country.

431   *Poverty, Rural Poverty and Minority Groups Living in Rural Poverty: An Annotated Bibliography.* Lexington, KY: Spindletop Research, 1969.

432   Tompkins, Dorothy Campbell. *Poverty in the United States during the Sixties. A Bibliography.* Berkeley: Institute of Governmental Studies, University of California, 1970.

During the 1960s increasing political interest was devoted toward the elimination of poverty in the United States. A massive literature detailing causes and various manifestations of poverty emerged, with at least two bibliographies providing improved access to the literature.

The first title is arranged in three main sections, entitled Poverty in the United States, Rural Poverty, and Minority Groups Living in Rural Poverty. Suitable subdivisions under these three sections aggregate material relating to specific, poverty-afflicted groups (the aged, black Americans, migrants, Indians, etc.) or problems of the poor (health, education, jobs, housing, etc.). All entries are annotated.

The Tompkins bibliography is an unannotated list of more than 8,000 citations to books, periodical articles, dissertations, mimeographed reports, conference proceedings, and other information material dealing with the various aspects of poverty in the United States during this period. The entries are arranged under broad headings, like "What is poverty?," "Who are the poor?," "Where do the poor live?," "Aspects of life of the poor," "What is being done for the poor," and "Proposed programs for the poor." Numerous subdivisions of these headings provide further classification of the entries. A list of the periodicals cited and an index are also included in the reference work.

433   Rock, James M. *Money, Banking, and Macroeconomics*. Detroit: Gale Research Company, 1977.

Like the previously listed bibliography by Jacob Cohen, this bibliography focuses on monetary economics and macroeconomic theories. The annotated entries for books, periodical articles, and government publications are arranged under five chapters as follows: (1) Overview of Money, Banking and Macroeconomics, (2) Financial Intermediation and Commercial Banking, (3) Macromonetary Theory, (4) Central Banking, (5) Stabilization Theory. Three separate indexes by author, title, and subject offer additional access to the listed material. The bibliography is an excellent source for identifying the literature by and about John Maynard Keynes, his contemporary critics, and post-Keynesian analysts.

434   Washington, DC. Joint Library of the International Monetary Fund and the International Bank for Reconstruction and Development. *Economics and Finance: Index to Periodical Abstracts 1947–1971*. Boston: G. K. Hall, 1972.

———. *First Supplement, 1972–1974*. Boston: G.K. Hall, 1976.

This reference set and its supplement provide selective listings of periodical articles and reports on international economics and finance with special emphasis on the member countries of the World Bank and International Monetary Fund. Material dealing with currency exchange rates, gold coverage, capital movements, and other aspects of international economics and finance is well represented in the bibliographic listings.

435   Wasserman, Paul. *Encyclopedia of Business In-* *formation Sources*. Detroit: Gale Research Company, 1980.

Mistitled as an encyclopedia, this book is a valuable subject bibliography of reference and other information sources about various kinds of economic activities, specific products and processes, private and government organizations offering business-oriented services. All entries are arranged alphabetically under subject headings and contain complete bibliographic information for the appropriate reference source (dictionary, handbook, bibliography, directory, yearbook, etc.), periodical, or organization. Some entries also offer brief annotations. A table of contents, listing all subject headings in alphabetical sequence, is also included.

Book Reviewing Media

Reviews of economic books published in periodicals can be identified with the help of several bibliographic instruments previously listed, namely,

- *Business Index*
- *Business Periodicals Index*
- *Economic Literature Index* (computerized)
- *International Bibliography of Economics*
- *Journal of Economic Literature*

In addition, the following title will be useful as a reference source for book reviews.

436   *The Wall Street Review of Books*. Pleasantville, NY: Docent Corporation, 1973–.

The quarterly publication contains lengthy review articles about significant books in economics. The reviewers are economists and other social scientists affiliated with American colleges and universities.

Dictionaries and Thesauri

437   Adam, J. H. *Longman Dictionary of Business English*. Harlow, England: Longman, 1982.

438   Ammer, Christine, and Dean S. Ammer. *Dictionary of Business and Economics*. New York: Free Press, 1977.

439   Auld, Douglas A. L. *The American Dictionary of Economics*. New York: Facts on File, 1983.

440   Bannock, Graham. *The Penguin Dictionary of Economics*. New York: Allen Lane/Viking Press, 1977.

441   Berenyi, John. *The Modern American Business Dictionary*. New York: William Morrow & Co., 1982.

442   Brownstone, David M., Irene M. Franck, and Gordon Carruth. *The VNR Dictionary of Business and Finance*. New York: Van Nostrand Reinhold, 1980.

443   Davis, William. *The Language of Money; An Irreverent Dictionary of Business and Finance*. Boston: Houghton Mifflin, 1973.

444   Eichborn, Reinhart von. *Business Dictionary*. Englewood Cliffs, NJ: Prentice-Hall, 1962.

445   French, Derek. *Dictionary of Management*. New York: International Publications Service, 1975.

446   Gilpin, Alan. *Dictionary of Economic Terms*. London: Butterworths, 1973.

447   Hanson, John Lloyd. *A Dictionary of Economics and Commerce*. London: McDonald & Evans, 1967.

448   Johannsen, Hano, and G. Terry Page. *The International Dictionary of Business*. Englewood Cliffs, NJ: Prentice Hall, 1981.

449   *The McGraw-Hill Dictionary of Modern Economics. A Handbook of Terms and Organizations*. New York: McGraw-Hill, 1983.

450   Moffat, Donald W. *Economics Dictionary*. New York: Elsevier, 1976.

451   Moore, Norman D. *Dictionary of Business Finance and Investment*. Dayton, OH: Investors Systems, 1975.

452   Nemmers, Erwin Esser. *Dictionary of Economics and Business*. Totowa, NJ: Littlefield, Adams, 1978.

453   Pearce, David W. *The Dictionary of Modern Economics*. Cambridge, MA: MIT Press, 1983.

454   Rosenberg, Jerry M. *Dictionary of Business Management*. New York: John Wiley, 1983.

455   Sloan, Harold Stephenson, and Arnold J. Zurcher. *A Dictionary of Economics*. New York: Barnes & Noble, 1970.

456   Taylor, Philip A. S. *A New Dictionary of Economics*. New York: A. M. Kelley, 1966.

457   Wyckoff, Peter. *The Language of Wall Street*. New York: Hopkinson and Blake, 1973.

The rich and varied vocabulary of economists and the business world is listed and defined in a large number of dictionaries, as cited above. While some of the dictionaries also offer references to original sources of information for a specific term, none of the existing dictionaries provides a complete inventory of economic terminology. This is particularly true for the vocabulary of political economy, which has received only fragmentary coverage in the dictionaries.

458   Eynern, Gert von. *Wörterbuch zur Politischen Ökonomie*. Opladen, West Germany: Westdeutscher Verlag, 1977.

459   Palgrave, Robert Harry Inglis. *Dictionary of Political Economy*. Detroit: Gale Research Company, 1976.

Dictionaries specifically oriented toward the vocabulary of political economy are rare. The first title is a modern German dictionary by a leading political economist in the Federal Republic of Germany. Its nearly 500 pages offer excellent definitions. The second title is a reprint of a 1910 reference work. It contains explanations of economic terminology as well as biographical sketches of prominent economists.

460   International Labour Office. *ILO Thesaurus: Labour, Employment and Training Technology*. Geneva: ILO, 1980.

This thesaurus offers a controlled inventory of English, French, and Spanish descriptors for improved subject retrievability of information about labor, laboring classes, labor-management relations, labor processes and policies as well as general conditions affecting wage- or salary-dependent employees throughout the world.

461   Kohls, Siegfried, et al. *Dictionary of International Economics: German, Russian, English, French, Spanish*. Leiden: A. W. Sijthoff, 1976.

The purpose of this dictionary is to identify 6,500 German economic terms and their Russian, English, French, and Spanish equivalents. Readers proceeding from an English, Russian, French, or Spanish term must use the respective indexes for these languages. The index entries provide the number of the corresponding German entry with its foreign-language equivalents.

462   Organization for Economic Cooperation and Development. *Macrothesaurus for Information Processing in the Field of Economic and Social Development*. Paris: OECD, 1979.

463   United Nations Industrial Development Organization. *Thesaurus of Industrial Development Terms.* Vienna: UNIDO, 1976.

The two thesauri have been designed to offer a controlled vocabulary for improved access to economic, industrial, and social development information as provided by catalogs, indexes, and other bibliographic instruments. The OECD thesaurus consists of four parts: (1) descriptors A−Z, (2) numerical subject grouping of descriptions, (3) hierarchical display, and (4) permuted KWOC descriptors index. The UNIDO Thesaurus provides an inventory of English and French access terms as used in the *Industrial Development Abstracts* and other bibliographic tools.

Directories

464   *America's Corporate Families: The Billion Dollar Directory.* Parsippany, NJ: Dun & Bradstreet, 1981−.

465   *Dun & Bradstreet Reference Book of Corporate Management.* New York: Dun & Bradstreet, 1967−.

466   *50,000 Leading U.S. Corporations.* New York: News Front/Business Trends, 1980.

467   *Fortune Double 500 Directory.* Chicago: Time, Inc., 1970−.

468   *Million Dollar Directory.* Parsippany, NJ: Dun & Bradstreet, 1959−.

469   *The North American Register of Business and Industry.* Tarzana, CA: Global Marketing Services, 1980.

470   *The Top 1,500 Companies.* New York: Economic Information Systems, 1981.

These directories may be used to identify the companies that by virtue of their assets or sales volume can be expected to have a major influence on the political economy. Listings offer alphabetical, geographical, SIC classification, or sales volume approaches to company identification. Brief information about the directors and selected officers for some 2,400 companies with 1,000 or more employees or annual sales of $20 million can be found in *D & B Reference Book of Corporate Management.* Once identified, company names may be checked against entries in the *CIS/Index* or the *PAC Directory* and other appropriate reference sources to determine the precise nature and dimension of the political influence of the companies.

471   Arpan, Jeffrey S., and David A. Ricks. *A Directory of Foreign Manufacturers in the United States.* Atlanta: Georgia State University, 1979.

472   *Directory of American Firms Operating in Foreign Countries.* New York: Uniworld Business Publications, 1979.

473   *Directory of Foreign Firms Operating in the United States.* New York: World Trade Academy Press, 1978.

474   *Principal International Businesses.* New York: Dun & Bradstreet, 1974−.

Companies operating across national boundaries are often the target of benevolent or malevolent political action in view of their importance to the national economy of the countries involved. The cited directories will be useful for the identification of companies with an American business connection. For additional bibliographic references, see the subject index under multinational corporations.

475   Hoopes, David S. *Global Guide to International Business.* New York: Facts on File, 1983.

The directory serves as a reference source for the identification of governmental agencies, commercial organizations, and various publications offering political, legal, financial, or economic information of value in international business operations. Entries are arranged in four main sections, entitled (1) General Information on International Business, (2) Personnel Information, (3) Information on Areas of the World, and (4) Information on Individual Countries. Section 1 includes listings for public policy organizations, and information sources for laws and business regulations, exporting and importing, financial and foreign exchange data, transportation and shipping, etc. Section 2 covers management and language training organizations, recruitment organizations, etc. The regional and country listings identify chambers of commerce, governmental trade and policy offices, publishers, major reference works and periodicals domiciled in the United States or foreign country. A separate index of publications is also included.

476   Ingham, John N. *Biographical Dictionary of American Business Leaders.* Westport, CT: Greenwood Press, 1983.

This multivolume directory provides biographical information on 1,159 individuals who are considered the historically most significant business leaders from colonial times to the present in the United States. Nearly all of them played a political role, either by serving in the legislature or in a governmental agency, or by acting as advisors or supporters in political issues. Each biographical entry summarizes the business leader's major achievements and political role, and concludes with one or more references to additional information sources. Eight appendices offer listings by industry, company, birthplace, principal business activity, religion, ethnicity, year of birth, and female sex.

477   *Who's Who in Economics.* Cambridge, MA: MIT Press, 1983.

The directory offers biographical entries for more than 1,000 living and dead economists in the world who have made major contributions in the field of economics. Each of the alphabetically arranged entries comprises the following information elements: name, year and place of birth, current and previous posts, degrees, prizes and honors received, professional affiliation, major field of interest, principal contribution, and chief publications. Two appendices include indexes of names by field of interest and country.

478   *World Directory of Chambers of Commerce.* Paris: ICC Services, 1981.

Chambers of commerce play a leading role in the political economy, acting as advisors to governmental agencies or facilitating the execution of governmental policies. This directory lists for each country of the world the name and address of national, binational, or provincial chambers of commerce, as well as regional associations of chambers of commerce. A pocket supplement offers new additional entries.

Encyclopedias

479   *The Encyclopedia of Economics.* Guilford, CT: DPG Reference Publishing, Inc., 1981.

480   Greenwald, Douglas. *Encyclopedia of Economics.* New York: McGraw-Hill, 1982.

Containing 1,000 and 303 articles, respectively, the two encyclopedias written by groups of social scientists offer concise explanations of various economic or political concepts, theories and practices, structures, techniques, programs, and policies. The individual articles may also contain bibliographic references for additional information.

The first-cited encyclopedia also provides 20 subject maps that show in a single display the interrelationship of the individual components of the major subject areas studied by economists. Of special interest to political economists are the subject area maps for antitrust policy, business cycles, economic systems, federal budget, labor

movement, monetary policy, and regulation. Each of the identified components in the subject maps is described in a separate article in the encyclopedia.

EDUCATION

Introduction

Every society needs an institutionalized system that indoctrinates children, adolescents, and adults with forms of knowledge and abilities sufficient for individual as well as societal survival and progressive development in a competitive world. In most countries of the world education by professional educators has been institutionalized as the predominant form of such indoctrination. This situation is, by its very nature, political because educators, whether they serve the interests of the state, their own interests as a class, or a specific ideal or ideology, cannot help but exert a dominating influence on the life of individuals and groups in society.

Massive amounts of information are produced about education, its content, methods and objectives, achievements and failures. Much of this information can serve as the raw material by which a better understanding can be gained of the role of education in various political processes. Access to educational information is provided by a full array of reference instruments that list, describe, define, or summarize information for a variety of research needs.

Bibliographic Instruments

GUIDEBOOKS

481   Baatz, Olga K., and Charles Albert Baatz. *The Psychological Foundations of Education. A Guide to Information Sources.* Detroit: Gale Research Company, 1981.

The annotated entries in this guidebook identify books, periodical articles, and other information sources that relate to

1. What the psychological sciences reveal about the human personality, and
2. What formally constitutes the science and art of educating the human person.

Specifically covered are intellectual education, moral education, affective education and poetic education. A separate chapter is devoted to the educational actors — learners, parents, and teachers. The political aspects of education are poorly covered, however. Author, title, and subject indexes are included.

482   Bebout, Lois. *Resources for Educational Issues*. Austin: National Educational Development Laboratory Publishers, 1979.

In its two parts this bibliographic guidebook identifies (1) basic sources of information in education and (2) resources for four specific issues in education — accountability, competency-based education, educational planning, and governance. The general part lists guidebooks, encyclopedias, statistical compendia, directories, biographical sources, indexing and abstracting services, databases, current awareness services and newsletters, information sources about federal programs, legal information sources, and sources of information on public response to education. Material in part 2 includes key works, bibliographies, legal sources, federal program sources, databases, directories, and lists of associations, research centers, and institutions.

483   Harman, G. S. *The Politics of Education. A Bibliographical Guide*. St. Lucia: University of Queensland Press, 1974.

One fascinating fact, observable in a number of countries including the United States, is the surprisingly widespread belief that education and politics are separate and unrelated activities, and that they should be so. The obvious role of education as a primary tool for political socialization and as an essential contributor to political literacy seems to have been lost in an antipolitical or nonpolitical atmosphere. Political education along with education in general is the stepchild of the political process in the United States and some other countries with a federal form of government. In those countries education comes under the control of financially strapped state or provincial governments whose primary interest is to please voters and not educational experts. The unfortunate result is a citizenry who is often ill prepared to cope adequately with the political needs and demands in a rapidly changing and dangerous world.

The guidebook offers an excellent assessment of the interrelationship between politics and education and its pertinent literature. The material is presented in nine chapters organized around specific countries (Australia, United States, Great Britain, other developed and undeveloped countries), specific topics and issues. The role of political socialization, pressure groups, the economics of education, state and federal government agencies, etc., is well covered. A separate chapter identifies the major reference works for each country. A subject index is also included.

484   Rufsvold, Margaret I., and Carolyn Guss. *Guides to Educational Media*. Chicago: American Library Association, 1977.

A large number of catalogs and other lists exist for educational media in audiovisual form, such as phonodiscs, phonotapes, videotapes, transparencies, films, filmstrips, etc. The guidebook, which is frequently revised and updated, identifies generally available catalogs as well as listings that were published since 1957 but are no longer available. Audiovisual media lists for political information may be identified in the index of the guidebook under political science, names of continents, ethnic studies, communism, civil rights, social sciences, and similarly suitable keywords. The guidebook also lists professional organizations in the educational media field and provides an inventory of selected periodicals covering audiovisual media.

485   Woodbury, Marda. *A Guide to Sources of Educational Information*. Arlington, VA: Information Resources Press, 1982.

The reference sources and other information services available in the field of education are listed and well described in this guidebook organized in five parts, as follows: (1) Effective Research, (2) Printed Research Tools, (3) Special Subjects, (4) Nonprint Sources, and (5) Follow Through. The first part presents a valuable outline of the research process. The second part identifies reference sources by type (dictionaries, encyclopedias, directories, bibliographies, handbooks, abstracts and indexes, data sources, etc.). The third part lists printed sources on finance and government, special education, instructional materials, and tests and assessment instruments. Part Four covers computerized retrieval sources, nonprint sources of educational information, governmental and financial information, special education, as well as institutional sources of information on instructional materials and tests, and state library services for educators. Part Five lists various writers' guides for aiding individuals in reporting the results of their education research. An index is also included.

CURRENT BIBLIOGRAPHIES

486   *Australian Education Index*. Hawthorn: Australian Council for Educational Research, 1957— .

487   *Bulletin Signaletique 520: Sciences de l'Education*. Paris: Centre de Documentation Sciences Humaines, 1947— .

488   *British Education Index*. London: British Library, 1954— .

489   *Canadian Education Index*. Toronto: Canadian Education Association, 1965— .

These reference instruments, published in countries other than the United States, offer author and subject access to educational articles in approximately 1,000 English- and French-language periodicals. Issued quarterly with annual cumulations, the reference works cover all topics including the politics of education. The French reference work also provides abstracts of the listed items.

490   *Current Index to Journals in Education (CIJE)*. Phoenix: Oryx Press, 1969–.

491   *Resources in Education (RIE)*. Washington, DC: U.S. Government Printing Office, 1966–.

492   *ERIC*. Bethesda, MD: ERIC Processing and Reference Facility, 1966–. (Vendor: BRS; Dialog — File 1; SDC)

Established by the U.S. Office of Education in 1964, the Educational Resources Information Center (ERIC) is a nationwide network of currently 16 clearing houses, each responsible for acquiring, selecting, abstracting, indexing, storing, retrieving, and disseminating educational documents in specific subject areas of education. The resulting centralization of reference functions offers the prospective user of educational information just three easy-to-use reference instruments, as cited above.

The *Current Index to Journals in Education (CIJE)*, issued monthly in printed form, provides author and subject indexing as well as abstract coverage for the educational literature published in more than 700 periodicals in the United States and other countries. *Resources in Education (RIE)*, also published monthly, complements the preceding reference work by indexing and abstracting the unpublished literature, consisting mainly of conference proceedings, federally funded research reports, professional papers, etc. Semiannual and annually cumulated indexes are also published. The computerized equivalent of the two printed reference sources is called *ERIC* and offers online display of bibliographic citations and abstracts from the RIE records since 1966 and the CIJE records since 1969.

All subject indexes of this printed and computerized retrieval system use a controlled vocabulary listed in the *Thesaurus of ERIC Descriptors*, currently published in revised annual editions by Oryx Press. Politically relevant subject terms most frequently utilized include civil rights, civil liberties, moral values, educational policy, policy formation, political affiliation, political attitudes, political influences, political power, political science, politics, politics of education, social factors, social history, social problems, social responsibility, social values, and many others.

Articles indexed and abstracted in the *Current Index to Journals in Education*, if unavailable in the local library, may be obtained from University Microfilms International in Ann Arbor, Michigan. All other ERIC documents are available in hard copy or microfiche either in libraries or from the ERIC Document Reproduction Ser-

vice (EDRS) in Arlington, Virginia. All ERIC documents carry an identifying number listed or displayed by the reference instruments.

493   *Educational Administration Abstracts*. Columbus, OH: University Council for Educational Administration, 1966–.

The reference work, issued three times a year, will be useful for retrieving information about the politico-administrative control of education. It offers nearly 1,000 abstracts annually for periodical articles published in American management and education journals. Entries are arranged under six topical categories, namely, tasks of administration, administrative processes and organizational variables, societal factors influencing education, programs for educational administrators, theory and research, planning and futurology.

494   *Education Index*. New York: H. W. Wilson, 1932–.

Periodical articles, conference proceedings, and government publications relating to all aspects of elementary, secondary, higher, and adult education can be identified by author and subject with the help of this printed reference tool. It is issued ten times per annum and indexes approximately 300 periodicals, most of which are of U.S. origin. Annual cumulated volumes are also available.

495   National Information Center for Educational Media. *Index to. . . .* Los Angeles: National Information Center for Educational Media, University of Southern California, 1966–.

496   *NICEM*. Los Angeles: National Information Center for Educational Media, University of Southern California, 1977–. (Vendor: BRS, 1977–1980; Dialog — File 70, current edition only)

The National Information Center for Educational Media (NICEM) indexes nonprint educational material and makes the frequently updated indexes available in book, microfiche, and online format. Currently published are 14 different indexes to free educational materials and to commercially available 16 mm educational films, 35 mm filmstrips, 8 mm motion picture cartridges, educational audiotapes, videotapes, records, overhead transparencies, slides, as well as to their producers and distributors. Also published are indexes to multimedia in psychology, technical, health/safety, and environmental studies education. Most indexed materials include brief abstracts of the contents. The audiovisual media are identifiable for all educational levels from preschool to professional and graduate school levels, and for all subject areas including political material.

The computerized database is searchable by media

type, grade level, keywords in the abstracts, subject headings, producer and distributor name and code.

497   New York (City). Public Library. Research Libraries. *Bibliographic Guide to Education.* Boston: G. K. Hall, 1978–.

The unannotated annual bibliography will be useful as a current awareness tool and research instrument for identifying the existence and call numbers of educational books and series. It lists in one alphabetical sequence by author, title, subject, and series entry new books and serials from all countries and in all languages. The subject matter encompasses American elementary and secondary education, higher education, history and philosophy of education, international and comparative education material, adult education, etc.

498   *Sociology of Education Abstracts.* Liverpool: Information for Education, Ltd., 1965–.

The scope of this quarterly index and abstract publication encompasses studies and other information material relating to sociological variables (race, class, socioeconomic status, etc.), sociological theories and methods, and empirical situations found in education. Entries cover books, periodical articles, conference proceedings, and reports issued throughout the world. Entries are arranged by author and are also accessible by five separate indexes, namely, (1) Theories Index, (2) Methods Index, (3) Empirical Situations Index, (4) Data Index (for variables and units of study), and (5) Form of Document Index. The latter index identifies bibliographies, conference reports, reviews of research, textbooks, etc. The indexes are also available in annual cumulations.

Dictionaries and Thesauri

499   Biswas, A., and J. C. Aggarwal. *Encyclopedic Dictionary and Directory of Education.* New Delhi: Academic Publishers, 1971.

Produced by two Indian educators, this reference work is a three-part compendium of dictionary, directory, and encyclopedic information oriented towards Indian, British, and European experience. The first part is a dictionary containing definitions and a glossary, the latter limited to national terms other than English. The second part is a biographical directory of educators and educational thinkers throughout the world. The third part offers encyclopedic coverage of the educational systems of the world, including education's relationship to politics and government.

500   Collins, K. T. *Keywords in Education.* London: Longman Group Ltd., 1973.

501   Dewey, John. *Dictionary of Education.* New York: Philosophical Library, 1959.

502   Good, Carter V. *Dictionary of Education.* New York: McGraw-Hill, 1973.

503   Hawes, Gene R., and Lynne S. Hawes. *The Concise Dictionary of Education.* New York: Van Nostrand Reinhold, 1982.

504   Hills, P. J. A *Dictionary of Education.* London: Routledge and Kegan Paul, 1982.

505   Page, G. Terry, and J. B. Thomas. *International Dictionary of Education.* New York: Nichols Publishing Company, 1977.

These dictionaries provide definitions, background information, and analysis of terms, concepts, or activities in the field of education.

506   Educational Resources Information Center. *Thesaurus of ERIC Descriptors.* Washington, DC: U.S. Government Printing Office, 1968–.

507   Educational Resources Information Center. *Thesaurus of ERIC Descriptors.* Phoenix: Oryx Press, 1982.

The frequently revised thesaurus provides an inventory of the subject descriptors used for the efficient retrieval of educational information from the various ERIC indexes. The listings include an alphabetical descriptors display with broader, narrower, and related terms, a rotated descriptor display, a hierarchical display, and a descriptor group display.

Directories

The large number of directories available in the educational field makes it inadvisable to offer listings of individual directories in this section. An inventory of American educational directories can be found in the guidebook listed below. Where additional directories need to be identified, consult the general guidebooks for the reference literature.

508   *Guide to American Educational Directories.* New York: B. Kein, 1963–.

Updated by new editions at irregular intervals, this guidebook lists American education directories by subject and title. The annotated entries encompass yearbooks and biographical dictionaries as well as the standard educational directories.

Encyclopedias

509   Dejnozka, Edward L., and David E. Kapel. *American Educators' Encyclopedia*. Westport, CT: Greenwood Press, 1982.

More than 2,000 articles based on the principal names, concepts, and topics found in the literature of professional education are offered by this one-volume encyclopedia. Covering elementary, secondary, and higher education in the United States, the encyclopedia includes articles on the administration and supervision in education, educational measurement, educational organizations, federal programs and legislation, school law, the history and philosophy of education, and the principal study areas, such as social studies, business and vocational education, library science, minority education, citizen education, and others. All articles include bibliographical references. There are 22 appendices in the encyclopedia, providing directory information on various government and professional organization officials, the state departments of education, the land grant colleges and universities, etc., as well as a chronological list of significant federal legislation for education. An index is also included.

510   *The Encyclopedia of Education*. New York: Macmillan, 1971.

In more than 1,000 articles, written by American university professors, the encyclopedia presents an overall view of the institutions and people, of the processes and products, found in educational practice. Noteworthy are the numerous comparative education articles that, under the name of a specific country, describe the educational system of more than 100 countries in the world. The role of the United States government and the various state governments in educational matters is also covered in a number of articles. With the help of the detailed index volume, it is possible to locate articles dealing with political activity, political conditions, political processes, political science, and politics. Another politically relevant key term is *social*, which provides access to a variety of articles in the encyclopedia dealing with social attitudes, social change, social class, social conditions, social consciousness, social control, social problems, social sciences, social status, social structure, social system, social work, socialization, and similar topics. Value-related information can be found under the terms *value conflicts*, *value judgment*, and *values*. The encyclopedia has been updated by the *Education Yearbook* issued by the same publisher in 1975.

511   *Encyclopedia of Educational Research*. New York: Macmillan, 1941– .

Almost completely rewritten every ten years, this encyclopedia attempts to assess contributions to educational knowledge and new areas of research interest and activity. Although the encyclopedia uses an alphabetical arrangement for its articles, it is best to use the detailed index, printed on yellow paper in the center of the volume, to locate information of specific interest. Useful summaries are presented about the politization of education and educational research, or the political development of emergent nations. Federal programs of the United States government relating to education are also covered in several articles. All articles close with detailed bibliographies of additional information sources. The encyclopedia is updated by the *Review of Educational Research*, published five times a year by the American Educational Research Association, which also prepares the encyclopedia.

512   *The International Encyclopedia of Higher Education*. San Francisco: Jossey-Bass: 1977.

Written by nearly 600 educational experts located in 69 countries, the multivolume encyclopedia presents some 1,300 alphabetically arranged entries for national systems of higher education, topical essays, fields of study, educational associations, centers of higher education research, and documentation and information centers. Two articles deal with the political persecution of academics and political science as a field of study. There are also separate articles about international law, public administration, and the various social sciences as fields of study in higher education. Several articles provide summary information about authoritative structures in higher education, such as governments, governing boards, and administrative organizations. The encyclopedia also provides a glossary of educational terms and an explanation of acronyms in Volume 1, and a detailed author and subject index in Volume 10.

Handbooks

513   Goodman, Steven E. *Handbook on Contemporary Education*. New York: R. R. Bowker, 1976.

The handbook offers 118 articles summarizing the current state of knowledge in education. Articles are grouped under eight parts, entitled: (1) Educational Change and Planning, (2) Administration and Management of Education, (3) Teacher-Faculty Issues, (4) Education and Training of Teachers and Administrators, (5) Students and Parents, (6) Special Interest Groups, (7) Teaching and Learning Strategies, (8) Alternatives and Options in Education. All articles include bibliographies of further reading material. Political education and theories of education are poorly covered. An index is provided.

514 *International Handbook of Education Systems.* New York: John Wiley & Sons, 1984.

Organized by regions and countries, the *Handbook* surveys the education systems of Eastern and Western Europe, Canada, Subsaharan Africa, North Africa, the Middle East, Asia, Australia, and Latin America. Each education system is examined in terms of its history, social structure, and economy. Information on relevant legislation and educational policies as well as statistical data are also provided.

515 Shulman, Lee S., and Gary Sykes. *Handbook of Teaching and Policy.* New York: Longman, Inc., 1983.

Many educators and parents will agree with Paul Copperman's recent conclusion, published in *The Literacy Hoax* (New York: William Morrow & Co., 1978), that "with skills down, assignments down, standards down and grades up" the American educational system perpetrates a hoax on its students and on their parents. This handbook examines the connection between effective classroom teaching and educational policy from a variety of perspectives. Twenty-one separate articles focus on such topics as teacher education, teaching competence, the lives of teachers, complexity and control of classroom activities, the interests of the student, the state, and the humanities in education, the courts and teaching, and other objects of educational policy. A subject index is included.

GEOGRAPHY

Introduction

Geography deals with some of the most difficult societal factors that a political system may be confronted with in its process or policy stage. Frequently escaping human control, land, climate, distance, and environmental hazards are the most powerful of all political rulers, even though many politicians and political scientists fail to acknowledge them. While it may have been recognized, for instance, that policies conceived in Kenya would not work very well in Great Britain, it took 70 years to prove that policies conceived in London are not effective in distant equatorial Africa. A curious deficiency of the political reference system excludes such geographical phenomena as the frozen lakes of Finland, the Russian winter of 1941–1942, the caves of North Vietnam, or the oil fields of the Middle East from the classification schemes and indexing vocabulary of even the best political reference works, despite the evidence that these facts of nature have been politically more decisive than the most powerful men of Moscow, Berlin, Paris, or Washington, DC.

Although not specifically designed for political inquiries, the reference instruments of geography must therefore be viewed as a crucial, often indispensable part of the retrieval mechanism for political information. The titles listed and described on the following pages will be most useful in all inquiries that focus on the geographical aspects of the political world.

Bibliographic Instruments

GUIDEBOOKS

516 Brewer, J. Gordon. *The Literature of Geography: A Guide to Its Organization and Use.* Hamden, CT: Linnet Books, 1978.

Organized in 13 chapters, the guidebook deals with (1) the scope, structure and use of the literature of geography, (2) the organization of geographical literature in libraries, (3) bibliographies and other reference works, (4) general geography periodicals, (5) general geography monographs, (6) cartobibliographies, (7) sources of statistics, (8) government and international organization publications, (9) the history of geography, (10) geographical techniques and methodology, (11) physical geography, (12) human geography, and (13) regional geography. The chapter on human geography provides separate listings for works in political and economic geography. A combined author, title, and subject index provides additional access to the text and bibliographic listings.

517 Burkett, Jack. *Concise Guide to the Literature of Geography.* Ealing, England: Ealing Technical College, 1967.

A well-annotated guide to bibliographies, catalogs, periodicals, geographical societies, encyclopedias, dictionaries, maps, atlases, and other reference sources in geography.

518 Harris, Chauncy D. *Bibliography of Geography: Part I, Introduction to General Aids.* Chicago: University of Chicago, 1976.

Divided into 16 chapters, the Harris guidebook lists and describes bibliographies of bibliographies, current and retrospective bibliographies, gazetteers, dictionaries, encyclopedias, statistical sources, and methodological works in geography. Serialized geographical publications can be identified in a separate bibliography by the author, entitled *International List of Geographical Serials* (Chicago: University of Chicago, 1980).

LIBRARY CATALOGS

519 American Geographical Society. *Research Catalogue.* Boston: G. K. Hall, 1962.

_____. *First Supplement, 1962–1971.* Boston: G. K. Hall, 1972, 1974.

_____. *Second Supplement.* Boston: G. K. Hall, 1978.

Well over 350,000 card entries for books, periodical articles, pamphlets, and government publications are contained in this multivolume research catalog and its supplements. The entries are arranged in two classification systems based on regional and topical divisions of the subject matter. The regional classification system divides the world into 52 geographical units. The topical classification consists of nine major classes, as follows: (1) general geography, (2) travel and exploration, (3) mathematical geography, (4) physical geography: biogeography, (5) human geography, (6) history of geography, (7) geographical teaching and institutions engaged in geographical work, (8) aids to geographical study, and (9) history. Under each of the nine classes further subdivisions are made to indicate narrower topics. Most useful for political inquiries will be the subdivisions under the human geography class, such as 501 — adjustment of man to geographical environment; 52 — geography of population, including movements, forms of settlement, economic geography, industrial geography, political geography, social and cultural geography, military geography, etc. The catalog will be updated by additional supplements, but all recent geographical publications are identifiable in *Current Geographical Publications*, listed and described below.

CURRENT BIBLIOGRAPHIES

520   American Geographical Society. *Current Geographical Publications.* New York: 1938–.

Issued monthly, except July and August, this unannotated bibliography lists books, pamphlets, government documents, periodical articles, and maps added to the collections of the American Geographical Society. Entries are arranged according to the classification of the Society's research catalog. Wherever possible, material is classified by region and further classified by subject. The first two digits of the subject classification are printed in the right-hand margin next to each bibliographic entry. A separate author and subject index inclusive of regional references is provided.

521   *Bibliographie Geographique Internationale.* Paris: A. Colin, 1894–; Paris: Centre Nationale de la Recherche Scientifique, 1947–.

The publisher and the title of this bibliography have varied over the years. As presently issued, the bibliography offers annual, comprehensive, annotated and classified listings of the world's geographical literature. Entries are arranged in two parts: Part 1 lists general works, and Part 2 arranges works by country with subject subdivisions. Author and subject indexes are included.

522   *Enviroline.* New York: Environment Information Center, 1971–. (Vendor: BRS; Dialog — File 40; SDC)

523   *Environment Abstracts.* New York: Environment Information Center, 1971–.

524   *Environment Index.* New York: Environment Information Center, 1973–.

The titles above refer to a wide-ranging reference system for information about all aspects of environmental phenomena, notably pollution, chemical or biological contamination, use and misuse of renewable and nonrenewable resources, solid wastes, etc. Bibliographic citations to and abstracts of periodicals, official publications, books, research reports, and conference papers can be obtained from the monthly updated *Enviroline* database and in manual searches of its two printed equivalents.

Environment Abstracts, published monthly and in an annual cumulation, lists and abstracts environmental documentation in 21 subject categories, as follows: 01 — air pollution, 02 — chemical and biological contamination, 03 — energy, 04 — environmental education, 05 — environmental design and urban ecology, 06 — food and drugs, 07 — general, 08 — international, 09 — land use and misuse, 10 — noise pollution, 11 — nonrenewable resources, 12 — oceans and estuaries, 13 — population planning and control, 14 — radiological contamination, 15 — renewable resources — terrestrial, 16 — renewable resources — water, 17 — solid waste, 18 — transportation, 19 — water pollution, 20 — weather modification and geophysical change, and 21 — wildlife. An additional section, entitled Issue Alert, summarizes the most significant information covered in the 21 categories.

Indexing is available in each issue of *Environment Abstracts* as well as in an annual cumulation, entitled *Environment Index*. Access to all abstracted material is provided by a subject index, SIC Code and industry index, geographical index, source index, and author index. The *Environment Index* also includes a list of major environmental impact statements submitted to the U.S. Environmental Protection Agency by various governmental departments and independent agencies. A directory of all federal and state agencies and nongovernmental organizations concerned with environmental affairs is also provided.

525   *Environmental Bibliography.* Santa Barbara, CA: Environmental Studies Institute, 1973–. (Vendor: Dialog — File 68)

526   *Environmental Periodicals Bibliography*. Santa Barbara, CA: Environmental Studies Institute, 1972—.

Bibliographic citations for the contents of approximately 350 environmental periodicals published in the United States and other countries are offered by this reference source available in computerized and printed format. The printed version, *Environmental Periodicals Bibliography*, is published in six issues per year plus an annual cumulative index. Each of the bimonthly issues offers the table of contents pages of the periodicals arranged under six major subject categories, namely: (1) general, human ecology; (2) air; (3) energy; (4) land resources; (5) marine and freshwater resources; and (6) nutrition and health. While this arrangement is useful for browsing, additional access to the listed articles is provided by an author index and a detailed subject profile index. The latter uses several keywords to profile more accurately the contents of the cited article. The computerized database, updated bimonthly, can likewise be searched by keywords and author names, as well as by names of political entities.

527   *Geoabstracts*. Norwich, England: University of East Anglia, 1965—.

Books and periodical articles are listed and abstracted in this reference work, which is published six times a year in six different series. Section C (economic geography) and section D (social geography and cartography) will be most useful for political inquiries since the listed material deals with social and economic phenomena, cultural and urban geography, regional studies, population studies, and similar material. Other sections of *Geoabstracts* deal with landforms and the quarternary (section A), biogeography and climatology (section B), sedimentology (section E), and regional and community planning (section F). Author and regional indexes appear in each issue, and annually cumulated indexes are also published.

528   *Pollution Abstracts*. Bethesda, MD: Cambridge Scientific Abstracts, 1970—.

529   *Pollution Abstracts*. Bethesda, MD: Cambridge Scientific Abstracts, 1970—. (Vendor: BRS; Dialog—File 41)

This reference work, available in printed and computerized versions, offers access to and abstracts from publications about all forms of environmental pollution, its sources and control by legislation, policy, or programs. Air, fresh water, marine, land, noise, and thermal pollution are covered. More than 2,500 foreign and U.S. sources, including books, periodicals, government reports, conference proceedings, and other publications are regularly scanned.

The printed version is issued bimonthly and includes separate subject and author indexes to the published abstracts. The computerized database permits online retrieval of the abstracts since January 1978 and bibliographic citations since 1970, both updated bimonthly.

530   Royal Geographical Society. London. *New Geographical Literature and Maps*. London: 1918—.

The semiannual bibliography, a counterpart to the American title, provides a subject listing of books, periodical articles, new maps and atlases arranged by regions and countries. Entries reflect accessions to the Library of the Royal Geographical Society.

RETROSPECTIVE BIBLIOGRAPHIES

531   Anglemyer, Mary. *Natural Resources in Foreign Countries*. Washington, DC: U.S. Department of the Interior, 1968.

532   Larson, Arthur W., Glen Clatterbuck, and Erwin Chemerinsky. *The Development and Allocation of World Resources*. Skokie, IL: National Textbook Company, 1975.

These two bibliographic works are devoted to a fundamental geopolitical problem, namely, the development and allocation of natural resources. The first title is an annotated bibliography of bibliographies listing publications about the natural resources in all parts of the world. The entries are arranged by regions and countries. The second reference work is an annotated list of books, periodical articles, and government publications useful for an academic debate on the allocation of world resources. The book is organized in six chapters, entitled (1) Research on the Allocation of World Resources, (2) World Food Resources, (3) Social Resources, (4) Energy and Mineral Resources, (5) Who's Who of Experts on World Resources, and (6) Select Bibliography on World Resources. Each of these chapters contains a discussion of the problem, an outline of the issues, and supporting evidence produced by the literature.

533   Barton, Roy. *Radical Geography: A Research Bibliography*. Leeds, England: School of Geography, University of Leeds, 1983.

Radical geography seeks to understand and change its real world subject matter through the use of models, concepts, and ideas substantially different from the established discipline. This bibliography lists books and periodical articles that reflect Marxist and other radical viewpoints on geographically oriented social or political processes, such as urbanization, planning, financing, developing, etc., or on geographically manifested societal problems, such as housing, transportation, and others. All entries are unannotated, but concise headnotes introduce the various listings. No index is included. Regrettably, the presented listings cover only a fraction of the vast literature produced throughout the world on this subject area.

534   Dolman, A. N., and D. S. M. Munro. *Author and Subject Index of the Publications of the Canadian Association of Geographers 1951–1967.* Montreal: McGill University, 1968.

535   *National Geographic Cumulative Index.* Washington, DC: National Geographic Society, 1899–1963.

536   Snipe, Ronald H. *A Guide to Geographical Periodicals: Annals of the Association of American Geographers, Geographical Review and Economic Geography.* Manitou Springs, CO: Ronald H. Snipe, 1969.

Some of the heavily used geographical periodicals have been cumulatively indexed for varying periods of time. The indexes listed above provide author, subject, and regional access to several thousand articles published in hundreds of periodical volumes.

537   Morrison, Denton, Kenneth E. Hornback, and W. Keith Warner. *Environment: A Bibliography of Social Science and Related Literature.* Washington, DC: U.S. Environmental Protection Agency, 1973.

In order to achieve the object of improved environmental quality, political actors are required to consider numerous social and philosophical factors and impacts. This bibliography contains nearly 5,000 entries for social science literature that is relevant, substantively, methodologically, or theoretically, to the political concerns for a better environment. The entries are arranged alphabetically by author with a subject by title index under 42 major categories. These categories include aesthetic, humanistic or philosophical factors, air quality, attitudes and opinions, climate, conflicts and issues, conservation, economics and economic growth, energy, history, law and property rights, natural resources, noise, pollution, population, migration and crowding, recreation, spatial behavior, transportation, waste, water, and others. Bibliographies, directories, and other reference works are listed in a separate category. All entries are unannotated.

538   Sanguin, A. L. *Geographie Politique.* Montreal: Les Presses de L'Université du Quebec, 1976.

This reference work identifies the fundamental literature of political geography. The unannotated entries list books and periodical articles dealing with geopolitics, civilization and culture, geography of races and peoples, geography of languages, geography of religions, nation and nationalism, the concepts of state, territory and frontiers, political geography of oceans, rivers and airspace, military geography, geography of international relations and international organizations, colonialism, decolonization, and other areas of interest in political geography.

539   Wasserman, Paul. *Encyclopedia of Geographic Information Sources.* Detroit: Gale Research Company, 1978.

This book is not an encyclopedia but an unannotated bibliography of reference publications and other information sources arranged under names of countries, provinces, and cities. Listed are abstracts and indexes, almanacs and yearbooks, bibliographies, biographical works, directories, lists of newspapers and periodicals, gazetteers, and other geographical reference works, government and trade offices, guides to doing business, periodicals, statistical sources, and other sources of diverse origin. The listings are incomplete or highly selective, and do not cover political and legal reference works for geographical inquiries adequately. Consulates and information centers maintained by other countries in the United States, for instance, are not fully recorded in this reference book.

Dictionaries

540   Allaby, Michael. *A Dictionary of the Environment.* New York: Van Nostrand, 1978.

The terminology, concepts, and major concerns of environmentalists are identified and defined in this dictionary.

541   *Columbia Lippincott Gazetteer of the World.* New York: Columbia University Press, 1962.

542   *Webster's Geographical Dictionary.* Springfield, MA: Merriam, 1962.

These reference works, also known as gazetteers, provide significant information about places, cities, countries, and geographic features of the world. The first title lists some 130,000 names and offers concise information concerning the geographical and political location, population, trade, industry, history, and cultural institutions of places. The second title contains some 40,000 geographical names with similar categories of information.

543   Johnston, R. J. *Dictionary of Human Geography.* New York: Free Press, 1981.

Initially a largely introspective discipline, human geography was one of the social sciences that enthusiastically adopted the nomothetic, positivist philosophy of the natural sciences, while introducing a variety of humanistic and structuralist approaches. The resulting linguistic explosion is well reflected in this dictionary, which offers detailed explanations and definitions together with bibliographic references for both new and older words, terms, and concepts. A separate index for terms and authors covered in the entries is also included.

544   Kurian, George Thomas. *Geo-Data. The World Almanac Gazetteer.* Detroit: Gale Research Company, 1983.

This reference work provides a wide range of geographical, economic, and political facts for the United States and other countries as follows: Part I, section 1 offers 20 items of information, including population, elevation, nickname, names of newspapers, crime rate, municipal revenues and expenditures, per capita income, and Moody's bond rating for each town and city in the United States with a population of 10,000 or more. Ten additional categories of data, such as percentage of families below poverty level, population density, percentage of foreign population, etc., are provided for larger cities. Section 2 presents for each of 3,142 counties such data as per capita income, population size, public school enrollment, county seat, etc. Section 3 supplies 100 items of information on the 50 states and the U.S. territories, including data on education and industry, physical quality of life index numbers, women in public office, percentage of civilian labor force in government, and others. Part II provides similar information for foreign countries. Part III presents geographical information on lakes, rivers, islands, mountains, and other physical features of the earth. Part IV offers a variety of rankings based on geographical extremes — the highest, widest, deepest, coldest, hottest, largest, most populous places on earth. An index by cities, countries, and major subject terms is included.

545   Larkin, Robert P., and Gary L. Peters. *Dictionary of Concepts in Human Geography.* Westport, CT: Greenwood Press, 1983.

Like political science, human geography is a hybrid discipline that incorporates terms and concepts from several academic fields and infuses them with meanings of its own. This dictionary presents an inventory of 140 key concepts in human geography, such as boundary, cultural landscape, distance, economic base theory, environmentalism, geopolitics, gerrymander, land use, migration, mobility, population density, region, social change, state, Third World, and others that are politically significant. Each concept is briefly described together with a history of its usage development and cross-references to other concepts. Bibliographical references to major and additional sources of information are also included in each entry.

546   Monkhouse, F. J. *A Dictionary of Geography.* Chicago: Aldine, 1970.

547   Stamp, Sir Dudley. *A Glossary of Geographical Terms.* New York: John Wiley and Sons, 1966.

The study of the geographical features of the earth has produced a significant number of specialized terms that are listed and defined in these two dictionaries. The second title attempts, wherever possible, to trace new terms back to their originators and to provide the original definition.

Directories

548   Association of American Geographers. *Directory.* Washington, DC: 1949– .

The irregularly revised directory lists the name, birth date, education, employment, geographic specialty, geographic area of interest, and language of proficiency of more than 700 geographers who are members of this association.

549   *Orbis Geographicus. World Directory of Geography.* Wiesbaden: Steiner, 1973.

This standard international directory is issued in two parts and provides information about societies, institutes, agencies, geography departments in universities, as well as individual geographers in the various countries of the world.

Encyclopedias

550   *The International Geographic Encyclopedia and Atlas.* Boston: Houghton Mifflin, 1979.

The more than 25,000 alphabetically arranged entries in this encyclopedia offer, apart from basic geographical data, a variety of information on the history, economic importance, and the educational, cultural, or political institutions of the cities, counties, and countries of the world. All country entries identify the names of the individual provinces or states and their respective capitals. The entries for the 50 U.S. states identify the names of all counties and the county seats. A 64-page atlas of four-color maps and more than 200 black-and-white maps shows the major physical and political features in every region of the world.

551   Parker, Sybil P. *McGraw-Hill Encyclopedia of Environmental Science.* New York: McGraw-Hill, 1980.

The one-volume encyclopedia contains more than 250 alphabetically arranged articles, including five feature articles, that provide a concise insight into the present state of scientific knowledge available, the governmental and commercial directions that must be taken, the laws and conservation procedures required to deal with the massive problems of environmental protection. A list of the major laws already enacted by the United States Congress is included. A detailed index offers additional access.

Handbooks and Digests

552   Fullard, Harold. *The Geographical Digest*. London: George Philip & Son, 1963—.

The annually published reference work offers population statistics for countries and large towns, production statistics for mineral, agricultural, and industrial products, gross domestic product and consumer price index numbers, as well as brief descriptive information about new sources of raw materials, new engineering projects, and new transportation facilities around the world.

553   Lock, C. B. Muriel. *Geography. A Reference Handbook*. Hamden, CT: Shoestring Press, 1968.

The handbook contains in alphabetical sequence entries for books, periodicals, atlases, societies, organizations, individual geographers, and libraries of potential interest in the study of geography.

554   Pounds, Norman J. G. *Political Geography*. New York: McGraw-Hill, 1972.

Essential information in political geography is summarized by this handbook under the following chapter headings: The State and the Nation, Area and Location of States, Frontiers and Boundaries, Territorial Sea, Population, Resources and Power, Core Areas and Capitals, The Geography of Administrative Areas, Geographical Aspects of Relations between States, The Geography of Foreign Trade, The Geography of Rivers, Colonies and Decolonization, The Developing World, etc. Bibliographic references conclude each chapter.

HISTORY

Introduction

Due to the availability of additional, previously unknown information sources and a broader time perspective, the historians, rather than the members of any other academic discipline, are able to provide more definitive evidence about the various political phenomena that had their origin in the recent or more distant past. This historical evidence assumes its greatest utility, however, in a better understanding and a more correct evaluation of most current political phenomena since their contemporary existence is invariably predicated on causal anteced-

ents in the past and a historical continuity in the present. Much of the irrationality of current political phenomena, for instance, can best be explained by the historical method, and this is true for the current division of Germany, the continuing conflict in the Middle East, the election primaries in the United States as well as most other puzzling political processes, policies, or ideas of the contemporary period.

The retrieval of historical evidence is facilitated by reference works that offer bibliographic and other access to as yet unpublished, archival resources as well as to published documentation material. Much of what has become known is summarized by abstracts, dictionaries, digests, and encyclopedias. These fact retrieval tools offer essential details in all substantive political reference categories, notably,

- specific areas and countries
- political and other events
- political actors
- political processes and policies
- political ideas and ideologies
- social conditions and societal factors

as well as their interaction within specific time frames.

Despite these positive features, the historical reference literature is still deficient in a more precise accounting of the lessons of history. There are indications that political decision-makers as well as the general public frequently ignore, overlearn, or underestimate the lessons of the past.* If the historical mistakes are to be truly understood and not merely repeated or exaggerated by each succeeding generation, it is vital that they are not buried in the historical literature, but more effectively highlighted against the background of changing conditions and opportunities.

Apart from the listings on the following pages, many important reference works of at least partial historical content may also be found in the various sections on International Relations, Comparative and Area Studies in Chapter 4 of this guidebook.

Archival Resources

A considerable amount of historical evidence remains buried and unpublished in the holdings of historical archives in the United States and other countries. In recent years the wealth of historical material has become more accessible to researchers as a result of microfilming, better inventories, and improved finding aids. Although it would be difficult to draw up a complete list of the world's

*See, for instance, Ernest R. May, *Lessons of the Past. The Use and Misuse of History in American Foreign Policy* (New York: Oxford University Press, 1973).

archival records, the following items are the most frequently used retrieval aids for historical records preserved in the U.S. and foreign repositories.

UNITED STATES REPOSITORIES: GUIDEBOOKS, CATALOGS, INVENTORIES

555   *National Inventory of Documentary Sources in the United States*. Teaneck, NJ: Chadwyck-Healey, 1983–1985, 1985–.

Archival and manuscript collections cannot be used without detailed finding aids that list the constituent parts of each collection down to box, folder, and document level. The purpose of the new *National Inventory* and its updating service is to bring together through reproduction on microfiche thousands of mainly unpublished or previously inaccessible finding aids, such as lists, registers, and collection guides in repositories throughout the United States. By also providing printed name and subject indexes, this single reference work enables the user to pinpoint the existence and location of specific documents without time-consuming research trips, calls, or correspondence.

The reference work is issued in four parts: (1) Federal Records; (2) Manuscript Division, Library of Congress; (3) State Archives, State Libraries and State Historical Societies; and (4) Academic and Research Libraries. Part 1 includes 428 current finding aids for the records of the executive, judicial, and legislative branches of the U.S. government as well as other governments in the National Archives. In addition, 886 finding aids are reproduced for the personal and official papers of presidents Hoover, Franklin D. Roosevelt, Truman, Eisenhower, Kennedy, Johnson, and Ford in the seven presidential libraries. Earlier presidential papers are identifiable in part 2. The official records of state governments as well as the documentation of businesses and organizations are listed in part 3, while a wealth of material on political figures and societal factors stored in libraries is made accessible in part 4. Parts 3 and 4 are open-ended series with continual additions. The entire reference work will eventually also be searchable online.

556   U.S. Library of Congress. *National Union Catalog of Manuscript Collections*, 1959–. Ann Arbor, MI: S. W. Edwards, 1962; Hamden, CT: The Shoestring Press, 1964; Washington, DC: Library of Congress, 1965–.

Only the existence, location, and general scope of the manuscript collections in United States repositories can be identified with the help of this catalog. The entries are arranged by author of the manuscripts and are indexed by name, subject, and repository. Each entry provides information about the location, scope, and content of the collection but does not furnish access to specific items in the collections.

557   U.S. National Archives. *National Archives Accessions*. Washington, DC: 1940–.

558   _____ . *Guide to the Records in the National Archives*. Washington, DC: U.S. Government Printing Office, 1948.

559   _____ . *Guide to Federal Archives Relating to the Civil War*. Washington, DC: 1962.

560   _____ . *Guide to Materials on Latin America in the National Archives*. Washington, DC: 1961.

561   _____ . *Handbook of Federal World War Agencies and Their Records, 1917–1921*. Washington, DC: 1943.

562   _____ . *Federal Records of World War II*. Vol. 1, *Civilian Agencies*; Vol. 2, *Military Agencies*. Washington, DC: 1950–1951.

563   _____ . *Guide to the Archives of the Government of the Confederate States of America*. Washington, DC: 1968.

The National Archives collect, preserve, and administer the permanently valuable records of the federal government of the United States. These records are organized in more than 400 groups, which consist of the official documentation produced or collected by a specific department, bureau, or other governmental unit. Many record groups contain documentation relating to other nations and their relationship with the United States. The documents may be textual records in handwritten, typewritten, or printed form as well as maps, sound recordings, motion pictures, microfilms, etc. Usage of these records is subject to restrictions imposed by the originating agency, Congress, or the Archivist of the United States of America. To assist users in their search for historical documentation, a number of guidebooks and other finding aids have been made available by the National Archives and Records Service.

New additions to the archival collections are listed and briefly described in an irregularly issued publication, entitled *National Archives Accessions*. A general description of the records collected by the National Archives can be found in the *Guide to Records in the National Archives*. Several other guidebooks exist that describe the archival records relating to a specific historical period (Civil War, World War I, World War II) or geographic area.

564   U.S. National Archives. *List of National Archives Microfilm Publications*. Washington DC: 1947–.

In order to make the holdings of the National Archives more accessible for a larger public, millions of pages of archival material have been put on microfilm available for purchase. The irregularly published list identifies series of archival records existing on microfilm. The microfilmed material relates to various periods of American history and also includes documentation originally produced in Europe, Latin America, and other parts of the world. Separate lists have been issued for microfilm publications of the diplomatic and consular correspondence of the U.S. Department of State and its embassies, consulates, or other diplomatic posts.

565   U.S. National Archives. *General Records of the Department of State*. Washington, DC: 1963. (#157)

566   _____ . *House of Representatives, 1789–1946*. Washington, DC: 1959. (#113)

567   _____ . *National Recovery Administration*. Washington, DC: 1952. (#44)

568   _____ . *Office of War Information*. Washington, DC: 1953. (#56)

569   _____ . *Selected Foreign Service Posts*. Washington, DC: 1953. (#60)

570   _____ . *Supreme Court of the United States*. Washington, DC: 1962. (#139)

571   _____ . *United States and Mexican Claims Commissions*. Washington, DC: 1962. (#136)

572   _____ . *United States Food Administration, 1917–1920*. Washington, DC: 1943. (#3)

573   _____ . *United States Participation in International Conferences, Commissions and Expositions*. Washington, DC: 1955. (#76)

In addition to the guidebooks and other lists previously cited, the National Archives and Records Service has made available nearly 200 preliminary inventories in book form that list and describe the archival records of a specific governmental unit. Included in the description are indexes, registers, and other bibliographic aids that may exist for this particular record group. The titles listed above represent a selection from the available inventories. Their content varies from a few pages to several hundred pages. Items available on microfilm or inaccessible because of restrictions are indicated in many instances.

574   U.S. National Historical Publications and Records Commission. *Directory of Archives and Manuscript Repositories in the United States*. Washington, DC: National Historical Publications and Records Commission, 1978.

Some 3,250 repositories of archival material in the 50 states of the United States of America, plus the District of Columbia, Puerto Rico, and the Panama Canal Zone are identified in this reference work. Entries are arranged by state and city and offer details about the location and content of the holdings.

FOREIGN REPOSITORIES: GUIDEBOOKS, LISTS, INDEXES

575   Carter, Charles. *The Western European Powers, 1500–1700*. Ithaca, NY: Cornell University Press, 1971.

This reference work offers a valuable description of the archives, historical records, and published reference sources relative to great Western European powers during a 200-year period at the beginning of the modern age. The main focus is on the historical records of Spain, France, England, and the Spanish Netherlands. A discussion of miscellaneous research problems, such as authenticity, bias, dating, and interpretation, is also included in the book.

576   Foster, Janet, and Julia Sheppard. *British Archives. A Guide to Archive Resources in the United Kingdom*. Detroit: Gale Research Company, 1982.

Archival holdings in the United Kingdom are among the richest in the world and include massive collections of governmental records. The guidebook contains 708 entries arranged alphabetically by town, giving information about the name, address, opening times, access, historical background, acquisition policy, major collections, facilities, finding aids, and publications of each repository. An alphabetical list of the repositories, a county list of repositories, a select bibliography, a general index to collections, and a key subject work index are also included.

577   Great Britain. Public Record Office. *Guide to the Contents of the Public Record Office*. London: Her Majesty's Stationery Office, 1963–1968.

578   _____ . *Lists and Indexes*. London: KTO Press, 1977.

579   *Index to British Foreign Office Correspondence 1920–*. Nendeln, Liechtenstein: Kraus-Thomson, 1969–.

British historical records in unpublished form are available directly from the Public Record Office in London. Several guidebooks and indexes have been produced to assist the researcher in the identification of desired documents.

The first item is a multivolume guidebook that describes the judicial or legal papers, state papers, and departmental records held in the Public Record Office

(PRO) up to 1966. All archival material is arranged in groups according to the courts and departments from which it emanates and is divided into classes corresponding to distinct series compiled and preserved as such in their place of origin. Brief descriptions are given for each group and class of records. Existing reference aids, such as numerical and descriptive lists, calendars, transcripts, indexes, or catalogs, are mentioned. More recent additions to the PRO collections of archival material are listed in supplementary volumes or special lists issued at irregular intervals.

A commercial publisher has reprinted 53 volumes of lists and indexes begun by the Public Record Office in 1892, together with an additional 70 volumes known as supplementary series. These lists, indexes, and other finding aids pertain to Foreign Office records, Colonial Office records, Admiralty records, War Office records, Board of Trade records, Treasury records, and numerous other official records and proceedings extending from the twelfth century to 1946.

British Foreign Office correspondence for the period after 1920 is identifiable with a massive index set originally prepared for restricted usage within the British Foreign Office. Due to the fact that the restricted period has been reduced from the last 50 years to 30 years, all official papers identified in the index now become publicly available, including the so-called green papers of previously secret or confidential classification. The index entries include a brief description of each document's contents as well as three numbers: a registry number, a subject file number, and a country number. Researchers desiring to order microfilmed documents must refer to separate *Purport Guides*, obtainable from the London Public Record office, for lists of microfilm volume numbers corresponding to the registry numbers by which documents are identified in the index.

580   Hill, Roscoe R. *The National Archives of Latin America*. Cambridge, MA: Harvard University Press, 1945.

This guidebook offers a description of the history, classification system, historical records, and publications of the national archives in 20 countries of Central and South America.

581   Low, D. A., et al. *Government Archives in South Asia*. Cambridge, England: Cambridge University Press, 1969.

Government archives in three Asian countries, Sri Lanka, India, and Pakistan, are described in this guidebook. Arranged by country, the information includes the location of the archive, rules of access, history of the collection, nature and extent of holdings, and available retrieval aids.

582   Thomas, Daniel H., and Lynn M. Case. *Guide to the Diplomatic Archives of Western Europe*. Philadelphia: University of Pennsylvania Press, 1976.

The guidebook describes the history and organization of the principal archival institutions in 15 Central and Western European countries. Valuable information is presented on how to use the archives and their collections. The book also identifies the major collections of published documents whose originals are kept in the European archives.

Published Resources

BIBLIOGRAPHIC INSTRUMENTS

Guidebooks

583   American Historical Association. *Guide to Historical Literature*. New York: Macmillan, 1961.

The AHA guidebook provides a selective inventory of the best historical writing at the time of publication. Entries include books and periodicals published in English and other languages throughout the world. The arrangement follows a classified order that is mainly regional, partly chronological, and frequently subdivided by special topics. Within each section the historical literature is listed in the following categories: bibliographies, library and museum collections; encyclopedias; geographies, gazetteers, and atlases; anthropologic, demographic, and linguistic works; printed collections of sources; shorter and longer general histories; histories of periods, areas, and topics; biographies; government publications; publications of academies, universities, and learned societies; and periodicals. The index contains mostly name entries, names of countries, and broad terms, like social conditions, legislative bodies, laboring classes, nationalism, etc. The lack of a more detailed subject index and supplement is a serious deficiency of this otherwise valuable guidebook to the world's historical literature.

584   Beers, Henry Putney. *Bibliographies in American History, 1942–1978. Guide to Materials for Research*. Woodbridge, CT: Research Publications.

The two-volume set lists in classified order more than 10,000 bibliographies in the field of U.S. history from World War II to the late 1970s. Separately published bibliographies as well as bibliographies in periodical articles are identified. Separate author and subject indexes are included.

585   Cassara, Ernest. *History of the United States of America A Guide to Information Sources*. Detroit: Gale Research Company, 1977.

Chronological access to historical information in book form is offered by this guidebook. Entries are annotated and are highly selective in comparison to other available guidebooks.

586   Frick, Elizabeth. *Library Research Guide to History: Illustrated Search Strategy and Sources.* Ann Arbor, MI: Pierian Press, 1980.

Organized in 12 chapters and 4 appendices, this guidebook offers illustrated instructions for locating information on historical topics and provides a list of basic reference sources in history. The listings are classified according to 21 major categories based on time frames (ancient history, medieval history, modern history), regions (North American history, Russian and East European, European, Middle Eastern and North African, Africa South of the Sahara, Asian, South Asian, South East Asian, Latin American, Australian and New Zealand history), selected countries (British Isles, Chinese, Japanese, Korean history) or general history sections. Within these categories various types of bibliographic or substantive reference sources are separately identified.

587   Freidel, Frank. *Harvard Guide to American History.* Cambridge, MA: Belknap Press of Harvard University Press, 1974.

588   Handlin, Oscar. *Harvard Guide to American History.* Cambridge, MA: Belknap Press of Harvard University Press, 1954.

The more recent edition of this guidebook, published in two volumes, provides topical (volume 1) and chronological (volume 2) access to informative books and periodicals published in American history. Volume 1 is organized in four parts, namely, (1) Research Methods and Materials; (2) Biographies and Personal Records; (3) Comprehensive and Area Histories; (4) Histories of Special Subjects. Volume 2 contains five additional parts, entitled (5) America to 1789; (6) United States, 1789–1860; (7) Civil War and Reconstruction; (8) Rise of Industry and Empire; (9) Twentieth Century. Numerous subdivisions within these nine parts aggregate appropriate material within narrower topical, geographical, or chronological boundaries. Additional access to the listed material is provided by separate indexes of names and subjects. No annotations accompany the bibliographic entries.

The older guidebook also follows a topical and chronological arrangement but contains brief historical summaries before the bibliographic sections. The index contains mostly name entries as well as some title and subject entries. The bibliographic entries are unannotated.

589   Higham, Robin. *A Guide to the Sources of United States Military History.* Hamden, CT: Archon Books, 1975.

590   Higham, Robin, and Donald J. Mrozek. *A Guide to the Sources of United States Military History, Supplement I.* Hamden, CT: Archon Books, 1981.

Prepared by professors of history and military historians, the guidebook presents bibliographic essays and selective lists of titles in chronologically and topically arranged chapters. Army, Navy, and Air Force history as well as defense policy and diplomacy for the period up to 1973 are covered in the various chapters of the base volume. The supplement identifies publications on military topics not adequately covered in the original guide, such as the U.S. Marine Corps, the Department of Defense and defense policy since 1945, nuclear war and arms control, military law, martial law, military government, and others.

591   Poulton, Helen J. *The Historian's Handbook. A Descriptive Guide to Reference Works.* Norman: University of Oklahoma Press, 1972.

A narrative description of the historical reference literature is offered by this guidebook. Library catalogs, bibliographies, encyclopedias, dictionaries, almanacs, newspaper directories, newspaper indexes, geographical aids, biographical, legal, and other information sources useful for historical studies are cited within a narrative text. The bibliographic information for the cited works is given in footnotes.

592   Tingley, Donald F. *Social History of the United States. A Guide to Information Sources.* Detroit: Gale Research Company, 1979.

The articulation of social needs for current policy purposes cannot be understood without reference to the history of social conditions. This bibliography identifies key works that trace the history of specific ethnic groups, social or occupational classes, social thought and reform, education, religion, and culture in the United States during the nineteenth and twentieth centuries. The annotated entries are arranged under 26 chapters that reflect the aforementioned historical topics. Author, title, and subject indexes are included.

593   Trask, David F., and Robert W. Pomeroy III. *The Craft of Public History. An Annotated Select Bibliography.* Westport, CT: Greenwood Press, 1983.

While most historians are active in academic settings, many historians are being called upon by government agencies and other organizations to practice their discipline for the management of archives, the preservation of oral communication, and the preparation of policy histories.

This reference work identifies and briefly describes the most representative works from each area of interest to the public historian. While several of the 11 chapters in the book are devoted to general matters such as research, writing, training, and management, separate listings are provided for political and social oral history, as well as various policy histories, including foreign policy, military and strategic policy, welfare policy, urban policy, and others. An author index is included.

Library Catalogs

594   Stuttgart. Library for Contemporary History and World War. *Catalogs*. Boston: G. K. Hall, 1970.

595   Munich. Institute for Contemporary History. Library.

Alphabetical Catalog.

Subject Catalog.

Regional Catalog.

Biographical Catalog.

Boston: G. K. Hall, 1967.

_____ . *First Supplement*. Boston: G. K. Hall, 1972.

These book catalogs are of special value to the researcher who is interested in the documentation of political and military phenomena of the twentieth century. The collection of the Stuttgart library on wars, international relations, and politics of the various countries of the world presently exceeds 170,000 volumes. Two catalog sets identify almost 90 percent of the present collection, of which 22 percent is in English. The Alphabetical Catalog contains 171,000 cards in 11 volumes, and the Classified Catalog encompasses 20 volumes with 237,000 cards in three parts — general, historical, and regional. The Regional Catalog section is subdivided by subject and period. The catalogs are not scheduled to be supplemented by the publisher, but more recent material acquired by the library may be identified in various bibliographical serials issued by the library.

The book catalog of the Munich library consists of 15 volumes containing more than 250,000 cards for author, subject, geographical, and bibliographical entries. The collection is particularly strong for the political history from 1918 to 1949, with heavy emphasis on the national-socialist era in Germany and Europe.

Current Bibliographies

596   *America: History and Life.* Santa Barbara, CA: American Bibliographical Center—Clio Press, 1964– .

597   *America: History and Life.* Santa Barbara, CA: American Bibliographical Center—Clio Press, 1964– . (Vendor: Dialog — File 38)

Bibliographic citations to and abstracts from articles published in more than 2,000 U.S. and foreign periodicals about the political, diplomatic, economic, cultural, social, and intellectual aspects of American and Canadian history are provided by this bibliographic service available in printed and electronic formats. The printed version is published in four parts:

Part A: Article Abstracts and Citations, issued quarterly and organized in five geographical or chronological sections and a sixth bibliographical section.
Part B: Index to Book Reviews, issued semiannually.
Part C: American History Bibliography, listing articles cited in part A, new books cited in part B, and dissertations.
Part D: Annual Index, with cumulative subject and author indexes to parts A, B, and C.

In addition, five-year cumulative indexes are available for the years 1964–1968 (vols. 1–5), 1969–1973 (vols. 6–10), 1974–1978 (vols. 11–15), 1979–1983 (vols. 16–20). All indexes offer biographical, geographical, author, and subject entries.

The electronic database corresponds to the printed version and can be searched by names of countries, places, authors and biographies, subject terms, chronological and publication dates, journal titles, etc.

598   The American Historical Association. *Writings on American History. A Subject Bibliography of Articles.* Millwood, NY: KTO Press, 1974– .

The historical documentation cited by this annual bibliography is limited to periodical articles published during the preceding year about American history in all periods. The unannotated listings are arranged chronologically, geographically, and by subject. The subject listings employ broad headings, like economic history, agriculture, banking and finance, labor history, diplomatic history, military and naval history, etc. An author index offers an additional approach to the listed entries. Approximately 500 periodicals serve as the database of this bibliography.

599   *Bibliographie zur Zeitgeschichte* (Bibliography for Contemporary History). Stuttgart: Deutsche Verlagsanstalt, 1953– .

Books and periodical articles written in English and other European languages about various political phenomena in modern history are listed in this quarterly bibliography published in each issue of the *Vierteljahreshefte für Zeitgeschichte*. The unannotated entries are arranged in several main sections that cover (1) general finding aids, (2) historical science (general, theory, methods, research, teaching), (3) society and politics, (4) biographies, and (5) European history. Separate subdivisions in the society and politics section aggregate listings for such topics as the environment, minorities, the work force, intellectuals, race problem, Christendom, Jewry, Islam, socialism, Marxism, communism, anti-Semitism, human rights, democracy, political parties, terrorism, foreign policy, international law, development policy, and others.

600   *Historical Abstracts*. Santa Barbara, CA: American Bibliographical Center—Clio Press, 1955—.

601   *Historical Abstracts*. Santa Barbara, CA: American Bibliographical Center—Clio Press, 1973—. (Vendor: Dialog—File 39)

Periodical articles relating to the economic, intellectual, social, or political history of countries other than Canada and the United States are indexed and abstracted in this bibliographic service available in printed and electronic formats. The printed version is issued since 1974 in two parts—Part A (Modern History Abstracts 1450—1914) and Part B (Twentieth Century Abstracts 1914 to the Present), both published in four quarterly issues as follows: No. 1—Abstracts and Citations with Index; No. 2—Abstracts and Citations with Index; No. 3—Abstracts and Citations; No. 4—Annual Index. In addition, five-year indexes have been published for the years 1955—1959 (vols. 1—5), 1960—1964 (vols. 6—10), 1965—1969 (vols. 11—15), 1970—1974 (vols. 16—20), 1975—1979 (vols. 21—25). All indexes carry place, personal name, and subject entries. Volumes 1—16 of *Historical Abstracts* were restricted to the period 1450—1914. All abstracts are classified in three main sections: general, topical, and geographical.

The computerized database is searchable by subject descriptors, names of persons and countries, chronological period, periodical title, and publication date.

602   *International Bibliography of Historical Sciences*. Paris: Librairie Armand Colin, 1926—. Reprint ed.: New York: Kraus Reprint Company.

This annual bibliography offers selective, unannotated entries for books and articles in a chronological and methodological arrangement developed by the Bibliographic Commission of the International Historical Sciences. Additional access to the listed material is provided by a geographic and author index. Most useful to the political researcher are the listings under social history of modern times, legal and constitutional history, as well as the regional entries under Asia, Africa, America, etc. The bibliography is presently published with a delay of four years.

603   New York (City). Public Library. Research Libraries. *Bibliographic Guide to North American History*. Boston: G. K. Hall, 1977—.

New books and series publications dealing with North American history can be identified with this annual unannotated bibliography. The listings reflect items that were cataloged by the Research Libraries of the New York Public Library and the Library of Congress during the preceding year. The entries are arranged in one alphabetical format by author, title, series title, and subject heading. All aspects of North American history are covered, including colonial history, state and local history, political and constitutional history, foreign relations history, and Indian history for the United States and Canada. The bibliographic entries include the call numbers of the listed items.

604   *Recently Published Articles*. Washington, DC: American Historical Association, 1976—.

Previously published as an integral part of the *American Historical Review*, the bibliography—issued three times per annum—offers current listings of new periodical articles under geographic sections, as follows: General and Unclassified; Ancient; Medieval; Modern Europe, General; British Commonwealth and Ireland; France; Spain and Portugal; Low Countries; Northern Europe; Germany, Austria, and Switzerland; Italy; Eastern Europe; Soviet Union; Near East; Africa; East Asia; Southeast Asia; South Asia; United States; Latin America. Further subdivisions are made under these main sections for individual countries or periods wherever necessary. Entries are arranged alphabetically by author within the various sections. No annotations or subject indexes are provided.

Retrospective Bibliographies: Worldwide Coverage

605   *Combined Retrospective Index to Journals in History, 1838—1974*. Arlington, VA: Carrollton Press, 1978.

This set of eleven volumes provides cumulative subject and author indexing to 150,000 articles published in 234 English-language journals in history since 1838. Four of the nine subject volumes are devoted to world history, while the remaining five volumes cover United States history. Entries in the world history volumes are arranged by keyword under names of countries and regions, for which suitable chronological subdivisions have been made wherever necessary. A large number of geographical headings also contain a separate subdivision for biographical and genealogical material. For U.S. history an entire volume (volume 6) contains the Biography and Genealogy Index to persons appearing in the titles of the indexed journal articles. Other subject categories appearing in the U.S. history volumes are black history, Civil War, economic history, foreign policy, and numerous chronological categories. An author index is published in two separate volumes. The set can also be used to identify book reviews.

606   Higham, Robin. *Official Histories. Essays and Bibliographies from Around the World*. Manhattan: Kansas State University Library, 1970.

A description of the origin, composition, and problems of official histories of military establishments and wars, the book provides historiographic and bibliographic information about the official histories of Austria, Australia, Belgium, Canada, Nationalist China, Czechoslovakia, Denmark, Finland, France, Germany, Greece, Hungary, India, Israel, Japan, Korea, Netherlands, New Zealand, Norway, Philippines, Poland, Portugal, Rhodesia, Romania, Russia, South Africa, Spain, Sweden, Turkey, United Kingdom, United States, Yugoslavia, and Latin American countries.

607   Roach, John. *A Bibliography of Modern History*. Cambridge, England: Cambridge University Press, 1968.

Since the *New Cambridge Modern History* encyclopedia contains no detailed bibliography (unlike the first *Cambridge Modern History*), this volume cites the principal printed sources on the major subjects treated in the encyclopedia. Most of the entries do not date back beyond 1961.

Retrospective Bibliographies: Regional Coverage

608   Griffin, Charles C. *Latin America. A Guide to the Historical Literature*. Austin: University of Texas Press, 1970.

A selective and critical bibliography of publications dealing with the history of Latin American countries. The arrangement of the entries is chronological, with main subdivisions for the colonial, independence, and post-independence periods. Within these sections further subdivisions are made for individual countries.

609   Kienast, Walther. *Literaturberichte über Neuerscheinungen zur Ausserdeutschen Geschichte* (Reports of New Publications in Non-German History). *Historische Zeitschrift* (Sonderhefte 1–5) Munich: R. Oldenbourg, 1962, 1965, 1969, 1970, 1973.

Five special supplements of a West German historical periodical offer excellent evaluative country surveys of new historical literature. Supplement 1 provides literature surveys for Italy, Hungary, Poland, Russia and the Soviet Union, the Scandinavian countries, Latin America, Southeast Asia, Japan, Great Britain, and France. Supplement 2 updates the surveys for Great Britain and France and contains new literature reports for the Netherlands, Belgium, Ireland, United States of America, and China. Supplement 3 offers literature reports on the history of Great Britain, the Scandinavian countries, Spain, Portugal, Slovakia, Yugoslavia, Russia and the Soviet Union, Spanish America, Brazil, the Byzantine Empire, and the Crusades. Supplement 4 is devoted to Czechoslovak history. Supplement 5 covers the literature for the history of the Netherlands, Italy, Poland, Rumania, Greece, Bulgaria, Islamic Persia, and Canada. The narrative text of these literature surveys is in German, but the cited sources are published in English and other languages.

610   *The Library of American Civilization*. Chicago: Library Resources, Inc., 1971.

This is a self-contained collection of microbook film cards providing more than 6,500,000 pages of material relating to all aspects of American life and literature. The documentation is divided into 25 subject areas, including politics and government, constitutional history, foreign affairs, military history, etc., and nine chronological periods ranging from the age of exploration to 1914. Separate printed catalogs, namely, an author catalog, title catalog, subject catalog, and a topical index called the Biblioguide, provide access to individual items in the collection. Many of the items in the collection are books that are ordinarily out of print now.

611   Morrison, Gayle, and Stephen Hay. *A Guide to Books on Southeast Asian History*. Santa Barbara, CA: American Bibliographical Center—Clio Press, 1969.

Books published between 1961 and 1966 on the history of Southeast Asia in general and ten individual countries of that region can be identified with this annotated bibliography. Entries are arranged by author within the regional and country divisions. Separate author and subject indexes offer additional access to the listed items. Books published before 1961 may be identified in a previously published bibliographic volume, entitled *Southeast Asian History: A Bibliographic Guide* (New York: Praeger, 1962), edited by Stephen N. Hay and Margaret H. Case.

BOOK REVIEWING MEDIA

Indexes

In addition to several previously listed indexes, such as

• *America: History and Life, Part B —Index to Book Reviews* and

• the *Combined Retrospective Index to Journals in History, 1838–1974,*

which identify reviews of historical books, the following index will be useful.

612   Brewster, John W., and Joseph A. McLeod. *Index to Book Reviews in Historical Periodicals.* Metuchen, NJ: Scarecrow Press, 1972–.

Each annual volume contains over 4,500 book review citations relating to 100 English-language periodicals. All citations are arranged by main entry. A title index but no subject or name index is provided.

Full-Length Reviewing Journals

613   *History: Review of New Books.* Washington, DC: Heldref Publications, 1972–.

This monthly reference publication offers authoritative and evaluative reviews of some 500 history books published annually. The reviews are written by qualified historians and appear within a three-month period after the publication date of the reviewed book. The reviews are arranged in geographical sections but may also be identified by author in a monthly and annual index.

614   *Reviews in American History.* Westport, CT: Redgrave Information Resources Corporation, 1972–.

A quarterly journal, exclusively devoted to lengthy reviews of books in American history.

History Journals with Book Review Sections

615   *Historische Zeitschrift.* Munich: R. Oldenbourg, 1859–.

616   *English Historical Review.* London: Longman Group Ltd., 1886–.

617   *Journal of American History.* Bloomington, IN: Organization of American Historians, 1914–.

618   *History.* London: Historical Association, 1912–.

619   *Revue Historique.* Paris: Presses Universitaires de France, 1876–.

620   *American Historical Review.* Washington, DC: The American Historical Association, 1895–.

621   *Journal of Modern History.* Chicago: University of Chicago Press, 1929–.

The reviews of historical books are scattered through a large number of periodicals. The periodical titles listed above illustrate the quantitative variation exhibited by the review literature. Listed in descending order of reviews

published, the *Historische Zeitschrift* offers more than 600 reviews annually, whereas the *Journal of Modern History* prints slightly over 100 reviews each year. Additional book review periodicals can be identified by scanning the history listings in *Ulrich's International Periodicals Dictionary.*

DICTIONARIES

Historical dictionaries ordinarily are not a reference source for terms and concepts. Instead, they usually offer brief statements or articles of varying length about notable persons, organizations, events, or activities. The arrangement of the material may be alphabetical, chronological, geographical, or a combination of various organizing categories. Several dictionaries also serve as bibliographic instruments by listing additional reading material for a given subject.

622   Adams, James Truslow. *Dictionary of American History.* New York: Charles Scribner's Sons, 1974.

The multivolume dictionary contains several thousand signed articles of brief length on specific occurrences in American history. Bibliographic citations are given at the end of each article wherever possible. A separate index volume offers additional access possibilities to the historical information in the dictionary.

623   Hochman, Stanley. *Yesterday and Today. A Dictionary of Recent American History.* New York: McGraw-Hill, 1979.

The alphabetically arranged entries in this dictionary briefly describe major and minor events as well as institutions in American political and cultural history since the end of World War II. Noteworthy congressional, judicial, or executive acts or decisions are well represented.

624   Martin, Michael, and Leonard Gelber. *Dictionary of American History.* Totowa, NJ: Littlefield, Adams & Co., 1978.

A one-volume dictionary containing brief articles about persons, events, and developments notable in American history. Historical material in economics, finance and banking, labor relations, constitutional, statutory, and administrative law, social welfare, literature, industry, science, religion, international relations, foreign policy, education, the arts, politics, and military affairs is well represented.

625   Palmer, A. W. *A Dictionary of Modern History.* London: Cresset Press, 1962.

This one-volume dictionary offers brief statements in alphabetical arrangement about persons, countries, cities, institutions, or movements that have been of historical significance all over the world.

626   Wetterau, Bruce. *Macmillan Concise Dictionary of World History*. New York: Macmillan, 1983.

Covering the entire course of recorded history, the dictionary is a convenient sourcebook for events, people, and places of historical importance. There are some 10,000 alphabetically arranged entries plus 7,000 chronologically arranged items under the textual entries.

DIRECTORIES

Large numbers of directories exist that provide biographical information about notable persons throughout history. These directories may be identified in the previously listed guidebooks to the general reference literature or in Robert B. Slocum's *Biographical Dictionaries and Related Works* (Detroit: Gale Research Company, 1967–), listed as item 2102 in this guidebook. Another source is the *Biography Index* (New York: H. W. Wilson, 1946–), which is more fully described under item 2100.

In addition, the following titles appear to be useful for inclusion in this section of history directories.

627   American Association for State and Local History. *Directory of Historical Societies and Agencies in the United States and Canada*. Columbus, OH: 1956–.

This irregularly published directory identifies more than 3,500 historical societies and agencies by state and city. Information about membership size, staff, publications, office hours, etc., is included.

628   Bidwell, Robin. *Bidwell's Guide to Government Ministers*. The Hague: Nijhoff, 1972.

This four-volume directory will serve as a quick reference tool for the identification of leading government ministers throughout the world for the period 1900 to 1971. The arrangement of the names is geographical, as follows: Volume 1—Great Britain and Western Europe; Volume 2—Arab States; Volume 3—Africa; Volume 4—Commonwealth.

629   Tunney, Christopher. *A Biographical Dictionary of World War II*. London: J. M. Dent & Sons, Ltd., 1972.

The directory provides brief biographical information about persons in all parts of the world who have made a noteworthy contribution to the prosecution of World War II. Listed are military persons, secret agents, politicians, propagandists, journalists, scientists, etc.

DOCUMENT COLLECTIONS

630   Commager, Henry Steele. *Documents on American History*. New York: Appleton-Century-Crofts, 1968.

This reference volume is a handy collection of significant acts, treaties, United States Supreme Court decisions, presidential messages, and other documents of importance in American history. Explanatory notes and bibliographic citations are provided for all documents.

631   *Historic Documents, 1972–*. Washington, DC: Congressional Quarterly, Inc., 1973–.

A series of annual volumes that contain in a chronological arrangement by month the texts of the most significant public documents of the United States issued during the preceding year. Documents refer to important presidential statements, government reports, speeches, treaties, court decisions, special studies, etc. Shorter documents are printed in full, but longer documents are generally excerpted. Each document is preceded by an introduction that describes the history and significance of the document. A comprehensive subject index provides access to each document.

ENCYCLOPEDIAS

632   Dupuy, R. Ernest, and Trevor N. Dupuy. *The Encyclopedia of Military History*. New York: Harper & Row, 1977.

The one-volume encyclopedia consists of a series of chronologically and geographically arranged narratives of wars, warfare, and military affairs that have occurred in all parts of the world from the earliest times to the twentieth century. The entire military history has been arbitrarily divided into 21 time periods, with one chapter devoted to each period. Each chapter begins with an introductory essay about military trends, weapons, tactics, and theories of warfare, and contains a chronological exposition of the major military events. An exhaustive general index lists names and events mentioned in the text. Battles and sieges as well as wars are listed in two separate indexes. A bibliography of additional works for further study is also included.

633   *Family Encyclopedia of American History*. Pleasantville, NY: Reader's Digest Association, 1975.

The encyclopedia contains alphabetically arranged articles about notable persons, organizations, events, or activities in American history. At the head of each article a brief summary of the core facts is given in italicized print to be followed by a more detailed account of salient information. Wherever possible a bibliographic reference to the most informative book on the subject is listed at the end of each article. The encyclopedia also includes a subject guide of 133 topical categories under which the pertinent articles are listed together with the page numbers in the encyclopedia. Topical categories have been made for the abolitionist movement, administrative agencies, armed forces, arms and arms control, business and industry, presidential cabinets, civil liberties, civil rights movements, civil service, civil war, colonial wars, colonies, communism and anticommunism, Congress, constitution, courts and jurists, major depressions, economics, espionage, government projects, immigration, Indians, international relations, Korean War, law, Mexican War, New Deal, political organizations, political parties, political scandals, political science and scientists, politicians, population growth, Reconstruction, religion, revolutionary war, riots and rebellions, secession movements, slavery, sociology and sociologists, states and state rights, suffrage, Supreme Court, taxation, treaties, United Nations, Vietnam War, women's rights, World War I and II, and other major topics.

634   Freeman-Grenville, G. S. P. A *Chronology of World History. A Calendar of Principal Events from 3000 BC to AD 1973*. Totowa, NJ: Rowman and Littlefield, 1975.

Significant historical events that have occurred during five thousand years of human history are chronologically identifiable with the help of this reference work. The book lists events chronologically within five geographical columns and a sixth column entitled religion and culture. The geographical divisions are wholly arbitrary and show some variation due the the availability of data. From about 3000 B.C. Europe is represented in two columns, and from the fifteenth century a separate column is reserved for events on the American continent. Wherever possible precise dates of the events are given. A detailed index of names and events lists the years under which a description of the event may be found in the book. No bibliographic references are given.

635   Langer, William L. *The New Illustrated Encyclopedia of World History*. New York: Harry N. Abrams, Inc., 1975.

This two-volume encyclopedia describes in brief, chronologically arranged articles significant events and people from the prehistoric period to the 1970s. The articles are illustrated with more than 2,000 photographs, maps, charts, and drawings. The encyclopedia also contains a list of Roman emperors, Byzantine emperors, caliphs, Roman popes, Holy Roman emperors, kings of England and France, presidents of the United States, founding dates of universities in Europe and the New World. A name and subject index is also included, but no bibliographic references are provided.

636   Magill, Frank M. *Great Events from History*. Englewood Cliffs, NJ: Salem Press, 1973.

The nine-volume set offers reference coverage for

more than 1,000 important events in world history. The information is organized in three series, namely, the Modern European Series, covering 336 European events from 1469 to 1969, the Ancient and Medieval Series, covering the period from 4000 B.C. to A.D. 1500, and the American Series, which begins with the arrival of immigrants from Asia and ends with the first moon landing. Each event is the subject of an article, consisting of four sections: (1) quick reference material showing type of event (military, economic, religious, etc.), time, locale, and principal personages; (2) summary of event; (3) essay reviews of the pertinent literature; (4) bibliography of additional reading. Six indexes provide a key to the events or the cited literature, namely, an alphabetical list of events, a keyword index of events, category index for type of event, an alphabetical listing of principal personages, author listings for the pertinent literature reviewed and for the literature cited for additional reading. The articles were written by 150 history professors who selected, summarized, and evaluated the events and their treatment in the literature.

637   Morris, Richard B. *Encyclopedia of American History*. New York: Harper & Row, 1982.

The frequently revised encyclopedia, currently in its sixth edition, provides in one volume (1) a chronological description of the major political and military events in American history, including domestic and foreign policies up to 1981, (2) a topical nonpolitical chronology of demographic, economic, scientific, and cultural trends, (3) biographical sketches on 400 notable Americans, and (4) a federal government section with listings of U.S. presidents and their cabinets, tables on party strength in Congress, a list of U.S. Supreme Court justices, and the text of the Declaration of Independence and the U.S. Constitution. An index is also included.

638   *The New Cambridge Modern History*. Cambridge, England: Cambridge University Press, 1957–1970.

The multivolume encyclopedia offers an authoritative interpretation of modern civilization in narrative form. The historical period interpreted by the encyclopedia extends from the renaissance to 1945. The encyclopedia is a successor to the original *Cambridge Modern History*, planned by the first Lord Acton in 1896 and completed in 1912. The new encyclopedia, however, no longer includes bibliographies or footnotes, and supporting reading material is listed separately in John Roach's *Bibliography of Modern History*.

639   Sharp, Harold S. *Footnotes to American History. A Bibliographic Source Book*. Metuchen, NJ: Scarecrow Press, 1977.

Three hundred and thirteen events of American history are described in narrative form in this reference work. The historical events are arranged in chronological order beginning with the Norsemen's discovery of North America and ending with the Patty Hearst affair. The book includes major historical events as well as those that are comparatively minor yet significant in terms of human interest. Each entry also offers, apart from the descriptive narration of the event, a bibliography of suggested reading material. The described events can also be identified with an index composed of names of specific persons, places, and subject terms.

NEWS DIGESTS: WORLDWIDE COVERAGE

Whereas the existing dictionaries and encyclopedias of history offer summary information for a limited number of events whose historical significance has withstood the test of time, news digests report events and developments of more current relevance. Political and economic developments as reported by newspapers, news agencies, radio broadcasts, and other mass media are presented in digest form for easy retrieval and retention of information. Several digests exist for worldwide coverage, but the majority of the available news digests focus on the news developments of a specific region or continent.

640   *The Annual Register of World Events: A Review of the Year*. London: Longmans, 1758 – .

Separate chapters are created in this annual digest for the review of developments in the United Kingdom, the Americas and the Caribbean, the USSR and Eastern Europe, the Middle East, Africa, East and Southeast Asia, Australasia, and various international organizations, such as the United Nations, the Commonwealth, European Community, etc. Other chapters are devoted to developments in religion, science, medicine and technology, law, the arts, and economics. A chronology of the principal events of the preceding year is also included.

641   *Archiv der Gegenwart*. Bonn: Siegler, 1961 – .

Similar to *Keesing's Contemporary Archives*, this German-language digest presents summarized information about events and developments in all parts of the world on a weekly basis. Political speeches are frequently included. Monthly and semiannual subject indexes and quarterly personal name indexes offer access to the digested information.

642   *Current History*. Philadelphia: Current History, Inc., 1943 – .

Each issue of the monthly periodical contains a chronology of the most important events in political affairs. Arranged by country or major subject, the entries are limited to a brief summary of the event. A chronological summary of events that have occurred during the preceding year is published in the *Current History Annual*.

643   *Facts on File*. New York: Facts on File, Inc., 1941 – .

644   *News Dictionary*. New York: Facts on File, Inc., 1965 – .

The first item is a weekly, loose-leaf news digest of world and United States affairs. The news coverage is brief but immediate. Cumulative biweekly, annual, and quinquennial indexes make it possible to locate reported news within these time frames back to 1941. The *News Dictionary* is an annual digest that records events of the preceding year alphabetically under name and subject headings. For online retrieval of news events items reported since 1975 by *Facts on File*, use *Nexis*.

645   *Keesing's Contemporary Archives*. London: Keesing's Publications, Ltd., 1931 – .

Important events and developments occurring throughout the world are reported in this weekly loose-leaf reference work. The individual reports, many of which are quite detailed, are arranged by country or international organization, and are based on data selected, condensed, translated, or summarized from newspapers, periodicals, official publications, and foreign news agencies. Reports frequently appear several weeks after the event, which permits a more accurate or fuller description of the events. Biweekly, quarterly, and annual cumulative indexes furnish access to the recorded events.

646   Leonard, Thomas M. *Day by Day, the Forties*. New York: Facts on File, 1977.

647   Merritt, Jeffrey D. *Day by Day, the Fifties*. New York: Facts on File, 1979.

648   Parker, Thomas, and Douglas Nelson. *Day by Day, the Sixties*. New York: Facts on File, 1983.

These decade-by-decade digests offer annual, monthly, and daily chronologies of political and other events that have occurred throughout the world since the 1940s. Events are concisely listed in chronological sequence in ten columns representing the following categories: A — World Affairs, B — Europe, including USSR, C — Africa and the Middle East, D — Latin America, the Caribbean, and Canada, E — Asia and the Pacific, F — U.S. Politics and Social Issues, G — U.S. Foreign Policy and Defense, H — U.S. Economy and Environment, I — Science, Technology and Nature, and J — Culture, Leisure and Life Style. A separate index of persons, countries, and subject headings identifies the dates and column letters in the book where the events are listed.

NEWS DIGESTS: REGIONAL COVERAGE

Africa

649   *Africa Confidential*. London: Research Publications Services, Ltd., 1960—.

A biweekly intelligence digest reporting background material on African events from undisclosed sources. Individual issues are printed on airmail paper and usually cover the political situation in a selected number of countries rather than the whole continent.

650   *Africa Digest*. London: Africa Bureau, 1953—.

A bimonthly news digest for events in Africa, arranged by country. English, French, and African newspapers and periodicals, official documents, and reports from international organizations serve as sources for the reported items.

651   *Africa Research Bulletin. Political, Social and Cultural Series*. Exeter, England: Africa Research Ltd., 1964—.

A monthly news digest reporting political, social, and cultural developments in Africa. Reports are based on newspaper articles, official news releases, and news agency bulletins. Index entries for subjects and names are arranged by country.

652   *African Recorder*. New Delhi, Tilak Marg, 1962—.

The news digest is a sister publication of the *Asian Recorder* and follows the same format and arrangement as that publication. It covers events in all African countries.

653   *Maghreb Digest*. Los Angeles: University of Southern California, 1963—.

A quarterly summary of political and economic events and developments in the Maghreb region of North Africa. Sources are French- and Arabic-language periodicals published in the area.

Asia

654   *Asia Research Bulletin*. Singapore: Asia Research Ltd., 1971—.

A sister publication to the *African Research Bulletin*, this digest provides monthly abstracts or summaries of political, economic, and social material appearing in over 300 English-, Chinese-, Malay-, and Thai-language newspapers, periodicals, news agency reports, and official documents. Indexing is available by country, regions, commodities, and products.

655   *Asian Almanac*. Singapore: P.O. Box 2737, 1963—.

A weekly news digest of events in 26 Asian countries ranging from Afghanistan to Japan. The information presented is derived from official and authoritative sources in the country of origin. An annual book with the same title contains statistical information in addition to the news reports.

656   *Asian Recorder*. New Delhi: Tilak Marg, 1955—.

A weekly news digest of events in Asia. All items in the digest acknowledge the source of information — newspapers, periodicals, government documents, broadcasts, etc. Entries are arranged by country and are indexed quarterly. All countries of Asia except the USSR are covered.

Latin America

657   *Latin America*. London: Latin American Newsletters, Ltd., 1966—.

A weekly news digest that reports political and economic developments in Latin American countries.

658   *Latin American Digest*. Tempe: Center for Latin American Studies, Arizona State University, 1966—.

A quarterly publication that summarizes for each Latin American country the political and socioeconomic events reported in periodicals.

659   *Latin American Index*. Washington, DC: Latin Research Group Ltd., 1973—.

A fortnightly digest of relevant up-to-date facts on important developments in the political, economic, and social life of Latin America. A quarterly cumulative index, called Guide, identifies all items reported in the digest.

660   *The Wagner Latin American Newsletter*. Cottonwood, MN: 1977—.

A biweekly summary of Latin American news concerning political, economic, and cultural events and developments. The news is summarized from unidentified Spanish-language sources.

Middle East

661   *Arab Report and Record*. London: Middle East Economic Digest. 1966—1979.

Issued twice monthly, this digest reports political, economic, and social events for each country of the Arab world. A separate subject index and personal name index is included.

662   *SWASIA. North Africa*. Washington, DC: National Council of Churches, 1974—.

A weekly digest of Southwest Asian and North African news focusing on the Israel-Palestine conflict, the Persian gulf area, and the developments in the various Middle Eastern countries from Iran to Morocco and from Turkey to the Sudan. The news summaries are prepared from leading newspapers in the United States, Europe, Israel, and the Arab world as well as from radio broadcasts.

Europe

663   *Radio Free Europe Research*. New York: Radio Free Europe, 1976– .

Separate series of research reports are prepared for each of the East European countries with summaries and detailed news of the political, economic, and other developments in the Communist party states. The information material is collected from a wide variety of news sources for use by the editors and the policy staff of Radio Free Europe but is available on subscription.

North America

664   *Canadian News Facts*. Toronto: Marpep Publishing Ltd., 1967– .

Current events in Canada, including political and other developments in Ottawa and the provincial capitals, are summarized and indexed in this biweekly loose-leaf digest. Its major sources of news events are 19 Canadian newspapers, the *New York Times*, and Canadian government publications.

POLITICAL SCIENCE

Introduction

Although politics is probably as old as mankind, the scientific study of politics is a very recent development. The scientific investigation of political phenomena apart from purely legal, historical, and economic inquiries began mainly in the United States and received its greatest impetus from the widespread consequences of World War I and II. In its relatively brief existence, the science of politics has undergone a series of developmental stages in which the focus of scholarly attention shifted from institutional phenomena to political behavior and more recently to policy studies. Due to its institutional, behavioral, and postbehavioral focus, political science has failed to become a truly integrative science for all political phenomena. While heavily culture-bound, political science has also failed to become universally accepted as a discipline essential for prosperous and peaceful coexistence in most countries of the world. Thirty years after the founding of the International Political Science Association, only 39 national political science associations belong to it, as compared to more than 150 member countries of the UN. Not surprisingly, the least developed and the least peaceful political entities have almost invariably the least developed political science discipline, primarily due to the tremendous power inherent in existing traditional belief systems and their institutional entrenchment. Unlike the discipline of medicine, political science

has not yet succeeded in finding effective antidotal processes for curing the major political ills of the world without widespread destruction of the societal fabrics involved.

Consonant with this situation, the reference literature of political science exhibits therefore the results of rather specialized inquiries that have proliferated within several subfields. The titles listed and described on the following pages represent those works of reference that aim at the identification of scholars and their writings within the framework of the entire discipline of political science. This framework is narrower than that of all the social sciences but broader than the structural limits of any individual subfield. Nevertheless, the cited reference sources do not displace the many specialized retrieval tools listed for a particular subfield, such as American Government and Politics, International Relations, or Comparative Government and Area Studies, in chapters 3, 4, and 5 of the guidebook.

Bibliographic Instruments

GUIDEBOOKS

665   Brock, Clifton. *The Literature of Political Science: A Guide for Students, Librarians and Teachers*. New York: R. R. Bowker, 1969.

The guidebook describes selected groups of reference publications, such as periodical indexes and abstracts, book review bibliographies, United States and United Nations publications, state government publications, statistical sources, and translation services. Descriptions are coupled with sample pages from various publications and suggestions for usage. There are also annotated listings of bibliographies and other reference publications in political science and several of its subfields. Regrettably, however, the listed reference literature is inadequately typologized, and no listings are included for political theory, federal and international law, history and other related social science fields.

666   Goehlert, Robert. *Political Science Research Guide*. Monticello, IL: Vance Bibliographies, 1982.

The guidebook identifies the principal reference publications for general as well as political science information. All entries are unannotated and arranged by field and/or form category. Separately listed are reference works for political theory, comparative politics, international relations, military affairs/peace research, state and urban politics, U.S. government publications, and international organizations. Also listed are the major political science journals and their indexing coverage by external index or abstract publications. A few computerized databases are identified. Brief introductory headnotes precede the various listings. Reference sources for legal information and societal data are inadequately covered. Apart from the table of contents, there are no author, title, subject, or other indexes in the guidebook.

667   Stoffle, Carla, Simon Carter, and Samuel Pernacciaro. *Materials and Methods for Political Science Research*. New York: The Libraryworks, a division of Neal-Schuman Publishers, 1979.

This excellent guidebook is designed to familiarize political science students with the basic types of information sources available in the discipline. The book consists of two sections — an instructor's manual and a workbook. The instructor's manual contains specific instructions for the use of the workbook together with assignment sheets and a checklist of titles used in the assignments. The workbook is divided into 13 chapters, entitled (1) Guides to the Literature, (2) Handbooks, (3) Yearbooks and Almanacs, (4) Subject Dictionaries and Encyclopedias, (5) Biographical Dictionaries and Directories, (6) Periodical Indexes and Abstracts, (7) Bibliographies, (8) Scholarly Journals, (9) Evaluation of Book-Length Studies, (10) Government Publications, (11) Legal Publications, (12) General Periodicals, Newspapers and Press Digests, and (13) Research Paper Mechanics and Methodology. Each of the first 12 chapters describes the objectives of the work assignment and the utility of one category or type of publication. Representative examples of the major reference or information sources are cited together with explanatory annotations. Each chapter concludes with a detailed assignment.

668   Wynar, Lubomyr R. *Guide to Reference Materials in Political Science*. Volume 1: Denver: Colorado Bibliographic Institute, 1966; Volume 2: Rochester, NY: Libraries Unlimited, 1968.

The two-volume set offers extensive, occasionally annotated title listings and brief introductory notes for the political literature within the social sciences, political science itself, and the subfields of political science. Reference works as well as scholarly monographs are listed. Noteworthy is a very detailed chronological and bibliographical table that lists the outstanding contributors and their major works in the field of political theory. No annotations are given for the monographs, but the reference publications are briefly described. The set includes an author and subject index as well as a list of important periodicals in political science.

CURRENT BIBLIOGRAPHIES

669   *ABC POL SCI (Advance Bibliography of Contents: Political Science and Government)*. Santa Barbara, CA: ABC-Clio, 1969 – .

The table of contents pages of some 300 journals published in the United States and foreign countries can be found in this bibliography, issued five times during the year with an annual index. Designed as an alerting mechanism for new scientific findings and other writings in political science and related fields, the bibliography also provides author and subject access to the principal periodical literature issued since 1969.

670   *International Bibliography of Political Science*. Volume 1 – . 1952 – . Paris: UNESCO, 1954 – 1961; Chicago: Aldine Publishing Company, 1962 – .

The bibliography is one of the four sections of the *International Bibliography of the Social Sciences* (sociology, political science, economics, social and cultural anthropology) and is prepared by the International Committee for Social Science Information and Documentation. It serves as a highly selective bibliographic tool for the political science literature by listing books, articles, reports, and other publications of true scientific character only. The unannotated entries follow a detailed plan of classification with the following major sections: (1) Political Science; (2) Political Thought; (3) Government and Public Administration; (4) Governmental Process; (5) International Relations; and (6) Area Studies. Numerous subdivisions within these sections aggregate material relating to general, comparative, or national studies or specialized topics. Entries for articles frequently include a reference (Abstract No.) to the *International Political Science Abstracts* if the article has been abstracted in one of the quarterly issues of that sister publication. Entries for books occasionally include a citation (Cr.) to periodicals that contain a review of the listed book. Additional access to the listed material is provided by separate author and subject indexes in English and French. The bibliography is published annually with a two-year lag but is truly international in its coverage. A list of more than 2,000 periodicals that are scanned but not necessarily completely indexed is included in each issue. As a result of its high selectivity, relatively narrow scope, and considerable publication delay the bibliography cannot be used for a comprehensive search of the current political literature without recourse to the following title and other reference tools.

671   *International Political Science Abstracts*. Oxford: Basil Blackwell, 1952 – .

This bibliography of abstracted periodical articles is prepared by the International Political Science Association in cooperation with the International Committee for Social Sciences Documentation. Its quarterly issues offer each year over 5,000 abstracts of articles published in 600 English-language and foreign-language periodicals. Less than a hundred of these periodicals, however, are completely indexed. Entries are arranged alphabetically by author under the six basic categories of the classification scheme of the *International Bibliography of Political Sci-*

ence. Abstracts are published in English for all English-language articles, but foreign-language articles are abstracted in French only. Each issue contains a separate subject index with broad subject terms and names of countries. There is also an annual index, but no cumulated indexes are available. Although there are a few other abstract publications available for special subject areas, this reference publication is the only major source of abstracts for all fields of political science. Regrettably, it has not yet been computerized for online information retrieval, nor has its reference volume been extended to a level comparable with similar tools in other disciplines.*

672 *Katalog Geisteswissenschaftlicher Fortschritts- und Übersichtsberichte — Politologie (List of Social Sciences Progress Reports — Political Science).* Berlin: Staatsbibliothek Preussischer Kulturbesitz, 1971 – .

Like other academic disciplines, political science requires a mechanism of self-correction that permits the correction of errors, half-truths, and omissions without the destruction of the basic body of knowledge. The above title refers to the information transfer arm of this mechanism of self-correction. It is a card service that provides a key to those articles in periodicals and collective works that give a critical evaluation, assessment, or progress report of specific political subject matter or the scientific literature of such subject matter. Citations are given to publications in English, German, and other Western European languages. The individual citation cards are classified according to several broad subject categories, such as political ideas, political parties, domestic policies, foreign policies, political systems of individual countries, public administration, etc.

673 *POL-DOK. Politische Dokumentation.* Munich: Verlag Dokumentation, 1966 – .

German-language periodical articles relevant to political scientists are indexed and abstracted in this monthly reference publication. Abstracts are arranged under seven major categories similar to the classification scheme used in the *International Bibliography of Political Science.* Four separate indexes provide access to the abstracted articles by name, geographic location or political entity, subject term, and classification term. The name index includes authors as well as persons cited in the articles. The indexes are cumulated in each monthly issue within an annual time frame. All indexed periodicals are published in the Federal Republic of Germany, Switzerland, or Austria.

*The principal reference tool in psychology, *Psychological Abstracts*, for instance, offers more than 20,000 abstracts each year.

674 *United States Political Science Documents.* Washington, DC: American Political Science Association, 1976 – .

675 *USPSD. (U.S. Political Science Documents).* Pittsburgh: University Center for International Studies, University of Pittsburgh, 1975 – . (Vendor: Dialog — File 93)

Scholarly articles published in approximately 120 political science journals in the United States can be identified or read in abstracted form with the help of this reference work, available in printed and computerized versions. Part 1 of the annually printed edition contains five indexes by author/contributor, subject, geographic area, proper name, and journal title. The subject index includes a rotated subject descriptor display located immediately before the subject listings. It lists in alphabetical sequence all words used as subject headings. The proper name index lists articles under organizational names or specific labels under which political objects, events, or activities have become popularly known, i.e., Watergate, B-1 bomber, Byrd amendment, clean air initiative, Johnson doctrine, Middle East war, Munich agreement, etc. Part 2 of the printed edition offers a content summary of the articles indexed in Part 1. In addition, each article is described in terms of special features (tables, figures, etc.), list of people cited in the article, and a list of key subject terms fitting the contents of the article.

USPSD is the name of the computerized version that can be searched online for bibliographic citations to and abstracts of the periodical literature. It is more current because of quarterly updates.

676 Universal Reference System. *Bibliography of Bibliographies in Political Science, Government and Public Policy.* Princeton, NJ: Princeton Research Publishing Company, 1968 – .

The Universal Reference System is a self-contained unique information retrieval system consisting of ten basic volumes with combined annual supplements and individual documentation services to scholars. The essential feature of the Universal Reference System is a master system of topics and methodological techniques expressed in various truncated descriptors that offer numerous access avenues to the scientific literature of books, articles, and selected unpublished papers only. The title listed above is base volume 3 of the series and offers annotated listings of some 2,550 bibliographies published in books, periodicals, and selected government publications. This listed material has received intensive indexing of 10 to 20 entries to permit more accurate retrieval of desired information than is possible with other bibliographies. All indexing descriptors are listed in a separate classification table (Grazian Index System) that contains 28 basic categories of topical and methodological approaches.

Since the annual supplements are issued in a single combined format for all ten base volumes, more recently published bibliographies are best identified by using the descriptors Bibliog and Bibliog/A, which cite unannotated and annotated bibliographies of more than 50 titles.

For a description of the other nine volumes in the Universal Reference System, see other entries in the appropriate sections of this guidebook. These entries can be identified in the Author Index under Universal Reference System.

RETROSPECTIVE BIBLIOGRAPHIES

677 American Political Science Association. *Cumulative Index to Proceedings of the Annual Meetings.* Washington, DC: 1971.

Important verbal and documented information exchange in political science occurs during the annual meetings of the American Political Science Association and the meetings of the various regional and state political science associations in the United States. Adequate indexing, however, is available only for the proceedings of the annual meetings of the American Political Science Association held between 1904–1912 and 1956–1970. The *Cumulative Index* provides access to all papers delivered at those meetings by panel, subject, or author. Copies of the 1,500 listed papers are not usually available in libraries but are obtainable on microfilm from University Microfilms in Ann Arbor, Michigan, which also sells hard copies of the more recent meeting papers.

Papers presented at the annual meetings of the regional and state political science associations have so far not been bibliographically controlled. Identification of the papers by title, subject, or author is especially difficult for nonmembers of the associations since titles are usually only listed in the official programs of the meetings. Copies of the papers are obtainable during the meetings and directly from the authors.

678 *A Bibliography for Students of Politics.* Oxford: Oxford University Press, 1971.

The bibliography is an attempt to transmit a fixed body of political knowledge with the help of a selected number of books and periodical articles. Although the bibliography is primarily intended as a reading guide for students at the Oxford Honour School of Philosophy, Politics and Economics, it is a valuable reference tool for all students of political science. The most important books and articles are listed in a classified arrangement including political institutions, political theory, international relations, political sociology, industrial sociology, social stratification, local government, etc. No annotations are given.

679 Bracher, Karl Dietrich, Manfred Funke, and Hans-Adolf Jacobsen. *Bibliographie zur Politik in Theorie und Praxis.* Königstein, West Germany: Droste, 1982.

This reference work is currently the only retrospective and most up-to-date bibliography that offers access to political publications in several European languages. Approximately 50 percent of the citations refer to English-language material. Theoretical as well as practical aspects of politics and policies are covered.

680 *Combined Retrospective Index to Journals in Political Science, 1886–1974.* Arlington, VA: Carrollton Press, 1978.

The purpose of this eight-volume set is to provide cumulative subject and author indexing for 115,000 articles published in some 180 English-language periodicals in political science since 1886. The index entries in the six subject volumes are arranged by keyword under one or more of 135 separate subject categories, including international relations, international law, international organizations, international trade and economics, methodology and theoretical approaches, political behavior and process, political ideologies, political systems, political thought, administration, economics in general, financial administration, management, organization, departments and functions, etc. Each entry provides a citation to the article title, author, publication year, volume number, page number, and code number of the periodical that contains the pertinent article. A separate list appearing in the endpapers of each volume contains all the journal code numbers in numerical sequence and identifies the title of the journal. Two volumes of the set are devoted to author entries. The entire set will be kept up by annual supplements.

681 Harmon, Robert B. *Developing the Library Collection in Political Science.* Metuchen, NJ: Scarecrow Press, 1976.

A convenient listing of English-language books about the major topics in political science is offered by this bibliography. The entries are arranged under subject headings in alphabetical sequence. Subject headings included are anarchism, authority, bureaucracy, campaign management, civil rights, communism, conservatism, democracy, diplomacy, equality, executive power, federal government, imperialism, international law, international relations, judicial process, liberalism, lobbying, minorities, nationalism, opposition, political participation, power, public opinion, separation of powers, socialism, voting, war, women in politics, and many others. The listings are primarily oriented toward conceptual topics and omit material about individual political actors, objects, laws, and directives. Various types of reference sources are listed separately. A combined author and title index is included. Brief annotations accompany the entries in the bibliography.

682   Harmon, Robert B. *Political Science. A Bibliographic Guide to the Literature*. New York: Scarecrow Press, 1965.

_____ . *First Supplement*. New York: Scarecrow Press, 1968.

_____ . *Second Supplement*. New York: Scarecrow Press, 1972.

_____ . *Third Supplement*. New York: Scarecrow Press, 1974.

The four-volume reference set will be most valuable as a reading list for the principal topics and subfields of political science. The bibliography offers a taxonomy of the political science literature with selected listings of monographs and pamphlets. There are brief introductory notes for the subchapters, but only a few brief annotations are provided for some titles. A limitation of the set is the fact that the periodical literature is not covered although a selective list of periodical titles in included.

683   Harmon, Robert B. *Political Science Bibliographies*. Metuchen, NJ: Scarecrow Press, 1973.

The aim of this reference work is to provide a convenient record of the separately published bibliographies in political science. The 790 entries are arranged under Library of Congress subject headings. In addition, separate author and title listings are also included. Some of the entries are briefly annotated.

684   International Political Science Association. *Synthesis Report in the I.P.S.A. 20 Years Activities*. Brussels: 1970.

The association was founded in 1949 to foster the development of political science by facilitating cooperation among national political science associations, institutions of higher learning, research workers, and professors throughout the world, by encouraging the creation and development of national associations of political science, organizing conferences and congresses, stimulating comparative research, publishing accounts of research, and preparing bibliographic publications. The title above contains a list of publications the association has sponsored, even though individual titles may have been published commercially. There is also a topical list of the papers presented during the triennial meetings or congresses sponsored by the association. IPSA also issues mimeographed lists of the papers presented at these meetings with

brief abstracts of the contents of each paper. The papers themselves are available for purchase directly from the association.

685   Janda, Kenneth. *Cumulative Index to the American Political Science Review*. Volumes 1–62; 1906–1968. Ann Arbor, MI: University Microfilms, 1970.

Cumulative indexing exists for this important periodical publication of the American Political Science Association. The index offers KWIC (keywords in context) listings of all articles published in the *American Political Science Review* during more than 60 years.

686   Pogany, Andras H., and Hortenzia L. Pogany. *Political Science and International Relations: Books Recommended for the Use of American Catholic College and University Libraries*. Metuchen, NJ: Scarecrow Press, 1967.

Nearly 6,000 books published between 1955 and 1966 have been selected for use in Catholic institutions of higher education by the authors of this bibliography. Entries are arranged in seven categories subdivided chronologically or geographically. No annotations are provided, but an author index and an alphabetical subject list of chapter, subchapter, and sub-subchapter headings is included. Bibliographic and other reference works are underrepresented. The list of recommended periodicals includes only 27 titles.

Book Reviewing Media

Book reviewing in political science fulfills important functions of evaluation, comparison, and content summarization of the published research of the discipline. Most of the book reviews are scattered throughout hundreds of periodicals, and no single periodical covers more than a small percentage of the annual political book production in its reviews. Although a few book titles receive a large number of reviews, a fairly substantial number of books is not reviewed at all. This is also true for the two full-length reviewing journals in political science, which cover only a portion of the published literature. This situation has a negative impact on the acquisition and circulation volume in libraries. In the absence of more comprehensive reviewing tools in political science, library administrators and academic users rely heavily on general reference tools, such as *Choice, American Book Publishing Record*, or *Current Book Review Citations*, when making decisions about the acquisition and usage of political books. An inevitable consequence of this procedure is the fact that the political literature is underutilized in comparison to the literature of other disciplines.

No separate indexing tool exists presently for the review literature in periodicals, but the following titles represent full-length and sectionalized reviewing journals in political science.

FULL-LENGTH REVIEWING JOURNALS

687   *Perspective*. Washington, DC: Helen Dwight Reid Educational Foundation, 1972—.

The publication is issued monthly and contains signed book reviews for some 600 books each year. The reviewers are political scientists affiliated with American universities and colleges. For easier identification of desired reviews, the titles are arranged in regional or field categories, such as United States politics and public policy, United States foreign policy and national security, Western Hemisphere, Africa and the Middle East, Europe and the USSR, international relations, law and organization, comparative politics, theory and organization, Asia, etc.

688   *The Political Science Reviewer*. Hampton-Sydney, VA: Hampton-Sydney College, 1971—.

This annual publication is devoted exclusively to lengthy critical and evaluative reviews of current studies in political science as well as textbooks, reprints, and the great classics of the political literature. The reviewers are political scientists currently teaching in American or foreign universities.

POLITICAL SCIENCE JOURNALS WITH BOOK REVIEW SECTIONS

689   *International Affairs*. London: Oxford University Press for Royal Institute of International Affairs, 1922—.

690   *American Political Science Review*. Washington, DC: American Political Science Association, 1906—.

691   *American Academy of Political and Social Science, Annals*. Philadelphia: American Academy of Political and Social Science, 1890—.

692   *Political Science Quarterly*. New York: Academy of Political Science, Columbia University, 1886—.

693   *Western Political Quarterly*. Salt Lake City: Western Political Science Association, Pacific Northwest Political Science Association, Southern California Political Science Association, 1948—.

694   *Public Administration Review*. Washington, DC: American Society for Public Administration, 1940—.

695   *American Journal of Political Science*. Detroit: Midwest Political Science Association, 1957—.

696   *Journal of Politics*. Gainesville, FL: Southern Political Science Association, 1939—.

697   *Polity*. Amherst, MA: Northeastern Political Science Association, 1968—.

The periodical publications issued by the various national or regional political science associations and research institutes often devote considerable space to book reviews. The titles listed illustrate the quantitative range of reviews published in a single year. Listed in descending quantitative ranking, *International Affairs* publishes more than 600 reviews annually as compared to less than 15 review articles published in *Polity*.

Dictionaries and Thesauri

The dictionaries presently existing for the entire discipline of political science have been improved by some valuable additions but continue to show significant weaknesses. Recent additions in this reference format are based on the attempt to arrive at a basic inventory of the political terms, their hierarchical and affinitive relationships, and their underlying concepts. These reference efforts are of fundamental importance not only for the retrieval of periodical information but also for a better understanding of political reality as expressed by political language.

In spite of the usefulness of these new dictionaries, political terminology and conceptualization continues to show major gaps in reference treatment. Political terminology even more than the vocabulary of the other social sciences needs to be analyzed as to content, ecology, or jurisdiction. While content analysis is readily available in the dictionaries of the natural sciences, the political dictionaries have so far ignored the analysis of conceptual components and the ecological or jurisdictional manifestations of the concept. Some examples will make this clearer. A frequently used but poorly defined word is *democracy*. *Democracy* is a word like *winter*. It is obvious that winter is different in the Soviet Union from winter in Costa Rica. It is equally obvious that winter is different in the countryside, the city, or inside a dwelling. Much confusion arises if the same word —*democracy* — is used for countries with different political systems, such as the United States and the German Democratic Republic. It is also inadequate to state that the United States is a democratic country because specific social relationships, like the parent-child, patient-doctor, teacher-student, factory owner-worker, police-civilian relationships, and others, are not governed by democracy. Practically all existing dictionaries fail to explain the terminology for the different types of democratic systems, such as centrifugal democracies, centripetal democracies, consociational democracies, depolitized democracies, etc. Likewise they fail to identify the countries exemplifying such democratic systems. This is also true for a concept like national self-determination. Presently existing dictionaries do not provide a record of the societies that currently struggle for a recognition of this concept, suffer under its denial, or are in the process of losing it through intervention by a foreign power. Even more dismaying is the lack of content analysis, which dictionaries would need to provide for terms like *people, equality, freedom, progress, power, groups*, etc., since these words require qualifying components to be meaningful.

Most of the titles listed in this section therefore illustrate the limited usefulness of the political reference literature in this form category. It should be noted, however, that numerous other dictionaries exist in the subfields of political science and related other social disciplines. The reader is therefore referred to the Typology Index for listings of other dictionaries that may provide the desired clarification missing from the more general political science dictionaries.

698   Back, Harry, Horst Circullies, and Gunter Marquard. *Polec. Dictionary of Politics and Economics*. Berlin: W. de Gruyter, 1964.

This is an example of the purely linguistic type of political dictionary. It aims to list English, French, and German equivalents of the most heavily used terms in politics and economics. About 14,000 equivalent terms are listed in a linguistically integrated arrangement. No definitions are provided for the listed words.

699   Beck, Carl, Eleanor D. Dym, and J. Thomas McKechnie. *Political Science Thesaurus II*. Washington, DC: American Political Science Association, 1979.

The thesaurus offers an inventory of the political science terminology together with scope notes, use references, broader and narrower terms. Also included is an inventory of geographical terminology, a rotated descriptor display, and a hierarchical display. With its 38 major concepts categories, the hierarchical index is the least successful of the presented word listings. Several of the listed key concepts, such as behavior, crime, or government, should have been consolidated into a broader concept. Several other key concepts like language (terminology) or societal factors are surprisingly omitted. Despite these limitations, the thesaurus is a most valuable reference tool for identifying access points to political information published in the literature. A revised edition of the thesaurus is planned.

700   Dunner, Joseph. *Dictionary of Political Science*. New York: Philosophical Library, 1964.

The dictionary is the result of an attempt by 195 political scientists to clarify the vocabulary of political science and to provide descriptive information about old and new nations, former and contemporary statesmen and politicians. Unfortunately, the attempt is not entirely successful since many definitions of political terms are incomplete and occasionally even misleading. Many important terms are also omitted. The entries for nations and politicians have insufficient content and have now been rendered obsolete by newer reference tools or recent developments.

701   Goldman, Ralph M., Philip G. Schoner, and DeVere E. Pentony. *The Political Science Concept Inventory*. Santa Barbara, CA: American Bibliographical Center—Clio Press, 1979.

The reference work provides an inventory of political science terms and concepts suitable for organized transfer to students within the framework of instructional courses and examinations. Nearly 22,000 terms and concepts used in dictionaries, textbook indexes, encyclopedias, periodical indexes, bibliographies, catalogs, and other reference works have been identified by the authors and classified into three transfer categories by a panel of experts. The panel agreed on 1,075 terms undergraduates should know well and on 8,399 terms undergraduates should be aware of. The remaining 12,453 terms need not necessarily be known by undergraduate students according to the panelists' consensus. The listed terms and concepts refer to beliefs, theories, events, policies, processes, groups, organizations, roles, names of persons and places, and titles of publications. An earlier edition of the *Information Sources of Political Science* was used by the authors for identification of the pertinent reference literature.

702   Lacqueur, Walter. *Dictionary of Politics*. Riverside, NJ: Free Press, 1971.

Only a very limited number of political terms and concepts are defined in this dictionary. Most of the entries refer to political personalities, institutions, or historical events. The value of this form of information packaging is questionable, however, as a result of the limitations imposed by the dictionary format. Since this is a one-volume directory, the reader, looking for information on the principality of Liechtenstein, will find only four lines on page 315 of the dictionary, whereas nearly two pages of information are provided in the annual editions of the *Statesman's Yearbook* together with a brief bibliography for further reading. Information on political institutions is likewise limited, as the very first entry in the dictionary—AAPSO—shows. Insufficient entries are furnished for the successors to this organization since neither AALAPSO is mentioned nor a cross-reference provided to OLAS, which is briefly identified on another page.

703   Plano, Jack C., Milton Greenberg, Roy Olton, and Robert E. Riggs. *Political Science Dictionary*. Hinsdale, IL: Dryden Press, 1973.

The dictionary lists and defines approximately 2,000 key terms believed to be building blocks of political science. The arrangement is alphabetical.

704   Roberts, Geoffrey K. A *Dictionary of Political Analysis*. London: Longman, 1971.

A dictionary of selected political terms, which are given modern usage definitions of varying length. Vagueness or multiplicity of definitions is pointed out by the author wherever applicable. The author also indicates his personal preferences for particular usages. Similar or closely related terms are listed with full cross-references. Regrettably, many important political terms are omitted.

Directories

A considerable number of individual and organizational experts are active in the advancement and dissemination of political knowledge as well as the advocation or execution of specific policies and programs of political significance. The following is a descriptive list of directories that provide valuable information about political scientists, scientific political institutions, and their work. Regrettably, many of these directories are not revised with sufficient frequency to reflect new developments.

INDIVIDUALS

705   APSA *Biographical Directory*. Washington, DC: American Political Science Association, 1983.

706   APSA *Directory of Members. Annual Supplement to the APSA Biographical Directory*. Washington, DC: American Political Science Association, 1974—.

The APSA *Biographical Directory* contains names and addresses of 12,500 individual members and biographical information on 7,000 political scientists. Appendices offer a classification of the members by field of interest, a geographical list of members for cities in the United States and foreign countries, as well as the dates of annual meetings held by the American Political Science Association. The directory is updated by annual supplements.

707   APSA *Directory of Department Chairpersons*. Washington, DC: American Political Science Association, to date.

The annual directory lists the names of persons who act as chairpersons in departments offering political science education in four-year institutions in the United States. The addresses of the listed chairpersons are also indicated.

708   *Directory of Librarians and Information Scientists in Political Science*. Washington, DC: American Political Science Association, 1983.

The directory contains biographical information on 124 librarians and political information scientists active in American colleges and universities.

709   European Consortium for Political Research. *Directory of European Political Scientists*. New York: Holmes & Meier, 1979.

Approximately 2,100 political scientists working in European countries are identified in this directory. Entries include birth date, nationality, career appointments, publications, and subject specialization. Indexing by subject field and area specialization is included.

710   *Policy Studies Personnel Directory*. Urbana, IL: Policy Studies Organization, 1979—.

The directory, issued on a serialized basis, identifies political and other social scientists involved in policy studies.

711   *Roster of Women in Political Science*. Washington, DC: American Political Science Association, 1969—.

The frequently revised directory offers biographical information on women active as political scientists.

INSTITUTIONS

712   American Political Science Association. A *Guide to Graduate Study in Political Science*. Washington, DC: 1972—.

The directory is an authoritative compilation of Ph.D. and master's programs in political science. It offers information on admissions policies, costs and financial aid, and fields of specialization.

713   APSA *Survey of Departments*. Washington, DC: American Political Science Association, to date.

Based on the results of an extensive questionnaire, this annual reference work offers information on the strength of political science departments in four-year institutions. Reported are enrollment, salary trends, and similar characteristics.

714   Nagel, Stuart, and Marian Neef. *Policy Research Centers Directory*. Urbana, IL: Policy Studies Organization, 1978.

Policy research centers are organizational units and groups of researchers, affiliated with academic or entrepreneurial institutions, whose primary function is to study public policy issues. The directory identifies more than 100 policy research centers and describes their policy concerns, clientele, funding, disciplinary background, type of decision-making procedure, and bibliographic reference material. The directory is arranged by the name of the parent institution, but a separate subject index is also included. There are also six essays that analyze the structure, function, style, control, impact, skill requirements, and the future of policy research centers.

715   Nagel, Stuart, and Marian Neef. *The Political Science Utilization Directory*. Urbana, IL: Policy Studies Organization, 1975—.

It has often been asserted that most of political science is irrelevant to the people operating within governmental settings. This reference work has been designed to show how political science has been and can be used in federal, state, and local government agencies. Based on the results of a questionnaire, the directory indicates the responses of governmental administrators, analysts, and specialists to six key questions about the most helpful publications, type of research needed, communication improvements, present hiring, future hiring, and improved training. The information is arranged under the names of the governmental agencies covered by the survey. Separate name and subject indexes are also included. Future editions of the directory are planned.

716   *Policy Grants Directory*. Urbana, IL: Policy Studies Organization, 1977—.

717   *Policy Publishers and Associations Directory*. Urbana, IL: Policy Studies Organization, 1980—.

718   *Policy Studies Directory*. Urbana, IL: Policy Studies Organization, 1973—.

These directories, published on a serial basis, identify funding organizations, publishers, periodicals, associations, and academic programs concerned with policy studies.

719   *Research Support for Political Scientists*. Washington, DC: American Political Science Association, 1981.

A detailed listing of public and private agencies that fund research fellowships, grants, and contracts for political scientists is offered by this reference work. A guide to preparing research proposals is also included.

Encyclopedias

720   *Handlexikon zur Politikwissenschaft*. Munich: Ehrenwirth, 1972.

721   *Staatslexikon*. Freiburg: Herder, 1957—1963.

These titles represent two major German-language encyclopedias in political science. The first title is a one-volume encyclopedia prepared by young German political scientists and qualified government officials. Its articles analyze political concepts in depth and offer factual information, critical evaluation, and bibliographies.

The second title is a multivolume set containing over 4,000 articles dealing with the legal, economic, and societal aspects of political science. The articles include useful bibliographies for pertinent works in major European languages.

722   Nagel, Stuart. *Encyclopedia of Policy Studies*. New York: Marcel Dekker, 1983.

Written by 41 contributors, the encyclopedia contains 34 chapters dealing with stages in policy formation and implementation, policy analysis across nations and disciplines, policy problems on various government levels, and policy problems with political, economic, sociological, and natural science emphases.

Handbooks

723   Andrews, William G. *International Handbook of Political Science*. Westport, CT: Greenwood Press, 1982.

The handbook presents an international survey of the development of political science since 1945. Most countries where political science is firmly established as a discipline are covered. In each of the 27 country chapters, a notable political scientist native to the country reviewed, examines the evolution of the discipline, its research, teaching and association activities, as well as its prospects for the future and the relationship between political science and politics. Each chapter also contains a concise bibliography. An introductory and four other essays by international specialists describe intellectual, institutional, and educational trends in political science throughout the world. Five appendices offer information on international political science associations. A separate bibliography of works on political science in 12 countries not included in this handbook is also provided. The index contains names of persons, organizations, and countries as well as some subject terms.

The most striking result of the international survey is the fact that the classification of the national political science professions might well follow the same terms as are used to classify the various countries of the world. Almost invariably the least developed countries have the least developed political science disciplines.

724   Garson, G. David. *Handbook of Political Science Methods*. Boston: Holbrook Press, 1976.

The handbook presents basic information on a wide range of conceptual approaches and techniques used in political science. In its 12 chapters the handbook covers Marxism, psychoanalytic approaches, structural-functional analysis, systems analysis, case studies and other approaches, survey research, scaling, statistical tests, association measures, correlation, regression and factor analysis, and causal modelling. Two appendices contain examples of computer routines and various mathematical tables. An index is included.

725   Greenstein, Fred I., and Nelson W. Polsby. *The Handbook of Political Science*. Reading, MA: Addison-Wesley Publishing Company, 1975.

The handbook partially fills the gap created by the lack of an English-language encyclopedia of modern political science. The eight volumes of the handbook bear the following titles: (1) Political Science: Scope and Theory; (2) Micropolitical Theory; (3) Macropolitical Theory; (4) Nongovernmental Politics; (5) Governmental Institutions and Processes; (6) Policies and Policymaking; (7) Strategies of Inquiry; and (8) International Politics. Each volume contains up to eight articles by distinguished scholars who summarize the current state of knowledge.

726   Ziegenhagen, Eduard A. *Techniques for Political Analysis. A Laboratory Manual*. Boston: Holbrook Press, 1971.

The handbook offers a descriptive survey of the basic techniques that researchers have found essential for political analysis. Separate chapters are devoted to the identification of political phenomena amenable to scientific inquiry and the procedures for their representation, including statistical methods, survey research techniques, indices and scaling techniques, gaming, simulation, experimental and ranking techniques.

Summaries of Teaching and Research Trends

Many questions frequently asked by students and professors of political science alike concern the content, value, purpose, or direction of political science as an academic discipline. The doubts and gaps in knowledge exposed by these questions are well justified for at least two reasons.

First, political science is a discipline still in search of its identity. Second, the literature that offers clarification of these questions has rarely been published in proper reference format for quick and easy consultation. It is true, of course, that the *International Encyclopedia of the Social Sciences* contains survey articles on political science and its subfields. Unfortunately the bibliographic references provided in these articles are not wholly satisfactory since most of the entries deal with phenomena of politics rather than with the science of politics.*

The following books offer descriptive, critical, or analytical summaries of political science as a field of scholarly inquiry. Some of these summaries are worldwide, some are limited to the United States, and others are limited to a particular subfield of political science. All of them provide an overview of the activities, conceptualizations, research trends, or directions within the discipline. At the same time, many of these books function as evaluative guides to important scholarly publications through extensive footnotes and selective bibliographies.

GENERAL

727   Finifter, Ada. *Political Science: The State of the Discipline*. Washington, DC: American Political Science Association, 1983.

728   Irish, Marian D. *Political Science. Advance of the Discipline*. Englewood Cliffs, NJ: Prentice-Hall, 1968.

729   Somit, Albert, and Joseph Tanenhaus. *The Development of American Political Science from Burgess to Behavioralism*. Boston: Allyn and Bacon, 1967.

730   Waldo, Dwight. *Political Science in the United States of America: A Trend Report*. Paris: UNESCO, 1956.

These publications survey the development and professional growth of political science and analyze the state of the discipline and its subfields from the early postwar period to the present. The books identify the main trends

*See, for instance, David Easton, "Political Science," *International Encyclopedia of the Social Sciences*, pp. 292–298; or Chadwick F. Alger, "International Relations," *International Encyclopedia of the Social Sciences*, pp. 60–69.

of study, current and past controversies or problems, and the main contributions made by political scientists to the advancement of the discipline. Footnotes and bibliographies cite the most important publications of the discipline.

731   Murphy, Robert E. *The Style and Study of Political Science*. Glenview, IL: Scott, Foresman, 1970.

732   Strum, Phillipa, and Michael Shmidman. *On Studying Political Science*. Pacific Palisades, CA: Goodyear, 1969.

These handbooks offer instructions on how to study political science, how to write term papers and book reports, and where to look for political data. They present brief information about the organizational structure of the discipline and describe some of the leading approaches and methodologies.

733   Dahl, Robert. *Modern Political Analysis*. New York: Prentice-Hall, 1970.

734   Strickland, Donald A., L. L. Wade, and R. E. Johnson. *A Primer of Political Analysis*. Chicago: Markham, 1968.

735   Van Dyke, Vernon. *Political Science: A Philosophical Analysis*. Stanford, CA: Stanford University Press, 1960.

The titles listed above represent a category of books that describe the basic analytical tools of the discipline. They explicate the central questions and concepts that concern political scientists. Typical issues raised by political scientists are analyzed by the application of basic conceptual schemes or hypotheses.

SPECIAL FIELDS

736   Butler, David. *The Study of Political Behavior*. London: Hutchinson University Library, 1958.

737   Jenkin, Thomas P. *The Study of Political Theory*. New York: Random House, 1955.

738   Macridis, Roy. *The Study of Comparative Government*. New York: Doubleday, 1955.

739   Murphy, Walter, and Joseph Tanenhaus. *The Study of Public Law*. New York: Random House, 1972.

740   Waldo, Dwight. *The Study of Public Administration*. New York: Random House, 1967.

741   Wright, Quincy. *The Study of International Relations*. New York: Appleton-Century-Crofts, 1955.

Political science has developed into a number of subfields, each of which exhibits a distinctive investigative focus. The books cited above describe the meaning and boundaries of each subfield, its main objectives, and its conceptual content. The principal issues and problems are described together with the available methodologies and approaches for their solution.

742   Davis, Vincent, and Arthur N. Gilbert. *Basic Courses in International Relations, an Anthology of Syllabi*. Beverly Hills, CA: Sage Publications, 1968.

743   Gurr, T. R., and F. J. Moreno. *Basic Courses in Comparative Politics*. Beverly Hills, CA: Sage Publications, 1969.

744   Hermann, C. F., and K. N. Waltz. *Basic Courses in Foreign Policy*. Beverly Hills, CA: Sage Publications, 1970.

745   Rohn, Peter H., L. Gordenker, and E. Miles. *Basic Courses in International Law, an Anthology of Syllabi*. Beverly Hills, CA: Sage Publications, 1970.

746   Rohn, Peter H., L. Gordenker, and E. Miles. *Basic Courses in International Organization*. Beverly Hills, CA: Sage Publications, 1969.

These reference books provide collections of syllabi that are considered representative, innovative, or exceptionally useful in the study of various subfields of political science. Course outlines and study requirements are given, together with bibliographies of books and articles required or recommended for reading.

Yearbooks

There is a definite need to assemble in an annual publication descriptive and statistical data about research developments and achievements in political science. In contrast to the situation in several of the subfields of political science, yearbook coverage of political science itself does not seem to be well developed. The following titles offer only a modest portion of the information that could be aggregated on an annual basis about the progression of scientific knowledge in politics.

747   Nagel, Stuart S. *Policy Studies Review Annual*. Beverly Hills, CA: Sage Publications, 1977 – .

Policy studies are an attempt to apply the concepts, methods, and findings of the social sciences to important policy problems. This series of annual publications brings together a selection of the best writing about policy research and the analysis of problems with a political science, economics, sociology-psychology, or natural science emphasis. Individual articles are written by scholars from various disciplines who explore the decision-making process and policy orientation in such areas as foreign policy, economic regulation, social legislation, taxation and spending policy, population control, energy policy, environmental protection, etc.

748   *Political Science Annual.* Indianapolis: Bobbs-Merrill, 1966–1975.

In spite of its title, this defunct reference series was not an annual publication during the decade of its existence. Each of the published volumes aimed to provide an inventory of theories and findings in political science, with no more than four to six review articles appearing in each volume. The articles were written by American political scientists and covered such topics as political socialization, legislative institutions and processes, public opinion and opinion change, education and political behavior, community power studies, crisis decision-making, internation alliances, and several others. Name as well as subject indexes are included.

PSYCHOLOGY

Introduction

Psychology is a subdiscipline of the social sciences that concentrates on the behavior of individuals as opposed to groups or organizations. In practice and in research, psychology covers every area of human activity that engages the mind and body of the individual. Mental processes and all forms of interpersonal relationships are the primary objects of scientific investigation. As a result of this investigative focus, psychology stands in close relationship to political science. Since the most important political decisions are ultimately made on the basis of personality and attitude factors, political science must include the scientific findings of psychology.

This field of study has produced a large body of literature that is rapidly expanding. In general, the mass of psychological information is covered by an excellent reference system that utilizes a minimum of instruments with considerable efficiency. If there is any marked deficiency in the reference literature, however, it is the lack of special bibliographic tools for the identification of psychological studies of political decision-makers.

The following pages contain listings and descriptions of the standard reference publications in psychology that are of major interest to political scientists.

Bibliographic Instruments

GUIDEBOOKS

749   Bell, James Edward. A *Guide to Library Research in Psychology.* Dubuque, IA: Wm. C. Brown Company, 1971.

The guidebook offers detailed listings of dictionaries, encyclopedias, handbooks, biographical sources, book reviews, test information material, abstracts and indexes, and bibliographies. Books, periodicals, newspapers, government publications, style manuals, and study guides of research value in psychology are also listed. Introductory chapters are devoted to a description of library classification systems and library research methods.

750   Borchardt, D. H., and R. D. Francis. *How to Find Out in Psychology.* A *Guide to the Literature and Methods of Research.* New York: Pergamon Press, 1984.

Two of the eleven chapters in this guidebook deal with what psychology is about and its major theories. Chapters 3–6 identify the bibliographic aids used by psychologists who want to find out about the literature of a subject. Principles and methods of research are described in chapters 7–10 while the final chapter is concerned with professional matters and organizations. Appendices include a detailed guide to library searches, instructions for report writing and self-testing for authors of empirical reports, as well as a reader's guide to assessing research reports. An author arranged list of the cited sources in the guidebook and a subject index are also included.

751   McInnis, Raymond G. *Research Guide for Psychology.* Westport, CT: Greenwood Press, 1982.

The guidebook offers lengthy detailed instructions about the use and characteristics of the bibliographic and substantive information sources available in psychology. Of the 17 (A–Q) parts in the guidebook 16 (B–Q) are devoted to subdivisions of psychology as classified in the *Psychological Abstracts* set. Part A presents descriptions of information sources covering all aspects of psychology, such as guidebooks, bibliographies and abstracts, biographical dictionaries, directories, book review citations, encyclopedias, handbooks, methodological works, and statistics sources. Parts H–N are of particular interest for politically related inquiries, as they focus on social processes; social issues; social psychology, including group processes and motivation; personality; psychological disorders, including antisocial behavior; treatment and prevention, including behavior modification, rehabilitation, and penology; educational psychology; and applied psychology, including personnel evaluation, organizational behavior, etc. All cited sources are listed in a separate bibliography. An index is also included.

752   Sarbin, Theodor R., and William C. Coe. *The Student Psychologist's Handbook: A Guide to Sources.* Cambridge, MA: Schenkman Publishing Company, 1969.

Major research areas in psychology and the sources of information commonly used by students of psychology are identified in this brief guidebook. Among the printed information sources, the guidebook lists mainly journals and handbooks. A glossary of statistical terms is also included.

CURRENT BIBLIOGRAPHIES

753   *Bulletin Signaletique 390: Psychologie et Psychopathologie, Psychiatrie.* Paris: Centre National de la Recherche Scientifique, 1947– .

An annotated bibliography of periodical articles, dissertations, conference proceedings, and reports published in psychology and related disciplines throughout the world. Entries are arranged under subject categories that include techniques and methods, social and applied psychology, personality, psychology of work, old age, psychoanalysis, and others. The bibliography is issued monthly with separate author and subject indexes that are also cumulated annually.

753a   *Catalog of Selected Documents in Psychology.* Washington, DC: American Psychological Association, 1971– .

Full bibliographic citations and 100–300 word abstracts are provided by this reference instrument for selected manuscripts and reports that are not published in periodicals or in book form. All listed manuscripts are deemed to be of high quality as judged by a panel of editors. Entries in this quarterly reference work are arranged by fields of psychology, including social psychology, personnel and industrial psychology, experimental psychology, etc. The listed material is available in paper or microfiche form from the publisher by payment of a small fee.

754   New York (City). Public Library. Research Libraries. *Bibliographic Guide to Psychology.* Boston: G. K. Hall, 1975– .

Based on the catalog entries of the Research Libraries of the New York Public Library and the MARC tapes of the Library of Congress, this series of annual, unannotated bibliographies lists books, pamphlets, and series publications published throughout the world on all aspects of psychology. The entries are arranged in an integrated format in alphabetical sequence and provide access by author or editor, title, series title, and subject heading. The bibliographies also identify the call numbers of all listed items.

755   *PsycALERT.* Washington, DC: American Psychological Association, 1983– . (Vendor: Dialog—File 140)

Full bibliographic citations for the latest articles published in more than 1,300 periodicals in psychology and related behavioral sciences are retrievable online with the use of this weekly updated database. Subject access is provided by a controlled vocabulary of descriptors listed in the *Thesaurus of Psychological Index Terms.* All bibliographic entries in this database are automatically deleted and transferred to the *PsycINFO* database, once the abstracting and final index processes are completed for each record.

756   *Psychological Abstracts.* Lancaster, PA: American Psychological Association, 1927– .

Cumulated Subject Index to Psychological Abstracts, 1927–1960. Boston: G. K. Hall, 1966.

———— . *First Supplement, 1961–1965.* Boston: G. K. Hall, 1968.

———— . *Second Supplement, 1966–1968.* Boston: G. K. Hall, 1971.

Cumulated Subject Index to Psychological Abstracts, 1969–1971, 1972–1974, 1975–1978, 1978–1980. Washington, DC: American Psychological Association, 1972, 1975, 1979, 1981.

Author Index to Psychological Index 1894–1935 and Psychological Abstracts 1927–1958. Boston: G. K. Hall, 1960.

———— . *First Supplement 1959–1963.* Boston: G. K. Hall, 1965.

———— . *Second Supplement 1964–1968.* Boston: G. K. Hall, 1970.

Cumulative Author Index to Psychological Abstracts, 1969–1971, 1972–1974, 1975–1978, 1978–1980. Washington, DC: American Psychological Association, 1972, 1975, 1979, 1981.

757   *Psycinfo.* Washington, DC: American Psychological Association, 1967– . (Vendor: BRS; Dialog—File 11; SDC)

The world's psychological literature, consisting of over 900 periodicals, 1,500 books, and numerous dissertations each year, is identifiable by author and subject and retrievable in English-language abstracts with the help of the printed *Psychological Abstracts* volumes and the computerized *Psycinfo* database, both updated monthly. Both reference tools may be used to locate behavioral studies and theoretical works that are of significant importance for an understanding of political phenomena. A large number of entries may be found under such behavioral terms as achievement, belief, conflict, conformity, hostility, motivation, opinion, personality, response, etc. Author and subject indexing in printed form is available monthly with semiannual, annual, and multiannual cumulations. All index citations offer numerical references to the individual volumes of the *Psychological Abstracts* set and the consecutively numbered abstracts in them.

Online display with offline printing of all citations and abstracts since 1967 is available with the computerized *Psycinfo* database. Like its printed counterpart, the computerized database also uses a controlled vocabulary that can be identified in the printed *Thesaurus of Psychological Index Terms*.

RETROSPECTIVE BIBLIOGRAPHIES

758   Coelho, George V. *Mental Health and Social Change. An Annotated Bibliography*. Rockville, MD: National Institute of Mental Health, 1972.

The rapid social changes occurring in this century have made behavioral adaptation problematical for many persons. This bibliography identifies the major sources of mental health information relevant to the subject of social change. Altogether, 730 abstracts of periodical articles and some books are compiled under five sections that illustrate scientific findings in the following areas: (1) biologically oriented approaches relevant to ethological and ecological aspects of behavior, (2) behavioral and social science approaches relevant to organism-environment relationships, (3) critical episodes of stress affecting behavioral adaptation, (4) group behavioral disorders and remedial approaches, and (5) new designs for improved human services. A computer-generated keyword title index and author index are also provided.

759   Crabtree, J. Michael, and Kenneth E. Moyer. *Bibliography of Aggressive Behavior: A Reader's Guide to the Research Literature*. New York: Alan R. Liss, 1977.

Aggressive behavior is one of the most intractable problems affecting the political systems of the world. The legal and administrative efforts to control human aggression are only moderately successful and frequently even exacerbate latent aggressive tendencies in society and political processes. Scientific inquiry has, however, contributed many valuable insights into the origin and prevention of human aggression. The bibliography cited above contains 3,857 unannotated entries for studies published between 1925 and 1975 on human and animal aggression. A code word index facilitates speedy identification of desired items.

760   Gottsegen, Gloria Behar. *Group Behavior. A Guide to Information Sources*. Detroit: Gale Research Company, 1979.

Anything that happens in the world politically could be termed an instance of group behavior. This bibliography will be useful for the identification of scholarly books and articles dealing with the psychology of group behavior, notably in respect of group influences, power in groups, and group conflicts. Reference sources, periodicals, and associations concerned with group behavior are separately listed.

761   Kirscht, John P., and Ronald C. Dillehay. *Dimensions of Authoritarianism, a Critical Review*. Lexington: University of Kentucky Press, 1967.

Authoritarianism is one of the key concepts for an understanding of political systems. A trail-blazing book by T. W. Adorno, E. Frenkel-Brunswik, D. J. Levinson, and R. N. Sanford, published in 1950 under the title *The Authoritarian Personality*, spawned an enormous literature, which Kirscht and Dillehay categorize and describe by major content areas. Separate chapters are devoted to studies focusing on the F scale; social and personality characteristics; political, religious, ethnic, and other beliefs related to authoritarianism; attitude change; group behavior; and similar topics. The reference book contains a separate bibliographic listing for all works cited in the text as well as a subject and personal name index.

762   National Institute of Mental Health, Rockville, Maryland. *Bibliography on Racism*. Washington, DC: U.S.Government Printing Office, 1972, 1978.

During the past several centuries the black, Indian, and several other ethnic population groups have been systematically subordinated by the white majority of the United States. The impact of this subordination on the minds of men may be termed racism or even a mental disease, as believed by some. The bibliography attempts to discern causes and cures of this attitudinal phenomenon by listing and abstracting the results of research on racism as published in books and periodicals. For best results it is advisable to use the author and subject index in the book for the identification of all conceptually related studies.

762a   Wilcox, Laird. *Bibliography on Political Psychology and Propaganda*. Kansas City, MO: Editorial Research Service, 1980.

This bibliography offers 432 partially annotated entries for books on various aspects of political psychology; including news media bias, persuasion, subliminal programming, brainwashing, propaganda and counterpropaganda.

Book Reviewing Media

763   *Contemporary Psychology: A Journal of Reviews.* Lancaster, PA: American Psychological Association, 1956—.

Lengthy signed reviews of psychological books are presented in this full-length reviewing journal. The reviews are written by competent scholars whose academic position and educational background is identified. The journal is issued monthly with an annual author and reviewer index.

Dictionaries and Thesauri

764   Chaplin, James Patrick. *Dictionary of Psychology.* New York: Dell Publishing Company, 1975.

765   Drever, James. A *Dictionary of Psychology.* Harmondsworth, England: Penguin, 1964.

766   Dorsch, Friedrich, et al. *Psychologisches Wörterbuch.* Hamburg: Meiner, 1970.

767   English, Horace B., and Ava C. English. A *Comprehensive Dictionary of Psychological and Psychoanalytical Terms. A Guide to Usage.* New York: McKay, 1968.

768   Glanze, Walter. *Dictionary of Psychology and Psychoanalysis.* Harlow, England: Longman, 1983.

769   Harre, Rom, and Roger Lamb. *The Encyclopedic Dictionary of Psychology.* Cambridge, MA: MIT Press, 1983.

770   Harriman, Philip Lawrence. *Handbook of Psychological Terms.* Paterson, NJ: Littlefield, Adams, 1969.

771   Hehlmann, Wilhelm. *Wörterbuch der Psychologie.* Stuttgart: A. Kroner, 1968.

772   Heidenreich, Charles A. A *Dictionary of Personality: Behavior and Adjustment Terms.* Dubuque, IA: W. C. Brown, 1968.

773   International Union of Psychological Science. *Trilingual Psychological Dictionary.* Vol. 1, *English/French/German*; Vol. 2, *Français/Allemand/Anglais*;

Vol. 3, *Deutsch/Englisch/Franzosisch.* Berne: Hand Huber, 1975.

774   Pieron, Henri. *Vocabulaire de la Psychologie.* Paris: Presses Universitaires de France, 1968.

775   Sury, Kurt F. *Wörterbuch der Psychologie und Ihrer Grenzgebiete.* Basle: Schwabe, 1967.

776   Warren, Howard Crosby. *Dictionary of Psychology.* Cambridge, MA: Houghton Mifflin, 1962.

777   Wolman, Benjamin B. *Dictionary of Behavioral Science.* New York: Van Nostrand Reinhold, 1973.

Psychological terminology and conceptualization is well served by dictionaries. The listed dictionaries identify and define terms and concepts in English, French, and German. Equivalent terms in the three languages are listed in a separate trilingual dictionary.

778   *Thesaurus of Psychological Index Terms.* Washington, DC: American Psychological Association, 1982.

The thesaurus offers an inventory of the descriptors used for the efficient indexing and retrieval of psychological information contained in the *Psychological Abstracts* set and the *Psycinfo database*. Three separate listings are provided, namely, a relationship section with broader, narrower, and related terms; a rotated alphabetical section; and a listing of postable terms and term codes.

Directories

779   American Psychological Association. *Directory.* Washington, DC: 1948—.

The annual directory provides alphabetical lists of fellows, members, and associates, alphabetical lists of new members and associates, a geographical list of members, lists of diplomates of the American Board of Examiners in Psychological Hypnosis. Also included are divisional membership lists.

780   Wolman, Benjamin B. *International Directory of Psychology: A Guide to People, Places and Policies.* New York: Plenum Publishing Company, 1979.

The directory surveys the state of the psychological profession in 70 countries and provides information about psychologists and professional societies.

Encyclopedias

781   Corsini, Raymond J. *Encyclopedia of Psychology.* New York: John Wiley & Sons, 1984.

Some 2,000 articles covering 1,200 major topics in all fields of psychology and 650 biographies (including 200 foreign psychologists) are presented in this encyclopedia written by 500 expert contributors. The encyclopedia describes all major psychological tests and also provides 222 summaries of psychology in foreign countries. A bibliography of 15,000 reference entries, as well as subject and person indexes, are included.

782   Eysenck, H. J., W. Arnold, and R. Merli. *Encyclopedia of Psychology*. New York: Herder and Herder, 1972.

The three-volume encyclopedia provides brief definitions of terms as well as more detailed articles about terms and concepts. The articles are written by well-known authorities and may range up to 4,000 words. Articles usually close with bibliographic listings.

783   Goldenson, Robert M. *The Encyclopedia of Human Behavior*. Garden City, NY: Doubleday, 1970.

All phases of psychology, psychiatry, and mental health are covered in this two-volume encyclopedia. It contains over 1,000 entries, many of which are of considerable length. Each article begins with a concise definition. Illustrative cases drawn from recognized sources are included in the articles on psychiatric disorders. The encyclopedia also includes a category index in which all topical articles are listed under broad headings, such as emotions, intelligence, motivation, personality, social behavior, etc. There is also a separate subject index that contains over 5,000 entries.

784   Wolman, Benjamin B. *International Encyclopedia of Psychiatry, Psychology, Psychoanalysis and Neurology*. New York: Van Nostrand Reinhold, 1977.

The twelve-volume encyclopedia offers the most ambitious and extensive summary of existing knowledge in the disciplines named in the title. There are more than 2,000 articles written by some 1,500 experts and 300 editor/consultants. Each article contains a bibliography of pertinent English-language works. Psychological subject matter of interest to political scientists is covered in articles entitled Aggression, Communication, Leadership, Motivation, Perception, Social Psychology, and others. Volume 12 of the set presents an alphabetical list of all entries, a name index, and a subject index.

Handbooks

785   Dunnette, Marvin D. *Handbook of Industrial and Organizational Psychology*. Chicago: Rand McNally College Publishing Company, 1976.

Politics, the formation and execution of authoritative directions within an entity, is fundamentally a group behavioral process in organizations. This handbook presents a detailed review and summary of psychological knowledge relating to individual behavior in organizations and group behavioral processes in organizations. The information is arranged in three parts, namely Part 1 — Theoretical and Methodological Foundations of Industrial and Organizational Psychology; Part 2 — Individual and Job Measurement and the Management of Individual Behavior in Organizations; and Part 3 — Description and Measurement of Organizations and of Behavioral Processes in Organizations. The three main parts are subdivided by major topical categories, such as aptitude, attitude, personality, decision-making, leadership, change processes, etc. Numerous bibliographic references accompany the text. Name and subject indexes offer additional access to the information presented in the book. For a more specific focus on the relationship between psychological processes and political behavior, see the following handbook by Jeanne N. Knutson.

786   Knutson, Jeanne N., et al. *Handbook of Political Psychology*. San Francisco: Jossey-Bass, 1973.

Political psychology is a comparatively new field concerned with understanding the relationship between psychological processes and political behavior. The handbook provides the first definite assessment of the scientific contribution made by psychology to political science. It examines past research findings, alternative strategies of inquiry, available models, and current research needs in all areas of political psychology. The material is presented in an introductory chapter and 15 individual articles arranged in four parts, as follows: Part 1 — Basic Psychological Constructs — examines the three basic methods by which political behavior is analyzed, i.e., personality, political attitudes, and political beliefs. Part 2 — Forming and Maintaining Stable Orientations — considers political socialization, authoritarianism, and anomie-alienation. Part 3 — Nexus of Individuality and Polity — covers leadership, aggression, violence, revolution and war, and international politics. Part 4 — Methods of Inquiry — evaluates psychobiography, survey research, experimentation, simulation and projective techniques. A detailed, comprehensive bibliography of more than 2,000 entries identifies further sources of information.

More recent information in this field is published in *Political Psychology*, a quarterly journal issued by the International Society of Political Psychology, which the author has founded.

787   Lindzey, Gardner, and Elliott Aronson. *The Handbook of Social Psychology*. Reading, MA: Addison-Wesley Publishing Company, 1968.

Social psychologists define their field as an attempt to understand and explain how the thought, feeling, and behavior of individuals are influenced by the actual, imagined, or implied presence of others. The current state of theories and knowledge is summarized in 45 articles written by distinguished scholars. The articles are arranged in five volumes that bear the following titles: (1) Historical Introduction and Systematic Positions; (2) Research Methods; (3) The Individual in a Social Context; (4) Group Psychology and Phenomena of Interaction; (5) Applied Social Psychology. Articles conclude with supporting bibliographies. Each of the five volumes of the handbook contains separate author and subject indexes.

788   Robinson, John P., Jerrold G. Rusk, and Kendra B. Head. *Measures of Political Attitudes*. Ann Arbor: University of Michigan, 1968.

789   Robinson, John P., and Phillip R. Shaver. *Measures of Social Psychological Attitudes*. Ann Arbor: University of Michigan, 1973.

For many years it has been known that political behavior is the result of attitudes developed in response to challenges experienced by the human body and psyche in interaction with the environment. The proliferation of scientific instruments for measuring human attitudes and the dispersal of information about them in many different publications has, however, created a significant impediment to the proper utilization of these instruments by students and other researchers.

The two handbooks for attitude measurements aim to include a complete list of relevant empirical instruments, their actual items and necessary scoring instructions, and a comprehensive assessment of the strengths and weaknesses of these instruments.

The information material in the handbook *Measures of Political Attitudes* is arranged under the following main headings: (1) Introduction; (2) Public Reaction to Government Policies; (3) Liberalism-Conservatism; (4) Democratic Principles; (5) Domestic Government Policies; (6) Racial and Ethnic Attitudes; (7) International Affairs; (8) Hostility-Related National Attitudes; (9) Community-Based Political Attitudes; (10) Political Information; (11) Political Participation; (12) Attitudes Towards the Political Process; (13) Individual Questions for Survey Research Center Election Studies. Appropriate subheadings identify specific scales, inventories, indexes, or other measurements and assessments. Bibliographic references are provided to the original publication of these instruments. A name index is also included.

The handbook *Measures of Social Psychological Attitudes* is arranged in eleven chapters, entitled (1) Introduction; (2) Life Satisfaction and Happiness; (3) The Measurement of Self-Esteem and Related Constructs;

(4) Internal-External Locus of Control; (5) Alienation and Anomia; (6) Authoritarianism, Dogmatism, and Related Measures; (7) Other Socio-Political Attitudes; (8) Values; (9) General Attitudes Towards People; (10) Religious Attitudes; (11) Methodological Scales.

While the two handbooks contain an overview and assessment of the measuring instruments for public attitudes, no attempt has been made to identify the numerous contradictions and illogical aspects in the various attitudes under measurement. The publisher has also issued a third handbook, entitled *Measures of Occupational Attitudes and Occupational Characteristics* (Ann Arbor: University of Michigan, 1969) which deals with work-related attitudes.

790   Sweetland, Richard C., and Daniel J. Keyser. *Tests: A Comprehensive Reference for Assessments in Psychology, Education, and Business*. Kansas City, MO: Test Corporation of America, 1983.

More than 3,000 tests for use by psychologists, educators, and human resource personnel are listed and described in this handbook. Each entry provides a statement of the test's purpose, a description of the test, relevant cost and availability information. Five separate indexes by test title, author, publisher, scoring service, and visual impairment are included.

791   Thomae, Hans. *Handbuch der Psychologie*. Göttingen: Hogrefe, 1959–1969.

Convenient summarization of psychological knowledge is also available in this 12-volume German-language set. Separate volumes are devoted to general psychology, motivation, genetic psychology, personality, expression, psychometrics, social psychology, industrial psychology, etc.

792   Triandis, Harry C., and William Wilson Lambert. *The Handbook of Cross-Cultural Psychology*. Boston: Allyn & Bacon, 1980.

Cross-cultural psychology is concerned with the systematic study of human behavior and experience as it occurs in different cultures. The handbook summarizes all reliable cross-cultural psychological knowledge in 52 chapters distributed over six volumes. Volume 1 examines the field in broad perspective, while volume 2 focuses on methodological difficulties. The remaining volumes concentrate on basic psychological processes, developmental processes, and psychopathological phenomena. Of special interest in political inquiries are the chapters on cross-cultural studies of attitudes, beliefs, values, alienation, and social change. Bibliographic references, name and subject indexes are included.

793   Wolman, Benjamin. *Handbook of General Psychology*. Englewood Cliffs, NJ: Prentice-Hall, 1973.

This handbook will be useful where the more extensive encyclopedic sets in psychology are not readily available. It offers a convenient overview of the subject matter of general psychology.

Yearbooks

794   *Annual Review of Psychology.* Palo Alto, CA: Annual Reviews, Inc. 1950–.

This annual reference publication is composed of articles that review the psychological literature within specific topics or bodies of knowledge. In recent years the articles covered such topics as individual decision behavior, attitudes and opinions, personality, mass communication, social psychophysiology, and personnel selection.

795   Buros, Oscar Krisen. *The Mental Measurements Yearbook.* Highland Park, NJ: Gryphon Press, 1938–.

796   *Tests in Print: A Comprehensive Bibliography of Tests in Education, Psychology and Industry.* Highland Park, NJ: Gryphon Press, 1961–.

The most recent edition of this irregularly published yearbook was issued in two volumes, consisting of three main parts: a section of tests and reviews, a section of books and reviews, and a section of indexes for publishers, book titles, test titles, and names. The main purpose of the MMYs is to provide information about separately published tests for measuring achievement, intelligence, aptitude, personality, cognition, etc. Critical reviews written by subject specialists and extensive bibliographies about the construction, use, and validity of specific tests are provided. Subject examination tests for political science and related social studies are included. *Tests in Print* functions as a master index to the entries and references in the earlier editions of the *Mental Measurements Yearbook* and provides information about the print status, number of available reviews, and the identity of the reviewer for the tests.

797   *Evaluation Studies Review Annuals.* Beverly Hills, CA: Sage Publications, 1976–.

The annuals offer a collection of outstanding articles published about evaluation theory, methods and studies in criminal justice, health services and other social services, public policy, etc., each year. A summary of evaluation research is presented in Marcia Guttentag and Elmer L. Struening's *Handbook of Evaluation Research* (Beverly Hills, CA: Sage Publications, 1975).

SOCIOLOGY

Introduction

As a subdiscipline of the social sciences, sociology is devoted to the study of the elements, processes, causes, and consequences of human contact and group living. It primarily investigates ethnic and race relationships along with other collective behaviors and analyzes the institutions, stratification, and mobility of society. Much of sociology is concerned with social change, social dysfunction, or social pathology as factors interfering with normal group relations. In addition, the study of population in patterns of aggregation, composition, spatial and temporal relationships occupies an important part of sociological inquiry. It is evident that these aspects of sociological inquiry are of great importance for the formulation and execution of social policy by governmental institutions.

Sociology has produced a voluminous literature with a distinct vocabulary but surprisingly only a limited and efficient reference literature of its own. The sociological bibliographies are particularly useful to the political researcher who is interested in using sociological findings for the illumination of political problems. For terminological and conceptual clarification the dictionaries and handbooks offer valuable assistance. The most important titles are listed and described on the following pages.

Bibliographic Instruments

GUIDEBOOKS

798   Bart, Pauline, and Linda Frankel. *The Student Sociologist's Handbook.* Glenview, IL: Scott, Foresman & Co., 1981.

While three of the six chapters in this excellent guidebook are devoted to a general discussion of the perspectives in sociology, the writing of sociological papers, and the mechanics of library research, the fourth and fifth chapters contain extensive descriptions of the periodical literature and principal reference works in sociology. Separately listed and described are periodicals concerned with social problems and social policies, radical and Marxist viewpoints, culture and ideas, and women's studies. The reference sources are listed by type, i.e., abstracts, indexes, bibliographies, handbooks, etc. The sixth chapter identifies governmental and nongovernmental sources of statistical data. Two appendices contain outlines of the Dewey and Library of Congress classification systems. An index is also included.

799   Mark, Charles. *Sociology of America. A Guide to Information Sources.* Detroit: The Gale Research Company, 1976.

The guidebook offers 1,861 entries for the monographic and periodical literature relating to American society as a whole, its social stratification, its private and collective behavior, and its formal political structures. Entries are grouped in 24 chapters, entitled: (1) Introduction, (2) Reference Works, (3) Periodical Literature, (4) American Society, (5) Population, (6) Regional and Rural Studies, (7) Urban Community, (8) Black America, (9) Jewish Community, (10) Ethnic Groups, (11) Religion, (12) Social Stratification, (13) Work and Occupations, (14) Marriage and the Family, (15) Women, (16) Youth, (17) Education, (18) Mass Culture, (19) Formal Organizations and Political Systems, (20) Collective Behavior, (21) Deviance, (22) Crime and Delinquency, (23) Health and Social Services, (24) Selected Works in American Sociology. All of the annotated entries can also be located with the help of the author, periodical and serial title, title, and subject indexes included in the guidebook.

800   McMillan, Patricia, and James R. Kennedy, Jr. *Library Research Guide to Sociology.* Ann Arbor, MI: Pierian Press, 1981.

Divided into 12 chapters and 3 appendices, this guidebook provides illustrated instructions for locating information on sociological topics, and presents an unannotated, selective list of major reference sources in sociology. The listings are classified according to 18 categories reflecting the scope of this discipline: (1) aging, gerontology, (2) cultural anthropology, (3) crime, delinquency, penology, (4) ethnic groups, race and minority relations, (5) industrial sociology, (6) marriage and the family, (7) organizational behavior, (8) population, demography, (9) research methods, (10) social change and progress, (11) social problems, (12) social stratification, (13) social work, (14) sociological theory, (15) sociology of religion, (16) urban sociology, (17) women, and (18) general. Where appropriate, different types of available reference sources are separately listed under these categories. Computerized databases and several important reference sources are, however, not included in the listings.

801   Wasserman, Paul, and Jean Morgan. *Ethnic Information Sources of the United States.* Detroit: Gale Research Company, 1983.

Ethnicity is one of the important societal factors in a political system. This guidebook lists organizations, agencies, institutes, government programs, religious organizations, publishers, libraries, book dealers, and radio stations offering information on ethnic affairs. The entries are arranged alphabetically by ethnic group. Annotations provide details on the information activities provided by each organization and included complete address data.

CURRENT BIBLIOGRAPHIES

802   *Abstracts on Criminology and Penology.* Deventer, The Netherlands: Kluwer B.V., 1961 – .

803   *Criminal Justice Abstracts.* Hackensack, NJ: National Council on Crime and Delinquency, 1968 – .

804   *Criminal Justice Periodical Index.* Ann Arbor, MI: University Microfilms International, 1975 – .

805   *Criminal Justice Periodical Index (Database).* Ann Arbor, MI: University Microfilms International, 1975 – . (Vendor: Dialog — File 171)

Crime prevention and law enforcement is an important political object in all countries. The scholarly literature about crime, including political, social, and industrial crime, crime prevention, law enforcement, and criminal justice is identifiable by author, subject term, and classification category in the printed and computerized bibliographic tools cited above.

Published six times a year with an annual author and subject index, *Abstracts on Criminology and Penology* indexes and abstracts articles appearing in some 450 periodicals published in English and other languages. Entries are arranged according to a detailed classification plan with separate sections for information dealing with such topics as social relations, socioeconomic processes, criminal and noncriminal behavior against public order, the state or society, military offenses, war crimes, and social and psychopathology. The causes of crime, control and treatment of offenders, criminal procedure, and the administration of justice are also well covered.

Criminal Justice Abstracts is a quarterly index and abstract publication for some 150 periodicals in law, criminology, and penology. The entries are arranged under subject categories and are additionally accessible by a subject index.

The *Criminal Justice Periodical Index*, available in printed and electronic formats, offers access to some 120 English-language periodicals. The printed version, published three times a year, has author and subject listings based on Library of Congress subject headings. Law enforcement programs, police work, prisons, court activities, and security systems are among the topics well covered. Book reviews are listed under a separate heading. The computerized database offers citations and abstracts, and is updated monthly.

806   *The Afro-American Studies Index.* Chicago: Chicago Center for Afro-American Studies and Research Program, 1979 – .

807   *Index to Periodical Articles by and about Blacks.* Boston: G. K. Hall, 1950 – .

These printed indexes will be useful for identifying scholarly information about the political, social, and economic life of the black population in the United States and other countries of the world. The *Afro-American Studies Index*, published annually, contains author and subject entries for books, dissertations, periodical articles, government publications, and book reviews about all aspects of the black experience. The second reference work, likewise issued annually, is an author and subject index to only 22 scholarly and popular periodicals publishing articles by and about blacks.

808   *Bulletin Signaletique: Sociologie, Ethnologie.* Paris: Centre de Documentation Sciences Humaines, 1947– .

A quarterly, French-language reference source that provides more than 4,000 abstracts annually for sociological material published in books, dissertations, periodical articles, and reports throughout the world. Approximately 500 periodicals are regularly scanned for appropriate material. Abstracts are arranged under 24 subject categories that include political and economic sociology, social problems and social work, leisure, work, communication and mass media, family, etc. Author and subject indexes are provided quarterly and annually. The ethnology section provides an additional 2,000 entries per year for publications relating to the social and economic life of ethnic groups, their religion, acculturation, social change, etc. Indexes by ethnic group and geography offer additional access.

809   *Current Sociology/La Sociologie Contemporaine.* Paris: Mouton & Co., 1952– .

Issued three times annually, this reference publication offers trend reports and annotated bibliographies on selected topics in sociology. Past issues were devoted to the sociology of international relations, community research, African development, public bureaucracies, expatriate communities, religious organizations, alienation, nationalism, industrial, military and political sociology, etc. The bibliographies cite books, periodicals, and unpublished material. The language of the annotations is French or English.

810   *International Bibliography of Sociology.* Paris: UNESCO, 1952–1959; Chicago: Aldine, 1960– .

The bibliography is one of the four sections of the annually published International Bibliography of the Social Sciences, which also includes separate volumes for political science, economics, and social and cultural anthropology. The bibliography selectively lists the scientific literature of sociology as it is published in books and periodicals throughout the world. Entries are arranged in

an elaborate classification scheme similar to but not identical with the classification of political science literature. The classification contains six major classes, namely (A) history and organization of social studies, (B) theories and methods of sociology, (C) social structure, (D) social control and communication, (E) social change, and (F) social problems and social policy. Numerous subdivisions of these classes offer a structural identity to the various aspects of sociological research. Entries are unannotated, but the presence of a book review article is indicated by the letters CR. The publication lag of the bibliography is one to two years.

811   *LLBA Language and Language Behavior Abstracts.* San Diego: Sociological Abstracts, 1967– .

812   *LLBA Language and Language Behavior Abstracts.* San Diego: Sociological Abstracts, 1973– . (Vendor: BRS; Dialog — File 36)

Available in printed and electronic versions, this reference source will be useful for identifying publications dealing with language policy, literacy programs, and various aspects of interpersonal communication, including rhetorical conduct in politics. Each issue of the quarterly printed edition contains a collection of abstracts from the world's literature in language behavior, linguistics, and related disciplines, including sociology, sociolinguistics, psychology, ethnology, and others. Author, source, and subject indexes are also included.

The computerized database can be searched by author, title, subject descriptors, journal name, and other file elements for the online display or printout of bibliographic citations and abstracts.

813   *Population Bibliography.* Chapel Hill, NC: University of North Carolina, 1966– . (Vendor: Dialog — File 91)

Human procreation is often the most decisive societal factor in political change, eclipsing by far the power of the sword in the political destiny of nations. The study of population trends is therefore an excellent method for gauging the direction of future political developments.

Updated bimonthly, the *Population Bibliography* is the largest single computerized database available for information on the socioeconomic aspects of population topics. Its scope is international with extensive coverage of Third World countries, notably in respect of such topics as abortion, demography, family and family planning, fertility, migration, population and development, population policy and law, etc. The bibliographic citations, retrievable online, relate to approximately 550 journals as well as books, conference papers, government publications, and other documentation items. Apart from author, title, and geographic name searches, access to the bibliographic citations is facilitated by subject descriptors that are listed in a printed edition of the *Population Family Planning Thesaurus II*.

814   *Population Index*. Princeton, NJ: Princeton University, 1935– .

815   *Population Index Bibliography. Cumulated 1935–1968*. Boston: G. K. Hall, 1971.

Population Index Bibliography. Cumulated 1969–1981. Boston: G. K. Hall, 1983.

The *Population Index* is a quarterly, annotated bibliography in printed form that lists new periodical articles, books, official statistical publications, and bibliographies dealing with various aspects of population studies. The entries are arranged within broad subject categories, entitled general population studies, regional population studies, spatial distribution, trends in population size, mortality, fertility, marriage, divorce and family, international migration, internal migration, population characteristics, demographic and economic interrelations, demographic and noneconomic interrelations, policies, population statistics, etc. Separate author and geographical indexes offer additional access to the listed material.

The two cumulated bibliographies contain approximately 190,000 entries for items originally listed in the *Population Index* for access by author, subject, and geographical names.

816   *Race Relations Abstracts*. Beverly Hills, CA: Sage Publications, 1978– .

A quarterly index and abstract publication for periodical articles and other information material dealing with racial relations in the United States and other countries. Annual cumulated author and subject indexes are also published.

817   *Sage Urban Studies Abstracts*. Beverly Hills, CA: Sage Publications, 1973– .

Information material dealing with urban conditions can be identified in this quarterly index and abstract publication. It covers books, periodical articles, government publications, pamphlets, significant speeches and reports. Entries are arranged under major subject categories, including urbanism, urban history, architecture and design, planning, growth management, urban finance, economic development and location theory, land use, environment and energy, transportation, housing, education, urban crime, social services, socioeconomic conditions, government and politics.

Separate author and subject indexes are included in every issue, but annual cumulations are also published.

818   *Social Work Research and Abstracts*. Albany, NY: National Association of Social Workers, 1965– .

A significant characteristic of Western industrialized countries is the fact that an inordinately high number of individuals requires for adequate social functioning special assistance from professional workers. Social workers are members of a profession that renders such assistance to a wide variety of groups and individuals who are unable to cope with their daily existence.

Previously published as *Abstracts for Social Workers*, this quarterly reference publication offers more than 1,000 abstracts annually of books and articles published in nearly 200 English-language periodicals. Abstracts are arranged under a classification scheme with the following categories: fields of service, social policy and action, service methods, the profession, history, related fields of knowledge. The fields of service category is subdivided by the nature of the clientele, namely, victims of the aging process, alcohol and drug addiction, crime and delinquency, economic (in)security, (un)employment, mental illness and retardation, housing problems, etc. Suitable subdivisions are also made under the other subject categories. Separate author and subject indexes, issued on a quarterly and annual basis, provide additional access to the listed material. For a summary knowledge of this field, see also the *Encyclopedia of Social Work*, listed as item 856 in this guidebook.

819   *Sociological Abstracts*. San Diego: Sociological Abstracts, Inc., 1953– .

820   *Sociological Abstracts*. San Diego: Sociological Abstracts, Inc., 1963– . (Vendor: BRS; Dialog—File 37)

Bibliographic identification and abstracts of the sociological literature are provided by this reference work that is available in computerized format as well as in five published issues per year. Over 1,200 periodicals published in 32 languages in 40 countries and unpublished material, like conference papers, are covered. The printed version arranges the abstracts under 32 major subject categories, as follows: 0100—methodology, 0200—sociology: history & theory, 0300—social psychology, 0400—group interactions, 0500—culture and social structure, 0600—complex organization, 0700—social change & economic development, 0800—mass phenomena, 0900—political interactions, 1000—social differentiation, 1200—urban structure, 1300—sociology of the arts, 1400—sociology of education, 1500—sociology of religion, 1600—social control, 1700—sociology of science, 1800—demography, 1900—family

and socialization, 2000—sociology of health, 2100—
social problems and welfare, 2200—sociology of knowledge, 2300—community development, 2400—policy,
planning, 2500—radical sociology, 2600—environmental interactions, 2700—studies in poverty, 2800—
studies in violence, 2900—feminist studies, 3000—
Marxist sociology, 3100—clinical sociology, and
3200—sociology of business. Numerous subdivisions are
made under these 32 classes to accommodate narrower
topics. Separate author, subject, and source indexes are
also included in each issue, while cumulated indexes are
available nine months after the last issue of each volume.
Decennial and quinquennial indexes are also published.
Online searches of the computerized database can be
made by author names, titles, and subject terms, but the
online display of abstracts is limited to the period after
1973. The publisher also operates a photocopying and
microfiche service for cited documents.

821   Universal Reference System. *Current Events
and Problems of Society*. Princeton, NJ: Princeton Publishing Company, 1968—.

As part of the ten-volume reference set of the Universal Reference System this unannotated bibliography lists
2,339 books, periodical articles, and other works dealing
with peacekeeping, race relations, urbanism, air pollution, drug abuse, overpopulation, and other sociological
problems and current events in all parts of the world.
Nearly 800 pages of the base volume are taken up by the
detailed index of topical and methodological terms,
which allows a more systematic identification of the pertinent literature. Annual supplementary volumes list more
recent publications in this and other subject areas covered
by the Universal Reference System.

822   *Women Studies Abstracts*. Rush, NY: Rush Publishing Co., 1972—.

This quarterly bibliographic publication will be useful for identifying scholarly periodical articles dealing
with the societal factor of women in the United States and
selected foreign countries. Political topics, like abortion,
affirmative action, civil rights, crime prevention, discrimination, family planning, drug abuse, government
employment, labor force participation, migration, racism, social mobility, social security, socioeconomic
status, women's liberation and other movements, etc., are
well covered. Not all cited articles are abstracted, however. Entries are arranged under broad subject headings,
but separate quarterly and annual indexes offer the best
access route to the listed material.

823   *World Agricultural Economics and Rural Sociology Abstracts*. London: Commonwealth Agricultural Bureau, 1959—.

Abstracts of books and periodical articles dealing
with agricultural economics and rural sociology can be
found in this monthly abstract publication. Topics relating to rural-urban relationships, attitudes and opinions,
standards and conditions of living and working are well
covered.

RETROSPECTIVE BIBLIOGRAPHIES

824   Antinoro-Polizzi, Joseph, and Joseph V. Versage. *Ghetto and Suburbia*. Rochester, NY: Great Lakes
Press, 1973.

825   Bryfogle, R. Charles. *City in Print: A Bibliography*. Agincourt, Ontario: General Learning Press, 1974.

———. *First Supplement*. Agincourt, Ontario: General Learning Press, 1975.

826   Hoover, Dwight W. *Cities*. New York: R. R.
Bowker, 1976.

827   Meyer, Jon K. *Bibliography on the Urban Crisis*.
Chevy Chase, MD: National Institute of Mental Health,
1969.

The conditions of urban living, particularly in the
United States, have been the subject of a massive literature. Much of this literature is concerned with the manifestations of urban pathology in such areas as housing,
ghetto and suburban patterns of settlement, transportation, poverty, civil unrest, etc. The titles listed above
represent a sampling of the available bibliographies that
offer annotated or unannotated entries for books and other
information material in this sociological subject matter.
Author and subject indexes in these reference works offer
additional access to the material, which is listed under
various subject categories.

828   Bienen, Henry. *Violence and Social Change: A
Review of the Literature*. Chicago: University of Chicago
Press, 1968.

829   Boston, Guy D., Kevin O'Brien, and Joanne
Palumbo. *Terrorism: A Selected Bibliography*. Washington, DC: U.S. Government Printing Office, 1977.

Group violence in the pursuit of social and political
change is indicative of serious flaws in the political system
of many countries. Scholarly writing about this problem
can be identified with the bibliographies listed above.

830   Bonjean, Charles M., Richard J. Hill, and
S. Dale McLemore. *Sociological Measurement. An In-
ventory of Scales and Indices*. San Francisco: Chandler
Publishing Company, 1967.

Measurements used or cited most frequently in the

sociological literature are reproduced in detail, and bibliographic citations are provided in this reference work. Entries for books and articles about scales and indices are arranged under 78 conceptual classes, including achievement, authoritarianism, consensus, interests, intergroup relations, leadership, personality traits, political attitudes, political behavior, small groups, status concern, urban areas, etc. Among the most frequently used or cited measurements are the Occupation Status (Edwards), the California F Scale, Occupational Prestige (North, Hatt), Stereotype Checklist (Katz, Braly), Indexes of Social Position (Hollingshead), Anomia (Srole), and Urbanization (Shevsky, Williams, and Bell).

831   Brode, John. *The Process of Modernization: An Annotated Bibliography on the Sociocultural Aspects of Development*. Cambridge, MA: Harvard University Press, 1969.

The theories and processes of social change, industrialization, urbanization, and rural modernization in all parts of the world are the subject of a significant portion of the sociological literature. The title above is an excellent, partly annotated bibliography that identifies pertinent books and periodical articles. Also included are a brief survey of the literature, a brief survey of regional studies, and separate indexes by author and geographic area. Annotated items are rated by the addition of one, two, or three stars according to the work's degree of relevance to an understanding of the process of modernization.

832   Bullough, Vern L., Barrett W. Elcano, W. Dorr Legg, and James Kepner. *An Annotated Bibliography of Homosexuality*. New York: Garland Publishing, 1976.

833   Parker, William. *Homosexuality: A Selective Bibliography of Over 3000 Items*. Metuchen, NJ: Scarecrow Press, 1971.

834   _____ . *Homosexuality Bibliography: Supplement, 1970–1975*. Metuchen, NJ: Scarecrow Press, 1977.

835   Weinberg, Martin S., and Alan P. Bell. *Homosexuality: An Annotated Bibliography*. New York: Harper & Row, 1972.

In many societies, homosexuals constitute a social minority that is, to a lesser or greater extent, subjected to discriminatory directives and other outputs of the political system. Several academic disciplines, notably medical science, psychology, legal science and sociology, have contributed to a better understanding of this rather complex minority problem and its political aspects. The bibliographies cited above provide an excellent account of the rather massive literature by source categories and type

of documentation. English- and foreign-language publications are listed, including books and articles dealing with the law and its application to homosexual behavior.

836   *Combined Retrospective Indexes to Journals in Sociology, 1895–1974*. Arlington, VA: Carrollton Press, 1978.

Some 85,000 articles published in 118 English-language sociology journals since 1895 can be identified in this cumulative subject and author index set of six volumes. Entries are arranged by keyword under one or more of 137 subject categories, which include culture, differentiation, group interaction, institutions, knowledge, research methods and techniques, rural systems and structures, social change and economic development, social disorganization, social ecology, theory of sociology, urban systems and structures, etc. A separate author index volume helps to locate the desired articles by author. All entries employ a journal code number for the listed periodicals. These code numbers appear in numerical sequence in the endpapers of each volume together with the title of the periodical to which they have been assigned. Annual supplements of this reference set are planned.

837   *Crime and Punishment in America*. Santa Barbara, CA: ABC-Clio Press, 1983.

Covering the scholarly periodical literature from 1973 to 1983, the bibliography identifies articles dealing with the issue of crime and punishment in America from the early colonial days to the present. Among the topics included are the sociological bases of criminal activity, the varied judicial responses, growth of the FBI and other investigative agencies, attempts at rehabilitation, civil rights of criminals and their victims, and capital punishment. A multiterm subject index is included.

838   Glenn, Norval D., Jon P. Alston, and David Weiner. *Social Stratification: A Research Bibliography*. Berkeley, CA: Glendessary Press, 1970.

A substantial amount of the sociological literature is devoted to aspects of social stratification. The bibliography identifies the important books and articles published in English about social stratification in the United States and other countries. The unannotated entries are arranged under various topics, such as class conflict, income distribution, role of minorities, characteristics of lower, middle and upper strata, and other politically important phenomena.

839   Harris, Diana K. *The Sociology of Aging: An Annotated Bibliography and Sourcebook*. New York: Garland Publishing, Inc., 1984.

Public attitudes towards the elderly, their needs, and the services provided for them are of perennial concern to policymakers and other political actors in the United States. This comprehensive bibliography lists and describes books and periodical articles that deal with various aspects of the societal factor of aging in the United States, including the governmental responses to it. Problems of social inequity, environmental conditions, and institutional activities are well covered. Periodicals and other data sources and agencies concerned with the elderly are listed. Author and subject indexes are included.

840   *Key to Journal Bibliography and Index to Sociology.* Vol. 1, 1971 – 1980. La Jolla, CA: Essay Press, 1983.

This inexpensive bibliography will be useful in all research situations where the more costly *Sociological Abstracts* set is unavailable. The bibliography identifies more than 6,800 sociological journal articles by author, publication source, and subject. Approximately 20 English-language periodicals published during the 1970s are covered.

841   Miller, Wayne Charles. *A Comprehensive Bibliography for the Study of American Minorities.* New York: New York University Press, 1976.

While in no way approaching definitiveness, this two-volume set contains 29,300 entries for the vast literature on American minorities. The entries are arranged by origin of the minorities, i.e., Africa, Middle East, Europe, Asia, Caribbean Islands, and North America. Appropriate subdivisions are made for the specific ethnic or racial group, such as black Americans, French-Americans, German-Americans, Chinese-Americans, Mexican-Americans, etc. Within these groups separate headings aggregate the listings by type of reference source or substantive focus, including economics, education, history, politics, religion, sociology, social issues, and other aspects of the minorities' experience. Entries are occasionally annotated. Author and title indexes are included. For a basic historical overview of these American minorities, their political and other experience, see also the author's *Handbook of American Minorities* (New York: New York University Press, 1976) which also provides basic bibliographic introductions.

842   Wolfgang, Marvin E., Robert M. Figlio, and Terence Thornberry. *Criminology Index.* New York: Elsevier Scientific Publishing Company, 1975.

Criminals exhibit an everpresent challenge to the law-and-order patterns created by a political system. Most governmental authorities have great difficulty applying scientific findings to a reduction of criminality and the treatment of offenders. The two-volume reference set cited above is an author and subject inventory of theoretical and empirical work in criminology published in the United States during the years 1945 to 1972. The subject

areas covered include crime types, kind of offenders, crime causation, etiology of crime, deterrence, prevention, gang delinquency, criminal statistics, victimology, etc. Listed are books, 3,132 periodical articles, dissertations, and reports of federally funded projects. The index is arranged in three parts: (1) a source document index with listings by author, editor, contributor; (2) a subject index that uses all keywords found in the titles of the published works; and (3) a criminology citation index that lists all those authors who are cited by authors listed in the source document index.

Book Reviewing Media

843   *Contemporary Sociology: A Journal of Reviews.* Washington, DC: American Sociological Association, 1973 – .

This bimonthly publication of the ASA is devoted entirely to the review of significant new books in sociology.

844   *Sociology: Review of New Books.* Washington, DC: Heldref Publications, 1973 – .

Like its sister publications, *Perspective* and *History: Review of New Books*, this full-length reviewing journal describes the content of new books and their major strength and weaknesses. The reviews are written by qualified sociologists whose institutional affiliation is indicated. The table of contents categorizes the reviewed books by subject, and a separate author index with annual cumulations provides additional access to the published reviews. The lapse in time between the publication dates of the books and the reviews averages approximately three months.

Dictionaries and Thesauri

845   Eichhorn, Wolfgang. *Wörterbuch der Marxistisch-Leninistischen Soziologie.* Cologne: Westdeutscher Verlag, 1969.

846   Fuchs, Werner, et al. *Lexicon zur Soziologie.* Opladen: Westdeutscher Verlag, 1973.

847   Hoult, Thomas Ford. *Dictionary of Modern Sociology.* Totowa, NJ: Littlefield, Adams, 1969.

848   Mitchell, G. Duncan. A *Dictionary of Sociology.* Chicago: Aldine, 1968.

849   Suavet, Thomas. *Dictionaire économique et social*. Paris: Économie et Humanisme, Editions Ouvrières, 1970.

850   Theodorson, George A., and Achilles G. Theodorson. *A Modern Dictionary of Sociology*. New York: Thomas Y. Crowell, 1969.

Sociology has produced a distinct vocabulary that has enriched scholarly writing in all areas of the social sciences. The titles listed above provide clarification of sociological terms in the English, French, and German languages.

851   Van de Merwe, Caspar. *Thesaurus of Sociological Research Terminology*. Rotterdam: Rotterdam University Press, 1974.

852   Viet, Jean. *Thesaurus for Information Processing in Sociology*. Paris: Mouton, 1972.

The two thesauri provide a controlled inventory of descriptive terms for the improved retrievability of sociological information. The Van de Merwe thesaurus is limited to the vocabulary of sociological method, however.

853   Williams, Vergil L. *Dictionary of American Penology*. Westport, CT: Greenwood Press, 1979.

This dictionary is not a wordbook but a factbook about various aspects of the American correctional system. The alphabetically arranged entries describe the prison systems of individual states or specific features of it, such as furloughs, homosexuality problems, lockdown, parole contracts, work release, etc. References to additional information are provided in all entries. Appendices list prison reform organizations, state planning agencies, prison system addresses, and U.S. government statistics pertaining to correctional activities. A bibliography and an index are also included.

Directories

854   American Sociological Association. *Directory*. New York: 1950–.

The directory presents an alphabetical listing of members of the American Sociological Association with information about year of birth, academic rank and employer, educational degrees, areas of sociological competence, and home address. A geographical listing provides a key to the ASA membership by state and city. An area of competence list indexes members according to 33 areas of specialization.

855   Bernsdorf, Wilhelm. *Internationales Soziologen Lexikon*. Stuttgart: Ferdinand Enke, 1959.

The directory was prepared by an international group of university professors and presents sketches of important sociologists of the past and the present. Each article contains a bibliography of the main works by the sociologist discussed.

Encyclopedias

856   *Encyclopedia of Social Work*. Washington, DC: National Association of Social Workers, 1977.

Social work is a profession that derives its justification from a number of critical problem areas in Western societies, such as alcohol and drug addiction, old age, crime and delinquency, stressful family life, inadequate health services, housing shortages, poverty, ethnic discrimination, etc. This frequently revised encyclopedia, presently issued in two volumes, provides summary and background information of the social and economic context in which the activities of social workers take place. It also contains biographical information on professionals who have played a significant role in social work. In addition, the encyclopedia is a source of statistical data in social work and welfare. Many of the articles, which are arranged in alphabetical sequence, include bibliographic references for further reading. A combined subject and name index provides a key to the information presented by the encyclopedia.

857   *Encyclopedia of Sociology*. Guilford, CT: Dushkin Publishing Group, 1974.

Summarization of existing knowledge in all areas of sociology is offered in alphabetically arranged articles by this one-volume encyclopedia.

858   Kadish, Sanford H. *Encyclopedia of Crime and Justice*. New York: Free Press, 1983.

Crimes, i.e., acts forbidden by (criminal) law, have been a persistent concern for all political systems because law created and enforced through the political processes articulates the basic values of society and prescribes citizen behavior. The encyclopedia brings together in four volumes all that is known about criminal behavior and the responses of societies to it. Specifically covered are the nature and causes of criminal behavior, the prevention of crime, the punishment and treatment of offenders, the functioning of the institutions of criminal justice, and the bodies of law that define criminal behavior and govern the processes through which criminal law is applied. The individual articles, written by political and other social scientists, summarize existing knowledge on each topic and also offer citations to pertinent laws or judicial decisions. A glossary and two separate indexes — a legal index and a general (name and subject) index — are included.

858a   Mann, Michael. *The International Encyclopedia of Sociology*. New York: Continuum Publishing Company, 1984.

The articles in this one-volume encyclopedia explain the important terms, concepts, and theories of sociology, summarize existing knowledge on various societal factors, and offer brief assessments of the contributions made by eminent sociologists or other scholars.

859   Ross, John A. *International Encyclopedia of Population*. New York: Free Press, 1982.

The two-volume encyclopedia offers 129 topical articles that summarize existing scientific knowledge on population matters, including trends and patterns not likely to change quickly. The articles cover one or more of the following subject areas: (1) the field of population, (2) data sources, measures, and methods, (3) population dynamics, (4) fertility determinants and regulations, (5) marriage and divorce, (6) morbidity and mortality, (7) distribution, migration, and urbanization, (8) population and natural resources, (9) population laws and policies, (10) world regions and countries, and (11) organizations and agencies. A topical outline index lists all articles in the encyclopedia under these subject headings. A name and topic index identifies all core articles and the individual topics covered in them. Bibliographic references are included in each article.

Handbooks

860   Brodsky, Stanley L., and H. O'Neal Smitherman. *Handbook of Scales for Research in Crime and Delinquency*. New York: Plenum Press, 1983.

The handbook offers critical, evaluative information about crime and delinquency research instruments to allow investigators to choose instruments based on their scientific merits. Included are scales that offer attitude measurements, behavior ratings, personality assessments, milieu ratings, predictions, and descriptions in connection with the law enforcement process, the judicial process, the correction process, and the social processes of law violation. Each review includes references for the publications cited in the text of the review. A separate bibliography on scales and an index are also provided.

861   March, James G. *Handbook of Organizations*. Chicago: Rand McNally, 1965.

862   Faris, Robert E. Lee. *Handbook of Modern Sociology*. Chicago: Rand McNally, 1964.

863   Coslin, David A. *Handbook of Socialization Theory and Research*. Chicago: Rand McNally, 1969.

864   Hare, A. Paul. *Handbook of Small Group Research*. New York: Free Press of Glencoe, 1962.

865   Ogburn, William F., and Meyer F. Nimkoff. *A Handbook of Sociology*. London: Routledge and Kegan Paul, 1960.

A number of handbooks have been published that summarize existing knowledge for the entire discipline or specialized areas of inquiry. The titles above represent a sampling of the available handbook literature.

866   Smigel, Erwin O. *Handbook on the Study of Social Problems*. Chicago: Rand McNally, 1971.

The resolution or amelioration of persistent social problems is the primary object of many governmental policies. Focusing on the difficulties encountered when dealing with social problems, the handbook presents 23 articles dealing with social problem solving. Specifically covered are problems of crime, education, industry, health, mental illness, race, and religion, as well as problems of scholarly methodology, social indicators, federal intervention, evaluation of social action, etc. Bibliographic references, name and subject indexes are included.

Chapter 3

American Government, Politics, and Public Law

INTRODUCTION

This chapter of the guidebook identifies and describes a variety of reference sources, in printed and electronic format, that offer or cite information about the

1. American government, i.e., the institutions of governing, such as Congress, the president and the offices of the executive branch, the independent agencies, the United States Supreme Court and other courts, the state and local governments, the political parties and other institutionalized bodies active in political affairs
2. American politics, i.e., the processes of governing, notably the legislative, executive-administrative, judicial, election, and communication processes, with the exception of the foreign affairs processes covered in Chapter 4 of the guidebook
3. Individuals involved in the institutions and processes of governing, notably the members of Congress and

their support staff, the cabinet officers and other officeholders in the executive and regulatory agencies, the justices and judges of the federal and state courts, the governors and other members of state and local governments
4. Public law of the United States, i.e., the federal and state constitutions, federal statutes, administrative regulations, judicial decisions, state laws, and international law
5. Language of American government and politics, notably the words, slogans, and concepts relating to institutions, processes, and activities in the American political system
6. Societal factors of the American body politic, notably statistical data about the American population and its activities, achievements, needs, and failures

As numerous and detailed as the reference sources listed on the following pages of this guidebook are, they do not cover all the information produced by federal government agencies. Sizable quantities of information remain poorly accessible or even totally unavailable as a result of

a. inadequate development of the reference literature and
b. legal restrictions.

The American political reference literature is noticeably weak in respect of policy-related information. Although such information is produced by a variety of political actors and purveyors of meaning, its access is at best made possible only by general and social science indexes that offer citations to appropriate books, periodical articles, newspaper reports, and other publications amidst massive quantities of nonpolitical material. There is hardly a reference work or set of reference works in existence that provides, in convenient format, a comprehensive inventory of all American policy-oriented information together with a summary and juxtaposition of policy options, justifications, and alternative policy objectives.

In spite of some recent improvements, these and other significant gaps in the reference literature are due in large measure to the existence of legal restrictions that limit public access to government information in several categories. The Freedom of Information Act (Public Law 89-487, as codified by Public Law 90-23 in 81 Stat 54 and amended by Public Law 93-502 in 88 Stat 1561) is a key element concerning the availability of information about the activities of the American government. This act permits nine categories of information to be withheld from the public, as follows:

1. *National Defense and Foreign Policy*. The basis for security classification is Executive Order 12356 (3 CFR Chapter IV), dated 2 April 1982, which permits the withholding of top secret, secret, and confidential information if the information concerns at least one of the following criteria:
   a. military plans, weapons, or operations;
   b. the vulnerabilities or capabilities of systems, installations, projects, or plans relating to the national security;
   c. foreign government information;
   d. intelligence activities (including special activities), or intelligence sources or methods;
   e. foreign relations or foreign activities of the United States;
   f. scientific, technological, or economic matters relating to the national security;
   g. United States government programs for safeguarding nuclear materials or facilities;
   h. cryptology;
   i. a confidential source; or
   j. other categories of information that are related to the

national security and that require protection against unauthorized disclosure as determined by the president or by agency heads or other officials who have been delegated original classification authority by the president.
Such information shall be classified when an original classification authority determines that its unauthorized disclosure, either by itself or in the context of other information, reasonably could be expected to cause damage to the national security.

2. *Internal Personnel Rules and Practices of an Agency*. Information may be withheld if disclosure is harmful to the legitimate function of an agency.

3. *Statutory Prohibitions*. There are many federal statutory regulations that interdict disclosure of information to the public. Many of these were listed in a committee print entitled, "Federal Statutes on the Availability of Information," U.S. Congress, House of Representatives Committee on Government Operations, 86th Congress, 2nd session, 1960. According to entry no. 8134 (June 1960) in the *Monthly Catalog*, this committee print itself is not available to the public.

4. *Information Given in Confidence*. This category includes a wide range of information that may be withheld on the grounds that a citizen must be able to confide in his government without fear of reprisal or disclosure of his sources.

5. *Interagency and Intra-agency Communication*. A considerable part of the internal communication process may be closed to the public in order to ensure free and frank interchange of ideas. Most internal staff reports or interagency memoranda are never published.

6. *Unwarranted Invasion of Personal Privacy*. With the exception of names, positions, titles, salaries, and assignments of government employees, a wide range of personnel, medical, and similar files are closed to the public. In recent years, however, information about financial interests of government employees has sometimes been made public and selected medical information about the president and other key figures has been disclosed.

7. *Investigations*. Criminal, civil, and regulatory investigation files are closed to the public unless specifically made available by law.

8. *Supervision of Financial Institutions*. Information regulating financial institutions or trading in securities and currencies may be withheld.*

*According to the Government in the Sunshine Act (90 Stat 1241, 5 U.S.C. 552 b) information may be withheld by an agency that regulates currencies, securities, commodities, or financial institutions if the disclosure of information is likely to (1) lead to significant financial speculation in currencies, securities, or commodities, or (2) significantly endanger the stability of any financial institution.

9. *Geological and Geophysical Information.* Information may be withheld in the interest of safeguarding geological trade secrets.

Unless withholding is otherwise authorized under applicable law, initially classified information can be released following a positive review for declassification by the original agency if (1) a request is made by a United States citizen or permanent resident alien, a federal agency, a state or local government, and (2) the request describes the document containing the desired information with sufficient specificity to enable the agency to locate it with a reasonable amount of effort. This possibility for a mandatory review for declassification does not exist, however, for information originated by a president, the White House staff, by committees, commissions, boards, or others acting on behalf of a president or providing advice and counsel to the president. Special procedures also exist for the review of classified information relating to cryptology, intelligence activities and sources.

All agencies of the executive branch of the United States government have issued regulations for implementing the provisions of the Freedom of Information Act. These regulations inform the public where and how certain types of information that are not normally published may be obtained. The regulations are printed in the *Code of Federal Regulations* and can be found by consulting the CFR index volume under Freedom of Information. A list of the Freedom of Information officers in each agency, showing the name and telephone number, is printed in the communications and media section of the *Washington Information Directory* (Washington, DC: Congressional Quarterly, Inc., 1975 –). This directory also identifies several nongovernmental organizations concerned with assisting individuals in their efforts to obtain official documents under the Freedom of Information Act.

To help fulfill its responsibility to inform the public on the policies and programs of the federal government, the United States Congress established the Depository Library Program. Under this program, currently nearly 1,400 congressionally designated libraries throughout the United States make available for the free use of the general public a selection of all government publications except those determined by their issuing agencies to be required

a. for official use only, or
b. for strictly administrative or operational purposes without public interest or educational value, or
c. classified for reasons of national security

Addresses and telephone numbers of all depository libraries, arranged by state and congressional district, are listed in a congressional committee print entitled *Government Depository Libraries: The Present Law Governing Deposi-* *tory Libraries* (Washington, DC: U.S. Government Printing Office, 1981 –).

The series and groups of government publications available for distribution, either in paper or microfiche format, to the depository libraries are identified in a special list entitled *List of Classes of United States Government Publications Available for Selection by Depository Libraries.* This list is published in quarterly revised issues by the U.S. Government Printing Office and furnished to all depository libraries. Items actually selected by the depository libraries are shown in the microfiche *Union List of Item Selections by Depository Libraries*, which identifies for each item number the depository libraries receiving the selected publication series.

A perusal and comparison of the two lists with Andriot's *Guide to U.S. Government Publications* (McLean, VA: Documents Index, 1973 –) discloses, however, that many government publications of value in political education are either not available for selection by depository libraries or have not been selected by them. To help fill this gap several commercial publishers have started ambitious programs for the publication of appropriate reference works and the delivery of the government documents cited in them. These programs are most effective for congressional and judicial publications but less so for certain categories of information and documentation emanating from the executive branch of the United States government.

Further details about the existing reference mechanism and the availability of political information from official and nongovernmental documentation sources are presented on the following pages.

FEDERAL GOVERNMENT

Official Publications

The official publications of the United States government sent to depository libraries or otherwise available to the public offer an enormous amount of information about the American government, politics, and policies. The United States Government Printing Office is probably the most prolific publisher in the world, but the mass and diversity of its publications make the use of bibliographic aids absolutely essential. The following entries identify and describe general guidebooks and bibliographies that provide a key to federal government publications by form, subject, issuing agency, and period.

GUIDEBOOKS

867   Andriot, John L. *Guide to U.S. Government*

Publications. McLean, VA: Documents Index, 1981 – (microfiche edition).

868   Andriot, John L. *Guide to U.S. Government Publications.* McLean, VA: Documents Index, 1973 – 1980.

869   Andriot, John L. *Guide to U.S. Government Serials and Periodicals.* Arlington, VA: Documents Index, 1959 – 1973.

As one of only two regularly updated guidebooks for United States government publications, this important reference work has undergone title and format changes over the years. The purpose of this guidebook, now issued annually in microfiche format only, is twofold: (1) to provide an annotated guide to the important series and periodicals currently published by the various U.S. government agencies as well as the important reference publications within these series, and (2) to present a complete listing of the Superintendent of Documents (SuDoc) classification numbers for all agencies currently in existence or abolished.

The basic arrangement of the entries for the various publication series is based on (1) the issuing agency, (2) the series or generic type of publication (bibliographies, handbooks, etc.), and (3) the individual publication within that type of series. The SuDoc classification scheme reflects this order in the arrangement of its symbols of letters and numbers. Entries indicate the series title, SuDoc number, frequency (weekly, monthly, irregular), beginning date, and occasionally the purpose of the publication.

Three separate finding aids are included in the guidebook, namely, (1) an agency class chronology, (2) an agency index, and (3) a title index. The agency class chronology shows in sequence of SuDoc numbers the dates and the names for an agency's existence.

The listing of a particular publication series in this guidebook should, however, not be taken as evidence that the series is actually available for depository libraries. To determine the selection availability for the various series, consult the quarterly updated *List of Classes of United States Government Publications Available For Selection By Depository Libraries*, published by the U.S. Government Printing Office in Washington, DC.

870   Boyd, Anne M., and Rae Elizabeth Rips. *United States Government Publications.* New York: H. W. Wilson Company, 1949.

This reference work has served as a standard guide to U.S. government publications for many years. It lists the official publications by type as well as by issuing agency or branch of government. Separate chapters are devoted to general catalogs, indexes, and other reference aids. The guidebook will be most valuable for the identification of publications that have been issued by agencies that are presently no longer in existence or for tracing the historical changes in the various publication series.

871   Jackson, Ellen. *Subject Guide to Major U.S. Government Publications.* Chicago: American Library Association, 1969.

872   Lu, Joseph K. *U.S. Government Publications Relating to the Social Sciences. A Selected Annotated Guide.* Beverly Hills, CA: Sage Publications, 1975.

A subject approach to specific categories of U.S. government publications is offered by the two guidebooks listed above. The Jackson guide will be valuable as a quick reference tool for identifying the most important publications under broad subject headings, such as foreign relations, history, parliamentary practice, president, treaties, etc. Similar subject access is provided by Lu's guidebook, which lists official publications under the following headings: (1) bibliographic sources, (2) American history, (3) business and economics, (4) communism, (5) Congress, (6) education, (7) foreign affairs, (8) foreign countries, (9) labor, (10) law, (11) the president, (12) social conditions and services, Appendix A — background readings, B — general guides, C — general ordering information, D — list of depositories.

Both guidebooks include the SuDoc numbers in their bibliographic entries.

873   *Government Reference Books.* Littleton, CO: Libraries Unlimited, 1968/1969 – .

Issued biennially, this guidebook lists and describes reference books published by the United States government. Listings are arranged in four parts, namely, (1) General Library Reference, (2) Social Sciences, (3) Science and Technology, and (4) Humanities. Within each part, further subdivisions group listings by type of reference work, e.g., bibliographies, directories, handbooks, etc., and major topics, such as American history, American political system, area studies and geography, economics and commerce, education, housing and urban development, law and the criminal justice system, sociology, statistics and demography, and others. All entries include Superintendent of Document (SuDoc) numbers, wherever available, as well as full bibliographic citations. An appendix lists more than 260 titles in the GPO's Subject Bibliography series. An author/title/subject index is also included.

874   Mason, John Brown. *Official Publications: U.S. Government, United Nations, International Organizations, and Statistical Sources.* Santa Barbara, CA: American Bibliographical Center—Clio Press, 1971.

Identification and brief description of U.S. government publications by issuing agency or branch of government is offered by this guidebook. The entries are limited to serial and monographic publications of reference value and are arranged in eleven chapters, as follows: (1) general guides to U.S. government publications, (2) U.S. Constitution, Supreme Court and Federal statutes, (3) Congress, (4) Library of Congress, (5) the presidency, (6) the executive branch: federal departments and independent agencies, (7) National Archives and Records Service, (8) American foreign policy, (9) Statistical sources: U.S. and foreign, (10) United Nations publications, (11) new and ceased publications. Three separate tables list the SuDoc classification symbols for boards or commissions, congressional committees, and congressional publications. Separate indexes by title, subject, and name provide additional access to the nearly 1,500 items listed in the guidebook.

875   Morehead, Joe. *Introduction to United States Public Documents*. Littleton, CO: Libraries Unlimited, 1983.

Organized in ten chapters, this guidebook describes in narrative prose the basic sources of information that comprise the bibliographic structure of federal government publications. The narrative begins with an overview of the issues and problems associated with the federal information transfer process. Chapters 2 through 4 describe the administrative machinery (GPO, Superintendent of Documents, Depository Library System) by which federal publications are made available. Chapter 5 deals with the technical report literature as distributed by NTIS, NASA, DOE, ERIC, and DocEx. Chapter 6 describes guides, indexes, and checklists. The remaining four chapters examine the types of publications and services provided by or relating to the legislative branch, the presidency and executive agencies, and the judicial branch. Two appendices present lists of (a) online databases for federal government publications, and (b) abbreviations, acronyms, and citations. Separate title/series and subject/name indexes are also included.

876   Palic, Vladimir M. *Government Publications. A Guide to Bibliographic Tools*. Washington, DC: Library of Congress, 1975.

Current and retrospective bibliographic aids to the official publications issued by the United States, international governmental organizations, and foreign countries are identified in this guidebook. Listings include catalogs, checklists, pricelists, indexes, accession lists, general and special bibliographies. LC catalog information including call numbers are given for all entries. Brief explanatory notes precede the entries for each state, country, organiza-

tion, and agency. The index is composed of names of individual or corporate authors, countries, and titles.

877   Schmeckebier, Laurence F., and Roy B. Eastin. *Government Publications and Their Use*. Washington, DC: Brookings Institution, 1969.

As one of the classic reference works for U.S. government publications, this book presents very detailed information about the existence, usage, and limitations of the official documentation activity in the United States. The material is organized under the following chapter headings: (1) Introduction, (2) Catalogs and Indexes, (3) Bibliographies, (4) Classification, (5) Availability of Publications, (6) Congressional Publications, (7) Federal and State Constitutions, (8) Federal Laws, (9) State Laws, (10) Court Decisions, (11) Administrative Regulations and Department Rulings, (12) Presidential Papers, (13) Foreign Affairs, (14) Reports on Operations, (15) Organization and Personnel, (16) Maps, (17) Technical and Other Departmental Publications, (18) Periodicals, (19) Microform Editions of Government Publications.

Since significant changes and developments have occurred in the official documentation of the United States in recent years, this guidebook will be most valuable for political inquiries of a historical nature.

878   U.S. Library of Congress. Special Division. *Popular Names of U.S. Government Reports. A Catalog*. Washington, DC: U.S. Government Printing Office, 1976.

During the past 80 years many significant government reports have been issued that have since become identified with personal or popular names. Since cataloging rules require the report to be listed under the name of the issuing department or agency, many reports present problems of retrieval to the researcher. While this irregularly revised listing is by no means complete, it constitutes an indispensable source for locating government publications by popular name.

879   Van Zant, Nancy Patton. *Selected U.S. Government Series. A Guide for Public and Academic Libraries*. Chicago: American Library Association, 1978.

While U.S. government publications in series format are identifiable by issuing agency in John Andriot's *Guide to U.S. Government Publications* (item 867), their subject identification is facilitated by a separate guidebook published by the American Library Association. The guidebook provides a selective listing of important series publications in 28 subject areas, including economics and business, general reference, government and international relations, history, law, military and defense, sociology and social service, statistics and demography, urban life and studies, etc. Excellent annotations accompany each entry. SuDoc numbers are listed for all cited works. A detailed index permits identification of the listed series publications by type, i.e., annual report, bibliography, handbook, as well as by subject category or title.

880   *Where's What. Sources of Information for Federal Investigators.* New York: New York Times Book Company, 1975.

This recently declassified reference manual identifies and describes sources of information on individuals or groups in official documentation maintained by the federal government and the subnational governments as well as in the records compiled by trade, industrial, or professional organizations. Specifically included are the sources of information in motor vehicle records, vital statistics, educational records, credit records, police records, insurance records, court records, and other records maintained by federal, state, county, and city government agencies. Facsimile copies of numerous application forms and questionnaires are included. A detailed subject index is also provided. Usage of the listed information sources will be reserved to federal investigators in most instances.

881   Wynkoop, Sally. *Subject Guide to Government Reference Books.* Littleton, CO: Libraries Unlimited, 1972.

Reference books issued as official U.S. government publications are listed and described in a subject arrangement by this guidebook. Listings are arranged in four parts, entitled (1) General Reference Sources, (2) Social Sciences, (3) Science and Technology, (4) Humanities. Numerous subdivisions within these four parts aggregate the available reference works within narrower subject or form categories. The guidebook also offers index entries for titles, authors, and subjects.

CURRENT BIBLIOGRAPHIES

882   *Declassified Documents Quarterly Catalog. Declassified Documents Quarterly Index.* Washington, DC: Carollton Press, 1975— .

Official documents of the United States government that have previously been classified top secret, secret, confidential, restricted, or official use only and have now become declassified can be identified with this reference source. Documents are listed by title in the quarterly catalog with entries arranged alphabetically under the names of the governmental agencies or offices that originated the documents. The entries contain references to access symbols on a series of microfiches with the complete text of the declassified documents. Separate quarterly and cumulative indexes provide name and subject

entries for all documents listed by title in the catalogs. More than 5,000 formerly classified documents are listed in a separate Declassified Documents Retrospective Collection volume. All documents listed in this reference work are made available on microfiche by the publisher.

883   *The Federal Index.* Washington, DC: Capitol Services, 1976— .

884   *FEDEX.* Washington, DC: Capitol Services, 1976— (Vendor: Dialog—File 20; SDC)

Legal and other political outputs of all three branches of the federal government, such as proposed rules, regulations, executive orders, contract awards, bill introductions, public laws, congressional resolutions, speeches, statements and reports, decisions by the U.S. Supreme Court, federal courts of appeal, U.S. district courts, and the U.S. Tax Court are identifiable in three different ways on a current basis with this index, available in a monthly printed version and in a weekly updated computerized database accessible for online searching. The indexed source documentation includes the *Congressional Record, Commerce Business Daily, Federal Register, Public Law Series, Congressional Bills, Weekly Compilation of Presidential Documents,* the *Washington Post,* and other official and nonofficial publications. All entries are arranged under

    agency, federal department, congressional committee, or federal court responsible for the action
31 major government functions (e.g., agriculture to veteran affairs) and over 375 subjects
appropriate SIC code for action affecting industry

Coverage of the electronic database partially overlaps with the scope of *Federal Register Abstracts,* created by the same producer and made available with the Dialog Information Retrieval Service as File 136.

885   *Index to U.S. Government Periodicals.* Chicago: Infordata International, 1970— .

Articles appearing in some 173 major periodicals issued by more than 100 agencies of the United States government are identifiable by author and subject in this quarterly and annually cumulated index. The majority of the indexed periodicals will be available in depository libraries, but many periodicals not sent to depository libraries or distributed by the U.S. Government Printing Office are also covered. Beginning in 1982 all cited articles and periodicals are made available on microfiche by the publisher of this index.

While all substantive articles of lasting research or reference value are indexed, the index is weak in respect of policy information. This is due to the facts that (a) with some exceptions (foreign policy, for instance) no specific index terms are used for the various policies, and pertinent information is at best listed under the object-related noun (example: monetary policy is listed under money), and (b) the official periodical literature itself does not contain much policy information.

886   New York (City). Public Library. Research Libraries. *Bibliographic Guide to Government Publications — U.S.* Boston: G. K. Hall, 1975–.

Federal, state, and local government publications in monographic or series format are identifiable under various approaches in this annual unannotated bibliography. Based on catalog entries of the Research Libraries of the New York Public Library and the MARC tapes of the Library of Congress, the bibliography provides, in an integrated dictionary format, listings by personal and corporate author, title, series title, and subject of the official literature published during the preceding year. All entries include the call numbers of the cataloged items.

887   U.S. Department of Commerce. National Technical Information Service. *Government Reports Announcements and Index (GRA & I)*.

888   _____ . *Government Reports Annual Index.*

889   _____ . *Abstract Newsletters.*

890   _____ . *Selected Research in Microfiche (SRIM).*

891   _____ . *NTIS,* 1964–. (Vendor: Dialog — File 6; SDC; BRS)
Springfield, VA: National Technical Information Service, 1946–.

The dissemination and bibliographic control of government-sponsored research, development, and other analytic reports prepared by federal agencies, their contractors or grantees is undertaken by the National Technical Information Service of the U.S. Department of Commerce. More than 1.2 million titles, usually not on hand in libraries, are presently for sale by NTIS in a variety of formats with about 70,000 new reports added annually.

All new reports are listed and abstracted biweekly in *GRA & I, Government Reports Announcements and Index.* Entries are arranged by COSATI classification using 22 broad subject categories and 178 subcategories, including the behavioral, social, and military sciences. Separate indexes by keyword, personal author, corporate author, contract number, and accession/report number provide additional access to the listed material. Complete order-

ing information, including telephone and telex numbers, is printed in each issue of *GRA & I.*

Annual cumulated indexes are also published. *Abstract Newsletters* are issued weekly in 26 subject categories, including behavior and society, business and economics, problem solving information for state and local governments, urban and regional technology and development, library and information sciences, energy, environmental pollution, transportation, etc. All newsletters carry author-prepared summaries (abstracts) of the reports. The last issue in each year is a subject index.

Selected Research in Microfiche (SRIM) is a biweekly service that delivers full reports on microfiche within specific subject areas selected by the researcher or subscriber.

NTIS is the computerized bibliographic database that is available for online searching on a customized basis directly from the National Technical Information Service and also through the facilities of two commercial vendors. The database is updated biweekly, but more than 1,000 prepackaged printed bibliographies are available as *Published Searches* directly from the National Technical Information Service.

892   U.S. Superintendent of Documents. *Monthly Catalog of United States Government Publications.* Washington, DC: U.S. Government Printing Office, 1895–.

893   *GPO Monthly Catalog.* Washington, DC: U.S. Government Printing Office, 1976–. (Vendor: Dialog — File 66; BRS; SDC)

894   *GPO Publications Reference File.* Washington, DC: U.S. Government Printing Office, 1971–. (Vendor: Dialog — File 166)

Available in printed and online searchable formats, the *Monthly Catalog* is at present the standard list for identifying U.S. government publications by issuing agency, author, title, subject, report or series numbers. Entries in the printed version are arranged by issuing agency and carry a consecutive entry number in addition to a SuDoc classification number. Libraries usually file microprint copies of United States government publications by entry numbers and the original issues of these publications by SuDoc numbers. Six separate indexes are included in the monthly and annual cumulative issues of the printed *Monthly Catalog.* The author index contains entries for personal and corporate authors, conferences, editors and co-authors. The title index lists titles, series titles, and subtitles or alternate titles. The subject index utilizes Library of Congress subject headings. The series/report index provides access by report numbers or series statements. The stock number index is a numerical list of

Superintendent of Documents stock numbers and their corresponding entry numbers in the *Monthly Catalog*. The title keyword index lists all important words selected from information in the title fields with the corresponding entry numbers. In addition to the annual indexes, two decennial indexes for the periods 1941–1950 and 1951–1960 and three quinquennial indexes for the periods 1961–1965, 1966–1970, and 1971–1976 have been issued. Cumulative author and subject indexes for longer periods have also been published commercially.

The *GPO Monthly Catalog* is the machine-readable equivalent of the printed catalog. The *GPO Publications Reference File* is a biweekly updated online file that can be used to identify, verify, or select U.S. government publications available for purchase. Availability, price, and stock number information is included.

895   U.S. Superintendent of Documents. *U.S. Government Books*. Washington, DC: U.S. Government Printing Office, 1982– .

Issued quarterly, this bibliography offers more than 1,000 annotated entries for books and serial publications available for sale by the Superintendent of Documents. Forms for ordering the publications are included in each issue of the bibliography. Listings of new books placed on sale during the preceding two months can also be found in a separate, unannotated bibliography, issued bimonthly by the Superintendent of Documents under the title *New Books*.

RETROSPECTIVE BIBLIOGRAPHIES

896   *Cumulative Subject Index to the Monthly Catalog of U.S. Government Publications, 1895–1900*. Washington, DC: Carrollton Press, 1977.

897   *Cumulative Subject Index to the Monthly Catalog of U.S. Government Publications 1900–1971*. Washington, DC: Carrollton Press, 1972.

898   Przebienda, Edward. *Monthly Catalog of U.S. Government Publications. Cumulative Personal Author Indexes, 1941–1975*. Ann Arbor, MI: Pierian Press, 1971–1978.

Due to the time limitations (i.e., annual or decennial) of the official indexes, the retrieval of federal publications may present a problem if the publication date is unknown. To facilitate author and subject identification of federal publications over an extended time period, three separate multivolume index sets have been commercially produced. Two cumulative subject indexes in two volumes and fifteen volumes, respectively, allow the subject identification of federal publications issued during

a 76-year period. The five-volume set for personal authors makes it convenient to identify U.S. government publications by personal author during a 35-year period. Citations in the index sets refer to the appropriate entries in the *Monthly Catalog of U.S. Government Publications*.

899   Parish, David W. *Changes in American Society, 1960–1978: An Annotated Bibliography of Official Government Publications*. Metuchen, NJ: Scarecrow Press, 1980.

This important bibliography identifies and briefly describes 1,157 government publications that best reflect the rapid transformation of the societal factors seen by the political system in the United States during the past two decades. The annotated entries are arranged by broad topical categories in the following subject areas for which governmental agencies have a legally mandated responsibility: (1) accidents and safety, (2) problems of the elderly, (3) children and youth, (4) crime, correction, and delinquency, (5) education, (6) employment, (7) discrimination, (8) health and environment, (9) housing, (10) military problems, (11) minorities, (12) demographic factors, (13) public welfare, (14) rural life, (15) science and technology, (16) general social issues, (17) sports and recreation, (18) transportation, (19) volunteerism, and (20) women. The listed items are reports and other official publications emanating from executive agencies and congressional committees. All entries include SuDoc numbers, which makes it possible to browse for additional, more recent publications on the shelves of depository libraries. Appendices list by subject area the federal and state periodicals that pertain to American society and culture, and by state the addresses of federal and state agencies and depository libraries.

900   U.S. Superintendent of Documents. *Catalog of the Public Documents of Congress and All Departments of the Government, 1893–1940*. Washington, DC: U.S. Government Printing Office, 1896–1945.

Generally known as the *Documents Catalog*, this multivolume bibliographic set, originally issued biennially, lists in dictionary arrangement (author, title, and subject entries) most congressional and departmental publications from the 53rd Congress to the 76th Congress. Although this reference series was in many respects the most comprehensive and detailed listing of official publications on the federal level, it did not survive because of high production costs and considerable publication lags. The last issue was published with a delay of five years.

901   U.S. Superintendent of Documents. *Checklist of United States Public Documents, 1789–1909*. Washington, DC: U.S. Government Printing Office, 1911.

902 _____ . *Checklist of U.S. Public Documents 1789–1975*. Washington, DC: U.S. Historical Documents Institute, 1976.

903 _____ . *Cumulative Title Index to United States Public Documents, 1789–1975*. Arlington, VA: U.S. Historical Documents Institute, 1976.

The first title represents a single bibliographic volume that lists official publications by Congress and executive departments. No index is available to the listings, but brief explanatory notes provide information about publishing policies. The value of this reference work is now largely diminished as a result of the availability of the second title.

Based on the active and inactive shelflists of the Superintendent of Documents' Public Documents Library in Washington, DC, the *1789–1975 Checklist* is the most comprehensive single bibliographic source for United States government documents. It provides full bibliographic citations and SuDoc classification numbers for all documents previously listed in various separate lists or catalogs. In addition, it contains references to thousands of publications that initially held security classifications and therefore did not appear in any lists or bibliographies. The *Checklist* is composed of 1,300,000 shelflist cards on microfilm and four computer-based indexes in bound volumes. Index One is essentially a table of contents for the microfilm segments and is arranged by author in SuDoc class order. Index Two provides an arrangement of some 3,000 government authors in alphabetical sequence regardless of SuDoc numbers. Index Three is an alphabetical listing of departments and agencies with alphabetical subdivisions for their publishing offices. Index Four lists some 18,000 U.S. government series titles in alphabetical order with SuDoc class numbers and microfilm reel numbers.

The *Cumulative Title Index* is a set of 16 hardcover volumes that list more than one million titles of U.S. government publications issued up to 1975. The entries include SuDoc class numbers, the date, and the microfilm reel section where full bibliographic data can be found in the *1789–1975 Checklist*.

Scholarly Publications

A massive scholarly literature exists about the American political system, but bibliographic control of this literature is somewhat fragmented and incomplete. Compared to the large number of bibliographies that list scholarly publications about the governments and politics in countries other than the United States, there is virtually no bibliography exclusively devoted to the identification of scientific publications about the American system of government. Most of the existing coverage is embedded in the general political and social science bibliographies, such as the *United States Political Science Documents*, the *Combined Retrospective Indexes to Journals in Political Science 1886–1974*, the *Public Affairs Information Service Bulletin*, and numerous other bibliographic instruments listed in Chapter 2 of this guidebook. In addition, several bibliographies are available that limit their scope to narrow segments of inquiry or specific topics relevant to the study of the American political system.

The following listings of guidebooks and bibliographies illustrate the pattern of available bibliographic coverage in this subfield of political science. Additional bibliographies can also be found in sections dealing with the American judicial system and state and local government reference works.

GUIDEBOOKS

904 *Administrative Histories of World War II Civilian Agencies of the Federal Government; Administrative Histories of U.S. Civilian Agencies: Korean War. A Guide to the Microfilm Collections*. Woodbridge, CT: Research Publications, 1979.

During World War II and the Korean War, the civilian agencies of the federal government dealt with the most stupendous set of problems in the management of public activities that the country ever faced. Properly preserved, this governmental expertise will again be useful when the country is confronted by a current emergency, such as an oil embargo or military conflict.

The guidebook identifies 423 microfilmed histories produced by well-known historians, economists, and political scientists about the wartime measures and activities of the various agencies. The listings include main entries (usually the name of the agency), added entries, title entries, and subject entries in dictionary order. The subject entries are all in upper case. All entries include the item number and reel number for locating the desired history in the microfilm collection.

905 Maurer, David J. *U.S. Politics and Elections. A Guide to Information Sources*. Detroit: Gale Research Company, 1978.

Covering the time period from 1607 to 1976, this annotated bibliography lists books dealing with politics on the federal or state level during specific historic eras. A general chapter identifies reference and other works that transcend individual historical periods. Author, title, and subject indexes are included.

906 Murin, William J., Gerald Michael Greenfield, and John D. Buenker. *Public Policy. A Guide to Information Sources*. Detroit: Gale Research Company, 1981.

Focusing almost entirely on American public policy

aspects and issues, the guidebook identifies and briefly describes more than 1,300 scholarly books and articles. The entries are arranged under eight chapters, as follows: (1) Theories and Concepts, (2) Decision Making, (3) National Policymaking Processes, (4) State and Local Policy Processes, (5) Urban Policy, (6) Intergovernmental Aspects of Public Policy, (7) Implementation and Evaluation, and (8) Policy Issues. Separately listed in the eighth chapter are such issues as business, labor, and economic policy; civil rights and criminal justice; education policy, health and welfare policy; housing and transportation; population and family policy; science, technology, energy, and environmental policy. Separate author and subject indexes to the listed material are also provided.

907   U.S. Library of Congress. A *Guide to the Study of the United States of America*. Washington, DC: U.S. Government Printing Office, 1960.

————— . *Supplement 1956–1965*. Washington, DC: U.S. Government Printing Office, 1976.

This richly annotated bibliography lists representative scholarly books reflecting the development of American life and thought. Entries are grouped into 32 chapters, of which the following are of special interest to students of political science: Diplomatic History and Foreign Relations, Constitution and Government, Law and Justice, Politics, Parties and Elections, General History, Military History, and The Armed Forces. This bibliography with its supplement does not claim, however, to be a complete listing of the scholarly literature about all aspects of American political life. Most noteworthy is the lack of bibliographic listings for the periodical literature.

908   Vose, Clement E. A *Guide to Library Sources in Political Science. American Government*. Washington, DC: American Political Science Association, 1975.

The material in this guidebook is presented in narrative form with reference works mentioned in the text identifiable in italic print. The cited reference works are also listed with full bibliographic information at the end of each essay. There are three parts, entitled (1) American National Government, (2) General Reference Books, and (3) The Political Scientist in the Library. Part 1 mentions reference sources about the U.S. Constitution and the three branches of the U.S. government. Sources for the American subnational governments are not covered. Part 2 identifies various almanacs, biographies, political dictionaries, and encyclopedias. Part 3 describes a variety of periodical and newspaper indexes as well as some archival and manuscript sources. There is no index to the listed reference material in the book.

BIBLIOGRAPHIES

909   American Enterprise Institute for Public Policy Research. *AEI Publications*. Washington, DC: AEI, 1943– .

The American Enterprise Institute for Public Policy Research is a publicly supported, nonpartisan research and educational organization. Its publications provide an objective analysis of American and international policy issues. The issues analyzed include defense policy, economic policy, energy policy, foreign policy, government regulation, health policy, legal policy, political and social processes, social security and retirement policy, and tax policy. The AEI publications are issued as books or as pamphlets in various series. An annual, annotated bibliography with author and subject indexes identifies all AEI publications.

910   Birch, Carol L. *Unity in Diversity: An Index to the Publications of Conservative and Libertarian Institutions*. Metuchen, NJ: Scarecrow Press, 1983.

Books and periodical articles published by 15 conservative research organizations, such as the American Enterprise Institute for Public Policy, the Cato Institute, the New American Foundation, and the Hudson Institute during the period 1970 to 1981 are identifiable by author and subject terms with the help of this index. Most of the periodicals are not indexed elsewhere, yet offer important analytical information about current political problems, policies, and policy options.

911   Buenker, John D., and Nicholas C. Burckel. *Immigration and Ethnicity. A Guide to Information Sources*. Detroit: Gale Research Company, 1977.

Information about U.S. immigration policy and the political influence of various immigrant groups can be found in many of the scholarly books and periodical articles as well as official publications listed and described in this bibliography. The nearly 1,500 entries are arranged by author under seven chapters, entitled: (1) General Accounts and Miscellaneous, (2) Old Immigration, (3) New Immigration, (4) Orientals, (5) Recent Ethnics: Post 1920s, (6) Acculturation, Assimilation, Ethnicity and Restriction, and (7) Repositories, Societies, Documents and Journals. Numerous subdivisions in these chapters aggregate listings by ethnic group, special topic, or issuing agency. Separate author and subject indexes are also included.

For more detailed analyses of U.S. immigration problems and policies, see also *Immigration: Special Studies, 1969–1982* (Frederick, MD: University Publications of America, 1983) and the *Papers of the Select Commission on Immigration and Refugee Policy* (Frederick, MD: University Publications of America, 1983).

912　*The Cato Institute Publications Catalogue.*
Washington, DC: Cato Institute, 1977–.

Founded in 1977, the Cato Institute is a nonpartisan
public policy research foundation named for *Cato's Letters*, libertarian pamphlets that helped lay the philosophical foundation for the American Revolution. The institute publishes a large number of books, periodicals, and
pamphlet-type studies, usually not listed in the standard
bibliographic tools, on various aspects of economic policy, monetary policy, commercial policy, natural resource policy, immigration policy, social policy, and
other policies and public issues. The *Catalogue*, issued
biannually, offers complete listings and descriptions of the
institute's publications and Cato policy conference tapes.
A review of new policy studies published by the Cato
Institute as well as by other research institutes, such as the
American Enterprise Institute, the Heritage Foundation,
the Brookings Institution, the Hoover Institution, the
Manhattan Institute, the Pacific Institute, and others can
be found in the *Policy Report*, the Cato Institute's
monthly newsletter.

913　*The Conference Board Cumulative Index.* New
York: Conference Board, 1971–.

The Conference Board is a global network of leaders
who exchange information on economic and public policy issues. The board's extensive examinations of social,
economic, and political trends and issues are published in
several serial publications. The *Cumulative Index*, issued
annually, identifies by subject all studies of continuing
relevance printed in the publications of the Conference
Board.

913a　Goehlert, Robert U., and Fenton S. Martin.
Policy Analysis and Management. A Bibliography. Santa
Barbara, CA: ABC-Clio Information Services, 1985.

Far more comprehensive than the recent bibliographies compiled by John S. Robey (item 917), this reference work offers some 9,400 citations for scholarly books,
journal articles, and research reports focusing on various
aspects of policy analysis. The unannotated listings are
arranged in seven sections and numerous subdivisions.
The first two sections cover concepts and theories of policy
analysis, while the remaining five sections deal with economic policy, political policy, social policy, technology
and science policy, and environmental policy. The section heading Political Policy encompasses a variety of
policies, including arms control, defense, development,
foreign, law enforcement, military, urban, and other
policies. Most of the citations refer to U.S. policy material, but policies of other countries are also covered.
Detailed access to the listings is provided by a separate
subject index, as well as an author index.

914　Johnson, George W. *American Political Science
Research Guide.* New York: IFI/Plenum Data Company,
1977.

This annotated bibliography lists books and articles
dealing with the executive, legislative, and judicial
branches of the federal government, state and local government. Entries are arranged under these headings by
author names. Separate author and subject indexes offer
additional access to the listed material. Regrettably, many
of the subject terms are too broad for quick retrieval of
desired information. There are 595 items listed under
economics, 626 items listed under law, and 450 items
listed under United States, 1945 to present. On the other
hand, some of the greatest policy problems of the U.S.
government, such as foreign policy in Indochina, Southern Africa, or international trade are represented by a
single entry or no entry at all. All entries have been
selected from the database of the Universal Reference
System.

915　Kotz, Arnold. *The Policy Analysis Source Book
for Social Programs.* Washington, DC: The National
Planning Association, 1975.

This two-volume reference set consists of 3,750
abstracts from significant books, periodical articles, and
reports concerned with policy issues and the analysis of
social programs in the United States. Entries are organized by major social policy areas, such as health,
manpower, education, housing, income security, consumer protection, and others. Numerous subdivisions are
made for entries focusing on specific services or policy
targets. Detailed author and subject indexes are included.

916　Raffa, Frederick A., Clyde A. Haulman, and
Djehane A. Hosni. *United States Employment and
Training Programs. A Selected Annotated Bibliography.*
Westport, CT: Greenwood Press, 1983.

Significant elements in United States employment
and social policies are the CETA (Comprehensive
Employment and Training Act) and PSE (Public Service
Employment) programs. This bibliography offers 248 citations for books, professional journal articles, reports by
private research organizations, and publications from federal agencies relating to these programs and their underlying policies. All entries carry lengthy annotations. An
introductory essay traces the history of the programs. A
directory of publishers, a detailed subject index, and an
author index are included.

917　Robey, John S. *Public Policy Analysis: An Annotated Bibliography.* New York: Garland Publishing, Inc.,
1983.

While American politics have always received considerable attention in the scholarly literature, detailed scholarly analysis of the various governmental policies is a comparatively recent phenomenon. This bibliography identifies many of the recently published journal articles and books as well as dissertations devoted to public policy analysis. The annotated entries cover agricultural policies, civil rights policies, economic policies, educational policies, energy policies, military and foreign policies, social welfare, and taxation policies. Publications dealing with policy-making activities are also listed. Subject and author indexes are provided.

See also the author's *The Analysis of Public Policy: A Bibliography of Dissertations, 1977–1982* (Westport, CT: Greenwood Press, 1984). It offers annotated listings for over 1,000 American, Canadian, and British doctoral dissertations about U.S. policies.

918   Rycroft, Robert W., Timothy A. Hall, Don E. Kash, and Irvin L. White. *Energy Policy-Making. A Selected Bibliography*. Norman: University of Oklahoma Press, 1977.

Since the 1973 oil embargo by the Organization of Petroleum Exporting Countries, the United States and other countries of the world have attempted to integrate the economic, environmental, and technical components of energy with energy politics in a public policy framework. These attempts are supported by a growing involvement of social scientists in the development of appropriate analytical approaches, methods, and techniques for subjecting energy policy-making to scholarly scrutiny. The main foci of scholarly analysis are identified in the bibliography as follows: (1) energy decision making, (2) energy economics, (3) energy industry, (4) energy self-sufficiency, (5) energy use and conservation, (6) energy regulation, (7) energy facility siting, (8) energy resources and technologies, (9) energy and the environment, (10) international energy policy, (11) energy research, (12) future energy policy, (13) energy bibliography. Books and periodical articles published until 1977 are listed under these research categories, but no annotations or indexes are included.

919   Szekely, Kalman S. *Electoral College: A Selective Bibliography*. Littleton, CO: Libraries Unlimited, 1971.

As the elections of John Quincy Adams, Rutherford B. Hayes, and Benjamin Harrison have demonstrated, a president may be elected in the United States who has lost the total popular vote. The reason for this undesirable eventuality is the constitutionally mandated system of electoral votes. In recent years criticism of the electoral college has intensified without gaining the necessary momentum to change a fundamental aspect of the American political system.

The bibliography contains some 800 entries for books, periodical articles, and unpublished dissertations dealing with the electoral college and its reform. Listings are arranged in six major categories: (1) historical background and organization, (2) arguments in favor of retaining the present system, (3) arguments against the present system, (4) proposals to reform the present system, (5) popular interest in reform, and (6) reapportionment of the electoral system. These categories are further subdivided, and all entries are briefly annotated.

920   Tompkins, Dorothy C. *Conflict of Interest in the Federal Government*. Berkeley: Bureau of Public Administration, University of California, 1961.

Government officials make binding decisions to resolve conflicts about valued objects among individuals and groups. It is widely believed that these decisions will have optimum effect if the government decision-makers are not themselves affected by conflicting interests of a financial or other nature. The unannotated bibliography lists official and scholarly publications dealing with the principles and problems of interest conflicts in the federal service. Specifically listed are publications about conflict-of-interest laws, persons exempted from conflict-of-interest laws, persons affected by conflict-of-interest laws, Congress and conflict-of-interest problems, executive appointments, outside employment of government employees, disclosure of financial interests, etc.

921   Universal Reference System. *Legislative Process, Representation and Decisionmaking*. Princeton, NJ: Princeton Research Publishing Company, 1967– .

The governmental decision-making process, in the legislature and other governmental bodies, is the subject of many scholarly publications that are intensively indexed according to the Grazian System of topical and methodological descriptors. The title listed above refers to one of the ten basic columns in the Universal Reference System. It contains entries for 2,134 books and periodical articles, most of which refer to the American system of government. The entries in the base volume and in the annual supplementary volumes of the Universal Reference System are conveniently retrievable as a result of the detailed indexing system, which uses numerous descriptors relating to governmental processes and practices.

HANDBOOKS AND ENCYCLOPEDIAS

922   Becker, Theodore L. *American Government: Past, Present, Future*. Rockleigh, NJ: Allyn & Bacon, 1976.

923   Burns, James M. *Government by the People*. Englewood Cliffs, NJ: Prentice-Hall, 1978.

924   Congressional Quarterly, Inc. *CQ Guide to Current American Government*. Washington, DC: Congressional Quarterly, Inc., 1961 – .

925   Cummings, Milton C., and David Wise. *Democracy under Pressure. An Introduction to the American Political System*. New York: Harcourt Brace Jovanovich, 1977.

926   Donovan, J. *Democracy at the Crossroads: An Introduction to American Government and Politics*. New York: Holt, Rinehart and Winston, 1978.

927   Ferguson, John H. and Dean E. McHenry. *The American System of Government*. New York: McGraw-Hill, 1977.

928   Lowi, Theodore J. *American Government: Incomplete Conquest*. New York: Holt, Rinehart and Winston, 1977.

929   Myers, James T. *The American Way: An Introduction to the U.S. Government and Politics*. Lexington, MA: D. C. Heath & Company, 1977.

930   Prewitt, Kenneth, and Sidney Verba. *An Introduction to American Government*. New York: Harper & Row, 1977.

931   Saffell, David C. *The Politics of American National Government*. Englewood Cliffs, NJ: Winthrop Publishing Company, 1978.

The titles cited above constitute a sampling of the many handbooks that apply scholarly findings for an explanation of the American political system. The books describe, under various approaches, the structural elements of the American political system and present recent illustrations of the continuing interplay of political actors in the process of authoritative decision making. With the exception of the semiannual Congressional Quarterly guidebook, most handbooks are published in frequently revised editions.

932   Gellhorn, Ernest. *Administrative Law and Process in a Nutshell*. St. Paul, MN: West Publishing Company, 1972.

933   Gellhorn, Ernest, and Glen O. Robinson. *The Administrative Process* St. Paul, MN: West Publishing Company, 1974.

The two handbooks offer a summary description of the administrative process in the United States. The first title is organized in 12 chapters, entitled: (1) Judicial Control, (2) Nonjudicial Controls, (3) Overview of Judicial Review, (4) Agency Jurisdiction, (5) Acquiring Information: Investigations, (6) Informal Administrative Process, (7) Formal Processes, (8) Formal Processes: Orders and Adjudications, (9) Requirements of a Hearing, (10) The Hearing Process, (11) Obtaining Judicial Review, (12) Scope of Judicial Review. The full text of the Administrative Procedure Act, a table of cases, and an index are also included.

The second title focuses on specific agency processes, such as licensing controls, control of business conduct, public land management, etc. The role of the public in the administrative process is also covered.

934   Gilbert, Neil, and Harry Specht. *Handbook of the Social Services*. Englewood Cliffs, NJ: Prentice-Hall, 1981.

During the past two decades the American political system has produced an enormous growth in and a significant transformation of the social services available to the American population. The handbook summarizes the current nature and status of the social service programs in the United States and reviews the methods of practice in the social services. The 30 articles in the handbook cover information services, home health services, day care services, recreation services, family services, services to the elderly, child welfare services, alcohol and drug abuse services, vocational rehabilitation services, social services for oppressed groups, criminal justice services, housing services, medical care services, social services in business and industry, income maintenance and social welfare programs, and others. Author and subject indexes are included.

935   Isaacson, Walter. *Pro and Con*. New York: G. P. Putnam's Sons, 1983.

Several American political processes, notably the communication, judicial, and legislative processes, have been struggling over many years with a number of political objects that have become key issues dividing the American population. This reference work presents a summary of the pro and con arguments relating to some 50 public issues. Included are such issues as abortion, affirmative action, arms sales, balanced budget amendment, busing, capitalism, capital punishment, the draft, ERA, flat tax, gay rights, gold standard, gun control, insanity defense, nuclear energy, nuclear freeze, one-term presidency, Palestinian state, press rights, rent control, schoolbook censorship, television, voluntary euthanasia, and others. Following the summary of the arguments, public opinion data and listings of published and unpublished information sources emanating from interest group and official organizations are provided.

Process-related information, however, is supplied only rarely, although some judicial decisions are occasionally cited.

936   Rosenbaum, Robert A. *The Public Issues Handbook: A Guide for the Concerned Citizen*. Westport, CT: Greenwood Press, 1983.

A large proportion of the public issues currently confronting legislators, policy-makers, and interest group actors in the United States is described in this handbook. The 24 issues covered include aging, armed forces, capital punishment, cities, civil liberties, civil rights, consumerism, crime, criminal justice, education, elections, energy, environment, family, health care, housing, immigration, Indians, juvenile justice, poverty, transportation, unemployment, welfare, and women. Each chapter in the book defines a single issue, provides historical perspective and other basic data, and presents the major opposing viewpoints. References to additional information sources as well as information about pertinent interest group organizations are also included.

937   Seidman, Edward. *Handbook of Social Intervention*. Beverly Hills, CA: Sage Publications, 1983.

Social intervention refers to an alteration of intrasocietal relationships, frequently planned or intended by political actors. The handbook describes the current nature and status of planned and unplanned social change, and reviews current research on social intervention issues. The 28 articles of the handbook are grouped into six parts, entitled: (1) Historical, Cultural and Value Perspectives, (2) Research Design and Measurement, (3) Strategies, (4) Educational, Psychological and Social Programs and Policies, (5) Economic and Environmental Programs and Policies, (6) Training Issues and Future Projections. Specifically covered are government interventions relating to criminal justice, income transfer, housing, environmental stress reduction, employment and business, energy conservation, education, and other policy areas. Bibliographic references, author and subject indexes are included.

938   *Worldmark Encyclopedia of the States*. New York: Harper & Row, 1981.

Written by political scientists, historians, and other scholars, the encyclopedia offers for the United States as a whole as well as for each of the 50 states, the District of Columbia, Puerto Rico, the U.S. Caribbean and Pacific dependencies 50 items of information, including location, size, population, ethnic groups, history, political parties, judicial system, state government and state services, local government, economics and public finance, taxation, the press, etc. A bibliography of additional information sources for each of these political entities is also provided. The encyclopedia also contains a chronological listing of U.S. presidents from 1789 to 1981 together with birth and death dates, residence at election, other major offices held, terms of presidential office, popular and electoral votes, notable events during the presidency, names of vice-presidents and chief justices of the U.S. Supreme Court.

Biographical and Organizational Information

Directories are the essential reference tools for identifying quickly the structure and functions of the organizational units in the United States government. Directories are also indispensable for the retrieval of basic information about governmental personnel and other political actors, such as interest and lobbying groups. In view of the principle of unwarranted invasion of privacy codified in category 6 of the Freedom of Information Act, directories are limited to basic biographical data, such as names, birth dates, addresses, positions, education, party affiliations, and achievements. While many directories are now issued annually, rapid changes and instability of their subject matter would require an even greater publication frequency.

The titles listed in the following sections represent the most useful directories for information about political actors.

GUIDEBOOKS

939   Larson, Donna Rae. *Guide to U.S. Government Directories, 1970–1980*. Phoenix: Oryx Press, 1981.

More than 800 directories issued by federal agencies can be identified with this guidebook. The directories are arranged by Superintendent of Documents (SuDoc) classification numbers and are described in terms of coverage, scope, arrangement, and available indexing. A subject index in the guidebook lists the title and publication date of the directory together with an entry number in the main entry section. Biographical directories are listed under the heading "Government Officials." Agency directories are listed under the name of the agency as well as by subject.

CURRENT DIRECTORIES: GOVERNMENTAL STRUCTURE

940   Barone, Michael, and Grant Ujifusa. *The Almanac of American Politics*. Washington, DC: National Journal, 1972– .

Currently issued annually, this reference work has undergone changes over the years in its contents, its publisher, and the frequency of its publication. It now offers up-to-date information on each state and congressional district, the senators, congressmen, and governors. Data include demographic and biographical summaries, interest group ratings, key votes, election results, campaign contributions and expenditures. Additional commentaries focus on the presidency, the Senate, the House, the governors and big city mayors, the people, and regions of the United States. Separate listings identify the membership of the various Senate and House committees. Three indexes — by topics, people, and places — are also included.

941   *Congressional Handbook*. Kensington, MD: Chamber of Commerce of the United States, 1981—.

The pocket-size directory lists congressional delegations by state and members of Congress alphabetically by name. Office locations, room numbers, and committee assignments are identified. Committee rosters are also included. New editions are published annually.

942   *Congressional Staff Directory*. Washington, DC: Congressional Staff Directory, 1959—.

The annual directory lists members and support staff of all congressional committees and subcommittees, key personnel of the executive departments and agencies, and staffs of miscellaneous offices of the Capitol. An alphabetical listing of 9,900 cities of 1,500 population, arranged by state, presents the latest population figure, the number of the congressional district, and the name of the member of Congress. Also included are biographical sketches for all key staff personnel. A prepublication supplement containing the latest biographical data and other recent information is issued under the title *Advance Locator for Capitol Hill*.

943   *Encyclopedia of Governmental Advisory Organizations*. Detroit: Gale Research Company, 1973—.

944   *Guide to Presidential Advisory Commissions, 1973–1981*. Westport, CT: Meckler Books, 1982.

Since the inception of the United States, advisory bodies, created by statute or established and utilized by the president or other officers of the federal government, have played an important role in shaping official decisions. These bodies may be constituted as committees, boards, councils, conferences, commissions, or other organizational units.

The first cited reference work, currently in its third edition, identifies over 3,400 advisory bodies under ten subject sections, as follows: (1) agriculture, (2) business, industry, economics, and labor, (3) defense, (4) education and social welfare, (5) environment and natural resources, (6) health and medicine, (7) history and culture,

(8) government, law, and international affairs, (9) science and technology, and (10) transportation. Up to 20 items of information are presented in each entry, including history, authority, membership, staff, meetings, program, etc. A list of committee management officers and an alphabetical and keyword index are also included. The basic volume is updated by periodic supplements, entitled *New Governmental Advisory Organizations*.

The second directory lists and describes in chronological sequence all presidential advisory commissions. It also includes a complete membership list of these commissions as well as a list of all titled reports issued, together with an abstract of their contents.

945   Ehrenhalt, Alan. *Politics in America. Members of Congress in Washington and at Home*. Washington, DC: Congressional Quarterly Press, 1982—.

The most important purpose of this reference book is to assess members of Congress in a way that official biographies and interest group ratings never do. Following an arrangement by state, the book presents a brief description of the state to be followed by evaluative articles on the governor, members of the U.S. Senate and the U.S. House of Representatives. The career of each politician in Washington and at home is described in terms of achievements, goals, and failures. Committee assignments, election and campaign finance data, voting studies, key votes, and interest group ratings are included. Membership lists of congressional committees, address directories for Senate and House offices, election data, and indexing to names and states are also provided. Updating editions are planned.

946   *Federal Executive Directory*. Washington, DC: Carroll Publishing Company, 1980—.

947   *Federal Staff Directory*. Mount Vernon, VA: Congressional Staff Directory, 1982—.

These two directories serve the information needs of persons and organizations that routinely interface with members of the executive branch. The *Federal Executive Directory*, published bimonthly, offers the most current listings in three sections. The alphabetical section lists federal executives by their names together with telephone numbers. The keyword section contains more than 18,000 subject entries with cross index numbers to the organization section. The latter shows every unit, section, division, or office within the executive branch and identifies the current officeholder and telephone number.

The *Federal Staff Directory*, published annually, is a less up-to-date source but offers adequate coverage on the 27,000 key executives and their staff assistants. Entries are arranged by keyword and include names of offices, officeholders, and job titles together with addresses and telephone numbers. A biographical section provides personal data on approximately 1,400 staff members.

948   *Federal Regulatory Directory.* Washington, DC: Congressional Quarterly, Inc., 1979– .

The federal regulatory process is vitally important for achieving a healthy environment, a safe workplace, a competitive marketplace, and many other essential political objects. The annually revised directory contains extensive profiles of 15 of the largest regulatory agencies as well as detailed information on 63 other important regulatory agencies, both independent and within executive departments. Summaries of responsibilities, lists of telephone contacts, citations to legislative authority, descriptions of organizational details, typologies of public participation, and listings of additional reference sources are included in each agency profile. An appendix contains material on the *Federal Register, Code of Federal Regulations,* the Administrative Procedure Act, and other pertinent legislative acts. A comprehensive index offers access to the listed material by subject and agency.

949   Kruzas, Anthony T., and Kay Gill. *Government Programs and Project Directory.* Detroit: Gale Research Company, 1983– .

Currently published in three issues per year, this reference work identifies and describes approximately 1,200 programs administered by federal executive departments and independent agencies. The individually numbered entries are arranged alphabetically by name of department-level and subordinate-level agency. Following the name of the agency, the program name, administrative location, and statutory authorization are identified. A separate paragraph in each entry describes the program and where applicable its relationship to other programs. The nature of the funding provided and the basis for its distribution are also indicated. The source for the listed information is identified. Indexing by program name and keyword offers additional access to the listed entries.

The reference work partially overlaps with the annual *Catalog of Federal Domestic Assistance.* It does not list all the assistance programs included in the *Catalog* but describes many programs not otherwise identifiable.

950   *National Roster of Black Elected Officials.* Washington, DC: Joint Center for Political Studies, 1970– .

While black participation in American politics has shown significant increases during the past decade, the total number of black elected officials still amounts to less than 1 percent of all officials elected in the country.

This annual directory currently lists some 4,000 black American men and women holding popularly elected offices in the United States. Entries are arranged alphabetically by state with subdivisions for federal, state, county, municipal, judicial and law enforcement, school district, and special district offices. The names, position titles, and addresses are listed for the officeholders. A brief summary of governmental offices in each state identifies the total number of elective positions and the percentage of the black population in the state or predominantly black congressional districts.

A further analysis of the nature and extent of black participation in American politics can be found in a separate publication entitled *The State of Black Politics,* issued by the same publisher.

951   *Official Congressional Directory.* Washington, DC: U.S. Government Printing Office, 1809– .

The annually published directory offers biographical, organizational, and statistical information about the members and administrative units of the United States government, international organizations, the diplomatic corps, the press, and other services. Biographical sketches are given for members of Congress, department secretaries, and the judiciary only. For all other governmental units, organizations, and services only the names, titles, and addresses of the personnel are given. An index of names and maps of congressional districts are also included.

952   *Taylor's Encyclopedia of Government Officials, Federal and State.* Dallas: Political Research, 1969– .

This is not an encyclopedia but a directory listing members of United States government departments and agencies as well as federal and state officials of each state. It also includes portraits of key officials and viewing charts for congressional and state senatorial districts. No biographical information is presented for the officeholders, however. Quarterly supplements are issued for additions, corrections, and adjustments of the listings.

953   U.S. Congress. House. Committee on Post Office and Civil Service. *United States Government Policy and Supporting Positions.* Washington, DC: U.S. Government Printing Office, 1960– .

This publication is issued in presidential election years and is designed to list the jobs that are the leading positions in the United States government. It is affectionately called the "Plum Book" because it is used by a new administration to make appointments in the executive branch that are based on political considerations rather than the merit system of the Civil Service. Entries in the directory are arranged by department or agency and identify the title and location of the position, its incumbent, if any, the type of appointment, grade or salary, tenure, if any, and expiration date, if applicable. Seven different types of appointment are listed, such as presidential appointments with or without the advice and consent of the Senate, and various position categories excepted from Civil Service rules. Approximately 2,200 positions were listed in the 1976 edition of the directory. Of this total some 500 positions are key policy-making posts.

954   U.S. Department of Commerce. *Commerce Business Daily.* Washington, DC: U.S. Government Printing Office, daily.

955   U.S. Department of Commerce. *Commerce Business Daily.* Chicago: U.S. Department of Commerce, 1982 – . (Vendor: Dialog — Files 194, 195)

Issued every weekday in its printed form and updated daily in the electronic version, *Commerce Business Daily* is a directory of U.S. government offices announcing procurement invitations for services, supplies, equipment, and material. Information is included for all proposed procurements of $5,000 or more by civilian agencies, all proposed procurements of $10,000 or more by military agencies, all federal contract awards of $25,000 from civilian agencies and $100,000 from military agencies. Surplus U.S. government property sales and U.S. government interests in specific research and development fields or programs are also announced.

The daily updated information material remains in the online file 195 for 60 – 90 days, at which time the oldest-month entries are transferred to backfile 194.

956   *The United States Directory of Federal Regional Structure.* Washington, DC: U.S. Government Printing Office, 1981 – .

Standard federal administrative regions have been established to achieve greater uniformity in the location and geographic jurisdiction of federal field offices. Agencies are now required to adopt the new uniform system when new offices are established. This directory provides a map of the standard federal regions as well as listings of the key officials, addresses and telephone numbers of the agencies conforming to the new system. Additional regional maps and listings for those agencies not conforming to the ten standard federal regions are also included. Updated editions of the directory are published.

957   *United States Government Manual.* Washington, DC: General Services Administration, 1935 – .

The reference work constitutes the official, annually published directory of the federal government that identifies all organizational units in the legislative, executive, and judicial branches of the United States government as well as quasi-official agencies, selected boards, committees, and commissions. For each administrative unit brief

information about the creation and authority, its functions and activities is presented. All principal officers of the various administrative units are identified, and their titles, responsibility, and authority are indicated. An appendix lists executive agencies and functions that were abolished, transferred, or terminated subsequent to March 4, 1933. A bibliographic list of representative publications of the various departments and agencies was included in a second appendix in editions up to 1970. Since then, a section entitled Sources of Information lists representative publications or the names of information officers under most administrative units described in the directory.

958   *Washington Information Directory.* Washington, DC: Congressional Quarterly, Inc., 1975 – .

There are, according to this directory, 16 functional areas involving political actors on the federal level. These political functions are (1) communications and the media; (2) Congress and politics; (3) economics and business; (4) education and culture; (5) employment and labor; (6) energy; (7) equal rights: minorities, women; (8) government personnel and services; (9) health and consumer affairs; (10) housing and urban affairs; (11) individual assistance programs; (12) international affairs; (13) law and justice; (14) national security; (15) natural resources, environment, and agriculture; and (16) science, space exploration, and transportation. For each of these functional areas the directory makes suitable subdivisions according to a more specific focus and identifies their institutionalized political actors in three categories: (1) agencies of the executive branch; (2) Congress; (3) private and nongovernmental organizations. Apart from the names, addresses, and telephone numbers of the responsible institutional actors, the directory also supplies a capsule description of the work performed by each organization. The names of the people acting in an executive or policy-making capacity in the listed organizations are also given. For additional access to the listed material, the directory includes a subject index, a department and agency index, a regional offices index, and numerous bibliographic lists for additional information. The bibliographic references usually relate to annual reports, statistical compendia, and other publications that summarize the progress in the various functional activities of the political system.

959   *Who's Who in American Politics.* New York: R. R. Bowker, 1967 – .

This directory presents biographical information on more than 15,000 political actors who play a leading role on the federal and state level in the United States. It provides for each politician the legal and mailing addresses, political party affiliation, birth place, education, family data, present and previous positions, and achievements. There is also a geographic index that lists political leaders by state. Revised editions of this directory are published at two-year intervals.

RETROSPECTIVE DIRECTORIES: GOVERNMENTAL STRUCTURE

960   *Black Enterprise—Black Political Leaders*. New York: Earl G. Graves Publishing Company, 1982.

961   Christmas, Walter. *Negroes in Public Affairs and Government*. Yonkers, NY: Educational Heritage, Inc., 1966.

The first directory identifies black Americans appointed to major posts in the Reagan administration and lists black political organizations operating at the state or city level.

Blacks who have held high positions in Congress, the judiciary, the diplomatic service, executive departments and agencies, or in United Nations organizations in earlier periods are listed in the second directory. Biographical information is provided for each listed person.

962   Brownstein, Ronald, and Nina Easton. *Reagan's Ruling Class: Portraits of the President's Top 100 Officials*. Washington, DC: Presidential Accountability Group, 1982.

Produced by a special research team formed by consumer advocate Ralph Nader, this reference work contains more biographical data and other information on President Reagan's top officials than the standard directories. Each entry includes a "Responsibility of Office" section describing the position and function of the officeholder along with background information on major issues. Information is also provided on financial and property status and links to corporate interests.

963   Delphos, W. *Washington's Best Kept Secrets: A U.S. Government Guide to International Business*. New York: John Wiley & Sons, 1984.

The reference work identifies and describes a large array of federal programs available to American companies for developing international business. Entries are organized by product or service rather than governmental agency.

964   Engelbarts, Rudolf. *Women in the United States Congress, 1917–1972: Their Accomplishments; with Bibliographies*. Littleton, CO: Libraries Unlimited, 1974.

965   Tolchin, Susan. *Women in Congress: 1917–1976*. Washington, DC: U.S. Government Printing Office, 1976.

No woman succeeded in becoming a member of Congress until 1916, and woefully few women have served in the United States Congress since then. The two reference books together present biographical information on 11 female senators and 85 women members of the U.S. House of Representatives. Party affiliation and other political service details are given. The Engelbarts volume also contains bibliographical listings for additional information material about each congresswoman and various subjects related to the study of women in politics.

966   Jablonski, Donna. *How To Find Information about Companies*. Washington, DC: Washington Researchers, 1979.

This reference work identifies local, state, and federal agencies in the United States that by virtue of their functional specialization will be a source of information relating to American companies. The entries contain brief explanatory annotations about the type of information available. An index offers additional access to the listed entries.

967   Lesko, Matthew. *Information U.S.A.* New York: Viking Press, 1983.

The federal government is by far the most comprehensive, yet the most unexplored source of information in the United States. This directory is an inventory of federal information sources, listed by department, board, commission, office, or other agency designation. For each agency the entries, arranged alphabetically by topic, describe the object of the information-gathering and dissemination program and identify the contact point or available publication. Contact point data include the address, room and telephone number of the organizational unit where further information can be obtained. An introductory sampler section and a keyword index offer additional access to the listed material.

For a list of federal government databases that can be used by the public either free or for a fee, see also *The Federal Data Base Finder* (Potomac, MD: Information USA, 1984).

968   Morris, Dan, and Inez Morris. *Who Was Who in American Politics*. New York: Hawthorn Books, 1974.

Brief biographical information can be found in this reference book about more than 4,000 men and women who were notable political actors during any period from the colonial days to the immediate past. Included are presidents, vice-presidents, governors, members of Congress and the state legislatures, the courts system, the diplomatic service, administrative agencies, and other political organizations.

969   Norback, Craig T. *The Computer Invasion*. New York: Van Nostrand Reinhold, 1981.

Many governmental agencies collect, store, and exchange information about the activities of private citizens. This reference work provides rudimentary information on most of the personal files, maintained by governmental agencies, to which an individual might desire access. Entries are arranged alphabetically by the names of the federal agencies and include the name of the file, who has the right of access to that file, and any special instructions concerning how a request for information should be made. For files maintained by state agencies less detailed information is given, under the name of each state. There is also a brief section in the book where consumer files maintained by credit, insurance, or other nongovernmental institutions are briefly described.

970   *Political Profiles*. New York: Facts on File, 1978–1979.

Each of the five volumes in the set is devoted to the men and women who were politically most influential during the administrations of five presidents, namely, Truman, Eisenhower, Kennedy, Johnson, and Nixon. Persons who achieved prominence in government service as well as those whose political, social, or scientific activities have helped shape public life are included. The individual profiles provide detailed biographical information in narrative form ranging from 400 to 2,000 words. More than 2,500 biographies written and edited by historians are included in the set, which also contains brief thematic introductions, extensive bibliographies, indexes, and appendices.

971   Robison, William C. *The Federal Employment Handbook*. New York: Julian Messner, 1981.

The federal government currently employs more than three million civilians to serve the community of citizens (politeia) in the United States and abroad. No other single employer offers as many diverse occupational fields and geographical locations for employment. This reference book contains occupational briefs for 450 white-collar occupations together with a directory of employment distribution by agency and by Standard Metropolitan Statistical Area (SMSA). Also included is an address listing of federal agencies, as well as several introductory chapters describing the federal workforce, position management, and hiring system.

972   Rutgers University Center for the American Woman and Politics. *Women in Public Office. A Biographical Directory and Statistical Analysis*. Metuchen, NJ: Scarecrow Press, 1978.

Women play a numerically small role in public office and comprise an estimated 8 percent of all officials in American government. The directory identifies over 17,000 women currently serving as public officials in local, state, and federal government. Entries are organized by state except for a separate section on women serving in federal offices. Within each state separate list-

ings are made under state executive and cabinet, state senate, state house, county commissions, townships, mayors, local councils, judges, state boards and commissions. Entries identify the name of the officeholder, position title, political party affiliation, service dates, education, birth dates, address, and telephone number. The directory also contains a statistical profile of women holding public office and a name index.

973   Sobel, Robert. *Biographical Directory of the United States Executive Branch 1774–1977*. Westport, CT: Greenwood Publishing Company, 1977.

Biographical information is provided by this directory about some 550 persons who have served or are serving in the executive branch of the United States government. Date of birth, education, personal and family data, career information, and brief bibliographical notes are given. Indexes offer a key to the listings by presidential administration, by government service, education, place and date of birth, and marital information.

974   Stineman, Esther. *American Political Women: Contemporary and Historical Profiles*. Littleton, CO: Libraries Unlimited, 1980.

This book presents biographical descriptions of 60 women, most of them serving as congresswomen, ambassadors, governors, lieutenant governors, mayors, special presidential assistants, or other major officeholders during the late 1970s and early 1980s. Each biographical portrait is accompanied by a selective listing of speeches and writings, as well as a bibliography of publications about the biographee. In addition, several separate bibliographies list reference and other publications about women in politics. Five appendices identify women serving in Congress, as ambassadors, chiefs of mission, federal judges, key departmental and White House officers.

975   U.S. Congress. *Biographical Directory of the American Congress, 1774–1961*. Washington, DC: U.S. Government Printing Office, 1961.

Members of the Continental Congress 1774–1789 and the Congress of the United States for any period from 1789 to 1961 as well as the executive officers of all administrations from 1789 to 1961 can be easily identified with the help of this directory. A separate section of the directory contains brief biographical information for each congressman, arranged alphabetically by name.

976   U.S. General Accounting Office. Comptroller General. *Federal Information Sources and Systems 1980: A Directory Issued by the Comptroller General*. Washington, DC: U.S. Government Printing Office, 1980.

Federal information sources maintained by departments of the executive branch and independent agencies, boards, and commissions are listed and described in this directory. The identified sources include publications, activities, and organizations oriented to central processing and dissemination of budgetary, fiscal, and program-related data. Each citation contains the title of the publication, database or other information activity, its budget function, public availability, if any, agency contact, and an abstract describing the object and content. Separate subject, agency, and budget function indexes offer additional access to the cited material.

977   Vexler, Robert. *The Vicepresidents and Cabinet Members*. Dobbs Ferry, NY: Oceana Publications, 1975.

Biographical sketches of the vice-presidents and cabinet members in the administration of each president from that of George Washington to that of Gerald R. Ford are presented by this two-volume set. A bibliography of books and articles offering further information is included at the end of each biographical sketch.

978   Whitnah, Donald R. *Government Agencies*. Westport, CT: Greenwood Press, 1983.

Over 100 in-depth profiles of federal government agencies are presented in this reference work, which is part of the *Greenwood Encyclopedia of American Institutions*. All cabinet-level departments as well as the majority of the bureaus, commissions, government corporations, and quasi-government entities are included. A few defunct bodies, particularly those from the New Deal era, are also covered. Appendices provide a chronology, genealogy, an organizational chart of various umbrella departments, and categories of agency services.

CURRENT DIRECTORIES: INTEREST STRUCTURE

Details of the American political scene are shaped not only by the legislative, executive, and judicial branches of the United States government but also by organized interests playing a decisive role in political decision making. Sometimes referred to as the fourth branch of government, organized interests constitute an institutional framework of political actors designed to safeguard the interests of specific groups of people active in industries, professions, domestic and foreign governments, or political associations. Many of these organized groups exert a quasi-monopolistic influence on the decisions of the federal government by virtue of the fact that countervailing positions are not articulated for lack of appropriate representation.

Reference treatment of the flow of information generated by organized interest groups leaves much to be desired, but the directories listed below will serve as useful starting points for research.

979   Christiano, David, and Lisa Young. *Human Rights Organizations and Periodicals Directory*. Berkeley, CA: Meiklejohn Civil Liberties Institute, 1983.

Human rights relate to a broad spectrum of conditions under which people treat one another legally, economically, or socially. Human rights in the United States include not only the civil rights and liberties under the U.S. Constitution and the Bill of Rights, but also a variety of economic and social rights embodied in international conventions, treaties, and other instruments of international law.

This directory identifies and describes interest group organizations as well as federal agencies involved in protecting or expanding human rights. Also listed are interest group organizations that advocate social and economic changes in the United States and other countries in order to strengthen or guarantee fundamental human rights. The book is composed of six sections: (1) alphabetical guide to nongovernmental organizations and periodicals, (2) federal agencies guide, (3) subject index, (4) periodical index, (5) geographical guide, and (6) compendium of resources from the Meiklejohn Institute.

980   *Encyclopedia of Associations*. Vol. 1, *National Organizations of the United States*; Vol. 2, *Geographic and Executive Indexes*; Vol. 3, *New Associations and Projects*; Vol. 5, *Research Activities and Funding Programs*. Detroit: Gale Research Company, 1956–.

981   *Encyclopedia of Associations*. Detroit: Gale Research Company, current year. (Vendor: Dialog—File 114)

Many nonprofit membership organizations, such as labor unions, political parties and other public affairs organizations, business and professional associations are politically active. Nearly 18,000 membership organizations in the United States, whether politically active or not, are listed and described in this reference work, available in annually revised printed editions and as a computerized database. Entries in the printed edition are arranged under 17 organizational categories, such as trade, business and commercial organizations, legal, governmental and military organizations, educational organizations, social welfare organizations, medical organizations, public affairs organizations, foreign interest organizations, religious organizations, veteran and patriotic organizations, labor unions, chambers of commerce, etc. Up to 18 items of information are included in each entry, notably address and telephone numbers, chief officials, founding date, membership size, regional, state, and local groups, purpose, publications, convention or other meeting dates. Additional access to the listed material is provided by separate name, geographic, and executive indexes. A separate interedition volume lists new associations. The electronic database contains current year entries only and can be searched by name, section category, geographic location, and other elements of the unit record.

982   *Directory of Business-Related Political Action Committees.* Washington, DC: The Business-Industry Political Action Committee, 1981.

The directory lists in alphabetical sequence the names of corporations, trade associations, business-related and health organizations that sponsor political action committees at the federal level. Entries include the address, telephone number, and name of the treasurer in addition to the name of the political action committee. Receipt and expenditure figures, but no amounts for contributions are also given.

983   Fine, Melinda, and Peter Steven. *American Peace Directory: 1984.* Cambridge, MA: Ballinger Publishing Co., 1984.

According to this directory there are more than 1,350 peace-oriented groups active in the United States. Included in the listings are national peace groups, educators' groups, local peace groups, and local chapters of national peace groups. Information is provided by type of organization, geographical location, primary focus of activity, and alphabetical listing. Names, addresses and telephone numbers are presented in all entries. An index is included.

984   Garling, Marguerite. *The Human Rights Handbook. A Guide to British and American International Human Rights Organizations.* New York: Facts on File, 1979.

Organized in three main parts—The United Kingdom, The United States, and International Non-governmental Organizations—this guidebook/directory identifies and describes in separate sections voluntary and professional organizations active in human rights affairs and organizations providing help for refugees. Subdivisions within these parts group entries according to a narrower focus of activity. In addition to addresses and telephone numbers, entries usually include a short description of the organization's history, activities, and finances as well as a list of publications if available. A bibliography of reference and general works on human rights and refugees as well as an index are also provided.

985   Gifford, Courtney D. *Directory of U.S. Labor Organizations.* Washington, DC: Bureau of National Affairs, 1982–.

986   *The Greenwood Encyclopedia of American Institutions.* Vol. 1, *Labor Unions.* Westport, CT: Greenwood Press, 1977.

987   Paradis, Adrian A., and Grace D. Paradis. *The Labor Almanac.* Littleton, CO: Libraries Unlimited, 1983.

Labor unions play a significant role in the political process stage through their lobbying efforts and by influencing federal elections through political action committees (PACs). The structure of labor unionism is a decisive determinant for the success of labor, wage-price, income, and other economic policies.

The first directory cited above reviews the structure of the labor movement in the United States, lists national unions and professional and state employee associations, provides membership estimates, lists commonly used abbreviations for unions and employee associations, and offers complete indexes to all listed organizations and their officers. The directory also identifies the publications issued by labor organizations and presents a variety of statistical data.

The second title cited above offers historical background and details of major achievements for each labor union.

The Labor Almanac is most useful for its directory information. The book identifies in separate sections prominent labor leaders, national labor organizations, federal government agencies concerned with labor relations, and state agencies concerned with labor. Also listed are the principal federal labor laws and executive orders affecting labor. Reference sources for statistical data are also listed.

988   Harrison, Cynthia Ellen. *Women's Movement Media: A Source Guide.* New York: R. R. Bowker, 1975.

Arranged by function, type, or special interest, the directory offers approximately 550 descriptions of organizations serving women's interests. Listings are arranged under five sections entitled: (1) Publishers, Distributors, News Services, and Products, (2) Women's Research Centers and Library Research Collections, (3) Women's Organizations and Centers, (4) Governmental and Quasi-Governmental Organizations and Agencies, and (5) Special Interests. Four indexes—a geographical, media title, name, and subject index—are included.

989   Roeder, Edward. *PACs Americana.* Washington, DC: Sunshine Services Corporation, 1982.

This reference book makes it possible to identify and compare nonparty political action committees (PACs) and their spending records. Section I lists PAC sponsors alphabetically by name and identifies the sponsored PAC. Section II contains listings by PAC name and details spending records. Section III offers a breakdown of the political or economic interests represented and lists PAC sponsors alphabetically within each group of interests. Appendices A and B provide cross-indexing of PACs by alternative names or sponsor's affiliate organizations. Appendix C lists 100 PACs in ranking order of contributions. Appendix D contains an alphabetically arranged list of states together with the number of representatives in the 97th Congress, the average campaign spending, and the average percentage raised from PAC contributions.

990   Schapsmeier, Edward L., and Frederick H. Schapsmeier. *Political Parties and Civic Action Groups.* Westport, CT: Greenwood Press, 1981.

Profiles on some 300 political organizations, currently in existence or now defunct, can be found in this reference book. Only organizations with historical significance or current relevance to the national political scene are included. Entries are arranged alphabetically and present information about the founding date, founding fathers, prominent officers and members, political objects pursued and attained, official publications, as well as other useful data. Wherever possible, one or more publications are listed for further information. Appendices contain listings of the organizations by function (e.g., business groups, civil rights groups, foreign affairs groups, good government groups, lobbies, peace groups, political machines, political parties, special interest groups, etc.) and by chronology of founding dates. A glossary and index are also included.

991   *Washington Lobbyists and Lawyers Directory.* Washington, DC: Amward Publications, 1977– .

992   *Washington Representatives: Lobbyists, Consultants, Registered Foreign Agents, Legal Advisors, Public Relations & Government Affairs.* Washington, DC: Columbia Books, 1977– .

Lobbyists, particularly those representing private sector interests, prefer to work anonymously. This fact and the weakness of the 1946 Lobby Registration Act make it difficult to prepare up-to-date listings of the membership of lobbying organizations.

The first directory identifies 9,500 individuals of which only 4,000 are registered under the 1946 Lobby Registration Act. Two separate listings are provided in the irregularly updated directory: Section 1 lists individuals in alphabetical sequence together with the name of the organization they represent. Section 2 is the reverse of the first section and provides names and addresses of the lobbying organizations together with the names of their representatives.

The second directory, updated annually, lists over 8,000 individuals and firms registered as lobbyists or foreign agents for interest groups. Representative and organizations represented listings show name, address, telephone numbers, registration date, and other background information. An organization index by subject of interest is included.

A third, very useful directory, not listed above, is the new *National Directory of Corporate Public Affairs* (Washington, DC: Columbia Books, 1985). It lists by corporations those officers and offices responsible for issue identification, lobbying activity, and other political action. Dollar amounts of PAC donations and contribution priorities are also included.

993   Weinberger, Marvin, and David U. Greevy. *The PAC Directory.* Cambridge, MA: Ballinger Publishing Company, 1982.

Political Action Committees (PACs) are an organizational device through which political parties, individuals, and business enterprises can raise and spend money to influence federal elections. *The PAC Directory* provides the following information under seven sections:

Section I: The Committees—Party & Non-Party PAC Contributions. Receipts and financial contributions are summarized for each of over 1,500 party and nonparty committees. Details are given of what candidates received $1,500 or more.
Section II: The PAC Directory. Names, addresses, contact people, phone numbers, sponsoring organization, etc., are given.
Section III: The Corporate PAC's. Lists all corporate PACs under standard industrial classification (SIC) numbers and identifies sponsors.
Section IV: PAC Independent Expenditure Support/Opposition. Amount of money spent for or against each candidate is given.
Section V: Selected Primary & General Election Candidates—Party and Non-Party Support. Lists by state the party and nonparty support given each candidate.
Section VI: Ratings of the Incumbents—95th & 96th Congress. Identifies by state and district the ratings given by 26 groups to all incumbents.
Section VII: Top Ranked Contributors and Recipients. Ranking of the top 200 PACs by amount of contribution, and ranking of the top Senate and House candidates by amount of contributions received.

Congressional Information

The following pages contain listings and descriptions of official and unofficial reference services that report and record action in the United States Congress. In view of the magnitude and diversity of congressional activities, no single reference instrument exists that offers access to all information produced by or about the legislative branch of the United States government. Which combination among the various existing reference instruments may have to be employed will, of course, depend on the problem to be studied. To assist the user, the available reference instruments are listed under the following categories of information:

1. Guidebooks
2. General Congressional Bibliographies
3. Debates and Proceedings
4. Bills and Resolutions
5. Reports and Documents
6. Committee Prints
7. Hearings
8. Unofficial Reporting and Reviewing Services
9. Other Legislative Branch Information

In several of these information categories there is overlapping coverage by two or more reference instruments. Wherever necessary one or the other reference instrument has been listed repetitively to demonstrate multiple coverage by competitive reference sources. The details of the retrieval mechanism provided by the various instruments will be found in the annotations of the listed titles.

GUIDEBOOKS

994   *Congressional Quarterly's Guide to Congress.* Washington, DC: Congressional Quarterly, Inc., 1982.

The guidebook explains in one volume how Congress developed and how it works today. Information is organized under numerous subheadings of the following seven parts: (1) Origins and Development of Congress, (2) Powers of Congress, (3) Congressional Procedures, (4) Housing and Support of Congress, (5) Congress and the Electorate, (6) Pressures on Congress, and (7) Qualifications and Conduct of Members. All sections include bibliographies for additional information. Several appendices provide a biographical index of Congress from 1789–1982, the text of the Budget Act of 1974, the U.S. Constitution and documents of the preconstitutional period, as well as congressional statistics, congressional rules, a glossary of congressional terms, information on unconstitutional acts and lobbying laws. A general subject and name index is also included. Revised editions of this guidebook are planned.

995   Congressional Quarterly, Inc. *Powers of Congress.* Washington, DC: Congressional Quarterly, Inc., 1976.

A detailed examination of the constitutional origins, the evolution, and current status of the major powers of Congress is presented by this guidebook. Information on the congressional powers is arranged under eight chapters, namely, (1) Fiscal Powers, (2) Foreign Affairs, (3) Commerce Power, (4) Impeachment Power, (5) Power of Investigation, (6) Confirmation Power, (7) Amending Power, and (8) Electoral Power. A bibliography of informative publications relating to each of these powers is presented at the end of each chapter.

996   Goehlert, Robert U., and John R. Sayre. *The United States Congress: A Bibliography.* New York: Free Press, 1982.

This exhaustive bibliography lists 5,620 English-language publications issued about the United States Congress during the past 200 years. Listings include books, periodical articles, dissertations, master's theses, and U.S. government publications. Entries are arranged under 14 topical areas, including the history and development of Congress, the congressional process, congressional reform, powers of Congress, committee structure, legislative analysis, pressures on Congress, and others. Subject and author indexes, as well as a detailed table of contents facilitate access to the listed material.

997   Goehlert, Robert. *Legislative Tracing and the Congress.* A *Bibliographical Guide to Research.* Santa Barbara, CA: American Bibliographical Center—Clio Press, 1980.

This guidebook is designed to help users trace congressional legislation and to familiarize them with the major sources of information about Congress. Apart from a general description of the legislative process the guidebook explains legislative tracing procedures and the congressional publications available for them. Separate bibliographic listings are provided for research on legislators, campaign finances, party strength, election results, and similar Congress-related topics. Personal name and title indexes are also included.

998   Zinn, Charles. *How Our Laws Are Made.* Washington, DC: U.S. Government Printing Office, 1978.

A revised and updated edition of this standard guidebook has recently become available to show the intricate process by which a bill becomes law or dies.

999   Zwirn, Jerrold. *Congressional Publications:* A *Research Guide to Legislation, Budgets, and Treaties.* Littleton, CO: Libraries Unlimited, 1983.

The guidebook offers a detailed description of the printed information sources that the United States Congress uses and creates in the pursuit of its legislative, research, and oversight processes. Organized in 11 chapters, the guidebook traces the purpose of each facet in the congressional processes, explains the procedures followed, and describes the nature and characteristics of the various publications issued. Specifically covered are hearings, committee reports, debates, voting, bills, resolutions, the federal budget, and U.S. treaties. A bibliography of related additional publications is found in each chapter. An appendix identifies all standing committees of Congress from 1789 to 1981. The guidebook is indexed by subject, type, and title of the listed congressional publications.

GENERAL CONGRESSIONAL BIBLIOGRAPHIES

1000   *CIS Index*. Washington, DC: Congressional Information Service, 1970–. (Vendor: Dialog—File 101; SDC)

Much of the fundamental work of Congress is performed by about 300 active committees and subcommittees. These committees hear expert testimony and gather facts to initiate or evaluate legislation and to oversee government operations. The committee findings are published in the following publications: House and Senate reports, House and Senate documents, committee prints, committee hearings, House and Senate special publications, Senate executive reports, and Senate executive documents. These publications total more than 700,000 pages annually. It is obvious that access to such massive amounts of information is best accomplished by computerized information retrieval.

Available by contract with the vendors listed above, the *CIS Index* database permits online identification of congressional information and documentation by one or more of 18 approaches. Online identification of documentation, as listed above, or online searches for abstracted information from the documentation can be made by title, bill number (if a bill has been the subject of a hearing, report, or other publication), report or document number, name of committee, subcommittee, or chairperson, name of witnesses or their affiliations, subject, keywords in the abstracts, congressional session, entry year, or SuDoc number. Any combination of these names, numbers, or words will suffice for a search command.

A printed version of this reference source is published monthly with annual and quinquennial cumulations. The printed *CIS Index* is issued in two sections, namely, an index and an abstracts part. For details of the coverage offered by the printed index and a better understanding of the retrieval capability of the online version, see the entries on the following pages.

1001   *Congress in Print*. Washington, DC: Congressional Quarterly, Inc., 1977–.

Published weekly when Congress is in session and monthly during long recesses, this reference source identifies all publications released by congressional committees. Included in the listings are hearings, prints, reports, calendars, and public laws. Separate listings are provided for the publications of the General Accounting Office and the Congressional Budget Office.

1002   *Library of Congress Information System (LOCIS)*. Washington, DC: Library of Congress, 1968–. (Vendor: none)

Accessible only from computer terminals located in congressional offices and in the reading rooms and the Computer Catalog Center of the Library of Congress, the *Library of Congress Information System (LOCIS)* offers automated retrieval of bibliographic citations and factual information according to file content. *LOCIS* presently consists of two major portions, namely,

I. MUMS (Multiple Use MARC System), and
II. SCORPIO (Subject-Content-Oriented Retrieval for Processing Information Online),

each of which contains several files, as follows:

I. MUMS Files
   a. Book File: Fully cataloged books in English since 1968, foreign-language books since mid-1970s, and books being processed. Access to bibliographic citations only, by author names, titles, LC subject headings, series, notes, often also by ISBN. Updated daily.
   b. Serials File: Periodicals, newspapers, and other serials fully cataloged since 1973, regardless of date of publication, but not specific articles in them. Access to bibliographic citations only, by corporate author, publication title, LC subject headings, notes, LC card number, often also by ISSN. Updated quarterly.
   c. Maps Files: maps fully cataloged since 1968, regardless of date of publication. Access to bibliographic citations only, by title, LC subject heading, series, notes, producer name. Updated quarterly.
II. SCORPIO Files
   a. Legislative Information Files (CG): Updated daily, this file is the computerized version of the printed *Digest of Public General Bills and Resolutions* (Washington, DC: U.S. Government Printing Office, 1936–), but with coverage from the 93rd Congress to the present only. Retrievable is an abstract and a lengthier digest for each bill, its date of introduction, sponsor and cosponsor, committee of referral, and current status. Access is by bill number, public law number (if applicable), subject, bill name, sponsor's name, committee of referral. The subject headings are called LIVT (Legislative Indexing Vocabulary Terms) and are available online and in printed volumes.
   b. Major Issues Files (ISSU): Updated daily, these files contain information on public policy issues authored by CRS specialists. Information retrieval consists of five parts:

1. a short, one-sentence definition of the issue
2. the background and analysis of the issue, including the context in which it developed, reasons for its emergence, and basic policy questions involved in any projected resolutions
3. the current congressional action affecting the issue: major pending legislation, associated reports, and relevant committee documents
4. a series of significant events providing insights into the present state of the issue
5. a listing of additional sources of information of academic, lobbyist, federal, state or local government origin

Access to these files is by LIVT, but restricted to authorized users.

c. Bibliographic Citation File (BIBL): Bibliographic citations are provided for congressional committee prints accessible by author and subject dating back to 1915, congressional documents accessible by issuing committee and subject dating back to 1935, and major serial publications, including articles in general and academic periodicals, U.S. GPO publications, UN publications, and material from 1,500 lobbying groups, accessible by author and subject for the three most recent years.

d. Citation File (CITN): Restricted to authorized users, this file contains bibliographic citations to reports and memoranda produced by the Congressional Research Service during the three most recent years. Access is provided by legislative indexing vocabulary terms.

e. National Referral Center Master File (NRCM): This file is a directory of some 13,000 organizations that are able and willing to provide scientific and technical information. Information in this directory is accessible by subject, organization name, and geographic location. It includes the name, address, telephone number of the organization, a description of its mission and area of interest, publications, and available services.

f. Congressional Record File (CR): Restricted to authorized users, this file offers the full text of abstracts from the *Congressional Record* from the 94th Congress to the present. Data are provided by Capitol Services, Inc., which makes a separate printed and computerized version available to the general public.

g. General Accounting Office Files (GAOE, GAOR, GAOS): These files are the computerized version of the printed *Federal Program Evaluations*, *Requirements for Recurring Reports to the Congress*, and the *Federal Information Sources and Systems*.

h. Latin American Legislation File (LAWL): Restricted to authorized users, this file contains abstracts of and citations to legislation of 22 Central and Latin American countries. Access is provided by name, subject, and title.

Although there has been some discussion about the possibility of making all SCORPIO files more widely available, the retrieval capability of this important reference system has so far not become fully accessible to researchers outside of Congress or the Washington, DC, area. Nevertheless, commercial vendors like the Dialog Information Retrieval Service, the Systems Development Corporation, and the Congressional Information Service are offering automated Retrieval for a wide variety of documentation produced or used by Congress, as the following pages of this guidebook demonstrate.

DEBATES AND PROCEEDINGS

The details of congressional proceedings and the texts of the debates and speeches in Congress have been reported in a variety of official and unofficial publications since 1789. Their titles and current or retrospective publishing dates follow:

1003   *The Congressional Record Scanner.* Washington, DC: Congressional Quarterly, Inc., 1973–.

This reference publication, issued daily, identifies the political process information contained in each day's *Congressional Record*, more fully described in a separate entry below. It lists all action taken by Congress in the following categories:

- legislation introduced
- legislation acted upon
- reports filed
- executive communications received
- treaties and nominations
- speeches and inserts
- procedural matters
- public laws approval

These categories are shown separately for the House and Senate, and contain entries for quick identification of the process information by subject or name together with page citations to the *Congressional Record*.

1004   *CSI Congressional Record Abstracts.* Washington, DC: Capitol Services International, 1976–.

1005   *Congressional Record Abstracts (Crecord).* Washington, DC: Capitol Services International, 1976–. (Vendor: Dialog—File 135; SDC).

Apart from the activities of congressional committees that are covered by the *CIS/Index*, Congress produces information on the floor of the House and Senate in the form of speeches, statements, motions, and other proceedings. This information is published in the *Congres-*

sional Record, which contains more than 50,000 pages each year. Access to this information is provided by the *Congressional Record*'s own indexes in printed form as well as by the reference works cited above. Available in printed and electronic versions, this reference tool identifies and summarizes congressional floor action as reported and inserted in the *Congressional Record*. The printed edition is organized by topics and subtopics, and issued daily. References and abstracts in the electronic database are updated weekly, and are retrievable by date, page number, bill number, subject term, and names of congressmen.

1006   U.S. Congress. *Debates and Proceedings in the Congress of the United States*. 1st–18th Congress, 3 March 1789–27 May 1824. Washington, DC: Gales and Seaton, 1834–1856.

1007   ———. *Register of Debates in Congress*. 18th–25th Congress, 6 December 1824–16 October 1837. Washington, DC: Gales and Seaton, 1825–1837.

1008   ———. *The Congressional Globe*. 23rd Congress–42nd Congress, 2 December 1833–3 March 1873. Washington, DC: The Globe.

1009   ———. *Congressional Record: Proceedings and Debates of the Congress*. 43rd Congress–, 1873–. Washington, DC: U.S. Government Printing Office.

1010   ———. *Daily Digest*. 80th Congress–, 1947–. Washington, DC: U.S. Government Printing Office.

1011   ———. *Proceedings of the United States Congress 1789–1970*. Washington, DC: U.S. Historical Documents Institute, 1971–.

The current source for debates and proceedings is the *Congressional Record*. It consists of four sections: (1) the Proceedings of the Senate, (2) the Proceedings of the House of Representatives, (3) the Extension of Remarks, and (4) the Daily Digest. Debates are printed in the Proceedings sections, but material such as excerpts from periodical and newspaper articles that a congressman wishes to have inserted in the *Congressional Record* is printed in the Extension of Remarks section. A resume of committee activities is found in the *Daily Digest*. The *Congressional Record* is not a complete record of all congressional activities since the texts of bills and resolutions introduced are not usually reported nor all details of proceedings included. These procedural details may be found in the journals of the two houses.

There are three editions of the *Congressional Record*, namely, a daily, biweekly, and permanent bound edition. These editions are not cumulative and completely identical since there are variations in the text as well as differences in the pagination.

Three separate printed indexes exist, namely, the index to the *Daily Digest*, a biweekly index, and the index to the permanent bound edition. The latter index appears with some delay, so that for several months during the current session of Congress information retrieval from the permanently bound volumes remains burdensome. The indexes in both the biweekly and permanent bound editions are made up of two parts: (1) the index to the Proceedings and Extension of Remarks sections of the *Congressional Record* arranged by subject or name, and (2) the History of Bills and Resolutions. Broad headings are used for subject indexing, making it difficult to identify the finer points in congressional debates. The Bills and Resolutions index is arranged by bill or resolution number but listed until recently only bills that have been reported out of committee or have progressed beyond that stage.

Prior to the publication of the *Congressional Record*, debates and proceedings were printed in three publications that are now available on microfilm. A new and combined set of all publications series has been published under the title *Proceedings of the United States Congress 1789–1970*. The set consists of 572 rolls of microfilm and 110 casebound reprint volumes containing the indexes to all 226 regular and special sessions, and histories of bills and resolutions.

1012   U.S. Congress. *House Journal*. Washington, DC: U.S. Government Printing Office, 1789–.

The *House Journal* is not available until the end of the congressional session and is issued in chronological order in one final volume for the entire proceedings in the House of Representatives. It contains information on all motions and actions taken in the House, as well as on the votes on roll calls but no debates and speeches. Two separate indexes are included: (1) History of Bills and Resolutions, arranged by number, and (2) an index by name and subject.

1013   U.S. Congress. *Senate Journal*. Washington, DC: U.S. Government Printing Office, 1789–.

Similar to the *House Journal*, this publication reports in chronological sequence all procedural matters in the Senate. There are two indexes, namely, (1) History of Bills and Resolutions, and (2) a name and subject index. The legislative history index lists all Senate bills and resolutions in numerical order, indicates the title of the bill, the action taken, and page citations to the appropriate entry. The *Senate Journal* also contains a list of Senate documents from which the injunction of secrecy was removed during the current session.

Senate action in closed sessions is reported in the *Journal of Executive Proceedings of the Senate*, which is printed in limited copies and restricted for official use only. Recorded in this journal are all motions that the president must refer to the Senate for approval, such as nominations to federal office or treaty proposals, etc. The journal is made public after the injunction of secrecy has been removed.

1014   *The Weekly Congressional Monitor.* Washington, DC: Congressional Quarterly, Inc., 1972– .

Published at the end of each week when Congress is in session, this reference source identifies present and future activities of congressional committees. Arranged by name of committee, the entries provide information on the date and place of scheduled meetings or hearings, their agenda, and scheduled witnesses. Separate chronological listings of scheduled floor action are also provided.

BILLS AND RESOLUTIONS

In each session of Congress many thousands of bills and resolutions are introduced. Only a tiny fraction of the number of bills introduced becomes law, however. Depository libraries throughout the United States maintain a set of printed bills and resolutions for the current session of Congress, but only a few major law libraries keep a collection of bills and resolutions for longer periods. In recent years microform copies of all bills and resolutions have become available from commercial publishers, thus making physical access to bills and resolutions less of a problem.

Intellectual access to bills and resolutions usually requires that bills and resolutions are identifiable by number, author or sponsor, subject matter, or status. The following reference works, listed in alphabetical sequence, will be useful for solving these and other access problems.

1015   *CIS/Index.* Washington, DC: Congressional Information Service, 1970– .

A separate index of bill numbers published in the monthly, cumulative quarterly and annual issues of this reference instrument lists the numbers of all bills that have become the subject of hearings, reports, or other publications abstracted in other parts of the printed *CIS/ Index.* References are provided to the serial numbers under which the abstracts together with full bibliographic information are arranged. The bills themselves are not abstracted in this reference work. The full text of bills and resolutions is available from the publisher in microfiche copies.

1016   *CIS Legislative History Service.* Bethesda, MD: Congressional Information Service, 1981– .

Complete legislative history citations for every major public law enacted by the United States Congress since

1981 are available with this loose-leaf reference publication. For each law, full citations are provided to all versions of all pertinent bills, all reports, all debates, all hearings, all committee prints, all documents and other publications, including the slip law, from both current and previous Congresses, provided the publications are directly related to the enactment. In addition to these citations, a concise summary of the public law's provisions is given. The arrangement of the reference material is by public law number.

1017   *Congressional Index.* Chicago: Commerce Clearing House, 1937– .

1018   *Electronic Legislative Search System (ELSS).* Chicago: Commerce Clearing House, 1981– . (Vendor: General Electric Information Service Company)

All public bills and resolutions are listed, indexed, summarized, and have their progress reported in this reference work, available in weekly updated, printed loose-leaf format and in daily updated electronic format. The printed version indexes all pending measures by subject, author, headline terms, and number. A numerical listing of all Senate and House bills identifies all sponsors and the subject of the bill. The voting record of congressmen on each House and Senate bill is given. House and Senate status tables report action on each bill in a numerical arrangement. A separate list of enactments arranged in sequence of public law numbers identifies the bill number, title, approval date for all bills enacted into law. All enactments are also identifiable by bill number, subject, and author.

The *Congressional Index* can also be used to identify congressional action on nominations, reorganization plans, and treaties. Entries for nominations are arranged by date of submission under agency names and identify the names of the nominees. Conversely, listings by name of nominee identify the agency. Reorganization plans are listed in sequence of their numbers together with essential details of each plan. Treaties are listed in alphabetical order for each session of Congress, and dates of ratification or numbers of reports, if any, are indicated.

Daily information on the legislative activities of the United States Congress and the 50 states is provided online by the computerized database. The *Electronic Legislative Search System* displays descriptions of bills and resolutions, and identifies their sponsors, dates of introduction, committee referrals, actions, and dispositions.

1019   *Legi-Slate.* Washington, DC: Legi-Slate, Inc., 1979– . (Vendor: I. P. Sharp; Source Telecomputing Corporation)

This online database contains the title, number, sponsor, and introduction date of every bill and resolution introduced in Congress since 1979. It also contains a synopsis of every legislative item and data of all committee and subcommittee actions, House and Senate floor actions, and all votes taken. All announcements and regulations published in the *Federal Register* are also retrievable.

1020   MLC, *Major Legislation of the Congress*. Washington, DC: Congressional Research Service, 1979–.

The *MLC* is an automated by-product of the CRS Legislative Issues Database. Copies of each monthly edition contain a concise summary of major issues facing Congress with information on key legislation introduced in response to those issues. The material is arranged under broad subject headings, such as agriculture, budget, civil rights, community development, consumer affairs, crime and law enforcement, education, environment, fiscal affairs, foreign affairs, government, health, housing, immigration, labor, national defense, natural resources, space policy, trade, welfare and social services, etc. Title and legislation indexes are included, but no information is provided on the interest and lobbying groups concerned with the issues.

1021   *Presidential Vetoes: List of Bills Vetoed and Action Taken Thereon by the Senate and House of Representatives, 1st Congress through 86th Congress, 1789–1976*. Washington, DC: U.S. Government Printing Office, 1978.

All bills vetoed by United States presidents up to 1976 are listed in the reference publication. Listings are chronologically arranged by congressional sessions and presidential administrations in which the vetoes occurred. Entries are by bill number with document number and citation to the *Congressional Record* where the veto message may be found.

1022   U.S. Congress. *Calendars of the United States House of Representatives and History of Legislation*. Washington, DC: U.S. Government Printing Office, to date–.

This reference publication is issued five times weekly while Congress is in session. It contains separate tables for bills that are in or through conference, on the Union calendar, private or consent calendar. House and senate conferees, House and Senate report numbers, and dates of action are identified. There is also a numerically arranged list of House and Senate bills and resolutions that have passed either or both houses, or are pending on the calendar. Legislative action and dates are identified. A separate subject index to all legislation that has been reported by the committees and acted upon by either one or both houses is also included in the *Calendar* once a week.

1023   U.S. Library of Congress. Legislative Reference Service. *Digest of Public General Bills and Selected Reso-*

lutions with Index. 74th Congress–, 1936–. Washington, DC: U.S. Government Printing Office.

The digest is published for each session of Congress in five or more cumulative issues, biweekly supplements whenever needed, and a final edition at the end of the session. Each cumulative and final issue is divided into five sections that offer (1) the status of bills and resolutions acted upon, (2) a numerical list of all enactments, (3) a separate digest of all public bills, joint resolutions, concurrent resolutions, and simple resolutions introduced in the Senate or House, (4) an author (sponsor) index to all measures introduced, and (5) a subject matter index.

REPORTS AND DOCUMENTS

House and Senate committees prepare detailed analyses of bills and analytical summaries of political issues to be handled by new legislation or revised federal agency procedures and policies. These are published as reports. Other congressional papers not necessarily related to legislation and covering a variety of topics are issued as documents. They may contain the text of committee-sponsored special studies or background information compilations. Frequently these documents record the text of presidential messages or communications from the executive departments and agencies. Another class of congressional publications is known as executive reports and executive documents. A Senate executive document relates to treaties and conventions and generally contains the text of the president's recommendation for ratification of the treaty and the text of the agreement itself. A Senate executive report is issued for committee recommendations regarding the ratification of a treaty or Senate confirmation of a presidential nomination.

The following reference instruments, listed in cohesive or alphabetical sequence, will be useful for identifying or locating congressional reports and documents.

1024   *CIS/Index*. Washington, DC: Congressional Information Service, 1970–.

All congressional reports and documents, except those concerning private bills, are abstracted and bibliographically described in this monthly and annual reference publication. Abstracts are arranged by title in the appropriate form category (reports, documents, executive reports, executive documents) under the name of the congressional committee. Indexing is provided monthly, quarterly, and annually by title, by subject, names of authors and committees, as well as numerically by report and document numbers. Microfiche copies of the full text of all listed publications are available from the publisher upon request.

1025   *CIS/U.S. Serial Set Index*. Washington, DC: Congressional Information Service, 1975.

1026   CIS/U.S. Serial Set on Microfiche. Washington, DC: Congressional Information Service, 1975.

1027   U.S. Congress. Documents Serial Set. Washington, DC: U.S. Government Printing Office, 1813– .

1028   U.S. Superintendent of Documents. Numerical Lists and Schedule of Volumes of the Reports and Documents of the 73rd Congress 1933/34– . Washington, DC: U.S. Government Printing Office, 1934– .

The full text of all congressional reports and documents issued between 1789 and 1969 is available in a microprint collection entitled CIS/U.S. Serial Set on Microfiche. In order to locate an individual report or document within the massive collection, a separate multivolume index set published by the Congressional Information Service must be used. The index provides access to the congressional papers by subject terms taken from the actual titles of the publications included in the serial set, by names of persons or organizations cited in publication titles as recipients of proposed relief or related actions, by numerical listings of reports and documents for each congressional session, and by numerical schedules of serial volumes.

A permanently bound collection of the congressional reports and documents in original print, entitled Documents Serial Set, was begun in 1813 and continues to date as the current source for these congressional publications. The set does not have continuous pagination and uses different numbering schemes for the report and document publications series within the various congressional sessions and the individual volumes of the serial set itself. For these reasons a separate locator tool, the Numerical Lists, must be used to determine the appropriate volume and serial number of the Documents Serial Set. For each session of Congress since the 73rd Congress separate numerical lists are made available for Senate reports, House reports, Senate documents, and House documents. The entries in the Numerical Lists are arranged in numerical sequence of the report and document numbers and contain the title of the listed publication together with a citation to the volume and serial number of the Documents Serial Set where the text of the report or document may be found.

1029   U.S. Congress. Congressional Record. Daily Digest. Washington, DC: U.S. Government Printing Office, 1947– .

This reference source may be used in legislative history research to identify the existence and the number of a House or Senate report issued for enacted legislation. The bound volumes of the Daily Digest contain a table entitled "History of Bills Enacted into Public Law" for the preceding session of Congress. For each bill enacted into public law, the House and Senate report numbers are listed in numerical sequence of public law numbers. Possession of the report number enables the researcher to use the previously listed reference instruments for locating the desired congressional reports.

1030   U.S. Superintendent of Documents. Monthly Catalog of United States Government Publications. Washington, DC: U.S. Government Printing Office, 1895– .

Before congressional reports and documents become available in the permanently bound Documents Serial Set, they are initially issued in pamphlet or unbound form. The Monthly Catalog offers separate listings for House and Senate reports and documents under the heading Congress. Full bibliographic information, including the report and document number, is given. The monthly and annual indexes of the Monthly Catalog provide access to the listed publications under broad subject terms and form headings, i.e., Senate reports, House reports, Senate documents, and House documents. No references are provided in the Monthly Catalog, however, to the physical position of the individual reports and documents in the permanently bound collection of the Documents Serial Set.

COMMITTEE PRINTS

Apart from legislative activities, congressional committees engage in fact-finding missions and other research activities. The results of these activities are frequently published as committee prints available in many instances as depository items in libraries. A large number of interesting committee prints, however, is issued for official use only and consequently not available to the public. Unlike reports and documents, the committee prints do not carry consecutive numbers and are identifiable by title in the following reference works.

1031   CIS/Index. Washington, DC: Congressional Information Service, 1970– .

Beginning in 1970 all committee prints, regardless of their designation as depository or official use items, are listed, indexed, and briefly abstracted in this reference work. Abstracts are arranged by title in the appropriate form category — prints — under the name of the congressional committee. Monthly, quarterly, and annual indexing is provided by title, subject, names of authors, and names of subcommittees. Microfiche copies of the publicly available committee prints are obtainable from the Congressional Information Service.

1032   CIS US Congressional Committee Prints Index.

Bethesda, MD: Congressional Information Service, 1980.

This index in five volumes predates the coverage of the current *CIS/Index* and offers multiple access to all committee prints published from the mid-1800s to 1969. The reference set consists of a Reference Bibliography and several indexes. The bibliography section presents full bibliographical data and lists assigned subject and author indexing terms for each committee print. An index by subject and names offers access by subject matter and names of individuals, organizations, bills, and public laws. Other indexes contain listings by title, by bill number, and by SuDoc number. All cited committee prints are available on microfiche from the publisher.

1033   U.S. Superintendent of Documents. *Monthly Catalog of United States Government Publications.* Washington, DC: U.S. Government Printing Office, 1895– .

Committee prints are listed by title under the name of the congressional committee. Entries contain full bibliographic information, including SuDoc numbers and symbols for availability or restriction to official use. The monthly and annual indexes in the *Monthly Catalog* provide numerical references to the entries under a limited number of subject terms or the name of the committee.

HEARINGS

Congressional committees considering specific pieces of legislation or investigating political issues hold public hearings for the purpose of gathering all pertinent information. The published hearings therefore offer the political researcher valuable texts of discussions and testimony by technical and academic experts, federal agency administrators, spokesmen for private interest groups, and other witnesses as well as statements or papers collected during the course of the committee's inquiry. Although not all hearings are immediately printed, libraries hold depository copies of the hearings or microform copies published by the Congressional Information Service or the Greenwood Publishing Corporation. The following finding aids will be useful for identifying copies of the published hearings.

1034   *Checklist of Congressional Hearings.* Washington, DC: Bernan Associates, 1958– .

Congressional hearings are listed by title in this bibliographic work, which is published in over 40 issues each year. Listings include complete bibliographic citation with concise explanation of the subject covered and the name of the congressional committee that held the hearings.

1035   *CIS US Congressional Committee Hearings Index, 1833–1969.* Bethesda, MD: Congressional Information Service, 1981–1985.

Predating the coverage of the *CIS/Index* this multivolume index in eight parts provides detailed, comprehensive access to more than 30,000 hearings published between the 1830s and 1969. The access mechanism comprises a number of individual indexes, a reference bibliography, and a document delivery service. Separate indexes contain entries for (1) subjects and organizations, (2) personal names, (3) bill numbers, (4) titles, and (5) Superintendent of Documents (SuDoc) numbers. Entries in the Reference Bibliography include the hearing's main title and subtitle, date of hearing, date of publication, Congress and session, SuDoc number, issuing committee and subcommittee, a listing of witness names and their affiliations, as well as brief annotations. All cited hearings are available on microfiche from the publisher.

1036   *CIS/Index.* Washington, DC: Congressional Information Service, 1970– .

All hearings published since 1970 are listed, indexed, and briefly abstracted in this reference work. Abstracts are arranged by title of the hearings under the name of the congressional committee. SuDoc numbers for the hearings are identified. The monthly, quarterly, and annual indexes of the reference set provide access to the listed hearings by subject of the hearings, subjects discussed by witnesses, names of witnesses, affiliations of witnesses, names of subcommittees holding or issuing the hearings, title of the hearings, bill numbers, and popular names of bills. Microfiche copies of the listed hearings are obtainable from the Congressional Information Service on request.

1037   Commerce Clearing House. *Congressional Index.* Chicago: Commerce Clearing House, 1947– .

The House and Senate Status Table section in this reference tool reports the availability of published hearings under the bill number. Hearings may also be identified under the name of standing committees in the sections "Senate Committee Hearings" and "House Committee Hearings." The subject matter of the hearings and the issuing date for the published hearings are identified. No SuDoc numbers are listed, however.

1038   U.S. Superintendent of Documents. *Monthly Catalog of United States Government Publications.* Washington DC: U.S. Government Printing Office, 1895– .

Published hearings are listed under Congress by the name of standing committee. Complete bibliographical information, including SuDoc numbers and availability symbols, is given. The monthly and annual indexes of the *Monthly Catalog* provide numerical references to each entry by subject or name of standing committee but not under the name of a subcommittee that may have held the hearings.

UNOFFICIAL REPORTING AND REVIEWING SERVICES

In addition to the previously listed official and unofficial reference sets for congressional documentation, there are several other unofficial publications that report, analyze, or review congressional activities. Some of these reference publications come closest to offering an issue-based information service to the academic researcher since a significant amount of information is devoted to public issues confronting the members of Congress. The following titles are considered the most useful publications in this category.

1039   *Budgettext*. Washington, DC: Data Resources, 1980– .

1040   *Budgetrack*. Washington, DC: Data Resources, 1980– . (Vendor: Data Resources)

As a result of international political and technological developments, the allocation of economic resources for defensive purposes is always of critical concern in the federal budgetary and political communication process. This digest, available in printed and computerized format, provides a current focus on the defense program elements in the United States budget. It allows an examination of the research, development, and procurement data in the defense and NASA portions of each year's federal budget from its inception as a presidential request until it becomes law. Source documents utilized include all appropriate governmental documents, as well as articles in *Aviation Week and Space Technology*.

The printed version is published three times during the budget cycle and offers data within specific defense categories. The computerized database offers full text retrieval of up to 3,000 defense program elements.

1041   *CIS Highlights*. Washington, DC: Congressional Information Service, 1970– .

A monthly bibliography that lists and briefly describes congressional publications issued during the previous month and considered to be of special reference, research, or news value. Entries are arranged under broad subject headings.

1042   *Congress and the Nation 1945 – 1964*. Washington, DC: Congressional Quarterly Service, 1965.

1043   *Congress and the Nation 1965 – 1968*. Washington, DC: Congressional Quarterly Service, 1969.

1044   *Congress and the Nation 1968 – 1972*. Washington, DC: Congressional Quarterly Service, 1973.

1045   *Congress and the Nation 1972 – 1976*. Washington, DC: Congressional Quarterly Service, 1977.

1046   *Congress and the Nation 1977 – 1980*. Washington, DC: Congressional Quarterly Service, 1981.

Most of the important national issues, policies, and political developments in United States governmental affairs since 1945 are summarized in these reference works that offer both detail and perspective in their descriptions. Separate chapters are devoted to foreign policy; national security; economic policy (including tax policy and financial regulations); commerce and transportation; agricultural policy; labor and manpower; housing and urban affairs; energy policy; environmental policy; health, education, and welfare; law and justice, as well as general government, congressional and presidential affairs. The excellent organization of the information material, the detailed table of contents, and careful indexing offer a chronology of and quick access to all reported facts. Supplementary volumes are published every four years.

1047   *Congressional Digest*. Washington, DC: Congressional Digest Corporation, 1921– .

The most significant political issues facing Congress are the results of powerful arguments advanced for or against congressional approval. This commercially published monthly periodical, which should not be confused with the *Daily Digest* or the *Congressional Record*, provides a detailed summary of the pro and con arguments in a current political controversy. During recent years the *Congressional Digest* dealt with such hotly debated political objects as the nuclear proliferation treaty, the military draft system, foreign military commitments of the United States, future U.S space exploration programs, major election campaign reform, etc. Only one controversy is covered in each monthly issue of the periodical. There is an annual index in the December issue, but the contents of this valuable reference source are also subject indexed in the *Reader's Guide* and the *Public Affairs Information Service Bulletin*.

1048   *Congressional Quarterly Almanac*. Washington, DC: Congressional Quarterly Service, 1945– .

The annually published reference volume offers a review of the latest congressional session, a description of major legislation enacted, in addition to special reports, voting studies, surveys of lobbying activities, information on House and Senate roll call votes, analyses of Supreme Court decisions, etc.

1049   *CQ Weekly Report*. Washington, DC: Congressional Quarterly Service, 1946– .

1050   *CQ Weekly Report*. Washington, DC: Congressional Quarterly Service, 1975 – . (Vendor: Mead Data Central)

Available in printed and electronic formats, this unofficial weekly news magazine provides concise and current information about the activities on the floor as well as in the committees of Congress. Voting records are presented for all major pieces of legislation. Since the 86th Congress voting records of each Congressman are also analyzed in two intervals on the basis of the preferred position of four major pressure groups, including the ACA (Americans for Constitutional Action) and ADA (Americans for Democratic Action). In addition, considerable information on lobbying activities as well as biographical and political background material is presented. A quarterly index printed on yellow paper contains name and subject entries by which currently debated political objects and other congressional activities can be identified.

The machine-readable version of the *CQ Weekly Report* is part of the *NEXIS* database permitting full text retrieval as well as KWIC, full text, and list-of-references searches and printouts.

1051   *National Journal*. Washington, DC: Government Research Corporation, 1969 – .

1052   *Public Policy 1980 – *. Washington, DC: Government Research Corporation, 1980 – .

The Government Research Corporation is a company whose staff of correspondents and research analysts specializes in information-gathering and analysis service to individual clients and the general public and matters of the American political process and public policy. Published weekly, except for the last week in August and December, the *National Journal* contains digests of recent developments and public issues in the areas of budget, business, defense, domestic and international economy, employment, energy, environment, financial institutions, foreign policy, health, housing, income security, legal and regulatory affairs, taxation, transportation, and other political objects. Weekly, nineweekly, and annual cumulative indexing is provided for all articles.

Issued in January each year, *Public Policy* offers two-page summaries distilling the background, status, and outlook for federal government action in each of 50 public policy areas. Each summary reflects expert advice and analysis of the underlying societal problems and the prospects of their resolution.

1053   *United States Code Congressional and Administrative News*. Saint Paul, MN: West Publishing Company, 1942 – .

Issued semimonthly during sessions of Congress and monthly when Congress is not in session, this news magazine provides a legislative history of most public laws with excerpts of committee reports on bills. It also furnishes the highlights of pending legislation and tables of major bills pending. Verbatim texts of presidential messages, proclamations, executive orders are also published. Each issue is cumulatively indexed.

1054   *The Washington Monthly*. Washington, DC: Washington Monthly Company, 1969 – .

Delayed or insufficient responses of Congress and other branches of the United States government to critical national problems are the subject of fact-finding analyses published by this monthly magazine. It also identifies political processes that need changing or additional support for increased effectiveness.

OTHER LEGISLATIVE BRANCH INFORMATION

1055   Deschler, Lewis. *Deschler's Precedents of the United States House of Representatives*. Washington, DC: U.S. Government Printing Office, 1981.

1056   Riddick, Floyd. *Senate Procedure: Precedents and Practices*. Washington, DC: U.S. Government Printing Office, 1981.

The relatively stable government that has prevailed in the United States for more than 200 years is to a considerable degree attributable to the strikingly effective parliamentary system developed by generations of legislators. These two reference works set forth and analyze the modern precedents and parliamentary practices in the House of Representatives and the Senate. The information is organized by chapters, each of which contains its own index to precedents. Numerous footnotes provide references to earlier compilations of precedents or other legal authority.

1057   *GAO Documents. Catalog of Reports, Decisions, and Opinions, Testimonies and Speeches*. Washington, DC: General Accounting Office, 1975 – .

The General Accounting Office (GAO), an agency of the legislative branch of the United States government, has the responsibility to investigate the financial operations of each agency in the executive branch for the purpose of determining whether national needs served by federal programs have been economically and efficiently fulfilled. Results of the investigations are made available in audit reports, staff studies, and other publications.

Issued monthly, *GAO Documents* indexes and abstracts all GAO publications. It is organized in two sections, containing bibliographic citations and detailed indexes. The citations section offers up to 15 items of information, including the name of the agency, accession number, title/subtitle, author, publisher, document number, date of publication, volume/pagination, sponsoring agency, program evaluated, budget function, program authorization, public availability, and an abstract of the document. The index section consists of eight different indexes, namely, a subject index, agency index, personal name index, budget function index, GAO issue areas index, congressional index, law/authority index, and document number index. Entries in the law/authority index are arranged under the legal reference source, such as the *Code of Federal Regulations, Federal Register, U.S. Code, U.S. Statutes at Large,* etc. All publications listed in *GAO Documents* are obtainable in paper or microfiche copies from the GAO Information Handling and Support Facility, Box 6015, Gaithersburg, MD 20877.

1058   *Immigration: Special Studies, 1969–1982.* Frederick, MD: University Publications of America, 1983.

1059   *Papers of the Select Commission on Immigration and Refugee Policy.* Part I, *Meetings, Consultations, Legal Materials, Selected Subject Files, and Staff Report with Appendices;* Part II, *Records of Regional Hearings.* Frederick, MD: University Publications of America, 1983.

Foremost in the documentation of U.S. immigration policy and problems are the *Papers of the Select Commission on Immigration and Refugee Policy,* prepared by a special commission created by Congress to reevaluate national immigration laws and policies in the light of large-scale population migration around the globe. The commission's papers, consisting of various subject files, records of meetings, consultations, and hearings, and a staff report together with appendices of research papers, provide detailed analyses, comments, and recommendations about present and future U.S. immigration policies and their implementation. Specific immigration problems, such as illegal or undocumented aliens, immigrant health conditions, immigrant crime, protection of the U.S. labor force, resettlement, language and education difficulties, employment and integration obstacles, bilingual education, political asylum, and many others are well covered.

Apart from the commission's papers, the special studies collection offers valuable research material prepared by prestigious organizations under contract with governmental agencies. These studies aim to assess the impact of specific laws and government policies on the resident and immigrant population.

Both collections are available on microfilm only and contain printed guides.

1060   *Major Studies of the Legislative Reference Service/Congressional Research Service: 1916–1974.*

————. *Supplement,* 1975–.

Frederick, MD: University Publications of America, 1975–.

1061   *CRS Studies in the Public Domain.* Washington, DC: U.S. Government Printing Office, 1982–.

The Congressional Research Service (CRS) is that department of the Library of Congress responsible for preparing special studies and reports relating to key legal, political, social, or international issues facing the United States Congress. Many of these studies are published by authority of Congress and are listed as depository items in the *Monthly Catalog of United States Government Publications.* Hundreds of significant studies are, however, not published by the U.S. Government Printing Office. The first title listed above refers to a commercially published microfilm collection that contains the text of all major studies prepared by the CRS since 1916. Access to the microfilmed studies is facilitated by printed guides containing title/author and subject entries. References are keyed to the microfilm by frame numbers. The collection is kept up to date with annual supplements.

GPO-issued studies are subject indexed in the *CRS Studies in the Public Domain.* Entries are arranged under broad headings, like economic affairs, education, foreign affairs, government and politics, immigration, international trade, law enforcement, national defense, and others. No SuDoc numbers are listed with the entries.

1062   Martis, Kenneth C. *The Historical Atlas of the United States Congressional Districts 1789–1983.* New York: Free Press, 1982.

The atlas is the first work to publish under one cover the maps of all congressional districts of the United States House of Representatives throughout American history. It also identifies all the representatives elected to Congress with their proper state and congressional district affiliations. The book is divided into three parts. Part 1, entitled Introduction, traces the history of congressional districting and discusses various aspects of geographical representation and their mapping. A bibliography of additional information sources is also included. Part 2 contains 97 national congressional district maps together with lists of the representatives. Part 3 provides the complete legal descriptions of every congressional district for every state from the 1st through the 97th Congress.

1063   Mason, Paul. *Manual of Legislative Procedure for Legislative and Other Governmental Bodies.* Sacramento, CA: Senate, California Legislature, 1979.

This manual was compiled to meet the need of all legislative and administrative bodies in the United States. The procedural rules are arranged in 10 parts, as follows: (1) parliamentary law and rules, (2) debate, (3) rules governing motions, (4) rules governing particular motions, (5) quorum, voting and elections, (6) legislative and administrative bodies, (7) conduct of business, (8) relations with the other house and with the executive, (9) sessions and meetings, and (10) investigations, public order, and apportionment. Numerous subdivisions by chapter and sections within the ten parts offer easy access to the appropriate rules. Separate tables of authorities and cases cited and a brief index are also included.

1064   National Transportation Policy Study Commission. *National Transportation Policies through the Year 2000*. Washington, DC: U.S. Government Printing Office, 1979.

The transportation needs and policies of the United States through the year 2000 were studied extensively by the National Transportation Policy Study Commission following a legislative mandate (PL 94-280, 90 Stat 448) in 1976. The final report of the commission, cited above, contains a detailed outline of current federal transportation policies and programs, comparative transportation policies in other countries, and major policy recommendations for the future, together with a description of present and future transportation needs and activities. Graphs, statistical tables, and an unannotated bibliography are also included.

1065   Ornstein, Norman J., Thomas E. Mann, Michael J. Malbin, and John F. Bibby. *Vital Statistics on Congress, 1982*. Washington, DC: American Enterprise Institute for Public Policy Research, 1982.

The compendium contains statistical tables for varying time frames up to 1981 on

1. Members of Congress (party strength, years of service, prior occupation, religious affiliation, blacks, women, etc.)
2. Elections (voter turnout, popular votes, seats changing party, incumbent's fate, ticket splitting, etc.)
3. Campaign Finance (expenditures, contributions, PAC data, etc.)
4. Committees (number, assignments, chairmanship, etc.)
5. Congressional Staff and Operating Expenses (size, mailing costs, allowances, etc.)
6. Activity (workload, ratio of bills passed to bills introduced, congressional mailings, etc.)
7. Budgeting (budgeted and actual revenues, uncontrollable federal outlays, supplementary appropriations, etc.)
8. Roll Call Voting (presidential victories, party unity, support for conservative coalition, etc.)

Several appendices offer data on individual members of Congress in 1980 and 1981.

1066   U.S. General Accounting Office. *Policy and Procedures Manual for Guidance of Federal Agencies*. Washington, DC: U.S. Government Printing Office, current.

Regulations and instructions of the Comptroller General relating to accounting principles, standards, and procedures to be observed by federal departments and agencies are published in this frequently revised manual. It also contains illustrative accounting procedures and methods for guidance purposes.

1067   U.S. General Accounting Office. *Requirements for Recurring Reports to the Congress*. Washington, DC: U.S. Government Printing Office, 1980.

Major sources of information about the objectives and activities pursued by federal agencies are the reports that agencies have to submit to Congress at annual or other recurring intervals. An inventory of the recurring reporting requirements is presented by this reference work. It provides details about the required reports, including the issuing agency, the public law requiring the report, and the congressional recipient. The listed information is made more accessible by separate agency, congressional law, budget function, and subject indexes.

1068   U.S. Library of Congress. Congressional Research Service. *A Congressional Handbook on U.S. Materials Import Dependency/Vulnerability*. Washington, DC: U.S. Government Printing Office, 1981.

The handbook brings together in one convenient compilation previously scattered items of information about the enormous dependency of the United States on foreign countries for the supply of fuels, metals, and other raw materials vital to the American economy. Written by qualified experts, the handbook presents a well-organized, objective analysis of the underlying issues, past policies, and future policy options together with statistical data on the production, importation, import reliance, stockpiling, and consumption of the strategically important minerals and fuels. While the principal import sources and trade routes are adequately identified in the handbook, consult also the serialized comparative and general reference sources, listed in this guidebook, for current information on the unstable, embattled, or hostile regimes in the supply and trade route areas that pose a threat to the continued importation by the United States of the needed raw materials.

Executive Branch Information

The various departments and agencies in the executive branch of the United States government produce prodigious quantities of information and documentation that is retrievable with the help of numerous reference

INFORMATION SOURCES OF POLITICAL SCIENCE

instruments compiled according to the following organizing principles:

1. *General bibliographies for U.S. government publications.* Considerable documentation material can be identified with the general bibliographies previously listed and described under items 867 to 903 in this guidebook.
2. *Legal reference sources.* Rules, regulations, and administrative decisions of executive branch agencies are retrievable with reference sources listed and described in the Public Law section of this guidebook, notably under items 1414–1443.
3. *Statistical reference sources.* The statistical information produced and disseminated by executive branch agencies is retrievable by agency name and subject term with reference instruments listed and described under the section Statistical Information in this guidebook.
4. *Foreign relations sources.* The documentation produced by the Department of State, the Department of Defense, and other agencies involved in the conduct of U.S. foreign relations is retrievable with the bibliographies and document collections listed and described in the International Relations sections of this guidebook.
5. *Other sources.* Some reference works for the documentation produced by executive branch agencies do not fit conveniently into the preceding four categories and are therefore listed and described below under three separate headings, namely: (1) Guidebooks, (2) Other Bibliographic Instruments, and (3) Document Collections.

GUIDEBOOKS

1069   O'Hara, Frederick J. *A Guide to Publications of the Executive Branch.* Ann Arbor, MI: Pierian Press, 1979.

This guidebook identifies and describes nearly 2,000 publications issued, frequently on a recurring basis, by 11 departments within the executive branch of the federal government. The annotated entries are arranged by issuing department and identify publications that (1) offer information on the purpose and activities of the agency, (2) contain listings of the agency's publications, (3) contain listings of other than agency publications, (4) offer information on career opportunities in the agency, (5) contain glossaries or other word listings, (6) contain statistical compilations, (7) contain histories other than agency histories, (8) contain directory information, (9) contain compilations of laws, regulations, or treaties, or (10) contain other useful information. A brief description of the agency's function and a list of the Superintendent of Documents (SuDoc) classification numbers relating to

each agency precede the listings. Four separate indexes, by agency, personal name, title, and subject, offer additional access to the listed material.

1070   U.S. Small Business Administration. *Catalog of Federal Paperwork Requirements.* Washington, DC: U.S. Government Printing Office, 1979.

This reference work is a first attempt to identify all business-related federal reports and record-keeping requirements that are mandated by law or required for benefits in the administrative process. The book is divided into six sections: (1) Reports and Recordkeeping Requirements by Industry Group, (2) Business-Related Federal Tax Forms, (3) Procurement Related Paperwork, (4) Compliance Related Paperwork (as a result of participation in a federally financed or assisted program), (5) International Business Related Paperwork (for imports, exports, investments, etc.), (6) Requirements Related to Applications for Federal Benefits. In each section information is presented on federal agency jurisdiction, report title, agency form number, frequency of requirement, authorization for the requirement, and other pertinent details.

1071   Weckesser, Timothy, Joseph R. Whaley, and Miriam Whaley. *Business Services and Information. A Guide to the Federal Government.* New York: John Wiley & Sons, 1978.

Federal government agencies assemble and disseminate information on a remarkably wide range of subjects relevant to the business world. Organized in four parts and ten chapters, this bibliographic guide identifies and describes the official publications and other information services for the following subject areas: (1) starting a business: opportunities, site selection, management, (2) money and financial management, (3) market research, marketing, government procurement, (4) business administration, (5) human resources management, (6) affirmative action, OSHA, product safety, (7) exporting, (8) energy and environment, (9) technical information and databases, and (10) minorities and the disadvantaged. An appendix lists the addresses and telephone numbers of the business-related agencies, and offers guidance for the usage of census data. A detailed index is included.

OTHER BIBLIOGRAPHIES

1072   *DOE Energy Data Base.* Oak Ridge, TN: U.S. Department of Energy, Technical Information Center, 1974– . (Vendor: BRS; Dialog — File 103; SDC)

1073   *Energy Abstracts for Policy Analysis.* Oak Ridge, TN: U.S. Department of Energy, Technical Information Center, 1975– .

1074   *Energy Research Abstracts*. Oak Ridge, TN:
U.S. Department of Energy, Technical Information Center, 1977—.

The Technical Information Center in Oak Ridge, Tennessee, has been the national center for scientific, technical, programmatic, socioeconomic, environmental, legislative/regulatory, and policy-related information for the Department of Energy (DOE) and its predecessor agencies since 1946. All energy-related information regardless of its source or format is bibliographically controlled by the computerized *Energy Data Base* and the two printed equivalents cited above.

Online access to bibliographic citations and abstracts for federal, state, and local government publications and reports, scientific publications in book, periodical, or other format, and journalistic publications in daily or weekly format can be obtained from the computerized *Energy Data Base* under a variety of approaches. The subject approach is facilitated by a printed thesaurus — *Energy Data Base Subject Thesaurus* — that identifies all energy-related keywords used for indexing.

All nontechnological or quasi-technological documentation irrespective of format or source is listed and abstracted in the monthly *Energy Abstracts for Policy Analysis* if it is of reference value for policy making and policy implementation. Entries are arranged by major subject category including economics and sociology, environment, commercialization, conservation, supply and demand, regulation, fossil fuels, synthetic fuels, and unconventional sources. Separate indexes by corporate and individual author, subject, and report number are included.

Energy Research Abstracts provides semimonthly abstracting and indexing coverage for all scientific and technical documentation in published and report format. *ERA* coverage of the nonreport literature is limited, however, to that generated by Department of Energy activity. The subject matter embraces all energy sources, supplies, safety and environmental topics and regulations. Cumulative indexes for this reference work are available on microfiche only.

1075   *Environmental Impact Statements (EIS)*. Arlington, VA: Information Resources Press, 1970—. (Vendor: BRS)

Required of federal agencies under the National Environmental Policy Act of 1969, the environmental impact statements identify positive and negative impacts of specific environmental programs relating to energy , defense, hazardous substances, land use, waste removal, or other objectives. The computerized database offers online retrieval of bibliographic citations to and abstracts of individual environmental impact statements.

DOCUMENT COLLECTIONS

1076   *Papers of the Federal Reserve System. Part 1. Legislation, Major Speeches and Essays, and Special Reports, 1913—1960. Part 2. Minutes of Meetings of the Federal Open Market Committee, 1923—1975*. Frederick, MD: University Publications of America, 1983.

1077   *The U.S. National Economy, 1916—1981: Unpublished Documentary Collections from the U.S. Department of the Treasury*. Frederick, MD: University Publications of America, 1983—1984.

Among all the functions of federal departments and agencies, none has greater political significance than the responsibility of the Federal Reserve System and the U.S. Department of the Treasury to shape and administer policies for the health of the American political economy. As the central bank of the United States, the Federal Reserve System is responsible for monetary policy, while the Department of the Treasury formulates and administers economic, financial and fiscal policies. Despite (or because of) the preeminent position of these agencies in monetary and economic matters, reference control of the documentary output in this important area of the federal administrative/executive process and policy has been poor until the publication of the documentary collections cited above.

Part 1 of the *Papers of the Federal Reserve System* contains documents from the legislative process pertaining to the evolution of the Fed's power, as well as speeches, essays, and reports by members of the Board of Governors and high-level staff of the Federal Reserve System relating to the various financial developments and crises with which this institution was confronted. Part 2 offers documents of the 12-member Federal Open Market Committee (FOMC) that determines the policy concerning the purchase and sale of governmental securities for the purpose of expanding or contracting the supply of money. The minutes of the FOMC reveal the frank discussions of this body about the basic assumptions, fiscal realities, and political pressures stemming from a specific situation of socioeconomic factors.

The document collections of the Treasury Department provide the text of press conferences, speeches, internal reports, policy memoranda, and other papers produced mainly in response to specific economic challenges, such as depression, recession, recovery, unemployment, inflation, trade deficits, national debt, or monetary devaluation that occurred in a seemingly endless progression of cycles during this century. The documentation provides not only valuable insights into the scope, success, or failure of the Treasury's policies but also shows how the financial load of the national economy was distributed during each presidential administration.

All document collections are available on microfilm

only but are accompanied by printed guides that offer chronological and topical access to the information material in the collection. More recent documentation will be published and referenced as it becomes available.

Judiciary Information

The United States judicial system, the source of official legal documentation, is the object of a considerable scholarly literature. The reference instruments covering official legal documentation are described under Public Law. This section deals with the bibliographic tools used to identify information about the United States Supreme Court and other units of the federal and state judicial system, its justices and judges.

During the past 20 years or more a significant number of political scientists and scholars from other disciplines have treated the United States Supreme Court and the federal and state judiciary as political units rather than as legal bodies. They visualize the courts as the prime means of authoritatively allocating values in the resolution of political conflicts and problems. The literature produced by these scholars therefore focuses on the concepts of political jurisprudence and judicial behavior as distinct from the purely legal evaluation of the opinions delivered by the courts.

The following reference works may be used as a source of biographical information as well as a starting point to identify political studies on judicial decision making, particularly those studies that analyze the attitudes and social background of the justices and judges.

GUIDEBOOKS

1078   Congressional Quarterly, Inc. *Congressional Quarterly's Guide to the U.S. Supreme Court*. Washington, DC: Congressional Quarterly, Inc., 1979.

Valuable assistance for increased understanding of the United States Supreme Court as an institution and as a vital force shaping the political life in the United States is offered by this guidebook. The guidebook's information is organized in seven parts, as follows:

I. *Origins and Development of the Court*. This part traces the history of the Court from an idea in the discussions of the Constitutional Convention in 1789 to the present role of the world's most powerful judicial institution.

II. *The Court and the Federal System*. The impact of the Court's decisions is analyzed in four chapters — The Court and the Powers of Congress, The Court and the Powers of the President, The Court and Judicial Power, and The Court and the States.

III. *The Court and the Individual*. The effects of the Court's rulings are examined in five sections — Introduction, Freedom for Ideas, The Rights of Political Participation, Due Process and Individual Rights, and Equal Rights.

IV. *Pressures on the Court*. The four principal factors influencing the work of the Court are described, namely congressional pressure, presidential pressure, public opinion, and the press.

V. *The Court at Work*. Past and present operations of the Court are described.

VI. *Members of the Court*. Personal background, career, and characteristics of the 101 Supreme Court justices are outlined.

VII. *Major Decisions of the Court*. Capsule summaries of the Court's major decisions from 1790 to 1979 are presented together with a statement of the significance of the ruling.

An appendix contains a variety of documents establishing the Court's framework as an institution. A detailed table of contents, a subject index, and a case index are also included.

BIBLIOGRAPHIES

1079   Dahl, Richard C., and C. E. Bolden. *The American Judge. A Bibliography*. Vienna, VA: Coiner Publications, 1968.

The bibliography identifies judicial biographies published in books and periodicals and also lists publications dealing with the character and temperament, selection, tenure and removal, powers, duties and functions, politics and relationships, criticism, and ethics of judges and similar topics of interest in the study of the judiciary. No annotations are provided, but the excellent subject index permits easy access to the content of the cited publications.

1080   Friedman, Leon, and Fred L. Israel. *The Justices of the United States Supreme Court 1789–1969: Their Lives and Major Opinions*. New York: R. R. Bowker, 1969.

1081   _____ . *The Justices of the United States Supreme Court*. New York: R. R. Bowker, 1978.

The two titles cited above refer to a five-volume set that offers biographical essays and representative opinions for each of the 101 justices of the United States Supreme Court active during the period 1789–1976. Many judicial cases are included more than once to permit the examination of dissenting, concurring, and majority opinions. Annotated and evaluative bibliographies of varying length are given for each biographee. An appendix contains charts, tables, and statistical data. A detailed index is also included.

1082   Rigby, Gerold, and James Witt. "Bibliographical Essay: Behavioral Research in Public Law 1963– 1967." *Western Political Quarterly* 22 (Sept. 1969): 622–636.

1083   Schubert, Glendon A. "Behavioral Research in Public Law." *American Political Science Review* 57 (1963): 433–445.

1084   _____ . "Judicial Process and Behavior, 1963–1971." *Political Science Annual* 3 (1972): 73– 280.

Three separately published bibliographies furnish a convenient record of the massive literature about judicial behavior and political jurisprudence. More than 1,500 articles, books, and other publications are listed in classified arrangements. In their evaluative comments and conclusions the authors elucidate the strength and weaknesses of the research findings.

1085   Stephenson, D. Grier, Jr. *The Supreme Court and the American Republic. An Annotated Bibliography*. New York: Garland Publishing, Inc., 1981.

In view of the virtually boundless information material available from and about the United States Supreme Court, this annotated bibliography provides much-needed guidance to the existing literature. It identifies and describes not only the standard casebook and other reference sets, but devotes special attention to the politically significant work of the Court as it relates to the powers of, and limitations on, government imposed by the Constitution and statutes. Entries are arranged under six chapters, as follows: (1) Research Aids, (2) General Works, (3) Origins, (4) Institutional Development, (5) Constitutional Interpretation, and (6) Biographical and Autobiographical Materials. In chapters 4 and 5 the bibliography contains numerous court case citations together with references to analytical material. Two appendices provide membership lists of the Court. Separate indexes by authors and case names are also included.

1086   Tompkins, Dorothy C. *The Supreme Court of the United States: A Bibliography*. Berkeley: Bureau of Public Administration, University of California, 1959.

While much of the more recent academic research has focused on the justices and their judicial behavior, an earlier body of literature concentrated on the institutional aspects of the United States Supreme Court. This bibliog-raphy identifies books, articles, reports, and other publications dealing with the organization of the Court, the relationship of the Court with other branches of government, the work of the court, and the Supreme Court as a center of controversy.

DIRECTORIES

1087   Barnes, Catherine A. *Men of the Supreme Court: Profiles of the Justices*. New York: Facts on File, Inc., 1978.

The book presents biographies of the 26 men who served as justices of the United States Court between 1945 and 1976. Each biographical profile contains information on the justice's educational background, his political, academic or legal work before joining the Court, and his judicial philosophy as a member of the Court. A scholarly assessment of the justice's contribution to the court and to the law is provided. The book also contains a capsule summary of the most important decisions of the Court in chronological sequence. In addition, a very detailed bibliography is presented for works about the justices, the Supreme Court, and the significant issues decided by the Court.

1088   Chase, Harold, et al. *Biographical Dictionary of the Federal Judiciary*. Detroit: Gale Research Company, 1976.

Biographical data are presented for judges of the following courts:

U.S. Supreme Court, 1789–1974
U.S. Courts of Appeals, 1801–1802 (now called the Circuit Court, 1891–1974)
U.S. District Courts, 1789–1974
U.S. Court of Claims, 1855–1974
U.S. Court of Customs and Patent Appeals, 1909–1974
U.S. Customs Court, 1926–1974
Commerce Court (now defunct), 1910–1913
Supreme Court of the District of Columbia (now the U.S. District Court for the District of Columbia), 1863– 1936.

An addendum offers biographies of judges appointed during the Nixon administration. An appendix lists judges according to appointing president.

1089   *Martindale-Hubbell Law Directory*. Summit, NJ: Martindale-Hubbell, Inc., 1868– .

The annually revised directory provides biographical and career information as well as organizational information about the American legal system, its courts, judges, attorneys, American Bar Association officials, etc.

1090   Reincke, Mary. *The American Bench: Judges of*

the Nation. Minneapolis: Reginald Bishop Forster & Associates, 1977 – .

The reference work contains a description of the federal and state court system as well as biographical information about 14,000 federal and state judges. The book is divided into 52 sections — one for U.S. courts, one for each state and the District of Columbia. Each section is subdivided into three parts: Part 1 has a description of the court system, including location, jurisdiction, names of judges, and method of judicial selection. Part 2 contains maps showing federal and state jurisdictional divisions. Part 3 consists of alphabetically arranged biographies of the judges. An index lists title, court, and state of each judge.

1091   *United States Court Directory*. Washington, DC: U.S. Government Printing Office, 1981 – .

The semiannually published directory lists names, addresses, and phone numbers of judges and clerks of the U.S. Supreme Court, Court of Appeals, Court of Claims, Court of Customs and Patents Appeals, and Court of Military Appeals. District court listings are arranged by state.

1092   Wasserman, Paul, and Marek Kaszubski. *Law and Legal Information Directory*. Detroit: Gale Research Company, 1980.

This reference work identifies more than 4,000 organizations, agencies, educational programs, libraries, research and information centers, publications, and other services and facilities available in the field of law. Entries are arranged under 14 chapters, as follows: (1) National and International Organizations, (2) Bar Associations, (3) Federal Court System, (4) Federal Regulatory Agencies, (5) Law Schools, (6) Continuing Legal Education, (7) Paralegal Education, (8) Scholarships and Grants, (9) Awards and Prizes, (10) Special Libraries, (11) Information Systems and Services, (12) Research Centers, (13) Legal Periodical Publications (including separate bar association publications index and law school publication index), (14) Book and Media Publishers. All entries are arranged alphabetically or by state, wherever appropriate, and contain descriptive annotations in addition to the address information.

1093   *Who's Who in American Law*. Chicago: Marquis Who's Who, Inc., 1978 – .

Current editions of this biannually revised directory provide biographical information on approximately 18,000 lawyers, judges, and educators in the United States. Included are the justices of the United States and state supreme courts, chief judges of the U.S. Courts of Appeal, judges of state appeal and district courts, the U.S. attorney general, the U.S. solicitor general and deputy solicitor general, counsel to departments and agencies of

the federal government, deans and eminent professors in leading law schools, American Bar Association officials and state bar association officials, general counsel for major industries, heads of major legal assocations, and principal counsel of prominent law firms. Each entry follows the familiar Who's Who format, containing biographical and career information as well as current addresses.

Presidential Information

The documentation of presidential information is not nearly as public and accessible as that of congressional information. Until recently, all presidents of the United States beginning with George Washington could regard their papers as personal. As presidents left office or died, their papers were stored in the Library of Congress or in special presidential libraries of the National Archives and Records Service, where they are handled according to the instructions and access limitations imposed by the donor. While the presidential papers deposited in the Library of Congress are currently free of access limitations, there are still many papers, notably on foreign affairs and political campaigns, not available to the users of the Roosevelt, Truman, Eisenhower, Kennedy, and Johnson libraries.

Presidential records created after January 20, 1981, now fall under the complete control and ownership of the United States as a result of the 1978 Presidential Records Act. Nevertheless, an outgoing president is still permitted to place mandatory restrictions of up to 12 years on the availability of six types of information, as follows:

1. Papers classified for reasons of national defense or foreign policy pursuant to executive order
2. Material related to presidential appointments
3. Documentary items exempted from disclosure by statute
4. Trade secrets and confidential business information
5. Confidential communication records between the presidents and their advisors
6. Information whose disclosure would result in an unwarranted invasion of personal privacy

As a result of the 12-year restriction rule for current records and the personal ownership of the older presidential papers, the dissemination of presidential information continues to be fragmentary. Only the public utterances of the presidents, such as speeches, press conferences, messages, etc., and certain types of legal directives, notably executive orders and proclamations, appear in some kind of current and regular reference format. Selected portions of the personal records of the persidents, including transcripts of telephone conversations, briefing papers, confidential files, etc., are made available in separate document collections on microfilm after 12 or more years.

For a better overview of the available reference mechanism, the entries for the individual retrieval tools, listed and described on the following pages, are arranged in five separate sections, namely, (1) Guidebooks, (2) Other Bibliographies, (3) Indexes, (4) Current Document Collections, and (5) Retrospective Document Collections. In addition, William A. DeGregorio's *The Complete Book of U.S. Presidents* (New York: Dembner Books, 1984) offers a detailed summary of salient facts about each president from George Washington to Ronald Reagan.

GUIDEBOOKS

1094   Goehlert, Robert U., and Fenton S. Martin. *The Presidency: A Research Guide*. Santa Barbara, CA: ABC-Clio, 1984.

Both primary and secondary sources available for the study of the presidency and the executive branch of the U.S. government are conveniently identifiable with the help of this guidebook.

OTHER BIBLIOGRAPHIES

1095   *The American Presidency. A Historical Bibliography*. Santa Barbara, CA: ABC-Clio, 1983.

More than 3,000 abstracts of periodical articles covering such topics as the growth of the executive branch, presidential elections, and the lives and activities of the presidents are offered in this bibliographic volume. The articles were published between 1973 and 1982 and relate to all facets of the U.S. presidency from George Washington to Ronald Reagan. A multiterm subject index with biographical, geographical, and chronological qualifiers, as well as an author index and a list of cited periodicals is included.

1096   Burns, Richard Deans. *Harry S. Truman: A Bibliography of His Times and Presidency*. Wilmington, DE: Scholarly Resources, 1984.

Approximately 3,000 books, articles, dissertations, and other documentation items dealing with Harry S. Truman's life, administration, and times are listed in this bibliography. The annotated entries are arranged in 11 chapters that focus on Truman's political life, his presidency, major personalities during his administration, domestic, foreign, and military affairs, and the Korean War.

1097   Greenstein, Fred I., Larry Berman, and Alvin S. Felzenberg. *Evolution of the Modern Presidency. A Bibliographical Survey*. Washington, DC: American Enterprise Institute for Public Policy Research, 1977.

Beginning with Franklin Roosevelt's administration, the American presidency has undergone a series of changes that distinguish it from the 30 traditional predecessors. This modern presidency is characterized by greater involvement in legislative action, direct policy making, a sizable presidential bureaucracy, and increased public attention to presidential virtues. A large number of scholarly books and articles bear on the evolution of the American presidency since 1932. The bibliography cited above contains approximately 2,500 entries, many of which are briefly annotated. The entries are arranged under 21 chapters, which include general discussions of American presidencies, presidential recruitment, comparison with other executives, comparison of American presidencies, presidential style and personality, advisory institutions and processes, presidential constituencies, presidential powers and restraints, etc. Separate chapters are devoted to the literature about the seven presidencies from Franklin D. Roosevelt to Gerald R. Ford. An author index completes the bibliography.

1098   Stewart, William J. *The Era of Franklin D. Roosevelt. A Selected Bibliography of Periodical and Dissertation Literature 1954–1966*. Hyde Park, NY: General Services Administration, National Archives and Records Services, Franklin D. Roosevelt Library, 1967.

As the first of the modern presidencies, Franklin D. Roosevelt's administration is noteworthy because of the incumbent's extraordinary leadership, a new public philosophy called the New Deal, and the United States' entry into World War II. The annotated bibliography appropriately devotes three of its four chapters to these three distinguishing features of FDR's presidency. A fourth chapter is entitled Archives, Bibliography and Historiography. Included are separate author and subject indexes as well as a list of all serials cited in the bibliography.

1099   Tracy, Kathleen. *Herbert Hoover—A Bibliography: His Writings and Addresses*. Stanford, CA: Hoover Institute Press, 1977.

Even after half a century has passed, the writings and addresses of Herbert Hoover, the last of the traditional presidents of the United States, find a strong echo in the popular political sentiments of today. More than 1,200 entries can be found in this bibliography for books, periodical articles, addresses, reports, letters, and other writings of Herbert Hoover. The entries are arranged in chronological order by form of publication.

1100   U.S. Library of Congress. General Reference and Bibliography Division, Bibliography and Reference Correspondence Section. *John Fitzgerald Kennedy, 1917–1963: A Chronological List of References*. Washington, DC: U.S. Government Printing Office, 1964.

1101   Newcomb, Joan I. *John F. Kennedy: An Annotated Bibliography*. Metuchen, NJ: Scarecrow Press, 1977.

Books published between 1940 and 1977 about John F. Kennedy or the Kennedy family can be conveniently identified with the help of these two bibliographies. The first title covers the literature up to 1963, including Kennedy's own four books and the reviews about them. The arrangement of the entries is chronological. The second bibliography lists books published after 1960 with entries arranged by author under nine form or subject categories. Separate listings are made for the writings of Kennedy, general material, campaigns and elections, the Kennedy administration, the assassination, tributes on Kennedy's death, poetry, fiction, and juvenile literature. The assassination material includes books about the official and unofficial theories connected with that event and also lists books on Lee Harvey Oswald and Jack Ruby. Author and title indexes are also provided.

1102   U.S. Library of Congress. General Reference and Bibliography Division. *The Presidents of the United States, 1789–1962*. Washington, DC: U.S. Government Printing Office, 1963.

This bibliography offers a chronological listing of works about the presidency, presidential elections, the White House, the vice-presidency, as well as individual presidents from Washington to Kennedy. Publications by and about each president are listed.

INDEXES

With one exception,* all of the papers of the 23 presidents whose manuscripts are in the Library of Congress have been microfilmed and indexed in order to make them more accessible and useful to scholars and other interested persons. The indexes are essentially name indexes that list the names of writers and recipients of letters, telegrams, messages, and other communications. There are no subject entries, but material such as speeches, debates, briefs, memoranda, petitions, invitations, orders, proclamations, etc., are identified under the name of the writer. The indexes supply date, reel and series numbers of the microfilms, and a general description of the papers of each president.

1103   U.S. Library of Congress. Manuscript Division. *Index to the George Washington Papers*. Washington, DC: U.S. Government Printing Office, 1964.

1104   _____ . *Index to the Thomas Jefferson Papers*. Washington, DC: U.S. Government Printing Office, 1976.

*No index exists for the papers of President Martin Van Buren.

1105   _____ . *Index to the James Madison Papers*. Washington, DC: U.S. Government Printing Office, 1965.

1106   _____ . *Index to the James Monroe Papers*. Washington, DC: U.S. Government Printing Office, 1963.

1107   _____ . *Index to the Andrew Jackson Papers*. Washington, DC: U.S. Government Printing Office, 1967.

1108   _____ . *Index to the William H. Harrison Papers*. Washington, DC: U.S. Government Printing Office, 1960.

1109   _____ . *Index to the John Tyler Papers*. Washington, DC: U.S. Government Printing Office, 1961.

1110   _____ . *Index to the James K. Polk Papers*. Washington, DC: U.S. Government Printing Office, 1969.

1111   _____ . *Index to the Zachary Taylor Papers*. Washington, DC: U.S. Government Printing Office, 1960.

1112   _____ . *Index to the Franklin Pierce Papers*. Washington, DC: U.S. Government Printing Office, 1962.

1113   _____ . *Index to the Abraham Lincoln Papers*. Washington, DC: U.S. Government Printing Office, 1960.

1114   _____ . *Index to the Andrew Johnson Papers*. Washington, DC: U.S. Government Printing Office, 1963.

1115   _____ . *Index to the Ulysses S. Grant Papers*. Washington, DC: U.S. Government Printing Office, 1965.

1116   _____ . *Index to the James A. Garfield Papers*. Washington, DC: U.S. Government Printing Office, 1973.

1117   _____ . *Index to the Chester A. Arthur Papers*. Washington, DC: U.S. Government Printing Office, 1961.

1118   _____ . *Index to the Benjamin Harrison Papers*. Washington, DC: U.S. Government Printing Office, 1964.

1119 _____ . *Index to the Grover Cleveland Papers*. Washington, DC: U.S. Government Printing Office, 1965.

1120 _____ . *Index to the William McKinley Papers*. Washington, DC: U.S. Government Printing Office, 1963.

1121 _____ . *Index to the Theodore Roosevelt Papers*. Washington, DC: U.S. Government Printing Office, 1970.

1122 _____ . *Index to the William H. Taft Papers*. Washington, DC: U.S. Government Printing Office, 1972.

1123 _____ . *Index to the Woodrow Wilson Papers*. Washington, DC: U.S. Government Printing Office, 1973.

1124 _____ . *Index to the Calvin Coolidge Papers*. Washington, DC: U.S. Government Printing Office, 1965.

CURRENT DOCUMENT COLLECTIONS

1125 *Public Papers of the Presidents of the United States*. Washington, DC: U.S. Government Printing Office, 1957– .

1126 *The Cumulated Indexes to the Public Papers of the Presidents of the United States*. Millwood, NY: KTO Press, 1977– .

The text of public messages, speeches and addresses, letters, statements, and other pronouncements of U.S. presidents is published in annual volumes of a document collection set issued for each president beginning with Herbert Hoover to the present with the exception of Franklin D. Roosevelt. Proclamations, executive orders, and similar legal material are not included in the set, but a list of these documents is provided together with references to the *Federal Register* where the text of these administrative regulations can be found. The annual volumes are issued with a delay of approximately one year. Each volume contains its own index of names and subjects, but a cumulated index set is available from a commercial publisher.

1127 U.S. Office of Management and Budget. *The Budget of the United States Government*, 1971/1972– .

1128 _____ . *Appendix*, 1971/1972– .

1129 _____ . *Special Analyses: Budget of the United States Government*, 1971/1972– .

1130 _____ . *The United States Budget in Brief*, 1971/1972– . Washington, DC: U.S. Government Printing Office, 1971– .

The United States budget is the single most important policy document in the nation. It is the president's proposed financial plan of operation for the federal government during the coming fiscal year beginning on October 1. Transmitted to Congress each January, the budget reflects the president's assessment of the state of the economy and his recommendations for allocating available resources between the private and public sectors of the economy. It details federal programs according to the following functions serving importaant national needs: (1) national defense, (2) international affairs, (3) general science, space, and technology, (4) natural resources, environment, and energy, (5) agriculture, (6) commerce and transportation, (7) community and regional development, (8) education, employment, and social services, (9) health, (10) income security, (11) veteran benefits and services, (12) law enforcement and justice, (13) general government, and (14) revenue sharing and general-purpose fiscal assistance.

Financial data and analyses relating to the budget are currently published in the four reference works as titled above. The *Budget of the United States Government* contains the president's budget message to Congress and an overview of the various spending programs designed to meet national goals and agency nations. The *Appendix* provides detailed information on the various appropriations and funds that comprise the budget. Alternative views of the budget, economic and financial analyses of governmental programs and operations are found in the *Special Analyses* volume. The *United States Budget in Brief* offers a more concise, less technical overview of the budget together with numerous tables and graphic displays.

Since the president's budget proposals require formal review and authorization by Congress, further information about the budgetary process as it relates to annual or permanent legislative authority is provided by the reference works listed under Congressional Information.

In interaction with congressional activities, the president or the Office of Management and Budget also issues numerous supplementary budget messages and other communications relating to budget matters. These can be identified with the help of the *Monthly Catalog of United States Government Publications*.

1131 U.S. Office of Management and Budget. *Catalog of Federal Domestic Assistance*. Washington, DC: U.S. Government Printing Office, 1965– .

1131a FAPRS *(Federal Assistance Programs Retrieval System)*. Washington, DC: U.S. Office of Management and Budget, current. (Vendor: Control Data Corporation/Business Information Services)

Apart from preparing the presidential budget proposals, the Office of Management and Budget serves as the principal management tool of the president for shaping the responses of the United States government to the socioeconomic needs of the American population. There are essentially three methods by which these needs can be responded to at the federal level, namely by public assistance, legal regulation, and manipulation. The titles cited above refer to printed and electronic versions of a basic reference work that details the public assistance programs and activities of federal government agencies.

Benefits and services of the assistance programs are provided through seven financial types of assistance (such as grants, direct payments, loans, insurance) and eight nonfinancial types of assistance (such as specialized services, counseling, dissemination of technical information, training, investigation of complaints, federal employment, use of property or facilities, sale or donation of goods or property). Recipients of the assistance programs fall into six categories: (1) individuals, groups, profit-making organizations; (2) local agencies, such as cities, towns, municipalities, counties, school districts, etc.; (3) nonprofit organizations; (4) state agencies, including institutions of higher education and hospitals; (5) U.S. territories (Puerto Rico, Virgin Islands, Guam, and others); (6) federally recognized Indian tribal organizations. The assistance programs address themselves to a wide range of needs in 20 basic functional categories, as follows: agriculture, business and commerce, community development, consumer protection, cultural affairs, disaster prevention and relief, education, employment, labor and training, energy, environmental quality, food and nutrition, health, housing, income security and social services, information and statistics, law, justice and legal services, natural resources, regional development, science and technology, and transportation.

The printed reference work is issued annually, usually in June with an update published in December. Its loose-leaf format consists of three basic sections: indexes, program descriptions, and appendices. The indexes identify the assistance programs by agency, applicant eligibility, deadline, functional category, and subject. The program descriptions provide detailed information about the programs, notably authorization, objectives, administrating agency, type of assistance, use and use restriction, eligibility requirements, application and award process, post-assistance requirements, financial information, available guidelines or literature, and information contacts. The appendices list programs requiring circular coordination, the legal authorizations, including public law numbers, budget functional categories, agency ad-

dresses, sources of additional information contacts, and historical profiles of programs.

FAPRS, available at designated access points in each state and by contract with the vendor, is a computerized question-and-answer system. Based upon the input (applicant data, type of desired assistance, functional category) supplied by the requestor, the database will provide a list of program numbers and titles, as well as the full text of the selected program.

1132   *Weekly Compilation of Presidential Documents.* Washington, DC: U.S. Government Printing Office, 1965 – .

1133   *Weekly Compilation of Presidential Documents.* Washington, DC: U.S. Office of the Federal Register, 1981 – . (Vendor: Mead Data Central)

This document collection, available in printed and machine-readable formats, is the most up-to-date source of information on presidential actions and policies. It contains the text of messages, statements, public speeches, remarks, and other nonlegal material released by the White House. The printed version is published every Monday and contains in each issue a cumulative index to prior issues of the publication. The machine-readable version is part of the *NEXIS* database that offers KWIC, full text, and list-of-references search possibilities as well as full text display and printout of all items contained in this document collection since 1981.

RETROSPECTIVE DOCUMENT COLLECTIONS

1134   A *Compilation of the Messages and Papers of the Presidents, 1789 – 1927.* New York: Bureau of National Literature, 1928.

This 20-volume set was prepared under the direction of the Joint Committee on Printing of the House and Senate pursuant to a congressional resolution and was supplemented with additional material and an encyclopedic index furnished by private enterprise. The encyclopedic index is in volumes 19 and 20 of this set and contains more than 25,000 page references to the official utterances of the presidents as well as some 800 encyclopedic articles about subjects discussed or handled by the presidents. The text of presidential proclamations, addresses, annual messages, veto messages, and other communications to Congress by presidents from Washington to Coolidge is given.

1135   Freidel, Frank, Richard S. Kirkendall, and Daun van Ee. *The Presidential Documents Series.*

Map Room Messages of President Roosevelt (1942 – 1945). Potsdam Conference Documents.

Map Room Messages of President Truman (1945–1946).

Minutes and Documents of the Cabinet Meetings of President Eisenhower (1953–1961).

President Kennedy and the Press (1961–1963).

Appointments Book of President Kennedy (1961–1963).

Daily Diary of President Johnson (1963–1969).

Minutes and Documents of the Cabinet Meetings of President Johnson (1963–1969).
Frederick, MD: University Publications of America, 1981.

For the first time in the history of publishing, this series of microfilm collections makes available to the public the hitherto top-secret documents of five United States presidents during the war and postwar era. Included in the collections are secret wartime messages, confidential conference files, minutes and supporting documents of cabinet meetings, records of telephone conversations, briefing papers, official reports, memoranda, and other items that document how the United States was managed during those challenging years. Identification of individual documents is facilitated by printed guides that are issued with each collection.

1136   Hoover, Herbert Clark. *The State Papers and Other Public Writings of Herbert Hoover.* Garden City, NY: Doubleday, Doran & Co., 1934. (Reprint edition: New York: Kraus Reprint Company, 1970)

Apart from the four Herbert Hoover volumes published officially as part of the *Public Papers* set, this two-volume set contains the text of the state papers and other public documents produced during the years of the Hoover administration from March 4, 1929, to March 4, 1933. The documents are arranged chronologically and include proclamations, press conference statements, addresses, messages, executive orders, letters and telegrams. All of the included documents were collected by William Starr Myers, professor of politics at Princeton University, at the suggestion of ex-President Hoover. Several other volumes also exist that contain the texts of President Hoover's campaign speeches and other addresses.

1137   *The Inaugural Addresses of the American Presidents, from Washington to Nixon.* Washington, DC: U.S. Government Printing Office, 1974.

The inaugural addresses of the presidents are a fertile ground for comparing rhetorical promises with actual achievements or exposing hopes and illusions in the light of subsequent reality. The present title is an anthology of inaugural addresses issued by the official government printer.

1138   *Presidential Press Conferences.* New York: Earl M. Coleman Enterprises, 1978.

Presidential statements made during press conferences constitute an important output of the American political system, clarifying and supporting the official position toward major political functions and objects. This three-volume set contains the full text of the press conferences held by three American presidents, Kennedy, Johnson, and Nixon. The material is arranged chronologically. Detailed indexing facilitates access to the various presidential statements by subject, major issue, and public figure.

1139   *The Presidential Campaign 1976.* Washington, DC: U.S. Government Printing Office, 1978.

As a result of developments in the telecommunications industry, presidential campaign rhetoric is of ever-increasing political importance. Regrettably, the existing reference treatment of this type of speech material remains fragmentary. This three-volume set contains the text of presidential candidates Carter and Ford's speeches, press conferences, debates, position papers, question-and-answer sessions with the media and special interest groups during the 1976 election campaign. The texts are arranged chronologically or by major topics and issues, such as foreign relations, economy, education, health and welfare, business and labor, energy and environment, national security, and others. Also included are the debates between vice-presidential running mates Dole and Mondale. Detailed indexing is provided for all included texts.

1140   Roosevelt, Franklin Delano. *FDR Press Conferences, 1933–1945.* Hyde Park, NY: Franklin D. Roosevelt Library, 1971.

1141   Roosevelt, Franklin Delano. *The Public Papers and Addresses of Franklin Delano Roosevelt, with an Introduction and Explanatory Notes by President Roosevelt.* New York: Random House, 1938–1950.

Since there are no FDR volumes in the official *Public Papers* set, the titles cited above constitute the main reference source for the public papers and addresses of President Franklin Delano Roosevelt. There were 1,011 press conferences during FDR's term of office, and their complete text can be found in a set of twelve microfilm reels as cited first above. Each reel contains its own subject index, but a consolidated index for the entire set is also provided.

A printed set in 13 volumes offers in chronological

sequence the text of the public messages, addresses, statements, proclamations, letters, and other public papers of President Roosevelt for the period 1933 to 1945. While each of the volumes is separately indexed, there is also a cumulative index in Volume 13. Only 48 press conferences are included in whole or in part in this set, but practically all of the prepared, formal addresses have been printed.

1142   *The State of the Union Messages of the Presidents, 1790–1966.* New York: Chelsea House, 1966.

Although the annual messages of the presidents may not be a full and accurate record of the state of the union, they are unquestionably documents of high historical and political signficance. This set provides the full text of 178 State of the Union messages with an introduction by Arthur M. Schlesinger, Jr.

1143   Weinstein, Stephen A. *The Nixon Administration.* Hyattsville, MD: National Educational Consultants, Inc., Greenwich, CT: Johnson Associates, 1976.

A significant feature of the presidency of Richard M. Nixon is the development and subsequent limitation of presidential power to gather political information. Wiretapping, tape recordings, burglaries, secret opening of first-class mail and other activities were used during the Nixon administration to obtain political information from and about political opponents, including the headquarters of the Democratic National Committee at the Watergate office building in Washington, DC. Public and official reaction to these activities resulted in the "Watergate affair," a series of congressional, judicial, and presidential actions that culminated in the resignation of President Nixon.

The title above refers to a comprehensive microfiche collection with analytical indexes of congressional, presidential, and judicial documents in the Watergate affair, including impeachment proceedings, the resignation and pardon of Richard M. Nixon.

1144   Windt, Theodore. *Presidential Rhetoric: The Imperial Age 1961–1974.* Dubuque, IA: Kendall/Hunt, 1978.

The transcripts of the speeches of presidents Kennedy, Johnson, and Nixon assembled in this collection have been reprinted from appropriate issues of the *Public Papers of the Presidents* and the *Weekly Compilation of Presidential Documents.* The selected speeches illustrate the exercise of presidential leadership in the protection of American interests or presidential power itself. Introductory commentaries and a bibliography of additional reading material about the three presidents are also included.

Statistical Information

Politics is not the art to administrate the present situation but the skill to formulate policies that anticipate future human needs and avoid emerging dangers at an early stage. To this end, quantitative data collected by the various governmental agencies of the United States serve as early warning signals and proof of developing problems, crisis areas, strengths and weaknesses in the life of the nation. Many of these data currently relate to unfavorable social and economic trends that could have been avoided by more astute political planning in the past. This is particularly evident in matters of energy supply, obsolescence of manufacturing capacity and transportation facilities, export growth, and budgetary deficits.

Statistical data are initially disseminated in as many as 7,500 different publications. Identification and location of the statistical information would, therefore, be most difficult without appropriate indexes and statistical compendia. The reference works listed on the next pages are arranged under the following subsections to facilitate convenient identification: (1) Socioeconomic Data — Guidebooks, Indexes, General Compendia, Demographic Compendia, Socioeconomic Compendia; (2) Election Data — Guidebooks, Current Compendia, and Retrospective Compendia.

SOCIOECONOMIC DATA

Guidebooks

1145   Andriot, John L. *Guide to U.S. Government Statistics.* Arlington, VA: Documents Index, 1973.

The guidebook lists by departments and agencies of the federal government all those publications that contain statistical data. A separate subject index identifies the type of statistics available and the period covered by the statistical data.

1146   Hoel, Arline Alchian, Kenneth W. Clarkson, and Roger LeRoy Miller. *Economics Sourcebook of Government Statistics.* Lexington, MA: Lexington Books, 1983.

Federal government agencies produce thousands of different statistics on a regular basis, but none are politically more sensitive than the many economic indicators of business and financial conditions.

This guidebook identifies and describes more than 50 of the most widely used economic statistics in the following categories: (1) measures of inflation, (2) profits: indicators of general business conditions, (3) interest rates and other financial indicators, (4) measures of employment, unemployment, and earnings, (5) indicators of international finance and trade, and (6) indicators of government influence. Entries in each of these categories contain information about the name of the statistic, its issuing agency, coverage, breakdown categories, frequency, data sources, limitations. publication title, and additional references. Four appendices offer information on (1) selected sources of business and financial information, (2) financial statements, (3) the standard industrial classification, and (4) value added and gross national product. A glossary and an index are also included. A major limitation of the guidebook is that computerized retrieval tools for the listed statistics are not indicated.

1147   U.S. Bureau of the Census. *Catalog of United States Census Publications 1790–1972*. Washington, DC: U.S. Government Printing Office, 1974.

1148   _____ . *Catalog of United States Census Publications (Monthly)*. Washington, DC: U.S. Government Printing Office, 1972– .

Census publications form a major and indispensable part of any collection of statistical data. A retrospective bibliography lists and describes all decennial census publications since 1790, and census publications other than decennial that were issued for various subject fields including government, business, industry, population, religious bodies, etc. The monthly listings offer current information about published and unpublished, printed and machine-readable statistical data, reports, indexes, and tabulations. The catalog also contains indexes that identify statistical reports by geographic area and subject.

1149   U.S. Bureau of the Census. *Directory of Federal Statistics for Local Areas*. Washington, DC: U.S. Government Printing Office, 1978.

1150   _____ . *Directory of Federal Statistics for States: 1967*. Washington, DC: U.S. Government Printing Office, 1968.

1151   _____ . *Guide to Recurrent and Special Governmental Statistics*. Washington, DC: U.S. Government Printing Office, 1976.

The three guidebooks function as useful finding aids for more than 200 current sources of federally published statistics relating to governmental and socioeconomic units below the national level, such as states, standard metropolitan statistical areas, counties, and cities. The last item cited above reproduces the title, table of contents, and one page from each statistical table in the major statistical reports issued by the Bureau of the Census on state and local governments. The other two guidebooks list the available data sources under main subject headings that include population, education, labor and employment, government, law enforcement, etc. The available subject and tabular detail as well as the area covered in the listed source documents is indicated in separate columns under the main headings.

1152   U.S. Bureau of the Census. *Directory of Non-Federal Statistics for States and Local Areas: 1969*. Washington, DC: U.S. Government Printing Office, 1970.

Apart from federally collected statistics, the quantitative data sources issued by state agencies, colleges and universities, or private organizations are also of great importance. Population, vital statistics, health, education, public welfare, employment, law enforcement, government, government finance, etc., are the subjects of these statistical sources, which the guidebook lists by state with information about the area to which the data apply.

1153   Wasserman, Paul, et al. *Statistics Sources. A Subject Guide to Data on Industrial, Business, Social, Financial and Other Topics for the United States and Internationally*. Detroit: Gale Research Company, 1980.

Some 26,000 citations to important statistical sources are presented in the latest edition of this frequently revised guidebook. In addition to a listing of major statistical publications under main entry, the guidebook identifies under alphabetically arranged subject headings the published and unpublished source of the pertinent statistics. If no published statistical material is available, the name of the organization, i.e., a government agency or a trade organization, from whom statistics on the desired subject may be obtained is indicated. Regrettably no SuDoc numbers are included with the bibliographic entries for federally published statistics.

Indexes

1154   *American Statistics Index*. Washington, DC: Congressional Information Service, 1973– .

1155   *ASI*. Washington, DC: Congressional Information Service, 1973– . (Vendor: Dialog — File 102; SDC)

By using the *American Statistics Index*, either in its printed or online version, available statistical information produced by more than 500 federal agencies or congressional committees and disseminated in as many as 7,500 different publications annually can be

- identified by name, subject terms, available breakdown categories, title or agency report number, and then
- located with the provided references, either in the original source document or in a microfiche facsimile of it supplied by the Congressional Information Service.

Statistical data are often available in one or more of 20 geographic, economic, or demographic breakdown categories, namely by census division, city, county, foreign country, outlying area, region, SMSA, state, urban-rural concentration, commodity, federal agency, income, industry, occupation, age, disease, educational attainment, marital status, race, and sex. A separate index of categories identifies the available statistical breakdown for each of 18 topical areas listed under the following subject headings: agriculture and food, banking, finance and insurance, communications and transportation, education, geography and climate, government, health and vital statistics, housing and construction, industry and commerce, labor and employment, law enforcement, natural resources and environment, population, prices and cost of living, public welfare and social security, recreation and leisure, science and technology, and veteran affairs.

Each entry in the various indexes provided by this reference work leads to an abstract of the referenced statistical publication with the help of a unique accession number. These accession numbers consist of four basic components that identify not only each individual publication but also the issuing agency and the type of publication, namely, current periodical, annual, series, etc. In many instances, the accession number is followed by an additional decimal number in order to identify sub-abstracts for parts, sections, or other subgroups of the main publication. The abstracts provide complete bibliographical information, including Superintendent of Documents (SuDoc) numbers, *Monthly Catalog* entry numbers, and ASI microfiche symbols. In addition, each abstract contains a narrative description of the available statistical data. This descriptive information identifies the statistical methodology, time span, geographic coverage, publication periodicity, arrangement, form, or other useful details.

The *American Statistics Index* is published in a retrospective edition, covering statistical publications issued from 1960 to 1973, in annual editions from 1974, and in monthly supplements for current coverage. Each edition is issued in two sections, namely, an index and an abstracts section.

Online searches of the computerized database are possible by any combination of search terms, including main and analytical index terms, main and analytical titles, keywords from the abstracts, name of issuing agency, agency report number, etc.

1156   *Disclosure Journal.* Bethesda, MD: Disclosure, Inc.; 1973 – .

1157   *Disclosure II.* Bethesda, MD: Disclosure, Inc., most recent 5 years. (Vendor: Dialog — File 100; Dow Jones News/Retrieval; others)

1158   *Disclo.* Bethesda, MD: Disclosure, Inc., current. (Vendor: Mead Data Central)
    A Bethesda, Maryland, publisher called Disclosure, Inc., is the nation's largest source of primary information about American business, its achievements, problems,

and failures. According to the Securities Act of 1933 public corporations are required to file with the Securities and Exchange Commission publicly available information in prescribed categories. Today more than 100,000 filings are made annually by nearly 9,000 companies. As a result of contractual arrangements with the SEC, these filings are made public and accessible in a variety of reference formats by Disclosure, Inc.

The *Disclosure Journal* is a reference system consisting of the SEC Corporate Profiles, the Index of Corporate Events, and the Company Filing Index. The SEC Corporate Profiles is published every fourth month on microfiche and delineates which filings a particular company has submitted and their contents. The Index of Corporate Events, issued monthly on microfiche, provides a subject approach to the information reported in the corporate filings. The Company Filing Index, issued monthly in printed form, lists by company all filings to the SEC, but without abstracting, indexing, or cross-referencing. Full text reproductions of all SEC corporate filings are made available by the publisher on a subscription basis as well as individual order basis. Corporate filings consist of annual business and financial reports (10-K), quarterly financial reports (10-Q), and other reports and statements. Apart from their value in economic studies, these reports are politically significant because they disclose politically amenable problems in the business community, such as availability of raw materials and labor; foreign exchange losses; foreign competition; effects of compliance with ecological, environmental, and other laws; inflationary, recessionary, and other negative market expectations; etc.

In addition to the microfiche and printed reference material, access to corporate filings is also provided by online reference tools available from several vendors. *Disclosure II* is a computerized database that contains extracts and narrative descriptions, annual balance sheets, and income statements taken from the 10-K, 10-Q, and other corporate reports. Updated weekly, the information in the database is retrievable by company name, SIC code, line of business, and key terms listed in the *Disclosure Financial Thesaurus*, published by the producer. *Disclo* is the name of the database that is part of the *LEXIS* computerized libraries. It offers full text retrieval of extracts and abstracts of all corporate reports filed with the Securities and Exchange Commission.

1159   Manheim, Jarol B., and Allison Ondrasik. *DataMap.* New York: Longman, 1983 – .

DataMap is a subject index to the statistical tables found in 28 of the most widely used statistical compendia, including: *Survey of Current Business, County and City Data Book, Congressional District Data Book, Criminal Justice Statistics, Characteristics of the Population: U.S.*

Summary, Handbook of Labor Statistics, International Financial Statistics Yearbook, Municipal Yearbook, Statistical Abstract of the United States, Social Indicators, Uniform Crime Reports, World Handbook of Political and Social Indicators, and others. Since many of these statistical compendia are published annually, *DataMap* itself will be updated annually to ensure access to current information.

1160   *Statistical Reference Index*. Bethesda, MD: Congressional Information Service, 1980—.

This companion set to the *American Statistics Index* offers multiple access to statistical data published by organizations other than the United States government. Private associations, business organizations, university and other research institutes, as well as state governments are among the sources of statistical data covered. *SRI* is published monthly and in annual cumulations in two parts: An index section contains several indexes by subject, name, issuing source, publication title, and breakdown categories. References are given to the abstracts section, where full bibliographic information and brief subject descriptions of the statistical publication can be found. The publisher also makes available a microfiche collection where 90 percent of the *SRI* cited publications are reproduced on microfiche.

General Compendia

1161   U.S. Bureau of the Census. *Congressional District Data Book*. Washington, DC: U.S. Government Printing Office, 1963—.

1162   _____ . *Supplement to Congressional District Data Book: Resdistricted States*. Washington, DC: U.S. Government Printing Office, 1965—.

1163   _____ . *Congressional District Atlas*. Washington, DC: U.S. Government Printing Office, 1960—.

The *Congressional District Data Book* is one of the small-area supplements to the *Statistical Abstracts of the United States*, listed and described below. It includes more than 300 items of statistical data for the 435 congressional districts. Statistical data are based on the latest decennial census and recent election returns. Special supplements are issued for states that have revised their congressional district boundaries. Maps and boundaries of the congressional districts are published in the *Congressional District Atlas*. The atlas also contains tables for each state that identify the congressional district number for each municipality and county. Revised editions or supplements of these reference works become available at irregular intervals as soon as the appropriate census data become available.

1164   U.S. Bureau of the Census. *County and City Data Book*. Washington, DC: U.S. Government Printing Office, 1949—.

Like the preceding title, this reference work is also a small-area supplement to the *Statistical Abstract of the United States*. Its irregularly revised editions contain more than 100 items of statistical data for each county, standard metropolitan statistical area, and incorporated city of the United States. The book publishes data obtained from the census of governments, census of business, manufacturers, and mineral industries, census of agriculture, and census of population and housing.

1165   U.S. Bureau of the Census. *Historical Statistics of the United States, Colonial Times to 1970*. Washington, DC: U.S. Government Printing Office, 1976.

A compilation of over 12,500 statistical time series covering the social, political, and economic life of the United States from 1610 to 1970. Source notes provide references to original published sources. A detailed subject index is also included.

1166   U.S. Bureau of the Census. *State and Metropolitan Area Data Book*. Washington, DC: U.S. Government Printing Office, 1979—.

This series of biannual books presents data for the United States as a whole, each state, and each standard metropolitan statistical area (SMSA). From the Census Bureau, data are presented on population, housing, governments, manufacturers, retail trade, wholesale trade, selected services, mineral industries, and agriculture. In addition, statistics from 60 other government and private agencies are shown, including data on defense outlays, elections, energy, public assistance, and other subjects. Also included are an explanation of geographic concepts and codes, source notes, several appendices, and a detailed subject index to the various tables.

1167   U.S. Bureau of the Census. *Statistical Abstract of the United States*. Washington, DC: U.S. Government Printing Office, 1878—.

This compendium is the standard source for the annual summarization of statistical information on the social, political, and economic situation in the United States. Statistical data are arranged under 32 sections entitled population; vital statistics; immigration and naturalization; education; law enforcement, federal courts and prisons; geography and environment; public lands, parks, recreation and travel; federal government finances and employment; social insurance and welfare services; national defense and veterans affairs; labor force, employment and earnings; income, expenditures, and wealth; prices; elections; banking, finance, and insurance; business enterprise; communications; energy; science;

transportation — land; transportation — air and water; agriculture; forests and forest products; fisheries; mining and mineral products; construction and housing; manufactures; domestic trade and services; foreign commerce and aid; outlying areas under the jurisdiction of the United States; comparative international statistics. A bibliographical note at the bottom of each statistical table identifies the original source of the statistics. The compendium also contains four appendices that list the standard metropolitan statistical areas (SMSAs) in the United States with their population, and the statistical time series appearing in the companion volume *Historical Statistics of the United States, Colonial Times to 1970*, additional sources of statistics, publications of recent censuses, state statistical abstracts, and information on statistical methodology and reliability. A detailed index provides access to the statistical tables by subject terms.

Demographic Compendia

1168   *NPADEMOG. National Planning Association Demographic Data*. Washington, DC: National Planning Association, 1967–. (Vendor: I. P. Sharp)

Demographic data for the United States can be retrieved online from this computerized database, which contains more than 550,000 time series. Population data are available by age, sex, and race for each of the 3,600 statistical areas in the United States based on divisions by regions, states, counties, Bureau of Economic Analysis areas, and Standard Metropolitan Statistical Areas (SMSAs). For each area there are 153 time series, covering historical data from 1967 to the present and projections to the end of the century.

1169   *Site II*. Arlington, VA; CACI, Inc., 1970 and 1980 census, plus projections. (Vendor: CompuServe; Control Data Corporation/Business Information Services; others)

Online access to this database is possible for personal computer users in homes and offices through the facilities of the Compuserve Information Service (MicroNet) or separate contract with other vendors. The database provides demographic data, obtained from the 1970 and 1980 census, in addition to annual updates and five-year projections. Population data can be retrieved by age, race and sex, as well as income level, educational attainment, or occupation for the entire United States or geographic or political divisons.

1170   U.S. Department of Commerce. Bureau of the Census. *1980 Census of Population and Housing*. Washington, DC: U.S. Government Printing Office, 1982–.

The decennial census of population and housing, conducted by the Bureau of the Census, is of great political significance because

1. the "one person, one vote" decisions of the U.S. Supreme Court require congressional districts within a state (as well as the state and local legislative districts) to be of nearly equal population
2. the allocation of revenue sharing and other federal and state funds among some 39,000 governments in the United States depends on census data
3. federal, state, and local planning for the socioeconomic and other needs of the American population would be impossible without reliable demographic data

The *1980 Census of Population and Housing* is issued in three major report series composed of the following parts:

A. Population and Housing Census Reports
  1. *Block Statistics* (C3.224/5: PHC-80-1- —). Population and housing unit totals as well as statistics on selected characteristics for all blocks in each census tract.
  2. *Census Tracts* (C3.233/11:980/ —; Cs 223/11; 980/ — /maps/sec. —). Data on population and housing subjects for all census tracts. Separate reports are issued for each SMSA, each state, and Puerto Rico.
  3. *Summary Characteristics for Government Units and Standard Metropolitan Statistical Areas* (C3.223/28:980/ —). Statistical data cover population, age, race, education, disability, ability to speak English, labor force, income, total housing units, housing value and age, and rent. Statistics are presented for states, SMSAs, counties, county subdivisions, and incorporated places.
  4. *Congressional Districts of the 98th Congress* (C3.223/20:80-4- —). Reports are issued for each state and the District of Columbia, presenting select data for congressional districts.
B. Population Census Reports
  1. *Volume 1: Characteristics of the Population*. The volume consists of four separately issued series of reports (e.g., chapters) with 57 separate reports in each series, covering a U.S. summary, one report for each state, the District of Columbia, and each dependent territory.
    a. *Chapter A: Number of Inhabitants* (C3.223/5:980/8 —). Final population counts by state, county, county subdivision, incorporated places, census designated places, standard consolidated statistical areas, SMSAs and urbanized areas.
    b. *Chapter B: General Population Characteristics* (C3.223/6:980/B —). Statistical data on household relationship, age, race, Spanish

origin, sex, marital status for each state, county, county subdivision, place of 1,000 or more, SCSA, SMSA, American Indian reservation, and Alaskan native village.

   c. *Chapter C: General Social and Economic Characteristics* (C3.223/7:980/C —). Statistical data on nativity, citizenship, language spoken, ancestry, fertility, family composition, group quarters, marital history, journey to work, education, disability, veteran status, labor force, income, poverty shown for each state, county, place of 2,500 or more, SCSA, SMSA, urbanized area, American Indian reservation, and Alaskan native village.

   d. *Chapter D: Detailed Population Characteristics* (C3.223/8:980/D —). Data shown in Chapter C are presented in greater detail by state, SMSA, and selected central cities within these SMSAs.

2. *Volume 2: Subject Reports* (C3.223/10: —). A series of separately issued reports, each focusing on a particular topic, such as persons in institutions, employment status and work experience, persons not employed, low-income population, low-income areas in large cities, veterans, Americans living abroad, journey to work, and others.

3. *Supplementary Reports* (C3.223/12:80-S1- —). Individually issued reports presenting special compilations of statistical data on specific population subjects.

C. Housing Census Reports

   1. *Volume 1: Characteristics of Housing Units* (C3.224/3:980/A —). The volume consists of different series of reports, called chapters (e.g., Chapter A: General Housing Characteristics; Chapter B: Detailed Housing Characteristics, etc.), each comprising 57 separate reports (one for each state, District of Columbia, and dependent territories with breakdowns by political or statistical entities).

   2. *Volume 2: Metropolitan Housing Characteristics* (3.224/4: —). Detailed housing census statistics by states, SMSAs, and cities of 50,000 or more with breakdown by race, Spanish origin where applicable.

   3. *Volume 3: Subject Reports* (Cs224/10: —). A series of separately issued reports dealing with a particular topic of housing.

With the exception of three report series — *Block Statistics*, *Detailed Population Characteristics*, and *Metropolitan Housing Characteristics* — that are available on microfiche only, all previously cited report series are re-leased as printed publications. In addition, the Census Bureau makes available extensive amounts of census data on computer tape. For a summary description of the printed and machine-readable data collections released by the Census Bureau, see the *User's Guide, 1980 Census of Population and Housing*, published by the U.S. Government Printing Office in 1982 (C3.223/22:80-R1A).

Socioeconomic Compendia

1171   *BLS Consumer Price Index.*

1172   *BLS Employment, Hours, and Earnings.*

1173   *BLS Labor Force.*

1174   *BLS Producer Price Index.*
Washington, DC: Bureau of Labor Statistics, U.S. Department of Labor, to date. (Vendor: Dialog — Files 175, 176, 177, 178)

These four computerized databases, accessible online with the Dialog system, contain numeric records for a variety of socioeconomic indicators useful for gauging the necessity for remedial political or governmental action. Prepared by the Bureau of Labor Statistics, the data measure changes in

- consumer prices
- employment and unemployment
- average hourly and weekly earnings
- weekly hours and overtime hours worked
- producer prices for manufactured commodities

for various areas, population and industry categories. All records are updated by new monthly data that are added to appropriate time series of up to 20 years of duration. All numeric data are displayed online or printed offline without narrative abstracts, but may also be found in several different BLS publications identifiable with the help of the *American Statistics Index*.

1175   U.S. Council of Economic Advisors. *Economic Indicators*. Washington, DC: U.S. Government Printing Office, 1948 – .

1176   U.S. Department of Commerce. Bureau of Economic Analysis. *Business Conditions Digest*. Washington, DC: U.S. Government Printing Office, 1961 – .

1177   U.S. Department of Commerce. Bureau of Economic Analysis. *Business Conditions Digest*. Washington, DC: 1946 – . (Vendor: ADP Network Services; Chase Econometrics/Interactive Data)

1178   U.S. Department of Commerce. Bureau of Economic Analysis. *Survey of Current Business*. Washington, DC.: U.S. Government Printing Office, 1921–.

1179   *USECON. U.S. Economic.* Ann Arbor, MI: ADP Network Services, 1947–. (Vendor: ADP Network Services)

1180   *U.S. Macroeconomic.* Bala Cynwyd, PA: Chase Econometrics/Interactive Data, 1945–. (Vendor: Chase Econometrics/Interactive Data)

1181   *U.S. Macroeconomic Forecast.* Bala Cynwyd, PA: Chase Econometrics/Interactive Data, 1960–. (Vendor: Chase Econometrics/Interactive Data)

These statistical compendia, available in printed and/or electronic formats, provide an excellent barometer of the state of the American economy and the success or failure of the economic policies of the United States government. For many years a system of leading, coincident, and lagging economic indicators has been widely used to appraise the health of the American economy and to detect at a very early stage the emergence or persistence of economic problems, notably inflation, unemployment, recession, and foreign trade imbalances. The leading indicators are essentially measures of new commitments or anticipations, including money supply figures and credit data. The coincident indicators measure economic performance, such as gross national product, income, employment, foreign trade, and savings. The lagging indicators are more sluggish in their reaction to economic processes, and are therefore most valuable for detecting real changes in the cyclical movement of aggregate economic activity.

The *Economic Indicators*, published monthly, provides summary data on total output, income, spending, employment, wages, prices, money, credit, and finance as well as merchandise exports and imports, foreign and domestic assets. The *Business Conditions Digest*, available monthly in printed as well as electronic format, offers more than 800 time series of cyclical indicators and other measures of economic activity. The *Survey of Current Business*, published monthly, presents more detailed statistical and descriptive data on the economic situation, including separate statistical tables for the various American industries, their products, workforce, domestic and international trade. There is some duplication (triplication?) of the published data in the three reference series and regrettably also some variation in the figures presented. The variations occur primarily in composite measures, ostensibly as a result of cumulative errors that are unavoidable when data from various sources are aggregated.

More than 22,000 historical time series on the U.S. economy are available for online display with the *USECON* database, which is updated as soon as data are released by a governmental agency. Historical, current, and forecast data on the U.S. economy are also available from the online databases prepared by Chase Econometrics.

1182   U.S. Department of Commerce. *Social Indicators*. Washington, DC: U.S. Government Printing Office, 1977 (1973–).

This irregularly published compendium offers, in statistical, graphic, or descriptive form, data in 11 social areas, namely, population; family; housing; social security and welfare; health and nutrition; public safety; education and training; work and income; wealth and expenditures; culture, leisure, and use of time; social mobility and participation. The material is presented in 11 chapters with separate sections for public perceptions and international comparisons. The public perception sections express the degree of satisfaction that the public feels in each of the eleven social areas. The international comparisons sections inform the reader how well or how badly the United States is doing in relation to the situation in selected foreign countries. Readers desiring further information are offered bibliographies for further reading in each of the 11 social areas. A subject index provides access to the listed material.

ELECTION DATA

Guidebooks

1183   Burnham, Walter Dean. *Sources of Historical Election Data, a Preliminary Bibliography*. East Lansing: Institute of Community Development and Services, Michigan State University, 1963.

This guidebook identifies publications for historical election data in the United States in the following categories: (1) general sources of election returns, (2) state publications of election returns, (3) elections reported below the county level, and (4) demographic material. All entries include explanatory annotations.

1184   Hall, Catherine M. *Sources of American Election Statistics by State and Territory*. Washington, DC: U.S. Library of Congress, 1980.

The most current sources of election statistics for the states and territories of the United States are listed in this guidebook. Since the most timely data are printed in the major newspapers of each state or territory on the day following the election, the guidebook usually identifies one newspaper, published in the largest metropolitan area or capital city, that contains the most complete election returns. Official state publications, blue books, or state manuals containing official election results are also listed.

Current Compendia

1185   *The Associated Press Political Service.* New York: Associated Press, 1977–. (Vendor: Mead Data Central)

Statistical and narrative information about U.S. Senate, U.S. House of Representatives, and gubernatorial elections, as well as state referendums and propositions can be retrieved online from the *NEXIS* database that contains all material disseminated by the AP Political Service and other AP wire services. In addition to the election results, the database also contains profiles of candidates, campaign descriptions, and a calendar of election events. Full text display and printout based on multiple search possibilities (KWIC, full text, etc.) is available 12 to 48 hours after dissemination of the material by the AP service.

1186   Congressional Quarterly Service. *Complete Returns of the . . . Elections by Congressional Districts.* Washington, DC: 1957–.

1187   _____ . *Guide to U.S. Elections.* Washington, DC: 1975.

_____ . *Supplement.* Washington, DC: 1977–.

Congressional Quarterly, Inc., is a major publisher of information material about United States elections. Complete election returns for presidential, congressional, as well as gubernatorial candidates are published quadrennially for each congressional district and state. In addition, a separate guidebook with supplements is published.

The *Guide to U.S. Elections* is a superb compendium of statistical and narrative information material on U.S. election history. Data are displayed under six major headings, as follows: (1) Political Parties, including national nominating conventions, convention ballots, political party nominees; (2) Presidential Elections, including history of the electoral college, electoral and popular votes, presidential primaries, list of candidates; (3) Gubernatorial Elections, including lists of governors and popular vote returns; (4) Senate Elections, including list of senators, senate candidates, and popular vote returns; (5) House Elections, including history of reapportionment and redistricting; and (6) Southern Primaries, including popular vote returns. Appropriate indexes and bibliographies are provided in each section. A separate appendix section contains tabular information on congressional sessions since 1789, political party affiliations in Congress and the presidency since 1789, U.S. Census of Population since 1790, immigrants by country since 1820, constitutional provisions on elections, political party abbreviations, and methods of selecting presidential electors. The election data have been obtained from the Historical Archive of the Inter-University Consortium for Political Research (ICPR), whose machine-readable data

are available to scholars. Supplements are issued for more recent elections as time progresses.

1188   Scammon, Richard M. *America Votes, A Handbook of Contemporary American Election Statistics.* New York: Macmillan; Pittsburgh: University of Pittsburgh Press; Washington, DC: Governmental Affairs Institute, 1956–.

The biennially issued compendium is a continuing source for the election statistics of presidential, gubernatorial, and congressional candidates. Each volume contains data for the population, total votes, votes for Republican and Democratic candidates, pluralities and percentages in each state, county, major city, and congressional district.

Retrospective Compendia

There are at least eight reference works that offer, in partially overlapping coverage, statistical compilations for presidential elections held between 1792 and 1980. Their chronological scope is as follows:

Presidential Elections	
	1789–1980 CQ's *Presidential Elections*
	1792–1980 Petersen
	1836–1892 Burnham
	1896–1944 Robinson
	1910–1970 Cox
	1920–1964 *America at the Polls*
	1948–1968 Runyon
	1952–1978 Miller

These reference works are listed below in alphabetical sequence.

1189   Burnham, Walter Dean. *Presidential Ballots 1836–1892.* Baltimore: Johns Hopkins University Press, 1955.

Statistical tables provide national, regional, state, and county returns for Democratic and Republican or other candidates for the presidency during elections held between 1836 and 1892. Narrative introductions to the statistical material elucidate the main trends of the election periods.

1190   Cox, Edward Franklin. *State and National Voting in Federal Elections 1910–1970.* Hamden, CT: Archon Books, 1972.

The compendium contains chronologically arranged tables of voting statistics for each state. The data consist of votes and percentages listed in four parallel columns, namely, (1) presidential, (2) senatorial, (3) representative, (4) average. In each table the votes and percentages are divided into three categories of Democratic, Republican, and other candidates. Following the statistical table of each state are notes that offer additional voting information. National voting statistics are also included.

1191   Governmental Affairs Institute. Election Research Center. *America at the Polls*. Pittsburgh: University of Pittsburgh Press, 1965.

Twelve presidential elections form 1920 to 1964 are reported in this compendium. The same breakdown by state and county is used as in the *America Votes* volumes. Total votes, pluralities, and percentages for Republican and Democratic candidates are listed.

1192   Miller, Warren E., Arthur H. Miller, and Edward J. Schneider. *American National Election Studies Data Sourcebook, 1952–1978*. Cambridge, MA: Harvard University Press, 1980.

This reference book has been compiled to enhance the understanding of individual elections and to provide a basis for broader generalizations on American politics since 1952. Personal face-to-face interviews with national full-probability samples of all citizens of voting age provided the data in the 14 American national election studies presented. Organized in six chapters, the data cover socioeconomic characteristics of various electoral groups, political partisanship, attitudinal positions on public policy issues, support of the political system, voter involvement and turnout, and presidential as well as congressional votes. Interpretation of the voluminous data requires a careful reading of the explanations provided by the authors in the introductory chapter.

1193   Petersen, Svend. *A Statistical History of the American Presidential Elections*. Westport, CT: Greenwood Press, 1981.

The compendium is one of only two sources of statistics for all presidential elections held during three centuries up to 1980. It contains 134 statistical compilations, including tables of votes and percentages for each election, each state, and each party. No county or city breakdowns of the votes are given.

1194   *Presidential Elections since 1789*. Washington, DC: Congressional Quarterly, Inc., 1983.

Like the Petersen compendium this reference book also offers presidential election statistics since 1789. Presidential primary returns, popular vote returns, and electoral college votes are presented in addition to details about the nominees of the political party conventions.

1195   Robinson, Edgar Eugene. *The Presidential Vote, 1896–1932*. Stanford, CA: Stanford University Press, 1934.

_____ . *The Presidential Vote 1936: Supplementing the Presidential Vote, 1896–1932*. Stanford, CA: Stanford University Press, 1940.

_____ . *They Voted for Roosevelt. The Presidential Vote, 1932–1944*. Stanford, CA: Stanford University Press, 1947.

Voting data by state and county may be found in this three-volume set for all presidential elections held between 1896 and 1944. Maps and statistical tables are used to portray various dimensions of the election results.

1196   Runyon, John H., Jennifer Verdini, and Sally S. Runyon. *Sourcebook of American Presidential Campaign and Election Statistics, 1948–1968*. New York: Ungar Publishing Company, 1971.

Detailed statistical data on presidential primaries, national party conventions, campaign staff and costs, as well as voting results are presented in this reference work for the presidential elections held during a 20-year period up to 1968. Bibliographic references to additional data sources are also included.

Terminological and Conceptual Information

The American political process has produced a rich and distinct vocabulary. Several dictionaries exist that provide definitions of American political terms according to linguistic, historical, legal, and other aspects. In addition, two encyclopedias offer brief but by no means comprehensive summaries of the subject matter of American government.

DICTIONARIES

1197   Elliot, Jeffrey M., and Sheikh R. Ali. *The Presidential-Congressional Political Dictionary*. Santa Barbara, CA: ABC-Clio, 1984.

More than 750 terms relating to the concepts, activities, and personalities that link Congress and the office of the president are defined in this dictionary. Each entry includes a paragraph that explains the significance of the listed item within the American system.

1198   Holt, Sol. *The Dictionary of American Government*. New York: McFadden-Bartell, 1964.

The small but useful dictionary contains over 1,000 entries for political terms, legal acts, Supreme Court decisions, executive departments, and other organizational units of the U.S. government. All entries are alphabetically arranged and carry a brief, compact description of the subject matter.

1199   McCarthy, Eugene J. *Dictionary of American Politics*. New York: Macmillan, 1968.

This dictionary by Senator McCarthy defines terms relating to the structure and form of the U.S. government as well as political processes. Emphasis is on the terminology most frequently used. The definitions reflect contemporary rather than historical usage. The arrangement of the entries is alphabetical.

1200   Plano, Jack C., and Milton Greenberg. *The American Political Dictionary*. New York: Holt, Rinehart and Winston, 1982.

Over 1,200 terms, agencies, court cases, and statutes that are most relevant for a basic understanding of American governmental institutions, practices, and problems are defined or described in this dictionary. The entries are arranged under 14 subject chapters with separate listings for important agencies, cases, and statutes. All entries include a statement about the listed item's significance to American government and citizenry. An index is also provided.

1201   Raymond, Walter J. *Dictionary of Politics*. Lawrenceville, VA: Brunswick Publishing Company, 1978.

There are over 4,600 entries in this volume, consisting of definitions of terms and concepts together with references to additional sources of information. There are also 46 appendices that offer a wide variety of information. Included are the texts of the Declaration of Independence, the Articles of Confederation, the U.S. Constitution; lists of U.S. presidents, vice-presidents, speakers of the U.S. House of Representatives, chief justices, secretaries of state; landmark cases of the U.S. Supreme Court; various statistical tables and charts. Ten political maps for the United States, Third World countries, Communist countries, and conflict areas are also provided.

1202   Safire, William. *The New Language of Politics*. New York: Random House, 1968, 1978; New York: Collier Books, 1972.

The prime purpose of this frequently revised and updated dictionary by a former reporter and practicing public relations man is to make readily available the words that worked for politicians. Emphasis is on modern catchwords, slogans, and rhetorical phrases that evoke desired images or produce political results. All entries consist of a brief definition followed by a frequently detailed description of the usage employed by politicians for the purpose of leading or misleading the public. The dictionary also contains an inventory of phrases coined by or associated with President Franklin D. Roosevelt or his successors. A good-sized bibliography and a separate name index are also included.

1203   Smith, Edward C., and Arnold J. Zurcher. *New Dictionary of American Politics*. New York: Barnes and Noble, 1968.

This dictionary has been frequently revised since its first appearance in 1888. It now contains almost 4,000 entries for American political terms, slogans, nicknames, governmental units, legal acts, Supreme Court decisions, and political ideas. All entries are signed by the scholars contributing to this standard reference tool.

1204   Sperber, Hans, and Travis Trittschuh. *American Political Terms*. Detroit: Wayne State University Press, 1962.

An attempt by two philologists to establish the historical facts for the usage of political terms. Arranged alphabetically, the entries contain a brief definition followed by identification of first usage and reference to time and source. Resembles Matthews' *Dictionary of Americanisms*, but limited to the political vocabulary.

1205   Whisker, James B. A *Dictionary of Concepts on American Politics*. New York: John Wiley, 1980.

The aim of this dictionary is to inform the reader, in as little space as possible, what the main ideas, events, concepts, and institutions of American government are and why they are important. Entries are arranged under 12 chapters, entitled (1) Political Ideas, (2) Founding of the Republic, (3) Federalism, (4) Politics and Political Parties, (5) Presidency, (6) Bureaucracy, (7) Congress, (8) Court System, (9) Civil Liberties, (10) Taxation and Fiscal Policy, (11) International and Military Affairs, and (12) State and Local Government. The texts of the Declaration of Independence and the U.S. Constitution as well as a detailed index are also included.

1206   Tallman, Marjorie. *Dictionary of American Government*. Paterson, NJ: Littlefield, Adams and Company, 1968.

The dictionary offers brief definitions of American political terms, governmental and judicial units, important legal acts, as well as sociological and economic terms frequently used in the political literature.

ENCYCLOPEDIAS

1207   *American Government 73/74 Encyclopedia*. Guilford, CT: Dushkin Publishing Group, 1975.

The encyclopedia consists of some 1,000 relatively short articles arranged in alphabetical sequence. Many of the longer articles contain study outlines. References to publications at the end of the article offer suggestions for further reading. Illustrations and diagrams accompany many articles.

1208   McLaughlin, Andrew C. *Cyclopedia of American Government*. New York: Appleton, 1914; Gloucester, MA: Peter Smith, 1963.

Although obviously much out-of-date this work remains the only multivolume encyclopedia for lengthy summarization of the subject matter of American government. All the articles fall within one or more of five basic categories of information, namely, (1) land and the people, (2) theory and principles, (3) history, (4) organization of government, and (5) functions of government. The arrangement of all articles is alphabetical by subject term. Larger subjects are subdivided as necessary. Articles rarely attempt an exhaustive treatment, but bibliographies for further reading are usually included. All articles are signed by the contributors. Volume 3 contains an index that discloses additional subjects treated within the context of larger subject matter.

STATE GOVERNMENT

Introduction

While there is no dearth of publications by or about state governments and politics, bibliographic control and other reference treatment for information about the political system at this subnational level continue to be in a stage of imperfection. There are virtually no current bibliographies that are specifically oriented toward scientific findings about state governments and politics. There is no abstracting service for scholarly books and articles published about the political institutions, processes, and problems at the state level. Much of the existing information material, therefore, has to be extracted from the general political and historical science bibliographies described in Chapter 2 of this guidebook.

The official publications issued by state governments are listed in individual state bibliographies and to some extent also in a nationwide checklist. Unfortunately, only a few libraries are able to collect all of these individual state bibliographies or the publications listed in them. Most academic libraries collect only the official documentation of the state in which they are located, but even within these limited collection programs bibliographic control is often less than perfect.

Biographical and organizational information is covered by a limited number of reference works on a nationwide basis. In many instances these reference works cannot offer the most current information because of the great instability of their subject matter.

Statistical information relating to states is available in federal as well as state publications. These statistical sources are identifiable in the guidebooks or directories that have been described in the Statistical Information section under Federal Government. No nationwide instrument exists for the oral argumentation in the legislatures of the 50 states. Even big states, like California, do not have a reference source for legislative debates comparable to the *Congressional Record* on the federal level. It is therefore difficult to obtain a current and accurate picture of the political objects under discussion in the legislative processes of the states.

Further details of the available reference mechanism for state government information are provided in the annotations for the reference works listed below.

Official Publications

GUIDEBOOKS

1209   Parish, David W. *State Government Reference Publications. An Annotated Bibliography*. Littleton, CO: Libraries Unlimited, 1981.

Now in its second edition, this bibliographic volume is the only complete guide to the official reference literature of the 50 state governments. The 1,756 annotated entries are arranged by form categories, as follows: (1) official state bibliography, (2) blue books, (3) legislative manuals and related references, (4) government finances, (5) statistical abstracts and other data sources, (6) directories, (7) tourist guides, (8) audiovisual guides, atlases, and maps, (9) bibliographies and general references. Within these categories listings are in alphabetical order of states. There are also four appendices: I. Bibliography: Suggested Readings; II. Bibliography: Reference Tools; III. A Subject Core of State Publications; IV. Agency Addresses. Title, personal author, and subject indexes are also included.

1210   Press, Charles. *State Manuals, Blue Books, and Election Results*. Berkeley: University of California, 1962.

1211   *State Blue Books and Reference Publications: A Selected Bibliography*. Lexington, KY: Council of State Governments, 1983.

Descriptive information about state agencies and a listing of their key personnel can ordinarily be found in a type of state publication that may bear the title manual, official register, legislative handbook, directory, roster, blue book, or almanac. Most of these reference publications are officially issued, although a few states have publications issued by commercial publishers only.

The first title above refers to an older guidebook that contains a state-by-state listing of these reference publications, whether officially or unofficially issued, together with an analysis and tabulation of their contents. The beginning date, frequency, and other useful details of these publications are reported.

The second title listed above refers to a current bibliography of blue books, legislative manuals, directories, statistical abstracts, and other state reference publications. The listings are arranged by state with subdivisions by reference type.

CURRENT BIBLIOGRAPHIES

1212   Council of State Governments. *Legislative Research Checklist*. Chicago: 1960 – .

New state publications related to state legislation are identifiable with this checklist. Entries are arranged alphabetically by subject and then by state, and provide information about the issuing agency, title, date, and pagination of the published material. All items in this checklist are available on microcard from Fall City Microcard of Louisville, Kentucky, or on microfiche from Microcard Editions of the National Cash Register Company.

1213   U.S. Library of Congress. Exchange and Gift Division. *Monthly Checklist of State Publications.* Washington, DC: U.S. Government Printing Office, 1910—.

The official publications of the states are usually listed individually for each state in an official bibliography produced by the state printer, but libraries ordinarily do not collect these bibliographies from other states. The title above refers to a monthly bibliography that functions as a useful although incomplete substitute for the individual state lists. The *Monthly Checklist* records only those publications that are received by the Library of Congress, but distribution of the official state publications to the Library of Congress is voluntary only. Very few states have enacted laws for the submission of at least one copy of each state publication. Entries are arranged by state and state agency. A subject index to the listed material is published annually.

Scholarly Publications

BIBLIOGRAPHIES

1214   Chase, Karen A. *Reorganization of State Government: A Selective Bibliography.* Berkeley: Institute of Governmental Studies, University of California, 1968.

It is difficult to talk collectively about the 50 state governments because of the great degree of variation exhibited by them. Consensus appears to exist among scholars, however, that state governments are in need of reorganization. This bibliography offers unannotated listings of books, periodicals, reports, special studies, and other information material dealing with specific reorganization plans or problems.

1215   Goehlert, Robert U., and Frederick W. Musto. *State Legislatures. A Bibliography.* Santa Barbara, CA: ABC-Clio Information Services, 1985.

More than 2,500 entries for books, journal articles, dissertations, and university research reports dealing with state legislatures are provided by this bibliography. The first part of the book lists theoretical and comparative legislative studies within 25 topical categories. The second part focuses on state legislatures in each of the 50 states. Subject and author indexes are included.

1216   *Selected Bibliography on State Government: 1959—1972.* Lexington, KY: Council of State Governments, 1972.

Publications on every aspect of state government issued during an earlier period can be identified with the help of this bibliography offering more than 1,000 entries.

Biographical and Organizational Information

HANDBOOKS AND DIRECTORIES

1217   *The Book of the States. 1. State Elective Officials and the Legislatures. 2. State Administrative Officials Classified by Functions. 3. Principal Legislative Staff Offices.* Chicago: Council of State Governments, 1935—.

This biennially revised set of reference works provides authoritative information on constitutions and elections, legislative structures and developments, state judiciary systems, administrative organizations, major state services, intergovernmental relations, financial and budgetary matters in the 50 states. Separate directories identify elective officials, legislative staff offices, and the administrative officials of each state. The latter are listed by state functions.

1218   Burns, John. *The Sometime Governments. A Critical Study of 50 American Legislatures.* New York: Bantam Books, 1971.

One of the weaknesses of the American political system is the limited decision-making capability of state legislatures. This handbook presents in easily retrievable form an evaluation of the legislatures together with itemized reform recommendations for each of the 50 states. An appendix contains a glossary of political terms and a list of organizations concerned with state government. A well-developed subject index is also provided.

1219   Glashan, Roy R. *American Governors and Gubernatorial Elections, 1775—1978.* Westport, CT: Meckler Books, 1979.

1220   Kallenbach, Joseph E., and Jessamine S. Kallenbach. *American State Governors, 1776—1976.* Dobbs Ferry, NY: Oceana Publications, 1977.

1221   Sobel, Robert, and John Raimo. *Biographical Directory of the Governors of the United States, 1789—1978.* Westport, CT: Meckler Books, 1978.

1222   Solomon, Samuel R. *The Governors of the American States, Commonwealths, and Territories, 1900—1980.* Lexington, KY: Council of State Governments, 1980.

There have been approximately 2,300 men and women who have served as state governors at one time or another since the American Revolution. Twenty-one of them have later become president or vice-president of the United States, while many others have subsequently been elected or appointed to other high political offices. Clearly the governorship is of central importance in the decision-making process that ultimately shapes national politics in the United States. There are at least four reference works that offer concise and handy gubernatorial information.

Following an arrangement by state, the first title offers a chronological listing of state governors together with information about their birthdate, birthplace, terms of office, political party affiliation, major occupation, residence, death date, and election returns. Quotations from speeches and writings of a few of the governors are also included in addition to general and state listings of important publications for further information.

The second title is a two-volume set. Volume I presents pertinent historical and political data regarding the practices and results of the efforts of each state to fill the office of the governor. The information is arranged by state and includes the names of all persons who were candidates in the gubernatorial elections together with their party affiliation and voting results. An introductory section informs about the mode of choice, term and reeligibility, time of election, beginning of term, qualifications, and removal and succession arrangements provided by state laws. The second volume contains biographical summaries for each of the governors listed in the first volume.

The third title above refers to a four-volume set offering brief information on the major decisions of each governor in addition to other biographical details. Entries are arranged by state and follow a chronological order. Each entry also contains bibliographical references to appropriate books and articles for further details about each governor. A separate name index is included.

The fourth title cited above is an inexpensive, 79-page booklet that presents basic data about the governors of this century. For each state governors are listed chronologically, and party affiliation, birth and death dates, terms of office, and residence are indicated. A short bibliography of works dealing with state governors is also included.

A notable weakness of all four reference works is the absence of information explaining why governors were able to win their elections.

1223   *The National Directory of State Agencies.* Washington, DC: Information Resources Press, 1974 – .

Issued biannually, the directory lists state agencies by state/function as well as by function/state. Nearly 100 different governmental functions, such as civil defense, community affairs, commerce, corrections, economic development, education, highways, liquor control,

police, social services, and others are identified. Entries provide the name of the administrator, his or her title, the name of the bureau and department, and the address and telephone number. Although elections, personnel shifts, and reorganizations may make some entries obsolete, the names, addresses, and telephone numbers of the vast majority of the agencies hold from edition to edition.

Process Information

NEWS DIGESTS

1224   *From the State Capitals.* Asbury Park, NJ: Bethune Jones, 1930 – .

Current and prospective legislative, administrative and judicial action at the state level is reported in this series of weekly or monthly digests. Each of the various digest series is devoted to a specific target of state control, primarily fiscal or administrative in nature, such as drug abuse control, highway financing, housing and development, liquor control, motor vehicle regulation, police administration, public assistance, public health, racial relations, school financing, urban transit and transportation, etc.

LOCAL GOVERNMENT

Introduction

According to the U.S. Bureau of the Census, there are more than 82,600 local governments in the form of municipalities, townships, counties, school districts, and special districts in the United States. Their purpose is to operate a variety of service delivery programs that provide the inhabitants with police protection, fire protection, judicial and legal services, public health facilities, transportation facilities, management of natural and human resources, control of land use and the environment, cultural and recreational facilities, and other essential activities.

As a result of their functional specialization to purely service-oriented activities, most of which are of a nonenterprise character, local governments suffer from an inadequate economic foundation that rarely provides the necessary opportunity for profitable operations or productivity increases due to technological improvements. Revenue sources must rely heavily on transfer funds, such as intergovernmental revenue sharing and taxation, including the unpopular method of property taxation. Most local governments therefore face increasing financial pressures, with operating costs and the need for new and expanded services rising faster than the willingness of the public to accept higher taxes or the necessary political reforms for improving the economic foundations.

Bibliographic control of the literature by or about local government has long been a stepchild of political science. In recent years several new or improved reference works have helped to make the retrieval of local government information somewhat easier. Significant gaps in coverage continue to exist, however, making it difficult to compare revenue sources and service levels across state and national boundaries.

An interesting and welcome feature of the present reference literature for local government studies is the existence of multipurpose reference works in the form of yearbooks that offer bibliographical, biographical, statistical, and other information categories within a single volume. These and other valuable reference works are listed and described below in classified order.

Bibliographic Information

GUIDEBOOKS

1225   *Municipal Government Reference Sources. Publications and Collections.* New York: R. R. Bowker, 1978.

This is a guidebook about the kinds of documents available from and about major municipalities in the United States. Arranged by state and city, the book lists and describes reference publications only but with specific indication of the institutions where municipal documents are made available. Typically included as reference publications are bibliographies, annual reports and budgets, directories, fact books, legal codebooks, local newpaper indexes, and similar reference works. The institutional listings describe public and academic libraries, associations, and governmental agencies that issue and collect municipal documents. A county-city cross-reference list and a detailed subject index are also included.

1226   Murphy, Thomas P. *Urban Politics.* Detroit: Gale Research Company, 1978.

1227   Palumbo, Dennis J., and George A. Taylor. *Urban Policy.* Detroit: Gale Research Company, 1979.

Urban politics and policies are political activities concerned with urban revitalization, i.e., the improvement of the living conditions in urban areas. Scholarly books and periodical articles describing or analyzing the process or policy stage of urban political activities are listed and annotated in the two guidebooks cited above. Entries follow a topical arrangement that focuses in the process stage on the urban governmental structure, political leadership, participatory decision making, socioethnic politics, metropolitan organization, and in the policy stage on the determinants, goals, formation, and evaluation of urban policies. Urban public interest and professional organizations are identified in *Urban Politics.* Both guidebooks include indexes by author, title, and subject.

CURRENT BIBLIOGRAPHIES

1228   *Index to Current Urban Documents.* Westport, CT: Greenwood Periodicals Company, 1972–.

Official documents issued by local governments in 286 of the larger cities, counties, and regions of the United States and Canada are listed geographically as well as by subject in this quarterly bibliography. The listed documentation comprises annual reports, audit reports, budgets, community development programs, master plans, criminal justice plans, demographic profiles, directories, economic base studies, environmental impact statements, evaluations, feasibility studies, minutes of proceedings, policy statements, public opinion polls, statistical tables, zoning ordinances, and other items. All cited documents are made available on microfiche by the publisher. The fiche number for locating the document in the microfiche collection is included in each bibliographic entry.

1229   *Sage Urban Studies Abstracts.* Beverly Hills, CA: Sage Publications, 1973–.

Much information relating to local governments and politics can be identified with this reference work. For a detailed description, see entry 817 in this guidebook.

1230   *Urban Affairs Abstracts.* Washington, DC: National League of Cities and United States Conference of Mayors, Department of Library Services, 1972–.

The weekly bibliography lists and abstracts articles on urban politics and other governmental activities in cities from nearly 1,200 periodicals. Entries are categorized under 50 major subjects, including community development, employment, environment, finances, municipal administration, social services, transportation, etc. Quarterly and annual cumulations are also published.

RETROSPECTIVE BIBLIOGRAPHIES

1231   Bollens, John C. *American County Government.* Beverly Hills, CA: Sage Publications, 1969.

The 3,000 county governments are numerically the smallest element of the local governments in the United States, but their existence and justification is poorly understood. This valuable reference work analyzes existing county research and future research needs. It describes new approaches in county research and offers a bibliographical commentary on the existing literature. Studies of individual counties are excluded, and only items of nationwide or statewide coverage are listed. An author and title index but no state or subject index is included.

1232   Booth, David Albin. *Council-Manager Government 1940–64: An Annotated Bibliography.* Chicago: International City Managers Association, 1965.

Probably no other innovation in municipal government has been more popular than the employment of a professional manager for the administrative work of the city. This annotated bibliography identifies books and articles that haave been published during a quarter-century on the council-manager and city-manager type of local government.

1233   Branch, Melville C. *Comprehensive Urban Planning. A Selective Annotated Bibliography With Related Materials.* Beverly Hills, CA: Sage Publications, 1970.

City planning is one of the most important functions of local government. The existing literature of books, articles, reports, and pamphlets on city planning is listed under the following headings: Background, Process, Theory, Information-Communication, Research-Analysis, Methodology, Institutionalization, Management, Decisionmaking, Effectuation, System Elements, Subsystems, and Particular Forms of Urban Planning. The book also contains a list of schools offering graduate courses and degrees in urban and regional planning. Separate author, title, and subject indexes are provided.

1234   Government Affairs Foundation, Inc., New York. *Metropolitan Communities: A Bibliography with Special Emphasis upon Government and Politics.* Chicago: Public Administration Service, 1956–1972.

The five-volume set contains partly annotated listings of books, periodical articles, and government reports dealing with (1) the function, problems, and the organization of metropolitan government, and (2) the socioeconomic background of metropolitan areas. More than 20,000 entries cover the literature published up to 1970.

1235   Hawley, Willis D., and James H. Svara. *The Study of Community Power. A Bibliographic Review.* Santa Barbara, CA: American Bibliographical Center—Clio Press, 1972.

The study of community power has produced much information and valuable insights on how local political systems operate. This bibliography identifies a substantial portion of the scientific literature on the subject of community power published during the 50 years preceding 1971. The well-annotated entries are arranged under five chapters: (1) a historical overview of the study of community power, (2) field studies of communities, (3) the methodology of community power research, (4) efforts at synthesis, general criticism, and other commentaries, and (5) defining and measuring social power. Citations to book reviews and an author index are included.

1236   Hutcheson, John D., Jr., and Jane Shevin. *Citizen Groups in Local Politics. A Bibliographic Review.* Santa Barbara, CA: Clio Books, 1976.

The attempts of citizen groups to influence local politics and decision making have been an important target of scholarly research. Following a general overview of the scholarly literature, this annotated bibliography lists books, periodical articles, and dissertations dealing with a general theory of citizen group participation, citizen group involvement in planning, community development and service delivery systems, voluntary associations and local politics, and local government reactions to demands for citizen participation. Also listed are guidebooks and handbooks for citizen group leaders and members.

1237   Michalak, Thomas J., and Robert Goehlert. *Reform of Local Government Structures in the United States, 1945–1971: Bibliography Index.* Greenwich, CT: Jai Press, 1976.

1238   White, Anthony G. *Reforming Metropolitan Governments: A Bibliography.* New York: Garland Publishing, Inc., 1975.

Pressing and rapidly increasing needs of a social, economic, and environmental nature require a restructuring of outmoded local governments in the United States. The two bibliographies facilitate the identification of the literature produced on reform efforts during the 30-year period since 1945.

1239   Shearer, Barbara Smith, and Benjamin F. Shearer. *Periodical Literature on United States Cities.* Westport, CT: Greenwood Press, 1983.

The bibliography can be used to identify periodical articles dealing with political and social conditions in American cities. It lists 4,919 articles on the 170 American cities with a population of 100,000 or more. Entries are arranged alphabetically by city and are divided into eight subject categories: (1) general, (2) architecture and the arts, (3) education and the media, (4) environment, (5) government and politics, (6) housing and urban development, (7) social and economic conditions, and (8) transportation. Separate subject and author indexes are also included.

Multiple Information

YEARBOOKS

1240   *The County Yearbook.* Washington, DC: International City Management Association and National Association of Counties, 1975–1978.

1241   *The Municipal Yearbook.* Washington, DC: International City Management Association, 1934– .

The two yearbooks combine various reference functions by offering bibliographical, organizational, and statistical information. The bibliographic listings identify general reference sources as well as books, periodical articles, and official publications dealing with each of the various functions of local governments. Organizational listings identify state municipal leagues, state agencies for local affairs, state associations of counties, professional organizations, special assistance and educational organizations that serve local governments. City officials in all cities of 10,000 or more population in each state, mayors, appointed administrators in cities of 5,000 to 10,000, appointed administrators in cities under 5,000 population, county clerks and other county officials, as well as Council of Governments (COG) directors are listed. Salary trends and patterns of employment are shown in statistical tables with accompanying summaries. Legislative, administrative, judicial, and financial trends are described in separate sections. The *County Yearbook*, currently no longer published, offered statistical profiles of individual counties. The *Municipal Yearbook* also contains a number of significant research article on the problems and conflicts facing local governments.

Organizational and Biographical Information

DICTIONARIES AND DIRECTORIES

1242   Andriot, John L. *Township Atlas of the United States: Named Townships*. McLean, VA: Andriot Associates, 1979.

The reference work identifies named townships in the 23 states that use this form of administrative subdivision by state statute according to the 1970 census of population. Arranged by state, the book contains a brief explanation of the state's township system, a county location index, a map of the state and its counties, and county maps showing the location of the townships. Also included is a detailed township index and unorganized territories index in alphabetical arrangement. Factual and statistical information on the townships, however, is not provided by this reference work.

1243   Holli, Melvin G., and Peter d'A. Jones. *Biographical Dictionary of American Mayors 1820—1980. Big City Mayors*. Westport, CT: Greenwood Press, 1981.

Following an alphabetical arrangement, the book provides biographies for 679 mayors of 15 leading American cities during a 160-year period. Information is included about political party affiliations, election results, and major political objectives or achievements. One or more sources of additional information material are listed at the end of each biographical article. There are also 12 appendices that provide various population statistics as well as listings of mayors by chronology, party affiliation, ethnic background, religious affiliation, and place of birth.

1244   Kane, Joseph Nathan. *The American Counties*. Metuchen, NJ: Scarecrow Press, 1972.

This directory is divided into an introductory chapter and eight parts that list counties alphabetically by name, by state, or by date of creation. Separately listed are counties whose names have changed, county seats, persons for whom counties have been named, independent cities, and Alaskan boroughs. The alphabetical listing of the counties is the heart of the work and provides information such as the parent state, date of creation, square area, the 1970 population, the county seat, the nickname of the county, the source of the county name, as well as author, title, and imprint information of books suggested for further reading about the county.

Statistical Information

1245   U.S. Bureau of the Census. *Census of Governments*.

Volume 1. *Governmental Organization*.
Volume 2. *Taxable Property Values and Assessments—Sales Price Rations*.
Volume 3. *Public Employment*. Part 1, Employment of Major Local Governments; Part 2, Compendium of Public Employment; Part 3, Management-Labor Relations in State and Local Governments.
Volume 4. *Governmental Finances*. Part 1, Finances of School Districts; Part 2, Finances of Special Districts; Part 3, Finances of County Governments; Part 4, Finances of Municipalities and Township Governments; Part 5, Compendium of Government Finances.
Volume 5. *Local Government in Metropolitan Areas*.
Volume 6. *Topical Studies*. Part 1, Employee Retirement Systems of State and Local Governments; Part 2, State Reports on State and Local Government Finances; Part 3, State Payments to Local Governments; Part 4, Historical Statistics on Governmental Finances and Employment; Part 5, Graphic Summary of the Census of Governments.
Volume 7. *State Reports*.
Volume 8. *Guide to Census of Governments*.

Washington, DC: U.S. Government Printing Office, 1957—.

Apart from the previously listed statistical sources of the federal government, this set of statistical compendia presents valuable data on local governments in the United States. The Census of Governments is taken at five-year intervals in years ending in 5 and 7, and covers four major subject fields—government and organization, taxable property values, public employment, and governmental finances. In addition to the quinquennial census volumes, annual, quarterly, monthly, and special surveys are undertaken. The results of the census and survey program are published in a series of preliminary reports and final reports, supplemented by a number of quarterly and annual publications. Beginning in 1974 the Bureau of the Census also began issuing a series of tapes in computer-readable form. Descriptive information and statistical data in tabular and graphic form provided by this massive publication program enable the user to identify the units of local government, their functions, manpower, expenditures, revenues, and interrelationships. Historical summaries extending back to 1902 show trends in all subject areas. Facsimiles of the questionnaires and other forms used in the census are also included, thus permitting the user to gauge the limitations of the information collected. Like many other statistical programs, the census measures only what is and not what ought to be. Gaps in quality of service, satisfaction of needs, and availability of revenues for all desired services are therefore not readily apparent. The presented data do show, however, that in spite of a decreasing trend local governments still rely to an astonishing extent on the questionable practice of property taxation to finance essential services, notably the education of school children. Readers desiring additional information are referred to Part 2 of the *Topical Studies* volume, which contains annotated bibliographies of additional publications issued by state agencies.

POLITICAL BEHAVIOR

Party and Interest Group Actors

According to the *Dictionary of the Social Sciences*, a definition embracing all phenomena that are regularly called *party* is a difficult task.* Nevertheless, it is probably accurate to state that political parties in the United States are primarily instruments for the organization of elections and other mass political behavior. To a significant degree the major American political parties are also depoliticizing instruments, acting as a filter for rising expectations and suppressing dynamic leadership that might stir up political passions in the country. In recent years, changing electoral and other political behavior has raised the question of whether the United States any longer possesses political parties.** It would appear that the traditional

---

* Julius Gould and W. K. Kolb, A *Dictionary of the Social Sciences* (New York: Free Press of Glencoe, 1964), pp. 482–483.
**Anthony King, *The American Polity in the Late 1970's: Building Coalitions in the Sand*, in Samuel H. Beer et al., *The New American Political System* (Washington, DC: American Enterprise Institute for Public Policy Research, 1978), p. 375.

role of parties is increasingly being replaced by movements funneled by issue or candidate enthusiasts. In addition to the established interest groups based on corporate self-interest, many new interest groups are constantly emerging that pursue only a single limited goal. Having achieved their mission or failed in it, there is nothing to hold these groups together, and they disappear again. During their relatively brief existence, however, these movements add a new dimension to the policy-forming process in the ranks of government.

Reference treatment of this phenomenon in American political behavior has so far failed to recognize the changing character of the American political system. Specialized reference instruments, for the most part, cover information by or about political parties only, and no comprehensive or current bibliography has emerged about political movements. A noteworthy exception is the women's rights movement, which, due to its long existence and potentially large interest sphere, has spawned several bibliographies of its massive literature.

BIBLIOGRAPHIES

1246   Argranoff, Robert. *Elections and Electoral Behavior: a Bibliography*. DeKalb: Center for Government Studies, Northern Illinois University, 1972.

The unannotated bibliography identifies over 300 publications dealing with electoral systems and voting rights, candidate selection, nominations, party conventions, voting behavior, and electoral interpretation.

1247   Garrison, Lloyd W. *American Politics and Elections*. Santa Barbara, CA: American Bibliographical Center—Clio Press, 1969.

1248   Garrison, Lloyd W., and Dwight L. Smith. *The American Political Process: A Bibliography*. Santa Barbara, CA: American Bibliographical Center—Clio Press, 1972.

1249   Schlachter, Gail A., and Pamela R. Byrne. *The American Electorate*. Santa Barbara, CA: ABC-Clio, 1983.

The American political process through partisan alignments, campaign and voting activities has received extensive treatment in the scholarly literature. More than 4,000 abstracts of periodical articles published between 1955 and 1982 can be found in the three bibliographic volumes cited above. The abstracts are arranged by major subject category, including partisan development, ideologies and alignments, political parties, political action groups, electoral issues and processes, ethnic politics, women in politics, public opinion, and similar topics. Additional access to the listed material is provided by detailed indexes containing topical, biographical, geographical, and chronological terms.

1250   Garza, Hedda. *The Watergate Investigation Index: Senate Select Committtee Hearings and Reports on Presidential Campaign Activities*. Wilmington, DE: Scholarly Resources, 1982.

The magnitude of the documentary material published as a result of the U.S. Senate's investigation into illegal or improper activities during the 1972 presidential election campaign presents unusual access problems to the researcher. While the *CIS/Index* is normally more than adequate for congressional information material, the index cited above offers extremely detailed access to the 27 volumes of hearings and reports published by the U.S. Senate Select Committee under the title *Presidential Campaign Activities of 1972, Senate Resolution 60, Watergate and Related Activities* (Washington, DC: U.S. Government Printing Office, 1973–1974). Virtually every person, event, or activity mentioned in the investigation is identifiable with the help of some 30,000 entries in the index.

1251   Kaid, Lynda Lee, Keith R. Sanders, and Robert O. Hirsch. *Political Campaign Communication*. Metuchen, NJ: Scarecrow Press, 1974.

The bibliography lists books, periodical articles, pamphlets, official documents, dissertations, and conference papers published about the communication process as it operated in a political campaign or similar context in the United States from 1950 through 1972. There are 1,539 entries arranged alphabetically by author names that are also topically accessible by a separate subject index. A supplement identifies French and German publications offering a foreign perspective on political communication. Also included are an annotated list of 50 books considered seminal to the study of political campaign communication, a list of professional and scholarly journals, and a list of professional and scholarly organizations.

1252   Krichmar, Albert. *The Women's Rights Movement in the United States 1948–1970*. Metuchen, NJ: Scarecrow Press, 1972.

1253   Stanwick, Kathy, and Christine Li. *The Political Participation of Women in the United States: A Selected Bibliography, 1950–1976*. Metuchen, NJ: Scarecrow Press, 1977.

1254   Tingley, Elizabeth, and Donald F. Tingley. *Women and Feminism in American History. A Guide to Information Sources*. Detroit: Gale Research Company, 1981.

The amount of information about the political role of women in the United States has increased dramatically in recent decades. A significant portion of the available literature can be identified with the help of the three bibliographies cited above.

The Krichmar bibliography offers unannotated listings for books, theses, pamphlets, periodical articles, and manuscript sources relating to the women's rights movement in the United States. Entries are arranged by author names under various subject headings, such as Legal and Political Status, Equal Rights Amendment, Suffrage, Economic Status, Women in Law, Women in Politics, Equal Wages, Education, Religion, Biography, Manuscript Sources, Selected References, anad Women's Liberation Serial Publications. Four separate indexes for manuscripts, serials, authors, and subjects provide additional access to the listed material.

The Stanwick and Li bibliography focuses on the political participation of women during a recent 25-year period. Entries are arranged by author names under headings that reflect the form categories of the publications, but no subject index is included.

The Tingley bibliography presents annotated listings for books arranged under 33 subject chapters. Separately listed are bibliographies, biographical directories, general works, and books dealing with specific historical periods, the contemporary feminist ideology, and selected topics, such as women in the labor force, women and crime, abortion, birth control, motherhood, child care programs, etc. The major periodicals in women's studies are also identified. Author, title, and subject indexes are included.

1255   Miles, William. *The Image Makers. A Bibliography of American Presidential Campaign Biographies*. Metuchen, NJ: Scarecrow Press, 1979.

Campaign biographies attempt, through a recounting of the lives of candidates or would-be candidates, to assist in the process of persuading the electorate to nominate and elect contenders for the presidency. Through their emphasis on biographical features most appealing to the American electorate, such works usually border on the mythical by creating pure political imagery. The bibliography initiates some control over this genre in the American political process and lists in chronological sequence of campaigns the books, pamphlets, magazines, or compendia that can be regarded as the most noteworthy examples of this type of campaign literature. The entries cover successful as well as unsuccessful candidates and include complete bibliographical description. Separate author/candidate and title indexes are also provided. Only works for the campaigns dating from 1824 to 1976 are included.

1256   Nelson, Barbara J. *American Women and Poli-*

tics: *A Bibliography and Guide to the Sources*. New York: Garland Publishing, 1983.

The bibliography contains more than 2,500 entries for books and periodical articles dealing with the political behavior of American women. Arranged in 13 topical chapters, the entries cover Women in Social Movements, Feminist Theory, Women as Political Leaders, Political Participation of Women, and the role of women in the family, at work, and in education. A chapter on research resources and an index are included.

1257   Pardo, Thomas C. *The National Woman's Party Papers 1913–1974. A Guide to the Microfilm Edition*. Sanford, NC: Microfilming Corporation of America, 1979.

Founded in 1913 by Alice Paul, the National Woman's Party (NWP) campaigned successfully for a federal amendment guaranteeing the enfranchisement of women, and unsuccessfully for a federal amendment guaranteeing equal rights for men and women. Although never large in size, the NWP succeeded in many other political efforts to equalize the status of women.

Access to the party's microfilmed papers is facilitated by this guidebook. It offers a description of the party's activities and its papers, together with a complete reel list and an index to the important correspondence. Two appendices list the national chairmen and presidents of the NWP, its national conventions and conferences.

1258   Schlachter, Gail A., and Pamela R. Byrne. *The Democratic and Republican Parties in America*. Santa Barbara, CA: ABC-Clio, 1983.

1259   Wynar, Lubomyr R. *American Political Parties: A Selective Guide to Parties and Movements of the 20th Century*. Littleton, CO: Libraries Unlimited, 1969.

A substantial portion of the voluminous monographic and periodical literature dealing with American political parties and their activities is identifiable with the two reference works cited above. The first item contains over 1,000 abstracts of periodical articles published between 1973 and 1982. Entries are arranged alphabetically by author names within major subject chapters and are made additionally accessible by a detailed multiterm subject index. The second item lists more than 3,000 books and dissertations in 18 major sections. General reference works and government publications are listed separately. Author and subject indexes are included.

1260   Walton, Hanes, Jr. *The Study and Analysis of Black Politics: A Bibliography*. Metuchen, NJ: Scarecrow Press, 1973.

Unannotated citations for books and periodical articles dealing with the political activities of black Americans are provided by this bibliography. The entries are ar-

ranged under broad headings, namely, Black Politics, Blacks and Major Political Parties, The Black Vote and National Elections, Black Political Pressure Groups, Black Political Candidates, Black Political Behavior, Blacks and Public Policy, and others.

DOCUMENT COLLECTIONS

1261   Chester, Edward W. *A Guide to Political Platforms*. Hamden, CT: Archon Books, 1977.

1262   Johnson, Donald Bruce. *National Party Platforms. V. 1. 1840–1956. V. 2. 1960–1976*. Urbana: University of Illinois Press, 1978.

1263   Johnson, Donald Bruce. *National Party Platforms of 1980: Supplement to National Party Platforms, 1840–1976*. Champaign: University of Illinois Press, 1982.

Political platforms are carefully prepared documents that evaluate the respective performance of opposing parties and spell out the party's own approach to current issues in foreign policy, defense policy, economic programs, labor policy, welfare, civil rights, management of resources, and other important matters. The Chester book provides a summary of the underlying issues and briefly describes the policy orientations in the party platforms as seen by contemporary journalism and retrospective scholarly assessment. The literal text of the party platforms adopted up to the 1980 campaign can be found in the Johnson volumes. All cited reference books arrange the information chronologically by campaign years.

1264   *Representative American Speeches*. New York: H. W. Wilson Company, 1937– .

1265   *Vital Speeches of the Day*. New York: City News Publishing Company, 1934– .

Unlike the speeches in Congress and the presidential press conferences, the speeches and addresses of American political actors in front of campaign, student, or other audiences have received poor reference treatment. On November 1, 1970, James Reston of the *New York Times* noted that not a single campaign speech on either side had been printed in full in a major newspaper.

The two serialized document collections cited above fill the void only partially. *Representative American Speeches*, issued annually, offers the text of selected political speeches on a variety of contemporary issues, such as U.S. foreign commitments, inflation, international economic policy, social change, governmental reform, education, consumer interests, and many others. Introductory essays, biographical notes about the speakers, and bibliographic references are included in the set.

Vital Speeches of the Day, issued twice monthly, contains the text of speeches delivered by politicians, interest group spokesmen, university professors, and other purveyors of meaning. Not all speeches refer to political topics, however, or are delivered in the United States. *Vital Speeches of the Day* is indexed in the *Reader's Guide to Periodical Literature* and the *Magazine Index*.

HANDBOOKS

1266   Bain, Richard C., and Judith H. Parris. *Convention Decisions and Voting Records*. Washington, DC: Brookings Institution, 1973.

1267   *National Party Conventions, 1831–1976*. Washington, DC: Congressional Quarterly, Inc., 1979.

Initiated by the Anti-Masonic Party in 1831, America's prominent political parties have met in conventions to nominate their presidential and vice-presidential candidates, and to adopt a party platform. While a written record of the convention proceedings is published by both major parties, these publications are usually not readily available in libraries. A useful summary and chronology of each convention held by the major parties is presented by the two reference works listed above. Included are listings for the presidential and vice-presidential nominees, brief biographical information on the principal convention participants, the results of convention ballots, historical profiles of the American political parties, excerpts from the party platforms, and presidential election data. CQ's volume is indexed, contains bibliographic listings, and is likely to be updated as time progresses.

1268   Long, Samuel L. *The Handbook of Political Behavior*. New York: Plenum Press, 1981.

The scientific study of political behavior focuses on political actors, their language, values, actions or series of actions (processes) in pursuit of political objects. As a scientific trend it is thus different from the purely institutional or legal focus of political inquiry. The handbook surveys and evaluates the voluminous behavioral research literature and identifies its principal authors. Since there is as yet no agreed-upon classification of behavioral research, the individual chapters of the handbook cover a motley group of topics, such as Administrative Behavior, Judicial Behavior, Presidential Behavior, Interest Groups, Social Conflict and Public Policy, Processing Framework for Politics, Political Learning, Political Disaffection, Sociopolitical Movements, Political Participation, and many others. All articles are written by political scientists or other social scientists and include lengthy bibliographic listings. Each of the five volumes in the set has its own index.

1269   Nimmo, Dan D., and Keith R. Sanders. *Handbook of Political Communication*. Beverly Hills, CA: Sage Publications, 1981.

Political communication has been defined as one of the intervening processes by means of which political influences are mobilized and transmitted. The study of political communication has produced a substantial literature that is summarized and evalutated in this handbook. Following an introductory essay by the editors, the handbook contains 22 survey articles under four parts, as follows: (1) Contemporary Theoretical Approaches, (2) Modes and Means of Persuasive Communication in Politics, (3) Political Communication Settings, and (4) Methods of Study. Appendices provide a summary of European research and a guide to the literature. The handbook is kept up to date by the *Communication Yearbook* (New Brunswick, NJ: International Communication Association, 1977–).

1270   Theis, Paul A., and William P. Steponkus. *All about Politics*. Ann Arbor, MI: R. R. Bowker, 1972.

This handbook provides answers to over 4,000 of the most frequently asked questions about American politics. The material is arranged in a 12-chapter, question-and-answer format, with each chapter devoted to a different aspect of the American political process. No bibliographic citations are provided with the answers.

1271   U.S. Congress. Senate. *Nomination and Election of the President and Vice President of the United States Including the Manner of Selecting Delegates to National Political Conventions*. Washington, DC: U.S. Government Printing Office, 1956– .

An analysis of the rules of the major political parties, federal and state laws governing the procedure of the nomination and election of the president and vice-president is presented in this official compilation of the Senate. The book identifies the states in which primaries are held together with the filing deadlines and dates of such primaries. The selection procedures for the delegates to the national conventions, including the number of delegates to be selected and the dates of the selections are also described.

Public Opinion, Propaganda, and Mass Communication

The idea that public opinion carries political authority is centuries old, but the systematic identification and study of public opinion, including its formation through the mass media, propaganda, and other promotional activities is a twentieth-century development. Many surveys of public opinion are available only in unpublished, machine-readable form maintained in separate data archives. A newsletter, entitled *SS Data* and more fully described under item 343 in this guidebook, provides a record of the available public opinion surveys in machine-readable form.

The following listings identify (1) bibliographies for books and articles relating to mass communication, the formation of public opinion, and political attitudes, and (2) data collections of public opinon surveys.

BIBLIOGRAPHIES

1272   Blum, Eleanor. *Basic Books in the Mass Media*. Urbana: University of Illinois Press, 1980.

Nearly 1,200 annotated entries for books dealing with various aspects of mass communication, including broadcasting and editorial journalism, are included in this bibliography. To identify politically relevant books, consult the subject index under such headings as government, Marxism and the media, press law, propaganda, public opinion, Radio Free Europe, socialism and the media, socialist press, Voice of America, and similar terms. An author/title index is also included.

1273   *Communication Abstracts*. Beverly Hills, CA: Sage Publications, 1978— .

Published quarterly, *Communication Abstracts* offers bibliographic citations for and abstracts of communication-related, scholarly articles, reports, books, and book chapters. All forms of communication are covered, notably speech, small group, and mass communication, either in the United States or other countries. Political communication, including political campaign coverage, is well represented. Author and subject indexes are included.

1274   *Communications Information (Comm)*. Guelph, Ontario: University of Guelph, 1960— . (Vendor: QL Systems)

Online access to bibliographic citations for publications dealing with the political, legal, and social aspects of mass communications and telecommunications is available with this database. Propaganda and the role of the mass media in foreign and domestic policy matters is well covered in the more than 10,000 records presently stored in the database.

1275   Gilbertson, Norma L. *Cumulative Index to the Public Opinion Quarterly*. Irvington on Hudson, NY: Columbia University Press, 1972.

The *Public Opinion Quarterly* is the organ of the American Association for Public Opinion Research and a principal information source for completed studies on public opinion. Cumulative indexing is available for the first 31 volumes of the publication from 1937 to 1967. The index provides author, subject, geographical, and book review entries for more than 2,500 published articles.

1276   Gitter, A. George. *Communication. A Guide to Information Sources*. Detroit: Gale Research Company, 1980.

1277   Gordon, Thomas F., and Mary Ellen Verna. *Mass Media and Socialization. A Selected Bibliography*. Philadelphia: Temple University, 1973.

1278   Mowlana, Hamid. *International Communications*. Dubuque, IA: Kendall/Hunt Publishing Co., 1971.

The three bibliographies may be useful for anyone seeking informative glimpses into the effects of the mass media on the formation of attitudes and public opinion. The Gitter bibliography contains annotated listings for books and articles dealing with political communication, attitude change, mass communication, and international communication.

The Gordon/Verna bibliography offers unannotated entries for periodical articles and dissertations about media effects on social norms, values, roles, and public opinion.

The Mowlana bibliography provides unannotated listings under 11 chapters that focus on propaganda, public opinion, communication and foreign policy, international laws on communication, and other related topics.

1279   Hansen, Donald A., and J. Herschel Parsons. *Mass Communication. A Research Bibliography*. Berkeley, CA: Glendessary Press, 1968.

Public opinion is shaped or expressed to a significant degree by media that as a result of their electronic dissemination or other efficient forms of circulation reach large population masses. These mass media, their social context, content, organization, audience, and effects have been the subject of more than 10,000 publications issued since 1945. This bibliography identifies nearly 3,000 books and articles, many of which relate to political issues, political imagery, and political attitudes. More recent publications can be identified in an annotated bibliography, entitled "Articles on Mass Communication in U.S. and Foreign Journals," which is published in every issue of *Journalism Quarterly*.

1280   Lasswell, Harold D., Ralph D. Casey, and Bruce Lannes Smith. *Propaganda and Promotional Activities*. Minneapolis: University of Minnesota Press, 1935; Chicago: University of Chicago Press, 1969.

1281   _____ . *Propaganda, Communication and Public Opinion*. Princeton, NJ: Princeton University Press, 1946.

1282   Smith, Chitra M., Berton Winograd, and Alice

R. Jwaideh. *International Communication and Political Warfare*. Santa Monica, CA: Rand Corporation, 1952.

1283   Smith, Chitra M., and Bruce Lannes Smith. *International Communications and Public Opinion: A Guide to the Literature*. Princeton, NJ: Princeton University Press, 1956.

A serious distortion of the public's view of political reality occurs as a result of propaganda activities. These bibliographies offer a descriptive inventory of the scholarly literature about propaganda and its effects on public opinion. Books, articles, dissertations, and reports issued during the first half of this century are listed in the following categories: (1) propaganda strategy and technique, (2) propaganda classified by the name of the promoting group, (3) propaganda classified by the response to be elicited, (4) symbols and practices that propaganda uses, (5) channels of propaganda, and (6) measurements of the effects of propaganda.

1284   National Opinion Research Center. Library. *Bibliography of Publications, 1941–1960*. Chicago: University of Chicago, 1961.

————. *Supplement, 1961–1971*. Chicago: University of Chicago, 1972.

The publications listed in these bibliographies are of three types: reports published by the National Opinion Research Center (NORC), books and papers published externally that report on NORC research, and unpublished papers reporting on NORC research. Entries are arranged in various subject categories that include political and international affairs. NORC reports and monographs are available for purchase or obtainable on loan from depository libraries.

1285   Shearer, Benjamin F., and Marilyn Huxford. *Communcations and Society*. Westport, CT: Greenwood Press, 1983.

Organized in nine chapters, this bibliography offers unannotated entries for books, periodical articles, and dissertations dealing with communications technologies and their social impact. Separate chapters are devoted to the social effects of mass media, their influence or reflection of public opinion, and their relationship to politics. Separate author and subject indexes are also included.

1286   Universal Reference System. *Public Opinion, Mass Behavior and Political Psychology*. Princeton, NJ: Princeton Research Publishing Company, 1969–.

A separate volume of the basic Universal Reference System (URS) set is devoted to studies of public opinion and political behavior. It contains an annotated listing of 3,456 books and articles, which are indexed according to the Grazian system of topical and methodological descriptors. Although each listed title has received up to 20 descriptors to enable the researcher to isolate desired information, the choice and frequency of the descriptors used is often less than ideal. There are, for instance, 732 entries under power, 354 entries under trend, 306 entries under USSR, 371 entires under social structure, and 1,003 entries under EDU/Prop (education, propaganda, persuasion), but no entries under authority, demonstrations, apathy, loyalty, and many other generally used terms in this field. The volume is updated annually by entries in a supplement to the entire URS set.

DATA COLLECTIONS

1287   *American Public Opinion Index*, 1981–. Louisville, KY: Opinion Research Service, 1983–.

The index provides access to the results of hundreds of scientifically conducted opinion surveys in the United States. It is arranged in two sections. Section 1 lists all questions under broad, alphabetically arranged subject headings. Apart from the question asked, each entry identifies the organization that conducted the poll, its date, and type of response solicited. Section 2 indicates the sources of the polling results, including the name of the polling organization, the universe of each poll (national, name of state or city, etc.), sample size, method of polling, and availability of the published results.

New editions of the *APOI* will be published annually. Due to its broad scope, the *American Public Opinion Index* will complement rather than supplant the monthly *Gallup Report*.

1288   Converse, Philip E., Jean D. Dotson, Wendy J. Hoag, and William H. McGee III. *American Social Attitudes Data Sourcebook, 1947–1978*. Cambridge, MA: Harvard University Press, 1980.

Based on data collected by the Survey Research Center at the University of Michigan, this compendium of texts, tables, and time series graphs documents the social and economic attitudes of the American population during the post–World War II era. Organized in nine chapters, the data cover attitudes toward self and others (business, labor unions, the military, policemen, various religious groups, etc.), racial attitudes, women's roles, family living, work and retirement, personal economic outlook, national economic outlook, government spending (on defense, foreign aid, education, welfare, low-cost housing, etc.), attitudes toward war and peace (Korea, Vietnam, bigger wars, etc.). An introductory chapter and two appendices provide details about the origin, nature, and usage of the massive data.

1289   *Current Opinion*. Williamstown, MA: The Roper Center, 1972–.

215

Recent information about the public's views on a wide range of important issues can be found in this monthly publication. Over 100 survey research organizations supply statistical information for this publication.

1290   Gallup, George H. *The Gallup Poll Public Opinions, 1935–1971.* Westminster, MD: Random House, 1972.

1291   _____ . *The Gallup Poll Public Opinions, 1972–1977.* Wilmington, DE: Scholarly Resources, Inc., 1978.

1292   _____ . *The Gallup Poll: Public Opinions.* Wilmington, DE: Scholarly Resources, 1978–.

1293   _____ . *The Gallup Opinion Index: Political, Social, and Economic Trends.* Princeton, NJ: Gallup International, 1965–1980.

1294   _____ . *The Gallup Report.* Princeton, NJ: Gallup Poll, 1981–.

Results of national public opinion surveys based on interviews of a minimum of 1,500 scientifically selected individuals are available in multiannual and annual collections as well as in monthly reports. The surveys cover such topics as the popularity of the United States president, domestic policy issues, response to international or foreign area conflicts, popularity of election candidates, relations between ethnic groups, and others. Many survey findings demonstrate the public's desire for alternatives to the policies pursued by individual or institutional political actors.

1295   *General Social Survey, 1972–1983 Cumulative Data Set.* Storrs, CT: Roper Center, 1983.

The *General Social Survey*, conducted each year from 1972 to Spring 1983 (except 1981), is a comprehensive investigation of the opinions, values, and cultural orientations held by the American population. Each survey has a scientifically determined sample size of 1,599 respondents and contains up to 500 variables. The complete data set in card image format augmented by control cards is available on magnetic tape only. A printed codebook is included in the data set.

1296   *A Guide to Roper Center Resources for the Study of American Race Relations.* Storrs, CT: Roper Center, 1983.

Covering 45 years of American public opinion, this compendium is a comprehensive index to all questions in the Roper Center data archive regarding black/white relations in the United States. Over 3,000 questions surrounding racial issues are presented chronologically within subject categories. Also included is an index by study that enables the reader to identify those data sets that are particularly rich in measuring racial attitudes.

1297   *The Harris Survey Yearbook of Public Opinion.* New York: Louis Harris and Associates, 1970–.

Survey results of the American public opinion polls conducted by the Harris organization during the preceding year are published in this yearbook. Current results of the Harris polls are published in *ABC News-Harris Survey,* issued twice weekly by the Harris organization, but are also reported in *Newsweek* and the *Washington Post.*

1298   *Public Opinion.* Washington, DC: American Enterprise Institute, 1978–.

This bimonthly publication features an "opinion roundup" that displays data from several public opinion research organizatons.

PUBLIC LAW

Introduction

The pattern of social control created by the American political system is foremost the result of the rule of law. Public law governs the relationships between private persons, between public officials and private persons, and between individuals and organizations by giving precise, binding, and enforceable directives.

Public law is usually subdivided into constitutional, statutory, administrative, decisional, and international law. It includes laws formulated by the founding fathers of the United Staes, those passed by Congress and other legislative bodies, as well as the judicial interpretations of the courts, decrees, orders, and opinions issued by administrative authorities, and the law created by international treaties, international courts, and customary rules of international behavior.

The reference literature of public law is published officially and unofficially and falls into two categories of effectiveness:

1. *Primary sources.* These are the officially published texts of the constitutions, statutes, court decisions, administrative rules and decisions, and other rulings that have legal authority.
2. *Secondary sources.* These are the officially or unofficially published bibliographies, dictionaries, encyclopedias, indexes, digests, casebooks, and other items that lack legal authority but are indispensable for locating or interpreting the primary sources of law.

In view of the volume and diversity of legal reference

literature, only those primary and secondary reference publications that are likely to be most frequently required in the political study of legal phenomena have been listed and described in the following sections. For the most part the listed reference sources refer to law enforced by federal authorities, and only a very limited number of reference instruments for state and municipal law is indicated. Where additional reference tools are desired, the available guidebooks to the legal literature will provide helpful informational leads in most instances.

Guidebooks

1299   Coco, Al. *Finding the Law: A Workbook on Legal Research for Lay Persons*. Washington, DC: U.S. Government Printing Office, 1982.

This excellent guidebook offers detailed explanations and illustrations for using legal reference sources to locate the law of federal authorities. The book is divided into four sections: (1) Introduction, (2) Statutory Law, (3) Case Law, and (4) Finding Tools. Subdivisions within these sections focus on specific reference sources. A section on research exercises and an index are also included. Online reference sources and retrieval tools for the decisions of regulatory agencies are not covered, however.

1300   Cohen, Morris L. *Legal Research in a Nutshell*. St. Paul, MN: West Publishing Company, 1978.

The use of judicial reports, case finding aids, collections of federal and state laws and statutes, loose-leaf services, United States treaty collections, and secondary legal materials is succinctly described in this brief guidebook. Most bibliographic detail has been omitted, however, in the interest of condensation.

1301   Henke, Dan. *California Legal Research Handbook. State. Federal*. Walnut Creek, CA: Lex-Cal-Tex Press, 1971 –.

This comprehensive and updated guidebook offers detailed instructions for the use of the legal reference literature for federal and California statutes, court decisions, and administrative regulations. The material is arranged under the following chapter headings:

1. California Law: California Constitutional Law, California Statutory Research, History of California Legislation, California Administrative Law, California Local Legislation, California Court Rules, Statutory Law of States, California Case Law
2. United States Law: United States Constitutional Law, Federal Statutory Research, History of Federal Legislation, Interstate Compacts, Federal Administrative Law, United States Treaties and International Law, United States Court Rules, Federal Case Law
3. Legal Research Aids: Legal Research with Secondary Aids, Reference Works, Loose-leaf Reports, Legal Periodicals, Court Briefs, Attorney General Opinions, Legal Research Technique

The guidebook is kept up to date with pocket supplements.

1302   Jacobstein, J. Myron, and Roy Mersky. *Fundamentals of Legal Research*. Minneola, NY: Foundation Press, 1981.

The legal research process and the use of encyclopedias, indexes, treatises, court reports, digests, citators, and other reference sources for federal, state, and international law is well described in this frequently revised guidebook. The latest edition contains a separate chapter for computers and microforms in legal research.

1303   Price, Miles O., and Harry Bitner. *Effective Legal Research: A Practical Manual of Law Books and Their Use*. Boston: Little, Brown & Company, 1979.

This standard guidebook, now in its fourth edition, explains the use of United States treaty collections, legislative history material, collections of federal and state statute books, law reports, administrative law sources, index and search books, digests, encyclopedias, treatises, legal periodicals, dictionaries, and other legal reference publications. The book also contains a list of legal abbreviations, Anglo-American legal periodicals, British and Canadian materials, and American law reports and digests.

1304   Sprowl, James A. *A Manual for Computer Assisted Legal Research — A Definite Guide to the Lexis and Westlaw Computer Systems*. Chicago: American Bar Foundation, 1976.

Computer-assisted legal research is presently in a stage of rapid development with at least two major full text retrieval systems being offered to academic and professional researchers. This guidebook describes the use of the *LEXIS* and *Westlaw* systems, which offer online retrieval of statutory and judicial material in federal and state law.

1305   Statsky, William P. *Legal Research, Writing and Analysis*. St. Paul, MN: West Publishing Company, 1982.

The technique of legal research and the use of legal reference materials is well explained in this guidebook with 25 sections that include

- a checklist of the legal research vocabulary
- a glossary of law and law books

- the form of legal citations
- the technique of using indexes and tables of content
- finding case law, statutes, constitutional law, administrative law, local law, court rules, and international law

Various illustrations, outlines, bibliographic references, and an index add to the usefulness of this guidebook.

Online Retrieval Tools

1306   *Laborlaw.* Washington, DC: Bureau of National Affairs, 1938 – . (Vendor: Dialog — File 244)

Online searches of this database, available with the Dialog system, will provide summaries of decisions and references to the source of the text of the decisions relating to labor relations, fair employment, wages and hours, and occupational safety and health. The database is the equivalent of several printed BNA reporter sets, such as *Labor Relations* (1966 –), *Labor Arbitration Reports, Fair Employment Practice Cases* (1938 –), *Wage and Hours Cases* (1961 –), *Occupational Safety and Health Cases* (1972 –), and *Mine Safety and Health Cases* (1970 –). Records are updated monthly.

1307   *Legal Resource Index.* Menlo Park, CA: Information Access Corporation, 1980 – . (Vendor: Dialog — File 150)

Index coverage for over 660 law journals, 5 law newspapers, and legal monographs from commercial and government publishers is offered by this computerized database. Online access is provided to citations for articles, book reviews, case notes, letters to the editor, obituaries, biographical pieces, editorials, and other secondary information material. Some primary sources, such as statutes and cases, are also indexed. Access is possible by author names, titles, and key subject terms. The printed version of this index is entitled *Current Law Index*, but relevant law articles from the *Magazine Index*, *National Newspaper Index*, and *Trade and Industry Index* are also included in the computerized version.

1308   *LEXIS.* Dayton, OH: Mead Data Central, 1973 – .

This online retrieval system enables the user to conduct a KWIC (keywords in context) or full text search through a variety of federal and state legal materials and obtain a full text display or hard copy printout within seconds. Searchable material at present available includes current versions of the *United States Code*, the *Federal Register* (since July 1980), the *Code of Federal Regulations*, as well as U.S. Supreme Court decisions since 1925, Courts of Appeal decisions since 1938, District Court decisions since 1960, Court of Claims decisions since 1960, and U.S. Supreme Court briefs since the fall term of 1979.

Specialized legal sources in the areas of taxation, securities law, trade regulation, patent, trademark and copyright law, including decisions and rulings of federal regulatory agencies, such as the Federal Communication Commission, National Labor Relations Board, or Federal Energy Regulatory Commission can also be searched. In addition, the decisions of state supreme courts and appellate courts, as reported in the official casebooks can be retrieved in case law searches for all states over varying periods of time. State constitutional and statutory law included in the database is limited to a few states, notably Kansas, Missouri, Ohio, and New York, but additional material will be added to the database as time progresses. Under agreement with Shepard's Division of McGraw-Hill, Inc., all federal, state, and regional case law citators are included in the database as well as the full text of legal treatises published by Matthew Bender & Company. Finally, authoritative accounting materials, such as statements of auditing standards and accounting series releases issued by the AICPA, the Securities and Exchange Commission, and other organizations, as well as abstracts and extracts of reports filed with the SEC by some 9,000 companies are made available for online searching. Users need to identify the specific compilation of statutory, decisional, or administrative law they wish to search. Searching is done on the basis of words, phrases, date, court, name of judge or litigants expected to occur in the materials being searched.

1309   *NCJRS.* Rockville, MD: National Criminal Justice Reference Service, 1972 – . (Vendor: Dialog — File 21).

All aspects of law enforcement and criminal justice programs considered, implemented, or discontinued in the United States are covered in this monthly updated computerized database. Citations and abstracts are retrievable for detailed descriptions of the various programs as well as for preliminary research disseminated in books, periodical articles, audiovisual presentations, or unpublished reports from courts, police, and correctional institutions. The database is an excellent source for identifying successful crime prevention programs and determining the extent of waste, fraud, and abuse in governmental programs.

For a printed and annotated list of bibliographies prepared by the National Criminal Justice Reference Service on a variety of criminal justice and law enforcement topics, see also John M. Ross's *National Criminal Justice Reference Service (NCJRS) Bibliographies: A Bibliography of Bibliographies* (Chicago: CPL Bibliographies, 1983), issued as number 103 of the CPL bibliography series. Copies of the bibliographies cited in the list are available free from NCJRS, Box 6000, Rockville, MD 20850, and all documents cited in the NCJRS bibliographies are made accessible to the public through interlibrary loan facilities. A bimonthly newsletter, entitled *SNI: Selective Notification of Information*, announces the most significant documents added to the NCJRS database. This newsletter can be obtained free by registering with the NCJRS as a user.

1310   *Patlaw*. Washington, DC: Bureau of National Affairs, 1970—. (Vendor: Dialog—File 243)

The computerized database contains records of reported judicial and administrative decisions pertaining to patents, copyrights, trademarks, and unfair competition law. The decisions originate from the U.S. Supreme Court, the U.S. Courts of Appeals, the District Courts, the U.S. Court of Customs and Patent Appeals, the Commissioner of Patents and Trademarks, the U.S. International Trade Commission, and selected state courts. Searchable records include case names, headnotes, subject descriptors, and, where applicable, case history or parallel citations. Records are updated monthly.

1311   *PHINet. Federal Tax Data Base*. Paramus, NJ: Prentice-Hall, 1983—. (Vendor: Prentice-Hall)

This computerized database, accessible by contract with the producer, enables the user to obtain online all appropriate document references for research queries on federal taxation law. Responses are activated by keywords, phrase, sentence, code section, regulation, committee report, or case name. Documents can be read on the screen, or document (paragraph) numbers jotted down from the screen can be used to look up desired items in the Prentice-Hall *Federal Taxes* loose-leaf reference set.

1312   *Westlaw/System II*. St. Paul, MN: West Publishing Company, 1925—. (Vendor: West Publishing Co.; QL Systems)

This legal database offers the user online access to the full text of federal statutory and administrative law, federal and state court decisions, West's case synopses, headnotes, and digest topic and key number classification, as well as *Black's Law Dictionary*, *Shepard's Citations*, and *West's Insta-Cite*. Specifically included in the database are the *United States Code*, *Code of Federal Regulations*, *Federal Register*, *IRS Cumulative Bulletin*, and IRS written determinations since 1954 in addition to

- U.S. Supreme Court cases since 1925
- U.S. Court of Appeals cases since 1945
- U.S. District Court cases since 1950
- U.S. Court of Claims cases since 1954
- U.S. Tax Court reported opinions and memo decisions since 1954
- U.S. Federal Trade Commission decisions since 1960

- U.S. Federal Communication Commission reports since 1975
- U.S. Federal Labor Relations Board decisions since 1972
- State Supreme Court and Courts of Appeals decisions for all 50 states with varying chronological coverage

Searches can be made by descriptive words or phrases, topic/key number, case names, legal citations, names of judges, lawyers, products, places, etc. Projected coverage of the *Westlaw* database will include presidential documents since 1936 and various European legal materials.

Current Bibliographies

1313   *Bibliographic Guide to Law*. Boston: G. K. Hall, 1974—.

Based on the Library of Congress law collection, this series of annual, unannotated bibliographic volumes lists new books, pamphlets, and serial publications for United States and foreign law, including international law. The entries, which reflect cataloging activities during the preceding 12 months, are arranged in one alphabetical order for access by author, editor, title, series title, and subject heading. LC call numbers and Dewey Decimal numbers are included in the bibliographic details supplied with each entry.

1314   *Current Law Index*. Menlo Park, CA: Information Access Corporation, 1980—.

1315   *Legal Resource Index*. Menlo Park, CA: Information Access Corporation, 1980—.

These printed indexes are equivalents of the computerized *Legal Resource Index* database previously described. The first title, cited above, is published in eight monthly, three quarterly, and annual printed editions. Each issue contains subject, author/title indexes, a table of cases, and a table of statutes. The second title is made available in microfilm only, to be used with a special viewer machine.

1316   *Index to Legal Periodicals*. New York: H. W. Wilson, 1908—.

1317   *Index to Periodical Articles Related to Law*. Dobbs Ferry, NY: Glanville Publications, 1958—.

Periodicals published by university schools of law, lawyers associations, and law institutes are an important source of persuasive authority. The titles listed above are the standard indexes that provide a key to the legal periodical literature by author and subject.

The *Index to Legal Periodicals*, published quarterly with annual cumulations, covers the legal periodical literature of the United States, Canada, Great Britain, Northern Ireland, Australia, and New Zealand. To qualify for indexing, articles must have a minimum length of five pages and contain legal material of high quality or permanent reference value. Author and subject listings plus tables of cases and a book review index are provided.

Articles not included in the *Index to Legal Periodicals* are subject indexed in the third reference publication cited above. It is published bimonthly with biennial and ten-year cumulations.

1318   Jacobstein, J. Myron, Meira G. Pimsleur, and Walter Rodino. *Law Books in Print*. South Hackensack, NJ: Glanville Publishers, 1970.

1319   _____ . *Law Books Published*. South Hackensack, NJ: Glanville Publishers, 1970–.

The legal literature in book form is identifiable by author and subject with these two reference publications. Current listings of new books available from the book trade are offered in three quarterly noncumulative issues and an annual clothbound volume of the bibliography. Not listed are statute books, law reports, digests, citators, loose-leaf services, and government publications.

1320   *Law Books 1876–1981*. New York: R. R. Bowker, 1981.

1321   *Law Information 1982*. New York: R. R. Bowker, 1982.

1322   *Law Information Update*. New York: R. R. Bowker, 1983–.

More than 180,000 law and law-related titles can be identified with the three reference sets listed above. The retrospective set in four volumes offers a subject arrangement of some 130,000 book titles. More recent listings can be found in the three-volume set published in 1982. It contains author, title, and subject listings for books as well as subject and title indexes for serials. A list of publishers and distributors of law and law-related materials is also included. Both sets are updated in monthly supplements, beginning in 1983.

1323   *Law Review Digest*. Boonton, NJ: Kimball Clark Publishing Company, 1951–.

1324   *Monthy Digest of Legal Articles*. Greenville, NY: Research and Documentation Corporation, 1969–.

Digests of articles from leading law periodicals are available in these two reference publications. The first title is published bimonthly and also offers subject indexing. The second digest is a monthly publication.

1325   *Legal Contents*. Wilmington, DE: Corporation Service Company, 1972–.

Formerly entitled *Contents of Current Legal Periodicals*, this biweekly publication reproduces the table of contents pages of all the leading legal periodicals issued during the current month. It also provides indexing by fields of law for the individual articles, comments notes, and court decisions listed in the contents pages. The publisher also offers a document delivery service for most of the items listed.

1326   Universal Reference System. *Law, Jurisprudence, and Judicial Process*. Princeton, NJ: Princeton Research Publishing Company, 1969–.

Volume 7 of the Universal Reference System's base set is an annotated and intensively indexed compilation of significant books, articles, and pamphlets in the field of law. More than 25,000 index entries for some 2,000 publications provide a detailed topical and methodological approach to the literature according to the Grazian system. The volume can also be used to identify 345 unannotated bibliographies and 213 annotated bibliographies pertaining to legal subject matter. Annual supplementary volumes of the URS system offer listings of the current legal literature.

Book Review Indexes

1327   *Abstracts of Book Reviews in Current Legal Periodicals*. Provo, UT: Brigham Young University, 1974–1977, 1980–.

Apart from the book review indexes in the *Index to Legal Periodicals*, the *Index to Foreign Legal Periodicals*, and the *Current Law Index*, this biweekly publication is a good source for reviews of legal books.

Dictionaries and Encyclopedias

In addition to the bibliographic instruments listed on the previous pages, law dictionaries and encyclopedias offer excellent starting points for research in legal and political matters. Precise terminology is very important in the field of law, but the words and phrases used by legal authorities frequently have a special meaning that may mystify the uninitiated user. Legal dictionaries and encyclopedias are not primary sources of law, but they are the preferred reference tools for obtaining precise definitions of legal terms and concepts with bibliographic citations to primary authority. The federal and state law encyclopedias also provide complete and integrated statements concerning existing law in its entirety, thereby supplying for most legal topics a concise and fairly comprehensive summary that would be difficult to obtain otherwise. To ensure coverage of current legal developments, all encyclopedias are kept up to date with annual cumulative supplements.

DICTIONARIES

1328   Ballentine, James A. *Ballentine's Law Dictionary, with Pronunciations.* San Francisco: Bancroft-Whitney Company, 1969.

Since many legal terms are based on Latin words, ensuing pronunciation difficulties can be overcome with this dictionary, which offers precise definitions together with correct pronunciation. The definitions are based on court decisions for which appropriate case citations are provided.

1329   Bieber, Doris M. *Dictionary of Current American Legal Citations.* Buffalo, NY: William S. Hein, 1981

The purposes of this work are (1) to give abbreviations for the legal publications of all United States jurisdictions, the international law publications, and privately published legal periodicals, and (2) to provide examples of the more commonly cited authorities. Included are some 1,300 examples of citations for American Law Reports, statutes, regulations, loose-leaf services, treaties, and other legal publications.

Entries are arranged in two columns. The left column lists alphabetically the full title of the publication for which a recognized citation exists. The right column contains the corresponding citation form. The citation form is accompanied by examples.

1330   Black, Henry Campbell. *Black's Law Dictionary.* St. Paul, MN: West Publishing Company, 1979.

A comprehensive inventory of the terms, phrases, and maxims used in American and English jurisprudence is supplied by this dictionary, available in irregularly revised printed editions and in online display format as part of the *Westlaw/System II* database. The dictionary offers precise definitions and correct pronunciation of legal terminology together with citations to court decisions and other legal authority. Numerous words taken from Roman law and European law as well as international law are also included. A separate list of legal abbreviations is also part of this dictionary.

1331   Burton, William C. *Legal Thesaurus.* New York: Macmillan, 1980.

The purpose of this reference work is to assist the user in finding the precise term to fit the nuances of a particular legal situation. Following an alphabetical arrangement,

all legally significant words are listed together with their definitions, synonyms, associated legal concepts, Latin or other foreign phrases and translations, and alternate parts of speech. A separate index lists the main entries under which the synonym is listed.

1332   Coughlin, George Gordon. *Dictionary of Law.* New York: Barnes & Noble, 1982.

This small dictionary defines over 1,200 terms from all branches of law. The definitions are expressed in everyday language for use by general readers. Numerous examples are given to show how terms apply to actual cases and situations.

1333   Egbert, Lawrence Deems, and Fernando Morales-Macedo. *Multilingual Law Dictionary.* Dobbs Ferry, NY: Oceana Publications, 1978.

The dictionary aims to give equivalents of legal terms in the English, French, German, and Spanish languages, when the concepts of these terms are the same or similar. If the concept of a legal term in the English language does not exist in the legal practice of French-, German-, and Spanish-speaking countries, a brief explanation or definition of its meaning is given in each of these languages. The dictionary consists of an English text section, indexes in the French, German, and Spanish languages, and four appendices. Readers proceeding from a foreign language term need to use the indexes, which provide references to the listed English-language terms where the foreign language equivalents are identified. The appendices contain a selected list of English-language definitions of legal terms, a list of law dictionaries in the four languages, a bibliography of legal reference books, and a list of UN organizations.

1334   Enslen, Richard A., Ralph C. Chandler, and Peter G. Renstrom. *The Constitutional Law Dictionary.* Santa Barbara, CA: ABC-Clio, 1984.

The dictionary offers access to two essential categories of information in the study of constitutional law. It provides a summary of about 300 important court cases and offers definitions of more than 200 terms in common legal usage. A separate paragraph in each entry identifies the significance of each item in the context of American constitutional law.

1335   National Criminal Justice Reference Service. *National Criminal Justice Thesaurus: Descriptors for Indexing Law Enforcement and Criminal Justice Information.* Rockville, MD: NCJRS, 1981.

The thesaurus offers an alphabetical listing of the subject descriptors available for accessing information in the law enforcement and criminal justice processes. This vocabulary is used in *NCJRS*, the computerized database of the National Criminal Justice Reference Service.

1336   Radin, Max. *Radin Law Dictionary*. Dobbs Ferry, NY: Oceana Publications, 1970.

This dictionary consists of three sections, namely: (1) a practical manual of standard legal citations, (2) the law dictionary, and (3) code of professional responsibility (Canon of Ethics) of the American Bar Association. The citations manual contains detailed instructions on how to cite statutory material, case material, treatises, reports, briefs, etc. The dictionary defines the meaning of legal words and phrases with case and statutory references.

1337   Redden, Kenneth R., and Enid L. Veron. *Modern Legal Glossary*. Charlottesville, VA: Michie Company, 1980.

While there are several good law dictionaries available, this dictionary is the only one devoted exclusively to a definition of legal terms and related concepts. Included are such items as professional organizations, government agencies, international organizations, names of popular cases and statutes, famous trials, classic law books, ancient codes, and biographies of outstanding people in the field of law. Specific governmental policies, such as the New Deal, Operation Bootstrap, and others, or legal doctrines and provisions are also defined. A separate chapter lists quotations on the law by famous people.

1338   Seide, Katharine. *A Dictionary of Arbitration and Its Terms, Labor, Commercial, International*. Dobbs Ferry, NY: Oceana Publications, 1970.

The terms, concepts, statutes, and cases used in commercial arbitration, labor arbitration, and international arbitration are defined in this dictionary. Citations to the source documents are provided. Also included are selective bibliographies for the various arbitration fields, as well as the text of international arbitration rules and conventions.

ENCYCLOPEDIAS

1339   *American Jurisprudence*. San Francisco: Bancroft-Whitney, 1962—.

The multivolume encyclopedia, currently in its second edition, aims at complete coverage of American federal and state law in over 400 alphabetically arranged treatises. Each treatise is preceded by a note indicating its scope and a table of contents. The textual material is supported by extensive footnote citations to legal authority, but not all cases in point are cited. Each volume contains its own index, but there is also a separate general index for the entire set. The general index also lists, under "Words and Phrases," topic and section reference where legal terminology is discussed or defined in the text. There

is no table of cases cited in the encyclopedia, but a table of statutes cited is included. The encyclopedia is kept up to date by annual cumulative pocket supplements. A separately issued desk book lists all articles in the *American Jurisprudence* encyclopedia and additionally offers a table of legal abbreviations and miscellaneous charts and statistics of interest to attorneys.

1340   *Corpus Juris Secundum*. New York: American Law Book Company, 1937—1960, 1961—.

The encyclopedia offers a complete restatement of American law under 433 main topics. Many, but not all of the topical headings are the same as those found in the *American Jurisprudence* encyclopedia. Each topical article is preceded by a scope note and a table of contents. The textual material is supported by complete citations to all cases in point. Each main topic is separately indexed in the volume containing it, but there is also a separate consolidated index for the entire set. In addition, each volume contains an index to the words and phrases defined in it. There is no table of cases, but a table of all legal abbreviations used in the encyclopedia is printed in each volume. The encyclopedia is kept up to date by annual cumulative pocket parts.

1341   *California Jurisprudence*. San Francisco: Bancroft-Whitney, 1952—.

1342   *Florida Jurisprudence*. San Francisco: Bancroft-Whitney, 1955—1961.

1343   *New York Jurisprudence*. San Francisco: Bancroft-Whitney, 1958—1970.

1344   *Ohio Jurisprudence*. San Francisco: Bancroft-Whitney, 1953—1964.

1344a   *Texas Jurisprudence*. San Francisco: Bancroft-Whitney, 1959—1966.

These state law encyclopedias offer a comprehensive textual statement of the constitutional, statutory, and decisional law of the state in alphabetically arranged topical articles. The textual material is supported by extensive citations to legal authority although not all cases in point are cited. Cross-references are provided to the *American Law Reports*, the *American Jurisprudence* encyclopedia, and other legal reference publications. Volumes are individually indexed, and there are also separate general index volumes supplied for each set. Updating is provided by annual pocket supplements.

Other state encyclopedias have been published by the West Publishing Company, St. Paul, Minnesota, for the law of Indiana, Illinois, Maryland, Michigan, and Pennsylvania.

1344b *The Guide to American Law. Everyone's Legal Encyclopedia.* St. Paul, MN: West Publishing Company, 1983.

The multivolume encyclopedia contains explanatory entries and signed articles about legal philosophies, principles, and concepts, important legislative acts, judicial decisions and famous trials, historical movements and events, federal regulatory agencies, legal organizations, and other facts of American jurisprudence. Biographies of prominent individuals and excerpts of landmark documents are also included. The text of an entry or signed article usually provides case and statutory citations for legal authority. Topical and general subject indexes, as well as quotation indexes by topic and author, illustration indexes, and name indexes are included in each volume.

1345 Zweigert, Konrad, et al. *International Encyclopedia of Comparative Law.* Dobbs Ferry, NY: Oceana Publications, 1971–1978.

Four hundred legal experts from many countries of the world contributed to this multivolume encyclopedia for comparative law. Its primary value lies in the fact that it offers political scientists, politicians, and lawmakers a multitude of models for the solution of recurring as well as novel problems. The encyclopedia describes, compares, and evaluates the typical solutions that the various legal systems in the world apply to any given social problem.

Constitutional Law

The difficult process of building and maintaining a nation in the face of ever-present conflicts of identity, integration, participation, and distribution in a world of international rivalry is the fundamental reason why most countries of the world, including the United States, revere constitutional documents. Constitutions not only provide certain basic rules for political behavior but also identify the proper locus of political authority. Constitutions serve as inspirational statements in a system of political myths that elicit continuous political support from present and future generations. As legal documents constitutions are designed to give permanence and stability to the rule of law by making deviations from certain basic principles more difficult.

Excellent reference coverage exists for the main ideas or legal points in the constitutional documents of the American political system. For ease of identification the following listings are arranged in three subsections, namely: (1) Bibliographies, (2) U.S. Constitution Texts, and (3) State Constitution Texts. Readers desiring to compare the texts of American constitutional documents with those of foreign constitutions are referred to the listings for

Comparative Legal Sources in the Comparative Government and Areas Studies section of this guidebook.

BIBLIOGRAPHIES

1346 Brown, Cynthia E. *State Constitutional Conventions: From Independence to the Completion of the Present Union, 1776–1959: A Bibliography.* Westport, CT: Greenwood Press, 1973.

1347 *State Constitutional Conventions, Commissions, and Amendments, 1959–1978: An Annotated Bibliography.* Washington, DC: Congressional Information Service, 1981.

Reapportionments, increased legislative power, executive reform, more effective judicial administration, increase in fiscal possibilities, expansion of natural and civil rights, changes in the structure and function of local governments, elimination of outmoded details, and simplification of constitutional provisions are among the main goals of constitutional revision. Historically and legally at least three devices have been used to bring about desired revisions of state constitutions, namely the state constitutional convention, the constitutional commission, and the amendment process. More than 200 constitutional conventions have been held since the early days of the states, and during the past 25 years a growing number of constitutional commissions have helped to rewrite constitutions. The amendment process involves legislative proposal and ratification by the electorate, but a number of states also authorize amendments by petition or constitutional proposition.

The listed bibliographies identify a variety of publications issued by conventions and commissions, such as reports, proceedings, minutes, proposals, hearings, studies, and rejected as well as approved amendments. The listed entries are generally arranged by state in chronological order. There are also alphabetical listings by author and title within each state, and a personal author index is also included. All listed items are available in a separate microfiche collection issued by the Congressional Information Service. The necessary accession numbers for the individual items in the collection are listed in the bibliographies. Since the bibliographies lack subject indexing, the object or issue orientation of the conventions, commissions, and amendments is identifiable only by careful reading of the bibliographic entries and their annotations. As these bibliographies are issued retrospectively only, the documentation of current efforts to revise state constitutions appears to be bibliographically uncontrolled.

1348 Equal Rights Amendment Project. *The Equal Rights Amendment: A Bibliographic Study.* Westport, CT: Greenwood Press, 1976.

Although first introduced in Congress in 1923, a proposed 27th amendment to the United States Constitution, titled "Equal Rights for Men and Women," has yet to become law after more than 60 years. As a constitutional issue and political object, the equal rights amendment has generated much research and considerable controversy, which has expressed itself in Congressional and other federal and state government publications, scholarly books and periodicals, newsletters, as well as mass circulation newspaper and periodical articles. The bibliography cited above identifies nearly 6,000 principal titles issued in these documentation categories within the first 50 years of the ERA struggle. All entries are unannotated, but the titles frequently give a clue about the nature of the political struggle and sociological arguments, or the envisioned impact of the ERA on existing statutory laws. An author and organization index, but no subject index, is included.

1349   Hall, Kermit K. A *Comprehensive Bibliography of American Constitutional and Legal History, 1896–1979*. Millwood, NY: Kraus International Publications, 1983.

The three-volume set lists institutional, doctrinal, and biographical works relating to the development of constitutional law in the United States during the twentieth century.

1350   McCarrick, Earlean M. *U.S. Constitution. A Guide to Information Sources*. Detroit: Gale Research Company, 1980.

1351   Millett, Stephen M. A *Selected Bibliography of American Constitutional History*. Santa Barbara, CA: Clio Books, 1975.

A large number of books and periodical articles has been published about the United States Constitution and its historical development. The two bibliographies are useful for identifying much of this literature.

The McCarrick bibliography offers annotated entries under 12 chapters. Chapter 1 identifies general sources, whereas chapters 2 and 3 are devoted to historical works. Interpretive materials and works on basic constitutional principles are listed in chapters 4 and 5. The remaining seven chapters cover works about the constitution itself and its various amendments. Separate author, title, and subject indexes facilitate access to the listed items.

Millett's bibliography identifies both primary and secondary sources relating to each of the seven articles of the U.S. Constitution, its origins, and its amendments.

1352   Mitchell, Ralph. *An Index to the Constitution of the United States with Glossary*. Kenosha, WI: Ralph Mitchell, 1980.

This reference book makes it easy to locate provisions of the United States Constitution. It contains an index with most terms necessary to find any article, amendment, section, or paragraph of the Constitution. It provides the full text of the Constitution along with all amendments, and also includes a glossary with definitions of almost 80 basic terms.

U.S. CONSTITUTION TEXTS

1353   Barrett, Edward L., Jr. and Paul W. Bruton. *Constitutional Law: Cases and Materials*. Brooklyn, NY: Foundation Press, 1968– .

1354   Beaney, William M., and Alpheus T. Mason. *American Constitutional Law*. Englewood Cliffs, NJ: Prentice-Hall, 1972.

1355   Cushman, Robert F. *Leading Constitutional Decisions*. New York: Appleton-Century-Crofts, 1971.

1356   Lockhart, William Bailey, et al. *The American Constitution: Cases and Materials*. St. Paul, MN: West Publishing Company, 1967.

1357   _____ . *Constitutional Law: Cases, Comments, Questions*. St. Paul, MN: West Publishing Company, 1975.

1358   _____ . *Cases and Materials on Constitutional Rights and Liberties*. St. Paul, MN: West Publishing Company, 1967.

1359   _____ . *Supplement for Use with Constitutional Law, American Constitution and Rights and Liberties*. St. Paul, MN: West Publishing Company, 1969– .

1360   Maddox, James L. *Constitutional Law: Cases and Comments*. St. Paul, MN: West Publishing Company, 1974.

1361   Saye, Albert B. *American Constitutional Law: Text and Cases*. Columbus, OH: C. E. Merrill Publishing Company, 1975.

The preceding titles are a few of the many casebooks that provide the full text or partial text of the United States Constitution, the text or abstracts of court decisions applying or construing the provisions of the Constitution, extracts from secondary authorities, and scholarly interpretations of constitutional law. Revised editions or supplements are issued to cover current developments in constitutional law.

1362   *United States Code Annotated*. St. Paul, MN: West Publishing Company, 1927– .

Seven volumes of the USCA contain the full text of

the United States Constitution together with thousands of case annotations or court decisions applying and construing the provisions of the Constitution. An alphabetical descriptive word index to the annotations and constructions by the courts is given under each clause. There is also a separate alphabetical index to the entire Constitution and amendments. The set is kept up to date by annual cumulative pocket parts inserted in the back of each volume.

1363   U.S. Library of Congress. Legislative Reference Service. *The Constitution of the United States of America, Analysis and Interpretation: Annotations of Cases Decided by the Supreme Court of the United States To....* Washington, DC: U.S. Government Printing Office, 1913–.

This publication, issued as a Senate document in new editions at irregular intervals with supplements every two years, is virtually an encyclopedia of constitutional provisions, their history and interpretation. It contains the full text of the Constitution together with case annotations and scholarly discussions. Also included are a section on acts of Congress and state laws held unconstitutional, a list of Supreme Court decisions overruled by subsequent decisions, a table of cases, and a subject index.

STATE CONSTITUTION TEXTS

1364   Columbia University. Legislative Drafting Research Fund. *Constitutions of the United States, National and State.* Dobbs Ferry, NY: Oceana Publications, 1974–.

1365   _____ . *Index Digest of State Constitutions.* Dobbs Ferry, NY: Oceana Publications, 1959–.

Unlike the United States Constitution, which through its brevity and simple language has made adaptation to the ever-changing social and economic conditions comparatively easy, the constitutions of the 50 states are often burdened by excessive length, unnecessary detail, inadequate amendments, and numerous restrictions, notably in the area of fiscal and regulatory power. As a result of this constitutional inflexibility or obsolescence, subnational governments find it increasingly difficult to respond in a timely, adequate, or balanced manner to the many challenges posed by major population shifts, fundamental changes in the economy, or profit-oriented applications of new as well as obsolete technologies.

The two reference sets listed above offer the researcher access to the complete literal text of the constitution as it presently exists in each of the 50 states. Access is provided by name of the state and subject term. The sets permit comparative analysis by subject of all pertinent constitutional provisions or individual points in the constitutions. Entries found in the *Index Digest* set serve to

locate the desired material in the four loose-leaf binders that hold the texts of the 50 constitutions and the United States Constitution. Supplements and revisions keep the material up to date.

Statutory Law

As elected and representative bodies of the American people, the United States Congress and the 50 state legislatures enact, subject to judicial review and interpretation, private and public laws. The private laws are passed for the benefit of specific individuals or groups. Public laws affect the general public. The texts of these enactments are published officially as well as commercially in various reference series that offer the researcher separate access to the law of each jurisdiction, either chronologically or by subject. Several finding aids issued separately or as an integral part of the statutory law collections make it possible to determine the current validity of a legislative act or to locate the statutory text by popular name or specific number. Further details of the reference mechanism available for statutory law research will be apparent from the annotations given with the following list of the principal reference sources.

FEDERAL STATUTES

Guidebooks

1366   U.S. Office of the Federal Register. *How To Find U.S. Statutes and U.S. Code Citations.* Washington, DC: U.S. Government Printing Office, 1980.

This frequently revised pamphlet is a "how to find" guide that should enable the user to locate the text of laws in the *United States Statutes* and the *United States Code*, even if only incomplete references are known. Multicolumn charts direct the user from a variety of approaches to the desired material.

Indexes

1367   *Shepard's Acts and Cases by Popular Names. Federal and State.* Colorado Springs, CO: Shepard's Citations, Inc., 1968–.

Federal and state acts and cases are often referred to or cited by popular names that frequently make the identification in statutory text compilations difficult. This bound reference volume and its paper-covered cumulative supplements list acts in alphabetical order of their popular names with references to the *United States Code* and the *United States Statutes at Large* or to the specific state codes and session laws where the acts concerned can be found. Federal and state cases are cited by popular names in a separate section with references to the *United*

States Supreme Court Reports, the *National Reporter System*, and other appropriate sources.

1368   *Shepard's United States Citations. Statute Edition*. New York: Frank Shepard Company, 1943.

————— . *Supplements*. Colorado Springs: Shepard's Citations, Inc., 1943–.

Shepard's citator system is the most complete and efficient tool for ascertaining the current validity of a statutory text or judicial decision. The title above is just one unit of the citator system and contains a compilation of citations in the form of references in later cases, statutes, or other legal sources to earlier statutory texts. It enables the researcher to verify the current status of a particular law by the existence or absence of citations to later enactments, repeals, amendments, or other legally binding decisions. For a more detailed description of this and other citators as well as notes on their usage, see Chapter 28 of Price and Bitner's *Effective Legal Research* (1303) or the pamphlet *How To Use Shepard's Citations* (Colorado Springs, CO: Shepard's Citations, Inc., 1968).

Compilations

1369   *Slip Laws (Public) . . . Congress*. Washington, DC: U.S. Government Printing Office, to date.

A slip law is the first official text of a newly enacted statute and is printed on a single sheet or in pamphlet form. Each slip law carries a consecutive number (public law number) according to the chronological order in which the congressional act was passed. All slip laws are listed in the *Monthly Catalog* as well as in several congressional reference sources shortly after their enactment. They are superseded as a reference source by their inclusion in the *United States Statutes at Large*, the first permanent and official edition of congressional session laws.

1370   *United States Code*. Washington, DC: U.S. Government Printing Office, 1926–.

The public, general, and permanent laws of the United States are officially compiled by subject under 50 titles in this multivolume set, which is published in a new edition every six years. In the intervening years bound supplements are issued annually. Each of the 50 titles is subdivided by parts, chapters, and sections to permit easier identification of the legal text. Title 34 is not currently used, however. Several General Index volumes in the set contain a table of title and chapter headings, a subject key to all sections, and a popular name index.

1371   *United States Code Annotated*. St. Paul, MN: West Publishing Company, 1927–.

The text of this commercially issued reference set is the same as in the *United States Code*, but annotations, editorial and analytical notes, and references to legislative history are added to the statutory text. These additions permit the user to learn how the courts have interpreted sections of the *United States Code* or what the lawmakers meant in the statutory text. Detailed indexes, parallel tables, and other retrieval aids are included in the set, which is supplemented by pocket parts.

1372   *United States Code Service*. Rochester, NY: Lawyers Cooperative Publishing Company, 1972–.

Like the preceding set, this commercially produced reference work offers a subject compilation of federal statutory law. In addition to the same statutory text as can be found in the official *United States Code*, legislative history and case notes are provided. A separate volume, entitled *U.S. Code Guide*, relates the entire code to pertinent material in the *American Jurisprudence* encyclopedia, the *American Law Reports, the U.S. Supreme Court Reports, L. ed.*, and other legal reference sets. The entire set is kept up to date with pocket supplements and advance service pamphlets.

1373   *The United States Law Week*. Washington, DC: Bureau of National Affairs, to date.

This loose-leaf publication is an unofficial but up-to-date source for the full text of those federal statutes that are of general interest or importance. In addition to the statutory texts, the publication also contains a summary and analysis of current legal developments, new court decisions, and agency rulings. Bimonthly and semiannually cumulated indexes offer access to the published material. The annual volumes of this publication contain an annual cumulative index.

1374   *United States Statutes at Large, Containing the Laws and Concurrent Amendments to the Constitution, and Proclamations*. Washington, DC: U.S. Government Printing Office, 1789–.

Private and public laws enacted by the United States Congress and approved by the president are reprinted and compiled in chronological order of their passage in this permanent and official edition of federal session laws. One or more volumes are issued for each legislative session, with a time lag of many months. Private laws are segregated from the public laws in a separate arrangement. In addition to the full statutory texts of the laws, several finding aids are included in the volumes. These include a subject index, an individual index listing persons and private entities mentioned in the statutory texts, a list of bills enacted into law with corresponding public or private law number, a list of public laws enacted during a given session of Congress with date of enactment and *U.S. Statutes* pages, a list of private laws enacted during a given session of Congress with date of enactment and page citations, a list of concurrent resolutions with dates of passage and page citations, tables of laws affected and a guide to legislative history of all bills enacted into law with bill numbers, corresponding public law numbers, report numbers, dates of enactments, and other legislative history details. These indexes and tables are, however, not cumulative beyond each congressional session, thus necessitating separate subject compilations and indexes as described in the preceding entries.

STATE LAWS

Enactments passed by the legislatures of the 50 states are printed in slip form and permanent chronological compilations similar to the *United States Statutes at Large*. The titles of these compilations vary but usually contain the name of the state. In most states the laws are also assembled by subject classification in codes that are either officially or privately published. Many states also have multivolume annotated sets. In addition, separate index volumes for the laws of the state may be available. Comparative, nationwide information retrieval for the statutory law of the 50 states is currently being developed by the *LEXIS* online system, which has previously been described. In addition, the following bibliography may profitably be used for the identification of statutory laws in the various states.

Guidebooks

1375   Foster, Lynn, and Carol Boast. *Subject Compilations of State Laws: Research Guide and Annotated Bibliography*. Westport, CT: Greenwood Press, 1981.

Persons who need to locate or compare the text of state laws are assisted by this reference work, which identifies and describes 1,242 compilations of state laws on 403 subjects. Following an alphabetical arrangement by subject, the entries cite officially or commercially published monographs or serial sets, loose-leaf services, legal treatises, and other appropriate items issued between 1960 and 1979. All citations include standard bibliographic information, including LC classification or Superintendent of Documents (SuDoc) numbers. Introductory chapters, an author and publisher index offer additional guidance.

Nationwide Summaries

1376   *Martindale-Hubbell Law Directory*. Summit, NJ: Martindale-Hubbell, Inc., 1868– .

Volume five of this annual multivolume reference set is entitled *Law Digests* and contains, under 100 principal subject headings and numerous subheadings, that portion of the law of the 50 states, the District of Columbia, Puerto Rico, the Virgin Islands, and 52 foreign countries which is considered the most useful for the legal profession. The uniform arrangement of the material, which is supported by citations to the appropriate code sections, the *National Reporter System*, and other legal sources, assures maximum accessibility to the law of each jurisdiction.

1377   Robinson, Joan. *An American Legal Almanac. Law in All States: Summary and Update*. Dobbs Ferry, NY: Oceana Publications, 1978.

Divided into four parts and twelve chapters, this reference book presents a popular restatement of the law in various subject areas. Part 1, entitled Law and the Family, covers basic relationships among family members. Part 2, entitled Law and Livelihood, deals with business law. Part 3, Law and Living, summarizes the law governing special interest relationships. Part 4, The Individual and Society, analyzes the law relating to basic rights, duties, and immunities of individuals in relation to their government and to each other. Wherever necessary, charts identify differences in the law by states. Updating material can be found in revised editions of the *Legal Almanac* series issued by the publisher.

Decisional Law

Case law or decisional law is important in the United States because federal and state statutes are interpreted and even declared invalid by court decisions. Based on a system of legal thought developed in England, the political system of the United States recognizes the right of the judicial branch of government not merely to apply the law, but to interpret and develop statutes by the rule of judicial precedent and in the light of constitutional and legislative intent. Since the courts hear a great many civil suits involving statutory laws on such matters as civil rights, management-labor relations, business-government conflicts, minority versus majority interests, and other public disputes, the decisions of the courts also serve important purposes in political education. They illuminate and rationalize the American democratic way and dispense with outmoded ideas and undesirable forms of behavior.

As the United States possesses both a federal government and 50 state governments, it also has a dual court system. At the top of the system is the United States Supreme Court. While many millions of cases are filed annually in American courts, only a few thousand cases reach the Supreme Court. The decisions of lower courts are, therefore, in most cases final. The full text of nearly all court decisions is available in officially and commercially published reference sets. Access to the voluminous information material is provided by a well-developed system of indexes, digests, tables of cases, topic numbers, and other finding aids.

To simplify the identification of all appropriate reference tools, entries are arranged in the following sections and subdivisions:

1. Citators, Digests, and Indexes
2. Casebooks: All Courts, U.S. Supreme Court Only, Tax Cases

Introductory headnotes and accompanying annotations provide further details of the reference mechanism.

CITATORS, DIGESTS, AND INDEXES

Three separate categories of finding tools exist for locating or evaluating individual decisions in case law. The citators show the current validity of a reported decision and identify all connected cases. Separate citator sets are published for the U.S. *Supreme Court Reports*, the *National Reporter System*, and the state court reports.

Digests are the appropriate reference tools for finding brief summaries (digests) of court decisions by topic, descriptive word, or case name. Most noteworthy are the digests published by the West Publishing Company. Their key number digests are issued for single states, groups of neighboring states, single courts, or court systems on the federal and state level. A research manual, *West's Law Finder*, issued by the publisher, describes special features and the usage of these digests.

Indexes published separately or as part of casebook (reporter) sets are useful for identifying and locating the text of court decisions by date, by names of litigants, justices, or judges, by subject, or by other approaches.

The most important reference works in the three categories are listed below in an alphabetical arrangement of their main entries.

1378   *American Digest*. St. Paul, MN: West Publishing Company, 1897– .

The *American Digest* is the master index to all the case law of the United States. It consists of several units, each a complete index to reported cases for a specific period of time. Court cases decided between 1658 and 1896 are indexed in the *Century Digest*. Beginning in 1897 a series of numbered *Decennial Digest* sets is available for all cases decided during each ten-year period up to the present time. All current court decisions are indexed in monthly pamphlets of the *General Digest* that cumulate every four months into bound volumes that in turn are superseded by a new *Decennial Digest* at the end of ten years.

Every digest contains a table of cases, a descriptive word index, and a table of contents in addition to the topic and key number arrangement of the digested cases. All case citations refer to volumes and pages in the various units of the *National Reporter System*.

Extractions from the *American Digest* are published separately as regional reporter and state digests. Such digests exist for the *Atlantic, Northwestern, Pacific, South Eastern,* and *Southern Reporter* units of the *National Reporter System*, and for all states, except Delaware, Nevada, and Utah. Each of these digests contains cases from the federal and/or state court system.

1379   Blandford, Linda A., and Patricia Russell Evans. *Supreme Court of the United States 1789–1980: An Index to Opinions Arranged by Justice*. Milwood, NY: Kraus International Publications, 1983.

Without this index, locating the opinions of a specific U.S. Supreme Court justice would require a tedious page-by-page search through each volume of the standard U.S. Supreme Court casebook sets published for the period during which the justice served on the Court. The two-volume set offers citations to the official *United States Reports* set arranged by justice for seven categories of opinions, namely: (1) majority opinions, (2) concurring opinions, (3) dissenting opinions, (4) opinions announcing judgement (as in plurality opinions), (5) separate opinions (which are concurring in part and dissenting in part), (6) opinions as circuit justice, (7) statements made through the Reporter of Decisions. A chronological list of all the U.S. Supreme Court justices together with brief biographical data is also included.

1380   Guenther, Nancy Anderman. *United States Supreme Court Decisions*. Metuchen, NJ: Scarecrow Press, 1983.

The decisions of the United States Supreme Court, originally published in officially or commercially produced reference sets, are reprinted or excerpted in hundreds of books and periodical articles. Because of the heavy use of the standard reference sets, these reprints or excerpts will be a welcome additional source for the text or discussion of Supreme Court decisions. The Guenther index offers complete citations to the appropriate book sections and periodical articles under several approaches. Section 3 of the index offers chronological access by year of decision and by volume and page numbers of the official *United States Reports*. Section 4 contains case name listings in alphabetical sequence. A subject index is provided in section 5. Two additional sections present a list of books indexed and periodical titles cited. The current edition of this reference work includes all works indexed in the first edition (Nancy Anderman. *United States Supreme Court Decisions: An Index to their Locations*. Metuchen, NJ: Scarecrow Press, 1976) and covers book and periodical publications issued between 1960 and 1980.

1381   *Digest of United States Supreme Court Reports, Annotated with Case Annotations, Dissenting and Separate Opinions since 1900, Collateral References*. Rochester, NY: Lawyer's Cooperative Publishing Company, 1948– .

1382 *United States Supreme Court Digest*. St. Paul, MN: West Publishing Company, 1944–.

All decisions of the United States Supreme Court since its beginning are identifiable by topic, descriptive word, or case name, and the applicable key sentences from the Court's decisions are retrievable with the help of these digest sets. Both digest sets also provide bibliographic citations to all three editions, (U.S., L.ed., and S.Ct.) of the U.S. Supreme Court casebook sets where the full text of the opinions can be found.

A special feature of West's digest is its key number system. It divides the legal subject matter into seven main topics, namely, (1) persons, (2) property, (3) contracts, (4) torts, (5) crimes, (6) remedies, and (7) government, all of which are broken down into 32 subtopics and about 400 digest topics. An identifying number called the key number marks each point of law within a topic, and all cases applying to this point are classified to that key number. By examining the topic and key number in the digest, it is possible to determine in what cases, if any, the Court has ruled on a particular point of law.

Both digest sets are kept up to date by bound volumes and cumulative pocket supplements.

1383 *Modern Federal Practice Digest*. St. Paul, MN: West Publishing Company, 1940–.

All federal case law reported from 1939 to the present from any jurisdictional area is identifiable by topic, topic key number, case name, descriptive word or phrases, and its key sentences from the courts' decisions are retrievable with the help of this digest set. In addition, bibliographic citations are provided to the appropriate casebook sets where the full text of the court decisions can be found. The citations may refer to the three editions for U.S. Supreme Court decisions or the various units of the *National Reporter System* reporting federal case law.

Three different series of the digest presently exist, namely the *Modern Federal Practice Digest* for decisions between 1939 and 1961, the *Federal Practice Digest 2d* for decisions between 1961 and 1975, and the *Federal Practice Digest 3d* for all decisions since 1975. Federal case law reported before 1939 is digested in the *Federal Digest*.

All digests have separate descriptive word index volumes, table of cases volumes, defendant-plaintiff table volumes, words and phrases volumes in addition to the topic and key number arrangement of the cases in the main parts of the digest.

1384 *Prentice-Hall Federal Taxes Citator*. Englewood Cliffs, NJ: Prentice-Hall, 1962–.

1385 *Shepard's Federal Tax Citations*. Colorado Springs, CO: Shepard's/McGraw Hill, 1981–.

The main purpose of Prentice-Hall's citator is to enable the user to find in an alphabetical arrangement of case names in a numerical listing of treasury decisions and rulings all the tax-related court cases, revenue procedures, and rulings that affect a given case or ruling. The citator shows the history of the case and turns up everything that has been said about a case or ruling. Sixteen single-letter symbols used with the citations identify the judicial history of the cases in terms of affirmation, dismissal, modification, reversal or other disposition; and ten single-letter symbols are used to indicate whether a cited case is followed, limited, criticized, questioned, overruled, or otherwise commented upon. Complete citations are given to all relevant cases and rulings in the *United States Reports*, the *United States Supreme Court Reports: Lawyers' Edition*, the *Federal Reporter*, the *Federal Supplement*, the *Court of Claims Reports*, the *American Federal Tax Reports*, the BTA, *Tax Court of the United States*, and *U.S. Tax Court Reports*, and the *IRS Cumulative Bulletin*. Where appropriate the citations also include the paragraph number of the syllabus to which the citing case relates. The Prentice-Hall citator set currently consists of three bound volumes of a First Series for decisons dated 1796–1954, a bound volume of the Second Series for decisions dated 1954–1977, and a loose-leaf volume for decisions after 1977.

Similar access is provided by *Shepard's* citator, which offers a compilation of citations to decisions of federal courts in tax cases, Treasury regulations and decisions, IRS rulings and procedures, etc.

1386 *Shepard's United States Citations: Case Edition*. Colorado Springs, CO: Shepard's Citations, Inc., 1974–.

The purpose of this reference instrument is to make available to the researcher every instance in which a reported decision has been cited in a subsequent case, thereby showing affirmation, dismissal, modification, reversal, criticism, or other change in adjudication. The cited materials are the *United States Supreme Court Reports* and the citing materials are the U.S., L.ed., and S.Ct. editions of the U.S. Supreme Court decisions, state reports of each state, the complete *National Reporter System*, and other court reporter sets.

Separate regional and state citators are published to cover cases in the various units of the *National Reporter System* and to locate cases and statutes for each state. Their titles are *Shepard's Federal Citations, Shepard's Atlantic Reporter Citations, Shepard's Pacific Reporter Citations, Shepard's South Western Reporter Citations, Shepard's South Eastern Reporter Citations*, and *Shepard's North Eastern Reporter Citations*. For state citator volumes, the first word in the title is the name of the state, as for instance *Alabama Citations, Alaska Citations*, etc.

CASEBOOKS

All Courts

1387 *American Law Reports.*

First Series, 1919–1948 (ALR).

Second Series, 1948–1965 (ALR 2nd).

Third Series, 1965–1980 (ALR 3rd).

Fourth Series, 1980– (ALR 4th).

Federal Series, 1969– (ALR Fed).
Rochester, NY: Lawyers' Cooperative Publishing Company, 1919– .

This massive set, issued and supplemented in separate series as cited above, is a collection of important court cases from various state and federal jurisdictions printed in full from the official texts. All reported cases are accompanied by annotations, many of which are of considerable length. The annotations contain an introduction with a scope note and a summary of the legal principles deduced from the cases together with any exceptions, limitations, qualifications, or other modifications in the application of the law. All cases in support of the individual points of law are cited, together with a factual summary. The annotations therefore offer a penetrating evaluation of the functionalism of American law in its applied form. Individual annotations for any point of law can be located in the set with the help of *Quick Index, Digest* or *Word Index* volumes supplied for each ALR series or the citations found in the *American Jurisprudence* encyclopedia. Note, however, that any ALR annotation may be subsequently supplemented or superseded. To determine if this has happened, consult either the *ALR Blue Book of Supplemental Decisions* or the Annotations History Table in the bound volumes and pocket supplements of the current *ALR 3rd–4th Quick Index*.

1388 *National Reporter System*. St. Paul, MN: West Publishing Co., 1879– .

The full text of federal and state court opinions can be found in this unofficial reporter set containing five multivolume units for federal cases and nine multivolume units for state court decisions. The five federal units and their beginning dates are:

1. The *Supreme Court Reporter* (S.Ct.), 1882–
2. The *Federal Reporter* (F., F.2nd), 1880– (U.S. Courts of Appeal, U.S. Court of Claims, U.S. Court of Customs and Patent Appeals)
3. *Federal Supplement* (F.Supp.), 1932– (U.S. District Courts, U.S. Customs Court)

4. *Federal Rules Decisions* (F.R.D.), 1940– (U.S. District Court decisions concerning federal rules of civil and criminal procedure)
5. *Military Justice Reporter* (M.J.), 1975– (U.S. Court of Military Appeals)

Two of the nine state court sets cover single states, namely, the *California Reporter* (Cal.Rptr.), 1959– and the *New York Supplement* (N.Y.S., N.Y.S.2nd), 1888–. The remaining seven state court sets are regionally organized, as follows:

1. The *Atlantic Reporter* (A., A 2nd), 1885– (Connecticut, Delaware, Maine, Maryland, New Hampshire, New Jersey, Pennsylvania, Rhode Island, Vermont, and the District of Columbia)
2. The *Northeastern Reporter* (N.E., N.E.2nd), 1885– (Illinois, Indiana, Massachusetts, New York, Ohio)
3. The *Northwestern Reporter* (N.W., N.W.2nd), 1879– (Iowa, Michigan, Minnesota, Nebraska, North Dakota, South Dakota, Wisconsin)
4. The *Pacific Reporter* (P., P.2nd), 1883– (Alaska, Arizona, California, Colorado, Hawaii, Idaho, Kansas, Montana, Nevada, New Mexico, Oklahoma, Oregon, Utah, Washington, Wyoming)
5. The *Southeastern Reporter* (S.E., S.E.2nd), 1887– (Georgia, North Carolina, South Carolina, Virginia, West Virginia)
6. The *Southern Reporter* (S.,S.2nd) 1887– (Alabama, Florida, Louisiana, Mississippi)
7. The *Southwestern Reporter* (S.W., S.W. 2nd), 1866– (Arkansas, Kentucky, Missouri, Tennessee, Texas)

Each case report in the various sets contains a summary of the case and the court's decision, key-numbered headnotes analyzing all legal points involved, the opinions with numbered paragraphs corresponding to the headnotes, the full text of the decision, and other pertinent details. Also included are tables of cases reported, tables of statutes construed, federal rules of civil and criminal procedure tables, tables of words and phrases, lists of all judges sitting on the courts, etc. All reporter sets are kept current by advance sheets issued weekly. Their pagination is identical to that of the bound volumes. There is, however, no subject matter index in any individual reporter volume, and subject access must be secured through separate digest sets.

U.S. Supreme Court Only

1389 *Decisions of the United States Supreme Court*. Rochester, NY: Lawyers' Co-operative Publishing Company, 1963/1964– .

Designed as a quick reference source for the work of

the U.S. Supreme Court in each term, this annual publication offers

- biographical sketches for each Justice serving during the term
- a narrative survey of the term
- summaries of every important decision
- a listing of the attorneys acting on behalf of the litigants
- a glossary of legal terms used in the decisions
- a table of cases and a detailed subject index

The narrative term survey is arranged by the major topical areas covered by the Court's decisions, such as abortion, antitrust law, aviation law, civil procedure, civil rights, criminal law and procedure, customs law, education, election and voting rights, energy law, federal taxation, firearms, freedom of information, international law, labor law, military law, natural resources, public employees, social security, state and local government, state taxation, and others.

1390   Kurland, Philip, and Gerhard Casper. *Landmark Briefs and Arguments of the Supreme Court of the United States: Constitutional Law*. Washington, DC: University Publications of America, 1975 – .

Issued in 80 volumes, this set contains the decisions of the U.S. Supreme Court together with briefs and transcripts of oral arguments on the major constitutional law cases from 1793 to 1973. Decisions issued during subsequent terms can be found in periodical supplements, entitled *Term Supplements*. The set and its supplements is one of the most important reference and information sources for the confrontations between the most influential political actors in the judicial process of the United States. Opposing political philosophies, economic principles, and moral and social ideals are well documented.

1391   *Preview of United States Supreme Court Cases*. Chicago: American Bar Association, 1973 – .

This reference source is published in about 30 issues from September through May. It presents for the major cases to be argued before the Court a summary of the legal issues, basic facts, background and significance, and principal arguments. It also contains separate alphabetical and subject indexes of the cases already decided during the current term with references to the slip opinion number and the *Preview* issue number.

1392   U.S. National Archives. Audiovisual Archives Division. Motion Picture and Sound Recording Branch. *Tape Recordings of Oral Arguments before the U.S. Supreme Court*. Washington, DC: 1955 – .

1393   U.S. Supreme Court. *Complete Oral Argu-*

ments of the Supreme Court of the United States. Frederick, MD: University Publications of America, 1969 – .

1394   U.S. Supreme Court. *Records and Briefs*. Washington, DC: 1832 – .

1395   *U.S. Supreme Court Records and Briefs*. Bethesda, MD: Congressional Information Service, 1897 – .

The written briefs of counsel and the transcripts of the oral arguments presented before the U.S. Supreme Court are essential documents for analyzing the highest level of the judicial process in the United States. The briefs and oral arguments show the line of reasoning taken by the opposing sides in a case and are useful for evaluating the final decision of the Court. Arguments presented orally by counsel have been recorded since 1955 and are available for purchase from the National Archives. The tape recordings are obtainable in either cassettes or seven-inch reel format. When ordering a tape, the case number, Supreme Court docket number, and the date of the oral argument must be specified. A letter must also be sent to the marshal of the United States Supreme Court requesting the Court's permission to release the tape. The complete text of the oral arguments is also available from a commercial publisher in microfiche format, together with printed indexes, from the 1969 term of the Court to the present.

All written briefs and other officially docketed materials are available in an official microcard edition as well as in a commmercially issued microfiche collection.

1396   *The United States Law Week*. Washington, DC: Bureau of National Affairs, Inc., to date.

Recent decisions and up-to-date details of the proceedings of the United States Supreme Court may be found in this loose-leaf commercial publication. It contains the following features in Section 3:

1. *Cases Filed Last Week*. Reports issues for which a Supreme Court review is sought.
2. *Summary of Cases Recently Filed*. Reports information concerning the nature of the case, ruling of the lower court, questions presented to the Supreme Court, and counsel for the petitioner.
3. *Journal of Proceedings*. Reports on Court orders granting or denying a review.
4. *Summary of Orders*. Provides a summary of cases.
5. *Arguments Before the Court*. Summarizes significant oral arguments presented to the Court.
6. *Argued Cases Awaiting Decisions*. Reports about scheduled hearings.
7. *Review of Court's Work*. An annual report series summarizing the Court's term.

8. *Review of Court's Docket*. A survey of cases awaiting decisions.

Section 4 of the *United States Law Week* contains opinions of the United States Supreme Court in full text, preceded by digest headnotes. An index is issued in October in the week after the first "order" day of the Court, and cumulative indexes are published at six-week intervals. Indexes offer topical references, docket number tables, and tables of cases.

1397   U.S. Supreme Court. *Supreme Court Reporter*. St. Paul, MN: West Publishing Company, 1883–.

The full text of United States Supreme Court decisions from 1882 to the present is available in this commercially produced multivolume reference set. The value of this set arises from the fact that it is a unit of the *National Reporter* System, for which efficient indexing is provided by key number digests, tables of words and phrases, and other finding aids. Each volume of the set contains a table of statutes construed that lists all statutes construed by the United States Supreme Court as well as all *United States Code* sections construed by state courts. A table of cases reported is also included. The most recent decisions are published in weekly advance sheets together with a cumulative key number digest for the cases included.

1398   U.S. Supreme Court. *United States Reports, Cases Adjudged in the Supreme Court (U.S.)*. Vol. 1–, 1790–. Washington, DC: U.S. Government Printing Office, 1922–.

1399   _____. *Preliminary Prints (Advance Sheets)*. Washington, DC: U.S. Government Printing Office, to date.

1400   _____. *Slip Opinions*. Washington, DC: U.S. Government Printing Office, to date.

The first official printing of the United States Supreme Court decisions is known as *Slip Opinions*, which are issued three days after the decisions without editorial material. The *Preliminary Prints* are issued 30 to 60 days after a Supreme Court decision has been announced. They contain the same information and the same pagination as the permanently bound volumes of the *United States Reports*, the official edition of all written decisions of the United States Supreme Court. The designation *United States Reports* began in 1875 (volume 91), and earlier volumes bear the name of the court reporter, namely, Dallas 1–4 (1790–1800), Cranch 1–9 (1801–1815), Wheaton 1–12 (1816–1827), Peters 1–16 (1828–1842), Howard 1–24 (1843–1860), Black 1–2 (1861–1862) and Wallace 1–23 (1863–1874). Prior to 1922 the volumes were published commercially with or without official sanction. Each volume contains a table of

cases reported and a table of cases cited. There are no cumulative tables or indexes and no annotatons or summaries included in the set.

Libraries frequently shelve the *Slip Opinions* under a SuDoc classification number in a different location from the *United States Reports* volumes. All *Slip Opinions* are listed in the *Monthly Catalog of U.S. Government Publications*.

1401   U.S. Supreme Court. *United States Supreme Court Reports. Lawyers' Edition*. Vols. 1–100, 1790–1955; Second Series, Vol. 1–, 1955–.

_____. *Advance United States Supreme Court Reports*.

_____. *Index to Annotations*.
Rochester, NY: Lawyers' Cooperative Publishing Company.

This commercial edition contains all decisions printed in the official reports as well as many per curiam decisions not reported in the official edition. The special value of this set lies in the fact that the majority, dissenting, and separate opinions of the justices are summarized and headnoted, and the briefs of counsel are summarized. All cases are also annotated for points of legal interest. These annotations are listed in a separate, unnumbered volume, entitled *Index to Annotations*. The most recent decisions of the Court can be found in the advance sheets, which are published biweekly while the Court is in session. Volume and page numbering in the advance sheets is the same as in the bound volumes.

1402   *U.S. Supreme Court Bulletin*. Chicago: Commerce Clearing House, 1936–.

As a weekly loose-leaf publication, this commercially issued reference set is—like the *United States Law Week*—a most valuable tool for

• getting fast access to the opinions of the United States Supreme Court
• identifying all pending cases

The set contains the full text of the opinions, numerous finding aids, such as a subject index, docket number index, status table for cases pending, etc., and sections offering a copy of the Court's docket and a tentative calendar for arguments.

Tax Cases

1403   *American Federal Tax Reports*. 1st Series. Englewood Cliffs, NJ: Prentice-Hall, 1924–1958.

1404   *American Federal Tax Reports*. 2nd Series. Englewood Cliffs, NJ: Prentice-Hall, 1958–.

1405   *United States Tax Cases*. Chicago: Commerce Clearing House, 1936–.

These casebook sets contain unabridged texts of court decisions from federal and state courts that settle problems of federal taxation. Included are the decisions from U.S. District Courts, the U.S. Court of Claims, U.S. Courts of Appeals, the U.S. Supreme Court, and certain state courts, but not from the Tax Court of the United States. The decisions arise out of suits or appeals brought by taxpayers or the United States for the recovery of taxes owed or overpaid. U.S. Supreme Court decisions are the only tax decisions that the commissioner of internal revenue is required to follow. They remain in effect until overruled by a later U.S. Supreme Court decision or replaced by a statute change passed by Congress.

While these decisions are usually printed in the general U.S. Supreme Court and National Reporter System sets, separate publication in the sets cited above improves their access by a tie-in with the subject treatment of the entire tax law in *Prentice-Hall Federal Taxes* and the Commerce Clearing House standard *Federal Tax Reporter* sets. The finding aids in these sets and the parallel and case tables of the bound volumes listed above provide a two-way reference link-up by subject, keyword, case name, code or regulation number.

1406   *Board of Tax Appeals Memorandum Decisions*. Englewood Cliffs, NJ: Prentice-Hall, 1928–1942

1407   *Tax Court Memorandum Decisions*. Englewood Cliffs, NJ: Prentice-Hall, 1943–.

1408   *Tax Court Reported Decisions*. Englewood Cliffs, NJ: Prentice-Hall, 1943–.

1409   *Tax Court Reporter*. Chicago: Commerce Clearing House, 1975–.

In 1928, the Board of Tax Appeals (BTA) began to issue memorandum opinions that are just as complete as the reported decisions, but are not published in sufficient quantity by the U.S. Government Printing Office. BTA and Tax Court memo opinions are disseminated commercially, however, by the casebook sets cited above.

Prentice-Hall prints all memorandum decisions in weekly loose-leaf reports, and each year's cases are published in bound volumes at the end of the year. Prentice-Hall paragraph numbers assigned to the memorandum decisions correspond to the numbers assigned to the cases by the Tax Court. Each bound volume contains a keyword index that coordinates the cases with the subject treatment of the complete tax law in the *Prentice-Hall Federal Taxes* set.

Officially reported decisions of the Tax Court are also published commercially by Prentice-Hall and Commerce Clearing House in separate casebook sets.

1410   U.S. Tax Court. *Reports*. Washington, DC: U.S. Government Printing Office, 1924–1942.

1411   U.S. Tax Court. *Reports of the Tax Court of the United States*. Washington, DC: U.S. Government Printing Office, 1942–.

The U.S. Tax Court was established as the Board of Tax Appeals (BTA) in 1924, renamed Tax Court of the United States (TC) in 1942 and United States Tax Court in 1969. Its decisions are rendered in response to petitions filed by taxpayers seeking to set aside or reduce a deficiency in income, excess profits, or other taxes as determined by the commissioner of internal revenue. The casebook sets cited above provide the official text of all reported BTA and TC decisions, composed of an official headnote, findings of fact, and the opinion. The bound volumes are published twice a year following initial monthly printings of the decisions in pamphlet form.

The official sets do not contain the text of the memorandum opinions issued by the Board of Tax Appeals and Tax Court since 1928. Likewise, the sets give no indication of the acquiescence or nonacquiescence by the commissioner of internal revenue in the reported decisions of the court.

Administrative Law

Administrative law consists of the legally binding and enforceable prescripts, orders, and decisions made and applied by administrative authorities. These administrative authorities are distinct organizational units of the federal government constituted as departments, boards, commissions, or services. A characteristic feature of all administrative authorities is their responsibility for implementing statutory law by specific rules, regulations, and decisions with broad functional effects on various segments of the population. Taxation, licensing, reparations, confiscation, destruction, or alteration of physical objects and modification of human behavior or situations are some of the most important effects of administrative rule and decision making.

In addition to the previously listed directories that identify administrative authorities and their functions, four different types of reference instruments exist for facilitating access to the massive amounts of information in administrative law. These are (1) guidebooks, (2) codebooks and other collections of administrative regulations, (3) casebooks for administrative adjudication, and (4) indexes and citators.

GUIDEBOOKS

1412   Nelson, Dalmas H. *Administrative Agencies of the USA. Their Decisions and Authority*. Detroit: Wayne State University Press, 1964.

The decisions of federal administrative agencies vary greatly in their functional intent. This book provides a description of administrative orders by subject content. It identifies the agencies responsible for assessment orders, penalty orders, social stigma orders, censorship orders, corporal orders, cease and desist orders, declaratory orders, benefactory orders, remissive orders, and others. Also included in the book are a table of cases and a bibliography.

1413   U.S. Office of the Federal Register. *The Federal Register: What It Is and How To Use It. A Guide for the User of the Federal Register – Code of Federal Regulations System.* Washington, DC: U.S. Government Printing Office, 1977.

Organized in five sections, the guidebook explains the historical background and current organization of the *Federal Register/Code of Federal Regulations* system and how to use it. It also discusses how the public can participate in the regulatory process. A list of depository libraries, GPO bookstores, and other distribution centers, as well as the text of the Federal Register Act and the Administrative Procedure Act are also included.

COLLECTIONS OF FEDERAL RULES AND REGULATIONS

1414   *Code of Federal Regulations.* Washington, DC: Office of the Federal Register, National Archives and Records Service, 1938–.

The general and permanent rules issued by the president, executive department, and federal agencies are codified in this multivolume reference set under 50 titles that represent broad areas subject to federal regulation. Titles are subdivided by chapters, parts, and sections to facilitate citing of the appropriate administrative regulations. The chapters within each title usually bear the name of the issuing agency. Title 3, for instance, refers to the president and contains the text of presidential proclamations, executive orders, reorganization plans, and other legal documents issued by the president under chapters I–IV.

A number of finding aids are included with the set to assist the researcher in locating the desired text of any administrative regulation. These finding aids are listed in Appendix C of Title 1 and include a separate general index volume, a table of CFR titles and chapters at the end of each CFR volume and at the beginning of the General Index volume, an alphabetical list of CFR subtitles and chapters at the end of each CFR volume, a list of sections affected, redesignation tables, parallel tables of presidential documents and agency rules, parallel tables of statutory authorities and rules, etc.

All volumes of the *Code* are revised once each year and contain the federal regulations in effect on January 1 of the year designated on the cover and title page. Regulations issued subsequently are printed in the daily issues of the *Federal Register*.

1415   *Codification of Presidential Proclamations and Executive Orders.* Washington, DC: U.S. Government Printing Office, 1981.

The full text of presidential proclamations and executive orders that have general applicability and continuing effect can be found in convenient form in this official reference publication revised in biannual intervals. The cited edition covers all legally binding documents issued during the Kennedy, Johnson, Nixon, Ford, and Carter administrations from January 20, 1961, to January 20, 1981. Each codified document is assigned to one of the 50 chapters representing broad subject areas similar to the title designations in the *Code of Federal Regulations* or the *United States Code*.

1416   *Federal Register.* Washington, DC: Office of the Federal Register, National Archives and Records Service, 1936–.

Issued daily except Sundays and Mondays, this reference publication serves as the most current source for federal administrative rules and regulations, proposed rule making, and notices. Since this material is arranged chronologically for the various administrative units, it is necessary to consult one or more of the finding aids printed either in each issue or published separately at monthly, quarterly, and annual intervals. These finding aids include contents tables in each issue, subject indexes issued separately, lists of CFR parts affected and CFR sections affected, published in each issue or separately.

In addition to these finding aids, two commercial publishers currently produce two other bibliographic instruments, namely, the *CIS Federal Register Index* and the *CSI Federal Register Abstracts*, more fully described in the Administrative Law index section. For online retrieval of the full text of the *Federal Register*, see the entries for *LEXIS* and *Westlaw/System II* in this guidebook.

1417   *Federal Tax Regulations.* St. Paul, MN: West Publishing Company, 1954–.

1418   Mertens, Jacob. *The Law of Federal Income Taxation.*

———. *Regulations.* Edited by Philip Zimet. Mundelein, IL: Callaghan & Company, 1961–.

Tax regulations constitute an official form of interpretation of the Internal Revenue Code developed by the Treasury Department, subject to invalidation only by court decision, or subsequent amendment by new regulations promulgated by the Treasury Department. All regulations are published in the *Federal Register* and the *Code of Federal Regulations*, but the reference sets cited above provide a more convenient collection of the regulations. *Federal Tax Regulations* is an annual multivolume series that preserves in permanent form the regulations adopted up to the end of the previous calendar year. The regulations relate to income, estate, gift, and employment taxes, and are arranged by sections of the *Code of Federal Regulations*, Title 26 and 31. A separate index using subject headings and key terms is also provided. Current changes to the regulations are published in *U.S. Code Congressional and Adminstrative News*.

Regulations relating to income taxes only can also be found in the bound and loose-leaf *Regulations* volumes of the Mertens set. Regulations are arranged numerically by section number of the Internal Revenue code. Separate regulations status tables show in which bound or loose-leaf *Regulations* volumes the current or prior text of any miscellaneous, general, or proposed regulations can be found. The entire Mertens set also contains additional finding aids by case name, code citation, or subject.

1419   U.S. Internal Revenue Service. *Internal Revenue Bulletin; Cumulative Bulletin*. Washington, DC: U.S. Government Printing Office, 1922 – .

――――― . *Index-Digest Supplement*. Washington, DC: U.S. Government Printing Office, 1953 – 1964.

――――― . *Index-Digest Supplement System*. Washington, DC: U.S. Government Printing Office, 1965 – .

1420   Mertens, Jacob. *The Law of Federal Income Taxation*. Mundelein, IL: Callaghan & Company, 1942 – .

――――― . *Rulings* edited by Philip Zimet and Leonard L. Silverstein. Mundelein, IL: Callaghan & Company, 1958 – .

It is the policy of the Internal Revenue Service to publish in the *Internal Revenue Bulletin* issues and answers involving substantive and procedural tax law affecting taxpayers' rights and duties. To this end chronologically numbered revenue rulings (rev. rul.), and revenue procedures (rev. proc.) as well as announcements of acquiescences, nonacquiescences, and miscellaneous other items are issued by the commissioner of internal revenue.

While the revenue rulings and procedures do not have the force and effect of Treasury Department regulations, they may be used as precedents for the application of the law in varying fact situations. The commissioner's acquiescences and nonacquiescences are issued in response to the reported decisions of the U.S. Tax Court only. Miscellaneous other announcements inform the public of the commissioner's position regarding treatment of gains, losses, expenses, and other taxation items.

The *Internal Revenue Bulletin (IRB)* is issued weekly. A consolidation of all items of a permanent nature published in the weekly bulletins is available in semiannual bound volumes, entitled *Cumulative Bulletin*. Access to all published items is facilitated by indexes included in the first *IRB* each month and cumulated on a quarterly and semiannual basis. In addition, the *Index-Digest Supplements*, currently consisting of four separate sections for income taxes, estate and gift taxes, employment taxes, and excise taxes, offer the following finding aids in a basic volume and cumulative supplements: (1) finding lists of items published in the *IRB*, (2) digests of revenue rulings, revenue procedures, and other published items, (3) indexes of public laws, Treasury decisions, and tax conventions.

Revenue rulings and procedures relating to income taxes only can also be found in the bound and loose-leaf volumes entitled *Rulings* that are part of the Mertens set. A code-rulings table links the revenue rulings, procedures, and miscellaneous announcements with the appropriate sections of the Internal Revenue Code. In addition, a topical index to the treatise volumes of the Mertens set offers a subject approach.

CASEBOOKS

1421   *Decisions of Federal Administrative Agencies and of Federal Courts in Agency Cases, Prior to 1958*. Westport, CT: Redgrave Information Resources Corporation, 1972.

The administrative decisions, findings, orders, and reports of the U.S. Bureau of Labor Statistics, U.S. Civil Aeronautics Board, U.S. Federal Communications Commission, U.S. Federal Power Commission, U.S. Federal Trade Commission, U.S. Immigration and Naturalization Service, U.S. National Labor Board, U.S. National Labor Relations Board, and the U.S. Securities and Exchange Commission for periods from 1912 to 1958 are available in full text in this microfiche collection. Eyelegible internal information frames (targets), as well as digests and indexes provide access to the desired information material.

More recent administrative decisions may be found in the official casebook sets, such as the items listed below.

1422   U.S. Civil Aeronautics Board. *Civil Aeronautics Board Decisions*. Washington, DC: U.S. Government Printing Office, 1938 – .

The decisions of the five-member board regulate airline routes, freight rates, and passenger fares. The board also approves or disapproves proposed agreements and corporate relationships between air carriers.

1423   U.S. Federal Communications Commission. *Federal Communications Commission Reports — Decisions, Reports and Orders*. Washington, DC: U.S. Government Printing Office, 1934—.

These decisions of the seven-member commission regulate civilian radio, cable, wire, and television communication. The commission also sets rates for interstate and international communication.

1424   U.S. Federal Power Commission. *Federal Power Commission Reports, Opinions and Decisions*. Washington, DC: U.S. Government Printing Office, 1931—.

The five-member commission regulates rates and practices in the interstate transmission of electric energy, and also regulates the transportation and sale of natural gas.

1425   U.S. Federal Trade Commission. *Federal Trade Commission Decisions*. Washington, DC: U.S. Government Printing Office, 1915—.

The decisions of the five-member commission apply laws preventing advertising misrepresentations, unfair competition, false packaging and mislabelling of products, price discrimination, and credit gouging. The commission also decides on antitrust violations.

1426   U.S. Immigration and Naturalization Service. *Administrative Decisions under Immigration and Nationality Laws of the United States*. Washington, DC: U.S. Government Printing Office, 1940—.

The decisions of this agency apply the immigration and naturalization laws relating to the admission, exclusion, deportation, and naturalization of aliens.

1427   U.S. Interstate Commerce Commission. *Interstate Commerce Commission Reports*. Washington, DC: U.S. Government Printing Office, 1887—.

The eleven-member commission regulates interstate surface transportation, including trains, trucks, buses, inland waterway and coastal shipping, freight forwarders, oil pipelines, and express companies. Regulation is exercised by certification of carriers, rate fixing, approval or disapproval of mergers and other consolidations, prescription of reparations, etc. The reports are presently issued in various subseries, such as *Finance Reports, Traffic Decisions, Water Carrier and Freight Forwarders Reports, Motor Carrier Cases*, etc.

1428   U.S. National Labor Relations Board. *National Labor Relations Board Decisions and Orders*. Washington, DC: U.S. Government Printing Office, 1935—.

The decisions and orders of the five-member board prevent and remedy unfair labor practices by employers and labor unions.

1429   U.S. Securities and Exchange Commission. *Securities and Exchange Commission Decisions and Reports*. Washington, DC: U.S. Government Printing Office, 1934—.

The decisions of the five-member commission regulate the operation of stock exchanges and activities of securities dealers and investment companies.

CITATORS AND INDEXES

Each of the previously listed casebook sets and collections of federal rules and regulations has its own index and/or digest coverage. In addition, the following external citator and index sets will be useful.

1430   *CIS Federal Register Index*. Bethesda, MD: Congressional Information Service, 1984—.

While the *Federal Register* does have its own index and other finding aids, the officially published indexes are neither published with sufficient frequency nor contain adequate depth of indexing. The *CIS Federal Register Index* is issued every week on Fridays, one week after the last *Federal Register* issue covered. The weekly issues are cumulated monthly, quarterly, and semiannually. It thus provides current access to all rules, proposed rules, notices, and presidential documents contained in each daily issue of the *Federal Register*. The index consists of three sections: (1) the subjects and names index, with citations for activities, industries, occupations, geographic areas, issuing agency, companies and organizations, etc., by subject term or name; (2) the CFR section index, with identification of the changes to a specific section or subsection of the *Code of Federal Regulations*; and (3) the agency docket number index, providing an easy way to identify cases, investigations, policy statements, interpretative rulings, or other regulatory actions, when an agency-assigned number is known. The entire reference set is issued in loose-leaf format.

1431   *Classification Outline with Topical Index for Decisions of the National Labor Relations Board and Related Court Decisions*. Washington, DC: U.S. Government Printing Office, 1982.

1432   *Classified Index of National Labor Relations Board Decisions and Related Court Decisions*. Washington, DC: U.S. Government Printing Office, 1935—.

1433   *Classified Index of Dispositions of Unfair Labor Practices Charges by the General Counsel of the National Labor Relations Board*. Washington, DC: U.S. Government Printing Office, 1968–1975, 1976—.

Separate and detailed indexing is available for the decisions of the National Labor Relations Board (NLRB), an independent agency established in 1935, as well as the advice and appeals memoranda and dispositions issued by the General Counsel, an organ of the NLRB, and related court decisions rendered in labor law cases. The *Classification Outline* provides a subject matter classification system for the procedural and substantive legal issues decided by the NLRB and the federal courts. The classification system contains eight classes, as follows: 100 — National Labor Relations Act as Amended; 200 — NLRB Jurisdiction; 300 — Investigation and Certification of Representative; 400 — Bargaining Units; 500 — Unfair Labor Practices; 600 — Remedial Order Provisions; 700 — General Legal Principles; and 800 — Court Proceedings. As many as seven levels of subheadings under each of the main headings may exist. The *Topical Index* is an alphabetical listing of terms and outline headings together with their respective classification numbers. The *Classified Index* provides, in classified order, citations by volume and folio number to the NLRB decisions set and appropriate units of the *National Reporter System* set. Advice memoranda, appeals memoranda, and dispositions issued by the General Counsel of the NLRB are separately indexed. All index publications are updated at biannual or other intervals.

1434   *CSI Federal Register Abstracts*. Washington, DC: Capitol Services International, 1977 – .

1435   *Federal Register Abstracts*. Washington, DC: Capitol Services International, 1977 – . (Vendor: Dialog — File 136)

Issued daily in its printed version and updated weekly in the electronic version, this index identifies and summarizes federal regulatory agency actions as published in the *Federal Register*. References are available to regulations taking effect each day, as well as to proposed rules, meeting and hearing notices. Also included are presidential executive orders, proclamations, and determinations. Online access to the electronic database is offered with the Dialog Information Retrieval Service.

1436   *Index to the Code of Federal Regulations*. Bethesda, MD: Congressional Information Service, 1977 – .

In view of their limited indexing vocabulary and lack of precision, the officially published finding aids to the *Code of Federal Regulations*, previously described, are often not much help. With a greatly expanded ratio of index pages to the nearly 100,000 *CFR* pages and an indexing vocabulary of more than 20,000 terms, the *Index to the Code of Federal Regulation* offers precision access to all regulations under several approaches. A detailed subject index with numerous see also references and scope notes provides citations to title, chapter, part, and page numbers in the *Code of Federal Regulations*. In addition to the subject index, there are two geographic indexes that identify regulations concerning cities and federally administered properties treated by name in the *CFR*. Also included are a List of Descriptive Headings and a List of Reserved Headings. The latter informs the user which parts of the *CFR* have been designated as "reserved" in anticipation of future use or because they have been vacated from previous use. The index is published in a cumulative edition for the years 1977 – 1979 and in annual editions since 1980.

1437   *Shepard's Code of Federal Regulations Citations*. Colorado Springs, CO: Shepard's/McGraw-Hill, 1981 – .

This publication is a compilation of citations to agency regulations, executive orders, presidential proclamations, and other administrative rules in the *Code of Federal Regulations*.

1438   *Shepard's Federal Energy Law Citations*. Colorado Springs, CO: Shepard's/McGraw-Hill, 1983 – .

The current validity of any aspect of energy law, regulation, or decision can be determined from references provided by this citator. Source documents include *U.S. Supreme Court Reports, Federal Power Commission Decisions and Orders, Federal Energy Regulatory Commission Decisions and Orders, CCH Energy Management, CCH Utilities Law Reporter*, the *U.S. Code*, and the *Code of Federal Regulations*.

1439   *Shepard's Federal Labor Law Citations*. Colorado Springs, CO: Shepard's Citations, Inc., 1959 – .

The value of any decision of the National Labor Relations Board as current authority can be determined and traced through all later citation usage by the board or the courts with the help of this citator set. Published with bimonthly cumulative supplements, the set consists of a case edition and a statute edition. The case edition covers federal labor law decisions since 1935 as reported in the *National Labor Relations Board Decisions and Orders* and the casebook sets of the federal court system, such as the three editions for the U.S. Supreme Court decisions, the *Federal Reporter*, and the Federal Supplement. Articles in labor relations periodicals, law journals, as well as the annotations in the *American Law Reports* are also covered.

1440   *Shepard's Federal Tax Locator*. Colorado Springs, CO: Shepard's Citations, Inc., 1974 – .

The obvious need for a comprehensive subject index to all the current sources of law relating to federal taxation is fulfilled by this reference set issued with quarterly supplements. The following sources are indexed:

1. Laws, rules and regulations: Internal Revenue Code, Treasury regulations, procedural rules (*26 CFR part*

601), Tax Court rules, treaties and conventions with other countries.
2. Rulings, bulletins, and other releases: Treasury decisions, Revenue rulings, cumulative bulletins, Internal Revenue bulletins, Treasury Department circulars, technical information releases, congressional committee reports.
3. Cases: *U.S. Supreme Court Reports, Federal Reporter, Federal Supplement, Federal Rules Decisions, Tax Court Reports, Court of Claims Reports, Board of Tax Appeals Reports*, etc.
4. Tax services: *CCH Federal Estate and Gift Tax Reporter, CCH Federal Excise Tax Reporter, CCH Standard Federal Tax Reporter, Prentice-Hall Federal Taxes*, Rabkin and Johnson's *Federal Income, Gift and Estate Taxation*, and the *Tax Coordinator*, published by the Research Institute of America.
5. Legal periodicals: A total of 122 different periodicals published throughout the United States is indexed.

Index entries are arranged alphabetically under subject headings and provide full bibliographic citations to the source document. Most subject headings include a brief introductory headnote explaining the nature of the subject matter. The quarterly cumulative supplements that update the basic volumes are inserted in a pocket at the back of each bound volume.

1441   *Shepard's Immigration and Naturalization Citations.* Colorado Springs, CO: Shepard's/McGraw-Hill, 1982 – .

Separate citator coverage is available for administrative decisions and regulations as well as court cases relating to immigration, naturalization, and deportation. Citing sources are the U.S. Supreme Court sets, the *Federal Reporter, Federal Supplement*, and selected law reviews. The quarterly updated citator is an excellent tool for determining the current validity of the law as it relates to problems of visas, asylum, illegal aliens, and other immigration and naturalization matters.

1442   *Shepard's United States Patents and Trademark Citations.* Colorado Springs, CO: Shepard's Citations, Inc., 1968 – .

Administrative decisions, court decisions, rules, and regulations relating to patents, trademarks, and copyright are analyzed separately in this citator set with quarterly cumulative supplements.

1443   *Shepard's United States Administrative Citations.* Colorado Springs, CO: Shepard's Citations, Inc., 1967 – .

All citations to the decisions of federal administrative departments, agencies, boards, or commissions as originally reported in their own casebook sets are listed in this

standard citator set for administrative law. The citing case can be found in the various casebook sets for federal and state court decisions. Citations appearing in law journals and various reporter sets are also shown. Citations involving labor relations, trademarks, patents, and copyrights are generally not included in this set and can be found in the special citator sets previously listed.

Special Areas of Law

Apart from the preceding reference sets, organized by categories of legal authority, there exists a large array of officially or commercially produced reporter, index, or abstracts sets that assemble, usually in loose-leaf format, detailed and up-to-date texts of the relevant statutory laws and their interpretation, implementation, or enforcement by judicial and administrative bodies in specific fields of public concern. These topical reference sets provide a systematic approach to all pertinent information by the use of classified arrangements of the subject matter or legal source and by a variety of finding aids, such as topical indexes, tables of cases, digests, numerical lists, etc.

The following selective list of topical reporter and similar reference sets will serve as a record of the most useful retrieval tools for research in specific areas of American law. In view of the large number of available reference sources, the listings have been divided into three sections, namely, (1) Tax Law, (2) Emergency Assistance Law, and (3) Other Law.

TAX LAW

Federal and state taxation is not only the principal revenue source for governmental operations but an important means for accomplishing political objectives of a social and economic nature. During the 1980s taxation has acquired a new significance as a result of increased federal spending, enormous revenue shortfalls, reduced federal aid flows, recessionary pressures on state and local government, and taxpayers' revolts. As currently practiced, taxation is based on an enormously complex web of legal directives that have prompted widespread demands for tax reform and simplification. The following reference sets serve as vital aids to all persons who need to know, apply, or reform the law of American taxation as presently constituted.

1444   *Federal Tax Coordinator 2nd.* New York: Research Institute of America, 1977 – .

Published in 28 weekly updated loose-leaf volumes, this reference set organizes the law of federal income, gift, estate, and excise taxation by subject matter or transaction. The entire area of taxation is divided into 30 self-contained chapters, each identified by a tab card. Each chapter begins with a detailed reference table that lists the subject matter or problems discussed and explained in the chapter. All explanations are supported by citation to authorities and followed by verbatim reprints of all pertinent code and Treasury regulations sections. Apart from this chapter approach, the *Federal Tax Coordinator 2d* also provides other finding aids to the published information. These include a topical index, arranged by subject and fact words, code tables, regulations and treasury decisions tables, rulings and releases tables, and cases and decisions tables. Also provided are a rapid code index that coordinates the IRC sections with the volumes and chapters of the reference set, a new law index, and parallel reference tables that link citations to the *U.S. Reports*, the *Federal Reporter Second Series*, and the *Federal Supplement* with the volume and page location in *U.S. Tax Cases* and *American Federal Tax Reports*. Cases decided before 1954, however, are not covered.

1445   *Prentice-Hall Federal Taxes.* Englewood Cliffs, NJ: Prentice-Hall, 1957–.

Consisting of 17 annually revised and weekly updated, loose-leaf volumes, *Prentice-Hall Federal Taxes* covers the federal tax law by editorial explanations, amplified by examples, supported by cases and rulings, and supplemented with the full text of the law and regulations, and with extracts from congressional committee reports relating to newly enacted laws. The basic arrangement of all law sections is in numerical order of the Internal Revenue Code with separate volumes devoted to income taxes, estate and gift taxes, and excise taxes. Numerous tab cards divide the material by code and regulations sections for easier access. For additional approaches, the income, estate and gift, and excise tax volumes have their own indexes. They offer access by subject heading and key term, transaction, number of ruling, and name of case. An index to tax articles in law journals and other periodicals is also provided.

Also included in the set are an AFTR 2nd Advance Sheets volume, with the full text of tax cases from courts other than the U.S. Tax Court, two Internal Revenue Code volumes with the full text of the code and proposed regulations, and a Current Matter volume.

The full text of the tax treaties concluded by the United States with other countries can be found in volume 8 for all income tax agreements and in the estate and gift tax volume for the estate and gift tax treaties.

1446   Rabkin, Jacob, and Mark H. Johnson. *Federal Income, Gift, and Estate Taxation.* New York: Matthew Bender, 1962–.

The multivolume, monthly updated, loose-leaf reference set offers a detailed subject description of the law of federal income, gift, and estate taxation, as well as the full text of the Internal Revenue Code together with legislative history and appropriate congressional committee reports.

The material is organized in eight chapters, entitled: (1) The Individual, (2) The Corporation, (3) Deductions: Expenses, (4) Deductions: Taxes and Losses, (5) Husband and Wife, (6) Foreign Transactions, (7) Aliens and Foreign Income, and (8) Foreign Corporation and Foreign Trade. Numerous subheadings within these chapters arrange the text according to topical categories. A detailed table of contents facilitates access to the subject sections of the set. The code volumes are arranged by subtitle, chapter, subchapter, and section number of the statutes. Immediately following the statutory sections, the full text of the relevant reports from the House Ways and Means Committee, the Senate Finance Committee, and the House Conference is reproduced. Federal income, gift, and estate regulations are set forth in separate volumes of the set, together with cross-references to the appropriate text and statute sections as well as the source of each original regulation. Other finding aids in the set include a table of statutory references, case tables, a tax rate table, and a self-contained index volume with all relevant key terms.

1447   *Standard Federal Tax Reporter.*

1448   *Federal Estate and Gift Tax Reporter.*

1449   *Federal Excise Tax Reporter.*
Chicago: Commerce Clearing House, 1945–.

These multivolume, weekly updated, loose-leaf reference sets offer a compilation of federal tax law on income, estate, gift, and excise taxes by reproducing the full text of the Internal Revenue Code, treasury decisions, court cases, revenue rulings, revenue procedures, and other IRS announcements together with detailed explanations and editorial comments. The basic arrangement of the compilation volumes is by code organization and section number. Appropriate tab cards divide the material for easier access. Additional access is provided by numerous finding aids that include

a topical index
a rapid finder index
case name listings for court decisions
title and numerical listings of rulings
numerical listings of regulations
checklists for income tax returns
various tables of contents for tax planning information

Also included are the full text of United States tax treaties with other countries, a dictionary of tax terms, a tax calendar, special tables for depreciation, annuities and savings bonds, income tax rates, etc.

1450   *State and Local Tax Service.* Englewood Cliffs, NJ: Prentice-Hall, 1941–.

Editorial explanations plus the full text of laws, regulations, and other official material relating to state and local taxes are available in this multivolume, weekly updated, loose-leaf reference set. The set is organized into three main parts: (1) Report and Legislative Bulletins; (2) Individual State Units; and (3) All States Tax Guide. The report bulletins offer news and feature articles on important new developments in the field of state and local taxes. The legislative bulletins inform about legislative meetings, governors' recommendations for tax legislation, and actions of the legislatures on tax measures. The individual state units sections are organized by subject or type of tax, notably income taxes, franchise taxes, sales or use taxes, property taxes, occupation taxes, gasoline taxes, and others. Finding aids for these sections include a chart of the state tax system, a calendar of tax and report dates, and a detailed subject index. The All States Tax Guide gathers in one volume all the essential tax information from all states. Multistate taxation as well as taxes for all states and thousands of localities are outlined. Cross-references, charts, and a master index facilitate access to and comparison of the available tax information, but the verbatim text of laws, regulations, and other official material can be found in the separate state volumes only.

EMERGENCY ASSISTANCE LAW

One of the prime functions of governments is to assist individuals and organizations in cases of emergency. Such government assistance is mandated by law, but due to the complexity of existing legal directives pertinent information has often been difficult to access. The following reference work will serve as an excellent finding aid in this important area of the law.

1451   *Federal Emergency Authorities Abstracts.* Washington, DC: U.S. Government Printing Office, 1979.

This abstracts publication contains the text of pertinent statutes, agency regulations, and executive orders relating to 20 categories of emergency and assistance programs of the federal government. These federal emergency programs are mandated by law as a government response to man-made or natural disasters. The response encompasses preparedness, mitigation, assistance, insurance, or other types of relief. The legal texts are arranged under 20 chapters, as follows: (1) Civil Defense, (2) Disaster Relief, (3) Earthquake Hazards Reduction/Dam Safety, (4) Transportation, (5) Fire Prevention and Control, (6) Educational Institutions Assistance, (7) Military Assistance, (8) Private National Organizations Assistance, (9) Federal Departments and Agencies, (10) Flood Control and Prevention, (11) Search and Rescue, (12) Pollution/Environmental Protection Assistance, (13) Hazardous Materials Assistance, (14) Energy Emergency Assistance, (15) Nuclear Materials Manage-

ment Assistance, (16) Housing and Urban Development Assistance, (17) Health and Medical Assistance, (18) Legal/Law Enforcement Assistance, (19) Business Assistance, and (20) Agricultural Assistance. A twenty-first chapter deals with various aspects of emergency management. All abstracts include complete bibliographic citations to the legal authority. A public law/regulation index and a subject index are also provided.

OTHER LAW

There are few areas of law that are not served by one or more topical loose-leaf or other reporter sets. Although very few libraries will have all of the available sets, most libraries will identify their holdings by the name of the publisher of the reporter sets. There are four major publishers of loose-leaf reporter sets, namely the Bureau of National Affairs (BNA), Commerce Clearing House (CCH), Prentice-Hall (PH), and the Rocky Mountain Mineral Law Foundation. Their most important sets are listed below.

1452   *Antitrust and Trade Regulation Report.*

1453   *Chemical Regulation Reporter.*

1454   *Criminal Law Reporter.*

1455   *Environment Reporter.*

1456   *Family Law Reporter.*

1457   *Housing and Development Reporter.*

1458   *Index to Government Regulation.*

1459   *Labor Relations Reporter.*

1460   *Media Law Reporter.*

1461   *Noise Regulation Reporter.*

1462   *Occupational Safety & Health Reporter.*

1463   *Product Safety and Liability Reporter.*

1464   *Securities Regulation & Law Reporter.* Washington, DC: Bureau of National Affairs, 1929– .

Since 1929 the Bureau of National Affairs, a commercial publisher, has been reporting and interpreting the decisions of federal authorities in the fields of business regulation, labor relations, consumer and environmental protecton. Full text treatment is provided for all pertinent administrative actions, legislative acts, judicial decisions, policy statements, and other political outputs. The listed titles represent a selection of this publisher's major reference works, which include three daily services and more than 40 weekly, biweekly, and monthly reporter sets.

1465   *Aviation Law Reports.*

1466   *Bankruptcy Law Reports.*

1467   *Federal Banking Law Reports.*

1468   *Federal Carrier Reports.*

1469   *Federal Immigration Law Reporter.*

1470   *Federal Securities Law Reports.*

1471   *Food Drug Cosmetic Law Reports.*

1472   *Labor Law Reports.*

1473   *Labor Arbitration Awards.*

1474   *Nuclear Regulation Reports.*

1475   *Trade Regulation Reports.*

1476   *Utilities Law Reports.*
Chicago: Commerce Clearing House, to date.

Several series of topical law reports, issued with varying frequency by this publisher, provide the text of statutory laws, administrative and judicial decisions relating to atomic energy, aviation, bankruptcy, banking, business and trade, labor relations, etc. Numerous finding aids for locating the desired information are provided with the sets.

1477   *Control of Banking.*

1478   *Government Disclosure.*

1479   *Securities Regulation.*
Englewood Cliffs, NJ: Prentice-Hall, to date.

The reporter sets, issued in loose-leaf format by this publisher, provide up-to-date coverage of the output of legislative, judicial, and administrative authorities in the area of banking, information disclosure by federal and state governments, and securities regulation. Suitable indexes, tables of cases, and other finding aids facilitate access to the published information.

Prentice-Hall also issues several loose-leaf reference publications in the area of taxation and the most important titles, such as the *American Federal Tax Reports*, the *Tax Court Reported Decisions*, and others have been previously listed in this chapter.

1480   *Gower Federal Service.*

_____ . *Mining Service.*

_____ . *Miscellaneous Land Decisions Service.*

_____ . *Oil and Gas Service.*

_____ . *Outer Continental Shelf Service.*
Boulder, CO: Rocky Mountain Mineral Law Foundation, 1955– .

Organized in 1955, the foundation publishes in loose-leaf format a series of reference works that contain the text and extensive finding aids for applicable federal laws, regulations, proposed regulations, orders, decisions of the Interior Board of Land Appeals, and certain Solicitor's memorandum opinions relating to natural resources law, including mining, public land, oil and gas, water, and environmental law.

International Law

The reference instruments for the retrieval of information material in international law reflect in varying degrees the continued uncertainty as to what in fact the sources of law are in the international community. Much of the uncertainty is based on Article 38 of the Statute of the International Court of Justice, which distinguishes four different sources of international law, namely:

1. International conventions or treaties, whether general or particular, establishing rules expressly recognized by the contesting states.
2. International custom, as evidence of a general practice accepted as law.
3. The general principles of law recognized by civilized nations.
4. Judicial decisions and the teachings of the most highly qualified publicists of the various nations, subject to the provisions of Article 59, as a subsidiary means for the determination of rules of law. (Article 59 states that the decision of the court has no binding force except between the parties and in respect of that particular case.)

Unfortunately, Article 38 exhibits profound ambiguities of terminology and conceptualization which have so far not been resolved in spite of repeated efforts by scholars and other experts.* A complete identification of all the generative forces or origins of international law and

*For a description of this problem, see Clive Parry, *The Sources and Evidences of International Law* (Dobbs Ferry, NY: Oceana Publications, 1965).

a precise, uncontradictory statement of the law in all situations does not exist.

The reference literature of international law therefore has both structural and functional deficiencies. Reference instruments are not consistently organized on the basis of international law sources, and this is particularly true as far as international custom and recognized general principles of law are concerned. Similarly, the functional efficiency of the retrieval tools leaves much to be desired, as any comparison with the reference instruments for the federal law of the United States will readily disclose. In view of the ambiguity, diversity, and incompleteness of international law, the reference literature needs to develop much greater sophistication in subject and cumulative indexing, encyclopedic treatment, worldwide digest analysis, and bibliographic coverage if time-consuming and frustrating search efforts are to be avoided.

The following sections describe the principal titles of reference literature in international law. Unless specifically indicated in the headnotes or annotations, the titles listed do not constitute a complete inventory of the existing retrieval mechanism, and additional titles may have to be identified from the general legal, political, and historical bibliographies.

GUIDEBOOKS

1481   Coplin, William D. "Current Studies of the Functions of International Law, Assessments and Suggestions." *Political Science Annual*, 1969–1970, pp. 149–207.

This publication offers an evaluative survey of the scholarly literature about international law. The author discusses works dealing with the theoretical framework for the study of international law, the operational aspects of the international legal system, notably legislation, adjudication, and enforcement, the allocation of legal competence, socioeconomic problems, the international political culture, etc. All the works mentioned in the text are listed in a separate bibliography arrranged by authors' names.

1482   Robinson, Jacob. *International Law and Organization*. Leyden: A. W. Sijthoff, 1967.

The partially annotated bibliography offers guidance to some types of reference publications for international law. Included are encyclopedias, dictionaries, treatises and textbooks of qualified publicists, bio-bibliographies of renowned international law scholars, bibliographies, periodicals, and yearbooks. Particularly useful are the extensive citations to book reviews and book notes that provide a critique or evaluation of the works listed. A separate chapter lists universities, institutes, and other agencies engaged in the study and research of international law. Regretta-

bly, the guidebook does not include treaty collections, indexes, digests, and casebooks for judicial decisions.

LIBRARY CATALOGS

1483   The Hague. Palace of Peace. Library. *Catalogue*. Leyden: 1916–; New York: Clearwater Publishing Company, 1980–.

The closest approximation to an exhaustive inventory of the literature and documentation of international law is offered by this catalog available in book and microfiche format. The catalog is based on the world's most outstanding collection of reference and research materials on international law, located at the Library of the Peace Palace, The Hague. These holdings are identified in the catalog in two separate sections, namely, (1) the Systematic Catalogue, and (2) the Universal Bibliographical Catalogue.

The Systematic Catalogue contains the Periodicals Reference Guide, a detailed subject index to the periodicals received by the library. Its 140,000 entries offer access to the contents of 2,300 periodicals. The arrangement under each subject heading is chronological and then alphabetical by author and title. This arrangement not only obviates the need to look in several separate index volumes but also provides an authoritative record for the evolution of thinking on a particular topic.

The Universal Bibliographical Catalogue contains approximately 350,000 entries for books, pamphlets, and other documentation material. This catalogue is also arranged by subject headings of the library's classification system and chronologically within each heading. A copy of the complete classification scheme together with more than 500 specific subject headings is available separately.

Updating entries for the *Catalogue* are available in microfiche supplements and are also listed in *Nouvelles Acquisitions* and *Nederlands Tijdschrift voor Internationaal Recht*.

1484   Harvard University. Law School. Library. *Catalog of International Law and Relations*. New York: K. G. Saur, 1983.

The Harvard Law School Library is the largest and oldest academic law library in the United States, and its collection in the field of international law and relations is second only to that of the Library of Congress. The catalog cited above contains 525,000 cards for author, title, and subject entries identifying the holdings of the library. The catalog is especially useful since publications can be identified by subject terms different from Library of Congress subject headings, thus offering the researcher additional access possibilities to the literature. Foreign-language titles are frequently entered under the English translation. Available on microfiche only, the catalog completely supersedes an earlier printed catalog (Cambridge, Mass: Harvard University Press, 1965–1966) since it includes all acquisitions of the library up to 1981.

CURRENT BIBLIOGRAPHIES

1485   *Public International Law: A Current Bibliography of Articles.* Berlin: Springer Verlag, 1975– .

Periodical articles in international law are listed by topic and indexed by names of persons and subject terms. The bibliography covers periodicals published in the major languages throughout the world.

RETROSPECTIVE BIBLIOGRAPHIES

1486   Doimi di Delupis, Ingrid. *Bibliography of International Law.* New York: R. R. Bowker, 1975.

The material in this unannotated bibliography is arranged under 14 main headings, which include a general section, nature and origin of international law, the relationship between international law and municipal law, sources of international law, subjects of international law, states and sovereignty, settlement of disputes, peace, war and armed conflicts, international criminal law, etc. Each main section is further subdivided by topical headings. The listed material comprises books and periodical articles in English and major European languages. A separate author index is included.

1487   Feldman, D. I. *Muzhdunarodnoe Pravo: Bibliographiia 1917–1972 (International Law: Bibliography 1917–1972).* Moscow: Turidicheskaia Literatura, 1976.

It is the official view of the Soviet government that international law serves important functions in the maintenance of peace and in the peaceful coexistence of contrasting social systems. This bibliography identifies Soviet sources on international law. Its entries are arranged in topical categories. The special value of the bibliography lies in the fact that it indicates translations and reviews in Western European languages, including English, wherever available.

1488   Gould, Wesley L., and Michael Barkun. *Social Science Literature. A Bibliography for International Law.* Princeton, NJ: Princeton University Press, 1972.

An annotated bibliography of books and articles published mainly between 1955 and 1965 with social science research findings of potential value to international law research. Entries are organized under eight chapters, namely, (1) Social Science Concepts and Methods, (2) Patterns, Structures and Units, (3) International Societal Development, (4) Conflict, Obligations, Reciprocity, Agreement, (5) Genesis, Functions, Dynamics, and Evolution of International Law, (6) International Procedures and Agents, (7) International Regulatory Problems, and (8) Humanitarian and Economic Affairs. Each of these chapters is subdivided according to the topics, concepts, or phenomena described or analyzed by the appropriate literature. The table of contents may therefore be used as a subject index to the relevant literature. A separate author index is also included.

1489   Grieves, Forest L. *International Law, Organization and the Environment. A Bibliography and Research Guide.* Tucson: University of Arizona Press, 1974.

Environmental demands frequently transcend national boundaries and need to be handled by arrangements on the basis of international law and organization. This reference book provides (1) a survey of the environment-related legal, political, and scientific literature; (2) a guide to international organizations involved in environmental affairs; and (3) some perspective on the scope and dimensions of the kinds of environmental work being done. The bibliographic listings are arranged under major topical categories, such as general material on the environment and specific sources for oceans and other waters, polar areas, air space and outer space, resources and land use, overpopulation, etc. An author index is also included.

1490   Heere, Wybe P. *International Bibliography of Air Law 1900–1971.* Dobbs Ferry, NY: Oceana Publications, 1972.

————— . *Supplement 1972–1976.* Leyden: A. W. Sijthoff, 1976.

The bibliography and its supplement offer an exhaustive, unannotated listing of books and articles in the field of air law, international and national. Entries are classified under 16 major subject categories with numerous subdivisions, namely, general subjects, organization in civil aviation, administration of national and international aviation, aviation industry, aircraft, aviation personnel, airports and air navigation facilities, air transport, damage to third parties, accidents, towage and salvage, insurance, criminal law (including hijacking and sabotage), acts on board aircraft, solution of disputes, military aviation, and miscellaneous subjects. Separate indexes by names and subject terms are also included.

1491   Lewis, John R. *Uncertain Judgement. A Bibliography of War Crimes Trials.* Santa Barbara, CA: ABC-Clio Press, 1979.

Over the past century an impressive number of international treaties and conventions has been created to regulate the conduct of war among nations. Violations of these treaties were handled as prosecutable offenses in numerous war crimes trials. This bibliography identifies the general and specific reference sources, official publications, scholarly books and articles that offer pertinent information about war crimes trials and their legal, political, and philosophical underpinnings. The trials conducted by international tribunals and national courts for German and Japanese war crimes are well covered, but material on the trials held in the aftermath of the wars in Algeria, Vietnam, Angola, and other areas is also included.

1492   Papadakis, Nikos. *International Law of the Sea. A Bibliography*. Germantown, MD: Sijthoff & Noordhoff, 1980.

Necessitated by political, scientific, and technological advances, the international law of the sea has undergone a tremendous revision and expansion in recent decades. Access to the widely scattered literature in this field is facilitated by the Papadakis bibliography, which identifies more than 4,500 publications under nine main headings, as follows: (1) Introduction — The Marine Environment and the International Law of the Sea; (2) Maritime Zones and Maritime Jurisdiction; (3) The Legal Regime of the Sea-Bed and Subsoil beyond the Limits of National Jurisdiction; (4) Marine Resources; (5) Protection and Preservation of the Marine Environment; (6) Marine Scientific Research; (7) Military Uses and Arms Control; (8) Ocean Policy Making; and (9) Settlement of Disputes. The unannotated entries within these sections are arranged by author under additional, narrower subject headings. An appendix lists bibliographies on the law of the sea and marine affairs. An index of documents, conferences, reports, declarations, and resolutions, as well as a subject and author index are also included.

1493   Schutter, Bart de, and Christian Eliaerts. *Bibliography on International Criminal Law*. Leyden: A. W. Sijthoff, 1972.

In its scope this bibliography is somewhat broader than the Lewis title (item 1491) and covers international criminal law including war crimes law. More than 5,000 unannotated entries for books, articles, and official documents are offered. The entries are divided into eleven chapters, which include general studies, studies on extraterritorial jurisdiction, extradition, status of foreign military forces, war crimes and other international crimes, humanitarian conventions, prisoners of war, etc. Additional subdivisions are made for the literature pertaining to specific countries. Separate author and subject indexes are also included. Like the bibliography by Lewis, this reference work is a major tool for identifying material on the Nuremburg, Tokyo, and Eichmann trials.

1494   White, Irvin L., Clifton E. Wilson, and John

A. Vosburgh. *Law and Politics in Outer Space. A Bibliography*. Tucson: University of Arizona Press, 1972.

The most significant works published up to 1970 about the legal and political problems in outer space can be identified in this unannotated bibliography. Following an introductory section, the entries are arranged under nine chapters based on the form of publication. The listed material is further subdivided by subject, country, and organization.

DICTIONARIES, ENCYCLOPEDIAS, AND HANDBOOKS

1495   Cheng, Bin. *General Principles of Law as Applied by International Courts and Tribunals*. London: Stevens and Sons, 1953.

One of the most nebulous and disputed source categories of international law is termed general principles of law. No adequate retrieval mechanism has been created for this source category, but the present title may be regarded as the only handbook for the identification of whatever general principles of law are applied in international judicial proceedings.

1496   *Dictionnaire de la Terminologie du Droit International*. Paris: Sirey, 1960.

The most comprehensive dictionary for all terms in international law. Bilingual tables for English-French, German-French, Italian-French, and Spanish-French provide equivalent terms in four languages for French international law terminology.

1497   Hyde, Charles Cheney. *International Law Chiefly as Interpreted and Applied by the United States*. Boston: Little, Brown and Company, 1951.

This three-volume set may be regarded as the nearest equivalent to an American encyclopedia of international law. It is a comprehensive restatement of international law as interpreted and applied by the United States up to 1944. The material is organized in seven parts, 38 divisions, and numerous subdivisions, which are outlined in the table of contents. Volume 3 contains a detailed subject index for the entire set. A table of all cases cited and a list of abbreviations are also included. Textual statements are supported by extensive citations to legal authority. The set has not been updated, but more recent developments in international law may be identified in the practice digests listed and described on the following pages.

1498   *Jurisclasseur de Droit International*. Paris: Editions Techniques, 1960 – .

The French-language encyclopedia contains articles about the sources of international law and international political, administrative, and jurisdictional organizations. Each article closes with a bibliography and alphabetical index.

1499 Schlochauer, Hans Jürgen. *Wörterbuch des Völkerrechts*. Berlin: de Gruyter, 1960–1962.

More than 150 scholars contributed to this German encyclopedia, which is a comprehensive source of information for leading cases and general topics in international law. Each article closes with a bibliography of relevant literature in English and other languages. Volume 4 is a separate index volume with a cumulative table of contents in English, French, and German.

1500 Schwarzenberger, Georg. A *Manual of International Law*. Littleton, CO: Fred B. Rothman, 1976.

The manual views international law as a system of fairly stable and interlocking rules of international customary law on which from time to time more ambitious superstructures have been grafted by way of treaties. The rules of international customary law as presented in the manual are based primarily on the application in international judicial and Anglo-American practice. The material is arranged under 12 major elements of international law with numerous subdivisions for the principal subject areas. The manual also contains separate study outlines, bibliographies of major scholarly works, treaty collections, textbooks, dictionaries, casebooks, and periodicals. There is also a glossary of terms and maxims, an index of persons and subjects, as well as numerous charts, diagrams, and tables.

1501 Sen, B. A *Diplomat's Handbook of International Law and Practice*. Boston: Martinus Nijhoff, 1979.

Diplomats must have a working knowledge of international law and practice on the matters of their concern. The handbook summarizes the fundamental elements of this knowledge in three parts, as follows: (1) Diplomatic Relations, Functions and Privileges, (2) Consular Functions, Immunities and Privileges, and (3) International Law — Selected Topics: (a) diplomatic protection of citizens abroad, (b) passports and visas, (c) asylum and extradition, (d) commercial activities, (e) recognition of states and governments, (f) treaty making. Appendices contain the text of the Vienna Conventions on Diplomatic and Consular Relations. Separate bibliographies of principal books, articles, reports, and treaties, as well as a detailed index are also included.

YEARBOOKS

A noteworthy characteristic of the reference literature for international law is the large number of yearbooks. With the exception of the United States, most major countries in the world have commercially issued yearbooks that contain significant information about annual developments in most source categories of international law. These national yearbooks of international law therefore provide current evidence of state practice, judicial decision making, doctrinal writing, problem areas, and other important events of international law as applied and interpreted in the various countries. Another category of yearbooks is issued by international organizations and thus offers an annual record of the legal activities performed by those bodies.

No attempt has been made here to furnish a complete inventory of all existing yearbooks, since these publications can be identified in the bibliographic instruments previously listed. The following section consequently lists only representative titles to illustrate the principal varieties in yearbook coverage.

1502 *Annuaire Français de Droit International*. Paris: Centre National de la Recherche Scientifique, 1955–.

The French yearbook contains doctrinal articles on current problems of international law, a chronology of international facts of legal relevance, a critical bibliography of new publications in international law, a classified bibliography of French-language books and articles in international law, as well as material concerning the French practice of international law. The yearbook also includes a chronological index of important international legal documents as well as a table of cases and a subject index. A selective English-language survey of the first ten volumes was published in the *American Journal of Comparative Law* 14 (1965): 364–367. Two decennial indexes have also been made available for the first 20 volumes of the yearbook, up to 1974.

1503 *The British Yearbook of International Law*. London: Oxford University Press, 1920–.

Issued under the auspices of the Royal Institute of International Affairs, this yearbook presents articles on general principles, cases, and problems of international law. Decisions of British courts involving questions of international law and decisions of the Court of Justice of the European Communities are well covered. The yearbook also includes an extensive book review section. Cumulative indexing by author, subject, and cases is available for the first 36 volumes of the yearbook.

1504 The Hague. International Court of Justice. *Yearbook*. The Hague: 1947–.

This yearbook offers information about the organization, jurisdiction, practice, and work of the International Court of Justice. A summary of the cases decided by the court during the year under review is given, and the present publications of the court are described. Until the 1963/1964 editions, the yearbooks also contained a bibliography of works and documents about the court, but beginning with number 19 these bibliographies are issued as separate fascicles.

1505   United Nations. International Law Commission. *Yearbook*. New York: 1949 – .

The object of the International Law Commission is the promotion of the progressive development of international law and its codification. Although information about the commission is scattered in hundreds of printed and unprinted documents, the yearbooks offer an annual record of the sessions of the 21-member commission together with extensive documentation about the subjects discussed in the sessions.

TREATIES AND AGREEMENTS

In the conduct of international relations, a treaty is the closest analogue to statutory legislation. It is primarily a compact between independent political entities, but the enforcement of its provisions, while lacking a supranational authority, depends ultimately on the honor and interest of the governments affected by it. Several interchangeable names are used for these international compacts, such as treaty, agreement, charter, convention, exchange of notes, etc. In the United States a distinction is made between treaties and agreements, but any differences that may exist do not have, in interpretation or intention, any international significance.* A significant difference exists, however, between bilateral treaties, which are simply a form of arrangement between two states, and multilateral treaties, which often have the force of general "legislation" for the international community.

Reference treatment for United States treaties and agreements is excellent as a result of appropriate indexes and treaty collection sets. Library access to the texts of treaties concluded by states other than the United States is greatly facilitated when the treaty is registered with the United Nations, but several recently published index and collection sets have greatly improved reference control for many historical treaty texts that have previously been hard to locate.

Indexes: United States

1506   *CCH Congressional Index*. Chicago: Commerce Clearing House, 1947 – .

A separate section in this index permits the researcher to check the status of newly negotiated United States treaties. Treaties are listed if they are being considered by Senate committee action, reported out of commit-

*Agreements are treaties for which consent of a two-thirds senatorial majority is neither sought nor obtained.

tee, ratified, or rejected. Citations are provided to published hearings and reports about the treaties.

1507   *Shepard's United States Citations, Statute Edition*. Colorado Springs, CO: Shepard's Citations, Inc., 1943 – .

Another method of evaluating the current validity of a United States treaty text is offered by citation indexing. Treaties are Shepardized (citation indexed) in the same way as federal statutes. All revisions, amendments, supplementation, extensions, and termination are cited by volume and page numbers of the *United States Treaties and Other International Agreements (UST)*, a current collection of American treaty texts listed and described as item 1518 in this guidebook.

1508   *United States Treaties and Other International Agreements Cumulative Index 1776 – 1949*. Buffalo, NY: William S. Hein, 1975.

1509   *UST Cumulative Index 1950 – 1970*. Buffalo, NY: William S. Hein, 1973.

1510   *UST Cumulative Index 1971 – 1975*. Buffalo, NY: William S. Hein, 1977.

1511   *UST Cumulative Indexing Service, 1976 – *. Buffalo, NY: William S. Hein, 1978 – .

1512   *Current Treaty Index. A Cumulative Index to the United States Slip and Agreements*. Buffalo, NY: William S. Hein, 1982 – .

Cumulative and current indexing for all treaties and other international agreements concluded by the United States with other countries or international organizations since 1776 is now available in the index sets listed above. Three multivolume sets cover treaties and other agreements up to the end of 1975. Volume 1 of each set offers a numerical listing; volume 2 presents chronological listings; volume 3 provides country listings; and volume 4 furnishes subject listings. Bilateral and multilateral treaty documents are separately indexed. Index references are made to several treaty collection sets, such as the *United States Statutes at Large*, Malloy's *Treaties*, including Redmond and Trenwith, Miller's *Treaties*, Bevans' *Treaties*, and the *UST* set. Current cumulative indexing is provided for all treaty documents published in the *UST* set since 1976. Current treaties and other international agreements not yet appearing in the bound *UST* volumes are identifiable by TIAS number, chronology, country, and subject in the annually updated *Current Treaty Index*.

1513   U.S. Department of State. *Treaties in Force: A List of Treaties and Other International Agreements of the*

United States in Force on January 1, 19—. Washington, DC: U.S. Government Printing Office, 1929—.

The purpose of this reference publication is adequately explained by its title. Listings of treaties and agreements currently in force are arranged in two parts. Part 1 includes bilateral treaties and other agreements indexed by country with subject headings under each country. Part 2 lists multilateral treaties under subject headings, together with the names of the states that are parties of the treaties. The date of signature, the date the treaty takes effect for the United States, and citations to the appropriate treaty collection are provided for each agreement. Treaty developments occurring between the annual publication dates of this index are reported in the *Department of State Bulletin*, a monthly publication available from the United States Government Printing Office in Washington, D.C.

See also Igor I. Kravass and Adolf Sprudzs's *A Guide to the United States Treaties in Force*. (New York: William S. Hein, 1983—1984).

Indexes: Worldwide

1514   Harvard University. Law School. Library. *Index to Multilateral Treaties*. Cambridge, MA: Harvard University Press, 1965.

Almost 4,000 treaty texts that have been signed by three or more states or international organizations between 1596 and 1963 can be located in official and unofficial collections with the help of this index. Its entries are arranged chronologically and provide citations to the appropriate treaty collection. Separate subject and regional indexes are also included. A supplement identifies treaties up to 1966.

1515   Parry, Clive, and Charity Hopkins. *An Index of British Treaties 1101—1968*. London: Her Majesty's Stationery Office, 1970.

Although the index was prepared with the encouragement and assistance of the British Foreign Office, it is not an official compilation. The three-volume index consists of (1) The Index of Multilateral Treaties (by subject), (2) The Index of Bilateral Treaties (by countries), (3) The Index of Bilateral Treaties (by subject), and (4) The Chronological List. Entries in Part 4 contain information about the place and date of signature, ratification, entry into force, duration, modification, and the location of the text.

1516   *World Treaty Index*. Santa Barbara: ABC-Clio, 1983.

The five-volume index set, now in its second edition, offers bibliographic citations for some 44,000 treaties published in the *League of Nations Treaty Series*, the *United Nations Treaty Series*, and more than 100 national sources. Volume 1 contains introductory material,

thesauri, and treaty profiles, offering a statistical analysis of treaties by parties, regions, topics, and dates. Volumes 2 and 3 contain chronological listings of the treaties by titles together with textual references and identification of the registering parties, treaty language(s), force dates, etc. Volume 4 provides an alphabetical index by parties, and volume 5 offers keyword indexing of treaty titles. The party index offers signature dates as well as bibliographic citations for the treaty text publications. The keyword index contains signature dates and party identification. Only treaties concluded in the twentieth century are included in the set.

American Treaty Collections: Current

1517   U.S. Department of State. *Treaties and Other International Acts Series* (TIAS). Washington, DC: U.S. Government Printing Office, 1946—.

New treaties and other international agreements of the United States are initially published as separate pamphlets after they have been signed and taken effect. Each treaty pamphlet carries a consecutive TIAS number. All treaties published in this series are listed under State Department in the *Monthly Catalog of United States Government Publications*, where they are also indexed by names of countries and by subject. Libraries usually discard these pamphlets as soon as the treaty texts become available in the permanent *UST* set.

1518   U.S. Department of State. *United States Treaties and Other International Agreements (UST)*. Washington, DC: U.S. Government Printing Office, 1952—.

This series provides a permanent record and legal evidence of the treaties and other international agreements of the United States since 1950. Treaty documents are arranged by TIAS number and contain the full text in English and foreign language. Separate volumes in one or more parts are issued each year. All volumes contain their own combined country and subject indexes, but only broad subject terms are used. Cumulative indexing to all entries in this set is available in a separate, commercially published index, listed previously.

American Treaty Collections: Retrospective

1519   *The Statutes at Large of the United States, Concurrent Resolutions, Recent Treaties, Conventions and Executive Proclamations* (STAT). Boston: Little, 1845—1873; Washington, DC: U.S. Government Printing Office, 1875—.

United States treaties were included in this set until 1950. An index to all treaties in the set is provided in Volume 64, Part 3. Although the set will remain a useful reference source for all statutory laws other than treaties, the availability of the Bevans set (item 1520) will obviate the use of this set for the retrieval of treaty texts.

1520 *Treaties and Other International Agreements of the United States of America 1776–1949.* Washington, DC: U.S. Government Printing Office, 1968–.

The text of all treaties and other international agreements entered into by the United States from 1776 to the end of 1949 can be found in this multivolume reference set. The cutoff date — December 31, 1949 — is the beginning date for the current treaty series, entitled *Treaties and Other International Agreements (UST)*, listed above.

The reference set was prepared under the direction of Charles I. Bevans and begins with several volumes of multilateral treaties and other international agreements arranged chronologically by date of signature. The remaining volumes contain the text of bilateral treaties arranged by country. Each volume includes an index, but the entire set also has a cumulative and analytical index for all volumes.

1521 *Treaties, Conventions, International Acts, Protocols and Agreements between the United States of America and Other Powers, 1776–1909 Compiled By William M. Malloy, 1910–1923 Compiled By C. F. Redmond, 1923–1937 Compiled By Edward J. Trenwith.* Washington, DC: U.S. Government Printing Office, 1910–1938.

1522 *Treaties and Other International Acts of the USA, Edited By David H. Miller, 1776–1863.* Washington, DC: U.S. Government Printing Office, 1931–1948.

These titles refer to two reference sets of altogether 12 volumes that contain bilateral as well as multilateral treaties entered into by the United States between 1776 and 1937. The two sets will be useful only where the more recently published Bevans set is unavailable.

World Treaty Collections: Current

1523 Lillich, Richard B. *Transnational Terrorism: Conventions and Commentary.* Charlottesville, VA: Michie Company, 1982–.

Terrorism is an imprecise, ambiguous term, but covers a host of violent acts, usually in a political communication process, made criminal by the national law of most states as well as by international agreements. The cited volume brings together the texts of (1) conventions proscribing terrorist acts, (2) multilateral extradition treaties and agreements, (3) conventions relating to asylum, in addition to draft and proposed conventions. A country-by-country list of ratifications and accessions is included in an appendix, and a country and subject index is also provided. The information flow in the first volume stops as of March 1, 1982, but regular supplements will keep the volume up to date.

1524 United Nations. *Treaty Series.* New York: United Nations, 1946–.

The continuing set contains the text of all treaties and other international agreements that were registered with the United Nation Secretariat according to Article 102 of the United Nations Charter or were filed and recorded with the Secretariat of the United Nations. The treaty texts are published in the official languages of the treaty and also in English and French translations where the original treaty text is not in these languages. Separate index volumes are issued at irregular intervals. Each index volume consists of three sections: (1) a chronological index that lists treaties by date of signature, supplementation, prolongation, or other modification; (2) a list of general international agreements, arranged chronologically by date; and (3) an alphabetical index that identifies treaties by party and broad subject terms. Almost one-half of all the treaties in this series were concluded by the United States and Great Britain with each other or with other countries.

World Treaty Collections: Retrospective

1525 *The Consolidated Treaty Series.* Dobbs Ferry, NY: Oceana Publications, 1969–.

Once completed, this massive collection in 140 volumes will contain the text of all treaties from the Peace of Westphalia in 1648 to 1918, the beginning date of the *League of Nations Treaty Series.* Arranged in chronological order, the treaties are printed in the original languages. Where the original language is not English or French, a contemporary translation or summary in English will be given. The history of each treaty is summarized in an annotation.

1526 Grenville, J. A. S. *The Major International Treaties 1914–1974: A History and Guide with Texts.* New York: Stein and Day, 1974.

1527 Israel, Fred L. *Major Peace Treaties of Modern History 1648–1967.* New York: McGraw-Hill, 1967.

While most treaty collections offer their treaty texts in a chronological arrangement, the two sets listed above offer the researcher a classified framework for the study of related treaty texts. Historical and analytical commentaries precede the textual sections. The Israel set contains two treaties — the Austrian State Treaty and the Geneva Agreement on Vietnam — that, legally speaking, are not peace treaties.

1528 *The League of Nations Treaty Series.* London: Harrisons and Sons, 1920–1946.

A collection in 205 volumes of all treaties and agreements that were registered according to Article 18 of the League of Nations Covenant by member states and some nonmember states from 1918 to 1945. Treaty texts are arranged according to the date of registration. Nine tables of contents provide a key to the treaty documents.

1529   Schindler, Dietrich, and Jiri Toman. *The Laws of Armed Conflicts. A Collection of Conventions, Resolutions and Other Documents.* Rockville, MD: Sijthoff & Noordhoff, 1981.

The present volume reproduces the text of all multilateral conventions on the law of armed conflicts, including those in force, those not entered into force, and those no longer in force. Also included are resolutions adopted by intergovernmental and nongovernmental organizations. The texts of the documents are printed in different fonts to distinguish the preceding categories of documentation under the following arrangement: (1) general rules concerning the conduct of hostilities, (2) methods and means of warfare, (3) air warfare, (4) protection of populations against the effects of hostilities, (5) victims of war (wounded, sick, prisoners, civilians), (6) protection of cultural property, (7) warfare on the sea, (8) civil war, (9) application of the law of armed conflicts to hostilities in which United Nations forces are engaged, (10) war crimes, and (11) neutrality. Introductory notes, text references, and lists of signatures, ratifications, notifications of continuity or reservations accompany the textual material.

1530   *Treaties and Alliances of the World.* Detroit: Gale Research Company, 1981.

The international relations of the countries of the world are shaped by a wide network of alliances based on multilateral treaties and other agreements. This reference work offers basic information on the various groupings of nations for purposes of defense, trade, or other cooperation. The material is arranged under 19 chapters based on the name or nature of the alliance, such as the United Nations, OECD, NATO, the Commonwealth, the Third World, the Communist world, the French Community, and others. Included are the text of treaties, and data on current membership and institutionalized organs. An index is also provided.

INTERNATIONAL LAW PRACTICE

Apart from treaties and other international agreements, the great bulk of international law appears to be customary law applied and practiced by the various countries of the world. It is therefore logical to assume that the reference literature of international law displays its greatest efficiency in the retrieval of relevant data for customary law practice by the international community. Regrettably, this assumption is not borne out by the facts.

Legal custom or practice data is retrievable for some countries but irretrievable for the international community as a whole. Ideally, the reference literature should provide topical digest coverage for all or most of the states in the world on a general or comparative basis.

The mass of diplomatic material and governmental secrecy are usually cited as major reasons for the lack of truly international digest coverage. But even the state practice digests, which are virtually the only tools for extracting evidence of customary international law, exhibit some astonishing deficiencies. There is, for instance, no adequate retrieval mechanism for protests that, as unilateral instruments, document state practice in conflict situations. There is also no key provided for the identification of state inaction, silence, toleration, or delayed response in relation to political acts that appear to have violated norms of international law.

Another set of deficiencies results from the differences in the nature of the documentation material utilized in the digests. The published digests do not utilize all international law sources in equal measure, thus making an evaluation of international practice problematical.

In spite of these deficiencies, the following digests are invaluable sources for the study of the international law practice of the United States, Great Britain, France, Italy, and international organizations.

Digests: United States

1531   Moore, John Bassett. *Digest of International Law.* Washington, DC: U.S. Government Printing Office, 1906.

1532   Hackworth, Green Hayword. *Digest of International Law.* Washington, DC: U.S. Government Printing Office, 1940–1944.

1533   Whiteman, Marjorie Millace. *Digest of International Law.* Washington, DC: U.S. Government Printing Office, 1963–1973.

1534   *Digest of United States Practice in International Law.* Washington, DC: U.S. Government Printing Office, 1974–.

Three completed sets and a continuing series of digests offer documentary evidence for the international law practice of the United States during the nineteenth and twentieth centuries. Each of the completed digest sets covers a chronological period ending with the date of publication. Beginning in 1974 new developments in the United States practice of international law are documented in annually issued digests. The material in each digest is arranged topically. All sources of international law are considered, and the digests specifically include diplomatic discussions and correspondence, treaties and other agreements, legislation, testimony before congressional and international bodies, court decisions, writings of jurists, published and unpublished documents issued by United States presidents and secretaries of state. Each of the completed digest sets contains comprehensive indexes, lists of cases, and detailed tables of contents. These finding aids are also included in the annual digests.

Digests: Other Countries

1535   Ago, Roberto. *The Italian Practice in International Law.* Dobbs Ferry, NY: Oceana Publications, 1971.

The digest set covers the Italian international law practice from 1861, the date of the proclamation of the Italian Kingdom, to the end of World War II. The text is in Italian with the table of contents in Italian, French, English, and Spanish. The set includes diplomatic documents, parliamentary debates, and legislative acts relating to international questions but omits Italian judgments of international law or Italian legal literature. The material is arranged under topical categories, including fundamental rights and duties of states, position of individuals, state territory, seas and space, state responsibility, peaceful settlement of disputes, use of force, the law of warfare, etc.

1536   Guggenheim, Paul. *Repertoire Suisse de Droit International: Documentation Concernant La Pratique De La Confederation En Matière De Droit International Publique 1914–1939.* Basle: Helbing and Lichtenhahn, 1975.

Due to Switzerland's special role in international relations, the documentation of Swiss practice in international law offers rewarding insights. The material is arranged according to major categories that include the sources of international law, relations of international law and domestic law, subjects of international law, diplomatic protection and status of aliens, territorial sovereignty, state succession, the organs of states and international organizations, state responsibility, settlement of disputes, the law of war, and the law of neutrality. Detailed lists of contents and a separate index volume in the multivolume set provide access to the published material.

1537   Kiss, Alexandre-Charles. *Repertoire de la Pratique Française en Matière de Droit International Publique.* Paris: Editions du Centre National de la Recherche Scientifique, 1962–.

French international law practice is of special significance because of France's position as a continental European and world power outside the Anglo-American system of law. The French set of digests exhibits important

methodological and material differences. Unlike the British and American digests, which view treaties as transactions under the law, the French digest set deals with treaties separately as a source of law. The material is therefore arranged in classified order by sources of law as well as by broad subject categories. Differences also exist in the nature of the documentary material used. Great emphasis is placed on published diplomatic correspondence, includng the 293 yellow books issued by the Ministry of Foreign Affairs. Unpublished material is limited to certain minutes of the ministry's legal department, from which names of states and individuals have been omitted. The decisions by French courts and administrative tribunals are used heavily.

1538   Parry, Clive. A *British Digest of International Law.* London: Stevens and Sons, 1965–.

As a result of Great Britain's unique worldwide role in modern history, this digest set assumes special importance for the study of international law practice. The set is divided into two chronological phases, namely, 1860–1914 and 1914–1960. Within the uwo phases the material is arranged in broad subject categories. The treatment of the material has the character of a narrative in which the full uexts of documents are woven. Eocumentary sources include the printed and unprinted papers of the British Foreign Office, reports of law officers of the crown, parliamentary and command papers, United Kingdom and colonies judicial decisions, treaties, and international judicial and arbitral decisions.

Digests: International Organizations and Courts

1539   *Digest of Legal Activities of International Organizations and Other Institutions.* Dobbs Ferry, NY: Oceana Publications, 1970–.

A current loose-leaf digest in English and French covering the legal activities of international organizations.

1540   Syatauw, J. J. G. *Decisions of the International Court of Justice: A Digest.* Leyden: A. W. Sijthoff, 1969.

The decisions of the International Court of Justice contained in this digest are arranged in three groups: (1) judgments, (2) cases removed from the list, and (3) advisory opinions. For each case, the digest provides the composition of the court, basis of the court's jurisdiction, facts and main issues, judgment and other decision, dates of the proceedings, original source of publication, and a bibliography if available. The digest also includes a subject index and a table of cases.

Casebooks: All Courts

1541   *Annual Digest and Reports of Public International Law Cases.* Vols. 1–16, 1919–1949. London: Butterworths.

1542   *International Law Reports.* Vol. 17–, 1950–. London: Butterworths.

This series contains the decisions of international courts and tribunals as well as of national courts applying public international law. Cases are arranged in classified order according to broad subject areas. The text of each judgment is preceded by a summary of the facts of the case, including the legal contentions of the parties, and a brief statement of the principles upon which the decisions are based. Each volume provides a table of cases in alphabetical order and a case list according to courts and countries. There is also a separate table of treaties cited in the decisions. Court decisions that were given in a language other than English are published in literal English translations.

Casebooks: Permanent International Courts

1543   Permanent Court of International Justice. A. *Collection of Judgements.* B. *Collection of Advisory Opinions.* A/B. *Judgements, Orders and Advisory Opinions.* C. *Pleadings, Oral Statements and Documents.* D. *Acts and Documents Concerning the Organization of the Court.* E. *Annual Reports.* F. *General Indexes.* Leyden: A. W. Sijthoff, 1922–1946.

This series of seven publications contains the texts of decisions, opinions, and orders of the court, pleadings and documentary evidence submitted by the contending parties, constitutional texts and regulations for the organization of the court, summaries of the activities of the court, and location aids.

1544   International Court of Justice. *Reports of Judgements, Advisory Opinions and Orders. Pleadings, Oral Arguments, Documents. Acts and Documents Concerning the Organization of the Court. Yearbook. Bibliography of the International Court of Justice.* Leyden: A. W. Sijthoff, 1946–.

These publications are issued for the decisions, opinions, and orders of the court, the pleadings and speeches of the contending parties, constitutional, statutory, and other rules for the organization of the court, information about the activities and judges of the court, and the scholarly or legal literature about the court and its activities.

1545   Council of Europe. *Yearbook of the European Convention on Human Rights.* The Hague: M. Nijhoff, 1955–.

The texts of selected decisions of the European Court of Human Rights as well as general information about European activities and developments in the field of human rights can be found in this annual reference work. The publication series also provides extensive bibliographic references and statistical charts relating to the exercise of human rights in European countries.

Casebooks: Special International Tribunals

1546   Dull, Paul S., and Michael Takaaki Umemura. *The Tokyo Trials: A Functional Index to the Proceedings of the International Military Tribunal for the Far East.* Ann Arbor, MI: University of Michigan Press, 1957.

1547   *International Military Tribunal for the Far East. Court Docket, Court Journal, Court Exhibits, Documents Rejected as Exhibits; Judgements, Sentences.* Wilton, CT: Micro 8 Publications, 1972.

1548   *International Military Tribunal for the Far East. Proceedings of the Tokyo War Crime Trials.* Wilton, CT: Micro 8 Publications, 1972.

1549   Pritchard, R. John, and Sonia Magbanua Zaide. *The Tokyo War Crimes Trial.* New York: Garland Publishing Company, 1983.

1550   *The Trial of the Major War Criminals before the International Military Tribunal, Nuremburg, Germany. 1945–1946.* Nuremburg: 1947; Wilton, CT: Micro 8 Publications, 1972.

1551   *The Trial of War Criminals before the International Military Tribunal, Nuremburg, Germany. 1946–1949.* Nuremburg: 1949; Wilton, CT: Micro 8 Publications, 1972.

These titles refer to the postwar attempt to create by special supranational judicial decision binding new international law for the control of international acts of aggression, violations of the rules of warfare, and actrocities. Although the attempt was largely unsuccessful, the trials and their supporting documentation offer unique insights into fundamental problems of international relations and international law. The published documentation, however, does not completely and accurately reflect historical reality since many secret documents were not released for publication and many trial documents remained unpublished. In the major war crimes trial at Nuremburg, for instance, 694 French documents were submitted but only 8 percent of them were published, and of 322 Russian documents only 15 percent were included in the publication. The German defense submitted 1,310 documents of which only 28 percent were completely and another 20 percent partially published.

Casebooks: International Arbitration

1552   *Digest of Case-Law Relating to the European Communities.* 1977–. Luxembourg: Research and

Documentation Division, Court of Justice of the European Communities, 1984 — .

Issued in loose-leaf form, the reference work provides digest information of the judgments of the Court of Justice relating to the general principles of the community legal order as well as the law of the three supra-national bodies collectively known as the European communities. All entries are arranged under subject headings and include citations to the official case reporter set. A subject index and chronological tables of cases are also included.

1553   United Nations. Office of Legal Affairs. *Reports of International Arbitral Awards. Recueil des Sentences Arbitrales*. Lake Success, NY: United Nations, 1948 — .

The first 11 volumes in this series contain awards rendered between 1902 and 1941. Beginning with Volume 12, texts of arbitral awards rendered since 1941 are made available following a circular letter by the secretary general, dated 25 September 1961, which requested governments to submit the texts of arbitral decisions. Awards are published in English or French, arranged chronologically, and preceded by headnotes. See also A. M. Stuyt, *Survey of International Arbitrations, 1794 – 1970* (Dobbs Ferry, NY: Oceana Publications, 1972) and the *Union Catalog of Arbitration* (Totowa, NJ: Rowman and Littlefield, 1974). The latter item is a three-volume bibliography that lists by author and subject official documentation sets and other publications relating to arbitration under international law.

Casebooks: National Courts

1554   Deak, Francis. *American International Law Cases*. Dobbs Ferry, NY: Oceana Publications, 1971 — .

A collection of American federal and state court decisions involving questions of international law during the period 1783 to 1968. Where appropriate, annotations and citations identify the treaties underlying the decisions.

1555   Germany. Max Planck Institute for Foreign Public Law and International Law. *Deutsche Rechtssprechung zum Völkerrecht 1879 – 1960* (Decisions of the Superior Courts of Germany Relating to Public International Law). Cologne: Carl Heymanns Verlag, 1931 — .

German international law decisions are available in this series of volumes for the periods 1879 – 1929, 1929 – 1945, 1945 – 1949, 1949 – 1960. The full text of the decision is given in German together with headnotes in German, English, and French. Separate subject indexes in these three languages are also provided.

1556   Parry, Clive. *British International Law Cases*. Dobbs Ferry, NY: Oceana Publications, 1964 — .

1557   _____ . *Commonwealth International Law Cases*. Dobbs Ferry, NY: Oceana Publications, 1975 — .

The texts of British and Commonwealth court cases involving questions and interpretations of international law can be found in these two reference sets. The second item listed above also includes decisions by British consular courts in China, Turkey, and other countries.

Document Collections

1558   American Society of International Law. *International Legal Materials, Current Documents*. Washington, DC: 1962 — .

Current documentation in several source categories of international law is selectively provided in this bimonthly publication. The texts of important treaties, court decisions, legislative acts, reports, etc., are reproduced. Annual and other cumulative indexes offer access to the published texts by author, subject, and area headings as well as by tables of cases.

1559   Brownlie, Ian. *Basic Documents in International Law*. Oxford: Clarendon Press, 1983.

This reference work contains the text of the most important documents relating to (1) international organizations, (2) the law of the sea, (3) the law of outer space, (4) diplomatic relations, (5) permanent sovereignty over natural resources, (6) human rights and self-determination, (7) the law of treaties, and (8) the judicial settlement of disputes.

1560   Friedman, Leon. *The Law of War: A Documentary History*. New York: Random House, 1972.

Documents on the origin, development, and enforcement of the laws on war are presented in this two-volume set. The information and documentation is arranged in three sections: (1) Hugo Grotius and the Law of War, (2) Treaties, Conventions, and Agreements, and (3) Trial of War Crimes. Each section is preceded by an introduction and contains the text of appropriate treaties, codes, court decisions, and other documentation. Both volumes have a table of contents, and volume II has a detailed index for the entire set.

1561   *Human Rights. A Compilation of International Instruments*. New York: United Nations, 1978.

The observance of human rights is an indispensable condition for the peaceful coexistence of nations. In recent years, leading statesmen, including the president of the United States,* have found it necessary to give strong

---

*In his inaugural address on January 20, 1977, President Carter emphasized American preference for those societies that share with the United States an abiding respect for individual human rights.

endorsement to the protection of individual human rights in the various countries of the world, even though many human rights appear to be well entrenched in international law. The compilation, cited above, is the latest in a series of United Nations document collections that offer in convenient form the texts of international conventions, declarations, and legal instruments relating to human rights. The documentary material is arranged under the following headings: (A) The International Bill of Human Rights; (B) The Proclamation of Teheran; (C) The Right of Self-Determination; (D) Prevention of Discrimination; (E) War Crimes and Crimes against Humanity; (F) Slavery, Servitude and Similar Practices; (G) Protection of Persons subjected to Detention; (H) Nationality; (I) Freedom of Information; (J) Freedom of Association; (K) Employment Policy; (L) Political Rights of Women; (M) Marriage and the Family; (N) Social Welfare; (O) Right to Enjoy Culture. A list of all included international instruments arranged in chronological order of adoption is separately provided in the reference work.

Chapter 4

International Relations and Organizations

INTRODUCTION

This chapter is devoted to a description of specialized reference sources that offer direct or indirect access to official and scholarly information about specific aspects of the organizations, individual actors, and processes involved in the interaction between independent political entities. These specialized reference sources—for reasons briefly indicated below—complement rather than supplant a variety of reference works that, while listed in other chapters of this guidebook, also yield significant information in the area of international relations.

As a subfield of political science, the study of international relations requires a number of more or less distinct approaches in order to produce meaningful explanations for the conduct of international relations. Some of these approaches may focus on only one or two of the nine elements of the political world, such as the systems characteristics of the individual political entities, the normative character of international law and institutions, or the effect of societal factors, specific events, and political ideologies. Other approaches will concentrate primarily on specific objects and developments in the policy and process stages of the international system. Most notable in this category are the inquiries relating to national security, the formulation and execution of foreign, military, and arms control policies, and the illumination of tension-reducing or -increasing activities within peace research and war studies. Finally, the role of international organizations will be the target of many inquiries. As a result of this specialization, the reference mechanism for international relations information has become excessively diffused and diversified.* The following table provides an overview of the diversification in the reference literature and indicates for each of the major foci of inquiry the most appropriate reference works listed in the other chapters of this guidebook.

Type of Inquiry	Appropriate Reference Source
1. American legislative and policy-making processes in foreign affairs	Congressional sources (items 994–1054, 1058–1061, 1967, 1968)
	Presidential sources (items 1094–1130, 1132–1144)
2. Analytical or descriptive exposition	Bibliographies, fact and knowledge retrieval tools in

* For a detailed description of the chaotic bibliographic situation, see E. Raymond Platig, *International Relations Research: Problems of Evaluation and Advancement* (Santa Barbara, CA: ABC–Clio Press, 1967).

Type of Inquiry	Appropriate Reference Source
of societal factors in the United States and other countries	the social sciences (items 274–866, 1929)
3. Biographical or organizational information	Worldwide biobibliographies and directories (items 2098–2120)
	U.S. sources (items 957, 958)
4. Comparative exposition of political phenomena	Comparative and area studies sources (items 1892–2097)
5. Events and developments	News digests (items 640–664)
	Newspaper indexes (items 140–187)
	Periodical indexes (items 244–256, 669–686)
	Historical sources (items 555–626, 632–639)
	Radio, TV, & other (items 257–272)
4. International Law	Digests, indexes, and compilations (items 1481–1561)
5. Political ideologies	Bibliographies and fact retrieval tools for political thought (items 1119, 2270–2324)
6. Public opinion	U.S. sources (items 1287–1298)
	Foreign sources (items 2223, 2246)
7. Statistical data	Compendia and indexes (items 1154, 1155, 1159, 1160, 1167, 2204–2222, 2224–2245, 2246–2254)
8. Systems characteristics of political entities	Encyclopedias and handbooks (items 1918–1922, 1928)

Researchers interested in

1. bibliographic citations for
   * the foreign relations of the United States and other countries,
   * specific topics, such as arms control, diplomacy, international economic relations, peace research, refugees, or war,
   * international organization structures and activities, or
2. fact retrieval tools in the field of international relations and organizations

will find the following listings in this chapter useful. It should be noted, however, that most of the listed sources are heavily history-oriented as a result of the secrecy restrictions under which the academic study of international relations labors and the unique environment in which the government decision-maker operates.

INTERNATIONAL RELATIONS

Bibliographies

GUIDEBOOKS

1562   LaBarr, Dorothy F., and J. David Singer. *The Study of International Politics. A Guide to the Sources for the Student, Teacher and Researcher.* Santa Barbara, CA: American Bibliographical Center–Clio Press, 1976.

The authors of this guidebook divide the English-language literature on international politics into eight major categories for which the most useful publications are listed. Specifically identified are publications within the framework of (1) Approaches to the Study and Teaching of International Politics (authored volumes, edited volumes, articles, course outlines), (2) Texts and General Treatises on International Politics (authored volumes, edited volumes, propositional inventories), (3) American and Comparative Foreign Policy (authored volumes, edited volumes), (4) Journals and Annuals in International Politics (largely data-based, largely traditional, largely policy analysis), (5) Special Series in International Politics, (6) Abstracts and Book Reviews, (7) Data Sources and Handbooks (Approaches, Attributive Data, Diplomatic, Political and Military Events Data, Collections of Documents), and (8) Bibliographies of International Politics. With the exception of the listings for journals and annuals, the bibliographic entries do not include annotations. An author index is provided.

1563   Mason, John Brown. *Research Resources: Annotated Guide to the Social Sciences.* Volume 1, *International Relations and Recent History.* Santa Barbara, CA: American Bibliographical Center–Clio Press, 1968.

Annotated listings of index and abstract publications, periodicals, books, national and trade bibliographies, United States government publications, American and foreign newspapers that might be of possible value in the study of international relations are presented by this guidebook. Approximately 1,300 items are listed, but only reference tools such as bibliographies, handbooks, directories, etc., are included in the book section, which does not list scholarly monographs. Of special value is the annotated list of over 500 periodicals with international relations content of varying degree. Regrettably, the index coverage for these periodicals is not indicated. Also of interest is a list of biographical publications arranged by region or country. Reference sources in international law and document collections are not included.

1564   Pfaltzgraff, Robert L., Jr. *The Study of International Relations. A Guide to Information Sources.* Detroit: Gale Research Company, 1977.

Differing slightly from the LaBarr and Singer guidebook (item 1562) in the categorization of the international relations literature, this reference book offers selective listings of books under the following chapters: (1) The Evolution of the Study of International Relations, (2) Approaches to the Study of International Relations, (3) The Nature of the International System, (4) Foreign Policy and Diplomacy, (5) Power and International Relations, (6) Military Strategy and Theories of Deterrence, (7) Theories of Conflict, and (8) Integration and Alliance Theories. An annotated list of major international relations journals and a list of recommended books for small and personal libraries are also included. Introductory essays precede the chapter listings. Separate author, title, and subject indexes are provided.

1565   Zawodny, Janusz Kazimierz. *A Guide to the Study of International Relations.* San Francisco: Chandler Publishing Company, 1966.

This guidebook is an earlier attempt to list and describe widely scattered sources for the study of international relations. There are approximately 500 entries for atlases, bibliographies, dictionaries, dissertation lists, document collections, encyclopedias, newspaper and periodical indexes, statistical compendia, treaty collections, yearbooks, international law sources, etc. Many of the entries may now be out of date or incomplete because of more recent publications. Nevertheless, the guidebook still offers valuable clues for research purposes.

LIBRARY CATALOGS

1566   Great Britain. Foreign and Commonwealth Office. Library. *Catalogue of the Colonial Office Library, London.* Boston: G. K. Hall, 1964.

_____ . *First Supplement, 1963–1967.* Boston: G. K. Hall, 1967.

_____ . *Second Supplement, 1968–1971.* Boston: G. K. Hall, 1972.

_____ . *Third Supplement, 1971–1977.* Boston: G. K. Hall, 1979.

1567   Great Britain. Foreign and Commonwealth Office. Library. *Catalogue of the Foreign Office Library, 1926–1968.* Boston: G. K. Hall, 1972.

In 1968 the formerly separate British Foreign Office was merged with the Commonwealth Office to form the Foreign and Commonwealth Office, and the libraries maintained by these offices were combined. During its separate existence, the Colonial Office Library has acquired all worthwhile publications — books, pamphlets, reports, official publications, periodicals, etc. — relating to dependent territories irrespective of subject with imprint dates from the middle of the seventeenth century to the twentieth century. For independent countries the collection is selective, with emphasis on external relations, public administration, and economic and social material. Many items concern countries never affiliated with Great Britain. The catalog is divided into two parts. A sheaf subject catalog with extensive geographical entries, followed by an author index, lists material acquired before 1950. The post-1950 catalog is in three sequences: (1) authors and titles (alphabetical), (2) subjects (alphabetical), and (3) all entries (classified).

The Foreign Office Library catalogue contains material reflecting not only the history of British diplomacy, but the international relations of all countries. The arrangement of the catalog is in four sequences — author, subject, title, and class. In contrast to the Colonial Office Library catalog's post-1950 acquisitions, which are listed in order of the Library of Congress system, the classification of the Foreign Office Library Catalogue is based on Dewey. A two-letter country symbol is used in conjunction with an amended numerical subject notation. The two catalogs and supplements contain more than 400,000 cards.

1568   Harvard University. Law School. Library. *Catalog of International Law and Relations*. New York: K. G. Saur, 1983.

One of the largest collections of published materials about international relations is maintained by the Law School Library of Harvard University. A 20-volume book catalog, published 1964, and its unpublished card supplement covering acquisitions from 1964 to 1981 has been reproduced on microfiche. This catalog is especially useful since publications can be identified, apart from author and title entries, by subject terms different from Library of Congress subject headings, thus offering the researcher additional access possibilities to the international relations literature. Foreign-language titles are frequently entered under the English translation. Approximately 525,000 author, title, and subject cards are included in the catalog.

1569   New York. Council on Foreign Relations. *Catalog of the Foreign Relations Library*. New York: 1969.

_____ . *First Supplement*. New York: 1979.

Approximately 55,000 volumes in the well-developed library collection of this prestigious advisory organization are represented by photographically reproduced catalog cards in this multivolume book catalog.

The catalog entries are by author and subject with some title listings and refer to all phases of international relations since 1918. Books, pamphlets, and documents issued by national governments and international organizations but no periodicals or documents of the League of Nations and the United Nations are included. The catalog can be kept up to date by referring to the listings of new publications printed in *Foreign Affairs*, a quarterly publication of the Council on Foreign Relations.

CURRENT GENERAL BIBLIOGRAPHIES

1570   *Current Bibliographical Service on International Affairs*. Paris: Centre d'Etude des Relations Internationales de la Fondation Nationale des Sciences Politiques, 1973 – .

Several European institutes of international relations created this index card service, which offers subscribers identification and brief content analyses of all articles appearing in 105 journals published throughout the world. Each periodical article is represented on an index card containing complete bibliographical references, an English analysis, an ordinal number, and a class number from the classification scheme of the FNSP's Centre de Documentation Contemporaine. As soon as the journals arrive in Paris, the index cards are prepared and sent to subscribers as rapidly as possible. More than 3,000 articles are analyzed and indexed each year.

1571   *Foreign Affairs*. New York: Council on Foreign Relations, 1922 – .

Each issue of this quarterly periodical contains an annotated bibliography of recent books on international relations. Entries are arranged under various topical and regional sections. There is also a separate unannotated list of recent documents from governmental agencies in the United States and other countries. A 50-year cumulative index for this periodical was published by the R. R. Bowker Company in 1972. Recent issues of the periodical also offer a chronology of foreign affairs events under topical and regional sections.

1572   Universal Reference System. *International Affairs*. Princeton, NJ: Princeton Research Publishing Company, 1969 – .

The Universal Reference System offers an annual annotated bibliography of books and articles that are intensively indexed according to the Grazian system of topical and methodological descriptors. The annual volumes update a set of ten base volumes, one of which is devoted to international relations. This international relations volume contains entries for 3,459 books and articles. To aid the researcher, the base set and the annual supplements provide a classified and alphabetically arranged list of the descriptors by which the listed literature is indexed.

The number of titles listed under each descriptor is also indicated. Not all keywords employed in the international relations literature, however, are represented by appropriate descriptors. Despite the large number of descriptors used, it is difficult to retrieve titles devoted to specific aspects or problems of international relations and foreign policy.

1573   U.S. Department of State. Office of External Research. Bureau of Intelligence and Research. *Government-Sponsored Research on Foreign Affairs.* Washington, DC: U.S. Government Printing Office, to date, currently suspended.

1574   U.S. Department of State. Office of External Research. Foreign Affairs Research Documentation Center. *Foreign Affairs Research Papers Available.* Washington, DC: U.S. Government Printing Office, to date, currently suspended.

The Office of External Research (XR) is the institutional unit charged by the Department of State to identify and meet the department's needs for timely professional research from the private sector. For this purpose XR manages a program of research contracts, conferences, and consultant studies. It also operates a collection and dissemination program for information on the products of government-sponsored research.

Government-Sponsored Research on Foreign Affairs is a quarterly publication that describes in project number sequence the research projects initiated during the fiscal year. For each project the description includes the title, funding agency, contractor/grantee, principal investigator, expenditure, and scope of research. Five separate indexes provide a key to the listed projects by subject matter, regional dimension, supporting organization, name of the investigator, and by the performing university or research organization. A monthly accession list of the mostly unpublished research papers collected by the Foreign Affairs Research Documentation Center of the Office of External Research is issued under the title *Foreign Affairs Research Papers Available.* In addition, annual cumulative listings of papers previously cited in *Papers Available* are published in various geographic series with separate volumes for the People's Republic of China, USSR, American republics, Near East, South Asia, North Africa, East Asia and Pacific area, Europe, Canada, and Sub-Saharan Africa. Regrettably, the two bibliographic serials have not been published since 1981 and 1979 respectively.

RETROSPECTIVE GENERAL BIBLIOGRAPHIES

1575   Dexter, Byron. *Foreign Affairs 50-year Bibliography: New Evaluations of Significant Books on Interna-*

tional Relations, 1920–1970. Ann Arbor, MI: R. R. Bowker, 1972.

The bibliography reviews 2,130 books and cites without review another 900 books published on international relations during a 50-year period ending in 1970. All the books have been selected by 400 American and foreign scholars as works of lasting scholarship that contribute to a better understanding of the ideas and events developed during that part of the twentieth century. Although many of the selected works have been previously listed in the *Foreign Affairs Bibliography*, the chief value of this bibliography lies in its lengthy annotations, which are almost brief essays. English-language as well as foreign-language books are included. An appendix contains an unannotated list of the principal collections of documents published during these 50 years by the United States and other major countries.

1576   *Foreign Affairs Bibliography.* Volume 1, 1919–1932 (William L. Langer and Hamilton Fish Armstrong); Volume 2, 1932–1942 (Robert Gale Woolbert); Volume 3, 1942–1952 (Henry L. Roberts); Volume 4, 1952–1962 (Henry L. Roberts); Volume 5, 1962–1972 (Janis A. Kreslins). New York: Harper, 1919–1952; R. R. Bowker, 1952– .

The annotated bibliographies in this series are issued at ten-year intervals. Each bibliographic volume is divided into three parts: (1) General International Relations, (2) The World Since 1914, and (3) The World by Regions. Bibliographic entries are therefore arranged analytically, chronologically, and regionally. The analytical arrangement identifies political factors (nationalism, ideologies, authority problems, etc.); social, cultural, and religious factors; geographic, ethnic, and population factors; economic factors; international legal factors; war and peace factors; etc. The bibliographies list only books, and many of the listed items are not solely concerned with foreign relations but deal with the internal affairs of individual countries.

1577   Groom, A. J. R., and C. R. Mitchell. *International Relations Theory.* New York: Nichols Publishing Company, 1978.

The theoretical and conceptual aspects of the international relations field are illuminated by a sizable monographic literature. This reference work offers 14 commentaries, each with a selected list of significant books about the following aspects of international relations research: (1) Methodology of International Relations; (2) Research Methods in International Relations; (3) International Relations Textbooks, (4) Systems Theory and International Relations; (5) International Stratification; (6) Theories of Power, Influence and Authority; (7) Conflict and War; (8) Strategy; (9) Order and

Change; (10) Integration; (11) Foreign Policy Analysis; (12) Psychological Aspects of International Relations; (13) Anthropology and International Relations; (14) Ways of Analyzing the World Society.

1578   Jones, Susan D., and J. David Singer. *Beyond Conjecture in International Politics. Abstracts of Data-Based Research*. Itasca, IL: F. E. Peacock Publishers, 1972.

The bibliography identifies that portion of the international relations literature which provides a numerical, data-based description or explanation of events or conditions in international politics. Abstracts are offered of articles in periodicals and yearbooks and of individual chapters in anthologies. The abstracts are arranged in three main groups, each of which is subdivided into smaller groups describing or accounting for behavior. Group 1 lists and abstracts studies that focus on the attributes of the international system or its regional or functional subsystems, including international bonds, links, and associations. Group 2 is composed of studies that focus on the attributes of individual nations, including events and conditions relevant to international politics. Group 3 listings refer to studies that focus on the behavioral and interactional patterns of nations. Each abstract identifies and describes the major question to which the study is addressed, the spatial-temporal domain, the key variables, the data sources, details of data manipulation and analysis, and the findings of the study. Brief citations are given to publications of related research value. In addition to the abstracts, there are several bibliographic appendices. Appendices A and B are fairly complete lists of empirical studies that were not included in the abstracts, primarily public opinion studies and book-length studies. Appendix C is an alphabetical listing of data-based articles published after the 1970 cutoff date. Appendix D is an alphabetical author listing of all studies included in the abstracts. Coverage extends from 1939 to 1970.

1579   The Royal Institute of International Affairs, London. *Index to Periodical Articles, 1950 – 1964, in the Library of the Royal Institute of International Affairs*. Boston: G. K. Hall, 1964.

_____ . *Index to Periodical Articles, 1965 – 1972, in the Library of the Royal Institute of International Affairs*. Boston: G. K. Hall, 1973.

_____ . *Index to Periodical Articles, 1973 – 1978, in the Library of the Royal Institute of International Affairs*. Boston: G. K. Hall, 1979.

The aim of the Royal Institute of International Affairs, London, is to advance the objective study of all aspects of international affairs. With more than 65,000 entries, the institute's index, available in a four-volume set, provides a well-organized record of articles published on international affairs in some 200 periodicals during almost 30 years. All entries are arranged according to a special classification scheme that includes designations for regions, political entities, and topics.

1580   Wright, Moorhead, Jane Davis, and Michael Clarke. *Essay Collections in International Relations. A Classified Bibliography*. New York: Garland Publishing, 1977.

One of the major forms in which scholarly research and analysis in international relations has appeared is the collection of essays by several authors. This bibliography identifies such essays in multi-author works published between 1945 and 1975 on international relations since 1870. Listings are classified in 22 major subject areas that include actors, area studies, arms control, communication and public opinion, economics and international politics, diplomacy, ethics, morality and values, foreign policy, international law, nationalism, peace and pacifism, and others. A separate list of essay collections, an author and subject index are also included.

BIBLIOGRAPHIES FOR U.S. FOREIGN RELATIONS

1581   Bemis, Samuel F., and Grace G. Griffin. *Guide to the Diplomatic History of the United States 1775 – 1921*. Washington, DC: U.S. Government Printing Office, 1935.

The reference work presents a very detailed bibliographic survey of the published and unpublished material relating to the diplomatic relations of the United States from the revolutionary period to the peace settlement of 1921. The book is divided into two main parts. Part 1 contains bibliographic chapters that are chronologically and topically arranged. Part 2 provides a description of the doumentary material by form, such as treaties, diplomatic correspondence, memoranda, printed state papers, etc. An author index and an index to collections of personal papers are included.

1582   Bryson, Thomas A. *United States/Middle East Diplomatic Relations 1784 – 1978. An Annotated Bibliography*. Metuchen, NJ: Scarecrow Press, 1979.

The bibliography lists 1,353 books, periodical articles, documents, and dissertations relating to the American diplomatic experience in the Middle East during nearly 200 years. The entries are arranged under 17 chapters based on chronological periods. General works and dissertations are listed in separate chapters. The major reference works and periodicals covering this area are identified in the preface. An author index is included.

1583   Burns, Richard Dean. *Guide to American Foreign Relations since 1700*. Santa Barbara, CA: ABC-Clio, 1983.

Updating the Bemis and Griffin guide (item 1581), this new reference volume, produced by the Society for Historians of American Foreign Relations (SHAFR), contains nearly twice as many entries as the work it supersedes. The enlarged chronological coverage that serves as the basic organizational framework of the book extends from the international experience of the Anglo-American colonies to the international relations of the United States since 1941. Conceptually, the new work lists books, dissertations, and periodical articles relating not only to the diplomatic history of the United States but also to the influences exerted on foreign policy decisions by public opinion, peace movements, international economic developments, intelligence operations, cultural and other factors. The extensively annotated entries are arranged under 40 main headings that, for the most part, reflect chronological and regional boundaries. Within those headings appropriate subsections aggregate listings by personalities, episodes, or special topics. Reference works and surveys are listed separately. Access to the listed entries is provided by the detailed table of contents, the author index, and a subject index. The latter is divided into three separate sections — topics; individuals, Americans; and individuals, foreigners. Appendices contain listings for the makers of American foreign policy as well as biographies of the secretaries of state, 1781–1982.

1584   Boyce, Richard Fyfe, and Katherine Randall Boyce. *American Foreign Service Authors: A Bibliography*. Metuchen, NJ: Scarecrow Press, 1973.

American foreign service personnel can be expected to have firsthand knowledge of the international relations of the United States. This bibliography identifies the published works of approximately 760 American foreign service authors. The rank of the writer, from ambassador to clerk, was considered irrelevant for the purpose of this bibliography, which applies no limitations to the subject matter included. The entries are arranged alphabetically by name of the author and include a brief biographical sketch of the author. The listed works are, however, not annotated. No subject index is included.

1585   Danaher, Kevin. *South Africa and the United States: An Annotated Bibliography*. Washington, DC: Institute for Policy Studies, 1979.

1586   El-Khawas, Mohamed A., and Francis A. Kornegay, Jr. *American–Southern African Relations. Bibliographic Essays*. Westport, CT: Greenwood Press, 1975.

Just as in the Middle Eastern area, the foreign relations of the United States with Southern Africa are dominated by vital economic, strategic, and political interests that clash with traditional American commitments to individual freedom, majority rule, and self-determination. Although considerable information is published about this area, it remains widely scattered and under poor bibliographic control. Danaher's bibliography lists and describes only 221 books and articles dealing with U.S. involvement in South Africa. The second bibliography cited above identifies publications that focus on U.S. policy toward Rhodesia and Namibia, U.S. investments in Southern Africa, and the role of black America in the U.S. relationship with Southern Africa. While the bibliographic essays are generally biased in favor of liberation policies, some material detailing opposing viewpoints is also included.

For recent information, albeit from a Marxist perspective only, on the issues and political organizations involved in the struggle over the separation of power in South Africa, see Rob Davis, Dan O'Meora and Sipho Dlamini's *The Struggle for South Africa: A Reference Guide to Movements, Organizations, and Institutions* (London: Zed Books, 1984).

1587   Fowler, Wilton B. *American Diplomatic History since 1890*. Northbrook, IL: AHM Publishing Corporation, 1975.

1588   Graebner, Norman A. *American Diplomatic History before 1900*. Arlington Heights, IL: AHM Publishing Corporation, 1978.

Nearly 5,000 books and articles about the foreign relations of the United States during 200 years are identified in the two unannotated bibliographies. Apart from a general reference section, both bibliographies arrange their entries in sequence of historical periods with subdivisions for specific countries, events, or topics. A detailed table of contents and an author index provide access to the listed material.

1589   Plischke, Elmer. *U.S. Foreign Relations. A Guide to Information Sources*. Detroit: Gale Research Company, 1980.

This selectively annotated bibliography is concerned with the U.S. foreign affairs process, not with diplomatic history, current events, world politics, or substantive foreign policy questions. It identifies scholarly books and periodical articles dealing with various aspects of diplomatic practice, foreign policy formulation, and crisis management. It also lists publications about the institutionalized political actors, such as the presidency, Congress, the Department of State, military and other agencies involved in the conduct of foreign relations. Official publications emanating from these agencies are listed separately. A list of memoirs, diaries, and biographical publications is also included. Since there is no subject index in the book, the detailed table of contents provides the best access to the listed material. An author index is also provided.

1590   Pourhadi, Ibrahim V. *Iran and the United States, 1979–1981: Three Years of Confrontation; A Selected List of References*. Washington, DC: Library of Congress, 1982.

When the 2,500-year Iranian monarchy was replaced by the Islamic Republic in Iran in 1979, U.S.-Iranian relations entered a three-year period of confrontation culminating in the seizure of the American embassy staff as hostages, U.S. sanctions against Iran, and an abortive U.S. military rescue attempt. This bibliography identifies and describes, under 12 separate headings, some 250 publications dealing with the Iranian revolution, its causes and effects, including the hostage crisis and its diplomatic, economic, legal, and military dimensions.

1591   Trask, David, Michael Meyer, and Roger Trask. *A Bibliography of United States–Latin American Relations since 1810: A Selected List*. Lincoln: University of Nebraska Press, 1968.

Meyer, Michael C. *Supplement to a Bibliography of United States–Latin American Relations since 1810*. Lincoln: University of Nebraska Press, 1979.

1592   Wolpin, Miles D. *United States Intervention in Latin America: A Selected and Annotated Bibliography*. New York: American Institute for Marxist Studies, 1971.

The literature on the international relations of the United States with specific countries or regions has received no better bibliographic control than is available for Latin America. The first title and its supplement contain more than 14,000 items in the following arrangement: (1) guidebooks and other aids, (2) basic works for the study of United States–Latin American relations, (3) United States and the period of Latin American independence, (4–10) works on specific chronological periods, (11) works on Pan-Americanism, (12) works on Pan-Hispanism, and (13–24) United States relations with specific countries. Bibliographic entries are unannotated.

The Wolpin bibliography contains mostly unannotated entries for books, periodical articles, unpublished dissertations, and government publications arranged under the following subject categories: (1) conceptual analyses of intervention and nonintervention, (2) intervention as a source of political conflict in the United States, (3) intervention as a source for anti-Americanism and struggle in Latin America, (4) instrumentalities of direct intervention, (5) beneficiaries or instrumentalities of indirect intervention, and (6) intervention in particular nations or areas.

1593   U.S. Congress. House of Representatives. Committee on Foreign Affairs. *Required Reports to Congress in the Foreign Affairs Field*. Washington, DC: U.S. Government Printing Office, 1973.

While Congress and the presidency share power to conduct the foreign affairs of the United States, most of the diplomatic, intelligence, and military information flows directly to the president. To offset this congressional information gap, various organizational units of the executive branch are required to submit reports to Congress. This congressional publication identifies most of the required reports that are presently received by congressional committees.*

1594   U.S. Department of State. Division of Publications. *Publications of the Department of State, 1930–1960*. Washington, DC: U.S. Government Printing Office.

1595   U.S. Department of State. Historical Office. *Major Publications of the Department of State: An Annotated Bibliography*. Washington, DC: 1977.

The Department of State issues a considerable amount of information material about the foreign relations of the United States. Three successive bibliographies list the numbered publications of the Department of State during a 30-year period up to 1960. Recently issued publications are regularly listed in the *Monthly Catalog of U.S. Government Publications* and in the monthly *Department of State Bulletin*. Serial publications, many of which contain important speeches and official policy statements by senior State Department personnel, can be identified, by series title only, in John Andriot's *Guide to U.S. Government Publications*. In addition, an annotated bibliography exists for the major publications of the Department of State. This bibliography, cited above, is published as an irregularly revised pamphlet, presently containing some 27 pages, which lists and describes all the publications considered to be of lasting value for research in United States foreign policy.

Large quantities of important information material, however, remain unpublished. Unlike the documentation of the British Foreign Office,** the unpublished documentation of the U.S. Department of State is not indexed by a single, continuously updated reference set. A description exists, however, of the unpublished records of the Department of State for the period 1789–1944 and their locator aids. It is a National Archives publication, entitled *General Records of the Department of State*,

---

*Note also that beginning in 1974 the Central Intelligence Agency cannot spend money on covert operations without reporting them to Congress, as required by the Hughes-Ryan Amendment.
**Index to British Foreign Office Correspondence 1920– (Mendeln, Liechtenstein: Kraus-Thomson, 1969–).

and was compiled by Daniel T. Goggin and H. Stephen Helton.

1596   Witherell, Julian W. *The United States and Africa: Guide to U.S. Official Documents and Government-Sponsored Publications on Africa, 1785– 1975.* Washington, DC: Library of Congress, 1978.

Unclassified publications on Africa issued by or for the United States government from the late eighteenth century to September 1975 are recorded in this massive bibliography totalling nearly 950 pages. With the exception of Egypt, all countries of Africa are covered. Entries are grouped in five chronological sections subdivided by regions and countries. In the final section, covering the last 25 years, the regional and country listings are further subdivided by subjects, including politics and government, foreign relations, economic conditions, military affairs, and others. All categories of official documentation are included, notably congressional and executive documents, diplomatic papers, commercial reports, translations issued by the U.S. Joint Publications Research Service, printed and mimeographed studies of American assistance programs prepared by or for federal government agencies. Full bibliographic information, including LC call numbers, is provided for all listed items. The availability of the listed documents from the Library of Congress, the Superintendent of Documents, or major research libraries is indicated by suitable symbols. Identification of the nearly 9,000 listed items is also facilitated by a detailed index with name entries, country and subject terms.

BIBLIOGRAPHIES FOR THE FOREIGN RELATIONS OF OTHER COUNTRIES

Africa

1597   DeLancey, Mark W. *African International Relations: An Annotated Bibliography.* Boulder, CO: Westview Press, 1981.

This annotated bibliography of African international relations covers books and periodical articles published during a 20-year period since 1960. Entries are arranged alphabetically by author names under eleven headings: (1) African International Relations: General Works; (2) African States Foreign Policies; (3) Inter-African Conflicts, Borders, and Refugees; (4) Sub-continental Regionalism; (5) The OAU, Pan-Africanism, and African Unity; (6) The UN and International Law; (7) Southern Africa; (8) The USSR, the PRC, the UK, and France: Relations with Africa; (9) The USA: Relations with Africa; (10) Other States: Relations with Africa; and (11) Economic Factors in African International Relations. A detailed index with country and subject headings is also included.

Asia

1598   Attar, Chand. *Bibliography of Indo-Soviet Relations 1947–1977.* New Delhi: Sterling, 1978.

The bibliography offers 1,166 entries for books, newspaper and periodical articles relating to the Soviet Union's relationship with India during the 30-year period up to 1977. The entries are arranged by subject and indexed by name. Indian, Russian, and Communist information sources are emphasized.

1599   Kozicki, Richard J. *International Relations of South Asia, 1947–80.* Detroit: Gale Research Company, 1981.

The bibliography identifies books, articles, and essays dealing with the foreign policies and international relations of India, Pakistan, Bangladesh, Sri Lanka, Nepal, Sikkim, Bhutan, and Afghanistan. It does not include Burma. The annotated entries are arranged by country and form category. A separate section lists bibliographies and reference works, as well as other publications for the entire region. Author and subject indexes are included.

Canada

1600   Page, Donald M. A *Bibliography of Works on Canadian Foreign Relations, 1945–1970.* Toronto: Canadian Institute of International Affairs, 1973.

1601   Page, Donald M. A *Bibliography of Works on Canadian Foreign Relations, 1971–1975.* Toronto: Canadian Institute of International Affairs, 1977.

1602   Barrett, Jane R., and Jane Beaumont. A *Bibliography of Works on Canadian Foreign Relations, 1976–1980.* Toronto: Canadian Institute of International Affairs, 1982.

Books and articles dealing with the foreign relations of Canada since 1945 are listed in this unannotated bibliography, currently updated at five-year intervals. The entries are arranged in three main parts: (1) Foreign Relations (by region or country), (2) Defense, and (3) Related Areas (Foreign Investment and Ownership, Immigration and Emigration, International Trade and Finance). Also included are separate indexes by author and subject, a chronological list of statements and speeches by the Department of External Affairs, and a cumulative index to the *Monthly Report on Canadian External Relations* and *International Canada*.

Latin America

1603   Finan, John J., and John Child. *Latin America: International Relations. A Guide to Information Sources.* Detroit: Gale Research Company, 1981.

The bibliography identifies over 1,400 basic and readily available books and periodical articles useful for the study of Latin American international relations. The annotated entries are arranged under 37 chapters in three parts: (1) Bibliographies and Aids, (2) General (Hemisphere; Caribbean; Central America; Organization of American States; Economic and Develoment Aspects; Strategic and Security Aspects; Cultural, Scientific, and Technological Aspects; Extra-Hemisphere Relations), and (3) Countries. The country listings contain separate entries for Canada and the United States to identify publications dealing with the inter-American system, as well as see also references to works covering the bilateral relations of the United States with individual Latin American countries. Separate author and subject indexes are also provided.

Middle East

1604   Khalidi, Walid, and Jill Khadduri. *Palestine and the Arab-Israeli Conflict*. Beirut: Institute for Palestine Studies, 1974.

The national consciousness of two distinct groups of Middle Eastern residents underlies one of the most persistent problems in the international relationships of the world. Commonly known as the Palestine question, the problem originated in the late nineteenth century and has so far defied a satisfactory solution. This annotated bibliography identifies significant books, newspaper and periodical articles, academic dissertations, pamphlets, reports, and government publications dealing with Palestine as a political problem during the period 1880 to 1971. Entries are arranged under nine categories, as follows: (1) general sources; (2) historical background; (3) development of the Palestine problem, 1880–1947; (4) the Palestine war, the establishment of Israel, and the expulsions of the Palestinians, 1947–1949; (5) the Palestinian people, 1948–1967; (6) the Palestine question, the Arab states, and Israel, 1948–1967; (7) the 1967 war; (8) the Palestine question, the Arab states, and Israel, 1967–1971; (9) the Palestinian people, 1967–1971.

For additional information, see also the appropriate reference sources in the documents collection section for international relations.

1605   Sherman, John. *The Arab-Israeli Conflict 1945–1971. A Bibliography*. New York: Garland Publishing Company, 1978.

Arranged by year of publication, this bibliography contains 3,694 mostly unannotated entries for books, pamphlets, periodical articles, and official documents in English relating to the Arab-Israeli conflict. Arab, Israeli, and other viewpoints are reflected in the cited publications. Separate author and subject indexes offer additional access to the listed material.

1606   Schulz, Ann. *International and Regional Politics in the Middle East and North Africa. A Guide to Information Sources*. Detroit: Gale Research Company, 1977.

The guidebook identifies important books dealing with the foreign policies of Middle Eastern states, the role of external powers in the Middle East, the Arab-Israeli conflict, the role of Middle Eastern oil in international relations, and other political phenomena in this region. The annotated entries are arranged by author under chapter headings and subheadings that reflect the aforementioned subject matter. Reference and serial publications are separately listed. Author, title, and subject indexes are included.

1607   Tamkoc, Metin A. A *Bibliography on the Foreign Relations of the Republic of Turkey, 1919–1967 and Brief Biographies of Turkish Statesmen*. Ankara: Middle East Technical University, 1968.

Turkey's relationship with foreign powers and Turkey's territorial and security problems during a period of almost 50 years are the subject of this unannotated bibliography. Its entries are arranged by Turkish and foreign source with separate listings for books, articles, theses, public documents, etc. The book also includes brief biographies of the prime ministers, presidents, and foreign ministers of Turkey.

Soviet Union and Eastern Europe

1608   Kanet, Roger E. *Soviet and East European Foreign Policy: A Bibliography of English and Russian Language Publications, 1967–1971*. Santa Barbara, CA: ABC-Clio Press, 1974.

1609   Remington, Robin Alison. *The International Relations of Eastern Europe*. Detroit: Gale Research Company, 1978.

More than 3,000 books and articles published during a five-year period up to 1971 about the foreign policy of the Soviet Union and its East European allies are listed in the Kanet bibliography. Its unannotated entries are arranged alphabetically by author, but separate subject, geographical, and chronological headings are provided in an index to the listed material. Additional publications can be identified in the Remington bibliography, which covers a larger time frame. Since both bibliographies are retrospective instruments, current publications on the foreign relations of the Soviet Union and Eastern European countries will have to be identified with the help of the *American Bibliography of Slavic and East European Studies*, more fully described as item 2044 in this guidebook.

1610   Saran, Vimla. *Sino-Soviet Schism. A Bibliography*. New York: Asia Publishing House, 1971.

1610a   *The Sino-Soviet Conflict*. Santa Barbara, CA: ABC-Clio, 1984.

Despite the fact that the Soviet Union and China are both Communist party states, the international relationship of the two countries is dominated by a deep ideological schism. The first item listed above is an unannotated bibliography that will be mainly useful for identifying English-language publications that illuminated at a very early stage the causes and manifestations of the Sino-Soviet schism. Works about the cult of personality, Maoism, Leninism, revisionism, and the conflicting objectives of the respective party programs of the two states are listed and subject indexed. The second item provides bibliographic identification and abstracts of more than 1,000 journal articles that describe or analyze the broad range of the ideological and political hostilities between China and the USSR. A detailed multiterm subject index is included.

Western Europe

1611   Aster, Sidney. *British Foreign Policy, 1918 – 1945*. Wilmington, DE: Scholarly Resources, 1981.

1612   Cassels, Alan. *Italian Foreign Policy, 1918 – 1945*. Wilmington, DE: Scholarly Resources, 1981.

1613   Kimmich, Christoph M. *German Foreign Policy, 1918 – 1945*. Wilmington, DE: Scholarly Resources, 1981.

1614   Young, Robert J. *French Foreign Policy, 1918 – 1945*. Wilmington, DE: Scholarly Resources, 1981.

This series of bibliographic volumes is intended for scholars doing research on European diplomatic history during the critical post–World War I period. Each volume contains an introductory chapter on the Foreign Ministry and foreign policy of the country. A second chapter describes available archives and libraries, newspaper collections and research institutes. The main part of each volume presents bibliographic listings for reference works, dissertations, document collections, memoirs, and various historical publications. Appendices offer biographical material on diplomats and other government officials. Separate name and subject indexes are also included.

1615   Carlson, Andrew R. *German Foreign Policy 1890 – 1914, and Colonial Policy to 1914: A Handbook and Annotated Bibliography*. Metuchen, NJ: Scarecrow Press, 1970.

The bibliography lists bibliographies, yearbooks, encyclopedias, newspapers, dissertations, diplomatic histories, archival and published document collections dealing with German foreign policy in general and Germany's foreign relations with specific countries, including the United States, during a 25-year period before the first world war. Also listed are important personalities whose influence or activities shaped German foreign policy. In addition, the book contains a chronological account of important events.

1616   *A Catalog of Files and Microfilms of the German Foreign Ministry Archives 1867 – 1920*. Washington, DC: American Historical Association, Committee for the Study of War Documents, 1959.

1617   Kent, George O. A *Catalog of Files and Microfilms of German Foreign Ministry Archives, 1920 – 1945*. Stanford, CA: Hoover Institution, 1962 – 1966.

Following the collapse of Nazi Germany at the end of World War II, the archives of the German Foreign Ministry came into Anglo-American custody. Most of the documentary material was microfilmed in the United States and is thus widely available for study purposes. Two separate bibliographic sets have been produced to serve as locator aids to the microfilms and original files of the captured German foreign policy documents for the period 1867 to 1945.

1618   Cortada, James W. A *Bibliographic Guide to Spanish Diplomatic History, 1460 – 1977*. Westport, CT: Greenwood Press, 1977.

Divided into 21 chronological chapters, the bibliography lists without annotations books, pamphlets, and periodical articles relating to Spanish diplomacy during more than 500 years. Suitable subdivisions within the main chapters aggregate the listings by countries or special topic. Publications in English, Spanish, and other European languages are listed. An author index is included.

SPECIAL SUBJECT BIBLIOGRAPHIES

Many bibliographies are devoted to special aspects, activities or problems in the conduct of international relations. Most noteworthy in this respect are the bibliographies that focus on the massive literature about the international political economy, diplomacy, national security, arms control and disarmament, war and peace. Although there is inevitably a certain amount of overlap in the bibliographic coverage offered, each of the bibliographies listed and described below provides access to published information for a wide range of subjects of major importance in the study of international relationships among the countries of the world.

Arms Control and Disarmament

Despite repeated arms control negotiations during more than three decades, governments throughout the world have spent more than $6 trillion for armaments since World War II. This militarization of the planet is continuing at the rate of $660 billion annually, with six leading countries — the United States of America, the Union of Soviet Socialist Republics, China, France,

Great Britain, and the Federal Republic of Germany — spending three-fourths of that total. It is obvious that the theoretical and practical foundations of the arms control efforts would have to be improved considerably before the massive diversion of resources to military ends can be effectively reduced.

1619   Burns, Richard Dean. *Arms Control and Disarmament*. Santa Barbara, CA: American Bibliographical Center — Clio Press, 1977.

The unannotated bibliography presently provides the most comprehensive and systematic access to the vast number of books, periodicals, reports, and official publications dealing with arms control and disarmament. The volume is organized in two parts, entitled (1) Views, Overviews and Theory and (2) Accords, Proposals and Treaties. The two main parts are subdivided into 13 chapters devoted to the following aspects of the subject matter: (1) research resources and arms control and disarmament organizations; (2) introduction to arms control and disarmament issues; (3) historical surveys and contemporary views; (4) League of Nations and United Nations; (5) inspections, verification, and supervision; (6) economic consequences, legal and psychological dimensions; (7) limitation of weapons and personnel; (8) the SALT era; (9) demilitarization, denuclearization, and neutralization; (10) regulating and outlawing weapons and war; (11) controlling arms manufacture and traffic; (12) controlling proliferation of nuclear weapons; (13) rules of war and stabilizing the international environment. Two separate, detailed indexes by subject and author offer additional access to the material listed in the 13 chapters.

1620   Clemens, Walter C. *Soviet Disarmament Policy, 1917 – 1963; An Annotated Bibliography of Soviet and Western Sources*. Stanford, CA: Hoover Institution Press, 1965.

The ideological, economic, legal, strategic, and historical aspects of Soviet disarmament policy have been the subject of numerous Western and Russian publications. The annotated entries of this bibliography cover the literature for the first five decades of the Soviet Union's existence and include official publications as well as scholarly books and articles.

1621   *Repertory of Disarmament Research*. New York: United Nations Publications, 1982.

A substantial portion of the information sources for disarmament research is identified in this reference work. Part I contains a general bibliography on the subject. Part II lists documents and publications issued between 1970 and 1980, by period and topical categories that include general disarmament, nuclear disarmament, biological and chemical disarmament, prohibited arms, reduction of military budgets, maritime disarmament, outer space disarmament, regional disarmament, and related topics. Part III offers a directory of international and national research institutes involved in disarmament research.

1622   United Nations. Dag Hammarskjold Library. *Disarmament: A Select Bibliography 1962 – 1967*. New York: United Nations, 1968.

_____ . *Disarmament: A Select Bibliography 1967 – 1972*. New York: United Nations, 1973.

_____ . *Disarmament: A Select Bibliography 1973 – 1977*. New York: United Nations, 1978.

Substantial progress toward curtailment of the qualitative arms race and military budgets requires international coordination and systematic planning with the participation of all states. This requirement predestines the United Nations to an effective role of guidance in the elaboration, specification, and adjustment of programs for the control of armaments. The unannotated but regularly updated bibliographies cited above identify pertinent information sources for each of the major topical areas, notably general disarmament, arms control, nonproliferation of nuclear weapons, cessation of nuclear weapons tests, peacekeeping operations, economic and social consequences of the arms race, mutual force reductions, European security, etc. More recent information can be found in two new United Nations publications, namely, the *United Nations Disarmament Yearbook* and *Disarmament: A Periodic Review by the United Nations*.

1623   U.S. Department of State. Bureau of Intelligence and Research. *Studies in Progress or Recently Completed: Arms Control and Disarmament*. Washington, DC: 196– .

Although the 1970s were proclaimed Disarmament Decade, bibliographic control for arms control and disarmament publications was discontinued by several agencies of the United States government during that period.* To acquaint officials of the U.S. Arms Control and Disarmament Agency and other governmental units with current privately conducted research on disarmament, arms control, and related subjects, the bibliography cited above is issued in series format. It includes three types of material: (1) studies in progress, (2) studies completed and unpublished, and (3) studies completed and published. The studies are listed under major subject or geographical categories. Separate author and subject indexes are included.

---

*Sadly missed will be U.S. Library of Congress, General Reference and Bibliography Division, Arms Control and Disarmament Bibliography Section, *Arms Control and Disarmament: A Quarterly Bibliography with Abstracts and Annotations*, which was discontinued in 1973.

Diplomacy

1624   Harmon, Robert B. *The Art and Practice of Diplomacy: A Selected and Annotated Guide*. Metuchen, NJ: Scarecrow Press, 1971.

Nearly 900 books, articles, and official publications dealing with the nature and objectives of diplomacy, the historical evolution of diplomacy, modern diplomatic methods, and the diplomatic and consular service of individual countries are listed in this annotated bibliography. A separate chapter lists bibliographies, indexes, directories, yearbooks, and other reference publications containing information about the art and practice of diplomacy. A number of diplomatic documents are reproduced in the book. Author and title indexes are also included.

1625   Moussa, Farag. *Diplomatie Contemporaine: Guide Bibliographique*. Geneva: Centre Europeen de la Dotation Cernegie pour la Paix Internationale, 1964; New York: Taplinger Publishing Company, 1964.

This bibliographic volume is arranged in two parts. Part 2 is a richly annotated bibliography of books, articles, pamphlets, and dissertations pertaining to contemporary diplomacy in all parts of the world. The items listed are arranged by author and refer to works written in English, French, German, Russian, Arabic, and other languages. Part 1 provides a topically arranged survey and commentary of the items listed in part 2. There are 31 topical sections dealing with diplomatic law and practice, bilateral and multilateral diplomacy, special diplomatic problems, Afro-Asian diplomacy, Soviet diplomacy, etc. All items listed in Part 2 are also indexed separately by country.

1626   Plischke, Elmer. *American Diplomacy: A Bibliography of Bibliographies, Autobiographies and Commentaries*. College Park: Bureau of Governmental Research, University of Maryland, 1957.

Bibliographies, autobiographies, and other works relating to diplomats active in the foreign service of the United States during the first half of this century are identifiable with the help of this briefly annotated bibliography.

International Economic Relations

1627   Amstutz, Mark R. *Economics and Foreign Policy. A Guide to Information Sources*. Detroit: Gale Research Company, 1977.

A close interrelationship exists between economics and foreign policy since states pursue economic objectives in foreign policy, which in turn reflects the domestic economic interests of the country. The nature and manifestations of this political-economic interrelationship are described or analyzed in numerous books and articles. More than 750 items of the available literature are identified in this annotated bibliography. Its entries are arranged under ten chapters as follows: (1) International Political Economy; (2) International Economic Relations; (3) Politics and Trade; (4) The Politics and Economics of Regional Integration; (5) Politics and the International Monetary System; (6) Politics and Foreign Aid; (7) Foreign Private Investment; (8) Imperialism; (9) Economics of War and Defense; (10) Other Reference Materials. Suitable topical subdivisions are made under these chapters. Brief introductory headnotes and an introductory section at the beginning of the book offer additional guidance to the nature of the available information sources. Author, title, and subject indexes are included in the book.

National Security and Defense

The prime fact influencing the foreign relations of all nations is the human realization that most of the world lies outside one's own national boundaries and is a world not of one's own making. This fact is as true for the tiny state of Israel, a nation of three million inhabitants, as it is for China, a nation with one billion people. The resultant concerns for national survival are of such overriding importance that all nations, to a greater or lesser extent, try to keep secret much of the information relating to their national security, including the information-gathering (intelligence) activities themselves. It is therefore not surprising that the bibliographic instruments for national security information are not well developed and heavily oriented toward historical information. Whether such bibliographic neglect is really in the interest of national security is a question frequently debated in academic and military circles, but the emergence of several new bibliographies prepared by professional experts seems to indicate a change in traditional thinking.

1628   *Abstracts of Military Bibliography*. Buenos Aires: Navy Publications Institute, 1968 – .

1629   *Naval Abstracts*. Alexandria, VA: Center for Naval Analysis, 1978 – .

The purpose of these two quarterly bibliographies is to identify and briefly abstract the contents of periodical articles dealing with political, strategic, or other subject matter affecting military forces. English-, French-, German-, Italian-, and Spanish-language material is abstracted. Access to the listed material is offered by personal name, country, and topic.

1630   *Air University Library Index to Military Periodicals*. Maxwell Air Force Base, AL: 1949 – .

1631   *Quarterly Strategic Bibliography*. Boston, MA: American Security Council Education Foundation, 1977 – .

Publications dealing with national security problems, military and strategic affairs are identifiable by author and subject with the help of these quarterly indexes.

1632   Arkin, William M. *Research Guide to Current Military and Strategic Affairs*. Washington, DC: Institute for Policy Studies, 1981.

The basic sources of information on worldwide military and strategic affairs are listed and succinctly annotated in this guidebook, arranged in five chapters, as follows: (1) introduction and user's guide; (2) general information sources — (a) reference tools, (b) statistical data sources, (c) descriptive sources for current events and developments; (3) U.S. government documents — (a) introduction, (b) congressional information, (c) executive branch information; (4) U.S. military — (a) Department of Defense organization and background, (b) defense policy and posture, (c) defense budget, (d) military-industrial complex, (e) military personnel, (f) local impact of military presence and spending, (g) overseas commitments; (5) worldwide military and strategic affairs — (a) armed forces and weapons, (b) regional and country defense issues, (c) Soviet Union, Eastern Europe, and the Warsaw Pact, (d) Western Europe and NATO, (e) arms control, (f) international organizations and international law. Two appendices list 400 important military periodicals and the research organizations active in this field. No index is included.

1633   Blackstock, Paul W. *Intelligence Espionage, Counterespionage, and Covert Operations: A Guide to Information Sources*. Detroit: Gale Research Company, 1978.

1634   Cline, Marjorie W., Carla E. Christiansen, and Judith M. Fontaine. *Scholar's Guide to Intelligence Literature: Bibliography of the Russell J. Bowen Collection*. Frederick, MD: University Publications of America, 1983.

1635   DeVore, Ronald M. *Spies and All that ... Intelligence Agencies and Operations: A Bibliography*. Los Angeles: California State University, Los Angeles, 1977.

As the role of the intelligence services has assumed greater importance for national security, it has become more institutionalized and more public. As a result, the publicly available literature on intelligence has grown to vast and varied dimensions. The three bibliographies cited above offer access by topic and country to thousands of books and periodical articles otherwise difficult to locate. The bibliography of the Russell J. Bowen Collection

at Georgetown University is of most recent vintage and identifies more than 5,000 titles under 372 headings and subheadings. Intelligence establishments, clandestine operations, counterintelligence, espionage, reconaissance, ciphers and codes, subversion, interrogation techniques, psychological warfare, unconventional warfare, and similar topics are well covered.

1636   *Defense Markets & Technology*. Cleveland, OH: Predicasts, 1982 – .

Multiple access to information published in leading defense industry and trade journals, government reports, newspapers, and annual company reports about

- land, sea and air weapons, their testing, production, and combat effectiveness,
- new weapons technologies,
- international arms trade,
- arms manufacturers,
- defense budgets, and
- related topics

is provided by this monthly and annually cumulated index and abstract publication. Each issue of *DM & T* contains approximately 1,500 abstracts grouped under ten major sections: (1) aircraft and parts, (2) ships and parts, (3) missils and space vehicles, (4) ordnance and ordnance vehicles, (5) fire control, search and detection, (6) navigation control and instrumentation, (7) C^3 equipment, (8) electronic components, (9) other components, and (10) defense finance and administration. Each of these sections is further subdivided for rapid scanning of related information. Four separate indexes by author, country, product, and organization offer references to the individually numbered bibliographic citations and abstracts in the reference set.

DM & T is also available in several computerized versions, but no online access is as yet offered by a commercial vendor.

1637   Greenwood, John. *American Defense Policy since 1945*. Wichita: University Press of Kansas, 1973.

American defense policy since World War II has primarily been a policy of containment of the Soviet Union with comparative neglect of other security problems. Approximately 3,000 books, periodical articles, government publications, published and unpublished papers have been selected by this bibliography for illumination of this complex subject matter. The bibliographic entries are listed under six major categories: (1) Bibliography of Bibliographies; (2) The Factual Context: Data and Descriptive Material; (3) Strategic Thought and Military Doctrine in the Nuclear Age; (4) The Defense Policymaking Process; (5) Defense Policy Output, Weapons Systems and Military Programs; (6) The Domestic Effects of Defense Policy. No annotations are provided, but a list of periodicals that regularly include articles on American defense policy is included.

1638   Larson, Arthur D. *National Security Affairs: A Guide to Information Sources.* Detroit: Gale Research Company, 1973.

Nearly 4,000 English-language books and articles dealing with national security affairs within the world setting and within the domestic setting of the United States and selected foreign countries are listed in this unannotated bibliography. All entries are arranged by author in major subject categories. Bibliographies, handbooks, periodicals, research and educational organizations concerned with national security affairs are separately listed. A keyword index to the listed material is included.

Peace Research

Based on the growing realization that war is a useless and unsuitable political method, much academic research has focused on the maintenance of peace in the international relations of the world. Perhaps the most notable outcome of peace research is the discovery that the maintenance of peace is an enormously complex process that needs to be better understood not only in each of its many elements but also in the many-faceted, frequently contradictory relationship of these elements. Several bibliographic instruments exist that identify the available literature for the key elements of peace maintenance.

1639   Boulding, Elise. *Bibliography on World Conflict and Peace.* Boulder, CO: Westview Press, 1979.

Some 1,000 books, articles, and anthologies dealing with conflict situations and peace are listed by author in this bibliography. Its entries include at least one subject code, but no separate subject index is provided. Bibliographies and serials are listed separately. The listings include all major publications issued between 1945 and 1978.

1640   Cook, Blanche Wiesen. *Bibliography on Peace Research in History.* Santa Barbara, CA: ABC-Clio Press, 1969.

The bibliography presents over 1,100 annotated entries for books, dissertations, manuscript collections, periodical articles, and institutional publications dealing with specific peace or antiwar activities of the past. The phenomena of pacifism, antimilitarism, and nonviolent conduct in political affairs are reflected in the majority of the listings.

1640a   Gray, Charles, Leslie Gray, and Glenn Gregory. *A Bibliography of Peace Research Indexed by Key Words.* Eugene, OR: General Research Analysis Methods, 1968.

The keyword in context (KWIC) method in indexing is very useful for uncovering many of the conceptual elements by which peace can be understood. This KWIC index identifies over 1,300 titles of peace research publications issued between 1957 and 1967. The entries are based on words occurring in the titles of the publications. Author access to the listed material is also possible.

1641   Huxford, Marylyn, and Sandra Schelling. *Perspectives on War and Peace in a Changing World.* St. Louis, MO: St. Louis University, Pius XII Library, 1975.

The bibliography identifies 60 subject categories, many of which are key elements in a peace setting or absence of peace setting. The unannotated entries list books only about aggression, armaments, assassination, atomic warfare, balance of power, civil disobedience, conscientious objection, disarmament, guerilla warfare, imperialism, militarism, nationalism, neutrality, peace movements, power, propaganda, revolution, social change, social conflict, sovereignty, Third World, violence, war criminals, etc. An author index is also included.

1642   *Peace Research Abstracts Journal.* Clarkson, Ontario: Canadian Peace Research Institute, 1964—.

In view of its frequency, detailed classification plan, and international coverage, this monthly publication ranks as one of the finest tools for the retrieval of peace-related information. Books and articles published on peace-related subjects since 1945 are indexed and abstracted. The entries follow a detailed classification plan that consists of ten main headings with numerous subdivision. The main subject headings include the military situation, limitation of arms, tension and conflict, ideology and issues, international institutions, nations, pairs of countries, international law, decision making and methods. A separate coding manual is provided to facilitate the retrieval of the listed material. Separate author and subject indexes are also included.

1643   Swarthmore College. *Catalog of the Peace Collection.* Boston: G. K. Hall, 1982.

Since 1930 the Swarthmore College Peace Collection has aimed to preserve primary and secondary source materials from organizations and individuals committed to establishing or maintaining world peace. The scope of subjects covered in the collection includes proposals for permanent peace, pacifism and conscientious objection, disarmament and arms control, protests against war or military preparations, military conscription and service, League of Nations and United Nations activities, and documentation about the moral, psychological, and economic costs of war. The catalog contains 42,500 entries for books, periodicals, and archival material ranging in date from 1642 to the present. All entries are arranged in dictionary format by author, title, and subject.

1644   Woito, Robert S. *To End War. A New Approach to International Conflict.* New York: Pilgrim Press, 1982.

This important reference book is the sixth edition of a work first published in 1967 as an annotated bibliography. The new edition contains detailed analytical essays as well as annotated book entries for helping the reader acquire sufficient end-war knowledge. The material is organized in three sections (A. Ideas, B. Contexts, C. Action), five parts (1. World Politics and War, 2. Conditions Essential to a World without War, 3. Actors in World Politics, 4. New Problems, 5. Developing Capacities), and 21 chapters that focus on specific topics. Among the topics covered are military strategy, weapons, causes of war, arms control, human rights, economic order, environment, social change, organizational and individual action, and others. Also included are a typology and select list of world affairs organizations, a selected list of world affairs periodicals, as well as action-oriented question-and-answer lists. Separate title and author indexes are also included.

Refugees

1645   *Refugee Abstracts.* Geneva: International Refugee Integration Resource Centre, 1982 – .

One of the persistent problems in international relations is the tremendous exodus of refugees from many countries in the world due to political persecution, wars, and other adverse conditions. This quarterly reference publication contains abstracts of official documents, books, and periodical articles relating to

1. laws, treaties, organizations, assistance programs, and conferences concerned with refugees
2. the national, social, cultural, and ethnic backgrounds of refugee groups
3. causes and means of exodus
4. problems and provisions of asylum
5. resettlement problems, provisions, and experiences.

Author and subject indexes and lists of publishers are included.

War

Several times in this century small groups of political actors attempted to achieve illegal or outlawed political objects by the application of military means across international boundaries. They thereby precipitated the major armed conflicts in the world, known as World War I and II, the Korean War and the Vietnamese War. All of these wars ended contrary to the expectations of their initiators. The two world wars brought about not only the most fundamental changes in the political systems of the world but also the afterwars in Korea, Vietnam, and other areas of the world. Massive numbers of official, academic, and other publications have accumulated about these wars and, with the exception of the more recently conducted afterwars, the causes and operational details of these wars are now fully known. The bibliographic instruments below offer excellent access to all relevant information material.

1646   Bayliss, Gwyn M. *Bibliographic Guide to the Two World Wars. An Annotated Survey of English-Language Reference Materials.* New York: R. R. Bowker, 1977.

The guidebook lists and briefly describes the general and specific bibliographies, guides and directories to libraries, museums, archives, societies and associations with war collections, dictionaries and encyclopedias, periodical lists, indexes, abstracts, biographies, document collections, and other reference works that offer access to the massive information material about the two world wars. Entries are arranged by categories that reflect the type, language, regional or subject coverage of the reference instruments. Also included are four separate indexes by author, title, region or country, and subject.

1647   Blanchard, Carroll H. *Korean War Bibliography and Maps of Korea.* Albany, NY: Korean Conflict Research Foundation, 1964.

The Korean War is only just now emerging from the security classification of its diplomatic and military information material, at least as far as United States involvement is concerned. For this reason a definite bibliography covering all relevant information about this war must still be awaited. The bibliography cited above is an extensive listing of books, articles, manuscripts, and government reports that had become available in the early 1960s.

1648   Bloomberg, Marty, and Hans Weber. *World War II and Its Origins. A Select Annotated Bibliography of Books in English.* Littleton, CO: Libraries Unlimited, 1975.

While the origins of World War II are documented not solely in English-language publications, this bibliography performs useful reference service for English-speaking readers. Its 1,603 annotated entries identify English-language books only about the causes of World War II and the military, political, social, cultural, and technological events of the war years. The listed material is presented in 12 chapters with subdivisions for major topics and countries. An author-title-biography index is also included.

1649   Burns, Richard Dean. *War/Peace Bibliography Series*. Santa Barbara, CA: American Bibliographical Center—Clio Press, 1973—.

The series consists of bibliographies on relatively narrow topics within the broad spectrum of war/peace studies. Focusing on specific wars, causes and instruments of war, and revolutionary upheavals, titles published to date in the series include:

1650   Denisoff, R. Serge. *Songs of Protest, War and Peace: A Bibliography* (No. 1).

1651   Divale, William Tulio. *Warfare in Primitive Societies: A Bibliography* (No. 2).

1652   Leitenberg, Milton, and Richard Dean Burns. *The Vietnam Conflict: Its Geographical Dimensions, Political Traumas, and Military Developments* (No. 3).

1653   DeVore, Ronald M. *The Arab-Israeli Conflict: A Historical, Political, Social and Military Bibliography* (No. 4).

1654   Blackey, Robert. *Modern Revolutions and Revolutionists: A Bibliography* (No. 5).

1655   Lewis, John R. *Uncertain Judgement: A Bibliography of War Crimes Trials* (No. 8).

1656   Schaffer, Ronald. *The United States in World War I. A Selected Bibliography* (No. 7).

1657   Smith, Myron J., Jr. *The Soviet Navy, 1941—1978* (No. 9).

1658   Smith, Myron J., Jr. *The Soviet Air and Strategic Rocket Forces, 1939—1980* (No. 10).

1659   Smith, Myron J., Jr. *The Soviet Army, 1939—1980* (No. 11).

1660   Smith, Myron J., Jr. *The Secret Wars: A Guide to Sources in English*. Vol. 1, *Intelligence, Propaganda and Psychological Warfare, Resistance Movements, and Secret Operations, 1939—1945*; Vol. 2, *Intelligence, Propaganda and Psychological Warfare, Covert Operations, 1945—1980*; Vol. 3, *International Terrorism, 1968—1980* (Nos. 12—14).

1661   Ball, Nicole. *World Hunger. A Guide to the Economic and Political Dimensions* (No. 15).

1662   Carroll, Berenice A., Clinton F. Fink, and Jane E. Mohraz. *Peace and War. A Guide to Bibliographies* (No. 16).

1663   Blackey, Robert. *Revolutions and Revolutionists. A Comprehensive Guide to the Literature* (No. 17).

1664   Burns, Richard Dean, and Milton Leitenberg. *The Wars in Vietnam, Cambodia, and Laos 1945—1982* (No. 18).

The publications listed in these bibliographies include books, periodicals, newspaper articles, and some government publications. The arrangement usually follows a topical classification. Author and subject indexes are usually included, and where appropriate glossaries and chronologies are provided in appendices.

1665   Enser, A. G. S. *A Subject Bibliography of the Second World War: Books in English 1939—1974*. Boulder, CO: Westview Press, 1977.

Like the Bloomberg bibliography (item 1648), this reference work limits itself to English-language books about World War II. Works issued during a 35-year period are listed if their contents exceeds 30 pages and does not include fiction, poetry, or humor. The entries are listed alphabetically by subject and do not include annotations. An author index and a list of the subject headings used in the bibliography are provided.

1666   Lane, Jack C. *America's Military Past. A Guide to Information Sources*. Detroit: Gale Research Company, 1980.

The United States military were decisive actors in the major international conflicts of this century. This guidebook identifies books and periodical articles dealing with the role of the U.S. armed forces during the two world wars, the Korean War, and the Vietnam War. Separate listings are also provided for U.S. military policy during the nuclear age. Author, title, and subject indexes provide a key to the annotated entries.

1667   Lang, Kurt. *Military Institutions and the Sociology of War*. Beverly Hills, CA: Sage Publications, 1972.

The bibliography offers a review of the literature, with an annotated list of publications, dealing with the military profession, military organization as a social structure, the interdependence of armed forces and society, civil-military relations, the study of war and warfare. Author, title, and subject indexes are included.

1668   Schaffer, Ronald. *The United States in World War I: A Selected Bibliography*. Santa Barbara, CA: American Bibliographical Center—Clio Press, 1978.

1669   *World War II from an American Perspective. An Annotated Bibliography*. Santa Barbara, CA: ABC-Clio, 1983.

United States involvement in the first and second world wars has been the subject of a vast scholarly literature focusing not only on the military operations themselves but also on the causes and effects of this involvement. The Schaffer bibliography offers a brief chronology of U.S. involvement in World War I and identifies relevant publications in the following chapters: (1) General References, (2) The European War, (3) The United States and World War I — General, (4) American Intervention, (5) Military Activity, (6) Unit Histories, (7) The War and American Society, (8) Peacemaking, and (9) Survivals and Precedents. Numerous subdivisions for narrower topics are made within these main headings. An author index is also included.

The second bibliography, dealing with World War II, contains more than 1,100 citations and abstracts selected from the periodical literature published during the decade 1971—1981. Entries are arranged alphabetically by author, but a detailed subject profile index offers access to the listed material.

1670   *The Two World Wars*. Oxford: Pergamon Press, 1964.

The bibliography is the result of an attempt by the International Commission for History Teaching to select from among 11,000 publications those works that provide original evidence and traces of historical facts about the origins and the conduct of the two world wars. Approximately 1,000 titles are listed in a classified arrangement based on chronology, names of countries, and major topics. The works selected included document collections, memoirs, testimony of witnesses, summaries, treatises on single historical subjects, chronologies, and general and specific bibliographies. Where necessary the entries have been briefly annotated. The cited works are published in English and other European languages.

1671   Ziegler, Janet. *World War II: Books in English, 1945—1965*. Stanford, CA: Hoover Institution Press, 1971.

Like the Bloomberg and Enser bibliographies, previously cited and described, this bibliography identifies English-language books about World War II. It lists 4,515 books published between 1945 and 1965 in classified order under these headings: general works, origins of the war, military, political, economic, and legal aspects of the war, its social impact, position of the neutral countries, and war crimes trials. Numerous subdivisions of these main headings by country, form of publication (memoir, biography, chronology, pictorial history, etc.) and broad subjects provide good access to individual citations. An index of authors and major series is also included. Works of fiction and statistical publications are omitted.

Dictionaries and Encyclopedias

The alphabetical approach provided by the following dictionaries and encyclopedias makes it possible in many instances to locate quickly concise information about specific terms, concepts, persons, organizations, conferences, events, ideas, and activities of significance in the international relationships of the countries of the world. Encyclopdic coverage is, however, limited to the foreign relations of the United States and the international participation in World War II.

DICTIONARIES

1672   Findling, John E. *Dictionary of American Diplomatic History*. Westport, CT: Greenwood Press, 1980.

The dictionary provides basic factual information about more than 500 persons associated with U.S. foreign policy as well as descriptions of over 500 nonbiographical items connected with American diplomacy. The chronological coverage extends from the American revolution through 1978. Entries include a statement about the historical importance of the person, organization, event, treaty, or other item listed. In addition, bibliographical references for additional information are given in each entry. The dictionary also includes five appendices: (A) Chronology of American Diplomatic History, (B) Key Diplomatic Personnel Listed by Presidential Administration, (C) Initiation, Suspension, and Termination of Diplomatic Relations, (D) Date and Place of Birth of the Biographees (United States, Foreign, and Unknown), (E) Locations of Manuscripts Collections and Oral Histories. The dictionary also includes a name and subject index.

1673   Gamboa, Melquiades J. *Elements of Diplomatic and Consular Practice. A Glossary*. New York: Oceana Publications, 1974.

The dictionary was prepared by a former ambassador and provides excellent definitions and descriptions of terms and topics prevalent in diplomatic practice.

1674   Haensch, Gunther. A *Dictionary of International Relations and Politics, Systematic and Alphabetical in Four Languages: German, English/American, French and Spanish*. Amsterdam, NY: Elsevier Publishing Company, 1965.

This dictionary of equivalent terms arranges entries in subject categories such as names of states, the state, international law, diplomacy, international negotiations, treaties and organizations, war, disarmament, history, etc. No definitions are given, and equivalent terms only are listed in four languages. Unfortunately, no Russian terms are included.

1675   Ostrower, Alexander. *Language, Law and Diplomacy. A Study of Linguistic Diversity in Official International Relations and International Law.* Philadelphia: University of Philadelphia Press, 1965.

This work is not a dictionary but a useful reference tool that analyzes the role of language in international relations, identifying official languages of diplomacy, international organizations, conferences, peace treaties, multinational federations, etc. Lengthy bibliography on pp. 825–923.

1676   Plano, Jack C., and Roy Olton. *The International Relations Dictionary.* Santa Barbara, CA: ABC-Clio, 1982.

The principal vocabulary of international relations is listed, defined, and its significance explained in 12 subject matter chapters entitled: (1) Nature & Role of Foreign Policy, (2) Nationalism, Imperialism & Colonialism, (3) Ideology and Communication, (4) Geography and Population, (5) International Economics, (6) War and Military Policy, (7) Disarmament & Arms Control, (8) Diplomacy, (9) International Law, (10) International Organizations, (11) American Foreign Policy, and (12) National Political Systems. A separate index listing all terms and other entries is also included.

1677   U.S. Department of State. Library. *International Relations Dictionary.* Washington, DC: U.S. Government Printing Office, 1980.

Intended only to supplement other dictionaries and reference works, this dictionary lists and defines terms, phrases, acronyms, catchwords, and abbreviations that may be difficult to locate otherwise. Most entries also include notes with authoritative information about the first use, significance, or other details of the listed item. No claim is made that any definition reflects Department of State policy.

1678   Vincent, Jack E. *Handbook of International Relations. A Guide to Terms, Theory and Practice.* Woodbury, NY: Baron's Educational Series, 1969.

All entries are arranged alphabetically by subject headings and provide explanation of terms, concepts, developments, structures, agreements, and rules relevant in international relations.

ENCYCLOPEDIAS

1679   Baudot, Marcel, et al. *The Historical Encyclopedia of World War II.* New York: Facts on File, 1980.

1680   Parrish, Thomas. *The Simon and Schuster Encyclopedia of World War II.* New York: Simon and Schuster, 1978.

1681   Snyder, Louis L. *Louis L. Snyder's Historical Guide to World War II.* Westport, CT: Greenwood Press, 1982.

World War II was the greatest prolonged mass tragedy in the history of the international relations process, causing the loss of 35-55 million lives. The three encyclopedias have assembled from literally millions of facts the most noteworthy items of information relating to the economic, political, social, cultural, psychological, and military phases of this war. Specifically covered are causes and consequences of the war, its major events and principal geographic locations, its leading personalities, organizations, and conferences, and its major military operations. Bibliographies for additional information are also included.

1682   De Conde, Alexander. *Encyclopedia of American Foreign Policy.* New York: Charles Scribner's Sons, 1978.

The three-volume set contains 95 essays by leading specialists exploring the concepts, theories, doctrines, and distinctive features of American foreign policy during the past 200 years. Among the topics covered are imperialism, anti-imperialism, colonialism, the Cold War, containment, detente, intervention and nonintervention, isolationism, the Marshall Plan, national self-determination, neutrality, peace movements, summit conferences, the Monroe, Eisenhower, Nixon, and Truman doctrines, and many others. Cross-references and a bibliography are included in each essay. A biographical appendix offers brief information on all important individuals in American diplomatic history. An analytical index enables the reader to trace any issue in American foreign policy through the appropriate essays in the encyclopedia.

1683   *Dictionaire Diplomatique.* Paris: Academie Diplomatique Internationale, 1957.

The seven-volume encyclopedic set was prepared with the collaboration of 27 chiefs of state, 49 foreign ministers, and 512 ambassadors and members of the academy, representing 91 countries. The individual articles are arranged by names of countries or under specific headings such as war, disarmament, capitulation, neutrality, etc. Excellent bibliographic references accompany each topical essay.

Digests

Most of the reference instruments for the study of international relations are heavily oriented toward history. Therefore there is a definite need for retrieval tools specifically designed to isolate information about current and future developments in world affairs. Such information is usually generated by four different occupational groups, namely, (1) the diplomatic services, (2) the intelligence services, (3) international business establishments, and (4) the press. The information produced by the first two groups is almost never available on a current basis for academic research. The information produced by international business establishments, notably international bankers, multinational corporations, and investment companies, is part of the economics literature and can be identified, albeit with some delay, with reference tools listed in the Economics section of this guidebook. The information collected by journalists presents special retrieval problems since it is disseminated in thousands of newspapers and periodicals and is buried in a mass of unrelated, extraneous information. Bibliographies and indexes that provide a key to newspaper and periodical information are not ideally suited for the retrieval of current information on world affairs because the publication delay may be too long or the coverage too broad. The most suitable retrieval instruments for current data are digests, which offer relevant information in a condensed and manageable format. A variety of news digests exists, but those dealing exclusively with events in all subject areas on a worldwide or regional basis are listed in the History section of this guidebook. The following titles represent digests that focus primarily on world affairs in their evaluations of current and future developments.

1684   *The Arms Control Reporter*. Brookline, MA: Institute for Defense and Disarmament Studies, 1982–.

Issued monthly in loose-leaf format, this digest offers current information on all international arms control negotiations and policy debates about weapons production and testing. For each negotiation, information is presented in four sections, as follows: (1) the status of talks, (2) a chronology of talks and events, (3) analyses and prospects of the negotiations, and (4) the texts of essential documents, treaties, conventions, etc. The analysis section utilizes critiques assembled from various newspaper and periodical publications. The chronology pages contain material from news agency transmissions, embassy press releases, personal interviews, and other sources. A calendar showing the dates of all negotiating sessions and related meetings is also included.

1685   *The Intelligence Digest*. Cheltenham, England: Ringrone Newspapers, Ltd., 1938–.

1686   *The Intelligence Digest — Weekly Review*. Cheltenham, England: Ringrone Newspapers, Ltd., 1952–.

The digest, issued as a monthly and weekly publication, offers an assessment of current and future trends in international relations prepared by unidentified observers in many parts of the world. Each issue is printed on thin paper to facilitate airmail dissemination. The weekly edition summarizes the most recent political developments.

1687   *Report on World Affairs*. London: Report on World Affairs, Ltd., 1919–.

The quarterly publication provides a summary of significant developments in the internal and foreign affairs of all countries. Political information is heavily emphasized, but economic and military developments are also well reported. An annual index is also issued.

1688   *Rundt's Country Risk Report*. New York: S. J. Rundt & Associates, 1956–.

1689   *Rundt's Weekly Intelligence*. New York: S. J. Rundt & Associates, 1956–.

1690   *S. J. Rundt World Risk Analysis Package*. New York: S. J. Rundt & Associates, current. (Vendor: I. P. Sharp)

Available in printed form or online, these digests offer current assessments of sociopolitical, domestic-economic, and external account developments in some 70 countries of the world. Each of the *Country Risk Reports* is devoted to a single country and consists of a frequently revised report containing the following items of information: (1) sociopolitical prognosis — (a) prospects for stability, (b) official attitudes toward foreign investment, (c) labor market trends, (d) role of the government in the economy; (2) domestic market forecast — (a) economic growth prospects, (b) market potential, (c) outlook for inflation and credit conditions, (d) monetary and fiscal policies; (3) external accounts projections — (a) current account balance of payments, (b) exchange reserves and foreign debt, (c) trade restrictions and collection reliability, (d) exchange control and currency outlook. A numerical risk rating grades the sociopolitical, domestic economic, and external account factors from 1 (best) to 10 (worst) and presents a numerical risk total for the country.

The *Weekly Intelligence*, issued weekly, contains up-to-date condensed information on current steps taken by governmental authorities to deal with pressing economic problems, and offers an assessment of the effectiveness of these governmental measures.

S. J. Rundt World Risk Analysis Package or WRAP is the name of the computerized database that offers online display of current textual and numerical information available in the printed reports.

1691   U.S. Department of Commerce. Bureau of International Commerce. *International Marketing Information Series*.

1. *Consumer Goods Research*.
2. *Country Market Survey*.

3. *Foreign Economic Trends and Their Implications for the United States.*
4. *Global Market Survey.*
5. *International Marketing Events.*
6. *International Marketing Newsmemo.*
7. *Overseas Business Reports.*
8. *Producer Goods Research.*

Washington, DC: U.S. Government Printing Office, 1962—.

The eight publications cited above constitute digests of political, economic, legal, and other information useful for promoting the sale of American products in foreign countries. Summary information is presented on the economic policy, trade regulations, government procurement, investment incentives, entrance and residence requirements, etc., of the major trading partners of the United States. U.S. Foreign Service posts and foreign government agencies are identified. Bibliographic listings for additional information are also provided. The cited publications are issued on a semiannual, annual, or irregular basis.

1692   U.S. Department of State. Bureau of Public Affairs. *Gist*. Washington, DC: 1970—.

1693   U.S. Department of State. Bureau of Public Affairs. *Issues in United States Foreign Policy*. Washington, DC: 1968—.

The first item is published monthly and offers brief outlines of United States foreign policy on major international problems, or questions of current public interest. The outlines are, however, not intended as comprehensive U.S. policy statements. The second title cited above is published irregularly and presents a summary of the principal elements of an international problem with which the United States is confronted. No solutions to the international problems are offered by this digest, which merely illuminates the context within which foreign policy decisions will have to be made.

1694   *World Political Risk Forecasts*. New York: Frost & Sullivan, 1979—.

Current assessments of future political risk to international businesses in over 70 countries are offered by this digest set published in four regionally organized binders. Political forecasts for each country are combined with economic data—some from public sources, other from country specialists—to form individual country reports that present an 18-month and 5-year estimate of the risk levels for 13 factors affecting international businesses. Totally revised annually and updated monthly, each country report contains a description of the individual and institutional political actors and a measurement of their influence on political stability, political turmoil, and re-

strictions on business establishments and trade, such as operations and repatriation requirements, taxation discrimination, foreign exchange controls, tariff and other import barriers, labor cost increases, fiscal/monetary expansion, and international debt problems.

Directories

This section lists directories and other reference sources that provide names, biographical data, and other useful information on members of the diplomatic and consular services of the United States and selected foreign countries.

UNITED STATES

1695   U.S. Department of State. *Biographic Register*. Washington, DC: U.S. Government Printing Office, 1870—.

1696   _____ . *Foreign Service List*. Washington, DC: U.S. Government Printing Office, 1929—.

1697   _____ . *United States Chiefs of Mission, 1778–1973*. Washington, DC: U.S. Government Printing Office, 1973.

Three separate directories offer information about United States personnel active in foreign affairs. Biographical information on the personnel of the Department of State and other federal agencies active in foreign affairs is presented in the *Biographic Register*. Data include birthdate, marital status, education, private and government experience, language proficiency, current assignment and title. Annual revisions keep the directory current.

Information relating to the assignments of foreign service personnel can be found in the *Foreign Service List*, published three times annually. Arranged by country and city, the entries include the names of chiefs of mission, foreign service officers, foreign service reserve officers, foreign service staff officers of class six and above. A separate listing provides data on United States missions to international organizations.

A retrospective list identifies ambassadors, secretaries of state, deputy undersecretaries of state, assistant secretaries of state for the United States during a period of nearly 200 years.

1698   U.S. Department of State. *Diplomatic List*. Washington, DC: U.S. Government Printing Office, 1893—.

1699   _____ . *Foreign Consular Offices in the United States*. Washington, DC: U.S. Government Printing Office, 1932—.

The diplomatic and consular representatives of foreign countries in the United States are listed in the two directories cited above. The quarterly published *Diplomatic List* provides the names, titles, and addresses of the diplomatic personnel of foreign embassies in Washington, D.C. The order of precedence and date of presentation of credentials of the diplomatic corps are also identified in this list.

Foreign consular offices in the United States are identified in a separate annually published directory bearing the same title. The jurisdictional area of the consulate as well as the names, ranks, and dates of recognition of all consular personnel are also indicated.

OTHER COUNTRIES

1700 *Annuaire Diplomatique et Consulaire de la Republic Française*. Paris: Imprimerie Nationale, 1858—.

1701 *The Diplomatic Service List*. London: Her Majesty's Stationery Office, 1966—.

1702 *The Foreign Office List and Diplomatic and Consular Yearbook*. London: Harrison, 1806—1966.

These directories list the diplomatic and consular officials of France and Great Britain throughout the world. Biographical notices and obituaries are also included.

1703 Crowley, Edward L. *The Soviet Diplomatic Corps 1917—1967*. Metuchen, NJ: Scarecrow Press, 1970.

The names and brief biographical data of Soviet diplomatic officials who have served in the Ministry of Foreign Affairs or Soviet missions abroad during the first 50 years of the Soviet Union's existence are listed in this directory. A chronology of the most noteworthy diplomatic acts and events, a list of UN Security Council vetoes, as well as schematic information about the organization structure of the USSR Ministry of Foreign Affairs is also included in the directory, which was compiled by the Institute for the Study of the USSR in Munich, Germany.

1704 *The Statesman's Yearbook*. New York: St. Martin's Press, 1864—.

This annual reference publication lists for each country of the world embassies and legations maintained abroad and identifies the names of ambassadors and the principal diplomatic officers of the embassies in London and Washington, D.C.

Handbooks and Yearbooks

1705 Day, Alan J. *Border and Territorial Disputes*. Detroit: Gale Research Company, 1982.

Border and territorial disputes are among the most difficult issues affecting the international relations process. This handbook offers summaries of more than 70 territorial disputes currently unresolved throughout the world. Summaries are arranged by continent and country. Each account presents an overview of the dispute, the historical background, recent exchanges and negotiations. Maps of the disputed borders and territories are included. A one-page bibliography provides highly selective references. A list of maps included, a name and subject index facilitate access to desired items of information in the country summaries.

1706 *Defense and Foreign Affairs Handbook*. Washington, DC: Copley and Associates, 1976—.

The general, political, economic, and military situation as it affects the international position of each country in the world is described in this annual handbook. Statistical data are given for the land area, major cities, total population, gross national product, balance of trade, the transportation and communication system, major newspaper circulation, available manpower, military forces, annual military expenditures, military organizations and equipment. Major producers of military equipment in each country are also identified. A separate section, entitled Who's Who in Defense and World Politics, presents brief biographical information on important persons. Various tables offer important military and political data.

1707 Feltham, R. G. *Diplomatic Handbook*. New York: Longman, 1977.

The handbook offers concise information for diplomatic practice. The information is presented under the following headings: (1) Diplomatic Relations (establishment, conduct); (2) The Ministry of Foreign Affairs; (3) The Diplomatic Mission; (4) Protocol and Procedure; (5) Diplomatic Privileges and Immunities; (6) Consular Officers and Consular Posts; (7) The United Nations; (8) International Organizations and agreements outside the United Nations; (9) International Law and Practice; and (10) Conferences. The handbook also contains a glossary of diplomatic terms, a list of abbreviations, and an organization chart of the Foreign and Commonwealth Office of Great Britain.

1708 *Jane's All the World's Aircraft*. Edited by John W. R. Taylor. 1909—.

1709 *Jane's Armour and Artillery*. Edited by Christopher F. Foss. 1979—.

1710 *Jane's Fighting Ships*. Edited by John Moore. 1898—.

1711 *Jane's Infantry Weapons*. Edited by John Weeks. 1974—.

1712   *Jane's Military Communications*. Edited by R. J. Raggatt. 1979–.

1713   *Jane's Military Vehicles and Ground Support Equipment*. Edited by Christopher F. Foss. 1978–.

1714   *Jane's Surface Skimmers*. Edited by Roy McLeavy. 1967–.

1715   *Jane's Weapons Systems*. Edited by Ronald T. Pretty. 1969–.
London: Jane's Publishing Company, varying dates.

Revised annually by leading commentators and analysts, these yearbooks constitute a current authoritative reference source for information on the instruments of defense policies, such as fighting ships, aircraft, weapons, and other military equipment in the world. The information is arranged by country or type of craft or weaponry, and typically includes building dates, technical descriptions, specifications, operational status, illustrations, and analytical tables for the various items of military hardware. Indexes, glossaries, and lists of advertisers are also provided. Even more current reports and analytical reviews of global defense subjects and military technology can be found in *Jane's Defense Review*, published bimonthly since 1980.

1716   Labrie, Roger P. *SALT Handbook. Key Documents and Issues 1972–1979*. Washington, DC: American Enterprise Institute for Public Policy Research, 1979.

Since November 17, 1969, the United States and the Soviet Union have conducted a series of negotiations for the purpose of control over the most destructive weapons ever devised by man. This document collection traces the history of the Strategic Arms Limitation Talks (SALT) and includes the texts of the SALT treaties and agreements. Also included are the statements and congressional testimony of presidents Ford and Carter, General Secretary Brezhnev, secretaries Rogers, Kissinger, and Vance, Soviet Foreign Minister Gromyko, secretaries of defense Laird, Schlesinger, and Brown, presidential advisor Brzezinski, and others. The volume also contains background essays, three annotated bibliographies, a glossary, and an index.

1717   London. Institute for Strategic Studies. *The Military Balance*. London: 1963–.

1718   _____ . *Strategic Survey*. London: 1967–.
The Institute for Strategic Studies in London is a prestigious research organization that publishes reliable information about the military aspects of international relations. The first title cited above offers an annual quantitative evaluation of the military relationship of the Western, Communist, and nonaligned countries. Estimates of comparative strengths, details of defense expenditures, and characteristics of armaments are given. The annual companion volume contains a description and analysis of strategic policies, problems of security, and issues in conflict in the various countries and regions of the world.

1719   McGowan, Patrick J. *Sage International Yearbook of Foreign Policy Studies*. Beverly Hills, CA: Sage Publications, 1973–.

The yearbook presents a number of essays by distinguished scholars who survey the current state of foreign policy studies. A publications list of recent comparative foreign policy studies is also included.

1720   Satow, Ernest Mason. *Satow's Guide to Diplomatic Practice*. London: Longman, 1979.

Currently in its fifth edition, this standard guidebook offers definition, description, and comment for the management of international relations by diplomacy. The book is arranged in 44 chapters that deal with diplomacy in general, diplomatic agents, consular matters, international transactions, and international organizations. Numerical subdivisions within the chapters focus on narrower aspects of the topic covered and allow precise access through appropriate entries in the index. Six appendices contain listings of definitions and terms, conferences, United Nations membership, specialized agencies, Commonwealth membership, and diplomatic specialists. A bibliography of important publications in the field of diplomacy is also included.

1721   Singer, J. David, and Melvin Small. *The Wages of War 1816–1965. A Statistical Handbook*. New York: John Wiley and Sons, 1972.

Although the literature on wars is huge, there are very few studies on the quantitative aspects of wars. This handbook remedies the deficiency by offering a variety of statistical data and numerical comparisons of wars waged during a 150-year period. The material is organized in four main chapters that provide (1) a description of the rationale and procedure, (2) an analysis of individual wars by magnitude, severity, and intensity, (3) generalizations about the incidence of war within the international system, and (4) data on the total amount of war experienced by various nations.

1722   Stockholm International Peace Research Institute. *World Armaments and Disarmament. Yearbook*. New York: Humanities Press, 1969–.

Like the reference works published by the London Institute for Strategic Studies the SIPRI yearbooks are a major source of information about the quantitative and qualitative changes in the world's military arsenals. Military expenditures, the international arms trade, the social and economic consequences of the arms race, the maintenance of military bases and forces in foreign countries, problems of European security, the Strategic Arms Limitation Talks, and the militarization of the deep ocean are the main subjects covered by the yearbooks.

1723   Yeager, Leland B. *International Monetary Relations: Theory, History and Policy.* New York: Harper & Row, 1976.

The problems of international relations are most obdurate and difficult in the area of money and banking. This handbook surveys the monetary side of international relations, and presents historical and theoretical summaries of specific problem spots, such as trade and payment imbalances, foreign exchange rates, intervention and adjustment policies, international liquidity, monetary reform, etc. A subject and name index is included.

Document Collections

The existing body of knowledge concerning the conduct of international relations is derived largely from diplomatic and other foreign policy documents. Less apparent, however, is the extent to which collections of foreign polcy documents reflect the reality of international relations.

A most serious weakness of all document collections is the ambiguity of documents resulting from the imprecision of human language and other factors. Most documents can be interpreted in different ways because they are abstract and sometimes incomplete. Documents are usually silent on what is taken for granted, and they are often based on unspoken assumptions and values. Thought processes are not documented, and the documentation for verbal communication in all its nuances is mostly incomplete. In addition, documents often reflect the closed language system imposed by the political system. Thus, the language of most documents hides the real intentions of political actors, whose purpose for writing or releasing them may be different from the written content. For these and other reasons, document collections should be regarded as "dependent" reference sources. That is, their proper usage depends on the concurrent use of other information sources, e.g., diaries, memoirs, and autobiographies produced by decision-makers in foreign affairs.

Practically all countries of the world restrict access to foreign policy records by time and category of information. The United States opens foreign policy records earlier than most other countries, but the governmental department most heavily engaged in the conduct of foreign relations, namely, the Department of State, still distinguishes two periods with respect to accessibility of its

records. Access to documents is generally barred during a closed period of approximately 20 years, after which time systematic declassification or review of U.S. government information takes place. Foreign government information is declassified or reviewed after 30 years. Apart from these time limitations, the records of the Department of State and other agencies engaged in the conduct of international relations are withheld from public scrutiny if disclosure in whole or in part can be expected to cause at least identifiable damage to national security. The current basis for security classification is Executive Order 12356 (3CFR Chapter IV) dated 2 April 1982, which permits the withholding of information in three grades of classification — top secret, secret, and confidential. Material to be classified must meet at least one of seven specific criteria as determined by the president or other officials with classification authority. The classification criteria cover military plans, weapons, and operations, foreign government information, intelligence activities, scientific, technological, or economic matters relating to national security, U.S. programs for safeguarding nuclear materials, foreign relations activities of the U.S. government, and other information related to national security. Foreign relations documents of the U.S. government are usually withheld from the public if (1) disclosure would tend to impede current diplomatic negotiations or other business, (2) disclosure would violate a confidence reposed in the Department of State by individuals or foreign governments, or (3) the publication would give needless offense to other nationalities or individuals.

It has been estimated in recent years that the Department of State accumulates classified documents at the rate of 200,000 per year, so that several million classified documents have accumulated in the central files of the Department of State during the last 30 years. Although some formerly classified documents are published after approximately 25 years in the *Foreign Relations of the United States* series, a considerable percentage* of these documents remains inaccessible, primaily because much of the material appears to be unimportant or has failed to attract the interest of the professional historians of the Department of State responsible for the publication of the documents.

There are special rules for the automatic or special declassification of restricted data when the information no longer requires the same level of protection. Thus, many formerly top secret or secret documents are made public as soon as changing circumstances permit. Many previously inaccessible documents have been made available to a

---

*Only 10 percent of the annual accumulation of records is published in the FRUS series. During 1977 the Department of State received 3,504 requests for the release of documents, most of which were granted.

wider public after declassification by extensive microfilm projects. Lists of available mircrofilms documenting diplomatic or consular activities of the United States with many foreign countries are published by the National Archives of the United States.

With few exceptions, the publication of foreign relations documentation in countries other than the United States remains considerably more restricted. Of 77 countries surveyed some years ago by the Department of State, three-quarters made no provision for serial publication of diplomatic correspondence even on a selective basis.

Bibliographic control of available document collections and supporting sources remains poor. The following list of major document collections is designed to fill the bibliographic gap only partially and should be regarded as a starting point for further searches in library catalogs, historical bibliographies, national bibliographies, guides to archives, and similar listings.

At the same time the reader is referred to the following guidebook, which contains an excellent survey and description of the diplomatic documentation relative to the origins of the first and second world wars.

1724   Toscano, Mario. *The History of Treaties and International Politics*. Baltimore: Johns Hopkins Press, 1966.

Although this book was originally designed for an international relations course at the University of Rome, it is indispensable for all students of international relations. The book describes the various types of diplomatic documents, public and private archives, treaty collections, colored books,* and other document collections relative to World War I and II, and the memoir sources for the two world wars. The description of the various document collections and memoir sources is arranged by country.

UNITED STATES

1725   Alexander, Yonah, and Allan Nanes. *The United States and Iran: A Documentary History*. Frederick, MD: University Publications of America, 1980.

Previously unprinted documents from the National Security Council, the Joint Chiefs of Staff, the OSS, the Central Intelligence Agency, the intelligence branches of the U.S. Department of State, as well as printed, but frequently unavailable documentation, such as presidential papers and diplomatic correspondence relating to the

---

*Colored books are special collections of diplomatic documents that a government publishes to inform the parliament of the action taken during an international crisis. The term derives from the fact that the covers of these document collections are traditionally the same color, i.e., French yellow books, British blue books, etc.

complex relationship between the United States and Iran from 1856 to 1980, can be found in this document collection.

1726   *American Foreign Relations*. New York: New York University Press, 1971–.

1727   *Documents on American Foreign Relations*. New York: Council on Foreign Relations, 1938–1970.

These sets of annual, commercially published volumes present an orderly, chronologically arranged assembly of official documents relating to the foreign relations of the United States throughout the world during the preceding year. The documents consist of the texts of treaties and agreements, communiques, speeches, statements, resolutions, and similar items released into public domain. Commentaries elucidate the meaning of the included documents. Cumulative indexes are available for periods of several years.

Classified documents are not included in these sets and following their release are reproduced in the U.S. Department of State's *Foreign Relations of the United States* series and other special collections listed and described separately in this section.

1728   Brockway, Thomas P. *Basic Documents in United States Foreign Policy*. Princeton, NJ: Van Nostrand, 1968.

1729   Goebel, Dorothy. *American Foreign Policy. A Documentary Survey, 1776–1960*. New York: Holt, Rinehart and Winston, 1961.

These reference works are an attempt to select from a large mass of documentation those items that would be crucial for a broad understanding of the foreign policy of the United States during its bicentennial existence. The collections include treaty texts, diplomatic notes, speeches, congressional resolutions, press releases, and similar items dealing with important issues in foreign policy. The documents are preceded by introductory and explanatory notes.

1730   *Crises in Panama and the Dominican Republic: National Security Files and NSC Histories (1963–1969)*. Frederick, MD: University Publications of America, n.d.

This microfilm collection of formerly top secret documents is valuable for an understanding of United States crisis management in two violence-ridden countries during the 1960s. President Johnson's options and judgment in the Panamanian riots and the U.S. military intervention in the Dominican Republic are covered fully in the documentation made accessible with a printed guide.

1731   *Documents of the National Security Council, 1947–1977.* Frederick, MD: University Publications of America, 1981.

1732   *Documents of the NSC: First Supplement.* Frederick, MD: University Publications of America, 1981–.

For well over 35 years the National Security Council (NSC) has been the most important governmental advisory organization in respect to the integration of domestic, foreign, and military policies relating to the national security of the United States. Supplemented at regular intervals, this document collection, available on microfilm only, is the first publication to collect all of the previously secret reports and action papers of the National Security Council. The more than 500 titles in the collection consist of assessments of U.S. strategic interests, policy options, and commitments in four areas of national concern, namely, (1) Asia, (2) the Middle East and Africa, (3) Latin America, and (4) Europe and the Soviet Union. Separate printed guides offer access to the individual items in the collection.

1733   Etzold, Thomas H., and John Lewis Gaddis. *Containment: Documents on American Policy and Strategy, 1945–1950.* New York: Columbia University Press, 1978.

American efforts to contain Soviet expansionism during the early Cold War period become apparent in this document collection. Many of the documents have recently been declassified and relate to national security policy, including contingency plans for war with the Soviet Union.

1734   *Israel: National Security Files (1963–1969).* Frederick, MD: University Publications of America, n.d.

This microfilm collection includes a wide range of documents about the conduct of the foreign relations between the United States and Israel. Included are regular and special messages from American diplomatic personnel in Tel Aviv, minutes of meetings of the U.S. ambassador with Israeli Prime Minister Levi Eshkol and Foreign Minister Abba Eban, background studies by the CIA and the National Security Council, and various briefings for President Johnson. A printed guide facilitates access to the documents in the collection.

1735   *Nuclear Weapons, Arms Control, and the Threat of Thermonuclear War: Special Studies, 1969–1981.* Frederick, MD: University Publications of America, 1982.

Of all the important political issues in the United States, none has surfaced with greater intensity than the controversy over nuclear policy. Considerable misunderstandings and doubts have been exhibited by the general public as well as scholars in regard to the nature and deployment of nuclear weapons, the prospects for controlling their proliferation, and the conditions under which nuclear arms can serve as instruments of national policy.

The cited document collection, available on microfilm only, contains numerous special studies prepared by prestigious private and official research organizations under contract with the Department of Defense and other governmental agencies. These studies have not previously been disseminated to depository libraries. Their availability in this collection now makes it possible to gain educated insights into such topics as postattack viability of American institutions; acceptable limits in strategic weapons; cycles, symmetries, and balance in U.S.-Soviet nuclear armaments; deterrence effectiveness of sea- and land-based nuclear missiles; the MX weapons system; trends in and control of nuclear proliferation, and many other related projections, problems, and policy options. Access to the individual studies in the collection is facilitated by a printed guide containing an abstract of each study and a subject index.

1736   *Official Conversations and Meetings of Dean Acheson (1949–1953)* Frederick, MD: University Publications of America, n.d.

1737   *Minutes of Telephone Conversations of John Foster Dulles and of Christian Herter (1953–1961).* Frederick, MD: University Publications of America, n.d.

1738   U.S. Department of State. *Press Conferences of the Secretaries of State, 1922–1974.* Wilmington, DE: Scholarly Resources, n.d.

The transcripts and minutes of the conversations, meetings, and press conferences of the U.S. secretaries of state, made available on 31 reels of microfilm, offer an authoritative insight into American foreign relations and policies during a 40-year period. The first two document collections contain considerable top secret material not previously available. Printed guides are supplied for each collection.

1739   *Public Statements by the Secretaries of Defense.*

Part 1. *The Truman Administration (1947–1953).*

Part 2. *The Eisenhower Administration (1953–1961).*

Part 3. *The Kennedy and Johnson Administrations (1961–1969).*

Part 4. *The Nixon and Ford Administrations (1969–1977).*

Part 5. *The Carter Administration (1977–1981).*

Frederick, MD: University Publications of America, 1982−.

Valuable information relating to the foreign relations, military affairs, and national security of the United States can be found in this collection of 71 reels of microfilmed documentation. Over 70,000 pages of press conferences, background briefings, press statements, official testimony, speeches, interviews, and other public pronouncements by the secretaries of defense during seven presidential administrations are included. Much of the collection pertains to the use of U.S. troops abroad and the defense posture of the United States in crisis areas throughout the world. Behind the coverage of regional affairs and individual conflicts, the documentation reflects the constant concern over the size of the military budget, the cost and effectiveness of weapons systems, and the power and intentions of the Soviet Union. Printed guidebooks, issued for each part of the collection, facilitate access to the documentation, which will be supplemented as time progresses.

1740   Schlesinger, Arthur M. *Dynamics of World Power. Documentary History of U.S. Foreign Policy 1945−1973.* New York: McGraw-Hill, 1973.

The five-volume set contains the texts of speeches, statements, policy papers, letters, and other documents relative to the foreign policy of the United States as a world power after World War II. Each volume is devoted to a specific geographic area — Western Europe, Eastern Europe and the Soviet Union, Latin America, the Far East, and the United Nations and Sub-saharan Africa. Introductions and commentaries by area and subject specialists are provided in all volumes, which are also individually indexed.

1741   Timberlake, Charles E. *Detente. A Documentary Record.* New York: Praeger Publishers, 1978.

The term *detente* has appeared as a label for a five-year period beginning in 1972 in which U.S.-Soviet relations passed from an era of confrontation to an era of negotiation. This document collection contains the text of all bilateral and multilateral agreements concluded during the detente era between the government of the USSR and the United States. Also included are important statements, communiques, messages, etc., relating to these documents. Full bibliographic references are provided to the original source of publication of the documentation included. A list of detente documents not included and a subject index are also part of this reference work.

1742   *U.S. Armed Forces in Vietnam, 1954−1975.* Frederick, MD: University Publications of America, 1983.

While history never repeats itself exactly and no army ever benefited from trying to meet a new challenge in terms of the old one, the study of the experiences, shortcomings, and achievements of the U.S. armed forces in Vietnam offers indispensable insights for handling or not handling a military conflict in international relations. This document collection is one of three major collections on the war in Vietnam. Its documentation was written by senior U.S., South Vietnamese, Laotian and Cambodian military officers and includes a 3,500-page contract study on the strategic lessons learned in Vietnam. The entire collection is organized in four parts, entitled: (1) Indochina Studies, (2) Vietnam: Lessons Learned, (3) Vietnam: Reports of U.S. Army Operations, and (4) Vietnam: U.S. Army Senior Officer Debriefing Reports. Although each of the four parts is available on microfilm only, the printed guides offer access to the individual items in the collection.

1743   U.S. Department of Defense. *United States − Vietnam Relations 1945−1967. Study.* Washington, DC: U.S. Government Printing Office, 1971.

In the middle of 1967, Robert S. McNamara, then United States secretary of Defense, commissioned a top secret study of the United States role in Indochina. The study resulted in 15 copies of a 47-volume set containing 3,000 pages of narrative history written by 36 anonymous government and civilian authors and more than 4,000 pages of appended documents.

In June 1971 the *New York Times*, which had obtained most of the 47 volumes without government authorization, began publishing a series of articles based upon the study. The U.S. Justice Department subsequently obtained a temporary restraining order against the further publication of the series. The department had contended that the nation's defense interests and security would suffer irreparable harm. On June 30, 1971, however, the U.S. Supreme Court in a 6−3 decision permitted the publication of the series.

The title cited above refers to the official set of the study, otherwise known as the Pentagon Papers, which have also become available in several other editions. Neither the original 47 volumes of the Pentgon Papers nor the officially and commercially published versions of the declassified 43 volumes of the original study contain a comprehensive collection of all pertinent documents. Four volumes of the original study, for instance, were not released because they contain the history of contacts for a peace settlement and the release of the prisoners. The Pentagon researchers did not have access to the complete files of the Department of State and the personal papers of the presidents nor to the documentation of the North Vietnamese Politbureau. The Pentagon Papers therefore cannot completely reflect historical reality. Incomplete as the published papers are, they nevertheless offer the political scientist the first good look into the inner workings of the executive branch in matters of foreign relations since the end of World War II.

1744   U.S. Department of State. *A Decade of American Foreign Policy: Basic Documents, 1941–1949*. Washington, DC: 1950. (Reprint edition: New York: Greenwood Press, 1968).

1745   _____. *American Foreign Policy: Basic Documents, 1950–1955*. Washington, DC: U.S. Government Printing Office, 1957.

1746   _____. *American Foreign Policy: Current Documents, 1956–1967*. Washington, DC: U.S. Government Printing Office, 1959–1969.

Foreign policy documents made public prior to the issuance of the volumes in the *Foreign Relations of the United States* series have been assembled in the three document collection sets, cited above. No previously classified documents are included in these sets, which contain mostly public statements, press releases, resolutions, treaties, and agreements delineating the scope and goals of United States foreign policy. A topical and chronological arrangement is used.

1747   U.S. Department of State. *Department of State Bulletin*. Washington, DC: 1939– .

1748   _____. *Selected Documents*. Washington, DC: to date.

1749   _____. *Speech*. Washington, DC: to date.

1750   _____. *Current Policy*. Washington, DC: to date.

1751   _____. *Special Report*. Washington, DC: to date.

1752   U.S. Department of State. Secretary of State. *Press Conference*. Washington, DC: to date.

The most current documentation of United States foreign policy can be found in the various publication series cited above. With the exception of the monthly *Department of State Bulletin*, individual issues in these series are published irregularly. The published material consists mainly of press releases, speeches, addresses, statements or summaries made by the president, the secretary of state, and senior government officials about the foreign policy of the United States.

1753   U.S. Department of State. *The Foreign Relations of the United States*. Washington, DC: U.S. Government Printing Office, 1861– .

This massive series of several hundred volumes constitutes the official printed record of the foreign policy of the United States. Issued presently with a delay of approximately 25 years, the volumes contain a selection of the diplomatic correspondence, notes, reports, memoranda, and other documents produced during one calendar year. Generally arranged by region and country, the selected documents, many of which were formerly classifed top secret, secret, or confidential, are reproduced in full text or significant sections. From time to time special volumes are issued that deal with specific countries or diplomatic conferences, such as those held at Paris, Malta, Yalta, Berlin (Potsdam), Cairo, Teheran, Casablanca, and Quebec. The selection of the published documents is designed to permit an understanding of the major foreign policy decisons within the range of the Department of State's responsibilities. No cumulative subject index exists for the entire series, but each volume contains a detailed table of contents and a separate index of names and selected subject terms. In addition, there are general indexes for the years 1861–1899, 1900–1918, and 1939–1945.

Although this series is a primary source for the study of United States foreign policy, it must be stressed that reliance on this source alone may be inadequate. There is, for instance, no indication of the numerical relationship the published documents bear by topic or chronological period to the unpublished documents. A large preponderance of unpublished documents must of necessity cause the published documents to be somewhat distorted in their information value. There is also evidence that some major foreign policy decisions did not emanate from the Department of State but rather from the president or some other federal agency. Appropriate documentation would therefore be missing from the series. For these and other reasons, the unpublished and microfilmed files of the Department of State and other federal departments as well as the archives of foreign governments must be consulted. Since these records are often unavailable to the public, however, the conduct of United States foreign relations in specific situations cannot be studied, understood, or evaluated with complete accuracy.

1754   *The War in Vietnam: Classified Histories by the National Security Council*. Frederick, MD: University Publications of America, 1982.

1755   *Transcripts and Files of the Paris Peace Talks on Vietnam, 1968–1973*. Frederick, MD: University Publications of America, 1982.

Far more comprehensive than the Pentagon Papers, this microfilm collection contains the text of more than 2,000 hitherto top secret documents from the upper level of the executive branch. Included are White House Situation Room reports, special reports to the president from cabinet officers, papers of the Vietnam Advisory Group, daily, weekly, and special reports from General Westmoreland, recommendations of the Joint Chiefs of Staff, studies by the CIA, instructions from the secretary of state to diplomatic officials in Vietnam, and many other documentary items relating to the United States involvement in Vietnam from 1964 through 1968.

Verbatim transcripts and other documentation of the Paris peace negotiations on Vietnam are available in a separate microfilm collection. Files on the informal talks between Henry Kissinger and Le Duc Tho are also included. Access to both collections is facilitated by printed guides.

AUSTRIA

1756   Mayrzedt, Hans, and Waldemar Hummer. *Dokumente — 20 Jahre Österreichische Neutralitäts- und Europapolitik, 1955–1975* (Documents — 20 Years Austrian Neutrality and European Policy). Vienna: Austrian Society for Foreign Policy and International Relations, 1976.

1757   Schilcher, Alfons. *Materialien zur Zeitgeschichte.* Vol. 2, *Österreich und die Grossmächte* (Documents on Contemporary History. Vol. 2, Austria and the Big Powers). Vienna: Geyer, 1980.

While there are many countries whose foreign relations are based on purely unilateral, revisable declarations of neutrality, there are only two European countries, Switzerland and Austria, that have their permanent neutrality firmly anchored in international law. Switzerland's neutrality policies after World War II have so far not been covered in a comprehensive collection of documents, but the two reference works cited above contain all the important documents leading up to Austria's neutrality status and the Austrian foreign policies pursued during the first 20 years of the country's neutral independence. The documentary material in the Mayrzedt/Hummer set is arranged in four sections, as follows: (1) foundations and development of Austrian neutrality policies, (2) Austria's multilateral policies toward Western Europe, (3) Austria's bilateral policies toward Eastern Europe, and (4) Austria's position in multilateral East-West relations. The published documents include treaties, communiques, protocols, speeches, and similar material. The Schilcher volume contains documents covering the period of the four-power occupation of Austria, illustrating the conduct of Austrian and Allied relations from the end of the Second World War to the conclusion of the Austrian state treaty, establishing Austria's neutral independence in 1955. Readers desiring additional information are referred to Alfred Verdross, *The Permanent Neutrality of Austria* (Vienna: Verlag für Geschichte und Politik,

1978) and to Lilly-Ralon Behrmann, Peter Broche, and Wolfgang Strasser, *Bibliographie zur Aussenpolitik Österreichs seit 1945* (Vienna: Wilhelm Braumuller, 1974).

CANADA

1758   Blanchette, Arthur E. *Canadian Foreign Policy, 1955–1965: Selected Speeches and Documents.* Toronto: McClelland & Stewart, 1977.

1759   Blanchette, Arthur E. *Canadian Foreign Policy, 1966–1976: Selected Speeches and Documents.* Toronto: Gage, 1980.

These volumes contain official pronouncements and documents on various aspects of Canadian foreign relations, including U.S.-Canadian relations, continental defense issues, the war in Vietnam, and other disputes.

1760   Canada. Department of External Affairs. *Documents on Canadian External Relations.* Ottawa: Queen's Printer, 1967– .

The documentation presented in this continuing series begins with the establishment of the Canadian Department of External Affairs in 1919 and presently covers Canada's foreign relations up to 1941. The individual volumes in the series are issued for specific time periods, with the documents arranged in topical or country chapters. Many of the reproduced documents are previously secret or confidential telegrams, despatches, memoranda, and other items of diplomatic communication. An analytical index in each volume offers references to the individually numbered documents by country, principal policy-maker, and subject.

1761   Swanson, Roger F. *Canadian-American Summit Diplomacy, 1923–1973: Selected Speeches and Documents.* Toronto: McClelland & Stewart, 1975.

This volume identifies and documents the summit meetings between Canadian prime ministers and U.S. presidents from 1923 to 1973. Separate chapters are devoted to each meeting, which is summarized in editorial headnotes. The reproduced documents include joint statements, addresses, press conferences, as well as the reports presented by the Canadian prime minister to the Canadian House of Commons.

FRANCE

1762   France. Commission de Publication des Documents Relatifs aux Origines de la Guerre 1939–1945. *Documents Diplomatiques Français 1932–1939.* Paris: Imprimerie Nationale, 1963.

Documentary records of the French Foreign Ministry have suffered great and lasting damage as a result of the war and German occupation. Although many of the most important documents have been lost forever, a special commission was able to collect and reconstruct a significant number of diplomatic papers. This documentary set contains a selection of important notes, instructions, memoranda, etc., arranged by country.

1763   France. Ministère des Affaires Etrangères. *The French Yellow Book. Diplomatic Documents 1938–1939.* New York: Reynal and Hitchcock, 1940.

A collection of the most important documents relative to the critical events and negotiations prior to the outbreak of World War II.

1764   France. Direction de la Documentation et Ministère des Affaires Etrangères. *La Politique Etrangère de la France. Textes et Documents.* Paris: Documentation Française, 1966– .

1765   _____ . *French Foreign Policy. Official Statements, Speeches and Communiques.* New York: Service de Presse et d'Information, Ambassade de France, 1966– .

The collection of texts and documents in French and in English translation is not intended to be an exhaustive inventory of documentation on French foreign policy, but rather presents the essential positions of the French government in foreign policy matters. The texts are arranged in chronological order and are preceded by a chronology of important events. The texts of treaties and agreements concluded and reports from the Council of Ministers are included in annexes. There are three indexes, namely a subject index, an index by country, and a table of texts reproduced.

GERMANY

1766   Brückner, Jens A., and Günther Doeker. *The Federal Republic of Germany and the German Democratic Republic in International Relations.* Dobbs Ferry, NY: Oceana Publications, 1979.

The three-volume set contains official documents and legal materials in English relating to the legal status, confrontation, and cooperation between the two German states, as well as their role in international organizations. Bibliographies and selected study texts on the problems and issues facing the two states are also included in the set.

1767   Deutsche Gessellschaft fur Auswärtige Politik. *Dokumente zur Auswärtigen Politik.* Bonn: 1945– .

1768   *Dokumente zur Aussenpolitik der Regierung der Deutschen Demokratischen Republik,* 1949– . Berlin: Rutten und Loening, 1954– .

Primary documentation in German of the foreign policies of the two Germanys is presented in the two sets cited above. The first item is a loose-leaf collection of foreign policy documents prepared in collaboration with the Ministry of Foreign Affairs of the Federal Republic of Germany. The second set consists of bound volumes of foreign policy documentation prepared by the East German government.

1769   Germany (Federal Republic, 1949–). Auswärtiges Amt. *Die Auswärtige Politik der Bundesrepublik Deutschland.* Cologne: Verlag Wissenschaft und Politik, 1972.

This reference work was produced by the German Foreign Ministry in collaboration with a council of scientists. The volume includes a 100-page summary of German foreign policy between 1949 and 1971, and the text of 336 important foreign policy documents, notably treaties, laws, memoranda, communiques, statements, correspondence, etc. Also included are a chronology of important events in international relations, 40 statistical tables, maps, and a bibliography of other official publications and document collections.

1770   Germany. Auswärtiges Amt. *Akten zur Deutschen Auswärtigen Politik 1918–1945: Aus dem Archiv des Auswärtigen Amts* (Documents on German Foreign Policy 1918–1945. From the Archives of the German Foreign Ministry).

Series A: 1918–1925 (German edition in preparation).
Series B: 1925–1933 (German edition only).
Series C: 1933–1937 (English edition only; German edition in preparation).
Series D: 1937–1941 (English, French, and German editions).
Series E: 1941–1945 (German edition only).

Washington, DC: U.S. Government Printing Office, 1949– ; Gottingen: Vandenhoeck und Rupprecht, 1950– ; Baden-Baden: Imprimerie Nationale, 1950– .

Although far from complete, the publication of these German foreign policy papers represents a unique event in the documentation of international relations. Never before has the foreign relations record of a vanquished state been presented by three victorious powers on the basis of the highest scholarly objectivity. During the final stages of World War II and shortly thereafter, the archives of the German Foreign Ministry came into Anglo-American custody. The governments of the United States, Great Britain, and France agreed to publish a selection from the 400 tons of captured documents for the period 1933–1941, based on the work of an international team of British, French, and American historians. By mutual agreement, the government of the German Federal Republic was to undertake, in German only, the publication of the document collections for the remaining years 1918–1933 and 1942–1945.

The published collections contain only those papers that are valuable for an understanding of German foreign policy. All document sets are published in chronological order and topical arrangement. An analytical list giving dates, number, and a brief subject description precedes the text of the documents.

From the political scientists' point of view, the document sets present special problems of evaluation. Not all German foreign policy documents fell into Anglo-American hands. Some came into possession of the Soviet government, and others disappeared, permanently or perhaps only temporarily. According to Dr. Wolfgang Mommsen, head of the Federal Archives in Koblenz, Germany, many documents from the Nazi era still remain under lock and key in the United States and Great Britain. Thus, for the politically and historically interesting period 1942–1945, only a few volumes of Series E have been published so far. The available documents sets should therefore be regarded as an excellent source for the study of international relations, but not as a final interpretation of history.

GREAT BRITAIN AND COMMONWEALTH

1771   Bourne, Kenneth, and D. Cameron Watt. *British Documents on Foreign Affairs: Reports and Papers from the Foreign Office Confidential Print*. Frederick, MD: University Publications of America, 1983–1988.

The Confidential Print papers of the British Foreign Office comprise diplomatic despatches and reports that were printed for limited internal circulation within the British government and until recently were unavailable to the public because their information content was of a sensitive nature. The papers are a unique source, not only for the study of diplomacy and international relations, but also for an evaluation of the political, economic, and social conditions of the various countries from which British diplomats reported.

The document collection set cited above contains a selection of the Confidential Print papers from the mid-nineteenth century to the Second World War to be published in 420 volumes until 1988. The set is divided into 2 parts and 18 series based on geographic regions and historical period. Each volume offers a general introduction and a chronology of important events, as well as a detailed table of contents for the included documents.

1772   Eayrs, James. *The Commonwealth and Suez. A Documentary Survey*. London: Oxford University Press, 1964.

A collection of documents that illustrate the reaction and attitude of the Commonwealth concerning nationalization of the Suez Canal Company, the invasion of Suez, the United Nations emergency force, and related aspects of the Suez conflict. Since this conflict is still within the closed period of British diplomatic documentation, the published material consists mainly of public speeches, statements, and messages from parliamentary debates, newspapers and periodical articles.

1773   Great Britain. Foreign Office. *British and Foreign State Papers*. London: Her Majesty's Stationery Office, 1814– .

A collection of the principal public documents relating to Great Britain's relations with other countries. Volumes are issued annually, with a delay of up to seven years, and contain a subject index and a chronological list of documents. There are also cumulative indexes covering various time spans. The series is comparable to the United States Department of State series *American Foreign Policy: Current Documents* and like its American counterpart does not contain confidential diplomatic papers.

1774   Great Britain. Foreign Office. *Documents on British Foreign Policy, 1919–1939*. London: Her Majesty's Stationery Office, 1946– .

This document set is issued in three series* covering various periods in British foreign relations during the interwar years. All chapter divisions are geographical, and documents are arranged in chronological order within each chapter. The published documents are mainly letters, telegrams, records of conversations, etc., from the Foreign Office files and occasional items from the personal papers of the diplomats. The texts of some documents are in French. All chapters contain a summary and a numerical listing of the published documents identified by author and title and briefly described by subject content. Volume 10 of the third series is a separate index volume.

Apart from the documents contained in these three series, massive numbers of documents of the British Foreign Office remain unpublished. These unpublished documents are, however, identifiable with a separate index set, entitled *Index to British Foreign Office Correspondence 1920–* (Nendeln, Liechtenstein: Kraus-Thomson, 1969–), which is kept current as time progresses in the 30-year period of secrecy for British foreign policy papers.

1775   Watt, D. C., and James Mayall. *Current British Foreign Policy. Documents, Statements, Speeches*. London: Temple Smith, 1971– . . .

This collection of selected documents, statements, and speeches on British foreign policy is not an official publication, but all the texts in it are taken from official sources. The published material is analyzed by chronological and subject indexes. Also included are a list

* 1st Series, 1919–1922; Series 1A, 1925–1927; 2nd Series, 1929–1933; 3rd Series, March 1938–September 1939.

of official publications on British foreign policy, debates on foreign policy in the House of Commons, speeches and statements by British spokesmen to the United Nations Security Council, as well as a separate index of speakers.

INDIA

1776   India. Lok Sabha Secretariat. *Foreign Policy of India: Text of Documents, 1947–1964*. New Delhi: Lok Sabha Secretariat, 1966.

1777   India. Ministry of External Affairs. *Foreign Affairs Record*. New Delhi, 1955–.

1778   Kumar, Satish. *Documents on India's Foreign Policy*. New Delhi: Macmillan of India, 1975–.

These reference sources are collections of official documents relating to India's foreign policy during various time periods after 1947. The *Foreign Affairs Record*, issued monthly, is the most current source for the text of speeches, statements, and agreements disseminated by the government of India.

MIDDLE EAST

1779   Agwani, M. S. *The Lebanese Crisis 1958: A Documentary Record*. New York: Asia Publishing House, 1965.

United States military intervention was a decisive element in the resolution of the severe political conflict experienced by Lebanon in 1958. This reference work offers a selection of Lebanese, Arab, American, and other documents relating to the local, regional, and international aspects of the Lebanese crisis during that period. The valuable compilation was issued under the auspices of the Indian School of International Studies in New Delhi.

1780   Hurewitz, Jacob Coleman. *Diplomacy in the Near and Middle East. A Documentary Record 1914–1956*. Princeton, NJ: Van Nostrand, 1956; New York: Octagon Books, 1972.

A collection of treaties, agreements, memoranda, reports, and other documents that relate to the diplomatic history of Middle Eastern countries during a 40-year period after the outbreak of World War I. Short introductory comments and bibliographies are given for each document.

1781   Magnus, Ralph H. *Documents on the Middle East*. Washington, DC: American Enterprise Institute for Public Policy Research, 1969.

This collection of treaties, diplomatic correspondence, messages, and other documents illustrates the origins of policies, United States relations with Arab states and the Northern tier states, the Palestine problem and the Arab-Israeli dispute, the 1967 war, and other developments in the Middle East.

1782   Moore, John Morton. *The Arab-Israeli Conflict*. Princeton, NJ: Princeton University Press, 1974.

One of the most persistent and explosive challenges to world order is posed by the continuing conflict in the relationship between Israel and certain Arab countries. Intended to promote a better understanding of this conflict this three-volume set presents a number of detailed expositions written by professional experts as well as the texts of the principal documents relating to the dispute. Included documents consist of resolutions, declarations, reports, letters, statements, and other diplomatic outputs. A detailed bibliography of important books and periodical articles dealing with the conflict and its possible settlement is also provided.

SOVIET UNION

1783   Clissold, Stephen. *Soviet Relations with Latin America 1918–1968: A Documentary Survey*. New York: Oxford University Press, 1970.

The documents included in this volume were drawn from a wide range of Soviet and Latin American sources, some of which are readily accessible, others less so. The arrangement is in three sections: (1) Antecedents, (2) The Comintern Period, and (3) War, Cold War, and Peaceful Coexistence. Documents are arranged by country in the last two sections. Most of the documents are press comments, but diplomatic notes, statements, and communiques by Communist parties are also included.

1784   Degras, Jane (Tabrisky). *Soviet Documents on Foreign Policy*. London: Oxford University Press, 1951–1953.

Issued under the auspices of the Royal Institute of International Affairs in London, this three-volume set contains English translations of documents on Soviet foreign relations from 1917 to 1941. The documents are arranged in chronological sequence and refer to all areas of the world. Footnotes identify the primary souce for each document included in the set, but a separate list of sources is printed at the end of each volume. Documents were selected from Russian and non-Russian sources. A comprehensive list of documents from which the items published in this set were selected is to be found in the *Calendar of Soviet Documents on Foreign Policy* (London: Royal Institute of International Affairs, 1948).

1785   Eudin, Xenia J., and Robert C. North. *Soviet Russia and the East, 1920–1927*. Stanford, CA: Stanford University Press, 1957.

1786   Eudin, Xenia J., and Harold H. Fisher. *Soviet Russia and the West, 1920–1927*. Stanford, CA: Stanford University Press, 1957.

1787   Eudin, Xenia J., and Robert M. Slusser. *Soviet Foreign Policy 1928–1934*. University Park: Pennsylvania State University Press, 1966.

These publications contain the text of documents useful for an understanding of the fundamental principles guiding Soviet relations with Asian and Western countries after the First World War. A total of 331 documents is included in the three collections. Most of the documents originated with the Soviet government and consist of official declarations, speeches, statements, letters, reports, and newspaper articles.

1788   Gittings, John. *Survey of the Sino-Soviet Dispute: A Commentary and Extracts from the Recent Polemics, 1963–1967*. London: Oxford University Press, 1968.

1789   Griffith, William. *The Sino-Soviet Rift; Analyzed and Documented*. Cambridge, MA: M.I.T. Press, 1964.

1790   _____. *Sino-Soviet Relations, 1964–1965*. Cambridge, MA: M.I.T. Press, 1967.

The three reference sets illustrate the failure of Soviet foreign policy to change the world's balance of power by maintaining friendly Sino-Soviet relations. Most of the documents are polemical articles from the Russian and Chinese press deepening the Sino-Soviet rift, but there are also resolutions, communiques, letters, and similar items issued by the Communist parties in the Soviet Union, China, and other countries.

1791   Hanak, H. *Soviet Foreign Policy since the Death of Stalin*. London: Routledge & Kegan Paul, 1972.

This collection of Soviet documents contains the text of speeches, interviews, newspaper articles, diplomatic notes, and treaties illustrating the Kremlin's foreign policy toward capitalist, socialist, and Third World countries since the death of Stalin.

1792   Jados, Stanley S. *Documents on Russian-American Relations, Washington to Eisenhower*. Washington, DC: Catholic University of America Press, 1965.

A useful compilation of basic documents illustrating the development of Russian-American relations during more than 150 years. The collection includes acts of Congress, addresses, aide-memoires, agreements, executive orders, letters, messages, notes, press conferences and releases, protocols, and similar items. As a result of the confidential nature of diplomatic exchanges during more recent years, many important documents are not included in the collection. The arrangement of the documents is chronological by presidential administration, with subdivisions for countries or form categories of documents.

1793   Jain, Rajendra. *Soviet-South Asian Relations, 1947–1978*. Atlantic Highlands, NJ: Humanities Press, 1978.

The two-volume set contains a compilation of official Soviet pronouncements and other statements on developments in South Asian countries. An appendix provides data on the Soviet Union's trade in that region.

1794   London. Instytut Historyczny Imienia Generala Sikorskiego. *Documents on Polish-Soviet Relations, 1939–1945*. London: Heineman, 1961.

Since its foundation in 1945, the General Sikorski Historical Institute in London has attempted to collect all available material on the political and military history of Poland. The present set contains a selection of documents from the institute's holdings as well as from British, American, and German sources relating to Soviet policy in Poland during the Second World War. Soviet documentary sources form only a small portion of the set since primary documents from the Soviet Union are scarcely available. Besides originals of hitherto unpublished documents, the set also includes extracts from other document collections.

1795   Moscow. Arkhiv Vneshnei Politiki SSSR. *Dokumenty Vneshnei Politiki SSSR*. Moscow: Izd-vo Politicheskoi Literatury, 1957–.

The Foreign Ministry of the Soviet Union maintains its own archival collections independent from the centralized system of state archives. The ministry's archives remain closed to Western scholars, although selected scholars from Communist bloc countries have been given limited access to certain files. The above title refers to an extensive publication series relating to the period 1917–1933.

1796   Russia. Komissiia po izdaniiu diplomaticheskikh dokumentov. *Correspondence between the Chairman of the Council of Ministers of the USSR and the Presidents of the USA and the Prime Ministers of Great Britain during the Great Patriotic War of 1941–1945*. Moscow: Foreign Language Publishing House, 1957–.

One of the few documentary collections available in English translation directly from the Soviet Union. Most of the documents are previously secret and personal messages transmitted through the embassies in Washington, London, and Moscow.

1797   Sontag, R. J., and J. S. Beddie. *Nazi-Soviet Relations 1939–1941*. Washington, DC: U.S. Department of State, 1948.

1798   *Documents and Materials Relating to the Eve of the Second World War.* Moscow: Foreign Languages Publishing House, 1948.

These document collections illuminate the conduct of Soviet foreign relations prior to the Soviet Union's entry into the Second World War. The first set cited above utilizes material from the archives of the German Foreign Office.

1799   *Vneshniaia Politika Sovetskogo Soiuza: Dokumenty i Materialy, 1945–.* Moscow: Izdatel'stvo Politicheskoi Literatury, 1949–.

1800   *Vneshniaia Politika Sovetskogo Soiuza i Mezhdunarodnye Otnosheniia: Sbornik Dokumentov, 1961–.* Moscow: Izdatel'stvo Instituta Mezhdunarednykh Otnoshenii, 1962–.

These documentary series cover the foreign policy of the Soviet Union after the Second World War.

MISCELLANEOUS

1801   Jacobsen, Hans-Adolf, and Arthur L. Smith, Jr. *World War II. Policy and Strategy. Selected Documents with Commentary.* Santa Barbara, CA: American Bibliographical Center–Clio Press, 1979.

This reference work is the result of an attempt to select from an unmanageable mass of documentation produced during the Second World War some 200 items that offer the best documentation of the war policies and strategies pursued by leading political actors. The documentary material is arranged in 17 parts based on chronological or topical phases of the war. It consists of speeches, directives, diplomatic notes, memoranda, press releases, protocols, treaties and agreements, etc. A glossary, maps and charts, an annotated chronology, and an index are also included in this valuable document collection.

1802   Jankowitsch, Odette, and Karl P. Sauvant. *The Third World without Superpowers: The Collected Documents of the Non-Aligned Countries.* Dobbs Ferry, NY: Oceana Publications, 1978.

1803   Sauvant, Karl P. *The Third World without Superpowers: The Collected Documents of the Group of 77.* Dobbs Ferry, NY: Oceana Publications, 1981.

During the past two decades the developing countries of the Third World have become an important force in world politics and a well-organized international pressure group for the reorganization of the international economic system. The ten volumes of the two sets cited above bring together the documents of the nonaligned countries and the Group of 77, the principal organ of the Third World. Included are the documents of the summit conferences, foreign minister conferences, and other special meetings. For the evolution and organizational structure of the Group of 77 see also Karl P. Sauvant's *The Group of 77, Evolution, Structure, Organization* (Dobbs Ferry, NY: Oceana Publications, 1981).

1804   Kertesz, G. A. *Documents in the Political History of the European Continent 1815–1939.* Oxford: Oxford University Press, 1968.

This collection contains the most important documents about the political developments in Europe from the Congress of Vienna (1815) to the outbreak of World War II. Included are peace treaties, proceedings of congresses and conferences, decrees, laws, proclamations, messages, telegrams, etc.

1805   Plischke, Elmer. *International Relations. Basic Documents.* New York: Van Nostrand, 1962.

The documents found in this collection do not illustrate the foreign policy of a particular country but have been selected to show how important activities or processes in international relations are reflected in specific diplomatic documents. Included are examples of diplomatic and consular credentials, treaty-making documents, documents relating to the recognition of states, territorial acquisitions, neutralization, mutual coexistence, declaration of war, collective sanctions, etc.

1806   Royal Institute of International Affairs. *Documents on International Affairs 1928–1963.* London: Oxford University Press, 1929–1973.

1807   _____ . *Survey of International Affairs 1920–1963.* London: Oxford University Press, 1925–1977.

1808   _____ . *Consolidated Index to the Survey of International Affairs 1920–1938 and Documents on International Affairs 1928–1938.* London: Oxford University Press, 1967.

The aim of the Royal Institute of International Affairs in London, an independent organization founded during the Versailles peace conference in 1919, is to advance the objective study of all aspects of international affairs. Along with three periodicals (*International Affairs, Report on World Affairs,* and *The World Today*) and a yearbook (*The Yearbook of World Affairs*), the Institute has published for many years an annual document collection. The document set contains speeches, letters, statements, communiques, conference resolutions, and similar public pronouncements on significant issues in international relations. A companion set, entitled *Survey of International Affairs,* offered interpretative analyses of international affairs. The consolidated index contains subject and personal name entries.

INTERNATIONAL ORGANIZATIONS

Introduction

States remain the basic units of action in international relations, but a considerable amount of politically significant intersocietal intercourse is conducted by international and multinational organizations. Some of these organizations function as instruments through which national governments pursue their foreign policy goals, and other organizations such as multinational or revolutionary organizations often escape governmental controls. Not surprisingly, it is more difficult to locate adequate information about organizations in the latter category. Brief information and bibliographic listings about the intergovernmental organizations can be found in a number of general reference instruments, but special reference tools exist for the United Nations and several other powerful intergovernmental organizations. The titles listed and described on the following pages complement the listings provided in Section E-1 of the *International Bibliography of the Social Sciences*.

Bibliographies

GUIDEBOOKS

1809   Atherton, Alexine L. *International Organizations. A Guide to Information Sources*. Detroit: Gale Research Company, 1976.

The guidebook identifies reference sources as well as books, periodicals, yearbooks, newspapers, and document collections dealing with international organizations and their work. The entries are partially annotated and arranged under 14 chapters. Some of these chapters are devoted to specific functions of the organizations, such as the struggle for peace and security, promotion of cross-national transactions, economic cooperation, welfare and human rights. Author, title, and subject indexes are provided.

1810   Baer, George W. *International Organizations 1918–1945. A Guide to Research and Research Material*. Wilmington, DE: Scholarly Resources, 1981.

This guidebook is designed to aid scholars doing research on the aims and activities of international organizations during the period from 1918 to 1945. Following a descriptive introductory chapter dealing with the various international organizations then existent, the book offers current information about the appropriate public and private archives, newspaper collections, libraries, and research institutes. The remainder of the book contains unannotated listings for primary and secondary materials arranged by major topics. These include problems of disarmament, major international crises (Manchuria, Ethiopia, etc.), minorities and refugees, social and humanitarian activities, wartime conference diplomacy, as well as general descriptions of the League of Nations, the Permanent Court of International Justice, the International Labour Organization, and other organizations. An index is also included.

CURRENT GENERAL BIBLIOGRAPHIES

1811   *International Bibliography. Publications of Intergovernmental Organizations*. New York: Unipub, 1973– .

The quarterly bibliography identifies publications issued by intergovernmental organizations in 40 subject areas, including commerce and business, communication, culture, development, education, energy, environment, finance, human rights, international economic relations, international law, international relations, labor, nonself-governing peoples, population, relief, social questions, social sciences, and others. All entries are annotated. Address lists of issuing agencies, periodical lists, title and subject indexes are also included.

RETROSPECTIVE GENERAL BIBLIOGRAPHIES

1812   Dimitrov, Theodore D. *World Bibliography of International Documentation*. Pleasantville, NY: Unifo Publishers, 1981.

Closely tied to international organizations, international documentation summarizes existing world knowledge on current world problems for use in global cooperation. Due to the proliferation of international organizations and meetings, the quantity of international documentation has increased dramatically, thereby posing problems of bibliographic control and accessibility.

The primary purpose of this bibliography in two volumes is to list those key publications from international organizations, research institutes, and global scholars that either summarize the structure and work of specific organizations or present information on current worldwide bibliographic or political problems and their solutions. The unannotated entries are arranged in several parts and chapters, entitled (1) International Organizations, Activities, Structure and Information Policies, (2) Bibliographic Control of International Documents, (3) Multilateral Diplomacy and International Relations (world politics, nuclear weapons, international control, disarmament, peace, peacekeeping operations, pacific settlement of international disputes), (4) International Periodicals — Union List, (5) Political Journals and Annuals Reviewing International Problems, and (6) Major International Conferences. Indexes by names of authors, organizations, and corporate bodies, and subject terms are included.

1813   Haas, Michael. *International Organization. An Interdisciplinary Bibliography*. Stanford, CA: Hoover Institution Press, 1971.

1814   Johnson, Harold S., and Baljit Singh. *International Organization. A Classified Bibliography*. East Lansing: Michigan State University, 1969.

Two classified bibliographies exist for tracing the massive scholarly literature published since 1945 about international organizations and their work. The first item lists scholarly books and articles under seven major sections and numerous subdivisions based on the identity or function of the organizations. The second bibliography contains no less than 4,000 entries for books and articles under a similar arrangement. Author and subject indexes offer additional access to the listed material.

1815   Speeckaert, Georges P. *Select Bibliography on International Organization, 1885–1964*. Brussels: Union of International Associations, 1965.

This bibliography will be useful for identifying older publications about the activities of international organizations during the late nineteenth and early twentieth centuries. About 350 publications are listed that deal with international organizations in general, and 730 publications are identified for 214 individual international organizations.

Yearbooks

1816   *The Europa Yearbook*. London: Europa Publications, 1950–.

Part 1 in Volume 1 of this annual two-volume set is devoted to international organizations, their aims and activities. Not every international organization is included, but the significant governmental organizations in all regions of the world are listed and briefly described. Publications issued by the international organizations are also included.

1817   *Statesman's Yearbook*. New York: St. Martin's Press, 1864–.

Part 1 of this yearbook lists international organizations and describes their history, structure, membership, purpose, activities, and publications. A bibliography of books for further information about each organization is also provided.

1818   *Yearbook of International Associations*. Union of International Associations. Brussels: Union of International Associations, 1948–.

1819   *International Associations*. Brussels: Union of International Associations, 1949–.

More than 4,000 governmental and nongovernmental organizations throughout the world are listed and briefly described in this yearbook. The listings are arranged alphabetically by the name of the organization, but several indexes offer additional access to the listings. There is an English and French name index, a classified list based on major activity, a list of acronyms, a subject list, and a geographical index. The descriptive information includes the founding date, aims, structure, finance, membership, present activities, and publications of the organizations. The yearbooks are kept up to date by monthly listings published in *International Associations*.

1820   *Encyclopedia of Associations*. Vol. 4, *International Organizations*. Detroit: Gale Research Company, 1983–.

The encyclopedia contains a separate volume offering detailed information on nonprofit organizations of international scope and membership that are headquartered outside the United States.

Document Collections

1821   Haas, Michael. *Basic Documents of Asian Regional Organizations*. Dobbs Ferry, NY: Oceana Publications, 1974–.

The three-volume set offers the texts of agreements and other documents for political, economic, military, and other international organizations in Asia.

1822   *International Organization and Integration*. Leyden: A. W. Sijthoff, 1968.

Basic documents of Western and Eastern European organizations, Arab, Asian, and African organizations can be found in this reference work. Constitutional documents of the United Nations, its various agencies, and the Organization of American States are also included.

1823   Peaslee, Amos Jenkins. *International Governmental Organizations: Constitutional Documents*. The Hague: Nijhoff, 1974.

This is the standard reference work for the text of the constitutional documents of international organizations created by governments. Where the constitutional document is in a language other than English, a translated text is provided. The documentary text is supported by brief summaries of the origin, history, functions, and membership of the organizations. Bibliographic references offer clues for additional information.

1824   Sohn, Louis B. *Basic Documents of African Regional Organizations*. Dobbs Ferry, NY: Oceana Publications, 1971–.

The four-volume set contains the text of all basic agreements, subsidiary rules of procedure, and other documents of African organizations, such as the Organization of African Unity, the African Development Bank, the Maghreb Permanent Consultative Committee, and others. Extensive bibliographies for supplementary documents, books, articles, and other publications in English and other languages are also provided.

Communist Organizations

It is a noteworthy feature of the international system that Marxist-Leninist parties operate legally or illegally in more than 90 countries of the world. Since a majority of these Communist parties is ideologically strongly committed to the Soviet Union and its political system, Soviet foreign policy is provided with internationally organized support on many crucial issues facing the world. Current assessments of the strengths and weaknesses of the Communist movements throughout the world can be found, along with background and other pertinent information, in the following reference works.

BIBLIOGRAPHIES

1825   Hammond, Thomas Taylor. *Soviet Foreign Relations and World Communism*. Princeton, NJ: Princeton University Press, 1965.

The bibliography lists with annotations more than 7,000 books in 30 languages, arranged in three parts: (1) Soviet foreign relations by chronological periods, (2) Soviet foreign relations and world communism by regions and countries, and (3) special topics.

1826   Sworakowski, Witold S. *The Communist International and Its Front Organizations: A Research Guide and Checklist of Holdings in America and Europe's Libraries*. Stanford, CA: Hoover Institution Press, Stanford University, 1965.

An unannotated list of publications in the Hoover Library and 47 other American and European libraries relating to the Communist Youth International and other front organizations such as the Communist International, the Red International of Labor Unions, etc. The guidebook is extremely useful for locating rare German, Russian, or French books and pamphlets.

YEARBOOKS

1827   U.S. Department of State. *World Strength of the Communist Party Organization*. Washington, DC: 1948 – .

The annual publication presents a survey of Communist party organizations and their activities in an alphabetical arrangement by country. Information is provided about membership size, ideological position, legal status, and principal activities.

1828   *Yearbook on International Communist Affairs*. Stanford, CA: Hoover Institution Press, Stanford University, 1967 – .

The yearbook provides a profile of individual Communist parties in all parts of the world as well as current descriptions of international Communist front organizations. Profiles are arranged by regions and countries and include the following information: founding date, domestic conditions of operation, membership figures, electoral support and government participation, if any, organization and leadership, role of auxiliary movements, domestic political programs and activities, positions on key problems of ideology, strategy and tactics, views on major international issues, orientation within the Marxist-Leninist movement, principal communication media, etc. Excluded are Marxist liberation movements and Marxist ruling parties that specifically disclaim being Communist. The book also contains a chronology of significant events in the various countries as well as an unannotated bibliography of books about Communist organizations and their activities. For a historical background of the various Communist organizations, see also *World Communism, A Handbook 1918 – 1965* (Stanford, CA: Hoover Institution Press, 1973).

European Organizations

In view of the political fragmentation of the European continent, the European international organizations constitute an indispensable political mechanism for effecting cooperation and integration in matters of common interest. Security and defense, control of terrorism, environmental protection, economic development, and human rights conventions are some of the major political goals pursued by the various international organizations or their member states. Access to information about the various European international organizations, their structures, procedures, officials, laws, and activities is presented by several different categories of reference instruments, namely, guidebooks, bibliographies, dictionaries, directories, document collections, handbooks, and yearbooks. The most important titles are listed and described below.

GUIDEBOOKS

1829   Collester, J. Bryan. *The European Communities. A Guide to Information Sources*. Detroit: Gale Research Company, 1979.

Annotated listings for books, doctoral dissertations, and pamphlets about the European Communities and European integration can be found in this bibliography.

Entries are arranged in 10 chapters: (1) Theoretical and Conceptual Studies of Integration and Cooperation, (2) General, Historical and Institutional Studies of Integration, (3) The European Communities, (4) European Communities and Member-State Relations, (5) European Communities and External Relations, (6) European Security, (7) Reference Sources, (8) Guide to Official Publications, (9) Relevant Periodicals, and (10) Recommended Holdings for Small and Private Libraries. Separate author and subject indexes are included.

1830   Jeffries, John. A *Guide to the Official Publications of the European Communities*. New York: Facts on File, 1978.

As a result of international treaties ratified by various European countries during the postwar years, three supranational entities, collectively known as the European Communities, came into being. The guidebook provides a brief history of the European Communities and their institutional organs. It identifies the official publications issued by the Commission (an administrative organ), the Council of Ministers (the cabinet), the European Parliament (the legislative body), the Court of Justice (the judicial organ), and other bodies of the European Communities. Dissemination of the official publications of these international institutions is facilitated by special European documentation centers and depository libraries throughout the world. A list of these is included in an appendix of the guidebook.

1831   Morris, Brian, Peggy Crane, and Klaus Boehm. *The European Community. A Guide for Business and Government*. Bloomington: Indiana University Press, 1981.

The guidebook contains alphabetically arranged entries that offer information on subject matter regulated within the European Communities and on contact points for further inquiries. These contact points include Community institutions, the national governments of Community member states, and industrial, trade union, consumer, and other representative organizations the Community consults. Addresses can be found either in the appropriate entry itself or in a general address section. The subject matter entries offer summary descriptions and figures as well as references to Community publications or relevant organizations. A detailed index is also included.

1832   Wood, David. *The Times Guide to the European Parliament*. London: Times Books, 1979.

In June 1979, 180 million voters in nine West European countries had the opportunity to vote in the world's first election for a multinational parliament that serves as the legislative body of the European Communities. The *Times Guide* presents detailed information on the results of this election, including the political party composition of the new parliament. The book also contains biographies and photographs of the elected members of the parliament as well as their committee assignments. Other chapters in the book describe the powers of the European Parliament, and summarize the main features of party manifestos and the historical development of the European Communities.

BIBLIOGRAPHIES

1833   *EC Index (European Communities Index)*. Maastricht, The Netherlands: Europe Data, 1985–; Bethesda, MD: Congressional Information Service, 1985–.

Published monthly in English and in French with quarterly and annual cumulation, the *EC Index* is the primary access tool for the official documents and other publications of the European communities. It provides complete abstracts coverage as well as indexing by subject, title, issuing source, or number. The abstracts offer analytic, in-depth summaries of some 2,500 documents resulting annually from EC procedural and legislative processes as well as other publications reflecting official policies or assessments of demographic, industrial, and social conditions in the EC member states. Judgments of the Court of Justice and opinions of the Advocates General are also covered.

1834   European Community Information Service. *Catalogue des Publications, 1952–1971*. Washington, DC: 1972.

———. *Publications of the European Communities*. Washington, DC: 1974–.

This monthly bibliography identifies the newly published monographs and series issued by the various institutions of the European Communities. Listings are arranged in three parts: Part 1 provides a subject classification of the titles; Part 2 contains full details of each current Community periodical in an alphabetical arrangement; and Part 3 offers indexes of titles and series. The listed publications are available in several European languages, including English. The retrospective *Catalogue* also includes a subject index.

1835   Gordon, Colin. *The Atlantic Alliance. A Bibliography*. New York: Nichols Publishing Company, 1978.

1836   U.S. Department of Defense. *Nuclear Weapons and NATO: An Analytical Survey of Literature*. Washington, DC: 1975.

1837   U.S. Department of Defense. *Nuclear Weapons and NATO*. Washington, DC: 1970.

The North Atlantic Treaty Organization (NATO) is the permanent organizational structure of the 15-nation Atlantic Alliance designed to promote national security, stability, and well-being in Europe and North America. Over the years its existence has been the object of considerable official, journalistic, and scholarly documentation.

The Gordon bibliography identifies nearly 3,000 English-language titles drawn from British, Canadian, U.S., Scandinavian, and Soviet sources. Listings are arranged to fall under four chronological periods from the late 1940s to 1977. Each period contains a brief historical outline of the main developments in addition to separate listings for books, reports, papers, and articles. These bibliographic listings are presented under five headings that aggregate the cited documentation according to its legal, economic, national and regional, politico-military, and military-strategic aspects. A general bibliographical introduction lists the principal reference sources and official document collections.

The other two bibliographies cited above focus on nuclear weapons and deterrence policies during the first 25 years of NATO's existence.

1838   Kujath, Karl. *Bibliographie zur Europäischen Integration* (Bibliography on European Integration). Bonn: Europa Verlag, 1977.

The bibliography presents classified, annotated listings of scholarly and official publications dealing with the organizational and political aspects of European integration. Specifically covered are community law, community institutions and bodies, common policies and activities, external relations, Council of Europe, Benelux Economic Union, European Free Trade Association, Organization for Economic Cooperation and Development, NATO, and other European organizations.

1839   Organization for Economic Co-operation and Development. *OECD Catalogue of Publications*. Paris: to date.

While European states compose the bulk of its membership, the Organization for Economic Co-operation and Development (OECD) also includes since 1961 five non-European member states, namely, Australia, Canada, Japan, New Zealand, and the United States. Its political objective is the promotion of economic and social welfare throughout the OECD area by assisting member governments in the formulation of appropriate policies.

The frequently revised and updated catalogue is an excellent reference source for identifying important statistical, analytical, and descriptive publications issued by the OECD on a variety of policy matters. Most notable are the publications relating to adjustment policies as a result of the energy crisis, competition policies in regulated sectors of the economy (energy, banking, transport, etc.), inflation control policies, economic growth policies, environmental policies, and others.

1840   *Register of Current Community Legal Instruments*. Luxembourg: Office for Official Publications of the European Communities, 1980—.

Legislation of the European Communities applies not only to all the citizens of the ten member countries, but is important for all organizations that pursue commercial or other interests in the European Community countries. New regulations, decisions, directives, and other legal instruments that supplement, repeal, amend, consolidate, or otherwise affect established laws are published every day in the *Official Journal of the European Communities*. For the identification of the current state of the legislation on any point, use of the reference work cited above is indispensable.

The *Register* is published annually in two volumes: Vol. 1, Information for Readers, Analytical Register; Vol. 2, Chronological Index, and Analytical Index to the Analytical Structure. The analytical register is the subject index that identifies all legal instruments applying to a particular subject area and provides references to their source. The analytical structure is a decimal classification scheme with 17 main headings, each applying to a particular area of Community law, such as social policy, transport policy, competition policy, economic and monetary policy, energy policy, industrial policy, environmental policy, and others. Supplements to the annual editions of the *Register* are published at semiannual intervals.

DICTIONARIES

1841   Parker, Geoffrey, and Brenda Parker. A *Dictionary of the European Communities*. London: Butterworths, 1981.

1842   Paxton, John. A *Dictionary of the European Economic Community*. New York: Facts on File, 1977.

Both dictionaries offer alphabetically arranged entries for organizational units, politicians, policies, or agreements relating to the European Communities.

DIRECTORIES

1843   *Who's Who in European Institutions and Organizations*. Zurich: Who's Who Verlag AG, 1982—.

Over 3,000 biographies of the top administrators, politicians, and other leading personalities working with European institutions and organizations are presented in this biannually revised reference work. An extensive appendix offers current information on the structure, function, and performance of the major political and economic organizations and contains address lists of European institutions and organizations by field of specialization.

DOCUMENT COLLECTIONS

1844   *COM Documents.* Luxembourg: Office for Official Publications of the European Communities, 1983–.

Documents issued by the Commission of the European Communities are the vehicle for initiating Community policy and legislation affecting individuals, companies, associations, and interest groups domiciled in the member states. All publicly available documents are collected in this set, either on microfiche or paper publication. Finding aids include monthly numerical lists and subject indexes, as well as annual cumulative indexes.

HANDBOOKS AND YEARBOOKS

1845   *Euroguide.* Luxembourg: Euroguide International, 1977.

Volume 1 of this multivolume reference set identifies and describes European-based international organizations with member states in Europe or throughout the world. The descriptive information, in English and three other European languages, includes details about the managing bodies, membership, principal aims and activities, publications, etc., of the organizations.

1846   *The European Yearbook.* The Hague: Nijhoff, 1955–.

The annual reference work is aimed at the scientific study of European international organizations and their work. The books provide a chronology of events, lists of members, information on formal decisions, bibliographies, etc. Also included are the text of documents issued by the organizations in French or English versions.

1847   Robertson, A. H. *European Institutions. Cooperation, Integration, Unification.* New York: Matthew Bender, 1973.

A description of the structure and functions of the more important European organizations with some information about their principal activities can be found in this handbook. Specifically described are the Council of Europe, OECD, European Communities, European Free Trade Association, NATO, and others. Appendices contain the texts of the principal treaties, conventions, and resolutions about these organizations.

Multinational Corporations

As a distinct subspecies in the family of international organizations, multinational corporations play an important national and international role that is frequently misunderstood by the general public as well as the policy-makers in many governments throughout the world. Many developing countries, for instance, have been brought to severe financial and economic hardships by misconceived development policies that shunned comparatively inexpensive development by multinational companies in favor of expensive foreign bank credits for state-owned or privately owned national enterprises. Other countries have curtailed the role of well-established multinational corporations for short-term price and revenue advantages that ultimately resulted in greatly increased risks of a social, economic, or military nature. Several countries have, however, used multinational corporations successfully for positive employment effects, efficient import substitution, increased export competitiveness, and other political benefits while neutralizing most of the concomitant negative side effects inherent in such economic policies. Not unexpectedly, therefore, the literature on multinational corporations is substantial and controversial. The following reference works offer bibliographic access or summary information in respect of multinational corporations, their role and activities.

BIBLIOGRAPHIES

1848   *Bibliography on Transnational Corporations.* New York: United Nations, 1979.

The bibliography lists books, dissertations, periodical articles, and conference proceedings dealing with multinational corporations, their investments, contracts, technology transfers, restrictive business or corrupt practices, and industrial activity. Its geographic coverage is worldwide. The bibliography is a product of the Information Analysis Division of the UN Center on Transnational Corporations in New York, which will undertake searches on request by special arrangement.

1849   Browndorf, Eric, and Scott Riemer. *Bibliography of Multinational Corporations and Foreign Direct Investments.* Dobbs Ferry, NY: Oceana Publications, 1978–.

The loose-leaf and updated volume contains more than 10,000 citations to English-language publications issued since 1970 on multinational corporations and foreign investments. Entries are grouped into four sections: (1) books, manuscripts and government publications on the activities of multinational corporations throughout the world, (2) periodical articles on the same topic, (3) case studies of foreign investment in specific countries, (4) studies about American multinational corporations operating in foreign countries.

1850   Burtis, David, et al. *Multinational Corporation — Nation-State Interaction. An Annotated Bibliography.* Philadelphia: Foreign Policy Research Institute, 1973.

1851   Hernes, Helga. *The Multinational Corporation*. Detroit: Gale Research Company, 1977.

The two annotated bibliographies identify a portion of the literature about the national and international relations of multinational corporations. The first item offers more than 700 entries for books and articles under a classified arrangement. English as well as foreign-language material is listed. The second bibliography lists books and articles arranged under three parts and 20 chapters, as follows: Part I, The Multinational Corporation as a Large Organization; Part II, The Multinational Corporation and the Nation State; Part III, Role of the Multinational Corporation in the International System. Separate chapters cover corporate relations with national governments, the impact on labor, the technology factor, the role of the multinational corporation in the international economy, the control of resources, and other related topics. Also included is a list of periodicals that are likely to contain information about multinational corporations. Separate author, title, and subject indexes are also provided for the listed material.

1852   Lall, Sanjaya. *Foreign Private Manufacturing Investment and Multinational Corporations*. New York: Praeger Publications, 1975.

In its 16 chapters the bibliography presents annotated entries for books, periodical articles, and official publications focusing on causes, determinants, and effects of foreign private investment, Marxist analyses of foreign investments, government policies on foreign investment, legal problems of foreign investment, restrictive practices and conflicts, and other topics in international economic relationships. Also included are area studies for developed and less-developed countries.

1853   Sagafi-nejad, Tagi, and Robert Belfield. *Transnational Corporations, Technology Transfer and Development*. A *Bibliographic Sourcebook*. New York: Pergamon Press, 1980.

The bibliography focuses on the important role that multinational corporations play in the needed transfer of technology from the home country to host countries, notably from highly developed industrialized countries to less-developed countries. Publications are listed without annotations by author under eight chapters, entitled: (1) The Setting: Science and Technology in Development, (2) The International Technology Gap and the NIEO, (3) Transnational Corporations and Technology, (4) The Anatomy of Corporate Technology Transfer: Modes, Costs and Management, (5) Technology Transfer and Host Countries: Appropriateness, Dependency and Sovereignty, (6) Sectoral Analysis: Technology Transfer Case Studies, (7) Technology Transfer and the Home Country, and (8) Regulating Technology Transfer: Control Systems and Mechanisms. Introductory headnotes

precede the bibliographic listings in each chapter. There is no country or subject index, but an author index is included.

DIRECTORIES

1854   Stopford, John M. *The World Directory of Multinational Enterprises*. Detroit: Gale Research Company, 1980 –.

The directory describes the 500 largest industrial corporations in the world that together control well over 80 percent of the total stock of foreign direct investment. Excluded are firms in banking, insurance, commodity broking, retailing and other service industries. Arranged alphabetically by company name, each profile identifies the principal subsidiaries in each country and offers summary information on the parent company, including addresses, names of directors, product lines, sales and financial performance data, major shareholders, historical background, and current situation. Two separate indexes identify companies by country and industry. Updating editions are published irregularly.

Organization of American States

The Organization of American States (OAS) was founded in 1948 to foster peace, mutual understanding, and cooperation among the nations of the western hemisphere. The scope of the OAS activities has expanded gradually over the years, with increasing attention also being devoted to the protection of individual human rights. In 1979, an Inter-American Court of Human Rights was established in San Jose, Costa Rica, with similar responsibilities as its European counterpart. Although its membership has now grown to 31 states, the organization was ineffective in recent years in maintaining peace in the western hemisphere, as the conflicts over the Falkland Islands, Grenada, and various Central American republics demonstrated. Further details about the activities of the OAS and its officials are retrievable from the following reference publications.

BIBLIOGRAPHIES

1855   Pan American Union. Columbus Memorial Library. *Indice Analytico y Lista General de los Documentos Oficiales de la OEA*. Washington, DC: 1960 –.

1856   _____ . *List of Books Accessioned and Periodical Articles Indexed in the Columbus Memorial Library*. Washington, DC: 1950 –.

1857   Pan American Union. General Secretariat of the OAS. *Catalog of Publications*. Washington, DC: n.d.

1858 _____ . *International Review of Bibliography*. Washington, DC: 1951 – .

The Pan American Union is the central organ of the OAS and also acts as the permanent General Secretariat. The Union's Columbus Memorial Library maintains, for purposes of public inspection and interlibrary loans, a sizable collection of official, scholarly, and other publications relating to the American states and the work of the organization. The monthly accession list of the library features a separate bibliography of the official documents of the OAS and the publications of the Pan American Union. Semiannual and annual indexes to the official documentation of the OAS are also issued. The publications of the OAS and its specialized organizations are also listed in an irregularly issued catalog and in the quarterly periodical *Inter-American Review of Bibliography*.

OTHER REFERENCE WORKS

1859 Pan American Union. *Organization of American States, a Handbook*. Washington, DC: 1977.

1860 _____ . *Organization of American States. Directory*. Washington, DC: 1951 – .

These reference publications are useful for identifying the organization structure of the OAS, its principal activities, and its officials.

Organization of Petroleum Exporting Countries

One of the most effective international organizations to emerge in recent years is the Organization of Petroleum Exporting Countries (OPEC), founded in 1960 by an international treaty registered with the United Nations in 1962, under no. 6363. The organization has achieved a leading but by no means universally accepted position due to the fact that its 13 member states control cheap and presently abundant fossil fuel resources while many industrial and developing countries* have so far been unable to pay for the high costs of the OPEC-controlled petroleum imports without devaluing their currencies. The organization seeks, in consultation and cooperation with the other countries of the world, the establishment of a new economic order** and has inspired, through the *Solemn Declaration*, the birth of the Conference on International Economic Cooperation (CIEC) — otherwise

---

*A notable exception is the Republic of South Africa, a country without any petroleum resources, which presently utilizes oil imports for less than 20 percent of its total energy needs, with prospects of becoming a net exporter of alternatively produced energy within the coming decade.

**Organization of the Petroleum Exporting Countries, *Information Booklet* (Vienna: 1977), p. 2. The term itself originated during the sixth Special Meeting of the U.N. General Assembly in 1974. It means a major restructuring of the present international trading and monetary system.

---

known as the North-South dialogue — between 19 developing countries and 8 major industrialized nations.

The following publications, obtainable from the Public Relations Department of the Organization of the Petroleum Exporting Countries in Vienna, Austria, offer a more detailed insight into the activities and policies involving OPEC member countries and their client states.

DIGESTS

1861 *OPEC Bulletin. Weekly Digest of World Press*. Vienna: Organization of Petroleum Exporting Countries, 1970 – .

The digest offers a selection of news and articles on energy and economics published in periodicals and newspapers throughout the world. Many of the articles deal with governmental policies. The news briefs are arranged under names of countries. The text of press releases issued by OPEC organs can also be found in the digest.

DOCUMENT COLLECTIONS

1862 OPEC. *Proceedings of the OPEC Seminar*. Vienna, 1977 – .

1863 OPEC. *Official Resolutions and Press Releases 1960 – 1980*. Oxford: Pergamon Press, 1981.

The present and future roles of the national oil companies and the options for global energy and development strategies are discussed in seminars held by the Organization of Petroleum Exporting Countries. Details of the work of the organization during its first 20 years of existence are reflected in a document collection offering the text of official resolutions and press releases.

1864 OPEC. *Selected Documents of the International Petroleum Industry*. Vienna: 1968 – .

A number of separate volumes have been issued at annual or irregular intervals that present significant documents relating to the petroleum industry in specific countries or throughout the world.

1865 *OPEC Review*. Vienna: Organization of the Petroleum Exporting Countries, 1977 – .

Recent issues of this quarterly publication contain a documentation section that presents statistical tables and graphs about oil production and economic development activities of the OPEC member countries. Also included are the full text and abstracts of articles about pricing and production policies pursued or contemplated by OPEC or its member states.

YEARBOOKS

1866 OPEC. *Annual Report*. Vienna: 1966 – .

Previously issued under the title *Annual Review and Record*, this annual publication presently reviews, in an expanded and revised format, the general situation in the world and in the OPEC countries. It surveys the main developments affecting the production and consumption of hydrocarbons and summarizes the activities of the OPEC Secretariat. Appendices contain statistical data, resolutions and press releases, and a list of the member countries' representatives.

1867 The OPEC Special Fund. *Annual Report*. Vienna: 1976—.

As part of its efforts to help establish the New International Economic Order, the OPEC Special Fund, established in 1976, supports new institutions and contributions to the development of new policies affecting the Third World. Presently endowed with more than $1.6 billion, the fund provides financial assistance on highly concessional terms to other developing countries. The annual reference work summarizes the activities of the OPEC Special Fund and presents concise information on the financial support granted individual countries of the Third World.

United Nations

A unique place in the study of international organizations is reserved for the United Nations Organization as a result of the magnitude of its activities and size or variety of its documentation output. The documentation of the United Nations consists of mimeographed and printed items that are made available through a comparatively small network of depository libraries in the United States and other countries. A list of these depository libraries is published in *UNDEX, United Nations Document Index*. Many other libraries also have sizable collections of United Nations publications either as part of the regularly cataloged material or arranged separately under the United Nations document symbols system.

The retrieval of information about the United Nations and its activities is facilitated by numerous reference instruments that make it possible to identify

- each UN document symbol by organ, nature of the document, subject, or country
- the country position on a particular political topic or object
- the political directives or action in the form of votes and resolutions
- the speeches, statements, and reports supporting or rejecting a particular political objective, by country, topic, or speaker
- member names of UN delegations and committees
- biographical information about UN officials
- basic laws, agreements, and rules of procedure governing the operation of the United Nations

- summaries of UN activities, and other UN-related information

Many of the functions presently carried out by the organs and subsidiary organs of the United Nations were originally begun by the League of Nations. The following list of the principal reference instruments for the United Nations therefore also includes a guidebook for the documentation of the League of Nations.

GUIDEBOOKS

1868 Aufricht, Hans. *Guide to League of Nations Publications*. New York: AMS Press, 1966.

The guidebook offers a detailed listing and description of the League of Nations publications from 1920 to 1947. Specifically covered are the Covenant and amendments, as well as the documentation of the principal organs and related agencies. League of Nations documents are available on microfilm from Research Publications, New Haven, Connecticut.

1869 Birchfield, Mary Eva. *The Complete Reference Guide to United Nations Sales Publications 1946—1978*. Pleasantville, NY: Unifo Publishers, 1982.

1870 *United Nations Publications in Print*. New York: Unipub, 1973—.

United Nations documents are frequently issued as sales publications if the information is of public interest with more than a minimal sales potential. Sales publications are issued in 22 numbered subject categories that include economics, economic development, world economy, African, Asian, European, or Latin American economy, social questions, international law, political and Security Council questions, international administration, human rights, public finance, international statistics, and others. Most sales publications bear a symbol called the sales number. It indicates the language of the publication, planned issue date, subject category, and item number.

The Birchfield guide offers a key to the sales publications issued during more than 30 years. Volume 1 of the guide identifies the sales publications in alphabetical sequence of UN document symbols, listing the title and sales number of each item. It also contains a list of sales publications in print (as of 1981), arranged in numerical sequence of the subject categories. Volume 2 offers keyword in context (KWIC), title, and sales number indexes.

UN sales publications that are currently in print can be identified in an annual checklist, entitled *United Nations Publications in Print*. Entries are arranged in numerical sequence of the subject categories and include prices as well as other ordering information.

1871   Fetzer, Mary K. *United Nations Documents and Publications. A Research Guide*. New Brunswick, NJ: Rutgers University Graduate School of Library Service, 1978.

1872   Hajnal, Peter I. *Guide to United Nations Organization, Documentation and Publishing*. Dobbs Ferry, NY: Oceana Publications, 1978.

1873   Winton, Harry, N. M. *Publications of the United Nations System. A Reference Guide*. Ann Arbor, MI: R. R. Bowker, 1972.

Three separate but complementary guidebooks offer practical hints and descriptive details for the use of United Nations publications. The Winton guidebook is arranged in three parts, namely, (1) The Organizations of the United Nations System and Their Publications, (2) Selected Reference Publications of the United Nations System, and (3) Periodicals of the United Nations System. Part 1 provides brief information on each agency, such as headquarters address, principal aims, number of member states, organization structure, and availability of publications. It lists all catalogs, bibliographies, indexes, and other reference publications of or about the agency. Part 2 is an annotated list of reference publications divided into 29 subject areas and including primarily statistical compendia, directories, collections of laws and treaties, dictionaries, bibliographies, etc. Part 3 is an annotated list of some 300 periodicals with information about the agency, frequency, beginning date, language of publication, etc. There is also a subject index to the selected reference publications and periodicals. The guidebook is kept up to date by entries in *International Bibliography, Information and Documentation*, a quarterly publication of the R. R. Bowker Company. Similar guidance with more recent coverage and different textual arrangement is provided by the other two guidebooks cited above. They identify primary and secondary sources of information about the United Nations.

INDEXES

1874   United Nations. Dag Hammarskjold Library. *Indexes to the Proceedings of the United Nations*. New York: 1946–; Millwood, NY: Kraus Reprint Company, 1973.

Four separate indexes exist in original print or reprint form for the proceedings and documentation of the principal organs of the United Nations, namely the General Assembly, the Security Council, the Economic and Social Council, and the Trusteeship Council. Each index volume has two sections, a subject index and a speech index. The latter identifies speech documents by country, speaker, and topic. The subject index identifies resolutions, reports, summary reports, voting records, and other documentation under standard subject headings. References refer to the printed record of the proceedings, issued as *Official Records* of each organ. No indexing is available for Security Council proceedings during the years 1950 to 1963, and listings for the proceedings of the Trusteeship Council and the Economic and Social Council during many years are taken from sections of the *Checklist of United Nations Documents* and *Disposition of Agenda Items*, which are the only indexes available.

1875   United Nations. Dag Hammarskjold Library. *List of United Nations Documents Series Symbols*. New York: United Nations, 1970.

This reference work may be of interest to researchers using libraries that shelve United Nations material in book- or microform by document symbol. UN document symbols consist of leading and secondary elements. The leading elements encompass a single letter or series of letters denoting the identity of the principal organs, such as A/- for General Assembly, ST/- for Secretariat, etc. The secondary elements follow the leading elements and denote subsidiary organs, the nature of the document and text modifications. Examples are -/AC.../- for Ad hoc committee, -/SR... for summary records, or -/Amend... for amendments. The book contains a list of all series symbols and a subject index to the symbols.

1876   United Nations. Dag Hammarskjold Library.

UNDI: United Nations Documents Index, 1950–1973.

UNDEX: United Nations Documents Index, 1974–1978.

UNDOC: Current Index, 1979–.
    New York: United Nations, 1950–.

1877   *UNBIS. United Nations Bibliographic Information System*. New York: United Nations, 1979–.

Official documents and sales publications issued by the United Nations since 1950 are identifiable by a printed index set that has undergone changes in title and arrangement over the years. Its current version, entitled *UNDOC*, is issued ten times a year with annual cumulations. Each issue contains a checklist of documents and publications with full bibliographic description arranged in alphanumeric order by series symbol and by session, as well as a list of official records arranged by Official Record designator, and a list of sales publications arranged by sales number. Separate author, title, and subject indexes are also included. The subject index lists names of countries as separate headings or subdivisions of other headings. The printed indexes are a product of *UNBIS*, an online database that is not yet available through the facilities of commercial vendors, but is accessible to outside qualified researchers in addition to official users within the United Nations organizations and their member governments.

1878 United Nations Industrial Development Organization, Vienna. *Industrial Development Abstracts*. New York: 1971 – .

This reference set supplements the previously listed indexes with specialized listings and descriptions of documentation on industrialization in developing countries. Indexed and abstracted are documents for the Industrial Development Board, reports and proceedings of expert working groups, workshops, and seminars, internal studies, feasibility studies, and similar published or unpublished documentation. Full bibliographic information, including the document symbol, is given for each listed document in addition to a brief summary of its contents. Author and subject indexes offer access to the documents, which may be obtained from UN offices in New York, Geneva, and Vienna. Most of the documents identify the governmental machinery and policies needed or already made available for the industrial development.

1879 *United Nations Publications, Periodic Checklist*. New York: United Nations, 1967 – .

Publications available from the United Nations are listed and indexed in this quarterly reference work. The indexes offer access to the listed items by subject, title, and sales numbers. Cumulative listings, entitled Catalog, are also published at irregular intervals for varying periods of time.

OTHER BIBLIOGRAPHIES

1880 Hüfner, Klaus, and Jens Naumann. *Zwanzig Jahre Vereinte Nationen: Internationale Bibliographie, 1945–1965* (Twenty Years United Nations: International Bibliography, 1945–1965). Berlin: de Gruyter, 1968.

1881 _____ . *The United Nations System – International Bibliography, 1965–1970*. Munich: Verlag Dokumentation, 1978.

1882 _____ . *The United Nations System – International Bibliography, 1971–1975*. Munich: Verlag Dokumentation, 1979.

The United Nations organization and its activities have been the subject of an enormous literature. The bibliographies cited above list no less than 13,300 books and other publications in English, French, and German for the first 30 years of the UN existence. Entries are arranged in subject categories that cover interpretations of the Charter, membership in the United Nations, UN diplomacy, problems of disarmament, process of decolonization, and human rights. An author index is included.

1883 Legault, Albert. *Peace-Keeping Operations. Bibliography*. Paris: International Information Center on Peace-Keeping Operations, World Veterans Federation, 1968.

The bibliography offers descriptive reviews of books, periodical articles, unpublished dissertations, reports, and some government documents dealing with various aspects of United Nations peace-keeping operations. The material is arranged alphabetically by author, but there is also a separate list by subject. The latter uses 27 subject headings, such as background of the conflicts, authorization of operations, objectives and performance of the operations, financing, host state relations, participating states agreements, political and executive control, military control, personnel and administration, applications of the laws of war, operational techniques, communications, permanent force proposals, etc.

HANDBOOKS AND YEARBOOKS

This section does not offer a comprehensive list of all yearbooks or handbooks issued by the United Nations, since many of these annual reference publications cover narrow categories of information, such as statistical, legal, or economic information. Many pertinent titles can therefore be found in other, more appropriate sections of this guidebook. The following list, consequently, includes only those reference works whose scope is of a more general nature.

1884 *Annual Review of United Nations Affairs*. Dobbs Ferry, NY: Oceana Publications, 1949 – .

This annual publication provides an introduction by the United Nations secretary-general to his annual report on the work of the United Nations. Also included are various messages, resolutions, addresses, communiques, etc., that relate to specific activities of the United Nations.

1885 Ku, Min-Chuan. *A Comprehensive Handbook of the United Nations*. New York: Monarch Press, 1978.

The handbook, in two volumes, contains the text of the basic laws, rules, and regulations dealing with substantive and procedural matters of all organs of the United Nations and its affiliated agencies. The material is organized in eight parts and a bibliography, as follows: Part I covers background information that led to the adoption of the Charter of the United Nations. Part II contains the basic laws, agreements, and statutes through which the United Nations operates. Part III lists the rules of procedure of the principal UN organs. Part IV describes the specialized agencies and their basic laws and agreements. Part V enumerates all nongovernmental organizations that have relations with the United Nations. Part VI describes the status of trust territories and trusteeship agreements. Part VII covers regional agencies and regional agreements. Part VIII contains important UN resolutions arranged under five categories. The bibliography consists mainly of projects, plans, and ideas for an ideal international organization resulting from research and study in universities.

1886   United Nations. Office of Public Information. *Yearbook of the United Nations*. New York: 1946–.

Issued with a delay of approximately three years, this annual reference book describes, with documentary citations, the proceedings and activities of the United Nations during a 12-month period. The information is presented in two parts, namely, (1) United Nations, and (2) Intergovernmental organizations related to the United Nations. Part 1 is subdivided into political and security questions, economic and social questions, questions relating to trust and nonself-governing territories, legal questions, and administrative and budgetary questions. A detailed subject index and index of names are included. The yearbook is kept up to date by the *United Nations Monthly Chronicle*.

DIRECTORIES

1887   *Delegations to the United Nations*. New York: United Nations, 1946–.

The annually published directory lists the names of all persons who serve as delegates of the member states to the General Assembly and other organs of the United Nations.

1888   *Directory of United Nations Information Systems*. Geneva: Inter-Organization Board for Information Systems, 1980.

The directory is intended to tell users what information systems and services are provided to the general public or to a specialized public by the United Nations family of organizations. More than 300 information systems, such as libraries, bibliographic systems, referral centers, clearing houses, information analysis centers, and data banks are described in volume 1 of the two-volume set. The description includes the address of the system, its subject scope, geographic coverage, working languages, access conditions, and other details. Volume 2 — printed in a single trilingual version — gives by country the addresses of United Nations organizations, UN information centers, input centers or contact points, and depository libraries where collections of United Nations publications can be found. When available, holdings data

for books, serials, and conference papers are given separately for each of the organizations within the United Nations family of organizations. Separate listings of UN symbols and organizations' acronyms are also included, as well as a subject index.

1889   *Who's Who in the United Nations and Related Agencies*. New York: Arno Press, 1975.

The biographical entries in this directory include the name, position or title, business, residence address and telephone number, nationality, languages spoken, date and place of birth, marital status, career positions, education, professional interests, publications, awards or honors, and avocational interests. Persons included are Secretariat staff members, members of permanent missions in New York and Geneva, members of the International Court of Justice, members on major commissions and committees, as well as representatives or officials of related associations. The directory also contains an organizational roster, a list of UN installations around the world, a list of the permanent missions in New York and Geneva, a list of the principal officials of the United Nations from 1946 to 1974, a list of UN depository libraries, addresses of member UN associations, and an index to the biographical listings by nationality.

DOCUMENT COLLECTIONS

1890   Djonovich, Dusan J. *United Nations Resolutions*. Dobbs Ferry, NY: Oceana Publications, 1972.

The multivolume set contains four series of resolutions together with supplementary documents and voting records for the General Assembly, the Security Council, the Economic and Social Council, and the Trusteeship Council. Resolutions and documents are photographically reproduced from the originals and arranged in chronological order. Each series includes subject indexes and cross-references for all related resolutions.

1891   *United Nations Documents and Official Records*. New York: Readex Microprint Corporation, 1946–.

The mimeographed and printed documents of the United Nations, including the official records of the four principal organs and several other bodies, are made available in microprint in this ongoing document collection. Included are the documents of all committees, commissions, and conferences connected with the main organs, but the documents of the UN Secretariat will be missing unless they carry, as they often do, the document symbol of the General Assembly or some other UN organ. Although the collection is periodically updated, there is a publication delay of many months.

Chapter 5

Comparative and Area Studies
of Politics and Government

INTRODUCTION

The reference literature described on the following pages serves as the information retrieval mechanism for comparative and area studies in politics and government. For the most part the existing bibliographies, handbooks, and other reference publications are organized spatially or geographically and are comparative in name only. With some notable exceptions, the accepted units for bibliographic coverage are works on individual countries, which are described and analyzed in purely intranational terms and concepts. To some extent this disappointing bibliographic situation reflects a gap in the scholarly literature that until recently has rarely used cross-national comparisons for analysis. Most of the scholarly literature concentrates on the institutional and behavioral aspects of a single country and leaves it up to the reader to discover similarities and differences among several societies, countries, or regions. Comparative government and politics is, however, a distinct subfield of political science that is unique because it has a methodological instead of a substantive label. The primary purpose of this methodological subfield is the scientific comparison of political ideas, processes, objects, and policies as well as institutional actors, even though there is no general agreement among political scientists concerning the correct methods of such comparisons. An increasing number of studies has appeared in recent years that provides a cross-national or diachronical comparison of innumerable social and political variables and indicators.

Bibliographic control of truly comparative works, however, is still inadequate, and many comparative studies remain buried among the noncomparative works listed in most bibliographic instruments. For example, there is no specific subheading "Comparative Studies" under any of the political subject headings in the *Library of Congress Subject Catalog* or other library catalogs based exclusively on Library of Congress cards. The general heading "Comparative Government" and the heading "Social Sciences — Comparative Studies" are too broad to properly identify comparative literature. Most of the comparative information, therefore, has to be extracted from regional or area studies bibliographies and handbooks through judicious use of clues provided by arrangement, titles listed, or index subject entries. In addition, those bibliographies that focus on such concepts as development, change, and population policies permit quick identification of comparative information. Regrettably, many other useful concepts, such as comparative response to multisectarian or multiethnic conflicts (South Africa, Yugoslavia, Northern Ireland, Lebanon, Nigeria, etc.), small country response to ideological or big power challenges (Korea, Vietnam, Austria, Germany, etc.), or government policy response to economic challenges (unemployment, energy shortage, inflation, monetary

devaluation, trade imbalances, etc.) have yet to be bibliographically treated. The bibliographic paucity in connection with information about political differentiation, similarity, and identity across national or chronological boundaries stands in odd contrast to the wealth of bibliographic instruments for national studies.

Each of the major continental areas of the world has a more or less developed set of reference instruments consisting of library catalogs, guidebooks, current bibliographies, retrospective bibliographies, document collections, and handbooks. Although no single reference work is exhaustive, the totality of the various regional reference publications comes close to offering a comprehensive inventory by author, title, and subject of the available information for each country of the world. Minor quantitative and qualitative differences and gaps persist, however, in this bibliographic retrieval mechanism. The bibliographic instruments for Africa south of the Sahara, for instance, are currently much better than those available for Western Europe, which continues to be neglected bibliographically.

The following pages contain listings for multiregional and regional reference instruments as well as a selective list of reference aids for biographical, legal, official, and statistical information.

MULTIREGIONAL OR WORLDWIDE SOURCES

Guidebooks

1892   Kennedy, James R., Jr., et al. *Guide to Reference Sources on Africa, Asia, Latin America and the Carribbean, Middle East and North Africa, and Russia and East Europe: Selected and Annotated.* Williamsport, PA: Bro-Dart Publishing Company, 1972.

The guidebook lists and describes bibliographies, handbooks, directories, and other reference works available for the study of areas other than Western Europe and North America. Entries are arranged by region, country, or subject. Separate author and title indexes are also provided. The guidebook is issued as an occasional publication (#17) of the Foreign Area Materials Center, State University of New York, which has also compiled bibliographies for East Asia, South Asia, South East Asia, the Middle East, and North Africa.

Current Bibliographies

1893   American Universities Field Staff. A *Select Bibliography: Asia, Africa, Eastern Europe, Latin America.* New York: American Universities Field Staff, Inc., 1960.

_____ . *Supplements*. New York: 1961 – .

The American Universities Field Staff (AUFS) is a nonprofit organization sponsored and financially supported by a number of universities and colleges in the United States. Staff associates of AUFS are chosen for their knowledge and personal experience in a particular area. They spend about 18 months out of every three years at their foreign post to observe and to analyze developments in the countries of Asia, Africa, Latin America, and Eastern Europe. Research results are published in books, articles and in various geographic series under the common title *Reports from Foreign Countries*. The individual items in the series are indexed in *Public Affairs Information Service Bulletin*.

The cited bibliography was prepared by AUFS scholars who listed what they regarded as the most helpful books and periodical articles for the college-level study of civilization in the various foreign areas. The arrangement of the entries is by major geographic area, divided into country sections and subdivided by subject. Titles that the compilers recommend for first consideration comprise about 10 percent of the total list and are identified by the letter A. Another 20 percent of the entries are considered of second priority and carry the letter B. All the A and B entries are briefly annotated. Separate author and title indexes are also provided.

1894   "Bibliography of Periodicals and Monographs." In *Journal of Developing Areas*. Macomb: Western Illinois University, 1966– .

The major industrialized nations, with a quarter of the world's population, still control three-quarters of the wealth, 95 percent of all research and development, and more than 90 percent of the world's industry. The modernization and development of the political, economic, and social infrastructure in the countries of the Third World constitutes therefore one of the most pressing problems of our times.

Each quarterly issue of the *Journal of Developing Countries* contains a bibliography that lists recent periodical articles and monographs dealing with the political, economic, and other problems of developing countries. All entries are unannotated and are arranged alphabetically by author under broad geographic headings.

1895   *International Bibliography of Political Science*. Paris: UNESCO, 1954–1961; Chicago: Aldine Publishing Company, 1962– .

This annual bibliography provides excellent access to comparative studies published in books and periodicals throughout the world. Comparative studies are listed separately from national studies under several sections within the main subject heading Political Systems (C.22, C.310, C.320, C.330, C.340, C.40, C.50, C.520, C.620, C.70, C.80) and Governmental Process (D.20).

No annotations are provided.

1896   "Recent Studies in Comparative Politics: An Annotated Listing." In *Comparative Political Studies*. Beverly Hills, CA: Sage Publications, 1968– .

The annotated listings in the quarterly periodical are intended to alert the scholar to recently published books and periodical articles in comparative politics. The entries are arranged alphabetically by author. Many of the works cited are not truly comparative, however, and deal with political phenomena in one country only.

1897   Universal Reference System. *Comparative Government and Cultures*. Princeton, NJ: Princeton Research Publishing Company, 1968– .

Volume 10 of the URS base set is an annotated bibliography of 3,466 titles intensively indexed according to the Grazian system of topical and methodological descriptors. The book can be used to identify 272 annotated bibliographies and 573 unannotated bibliographies of 50 items or more dealing with the subject matter of comparative government and cultures. The volume also contains 705 entries for political parties, 161 entries for political processes, 210 entries for local government, and 445 entries for nationalism. Books and articles can also be geographically identified, although the largest number of entries (342) refer to the Soviet Union. Politically active ethnic groups or minorities are only occasionally identified in the index or represented by pertinent publications in the bibliography, but a total of 406 items refers to intergroup relations and 244 items to power-dominant groups. The base volume is updated by yearly supplements to the entire URS set.

Retrospective Bibliographies

1898   Ashford, Douglas E., Peter J. Katzenstein, and T. J. Pempel. *Comparative Public Policy: A Cross-National Bibliography*. Beverly Hills, CA: Sage Publications, 1978.

Publications issued during the past two decades about policy making and specific policy issues in Great Britain, France, West Germany, Japan, and the United States are recorded in this annotated bibliography. The listed items are arranged under eight chapters, entitled Administrative Reform, Economic Management, Local and Regional Reorganization, Labor Relations, Race Migration, Social Security, Higher Education, Science and Technology. An appendix identifies official sources of current policy information.

1899   Beck, Carl, and J. Thomas McKechnie. *Political Elites: A Select Computerized Bibliography*. Cambridge, MA: M.I.T. Press, 1968.

In all large-scale societies, the key political, social, and economic decisions are made by tiny minorities or elites. This unannotated bibliography provides an extensive account of the scholarly literature published in books and periodicals from 1945 to 1967 on the subject of elite behavior in all parts of the world. The bibliography is organized in three parts. The first part is a KWOC (keyword out of context) title listing of books and articles with reference codes to a complete citation listing found in Part 2. The third part is a list of authors. The citation listings in Part 2 also include acronyms for classifying each study according to its relevance to one or more of the following topics of elite analysis: (1) GNELTH — general elite theory; (2) DEFEL — definition of elite groups or elite concepts; (3) COMEL — social and political composition of elites; (4) ELEL — structural and behavioral relationships between elites; (5) ELNOEL — structural and behavioral relations between political elites and non-elites; (6) ELPRNOR — elite perceptions, norms, and attitudes; and (7) METEL — methodology of elite analysis. Publications relating to elite behavior in specific countries are identifiable in the KWOC listings under the name of the country.

1900   Bergquist, Charles W. *Alternative Approaches to the Problems of Development: A Selected and Annotated Bibliography*. Durham, NC: Caroline Academic Press, 1979.

Since the way one understands a problem structures the solutions one proposes to deal with it, the distinction between two different schools of thought relating to problems of development in the Third World is important. Separate prescriptions are advocated by the modernization school and the alternative or Third World school.

The bibliography offers 35 critical annotations for books and articles by the major contributors to the alternative perspective of development theory. The listings include works containing critiques of the modernization theory, as well as publications dealing with the alternative approach to problems of dependency, foreign aid, imperialism, multinational corporations, world capitalism, etc. Entries are arranged by author, but a separate subject index is included.

1901   Bloomfield, Valerie. *Commonwealth Elections 1945–1970. A Bibliography*. Westport, CT: Greenwood Press, 1976.

The Commonwealth provides an area of exceptional interest for the comparative study of elections and political parties. This bibliography identifies unpublished sources, official publications, electoral studies in book or periodical form, and political party documents for over 760 elections held in the various member countries of the Commonwealth during a 25-year period until 1970. Entries are arranged by regions, countries, and provinces in chronological sequence of election dates. An author and name index is included.

1902   Carnell, Francis. *The Politics of the New States: A Select Annotated Bibliography with Special Reference to the Commonwealth*. London: Institute of Commonwealth Studies, 1961.

1903   Frey, Frederick W. *Survey Research on Comparative Social Change. A Bibliography*. Cambridge, MA: M.I.T. Press, 1969.

1904   Requa, Eloix G. *The Developing Nations, A Guide to Information Sources Concerning Their Economic, Political, Technical and Social Problems*. Detroit: Gale Research Company, 1965.

1905   Spitz, Allan A. *Developmental Change. An Annotated Bibliography*. Lexington: University Press of Kentucky, 1969.

During the 1950s and 1960s, the countries of Africa, Asia, and Latin America, feeling themselves freed from direct or indirect control by the colonial powers, pursued policies that, it was hoped, would eliminate many of their most pressing economic, social, and technological problems. One or two decades later, it is apparent that the desired developmental changes, for the most part, did not eliminate the old problems and, in fact, exacerbated them in many respects.

The four bibliographies cited above offer an excellent introduction to the earlier scholarly literature that today provides the necessary background against which the more recently completed studies need to be evaluated. The listed material is accessible under numerous subject categories and separate author and title indexing.

1906   Colleta, Nat J., and Trudy A. Todd. *Human Resource Development. An Annotated Bibliography on Social and Cultural Influences*. South Salem, NY: Redgrave Publishing Co., 1982.

Over the past three decades development policies aimed at alleviating poverty focused on purely economic variables as a means of achieving economic growth. This narrow focus overlooked the importance of belief systems and noneconomic societal factors for the success of developmental policies.

The Colleta/Todd bibliography identifies books and periodical articles relating to required changes in the belief and value systems and the improvement of such societal factors as motivation, health, family planning, basic education, and agricultural efficiency as a complementary aspect of broader economic development policies. The annotated entries are grouped into four parts, entitled (1) General Works, (2) Social Structure (organization, stratification, social change), (3) Ideology (beliefs, values, and behavioral change), and (4) Social and Cultural Influences on Human Resource Development (a. agriculture and rural development, b. health and nutrition, c. family planning, d. basic education and communication). Regrettably, no index by country and subect terms is included in the bibliography.

1907   Collison, Robert L. *World Bibliographical Series*. Santa Barbara, CA: ABC-Clio Information Services, 1979– .

The multivolume series features selective, annotated bibliographies of those publications that bring to light the essential characteristics of each country in the world. Entries in each volume are arranged in topical order focusing on the various aspects of the history, social and cultural life in the country, including its political phenomena. The cited publications include reference and other scholarly works in the form of books, periodical articles, or dissertations. The following titles have been published to date: Albania, Algeria, Bangladesh, Belize, Brazil, Canada, China, Cyprus, Finland, France, Greece, Guatemala, Haiti, Hungary, Iceland, India, Italy, Iraq, Jamaica, Kenya, Lebanon, Lesotho, Luxembourg, Malawi, Malaysia, Mexico, Morocco, Nepal, New Zealand, Nicaragua, Oman, Pakistan, Panama, Poland, Qatar, Rhodesia/Zimbabwe, Russia/USSR, Saudi Arabia, Scotland, South Africa, Sri Lanka, Sudan, Swaziland, Tunisia, Turkey, Uganda, United Arab Emirates, United States of America, Vatican City State, Yugoslavia.

1908   Driver, Edwin D. *World Population Policy: An Annotated Bibliography*. Lexington, MA: D. C. Heath & Company, 1971.

Many of the most intractable problems in domestic and international politics are the result of changes in the size and composition of human population. Political scientists and other scholars are therefore exhibiting increasing interest in the study of population policies. The present bibliography permits a cross-national and interregional comparison of two types of population policies: general population policy, and measures affecting fertility and family size. General population policies are defined as all those legislative, administrative, and other governmental or institutional measures that may influence the size, distribution, or composition of the population.

The cited bibliography includes more than 3,500 entries for these two categories of population policies,

arranged interregionally as well as regionally for individual countries. The various concepts inherent in the population policies may be identified in the detailed subject index, which provides a key to the bibliographic entries. An author index and a list of the journals indexed are also included. The bibliography may be updated by recent entries in the *Population Index* and the *Public Affairs Information Service Bulletin*.

1909   International Monetary Fund. *The Developing Areas: A Classed Bibliography of the Joint Bank-Fund Library*. Washington, DC, 1976.

The more than 37,700 cards reproduced in this three-volume set constitute the most encompassing inventory of printed information about the economic and social conditions and trends in the developing countries. The card entries identify monographs and serial publications in a geographical arrangement. Volume 1 lists publications for Latin America and the Caribbean area. Volume 2 offers material for Africa and the Middle East, while volume 3 covers the literature for Asia and Oceania.

1910   Mickolus, Edward F., *The Literature of Terrorism: A Selectively Annotated Bibliography*. Westport, CT: Greenwood Press, 1980.

1911   Norton, Augustus R., and Martin H. Greenberg. *International Terrorism: An Annotated Bibliography and Research Guide*. Boulder, CO: Westview Press, 1980.

Acts of terrorism, such as assassinations, bombings, hostage and hijacking incidents, are frequently the visible symptoms in the pathology of political communication processes and as such evidence of unresolved political issues in many countries of the world. Terrorism has spawned a massive literature, documenting both the incidence and causes of terrorist activities as well as the legal and other responses to it. The Mickolus bibliography identifies much of the monographic and periodical literature under subject chapters that focus on the tactics of terrorists and their philosophies, the geographic distribution of terrorism, the legal, psychological, and medical approaches to terrorism as well as the media response to it. The Norton/Greenberg bibliography also aggregates the listed material by geographic area as well as by topical categories that cover the ideological, moral, and biographical aspects of terrorism in addition to micro and macro perspectives in the response patterns. Both volumes include listings of additional bibliographies as well as indexes.

Another recent reference source is Laird Wilcox's *Bibliography on Terrorism and Assassination* (Kansas City, MO: Editorial Research Service, 1980), offering 485 partially annotated entries for books published since 1960.

1912   O'Connor, Barry. *International Human Rights. A Bibliography 1970–1975*. Notre Dame, IN: University of Notre Dame Law School, 1980.

1913   Young, Thomas D. *International Human Rights. A Selected Bibliography*. Los Angeles: California State University, Los Angeles, 1978.

Whereas Western Europe is a world leader in promoting and safeguarding human rights, the rest of the world exhibits an uneven record in the enforcement of human rights. The two bibliographies increase the accessibility of written materials that focus on the legal, philosophical, moral, and practical foundations of human rights in the world. The first item cited above is a revision of earlier editions that lists in alphabetical sequence of author names or titles periodical articles and monographs published in English. The unannotated entries are separately indexed by subject, country, and area. An index to collections is also included. The Young bibliography identifies books, periodical articles, and official publications under six chapters that deal with (1) basic issues, (2) human rights conventions, (3) the Helsinki Conference and Accord, (4) President Carter's human rights policy, (5) geographic regions, and (6) reference sources.

1914   Powelson, John P. A *Select Bibliography on Economic Development: With Annotations*. Boulder, CO: Westview Press, 1979.

This annotated bibliography will be useful for identifying the various challenges and objects that Third World countries face in their economic development. The more than 2,000 books and periodical articles listed in the book are arranged in topical and country sections. Among the object-related topics separately identified are agricultural reform, debt, economic intergration, energy, fiscal and monetary policy, foreign investment, hunger, import substitution, income distribution, industrial development, labor, militarism, modernization, multinational corporations, the new international economic order, poverty, United States policy, and other political matters. The country listings are arranged under names of continents. Periodicals and reports issued by international organizations and research institutes with worldwide or regional coverage of economic development are listed in the beginning of the book. No indexes are included.

Document Collections

1915   *Amnesty International. Section A: Country Dossiers 1975–1982; Section B: Publications 1962–1982*. Zug, Switzerland: Inter Documentation Company, 1983.

1916   *Human Rights Documents 1980–*. Zug, Switzerland: Inter Documentation Company, 1983–.

Published and unpublished documentation relating to a broad spectrum of human rights, their attainment and violation in the various countries of the world has been assembled in the two collections cited above. Amnesty International's collection consists of AI's comprehensive files of research on 130 countries in addition to AI's annual reports, newsletters, international briefings, and other publications. More than 200 human rights organizations throughout the world supply their documentation — newsletters, pamphlets, reports, press releases, books, manuscripts, etc. — for the second collection. Both collections are organized by region and country, but are available on microfiche only. Separate finding aids facilitate access to individual items in the collections by region, country, or subject. As both collections are updated annually, they constitute a current reference source for important information about the health and pathology of political processes occurring in the nations of the world.

See also items 1933 and 1934 for additional information on the human rights situation.

Encyclopedias

1917   *The Current History Encyclopedia of Developing Nations*. New York: McGraw-Hill Book Company, 1982.

The encyclopedia evaluates 93 developing countries in terms of the ways in which they are able to satisfy the basic human needs of their population. Arranged by region and country, the individual articles discuss briefly the culture, history, and politics of each country together with an evaluation of each country's potential for development. Statistical data for population, growth rates, and gross national product are included in addition to illustrations and maps. A detailed index is also provided. Regrettably, the encyclopedia does not offer sufficiently detailed information about each country's development policies, including government regulations concerning foreign investment, multinational corporations, tax incentives, business or trade restrictions, etc.

1918   Delury, George. *World Encyclopedia of Political Systems*. Harlow, England: Longman, 1983.

The encyclopedia offers a country-by-country survey of the political systems of the world. Each country chapter covers the political institutions, major and minor political parties, and other political organizations. Information is provided about the history, current and past leadership, policies and programs, electoral and other processes of the system.

1919   Kernig, C. D. *Marxism, Communism and Western Society*. New York: McGraw-Hill, 1973.

A scientific comparison of the contrasting intellectual positions taken by the Soviet and Western political systems toward social, economic, and other political questions is presented by this eight-volume encyclopedia. Each of the articles in the encyclopedia is divided into sections and subsections that (1) define the subject, (2) report on research conducted by scholars not influenced by Marxism, (3) report on research conducted by Marxists, and (4) give a critical comparison of the Marxist and non-Marxist positions or interpretations. In addition, each article closes with a lengthy bibliographic list of Communist and non-Communist works. The encyclopedia was prepared by 700 scholars from 15 countries.

1920   Kurian, George Thomas. *Encyclopedia of the Third World*. New York: Facts on File, 1982.

The Third World is defined as the politically nonaligned, economically developing, and less industrialized nations of the world. The encyclopedia provides objective descriptions of the dominant political, economic, and social systems of 122 Third World countries. Information presented for each country includes a basic fact sheet (heads of state, nature of government, population, ethnic majority, date of independence, etc.), as well as details on location and area, population characteristics, ethnic composition, constitution and government, freedom and human rights, civil service, local government, foreign policy, parliament, political parties, economy (type, principal economic indicators, GNP, CPI, etc.), budget, finance, agriculture, industry, energy, labor, foreign commerce, mining, defense, education, legal system, law enforcement, health, media and culture, and social welfare. A chronology, a bibliography, and a map are also included in each country article.

1921   *Worldmark Encyclopedia of the Nations*. New York: Worldmark Press, 1984.

The five-volume encyclopedia offers descriptive and statistical profiles, encompassing 50 categories of information, for each of more than 170 countries in the world. Updated data can be found on the land area and population, ethnic and linguistic groups, principal religions, history, government, political parties, judicial system, armed forces, economy, foreign investment, and other important characteristics. A short bibliography of important titles for further reference is included in each country profile.

Handbooks

1922   American University (Washington, DC). *Foreign Area Studies*. Washington, DC: U.S. Government Printing Office, various dates.

Each volume in this continuing series of handbooks, now called country studies, describes and analyzes the political system of a particular country in the world in its historical, societal, and economic setting. National security institutions, policies, and options are also covered. Statistical tables, detailed bibliographies, glossaries, and indexes are included in each volume.

1923   Banks, Arthur S., et al. *Economic Handbook of the World: 1981*. New York: McGraw-Hill, 1981.

Intended as an economic counterpart of the *Political Handbook of the World*, this handbook contains descriptive writeups of the economic characteristics of the countries of the world and selected intergovernmental organizations. Each country article provides general economic data (monetary unit and value, GNP, international reserves, external public debt, exports, imports, government revenues and expenditures, etc., as well as a description of the structure of the economy, domestic trends, trade and foreign investments, future direction, and principal economic institutions. The entries on international organizations describe the background and activities of monetary institutions, multilateral development agencies, trade and cooperative groups, and commodity organizations. Appendices offer a chronology of selected international economic events, and a membership list of the United Nations and selected specialized agencies.

1924   Blum, Albert A. *International Handbook of Industrial Relations*. Westport, CT: Greenwood Press, 1981.

1925   *International Labor Profiles: Comprehensive Reports on the Labor Forces of 40 Key Nations*. Detroit: Grand River Books, 1980.

While government involvement in industrial relations occurs in all countries, it is the group structure of labor unionism that has the most profound effect on equality of income distribution and economic productivity. This group structure varies from country to country, ranging from deeply fragmented in the United States to all-encompassing in Sweden or Austria.

The cited handbook offers 27 country essays by specialists who detail the nature and extent of unionism, employer interest organizations, and state intervention as well as the interrelationships among these three political actors in each country. The effects of labor politics and policies on the economy, notably in the area of strikes, industrial peace, productivity, income distribution, social security, etc., are described and supported by statistical data. Selective bibliographies for additional information conclude each country chapter. The usefulness of the handbook is marred by the omission of several countries, such as Austria or Switzerland, that have exemplary industrial relations and coherent labor, wage, or industrial policies.

Additional labor profiles are available in the second title cited above. Each of the reports is prepared by the U.S. Department of Labor and provides an overview of a country's government, labor force, labor organization, employer organizations, industrial relations, labor standards, social programs, government regulations and policies. As more reports become available for additional countries, an updated second edition will be published.

1926   Caiden, Gerald E. *International Handbook of the Ombudsman*. Vol. 1, *Evolution and Present Function*; Vol. 2, *Country Surveys*. Westport, CT: Greenwood Press, 1981.

The institution of ombudsman is designed to provide protection to both the public and the government against the misuse and abuse of governmental power by public officials. Volume 1 of the handbook analyzes the foundation, evolution, and current role of the ombudsman. Volume 2 presents in-depth studies of individual countries now using the ombudsman. Selected bibliographies for additional information are also provided.

1927   Cook, Chris, and John Paxton. *Commonwealth Political Facts*. New York: Facts on File, 1979.

The Commonwealth is a remarkable and unique grouping of countries scattered throughout the continents of the world. This handbook presents the following political facts about the Commonwealth: (1) evolution of the Commonwealth; (2) head of commonwealth, heads of state, governors general, governors and high commissioners; (3) constitutions and parliaments; (4) ministers; (5) elections; (6) political parties; (7) justice; (8) defense and treaties; (9) population; and (10) trade unions. An index is also included.

1928   Inter-Parliamentary Union. *Parliaments of the World*. Berlin: Walter de Gruyter, 1976.

The parliamentary systems existing throughout the world are characterized by their great variety. This handbook provides a detailed survey of the composition, organization, and operation of 56 parliaments in the world and contains a series of 70 tables with country-by-country entries. The information is arranged under six major headings, namely, (1) Composition of Parliament, (2) Organization and Operation of Parliament, (3) Legislative Function of Parliament, (4) Powers of Parliament, (5) Control of the Executive by Parliament, (6) Other Functions of Parliament. Bibliographic listings of comparative and general studies as well as publications about the parliaments in individual countries are also included. The information presented by this valuable reference work was gathered during an international inquiry by the International Centre for Parliamentary Documentation, a department of the Inter-Parliamentary Union.

1929   *Political Risk in 35 Countries*. London: Euromoney Publications Ltd., 1983.

The book analyzes the risks to financial and business operations from political instability, government restrictions, ideological and other factors in 35 industrialized, newly industrialized and developing countries. Risks are quantified, and countries are ranked according to risk exposure. The countries are: Argentina, Belgium, Bolivia, Brazil, Canada, Chile, China, Costa Rica, France, Greece, India, Indonesia, Iran, Ireland, Israel, Italy, Mexico, Nigeria, Pakistan, Peru, Philippines, Portugal, Saudi Arabia, Singapore, South Africa, South Korea, Spain, Sweden, Taiwan, Thailand, Turkey, Venezuela, Yugoslavia, Zaire, Zambia.

1930   Rose, Richard. *Electoral Behavior. A Comparative Handbook*. New York: Free Press, 1974.

Based on contributions from distinguished political scientists throughout the world, the handbook contains narrative and statistical summaries of electoral behavior in continental Europe and Anglo-American countries. Among the topics that are given special emphasis are the evolution of the party systems, the mechanics of electoral systems, the political importance of class, religion, region, national identity, age, education, sex, the role of election laws, and others. The information is presented under country headings with separate introductory and concluding chapters. The sources of the electoral statistics used in the handbook are identified.

1931   Szajkowski, Bogdan. *Marxist Governments. A World Survey*. London: Macmillan Press, 1981.

The growth in the number, ideological and political impact of countries ruled by Marxist-Leninist parties is a puzzling development in the world. This three-volume reference set offers an analytical survey of 25 countries whose government and politics are based on the principles of Marxism-Leninism. Each country article provides a summary of the historical developments, government and party characteristics, the economy, domestic and foreign policies. In addition, biographical information about the principal politicians, basic data about the country, and a bibliography of additional information sources are included. Two introductory articles comment on the Communist movement and the nature of Marxist regimes. A cumulative index is included in volume 3.

1932   U.S. Social Security Administration. Office of Research and Statistics. *Social Security Programs throughout the World*. Washington, DC: U.S. Government Printing Office, 1958– .

Although nations differ widely in their political, social, and economic settings, social security programs have achieved near-universal acceptance as prime political objects in all countries. This frequently updated handbook presents for each country a summary of the national social security system in the form of a two-page chart. Each chart is divided into eight vertical columns showing dates of basic laws and types of programs, coverage, source of funds, qualifying conditions, cash benefits for insured workers, permanent disability and medical benefits for insured workers, survivor benefits and medical benefits for dependents, and administrative organization. Five horizontal rows delineate the major social security branches, namely, old age, invalidity, death; sickness and maternity; work injury; unemployment; and family allowances. An introductory section highlights the principal features of the social security programs throughout the world.

Yearbooks

1933   *Amnesty International Report.* London: Amnesty International Publications, 1962–.

1934   Gastil, Raymond D. *Freedom in the World: Political Rights and Civil Liberties.* New York: Freedom House, 1978–.

Extensive and entrenched violations of human rights — often sanctioned at the highest level of government and practiced with acts of unspeakable cruelty — are manifestations of pathological political processes that occur in an ever increasing number of countries with widely differing ideologies. The two sets of yearbooks cited above complement each other in their country-by-country assessment of the human rights situation. The first title reports for each country the specifics of human rights violations. The second title contains (1) a comparative survey of political rights and civil liberties throughout the world, (2) several essays on particular countries or problems, and (3) individual country summaries, describing political rights and civil liberties together with a comparative ranking in terms of the status of freedom. The country summaries also offer population figures and a capsule description of the ethnicity, economy, and polity of each country.

For the texts of international conventions, declarations, and other legal instruments that mandate the observance of human rights, see *Human Rights: A Compilation of International Instruments* (New York: United Nations, 1978), described under citation 1561 in this guidebook.

1935   *Annual of Power and Conflict.* London: Institute for the Study of Conflict, 1972–.

It is a disturbing fact of the political life in many countries of the world that the existing system of legitimate imperative control is being challenged by revolu-

tionary, secessionist, or guerilla movements. This annual reference work offers regional as well as country-by-country surveys of political conflict with heavy emphasis on the revolutionary and nonrevolutionary challenges to established authority. The legitimate instruments of power, such as armed forces personnel, are described and contrasted with the strength of revolutionary movements. A chronology of events in the various conflict situations is given. A list of additional publications issued by the institute on conflict situations is printed in each issue of the yearbook.

1936   Dupuy, Trevor Nevitt. *The Almanac of World Military Power.* Dunn Loring, VA: T. N. Dupuy Associates, 1970; Ann Arbor, MI: R. R. Bowker, 1972–.

Prepared by military historians, political scientists, and soldiers, this frequently revised reference work provides a geopolitical appraisal and impartial assessment of the military power capabilities of the nations of the world. Entries are arranged by regions and countries and include information about the power potential, defense structure, politico-military policy, strategic problems, alliances, and armed forces of each country. For additional information, see also the *Defense and Foreign Affairs Handbook*, previously described as item 1706 in this guidebook.

1937   *The Europa Yearbook.* London: Europa Publications, 1959–.

1938   Mallory, Walter H. *Political Handbook and Atlas of the World.* New York: Council on Foreign Relations, 1927–.

1939   Stebbins, Richard P., and Alba Amoia. *The World This Year.* New York: Simon and Schuster, 1971–.

Brief descriptive and current information about the political system of each country can be found in the three reference works cited above. Partially overlapping but complementary information is presented about the consitutional background, governmental institutions, including parliament, cabinet, judicial systems, political parties, financial, commercial and educational institutions, news media, etc. The *Europa Yearbook* also provides statistical data on population, agricultural, mining, and industrial activities, balance of payments, external trade, and tourism, among similar topics.

1940   *Price Waterhouse Information Guide: Foreign Exchange Information. A Worldwide Summary.* New York: Price Waterhouse, 1972–.

This annually issued handbook will be useful for the international comparison of foreign exchange policies. It provides for each country basic information about the foreign exchange regulations, notably in respect of investments and repatriation of capital, settlement of debts, remittances of interests and profits, etc. While a pegged dollar exchange rate exists in many countries, see the foreign exchange table in the business section of your metropolitan newspaper for a daily quotation of floating foreign exchange rates.

1941   U.S. Central Intelligence Agency. *The World Factbook*. Washington, DC: U.S. Government Printing Office, 1977—.

1942   U.S. Department of State. *Background Notes*. Washington, DC: U.S. Superintendent of Documents, to date.

Concise descriptive profiles of the countries of the world are presented in two separate series of official reference works. The first item is an annually revised handbook, whereas the second item is a collection of approximately 150 pamphlets, half of which are revised each year. Both series offer information about the land area, population, government institutions and personnel, political parties, economic and political conditions, and other characteristics of each country. A reading list of useful publications about each country is also included. A reprint edition of the *Background Notes* is published under the title *Countries of the World* by Gale Research Company in Detroit.

1943   *What They Said*. Beverly Hills, CA: Monitor Book Company, 1969—.

Words casually or purposefully uttered in speeches, lectures, interviews, news conferences, or radio and television addresses by political actors constitute a most significant output of the political systems throughout the world. This annual reference work presents the highlights of vital views from the lips of prominent people on virtually every aspect of contemporary civilization. The quotes are arranged under three parts, entitled (1) National Affairs, (2) International Affairs, and (3) General. Suitable subdivisions within these three parts aggregate the material according to major topics or geographic entities. The occupation, position, or title of the speaker as well as the used source document are identified with all quotes. Separate indexes to speakers and subjects are also provided.

1944   *The World Today Series*.

Africa, 1966—.

The Far East and Southwest Pacific, 1968—.

Latin America, 1967—.

Middle East, 1967—.

The Soviet Union and Eastern Europe, 1970—.

Western Europe, 1982—.
    Washington, DC: Stryker-Post Publications.

This series of yearbooks is issued in six regional volumes with revised editions published each August. Following an introductory survey of the region, each volume provides updated descriptive information about the history, political system, economy, and culture of each country in the region. A separate bibliography lists key English-language books by country for additional information.

1945   *World View 1983*. New York: Pantheon Books, 1982—.

Initiated and first published in France, this yearbook presents

- a chronology of world events during the preceding year
- background information on the principal strategic questions
- summary reports on controversial issues, areas of tension and controversy
- analytical profiles of the principal economic and political developments in 34 major countries of the world
- economic, geographical, and cultural analyses of 35 regions in the world
- a directory of international and national organizations, including a list of publishers and information sources

Several of these sections also provide bibliographical references to books and articles. In addition, a section of statistical information and a subject index are included.

AFRICA

Library Resources

1946   Duignan, Peter. *Handbook of American Resources for African Studies*. Stanford, CA: Hoover Institution Press, Stanford University, 1967.

Published and unpublished resources for a detailed study of Africa are scattered through a number of libraries and other institutions in the United States. This reference book describes the holdings of 95 library and manuscript collections, 108 church and missionary libraries and archives, 95 art and ethnographic collections, and 4 business archives. An index is included containing the names of countries, individuals, and institutions.

1947   International African Institute. London. *Cumulative Bibliography of African Studies*. Boston: G. K. Hall, 1973.

Books and periodical articles previously listed in the bibliography published in the journal *Africa* from 1929 to 1970 and in the *International African Bibliography* during 1971 and 1972 are recorded in this book catalog containing author and subject sections. The classified cards are arranged geographically with subdivisions by ethnic groups, languages, and subjects. The main focus of the institute's collection is on tropical Africa. For current material see the *International African Bibliography*, published quarterly since 1971.

1948   Northwestern University. Library. *Africana Conference Paper Index*. Boston: G. K. Hall, 1982.

1949   Northwestern University. Library. *Catalog of the Melville J. Herskovits Library of African Studies*. Boston: G. K. Hall, 1972.

————— . *First Supplement*. Boston: G. K. Hall, 1978.

1950   Northwestern University. Library. *Joint Acquisitions List of Africana*. Evanston, IL: Northwestern University Library, 1962–; Boston: G. K. Hall, 1980–.

One of the major library collections of Africana is maintained by the Northwestern University Library. Three separate bibliographic sets are available from this library. The *Africana Conference Paper Index* identifies more than 12,000 conference papers presented throughout the world since 1945 and held by the Herskovits Library. Since the vast majority of African Studies research is rarely published and appears only in conference paper format, the index offers the only access to this valuable research material.

More than 60,000 books and 600 periodicals and newspapers held by the Herskovits Library are listed by author and title in an eight-volume book catalog. The geographical emphasis of this collection continues to be Sub-Saharan Africa, but material relating to North Africa is also included. The catalog is supplemented at five-year intervals. The *Joint Acquisitions List of Africana*, issued bimonthly and in five-year cumulations, provides a record of acquisitions not only of the Herskovits Library at Northwestern University, but lists also material cataloged by the Library of Congress, the New York Public Library, and the libraries of the Princeton, Stanford, and Yale universities. The cumulated editions also present entries by geographic area.

Guidebooks

1951   Duignan, Peter, et al. *Guide to Research and Reference Works on Sub-Saharan Africa*. Stanford, CA: Hoover Institution Press, 1972.

With more than 3,000 annotated entries, this guidebook offers a comprehensive inventory of guidebooks, bibliographies, indexes, encyclopedias, dictionaries, handbooks, yearbooks, directories, and other reference works available for the study of Africa south of the Sahara. Material is arranged in four parts: (1) guides to research organizations, libraries and archives, and the book trade, (2) bibliographies for Africa in general, (3) subject guide in general, including subdivisions for politics and government, international relations, history, law, etc., (4) an area guide by former colonial power, region, or country.

1952   Hartwig, Gerald W., and William M. O'Barr. *The Student Africanist's Handbook. A Guide to Resources*. New York: John Wiley & Sons, 1974.

The guidebook is organized in six chapters: (1) The Nature of African Studies — Disciplines with African Interests; (2) Understanding Africa; (3) A Guide to African Bibliography: General References and Disciplinary Sources; (4) A Guide to African Bibliography: Regions and Countries; (5) Aids for Intensive Research; and (6) Special Topics and Needs. The individual entries are unannotated, but extensive introductory sections and headnotes offer excellent guidance.

1953   McGowan, Patrick J. *African Politics. A Guide to Research Resources, Methods and Literature*. Syracuse, NY: Maxwell Graduate School of Citizenship and Public Affairs, Syracuse University, 1970.

1954   Shaw, Robert B., and Richard L. Sklar. *A Bibliography for the Study of African Politics*. Los Angeles: University of California, 1973.

Unlike the more comprehensive guidebook by Peter Duignan, the two guidebooks cited above are devoted exclusively to political information sources. Entries in the McGowan guidebook are arranged in nine chapters: (1) reference books, (2) problems of research conceptualization, (3) research methods, (4) bibliographies, indexes not listed in the first chapter, (5) checklist of scholarly journals for African political studies, (6) quantitative data sources, (7) qualitative data sources, (8) methods of data analysis and report writing, and (9) political change in Africa. Each of these chapters has numerous subdivisions for country, topic, or form of publication. The lack of an index and the somewhat overlapping arrangement mars the usefulness of this guidebook. The Shaw/Sklar guidebook lists annuals, symposia, surveys, histories, periodicals, and publications dealing with social change, African nationalism, biographical material, and international relations. There are also listings by countries. All entries are unannotated.

1955   Skurnik, W. A. E. *Subsaharan Africa. A Guide*

to Information Sources. Detroit: Gale Research Company, 1977.

This guidebook is useful for updating and complementing the preceding guidebooks since it is neither limited to reference works nor political information sources. It includes author, title, and subject indexes.

Current Bibliographies

1956   *Africa Index to Continental Periodical Literature*. Oxford: Hans Zell Publishers, 1976–.

Published annually on behalf of the African Bibliographic Center in Dar es Salaam, the index identifies articles in selected scholarly and semischolarly periodicals issued on the African continent, excluding South Africa.

1957   *Africana Journal*. New York: Africana Publishing Corporation, 1970–.

New and forthcoming books, pamphlets, and other monographic publications in English, German, and French are listed in each issue of this quarterly periodical. Government publications and periodical articles are not included. Listings are arranged by author in two sections. Part 1 is a subject section in which entries are grouped under broad headings, such as politics, law, race relations, colonialism, history, economics, sociology, etc. Part 2 is a geographic section with subdivisions for individual countries. A separate author index is included. The periodical also features retrospective bibliographies and bibliographic essays on selected topics in addition to news about publishing activities of interest to the Africanist scholar.

1958   *ASA News*. Los Angeles: African Studies Association, 1968–.

Formerly published as *African Studies Newsletter*, this bimonthly publication identifies research in progress, recent bibliographies and other publications, past and future meetings of Africanist scholars, and other developments in African studies. The association also issues the *African Studies Review*, a source of book reviews and list of books received but not reviewed.

1959   Cape Town. South African Public Library. A *Bibliography of African Bibliographies, Covering Territories South of the Sahara*. Cape Town; 1961–.

1960   ————. *Quarterly Bulletin (Kwartaalblad)*. Cape Town: 1946–.

Bibliographies on all subjects of interest in the study of Africa are identifiable on a current and retrospective basis with the help of these reference publications. Bibliographies compiled in all parts of the world in English,

Afrikaans, German, Portuguese, and other languages are listed. Entries are arranged according to the Universal Decimal Classification. The cumulated listing contains approximately 1,100 bibliographies.

1961   *Current Bibliography on African Affairs*. Washington, DC: African Bibliographic Center, 1962–1967; Westport, CT: Greenwood Periodicals Company, 1968–1972; Farmingdale, NY: Baywood Publishing Company, 1973–.

New periodical articles and books of value in African studies are listed quarterly in this bibliography. Entries are arranged by author in two sections. The first section lists items under broad subject headings, such as politics and government, relations with foreign countries, interstate relations, foreign economic relations, historical studies, economic studies, etc. The second section lists regional studies under regions and individual countries. An author index to all listed publications is included, as well as various bibliographic essays and book reviews.

1962   *Current Contents Africa*. Oxford: Hans Zell Publishers, 1976–.

Formerly issued as *CCA, Current Contents Africa*, this quarterly publication reproduces the contents pages of some 200 serials held by the Stadt- und Universitätsbibliothek in Franfurt am Main, Germany. The identified articles reflect worldwide coverage in English and other European languages.

1963   *Documentatieblad. The Abstracts Journal of the African Studies Centre Leiden*. Leiden: Afrika-Studiecentrum, 1968–.

Books and periodical articles published in English, French, Dutch, and German throughout the world are listed and abstracted in this quarterly bibliography. Entries are arranged by country within regions (North Africa, West Africa, East Africa, Southern Africa, etc.) and include extensive content summaries in addition to full bibliographic citations. The abstracts are in the language of the cited publication. Subject coverage includes general information, religion/philosophy, culture and society, politics (domestic, foreign policy, and international relations), economics, law, education/socialization, psychology, anthropology, medical care and health services, rural and urban planning, history, and other topical areas. Geographical and subject indexes are included in each issue.

1964   *International African Bibliography*. London: International African Institute, 1971–.

Tropical Africa is the main focus of interest in this bibliography, which lists new periodical articles and books at quarterly intervals. More than 3,000 titles are listed annually under broad subject headings, including political science, law, economics and development, etc. The institute also published *African Abstracts* during the years 1950–1972.

Retrospective Bibliographies

1965   Alderfer, Harold F., and L. M. Stevens. *A Bibliography of African Government 1950–1966*. Lincoln, PA: Lincoln University Press, 1967.

1966   Drabek, Anne Gordon, and Wilfrid Knap. *The Politics of African and Middle Eastern States*. New York: Pergamon Press, 1976.

1967   Hertefelt, Marcel d'. *African Government Systems in Static and Changing Conditions*. Tervuren, Belgium: Musée Royal de l'Afrique Centrale, 1968.

The scholarly literature on the political systems of Africa is selectively identified in two unannotated bibliographies for books and articles and one annotated bibliography for books, as cited above. The Drabek/Knap bibliography is an annotated list of books dealing with political history, political parties, interest groups, governmental institutions, and other elements of African political systems. Biographical publications, memoirs, and speech collections of African political leaders are also included. The listings are arranged by regions, namely Central Africa, Eastern Africa, Former Portuguese Africa, Southern Africa, West Africa, North Africa, and several Middle Eastern regions. No indexes are included.

The Alderfer/Stevens bibliography offers unannotated listings for books and articles written during the early years of the decolonialization process. Entries are arranged by regions and countries under separate form headings. The Hertefelt bibliography focuses on indigenous African governmental systems. The author-arranged entries are made accessible by separate indexes for ethnic groups and subjects.

1968   Duignan, Peter, and L. H. Gann. *Colonialism in Africa 1870–1960*. Volume 5, *A Bibliographical Guide to Colonialism in Subsaharan Africa*. Cambridge, England: Cambridge University Press, 1973.

An assessment of the colonial rule in Sub-Saharan Africa during nearly 100 years is facilitated by this bibliography, which offers the researcher multiple access to published evidence. Part 1, entitled Guide to Reference Materials, surveys libraries and archives in Western Europe, the United States, and Africa. It also lists centers of research as well as various kinds of general bibliographies. Part 2 is a subject guide to the literature of politics, economics, law, history, etc. Part 3 is an area guide

arranged by colonial power, region, and country. The bibliographic entries include material published up to 1971.

1969   Miller, E. Willard, and Ruby M. Miller. *Northern and Western Africa. A Bibliography on the Third World*. Monticello, IL: Vance Bibliographies, 1981.

1970   Miller, E. Willard, and Ruby M. Miller. *Tropical, Eastern, and Southern Africa. A Bibliography on the Third World*. Monticello, IL: Vance Bibliographies, 1981.

These two bibliographies present unannotated entries for books and periodical articles relating to the political and social conditions of Third World countries in Africa.

1971   Paden, John N., and Edward W. Soja. *The African Experience*. Evanston, IL: Northwestern University Press, 1970.

This multivolume set represents an integrated reference system for the study of the African continent, its peoples and problems. Volume 1 contains 31 essays that synthesize existing information about Africa. Volume 2 consists of summaries of information on 100 topics, and Volume 3b provides a bibliography of 4,000 books and periodical articles arranged to parallel the 10 topic summaries in Volume 2. The 100 subject categories are grouped into five parts, namely, (1) African Society and Culture, (2) Perspectives on the Past, (3) Processes of Change, (4) Consolidation of Nation-States, and (5) Africa and the Modern World, in addition to a prologue entitled "The African Experience" and an epilogue entitled "Social Science and Africa." Within each of the 100 subject categories five classes of references are indicated, namely, (1) introductory references, (2) supplementary references, (3) general theory references, (4) less accessible sources, and (5) case study references. The entries arranged under the introductory references are considered major information sources for a broad understanding of each subject and are critically annotated. Although the set is geared to the undergraduate level, Volume 3b is a guide to information sources for more advanced courses in African studies.

1972   Smaldone, Joseph P. *African Liberation Movements: An Interim Bibliography*. Waltham, MA: African Studies Association, 1974.

A significant element in the political struggles of Africa is the activity of nationalist and revolutionary organizations that in the past have successfully challenged the established political order in many parts of Africa. This bibliography offers a preliminary listing of books, reports, articles, pamphlets, and other publications issued by or about these organizations.

1973   U.S. Department of the Army. *Africa: Problems and Prospects. A Bibliographic Survey.* Washington, DC: 1967.

1974   _____ . *Africa, A Bibliographic Survey of the Literature.* Washington, DC: 1974.

Two separate bibliographic surveys of the political literature on Africa offer richly annotated listings of books and periodical articles. The listings are arranged by regions, states, or topics and identify the literature on past and present problems, notably the issue of self-determination, the search for unity and stability, Africa's relationship with the West and Communist countries, etc. Additional reference sources and valuable maps are included.

1975   U.S. Library of Congress. African Section. *Africa South of the Sahara. Index to Periodical Literature 1900–1970.* Boston: G. K. Hall, 1971.

_____ . *First Supplement.* Boston: G. K. Hall, 1973.

With its more than 100,000 entries, this multivolume reference set constitutes a comprehensive international record of the periodical literature published, since the beginning of this century, about the countries south of the Sahara. The entries are arranged by countries and regions with subdivisions for major subject fields, such as politics and government, economics, anthropology, etc. Citations have been gathered from numerous sources, notably the bibliographic card services of the Centre d'Analyse et de Recherche Documentaires pour l'Afrique Noire (CARDAN) in Paris, the Centre Internationale de Documentation Economique et Sociale Africaine (CIDESA) in Brussels, and the Fondation National des Sciences Politiques, Centre de Documentation Contemporaine (FNSP/CDC) in Paris. Entries from the services of these important European research and documentation orgnaizations are annotated. The citations refer to more than 1,500 periodicals published throughout the world and usually not covered in the standard periodical indexes.

Dictionaries

1976   Phillips, Claude S. *The African Political Dictionary.* Santa Barbara, CA: ABC-Clio, 1983.

The most significant terms of the African political language are defined in this dictionary. Terms dealing with major events as well as the theories and structural components of politics throughout Africa are included. Each definition is followed by a paragraph that places the term in its context with the overall political situation in Africa. Maps, tables, a select bibliography, and a comprehensive index are also included.

Document Collections

1977   *CIA Research Reports, Africa 1946–1976.* Frederick, MD: University Publications of America, 1982.

1978   *Special Studies, Africa 1962–1980.* Frederick, MD: University Publications of America, 1982.

Available to the general public for the first time, albeit with some delay, these collections of reports and special studies contain expert analyses of contemporary political phenomena in various African countries. Prepared by experts in the Central Intelligence Agency and major research organizations, such as the Rand Corporation, the Naval War College, the National Defense University, and other prestigious institutions, the reports and studies focus on such problems as apartheid in South Africa, the failure of civil leadership in black African countries, political parties in Africa, the Soviet Union's role in Angola, patterns of conflict in the Horn of Africa, and many others. All reports and studies are available on microfilm only together with printed guides.

1979   Marshall, H. H. *From Dependence to Statehood in Commonwealth Africa: Selected Documents, World War I to Independence.* Dobbs Ferry, NY: Oceana Publications, 1980– .

This collection of documents pertains to the steps by which the African territories of the British Empire progressed from colonies or protectorates to independence. Documentation in the four-volume set is arranged by region and country and preceded by a general historical introduction.

Handbooks and Yearbooks

1980   *Africa South of the Sahara.* London: Europa Publications, 1971– .

The irregularly revised handbook presents scholarly surveys of the economic, political, and social development in all countries south of the Sahara. The information material is arranged in four parts: Part 1 offers general background information for the entire continent. Part 2 is devoted to the regional organizations of Africa. Part 3 provides individual country surveys, which also include a statistical section, a directory of the political, financial, commercial, and educational institutions and their principal officeholders, and a select bibliography. Part 4 contains additional reference material, such as a Who's Who section, a list of research institutes concerned with Africa, and a select bibliography of periodicals publishing information material about Africa.

1981   *Africa Yearbook and Who's Who*. London: Africa Journal Ltd., 1976– .

The yearbook contains a diary of important events in political, military, economic, diplomatic, educational, and sundry affairs as well as six major descriptive parts for the geography, the people, the economy, and the communication system of Africa, its individual countries, and international organizations. A bibliographical section describes African personalities from various walks of life. Portraits, maps and statistical tables frequently accompany the textual presentation.

1982   Cook, Chris, and David Killingway. *African Political Facts since 1945*. New York: Facts on File, 1983.

This handbook offers a convenient collection of facts relating to the political conditions in all of the countries in Africa. Details are provided about the political actors and processes, including elections and international relations. Societal factors, such as famine, conflicts, exploitation of natural resources, etc., are also covered. Statistical tables, bibliographic listings, and an index are included.

1983   *Global Studies: Africa*. Guilford, CT: Dushkin Publishing Group, 1984.

The handbook contains regional essays and country reports that summarize the geographical, cultural, economic, and sociopolitical characteristics, differences, and similarities of the regions and countries of Africa. A large number of noteworthy articles from newspapers and periodicals are reprinted in a separate section. A glossary, a bibliography, and an index are also included.

1984   Legum, Colin, and John Drysdale. *Africa Contemporary Record. Annual Survey and Documents*. London: Africa Research Ltd., 1969– .

Each of the annual volumes is organized in three parts: Part 1 contains essays on current issues with emphasis on the role of foreign, non-African countries in Africa. Part 2 offers a country-by-country review. Part 3 presents important reports, statements, conference summaries, and other documents pertaining to political and foreign policy issues, social developments, economic trends, etc. Maps, statistical tables, and a subject and name index are also included.

1985   Morrison, Donald George, et al. *Black Africa, A Comparative Handbook*. New York: Free Press, 1972.

This truly comparative handbook is arranged in three parts. Part 1 presents 172 tables of comparative quantitative data for 32 black African countries in matters of ecology, demography, cultural pluralism, social and economic development, political development (political regime characteristics, political parties and elections, military and security systems, political instability, international relations, etc.), urban and ethnic patterns, etc. Part 2 offers individual country profiles on ethnic patterns, language patterns, urban and political patterns, national integration, and so forth. A list of additional references is given for each country. Part 3 discusses the problems, usage, and data reliability of cross-national research.

ASIA

Library Resources

1986   London. University. School of Oriental and African Studies. Library. *Library Catalogue*. Boston: G. K. Hall, 1963.

————— . *First Supplement*. Boston: G. K. Hall, 1968.

————— . *Second Supplement*. Boston: G. K. Hall, 1973.

————— . *Third Supplement*. Boston: G. K. Hall, 1979.

The London University catalog and its supplements contain more than one million card entries for published and unpublished material relating to politics, law, history, economics, and other subject matter in all parts of Africa, Asia, and Oceania. Separate volumes exist for author, title, and subject listings as well as for Japanese, Chinese, and manuscript or microfilm holdings.

1987   University of Michigan. *Catalogs of the Asia Library*. Boston: G. K. Hall, 1978.

The Asia Library of this university contains more than 300,000 volumes and 18,000 reels of microfilm of Chinese, Japanese, and Korean publications. The collection is particularly strong in materials on post-1949 developments in economics and politics, but special holdings relate to the war in the Pacific and the postwar occupation of Japan.

1988   U.S. Library of Congress. Orientalia Division. *Southeast Asia Subject Catalog*. Boston: G. K. Hall, 1972.

A reproduction of approximately 65,000 cards for books, periodicals, periodical articles, manuscripts, dissertations, pamphlets, microfilms, documentary materials, etc., dealing with political, historical, socioeconomic, and other subject matter in the study of Southeast Asia. The catalog is divided by countries, namely, Brunei, Burma, Cambodia, Indonesia, Laos, Malaysia, Philippines, Singapore, Thailand and Vietnam.

Guidebooks

1989   Embree, Ainslee Thomas, et al. *Asia: A Guide to Basic Books*. New York: Asia Society, 1966.

1990   _____ . *Asia: A Guide to Paperbacks*. New York: Asia Society, 1968.

The two guidebooks may be used to identify, with the exception of the more recent scholarship, cloth and paperbound editions of significant works on Asia in general and specific countries east of Afghanistan. Listings are grouped according to a regional and country arrangement with some subdivisions for political, economic, historical, and philosophical subject matter.

1991   Johnson, Donald Clay. *A Guide to Reference Materials on Southeast Asia*. New Haven, CT: Yale University Press, 1970.

The guidebook lists approximately 2,200 reference works by form of publication or subject field, including law and political science, economics, history, etc. In each form or subject category the reference works are arranged by country in chronological order of publication dates.

1992   Littlefield, David W. *The Islamic Near East and North Africa. An Annotated Guide to Books in English for Non-Specialists*. Littleton, CO: Libraries Unlimited, 1977.

English-language books dealing with the history, politics, international relations, civilization, language and literature, society, economy, and religion of the Islamic countries of the Middle East and North Africa are conveniently identifiable with the help of this guidebook. General works for the entire region as well as specific works relating to individual countries are listed and described. Author, title, and subject indexes offer additional access to the listed material.

1993   Nunn, G. Raymond. *Asia, A Selected and Annotated Guide to Reference Works*. Cambridge, MA: M.I.T. Press, 1971.

Nearly 1,000 directories, bibliographies, indexes, encyclopedias, dictionaries, yearbooks, and other reference works dealing with specific Asian countries or regions in Asia are listed in this guidebook. Soviet Asia and Asian countries west of Pakistan are not represented in the book. Two-thirds of the works listed are published in English, but reference sources in Japanese, Chinese, and other Asian or European languages are also included.

1994   Simon, Reeva S. *The Modern Middle East: A Guide to Research Tools in the Social Sciences*. Boulder, CO: Westview Press, 1978.

The guidebook identifies reference sources written in English and other Western languages, Arabic, Hebrew, Persian, and Turkish. The emphasis is on works in the social sciences dealing with the situation in the Middle Eastern countries, Iran, Afghanistan, and Turkey from the turn of the century to the present. The arrangement of the entries is by type of reference work rather than by discipline. There are separate listings for bibliographies of bibliographies, printed library catalogs, current bibliographies, subject and country bibliographies, machine-readable databases, periodical indexes and abstracts, document collections, guides to statistical sources, newspaper guides and indexes, news digests, data files, oral history collections, encyclopedias and handbooks, almanacs and annuals, directories, biographical sources, geographical sources, and listings of reports. An index is also included.

1995   Wagle, Iqbal. *Reference Aids to South Asia*. Toronto: University of Toronto, 1977.

The reference literature for five South Asian countries — Bangladesh, India, Pakistan, Nepal, and Sri Lanka — is listed and described in this guidebook. The bibliographic entries are arranged by country and then by subject, and include catalogs, bibliographies, biographies, handbooks, and other reference sources.

Current Bibliographies

1996   *Articles on the Middle East, 1947–1971*. Ann Arbor, MI: Pierian Press, 1972.

1997   "Bibliography of Periodical Literature." In *Middle East Journal*. Washington, DC: Middle East Institute, 1947– .

Each issue of the quarterly *Middle East Journal* contains a bibliography of important articles dealing with North Africa, Muslim Spain, the Arab world, Israel, Turkey, and Transcaucasian states of the USSR, Iran, Afghanistan, Pakistan, and Turkestan. Listings are arranged under geography, history and politics, economic conditions, science, philosophy and religion, language, literature and the arts, law, biography, bibliography, and book reviews. No attempt is made to segregate the listings by country. A two-volume set offers cumulative listings for the period 1947–1971.

1998   *Cumulative Bibliography of Asian Studies, 1941–1965; 1966–1970*. Boston: G. K. Hall, 1969, 1972.

1999   "Bibliography of Asian Studies." In *Journal of*

Asian Studies. Ann Arbor, MI: Association for Asian Studies, 1956– .

Significant books, periodical articles, pamphlets, and other publications dealing with Asia in general and specific countries of Asia are recorded annually in the *Bibliography of Asian Studies*. Entries are arranged alphabetically by author under names of countries subdivided by fields of inquiry, including politics and government, foreign relations, history, etc. A separate listing of pertinent periodical titles is given for each country. Although the countries of Western Asia are not represented in the listings, the bibliography now contains more than 14,000 entries annually. Two cumulative bibliographic sets with separate author and subject listings offer nearly 350,000 entries.

2000   *The Middle East: Abstracts and Index*. Pittsburgh: Library Information and Research Service, 1978– .

The quarterly reference publication indexes and abstracts current books, dissertations, major newspapers, periodical articles, government documents, and other publications as they pertain to the Middle East area. The subject matter covered includes politics, economic affairs, historical and sociological material, religion, philosophy, and related fields of interest. Entries are arranged in 18 sections based on the names of the countries in the area. Material relating to Iran but not to Turkey is included. Annual cummulated indexes by author and subject are also published.

2001   *The Mideast File*. Oxford: Learned Information, 1979– .

2002   *The Mideast File*. Oxford: Learned Information, 1979– . (Vendor: Dialog — File 249)

Available in printed and electronic versions, this monthly updated index identifies political, economic, military, historical, legal, and other information published about Middle Eastern countries in books, periodicals, official gazettes, and other media. 65 percent of the cited material is in the English language, 20 percent in Arabic, and the rest in European languages, notably French and German.

Retrospective Bibliographies

2003   Atiyeh, George Nicholas. *The Contemporary Middle East 1948–1973. A Selective and Annotated Bibliography*. Boston: G. K. Hall, 1975.

Significant publications dealing with the political, economic, religious, and social conditions of Middle Eastern countries, including their foreign relations, can be identified with this bibliography. The annotated listings are arranged under appropriate subheadings of the following main headings: (1) the Middle East, (2) the Arab-Israeli conflict, (3) the Arab countries, (4) the Arabian peninsula, (5) the Fertile Crescent, (6) the Nile Valley, (7) the Maghrib, (8) Turkey, and (9) Iran. The 6,491 annotated entries also include some works on education, architecture, arts, literature, and science. Bibliographies and other reference works are listed separately. Apart from the detailed table of contents, access to the listed entries is facilitated by separate author and subject indexes.

2003a   *The Middle East in Conflict*. Santa Barbara, CA: ABC-Clio, 1984.

More than 3,000 abstracts of journal articles published worldwide between 1973 and 1982 can be found in this reference work, covering the political and social turbulence in the Middle East from 1914 to 1982. A detailed subject index offers access by biographical, geographical, and chronological aspects of subject terms.

2004   Nicholas, David. *The Middle East, Its Oil, Economics and Investment Policies*. Westport, CT: Greenwood Press, 1981.

2005   Selim, George Dimitri. *Arab Oil: A Bibliography of Materials in the Library of Congress*. Washington, DC: Library of Congress, 1983.

With Western industrialized countries becoming increasingly dependent on Middle Eastern oil resources, economic development, and investment policies, a wide variety of information sources about the Middle East and its political and economic relationships with other countries has become available. The first title cited above identifies nearly 900 directories and other reference works, major periodicals, books, reports, and pamphlets for the Middle East in general, its individual countries, and major international trading partners. Entries are frequently annotated. Author, title, and subject indexes as well as a directory of publishers are included. Publications in Western languages held in the Library of Congress are listed in the second title cited above. Entries are arranged in four sections: (1) Arab World and Middle East as a Whole; (2) Political and Geographical Entities; (3) OPEC; (4) Dictionaries Relating to the Oil Industry. Name, title, and subject indexes offer additional access to the listed material.

2006   Nunn, G. Raymond. *Asia: Reference Works*. London: Mansell, 1980.

More than 1,500 directories, bibliographies, indexes, encyclopedias, dictionaries, yearbooks, and other reference works dealing with specific countries or regions in Asia are listed and annotated in this guidebook. Soviet Asia, Afghanistan, and Middle Eastern countries are not represented in the book. All subject areas, including political and other social sciences, are covered. Author and title indexes are included.

2007   Johnson, Donald Clay. *Index to Southeast Asian Journals 1960–1974: A Guide to Articles, Book Reviews, and Composite Works.* Boston: G. K. Hall, 1977.

2008   Tregonning, Kennedy G. *Southeast Asia: A Critical Bibliography.* Tuscon: University of Arizona Press, 1969.

Due to the Vietnam conflict, Southeast Asia has received increased scholarly attention during the 1960s. Johnson's index offers multiple access to articles and book reviews published about Southeast Asia during a 15-year period up to 1974. The citations to the articles are arranged by subject and indexed by author. Book reviews are arranged by main entry and indexed by title. The Tregonning bibliography identifies reference works and scholarly publications within a topical country arrangement.

2009   UNESCO. *South Asia Social Science Bibliography.* New Delhi: Research Centre on Social and Economic Development in Southern Asia, University Enclave, 1954–1965.

The 12-volume set presents bibliographic listings with annotations and abstracts of the social science literature on South Asia. Entries are arranged under broad subject headings and are also made accessible by detailed subject and geographic indexes. Earlier volumes in the set cover only India and Pakistan.

2010   U.S. Department of the Army. *Communist China, A Bibliographic Survey.* Washington, DC: 1971.

2011   _____ . *Communist North Korea, A Bibliographic Survey.* Washington, DC: 1971.

2012   _____ . *Insular Southeast Asia, A Bibliographic Survey.* Washington, DC: 1971.

2013   _____ . *Japan; Analytical Bibliography with Supplementary Research Aids and Selected Data on Okinawa, Republic of China (Taiwan), Republic of Korea.* Washington, DC: 1972.

2014   _____ . *Middle East: The Strategic Hub and North Africa. A Bibliographic Survey of the Literature.* Washington, DC: U.S. Government Printing Office, 1973.

2015   _____ . *Pacific Islands and Trust Territories. A Selected Bibliography.* Washington, DC: 1971.

2016   _____ . *Peninsular Southeast Asia. A Bibliographic Survey.* Washington, DC: 1972.

2017   _____ . *South Asia: A Strategic Survey.* Washington, DC: 1966.

2018   _____ . *Southasia and the Strategic Indian Ocean.* Washington, DC: 1973.

These extensively annotated bibliographies list books, periodical articles, and other publications dealing with the political, social, economic, and military situation as it existed a decade ago in specific regions and countries of Asia.

2019   Zuwiyya, Jalal. *The Near East (Southwest Asia and North Africa).* Metuchen, NJ: Scarecrow Press, 1973.

The unannotated bibliography offers subject, country, title, and author access to more than 3,600 English-language publications about the Middle East. Entries are arranged by author in two parts. Part 1 lists material in 13 subject categories, including political structures, economic structure, history, law, social organizations, etc. Part 2 contains listings for 13 individual countries, with subdivisions by subject categories, including politics and government. Separate indexes by authors and titles are also provided.

Book Reviewing Media

2020   *Gazelle Review of Literature on the Middle East.* London: Ithaca Press, 1977– .

This reference publication, issued twice yearly, presents lengthy reviews of English and French books dealing with the Middle East. Reviews are written by leading scholars, writers, and journalists. The subject matter covered by the literature includes political, economic, cultural, and historical aspects of the Middle East situation. The reviews reflect a variety of viewpoints.

Dictionaries

2021   Shimoni, Yaacov, and Evyatar Levine. *Political Dictionary of the Middle East in the 20th Century.* Jerusalem: Jerusalem Publishing House, 1972.

2022   Ziring, Lawrence. *The Middle East Political Dictionary.* Santa Barbara, CA: ABC-Clio, 1983.

2023   Ziring, Lawrence, and C. I. Eugene Kim. *The Asian Political Dictionary.* Santa Barbara, CA: ABC-Clio, 1984.

The three dictionaries offer concise definitions and other information for past and current political phenomena of the Asian world.

Document Collections

The standard bibliographic instruments for the book and periodical literature about the Middle East may frequently be insufficient for a thorough assessment of the complex developments and opportunities in this important area. For this reason a number of document collections have been developed that constitute a more penetrating reference source for essential information in economic, financial, military, and other political matters.

2024   *CIA Research Reports: The Middle East, 1946–1976.* Frederick, MD: University Publications of America.

2025   *The Middle East, Special Studies, 1970–1980.* Frederick, MD: University Publications of America.

————. *Supplement, 1980–1982.* Frederick, MD: University Publications of America.

Prepared by CIA experts and major research organizations, these document collections contain reports and special studies, not previously accessible to the public, about various contemporary political phenomena in Middle Eastern countries. Topics covered in the research works include Moslem fundamentalist movements, Palestinian guerilla organizations, Israeli reprisal policy, Israel's treatment of major ethnic groups, the political impact of U.S. military force in the Middle East, Arab perceptions of regional security issues, the impact of modernization in Saudi Arabia, as well as situation reports for individual countries and biographical assessments of political leaders. All reports and special studies are available on microfilm only, but printed guides provide access to the individual items in the collections.

2026   *Middle East Data File.* Ann Arbor, MI: Xerox University Microfilms, 1975–.

Access to primary documentation is offered by this microfiche collection of documents procured from government ministries, political parties and organizations, trade unions, chambers of commerce, banks, research institutes, and similar institutions. Documents are in English or French and cover a variety of subjects, including law, politics, economics, defense, urban planning, the oil industry, religion, etc. Geographic coverage encompasses the countries of North Africa, Northwest Asia (Northern Tier), the Levant and Mediterranean area, the Central Arab region, and Central Africa. Document and information retrieval is facilitated by a hard copy index containing a specially developed thesaurus, subject entries, and document guides. This reference set is also available in separate subject packages and regional packages, all of which are continuously updated.

2027   *Middle East Development Documents on Microfiche.* Zug, Switzerland: Inter Documentation Company, 1975–.

The continuously updated collection consists of microfiche documents in English and French relating to the economic, social, legal, and political developments in the Middle East. The collection covers 13 countries of the area, namely, Algeria, Egypt, Iraq, Jordan, Kuwait, Lebanon, Lybia, Morocco, Persian Gulf States, Saudi Arabia, Sudan, Syria and Yemen. Documents on Iran, Tunisia, and Israel are separately available. Access to the documents in the collection is provided by a sales catalog that lists titles by country, and a detailed subject index. In addition, regular catalog cards containing the same information as the sales catalog are issued by the publisher. Much of the information material in the document collection deals with policy decisions in matters of trade, oil production, labor utilization, public finance, etc., but considerable statistical and other survey material is also included.

Handbooks and Yearbooks

2028   *Asian Annual: The "Eastern World" Handbook.* London: Eastern World, 1954–.

Annually updated information is presented by this handbook for the area, population, constitution, diplomatic representation, trade, industry, education, communication media, etc., of individual Asian countries. Only countries east of Afghanistan are included.

2029   *The Far East and Australasia.* London: Europa Publications, 1969–.

This annual handbook provides a survey of the economic, social, and political situation in countries extending eastward from Afghanistan to the Pacific Islands including Soviet Asia. The information is arranged in four regional sections, a section on the regional organizations, and a section on reference material. The latter offers biographical information on political and other personalities, a list of research institutes, and a bibliography of periodicals. The political information supplied by the handbook includes descriptive and statistical data on the constitution, government, parliament, political parties, diplomatic representation, and other institutions in each country.

2030   Henderson, John W., et al. *Area Handbook for Oceania*. Washington, DC: U.S. Government Printing Office, 1971.

Basic details about the social, economic, political, and military institutions of the various countries and territories of Australasia are supplied by this handbook, which was prepared by the Foreign Areas Studies Department of the American University. A bibliography of recommended publications as well as tables and maps are also included.

2031   Legum, Colin. *Middle East Contemporary Survey*. New York: Holmes & Meier Publishers, 1978—.

Annual summaries of Middle Eastern affairs are presented by this reference work, along with a country-by-country analysis of political, economic, and social trends. Developments in the Arab-Israeli conflict are also reported. This series is also an excellent source for statistical information.

2032   Mansfield, Peter. *The Middle East. A Political and Economic Survey*. New York: Oxford University Press, 1980.

A broad spectrum of information on the land, people, history, politics, government, and economic conditions of Middle Eastern countries except Turkey can be found in this handbook. It is organized into ten chapters based on the individual countries of the region. An introductory chapter provides information on the entire region and the oil industry in the Middle East. Statistical appendices contain general data and oil industry figures. A reading list and index are included in addition to a map of the region.

2033   *The Middle East*. Washington, DC: Congressional Quarterly, Inc. 1981.

The handbook contains country profiles for 16 states in the Middle East area, a chronology of events during 1945 to 1981, biographies of key figures, and six articles on the Middle East, its history, religion, conflicts, and problems. Also included is the text of the Camp David accord and other peace agreements. A bibliography of books, articles, and government publications on the Middle East provides access to additional information. Various tables, charts, maps, and a detailed index are also provided in the frequently revised handbook.

2034   *The Middle East and North Africa: A Survey and Directory of the Countries of the Middle East*. London: Europa Publications, 1948—.

The annual reference work offers information about 37 countries and territories of Asia and Africa. Each volume includes a calendar of events, a general survey of the region, sections on regional organizations, and separate chapters on each country covering history, constitution, government, foreign relations, judicial system, etc. There is also a biographical section of Who's Who in the Middle East and North Africa, and a bibliographic section with listings of books on the Middle East and North Africa, as well as a list of periodicals publishing information on the area.

2035   *Middle East Record*. Tel Aviv: Reuven Shiloah Research Center, 1960—.

This unique reference work, prepared by a prestigious Israeli research center, provides a detailed annual account of the politics and international relations of the countries of the Middle East. Information is arranged in three parts: (1) the Middle East in World Affairs, (2) Relations between the Countries of the Middle East, and (3) Internal Political Affairs and International Relations of Cyprus, Iraq, Israel, Jordan, Lebanon, Saudi Arabia, Sudan, Syria, Turkey, Egypt, Yemen, and other states in the area. A very detailed index and list of information sources is included. Unfortunately, the publication lag is considerable.

2036   *Middle East Yearbook*. London: Middle East Magazine, 1977—.

The yearbook is an annual source of statistical information on population, education, oil production, agriculture, and other economic activities. It also provides general information about the Middle East area as well as a country-by-country survey.

EUROPE

Library Resources

2037   Horecky, Paul L., and David H. Kraus. *East Central and Southeast Europe*. Santa Barbara, CA: ABC-Clio Press, 1978.

Scholars dissatisfied with the inadequacies of local library holdings will find in this reference work a detailed description of the extensive East European collections in the Library of Congress and some 40 major university libraries and research institutes in the United States and Canada. Arranged alphabetically by the name of the institution and then by country, the descriptions, ranging from 2,000 to 5,000 words in length, identify bibliographic guides and other reference works, as well as the subject and area content of significant holdings in books, periodicals, newspapers, manuscripts, and other collected materials in a specific library. Subjects with strong research holdings are mentioned prominently. The described library collections focus mainly on the socioeconomic and political sciences as well as the humanities and cover nine countries, namely, Albania, Bulgaria, Czechoslovakia, East Germany, Greece, Hungary, Poland, Romania, and Yugoslavia. An area and subject guide in the book provides additional access to the collection descriptions.

2038   New York. Public Library. Slavonic Division. *Dictionary Catalog of the Slavonic Collection, The New York Public Library Reference Department*. Boston: G. K. Hall, 1974.

The catalog refers to one of the major Baltic and Slavonic collections in the western hemisphere, totalling some 200,000 volumes in all fields of knowledge. Approximately 65 percent of the holdings are in Russian, with 60 percent of the cards in the Cyrillic alphabet. There are approximately 727,000 card entries for authors, titles, and subjects, including many references to periodical articles and official documents. Microfilm, photostats, and electrostatic reproductions of the listed material can be obtained from the library. Revised editions of the catalog are published at irregular intervals.

Guidebooks

2039   *European Markets. A Guide to Company and Industry Information Sources*. Washington, DC: Washington Researchers, 1983.

While its scope is considerably broader than its title indicates, *European Markets* is a guidebook to official and private sector sources of information about the economic and political situation in 24 non-Communist countries of Europe. The sources include international organizations, European government agencies, including their representations in the United States, U.S. federal, state, and local government agencies, as well as private sector organizations (banks, accounting firms, etc.), and reference sources, such as computerized databases, directories, indexes, etc. The guidebook is most valuable for identifying persons, organizations, and publications that offer information about the various economic policies, government regulations of products, industries and commercial transactions, and societal factors in Western European nations.

2040   Horak, Stephan M., and Rosemary Neiswender. *Russia, The USSR, and Eastern Europe. A Bibliographic Guide to English Language Publications, 1964–1974*. Littleton, CO: Libraries Unlimited, 1978.

The guidebook updates the Horecky guidebooks, cited below. It is organized in 11 chapters within three main parts, namely, (1) General and Interrelated Themes; (2) Russian Empire to 1917 and USSR, Non-Russian Republics, Jews; and (3) Eastern Europe. Chapters with

suitable subdivisions aggregate the material by field of study (economics, history, government and law, international relations, military affairs, foreign policy, sociology, language and literature, etc.), and by country, namely, Russia and Soviet Union, Albania, Bulgaria, Czechoslovakia, German Democratic Republic, Hungary, Poland, Romania, and Yugoslavia. Reference books are listed separately within these divisions. All entries refer to English-language books and are accompanied by critical annotations usually excerpted or adapted from reviews. Two separate indexes, author/title and subject, provide access to the listed material.

2041   Horecky, Paul L. *East Central Europe. A Guide to Basic Publications*. Chicago: University of Chicago Press, 1969.

2042   _____ . *Southeastern Europe. A Guide to Basic Publications*. Chicago: University of Chicago Press, 1969.

The two volumes offer an annotated guide to basic books, periodicals, and periodical articles published in English and other languages about the political, socioeconomic, and intellectual life in Eastern European countries.* The volume on East Central Europe deals with the literature for Czechoslovakia, East Germany, Hungary, Poland, and the East Central European area in general. The volume on Southeastern Europe covers the literature for Albania, Bulgaria, Greece, Romania, and Yugoslavia. In both volumes the country chapters are subdivided into eight or nine categories that focus on the land, the people, the history, the state, the economy, the society, and the intellectual life of the country. General reference aids, bibliographies, and survey works are listed separately. The excellent indexes include names of authors, compilers, editors, translators, sponsoring organizations, titles, and principal subjects. Both volumes are the result of a cooperative effort by more than 50 distinguished scholars to prepare single-volume guides to essential publications from an aggregate book output of more than 600,000 titles covering the area.

2043   Slavic Bibliographic and Documentation Center. *Research Materials for Slavists: U.S. Government Sources*. Washington, DC: Association of Research Libraries, 1970.

This booklet describes United States government agencies that produce, process, or maintain records of research materials in the Slavic field.

*A separate guidebook by Paul L. Horecky exists for Russia under the title *Russia and the Soviet Union: A Bibliographic Guide to Western Publications* (Chicago: University of Chicago Press, 1965).

Current Bibliographies

2044 *The American Bibliography of Slavic and East European Studies.* Columbus: Ohio State University Press, 1956– .

Books and articles published in the English language on Russia and Eastern Europe during the course of a year are listed without annotations in this annual bibliography. Entries are arranged by subject fields, which include history, international relations, public affairs, law and government, sociology, philosophy and ideology, anthropology, geography, economics, science, education, literature and the arts, etc. Within each subject field further subdivisions are made by country or topic. Bibliographies and other reference works are listed separately. Individual countries covered by the bibliography are the USSR, Bulgaria, Czechoslovakia, Hungary, Poland, Romania, and Yugoslavia. In recent years the bibliography has been issued with a considerable time lag.

2045 *Britain and Europe since 1945.* Brighton, England: Harvester Press, 1973– .

This is a microfiche collection, with hard copy indexes, of newspapers, journals, pamphlets, leaflets, reports, memoranda, press releases, transcripts of speeches and public broadcasts emanating from interest groups and political or social movements. The collection, which is updated and enlarged annually, deals with the issues raised by the entry of Great Britain into the European Economic Community on January 1, 1973. Individual items in the collection can be identified with a hard copy index with chronological, author, and title entries offering full bibliographic details and fiche references. Most of this material cannot be otherwise traced or located because of the ephemeral nature of the documentation. The collected documents reflect the views of the issuing organizations and special interest groups and do not document Great Britain's offical position in this matter.

2046 Council for European Studies. *European Studies Newsletter.* Pittsburgh: University of Pittsburgh, 1972– .

In contrast to the extensive study programs for Africa, Eastern Europe, and Latin America, the study of political phenomena in Western European countries continues to be somewhat neglected in American colleges and universities. A modest reorientation of study interests is discernible from the formation in 1970 of the Council for European Studies, whose members are West European study programs at eight American universities, namely Berkeley, Columbia, Harvard, Princeton, Massachusetts Institute of Technology, Michigan, Wisconsin, and Yale. The *European Studies Newsletter* is published four times a year and contains information about bibliographies and other reference services of interest to the scholar and student of West European affairs.

2047 *Südosteuropa Bibliographie.* Munich: R. Oldenbourg, 1945–1950– .

2048 *OD. Ost-Dokumentation.* Vienna: Osterreichisches Ost und Südosteuropa Insitut, 1972– .

The two bibliographies expand on the previously listed, purely English-language reference tools by offering access to a wide variety of European publications. The first item is a series of unannotated bibliographies, issued with a time lag of several years, covering books and articles in German, English, and other European languages about the history, land and people, politics, religion, church-state relations, economics, and intellectual lfe in Eastern Europe. The bibliographies are issued in sections relating to Albania, Bulgaria, Hungary, Romania, Slovakia, and Yugoslavia.

The second bibliography cited above lists and abstracts in German a variety of periodicals and newspapers published in Eastern Europe. The listed material focuses mainly on economic phenomena under state direction. The bibliography is published ten times a year with annually cumulated name and subject indexes. State laws and regulations covering economic activities are listed separately in *DGVO: Dokumentation der Gesetze und Verordnungen Ost-und Südosteuropas.*

Retrospective Bibliographies

2049 Byrnes, Robert F. *Bibliography of American Publications on East Central Europe 1945–1957.* Bloomington: Indiana University Publications, 1958.

Scholarly and semischolarly works published by Americans in book or periodical form between 1945 and 1957 are listed in this bibliography without annotations. The area covered includes Albania, Bulgaria, Czechoslovakia, Finland, Hungary, Poland, Romania, Yugoslavia, and the three Baltic states under Soviet rule, i.e., Estonia, Latvia, and Lithuania. Entries are arranged by country and region, subdivided by major subject fields. A separate author index is included.

2050 *Index Nordicus: A Cumulative Index to English-Language Periodicals on Scandinavian Studies.* Boston: G. K. Hall, 1978.

The index offers author and subject access to the English-language periodical literature about the Scandinavian countries.

2051   Merritt, Anna J., and Richard L. Merritt. *Politics, Economics and Society in the Two Germanies, 1943–1975: A Bibliography of English-Language Works.* Urbana: University of Illinois Press, 1978.

More than 8,500 English-language publications, identified by this bibliography, describe or analyze the political, social, and economic situation in the waning years of the Third Reich and its two successor states. The entries are divided by major subject categories made for general works, demography, Allied occupation, West German politics and behavior, East German government and politics, etc.

2052   U.S. Department of the Army. *Communist Eastern Europe. Analytical Survey of Literature.* Washington, DC: 1971.

2053   _____ . *Scandinavia, A Bibliographic Survey of Literature.* Washington, DC: 1975.

The two bibliographies offer well-annotated listings of the literature on the Eastern European and Scandinavian countries. The listed material focuses on political, economic, and military affairs.

2054   Vesala, Heimo. *A List of Reference Books about the Soviet Union and Eastern Europe Including Selected Reading Lists.* Helsinki: Institute of Political Science, University of Helsinki, 1973.

This unannotated list identifies bibliographies, encyclopedias, dictionaries, handbooks, yearbooks, biographical dictionaries, calendars, document collections, and newsletters useful for the study of the Soviet Union and Eastern European countries. The reference works listed are published in English, German, and Russian. Also included are selected reading lists of books and articles dealing with the methodological problems of Communist studies, Kremlinology, totalitarianism, historiography, political science, and sociology in socialist countries.

Dictionaries

2055   McCrea, Barbara P., Jack Plano, and George Klein. *The Soviet and East European Political Dictionary.* Santa Barbara, CA: ABC-Clio, 1983.

2056   Rossi, Ernest E., and Jack C. Plano. *The European Political Dictionary.* Santa Barbara, CA: ABC-Clio, 1984.

The two dictionaries are a quick and up-to-date reference source for definitions, interpretations and other information of the political phenomena in Eastern and Western Europe.

Document Collections

2057   *CIA Research Reports: Europe, 1946–1976.* Frederick, MD: University Publications of America, 1982.

2058   *Europe and NATO: Special Studies, 1970–1980.* Frederick, MD: University Publications of America, 1982.

2059   *CIA Research Reports, Soviet Union, 1946–1976.* Frederick, MD: University Publications of America, 1982.

2060   *The Soviet Union, 1970–1980: Special Studies.* Frederick, MD: University Publications of America, 1982.

_____ . *The Soviet Union, 1980–1982 Supplement.* Frederick, MD: University Publications of America, 1983.

These document collections, available to the general public for the first time, albeit with some delay, offer reliable contemporary data and expert analyses of the most important political phenomena in various European countries and the Soviet Union. Prepared by experts in the Central Intelligence Agency and major research organizations, such as the Rand Corporation, the Army War College's Strategic Studies Institute, the National Defense University, and other prestigious unversities, the reports and studies focus on such topics as European security, attitude toward NATO, Britain's economy, the readiness of U.S. Forces in Europe, contemporary Italian terrorism, Soviet-Finnish relations, Soviet military weaknesses, political control of the Soviet armed forces, emergent nationality problems in the USSR, the politics of balance in Tito's Yugoslavia, NATO in the year 2000, Italian communism, the French Left, and many others. All reports and studies are available on microfilm only together with printed guides.

Handbooks

2061   Cook, Christopher, and John Paxton. *European Political Facts, 1918–1972.* New York: St. Martin's Press, 1973.

The most important political, social, and economic facts for 35 European countries since the end of World

War I are easily retrievable from this handbook. It names the heads of state and gives information about the parliament, ministers, elections, political parties, and the judicial system of each country. Population trends, economic planning, trade unions, education, the press, membership in international organizations are also detailed.

2062   *Euroguide*. Luxembourg: Euroguide International, 1977.

For each of the European countries, the multivolume reference set presents information in the following categories: history, constitution, judiciary system, economy, tax system, geography, size and population, ethnic groups, education, work and social insurance, energy sources, diplomatic representation, the state and government, universities, political parties, trade unions, industrial and financial organizations, the press, religions, etc.

2063   Merkl, Peter H., and Zane T. Reeves. *Western European Governmental and Political Organization: An Outline*. Pasadena, CA: Current World Leaders, 1975.

A comparison of the political institutions in Western European countries is facilitated by this reference work. It presents in handy tabular form facts and figures about the constitution, the executive, legislative, and judicial branches of government, political parties, elections, and armed forces of each country.

2064   *Scandinavian Political Studies*. New York: Columbia University Press, 1966–.

The annual handbook of the Political Science Associations of Denmark, Norway and Sweden contains various essays and reviews for government and political processes in Scandinavian countries. There are also bibliographical surveys of the political literature published in or about the Scandinavian countries.

2065   Staar, Richard F. *The Communist Regimes in Eastern Europe*. Stanford, CA: Hoover Institution Press, Stanford University, 1982.

The handbook, now in its fourth edition, describes the governmental structure, constitutional framework, systems of elections, ruling party, domestic and foreign affairs of each of the European countries under Communist rule. Information is also presented about the military and economic integration of the area. The book also provides a bibliography of books and pamphlets as well as a list of periodicals and newspapers containing information about the area. Previously independent countries, like the Baltic states now incorporated into the Soviet Union, are not covered in this work.

LATIN AMERICA

Library Resources

2066   Haro, Robert P. *Latin Americana Research in the United States and Canada: A Guide and Directory*. Chicago: American Library Association, 1971.

The systematic acquisition of books published in Latin America shows a pattern of country responsibility according to which a single library in the United States undertakes to acquire all the publications of a specific country. This reference work offers a list of Latin American countries with the names of the libraries responsible for the acquisition of their publications output. Also included are lists of Latin American library collections in the United States, Puerto Rico, Virgin Islands, and Canada with information about subject strengths, special collections, interlibrary loan facilities, etc. Libraries with printed book catalogs of their collections are separately listed. Finally, the book provides a list of Latin American research centers as well as indexes by country, subject, and library specialists.

2067   Miami. University of Miami. *Catalog of the Cuban and Caribbean Library*. Boston: G. K. Hall, 1978.

The six-volume set contains an estimated 102,000 cards for author, title, and subject entries relating to publications about the entire Caribbean area, including Mexico and Colombia.

2068   New Orleans. Tulane University. Library. *Catalog of the Latin American Library*. Boston: G. K. Hall, 1971.

————— . *First Supplement*. Boston: G. K. Hall, 1973.

————— . *Second Supplement*. Boston: G. K. Hall, 1975.

————— . *Third Supplement*. Boston: G. K. Hall, 1978.

Tulane University houses another important library collection of Latin American material for which a book catalog is available. The base catalog comprises approximately 152,000 cards for books, periodicals, newspapers, manuscripts, microfilms, church documents, etc. Central America is the strongest geographical area of concentration, with subject emphasis in the social sciences and humanities.

2069   Texas. University at Austin. Library. *Catalog of the Latin American Collection*. Boston: G. K. Hall, 1969.

————— . *First Supplement*. Boston: G. K. Hall, 1971.

_____. *Second Supplement.* Boston: G. K. Hall, 1973.

_____. *Third Supplement.* Boston: G. K. Hall, 1975.

_____. *Fourth Supplement.* Boston: G. K. Hall, 1977.

This catalog and its supplements represent one of the most important Latin American collections in the United States. The 31-volume base set lists some 175,000 books, pamphlets, periodicals. microfilms, and newspapers providing information about virtually any subject relating to Latin America. The publications output of Mexico, for which the library has country responsibility, is well reflected in the listings. The entire collection is made accessible with 768,500 card entries by author, title, subject, and numerous cross-references. More current acquisitions of this library appear annually in the *Bibliographic Guide to Latin American Studies*, published by G. K. Hall since 1979.

Guidebooks

2070   Sable, Martin H. *Guide to Latin American Studies.* Los Angeles: Latin American Center, University of California, 1967.

2071   Wilgus, Alva Curtis. *Latin America, Spain and Portugal: A Selected and Annotated Bibliographical Guide to Books Published in the United States, 1954 – 1974.* Metuchen, NJ: Scarecrow Press, 1977.

The two guidebooks present two different approaches to a substantial portion of the scholarly literature about Latin American countries. The first guidebook, a two-volume set, provides annotated listings of books and periodicals in English, Spanish, Portuguese, and other languages, whereas the second guidebook lists English-language books and pamphlets only. Entries in the Sable guidebook are arranged by major subject fields, including political science, anthropology, commerce, economics, history, education, etc. The largest number of entries is in political science, with subdivisions for armed forces, church and state, communism, democracy, elections, nationalism, political leaders and parties, etc. Within these divisions the listings are broken down by country. The Wilgus guidebook uses an area and country approach for its listings, which are then subdivided by subject. Approximately 1,700 titles are listed with annotations.

Current Bibliographies

2072   *Bibliographic Guide to Latin American Studies.* Boston: G. K. Hall, 1980 – .

Published annually, this bibliography lists books, serials, and nonbook materials cataloged during the preceding year by two of the world's most comprehensive Latin American collections — the Library of Congress and the University of Texas Library in Austin. Entries are arranged in one alphabetical sequence for main entries, added entries, titles, series, and subject headings. The listed material may originate anywhere in the world and covers virtually any topic related to Latin America. English-language as well as foreign language publications, including items in Indian dialects, are listed, but no annotations are provided.

2073   *Handbook of Latin American Studies.* Gainesville: University of Florida Press, 1935 – .

All important publications on Latin America are listed and annotated in this annual bibliography in a classified arrangement by academic discipline — anthropology, economics, geography, history, government and international relations, etc. Within each discipline entries are subdivided by countries and preceded by a brief survey of major trends in the literature. Separate author and subject indexes are provided, but the latter includes primarily references to countries, regions, and institutions.

2074   *HAPI. Hispanic American Periodicals Index.* Los Angeles: University of California, 1974 – .

Periodical articles of interest to Latin Americanists can be identified by subject and author with the help of this annually published index. Approximately 200 periodicals published in Central and South America, Mexico, the United States, Europe, and the Caribbean area serve as a database for the entries. All subject areas and disciplines in the social sciences are covered. Book reviews are also listed and can be found in the subject section under the author of the book. Due to its annual publication schedule, the index cannot be used to track down very recent periodical articles on the current political situation in Latin American countries.

2075   *Interamerican Review of Bibliography.* Washington, DC: General Secretariat of the Organization of American States, 1951 – .

The quarterly bibliography identifies books about Latin America under 21 broad subject and form headings, including political science, international relations, history, law, bibliography, reference works, etc. The listings are based on the acquisitions of the Columbus Library of the Pan American Union, the Library of Congress, the U.S. National Agricultural Library, and the libraries of Harvard and Columbia universities. The delay in the listings of new books varies between one and two years.

2076   Latin American Studies Association. *Latin American Research Review*. Gainesville, FL: 1965– .

This publication, issued three times yearly, contains an inventory of postdoctoral research projects concerned with Latin America that are currently undertaken in the United States, Canada, and Latin America. For each project the name of the principal and other researchers, the title, beginning date, expected date of completion, and a general description is provided. Newly received bibliographies, directories, and other reference works are also listed.

Retrospective Bibliographies

2077   Bayitch, S. A. *Latin America and the Caribbean: A Bibliographical Guide to Works in English*. Coral Gables, FL: University of Miami Press, 1967.

Books, periodical articles, and other publications in English about economic, political, and legal matters in Central and South American countries, including the Caribbean area, can be identified under various approaches in this bibliography. The unannotated listings are arranged in six parts: (1) Bibliographies and Reference Works, (2) General Information, (3) Fundamentals and Backgrounds, (4) Guide by Subjects, (5) Guide by Countries of Central and South America, (6) Guide by Countries of the Caribbean Area. The country listings are also subdivided by subject categories, including administration, armed forces and defense, constitutional law, elections, foreign relations, history, law, municipal government, politics, etc. There is no author index, but a brief subject index is included.

2078   Chilcote, Ronald H. *Revolution and Structural Change in Latin America. A Bibliography on Ideology, Development and the Radical Left*. Stanford, CA: Hoover Institution on War, Revolution and Peace, Stanford University, 1970.

The unannotated bibliography focuses on revolution, structural change, and radical political thought in Latin America. It identifies 10,000 books, pamphlets, periodical articles, and other publications in a country arrangement with author and title entries under three bibliographic form categories. The two-volume set also contains entries for general bibliographies, bibliographies of periodicals, as well as for general books, pamphlets, and articles. A subject, author, and periodical index is included.

2079   Comitas, Lambros. *The Complete Caribbeana 1900–1975: A Bibliographic Guide to the Scholarly Literature*. Millwood, NY: KTO Press, 1978.

The unannotated but comprehensive bibliography contains over 17,000 entries for books, articles, reports, dissertations, and other information material issued during a 75-year period about the Caribbean area. Entries are arranged topically by author. Topics include poltical issues, socioeconomic activities, economic and social prospects, elements of culture, population, race relations, etc. Separate indexes are provided by author, geographic area, and names of persons who appear as subjects in the works.

2080   Dahlin, Therrin C., Gary P. Gillum, and Mark L. Grover. *The Catholic Left in Latin America: A Comprehensive Bibliography*. Boston: G. K. Hall, 1981.

Oriented as it is toward educational, economic, and social reforms, the Catholic Left movement in Latin America is an intriguing political phenomenon that until recently has received scant bibliographic attention. The bibliography cited above offers comprehensive bibliographic coverage of the existing literature by listing nearly 4,000 books, journal and newspaper articles published between 1960 and 1978. The unannotated entries are arranged in 15 sections devoted to Latin America, Caribbean, Central America, and 12 specific countries. Within these sections subdivisions are made for major topics that include Catholic church and social change, Catholic church and state, Christian democracy, liberation, labor and laboring classes, Marxism, revolution, socialism, violence, and other political manifestations. Publications about Helder Camara and Camillo Torres, two prominent Catholic Left figures, are separately listed. English-language material as well as publications in Spanish, Portuguese, and other European languages are cited. Separate author and title indexes are provided, but no subject index is included.

2081   Delorme, Robert L. *Latin America, 1967– 1978: A Comprehensive Social Science Bibliography and Research Guide*. Santa Barbara, CA: American Bibliographical Center–Clio Press, 1979.

2082   Weaver, Jerry L. *Latin American Development, A Selected Bibliography*. Santa Barbara, CA: American Bibliographical Center–Clio Press, 1969.

The two bibliographies offer access to a substantial portion of the scholarly literature published during a period of almost 30 years about the Latin American area. Books, articles, and some dissertations are listed if they pertain to the political, economic, and social situation in Latin America. The unannotated entries are arranged by author under countries or regional headings. The Delorme bibliography contains separate listings for 3,500 journal articles and 1,500 books with separate topical indexes. Its coverage includes new research areas developed over the past decade.

2083   Gropp, Arthur E. *A Bibliography of Latin American Bibliographies*. Metuchen, NJ: Scarecrow Press, 1968.

————. *Supplement*. Metuchen, NJ: Scarecrow Press, 1971.

2084   ————. *A Bibliography of Latin American Bibliographies Published in Periodicals*. Metuchen, NJ: Scarecrow Press, 1976.

Bibliographies published about Latin America in book or periodical form during a period of some 30 years can be identified by subject with the help of these reference works. Many of the listed bibliographies cover topics in political science, its subfields, and auxiliary sciences. The subject listings are subdivided by countries. Detailed indexes of names, subjects, and countries are included.

2085   *Index to Latin American Periodical Literature, 1929–1960*. Boston: G. K. Hall, 1962.

————. *First Supplement*. Boston: G. K. Hall, 1968.

2086   *Indice General de Publicaciones Periodicas Latino Americanos: Humanidades y Ciencias Sociales* (Index of Latin American Periodicals: Humanities and Social Sciences). Metuchen, NJ: Scarecrow Press, 1961–1971.

The two bibliographic sets provide author and subject access to articles about the political, economic, legal, and cultural affairs of Latin American countries. All entries refer to periodicals published in Latin American countries, the United States, and other parts of the world during a period of some 40 years. A large number of the 300,000 entries in the first index cited above refer to official action published in government gazettes. The supplement does not include periodicals cited in the *Index to Latin American Periodicals*.

2087   Inter-American Development Bank. Washington, DC. *Inter-American Bank Index of Periodical Articles on the Economics of Latin America*. Boston: G. K. Hall, 1983.

In no other part of the world are the political economies of many nations in such disarray as in Latin America. Unbearably high rates of inflation, unemployment, external debt, and stagnation characterize the economic conditions of most countries south of the United States border. This index identifies most of the existing periodical literature bearing on this political phenome-

non. It cites nearly 12,000 articles selected from some 800 scholarly and official periodicals published in English or Spanish during a 20-year period up to 1980. Coverage includes monetary, fiscal and economic policies pursued or contemplated by the various countries as well as other political and sociological information related to Latin American economies. Access is facilitated by separate author, title, subject, and country listings.

2088   Sable, Martin H. *Latin American Studies in the Nonwestern World and Eastern Europe*. Metuchen, NJ: Scarecrow Press, 1970.

Books, pamphlets, dissertations, periodical articles, conference proceedings and government documents published in more than 20 languages in Africa, Asia, the Middle East, and Eastern Europe are listed in this bibliography if they relate to the Latin American area.

2089   U.S. Department of the Army. *Latin America and the Caribbean: Analytical Survey of Literature*. Washington, DC: U.S. Government Printing Office, 1975.

Political change, economic and sociological trends, foreign power interests, defense and security in the Caribbean area and South America, including Mexico, constitute the focus of this annotated literature survey. Listed are books, periodical articles, unpublished theses, research studies, and official publications. The reference work also includes a collection of maps for the various countries on which the location of economic activities is indicated.

2090   Zimmerman, Irene. *Current National Bibliographies of Latin America*. Gainesville: University of Florida, 1971.

The reference book provides a narrative description of the national bibliographies published in Latin American countries. Following an introductory section, the material is presented in two parts, South America and the Caribbean area, with separate chapters devoted to each country. The titles of bibliographic publications are interwoven in the text, which offers detailed information and a summary of the bibliographic situation as it existed up to a decade ago in each country.

Dictionaries

2091   Rossi, Ernest E., and Jack C. Plano. *The Latin American Political Dictionary*. Santa Barbara, CA: ABC-Clio, 1980.

The dictionary is a quick reference source for answering inquiries about political phenomena in Latin American countries.

Document Collections

2092 *CIA Research Reports: Latin America, 1946–1976.* Frederick, MD: University Publications of America, n.d.

2093 *Latin America, Special Studies, 1962–1980.* Frederick, MD: University Publications of America, n.d.

_____ . *Supplement, 1980–1982.*

Although released to the public with some delay, the *CIA Research Reports* and the *Special Studies* prepared by private and official organizations, such as the Rand Corporation, the Army War College's Strategic Studies Institute, the National Defense University, and other research institutions constitute a valuable research resource for evaluating policy options and responses to political challenges surfacing in Latin American countries. The 459 titles in the CIA collection and the 135 titles in the second collection cited above deal with such topics as Cuban training of Latin American subversives, the role of the military, problems of progress, political consequences of U.S. military assistance to Latin American countries, radicalism in the Caribbean, prospects for a U.S.-Mexican energy relationship, patterns of economic policy making, guerillas and politics, the role of the church, and other political phenomena typical for this region. All reports and studies are available on microfilm only, but printed guides provide access to the collections.

Encyclopedias

2094 *Encyclopedia of Latin America.* New York: McGraw-Hill, 1974.

The encyclopedia is a comprehensive yet concise reference book offering authoritative information on the leading personalities as well as the history, economy, politics, arts, and other aspects of Latin America. Political parties and political actors, including guerilla leaders, are well covered. The most important articles in the encyclopedia include bibliographical references for additional information. A separate select bibliography of bibliographies for general and special topics and individual countries is also provided.

Handbooks and Yearbooks

2095 *Global Studies—Latin America.* Guilford, CT: Dushkin Publishing Group, 1984.

The handbook offers regional essays and individual country reports describing the geographical, cultural, sociopolitical, and economic characteristics, differences,

and similarities of the countries and regions of Latin America. In addition, reprints of important periodical and newspaper articles are provided. A glossary, a bibliography, and an index are also included.

2096 Hopkins, Jack W. *Latin America and Caribbean Contemporary Record.* New York: Holmes & Meier, 1983– .

Current and well-documented surveys of Latin American and Caribbean affairs are provided by this yearbook. Part 1 contains essays on important regional and area topics, while part 2 consists of individual country reports summarizing recent developments. The text of international treaties and other documents can be found in part 3. Economic, social, and political data for varying periods of time are offered in part 4. A final section provides an annotated bibliography of recent books on Latin America.

2097 *Latin America & Caribbean.* Saffron Walden, England: World of Information, 1980– .

Latin American development and policies are surveyed in this yearbook, which also offers statistical data on current economic activities.

BIOGRAPHICAL AND ORGANIZATIONAL SOURCES

Introduction

The evaluation of political situations and developments in various countries and time periods is rarely possible without biographical and organizational information for statesmen, cabinet members, politicians, and other political actors. Unfortunately, such information is rarely available in sufficient detail unless supplied by memorialists or historians. Political figures who have only recently emerged into political prominence or influence seldom have adequate biographical detail known for correct assessment of their actions and capabilities. With few exceptions, biographical information is usually not available on a comparative basis. Students looking for comparative information about the socialist statesmen of Europe, the juntas of Latin America, or the guerilla leaders of the Third World, for instance, face time-consuming problems of information retrieval. Similarly, comparative studies between different kinds of political personalities, such as aggressive "can do" leaders and cautious doubters, are hard to identify.

Considerable biographical information can be located with the help of newpaper indexes and general periodical indexes. New digests, some dictionaries, and the regional handbooks are also useful reference sources.

There are, however, two types of reference instruments — biobibliographies and directories — that are most suitable for the retrieval of biographical information. It would be impossible to present, in the context of this guidebook, a comprehensive listing of the many biographical and organizational directories in existence for all parts of the world, but the following titles are considered excellent starting points in the search for information on the political actors of all countries.

Bibliographies

2098   *Biography and Genealogy Master Index*. Detroit: Gale Research Company, 1981.

_____ . *Supplement*. Detroit: Gale Research Company, 1982–.

2099   *Biography Master Index*. Detroit: Gale Research Company, 1981–. (Vendor: Dialog — File 88)

The printed and computerized versions of this index offer bibliographical citations to over 3,200,000 biographical sketches in more than 350 general or regional biographical reference works. Coverage includes historical and contemporary personages in all countries with political actors well represented. The cited sources are Who's Who type publications as well as regional handbooks, like *Africa South of the Sahara*, *The Middle East and North Africa*, and similar works.

2100   *Biography Index*. New York: H. W. Wilson, 1946–.

Biographical material published in books and periodicals about people from every age, country, or vocation can be identified with the help of this quarterly index. Entries are arranged by name of biographee and include, apart from full bibliographic citations, birth dates and death dates, if applicable. A separate name index by professions or occupations makes it possible to identify the names of various kinds of political actors who are the subject of biographical information cited in the index.

2101   *Chicorel Index to Biographies*. New York: Chicorel Library Publishing Corporation, 1974.

The index provides access to biographical books by name of biographee as well as by subject category. The subject categories include terms for professions, occupations, nationalities, and historical periods. It is possible to identify biographies of politicians, diplomats, military leaders, government officials, civil rights leaders, dictators, governors, judges, political reformers, political scientists, political theorists, presidents, revolutionaries, socialists, and many other political actors. An alphabetical list of biographees is also included. Updated editions of this reference work are planned.

2102   Slocum, Robert B. *Biographical Dictionaries and Related Works*. Detroit: Gale Research Company, 1967.

_____ . *First Supplement*. Detroit: Gale Research Company, 1972.

_____ . *Second Supplement*. Detroit: Gale Research Company, 1978.

Biographical reference works are usually published by vocation, country of residence, geographic region, or on a worldwide basis. This annotated bibliography, updated at irregular intervals, lists many thousands of biographical reference works by their organization form. Separate indexes by author, title, and subject offer additional access to the listed reference sources.

Current International Directories

2103   *Current World Leaders — Almanac, Biography and News, Speeches and Reports*. Santa Barbara, CA: International Academy at Santa Barbara, 1957–.

Published eight times a year, the *Almanac* offers biographical information about leading government officials, including chief delegates to the United Nations, ambassadors from foreign countries to the United States, etc. Speeches and other significant political comments made by governmental leaders are published in *Speeches and Reports*, issued five times yearly since April 1972. More recent biographical information and news are published in *Biography and News*, also issued five times per annum.

2104   *International Who's Who*. London: Allen and Unicorn, 1935–.

Influential political actors and other not necessarily politically active personalities who have achieved international fame are listed in this irregularly updated directory. All entries offer brief biographical information. A separate section is devoted to reigning royal families.

2105   *The International Yearbook and Statesman's Who's Who*. London: Burke's Peerage Ltd., 1953–.

The annually published directory offers biographical sketches about personalities prominent in government, administration, diplomacy, international organizations, and other fields.

2106   U.S. Central Intelligence Agency. *Chiefs of State and Cabinet Members of Foreign Governments*. Washington, DC: 1972–.

Information about the persons who currently occupy leading government positions throughout the world is highly unstable as a result of frequent governmental changes. This monthly reference work is the most current source for identifying in convenient form the names of the chiefs of state and cabinet members of all governments throughout the world. Entries are arranged by state but do not include biographical information. Governments with which the United States maintains no diplomatic exchanges are indicated by the initials NDE. The CIA also issues a number of more specialized directories for Communist party states, such as *Directory of Albanian Officials, Directory of Cuban Officials, Directory of Soviet Officials, Appearances of Soviet Leaders*, and several others.

Retrospective Directories

2107 Alexander, Robert J. *Political Parties of the Americas. Canada, Latin America, and the West Indies*. Westport, CT: Greenwood Press, 1982.

2108 Fukui, Haruhiro. *Political Parties of Asia and the Pacific*. Westport, CT: Greenwood Press, 1983.

2109 LeVine, Victor T. *Political Parties of Africa*. Westport, CT: Greenwood Press, 1983.

2110 McHale, Vincent. *Political Parties of Europe*. Westport, CT: Greenwood Press, 1982.

A description of the historical role and range of the political parties in each country of the world together with summarized information about each individual political party can be found in this multivolume reference set. The founding dates, principal leaders, political objects pursued or attained, and the current status of each party are identified. Detailed election statistics or membership data, the information on party newspapers and other party publications are usually omitted, but references to additional information sources are provided. Three appendices offer a chronology of party developments, a genealogy of the political parties, and two listings for ideological and interest group parties. An index is also included.

2111 Day, Alan J. *State Economic Agencies. A World Directory*. Harlow, England: Longman, 1983.

The directory offers detailed information on some 2,000 state agencies currently active in economic affairs throughout the world. Entries are arranged by country and include not only the name, address, and top officials of each agency, but also its history, aims, current policies, and financial structure. These entries are preceded by a brief introductory section that describes the prevailing economic conditions in the country.

2112 Day, Alan J., and Henry W. Degenhardt. *Political Parties of the World*. Detroit: Gale Research Company, 1980.

Arranged by country, the entries in this handbook offer concise factual data on all of the world's active political parties. Apart from basic information on the name, address, and leadership, a brief account of the history, orientation, structure, and membership of each party is presented. Introductory headnotes describe the prevailing constitutional and political situation in which the country's political parties operate. Appendices provide listings for international groupings of political parties. Separate indexes of names and publications are also included. Updating information may be found in *Keesing's Contemporary Archives*.

2113 Degenhardt, Henry W. *Political Dissent. An International Guide to Dissident, Extra-Parliamentary, Guerilla and Illegal Political Movements*. Harlow, England: Longman, 1983.

Offering a worldwide survey of illegal political opposition movements, this reference work provides details of the leadership, history, and political orientation of approximately 1,000 organizations. Both violent and nonviolent opposition groups are covered, and where applicable, the international affiliations of the organizations are identified. Entries are arranged by country under nine geographical sections, with further grouping by broad categorization — e.g., internal, external, secessionist, Islamic fundamentalist, etc. A general introduction for each country sets out the prevailing political and security situation in which the illegal movements operate.

2114 Hrabak, Diane E. *Lambert's Worldwide Government Directory with Inter-Governmental Organizations*. Washington, DC: Lambert Publications, 1981.

The directory identifies heads of state, chief executive and cabinet officers in 168 countries. Also listed are heads of defense and police forces, and the leadership of the national court system, central bank, major financial entities, and public enterprises. Apart from the names of the officeholders, address, telephone, telex, and cable information is provided for each office. Similar information is supplied for intergovernmental organizations. The frequency of updating editions, if any, is not indicated.

2115 Janke, Peter. *Guerilla and Terrorist Organizations: A World Directory and Bibliography*. Brighton, England: Harvester Press, 1983.

Guerilla and terrorist organizations are political actors that pursue political objects — often in skillful exploitation of the mass communication media — outside the established legislative, administrative, or judicial processes in violation of existing legal norms. This reference work identifies and briefly describes, in an arrangement by continent and country, the various guerilla and terrorist organizations operating in a particular country. The country entries are preceded by introductory headnotes that summarize the extent of terrorist activities in each country and offer a descriptive bibliography of the best official and scholarly publications on these illegal activities. An alphabetical index of the terrorist groups and a list of their acronyms are also included. Annual summaries of the guerilla and terrorist activities can be found in the *Annual of Power and Conflict*, cited under item 1935 in this guidebook.

2116   Gabriel, Richard A. *Fighting Armies*. Vol. 1, *NATO and the Warsaw Pact: A Combat Assessment*; Vol. 2, *Antagonists in the Middle East: A Combat Assessment*; Vol. 3, *Nonaligned, Third World, and Other Ground Armies: A Combat Assessment*. Westport, CT: Greenwood Press, 1983.

2117   Keegan, John. *World Armies*. New York: Facts on File, 1979.

While armies are important institutionalized political actors throughout the world, their actual role or influence is different in every country. There is only one situation that tests an army's performance — battle. Consequently, any theoretical or predictive assessment of an army's combat performance is a risky endeavor, usually limited to easily quantifiable factors, such as number of troops, weapons, or weapons systems.

In its three volumes, *Fighting Armies* offers a politically valuable assessment of the various armies, not only in terms of quantifiable data and publicly announced posturing, but also based on considerations of the value systems, morale, codes of ethics, and leadership qualities of the combatants. Information is organized in individual country chapters, each written by an expert in the field.

World Armies provides a descriptive portrait of each country's army in terms of its history, strength, budget, role, deployment, recent operations, organization, recruitment, training, reserves, equipment, ranks, and current developments.

2118   Korman, Richard I. *Government Organization Manuals 1900–1980*. Teaneck, NJ: Chadwyck-Healey, 1981–1983.

Government organization manuals are serially issued directories that outline and describe, often with considerable detail, the authority, structure, and function of the various organs in a nation's government together with lists of the principal officials. These directories also serve as an authoritative guide to the different sources of official publications issued in any one government.

The title cited above refers to a microfiche collection of government organization manuals, selected from 73 countries throughout the world with varying imprint dates from 1900 to 1980. The collection reproduces the full text of the original volumes from the holdings of the Library of Congress, the largest collection of government organization manuals in the world. Although many countries issue these directories at annual or other frequent intervals, this collection contains reproductions of the original volumes for selected years only, for example, every fifth or every alternate year. These selections have been made, not only in the interest of publishing economy, but also to show the different development stages in a nation's government over the years.

2119   Kuehl, Warren F. *Biographical Dictionary of Internationalists*. Westport, CT: Greenwood Press, 1983.

Until recently, biographical information about political actors who either held important positions in international organizations or otherwise actively promoted cooperation with existing or yet-to-be-created transnational bodies was difficult to retrieve. This dictionary fills the previous reference gap by offering more than 600 biographical sketches for the major proponents of world organization and cooperation from the Napoleonic era to the present. Each entry in this worldwide directory concludes with bibliographical references for additional information. Appendices list internationalists by birthplace and by career. An index is also included.

2120   Lewytzkyj, Borys, and Juliusz Stroynowski. *Who's Who in the Socialist Countries*. New York: K. G. Saur Publishing, 1978.

Brief biographical information is presented in this reference book on some 10,000 leading personalities in the Soviet Union and 15 other countries. Included are party and political officials as well as leaders in the field of economics, the military, religion, arts, and sciences.

COMPARATIVE LEGAL SOURCES

While the public law of the United States is generally retrievable without undue difficulty, access to the law of foreign countries is often problematical in the United States due to insufficient library holdings, the foreign-language barrier, or inadequate reference coverage. The following reference works will therefore be useful as

- textual sources in English for the law of individual foreign countries
- identifying tools for the scholarly publications in English and other languages relating to the law of specific countries or offering a comparison of the domestic law of several countries

For a better overview of the available reference sources,

the listings are arranged within five subsections, namely, (1) Current Bibliographies, (2) Retrospective Bibliographies, (3) Constitutional Document Collections, (4) Other Law Collections, and (5) Yearbooks.

Current Bibliographies

2121   *Index to Foreign Legal Periodicals*. London: Institute of Advanced Legal Studies, University of London, 1960–.

The quarterly reference publication offers multiple access to the legal periodical literature dealing with international law, comparative law, and the law of all countries of the world other than the United States, Great Britain, and the Commonwealth countries. Entries are arranged by subject terms, but separate geographical, author, and book review indexes are also provided. Annual and triennial cumulations are also published.

2122   Szladits, Charles. *A Bibliography on Foreign and Comparative Law: Books and Articles in English*. Volume 1: *1790–1953*. Dobbs Ferry, NY: Oceana Publications, 1955.

———. *Volume 2: 1953–1959*. Dobbs Ferry, NY: Oceana Publications, 1962.

———. *Volume 3: 1960–1965*. Dobbs Ferry, NY: Oceana Publications, 1968.

———. *Supplements*, 1966–. Dobbs Ferry, NY: Oceana Publications, 1970–.

This bibliographic set is an attempt to list all books and periodical articles in the English Language dealing with non–common law legal systems and with general subjects bearing upon the comparative study of law. Listings are arranged in ten parts, namely, (1) comparative law in general, (2) general, (3) private law, (4) commercial law, (5) labor law, (6) law of procedure, (7) criminal law, (8) criminal procedure, (9) public law, and (10) private international law. Separate indexes provide a key to the listed material by author, country, or legal system (Hindu law, Jewish law, Roman law, Roman-Dutch law, etc.). The set is kept up to date by annual supplements and by a bibliography, entitled "Foreign Law in English," published annually in the *American Journal of Comparative Law*.

Retrospective Bibliographies

2123   Harvard University. Law School. Library. *Foreign and Comparative Law Subject Catalog*. New York: K. G. Saur, 1984.

It is the area of foreign legal materials that most library holdings are deficient. As the largest and oldest academic law library in the United States, the Harvard Law School Library, however, possesses the second largest legal collection in the world — after that of the Library of Congress. The cited catalog, available on microfiche only, identifies by subject headings the library holdings relating to the law of all countries outside the common law system. It also contains cards for materials that compare the domestic law of any three or more countries, as well as for materials in the ancient, canon, Moslem, and Roman law collections.

Researchers interested in identifying Anglo-American legal materials are referred to a separate *Anglo-American Subject Catalog* (New York: K. G. Saur, 1984) for the Harvard Law School's collection of the laws of the United States, Great Britian, and all other countries with a common law system.

2124   International Association of Legal Science. *A Register of Legal Documentation in the World*. Paris: UNESCO, 1957.

This reference work lists for each country of the world the principal sources of documentation for constitutional, statutory, and decisional law as well as major law libraries, legal societies, legal periodicals, and legal bibliographies.

2125   Stollreither, Konrad. *Internationale Bibliographie der Juristischen Nachschlagewerke* (International Bibliography of Legal Reference Books). Frankfurt: Klostermann, 1955.

Regrettably much out of date, this unannotated bibliography may be used to identify general and legal bibliographies as well as other legal reference books. The entries are arranged in three parts — general, legal, and special fields. Headings are in four languages, including English. A combined author, title, and subject index is included.

2126   U.S. Library of Congress. *Index to Latin American Legislation, 1950–1960*. Boston: G. K. Hall, 1961.

———. *First Supplement, 1961–1965*. Boston: G. K. Hall, 1970.

———. *Second Supplement*. Boston: G. K. Hall, 1973.

———. *Third Supplement*. Boston: G. K. Hall, 1978.

All statutory laws as well as administrative decrees, regulations, and rulings issued in 20 Latin American countries since 1950 are available from the Library of Congress. The cited index and its supplements offer access to this legal collection with entries arranged by country and listed by subject for each jurisdiction in chronological sequence.

Constitutional Document Collections

2127   Blaustein, Albert P., and Eric B. Blaustein. *Constitutions of Dependencies and Special Sovereignties*. Dobbs Ferry, NY: Oceana Publications, 1977–.

The constitutional documents of semi-independent territories, such as the dependencies of the United States, Great Britain, and other countries, can be found in this reference set, composed of separate booklets for each governmental entity. Each booklet provides the text of the constitution, a historical introduction, and a bibliography. More than one-third of the dependencies are in the British sphere (Hong Kong, Gibraltar, Bermuda, Northern Ireland, etc.), and the second largest group is under United States jurisdiction, notably, Puerto Rico, Guam, Virgin Islands, etc. The remaining territories are under French, New Zealand, Australian, South African, Danish, Portuguese, Finnish, Norwegian, Spanish, and Netherlands jurisdiction. Also included is the Turkish federated state of Cyprus and the Vatican City state. As new dependencies are established, such as the new homelands in South Africa, for instance, new booklets are added to the collection.

2128   Blaustein, Albert P., and Gisbert Flanz. *Constitutions of the Countries of the World*. Dobbs Ferry, NY: Oceana Publications, 1971–.

The constitutions of the independent countries of the world are available in full text in this ten-volume loose-leaf set. It contains regularly updated constitutional documents together with chronologies and bibliographies. In instances where no official English translation was available, the editors have provided expert translations. The loose-leaf format permits flexibility in arrangement, alphabetically or by region, as well as the discarding of obsolete constitutional texts.

2129   Blaustein, Albert P., Jay Sigler, and Benjamin R. Beede. *Independence Documents of the World*. Dobbs Ferry, NY: Oceana, 1977.

The two-volume set offers the text of documents that mark the founding of 155 independent nation states in existence today. All documents have been translated into English, wherever necessary, but for many states documents are also provided in original languages. Brief historical introductions precede each document.

2130   Peaslee, Amos Jenkins. *Constitutions of Nations*. The Hague: M. Nijhoff, 1965–.

The multivolume set presents a comprehensive but not necessarily up-to-date compilation of the constitutions of the countries throughout the world. Only the literal text in English translation is given, but a brief summary of the international status, the form of government, the rights of the people, the legislative, executive and judicial departments, etc., for each country precedes the text of the constitution.

Other Law Collections

2131   *African Tax Systems*. 1971–. Quarterly.

2132   *Corporate Taxation in Latin America*. 19–. Quarterly.

2133   *Guides to European Taxation*. 1963–.

Vol. 1. *The Taxation of Patent Royalties, Dividends, Interest in Europe*. 3 times p.a.
Vol. 2. *The Taxation of Companies in Europe*. Bimonthly.
Vol. 3. *The Taxation of Private Investment Income*. 3 times p.a.
Vol. 4. *Value Added Taxation in Europe*. Quarterly.
Vol. 5. *Taxation in European Socialist Countries*. Annually.

2134   *Supplementary Service to European Taxation*. 1963–. Monthly.

2135   *Taxes and Investment in Asia and the Pacific*. 1978–. Bimonthly.

2136   *Taxes and Investment in the Middle East*. 1977–. Quarterly.
Amsterdam: International Bureau of Fiscal Documentation.

The International Bureau of Fiscal Documentation (IBFD) is a nonprofit research institute founded by the International Fiscal Association in 1938 and supported by grants from governments and international corporations. It publishes, as cited above, several series of loose-leaf reference works that provide complete English-language documentation on taxes imposed and tax incentives offered by the various countries on four continents. Updated monthly or at other intervals by airmailed supplements, each series is divided into several sections that contain

- the legal provisions of each country's foreign exchange regulation
- the legal provisions of each country's tax treatment of individuals, companies, property, wealth, goods, services, investments, and other transactions

- comparative surveys and statistical summaries of the tax systems, revenue sources, and fiscal policies on each continent
- the texts of double taxation treaties
- detailed bibliographies of books, periodical articles, and official publications offering additional information on taxation and economic regulation

A separate publication, entitled *Tax News Service*, issued twice monthly since 1980, reports concisely on all tax changes and new fiscal developments. In addition, a monthly journal — the *Bulletin for International Fiscal Documentation* — which is the official organ of the International Fiscal Association (IFA), reports on worldwide developments in the field of taxation.

The entire IBFD set is one of the most important political reference sources for identifying the possibilities and limitations of fiscal policies and for determining why some countries are more successful than others in managing their economies.

2137   *Commercial, Business and Trade Laws of the World*. Dobbs Ferry, NY: Oceana Publications, 1982 – .

Organized by country and region, this loose-leaf collection contains the actual texts, translated into English, of the national legislation affecting business and trade activities within and between nations. While not yet complete for all countries, the collection is updated as needed.

2138   *Commercial Laws of the Middle East*. Dobbs Ferry, NY: Oceana Publications, 1980 – .

Available separately or as part of the previously listed *CBTL* set, this loose-leaf collection focuses on the law of Middle Eastern and North African countries. The set not only includes code and statutory material but also covers leading case law and recent administrative rulings.

2139   *Digest of Commercial Laws of the World*. Dobbs Ferry, NY: Oceana Publications, 1965 – .

The digest currently consists of seven loose-leaf binders containing removable booklets on the commercial laws of 67 countries, special notes on the maritime law of 10 nations, and the law governing international commercial arbitration.

2140   Durante, Francesco. *Western Europe and the Development of the Law of the Sea: National Legislation*. Dobbs Ferry, NY: Oceana Publications, 1979 – .

2141   Nordquist, Myron H., and Choon H. Park. *North America, and Asia-Pacific and the Development of the Law of the Sea*. Dobbs Ferry, NY: Oceana Publications, 1981 – .

2142   Sebek, Victor. *Eastern European States and the Development of the Law of the Sea: Regional Documents, National Legislation*. Dobbs Ferry, NY: Oceana Publications, 1977 – .

2143   Simmonds, K. R. *Cases of the Law of the Sea*. Dobbs Ferry, NY: Oceana Publications, 1976 – .

2144   Szekely, Alberto. *Latin America and the Development of the Law of the Sea: Regional Documents and National Legislation*. Dobbs Ferry, NY: Oceana Publications, 1976 – .

Each of these loose-leaf collections contains analytical essays, regional documentation, and the text of national legislation relating to the law of the sea. The material covers the law of all countries in the region and is arranged in various subject categories, such as the territorial sea, fishing, offshore activities and continental shelf, pollution and high seas, etc.

2145   Henderson, Hamish McN., et al. *Oil & Gas, the North Sea Exploitation*. Dobbs Ferry, NY: Oceana Publications, 1979 – .

The laws relating to the exploration and exploitation of oil and gas in the waters surrounding Norway, the United Kingdom, and other North Sea coastal states can be found in this loose-leaf collection. Much of the legal material pertains to the rules for licenses and concessions, state participation, and taxation, including fiscal measures applied to companies operating in the North Sea.

2146   *International Tax Agreements*. New York: United Nations, 1948 – .

Issued in loose-leaf format, this reference work contains the text of international tax agreements arranged in 11 broad categories. Finding aids include a cumulative table of contents and a separate *World Guide* that indicates for each country the status of all tax agreements, including those under negotiation.

2147   *Investment Laws of the World*. Dobbs Ferry, NY: Oceana Publications, 1973 – .

National legislation and international treaties of interest to foreign investors have been assembled and classified in this loose-leaf collection of investment laws. Coverage presently extends to more than 60 countries of the world.

2148   *Mining and Petroleum Legislation of Latin America and the Caribbean*. Dobbs Ferry, NY: Oceana Publications, 1978 – .

The mining and petroleum laws of 24 countries that are member states of the Organization of American States are assembled in English in this loose-leaf set. Material for each country is organized within a similar structure to allow easy comparison.

2149   Simmonds, Kenneth R. *Multinational Corporations Law*. Dobbs Ferry, NY: Oceana Publications, 1981 – .

Arranged by region and country, this loose-leaf set offers a collection of laws affecting foreign investment and the operations of multinational corporations. When not available in English, laws have been translated into English, and important legal points are illustrated with case studies.

Yearbooks

2150   *Yearbook on Human Rights*. New York: United Nations, 1946 – .

Issued annually, the yearbook presents concise accounts of the national and international developments relating to human rights. Information on national legislative and legal developments is arranged by country with subdivisions based on pertinent articles of the Universal Declaration of Human Rights. The international coverage focuses on various UN activities in this subject area. A separate section is devoted to trust and nonself-governing territories and their right to self-determination. A table showing the current status of certain international agreements relating to human rights and an index are also included.

OFFICIAL PUBLICATIONS

The official publications of the various countries of the world produce considerable information material to support comparative and area studies of politics and governments. In fact, few significant topics can be studied without recourse to official reports, surveys, debates, gazettes, and other documentation issued by national governments.

Unfortunately, the official publications of foreign countries are often inaccessible to the student and researcher. Most libraries lack the resources for maintaining a comprehensive collection of foreign government documents. Furthermore, bibliographic control of official publications is deficient in many countries of the world. It is often difficult to identify, much less to acquire, foreign official documentation because of the lack of adequate retrieval mechanisms. Even in libraries with good collections of foreign government documents, insufficient familiarity with the titles, series, or forms of foreign official publications restricts retrieval of desired material.

The following guidebooks, library catalogs, and other bibliographies of official publications attempt to assist the researcher who wishes to identify or locate the official documentation issued by the various governments in the world.

Library Resources

2151   Boston University. Libraries. *Catalog of African Government Documents*. Boston: G. K. Hall, 1976.

This appears to be the only separate catalog that exists for a collection of official government documents of a specific region of the world. The catalog lists approximately 13,500 monographs and serials issued by governments in various parts of Africa. The African area index provides a subject key to the book material, which is listed by country.

2152   New York. Public Library. The Research Libraries. *Catalog of Government Publications in the Research Libraries*. Boston: G. K. Hall, 1972.

_____ . *Supplement 1974*. Boston: G. K. Hall, 1976.

While the official publications issued currently throughout the world can be identified in the annual *Bibliographic Guide to Government Publications: Foreign* and the *Bibliographic Guide to Government Publications: U.S.*, this massive catalog of 42 volumes serves as the retrospective record for the world's government publications up to the end of 1974. The catalog includes official gazettes, parliamentary papers, session laws, departmental reports, correspondence on foreign relations, treaties, statistical yearbooks, and other official documentation from national, colonial, state, provincial, and local governments. All parts of the world are well represented with major emphasis on official documents of the United States, Great Britian, and Western European countries. All catalog entries are arranged under political units and subdivided by agencies.

Worldwide Guidebooks

2153   Childs, James Bennett. "Government Publications." In *Encyclopedia of Library and Information Science*, v. 10 (1973): 36 – 140; and *Library Trends* (Jan. 1967): 378 – 397.

The author identifies for each country of the world national bibliographies, catalogs, and other publications that list official publications either separately or in combination with unofficial publications. Regrettably, the listed sources are seriously incomplete for several countries and do not reflect the true extent of bibliographic control existing in those countries.

2154   Palic, Vladimir M. *Government Publications: A Guide to Bibliographic Tools Incorporating Government Organization Manuals: A Bibliography*. New York: Pergamon Press, 1977.

Apparently the first in a new series of guides to government publications, this guidebook attempts to list existing reference instruments by which official publications, official personnel, and official organizations in the various countries of the world can be identified. The listings are arranged in three parts: (1) United States of America (Federal Government, State, Territorial and Local Government): (2) International Governmental Organizations (General, United Nations, League of Nations, Other Organizations); (3) Foreign Countries (General, Western Hemisphere, Europe, Africa, Near East, Asia and the Pacific Area). A separate chapter lists government organization manuals. Where such organization manuals do not exist, more general works, such as the Department of Defense Area Handbooks, are listed. Introductory headnotes and brief annotations provide guidance to the listed material. Although this guidebook lists more than 3,000 titles, it is still seriously deficient in its coverage of the true extent of bibliographic control existing in many countries. Parliamentary papers and legal material are often omitted.

2155   Wynkoop, Sally. *Government Reference Books*. Littleton, CO: Libraries Unlimited, 1970– .

A large number of official handbooks about individual foreign countries is published by the United States Government Printing Office. Identification of these handbooks and other useful reference publications may be made by subject, form category, or country in this biennially updated reference work.

Regional or Country Guidebooks

AFRICA

2156   Alman, Miriam. *Debates of African Legislatures*. Cambridge, England: W. Heffer and Sons, Ltd., 1972.

This is a holdings list of published debates and proceedings of African legislative bodies available in 21 libraries in the United Kingdom, 23 libraries in Africa, 6 libraries in the United States, and 4 libraries in Australia, Germany, India, and Sweden. Entries are arranged alphabetically by countries and preceded by a brief resume of the main constitutional changes that have occurred in the country. All entries include the name of the issuing

body, title, beginning or closing dates, language of the publication, etc.

2157   U.S. Library of Congress. Reference Division. *Botswana, Lesotho and Swaziland: A Guide to Official Publications, 1868–1968*. Washington, DC: 1971.

2158   _____ . *East Africa. A Guide to Official Publications of Kenya, Tanzania and Uganda*. Washington, DC: 1972.

2159   _____ . *East African Community; Subject Guide to Official Publications*. Washington, DC: 1976.

2160   _____ . *French-Speaking Central Africa; A Guide to Official Publications in American Libraries*. Washington, DC: 1972.

2161   _____ . *French-Speaking West Africa; A Guide to Official Publications*. Washington, DC: 1967.

2162   _____ . *Ghana: A Guide to Official Publications 1872–1968*. Washington, DC: 1963.

2163   _____ . *Kenya. Official Publications*. Washington, DC: 1978.

2164   _____ . *Liberia. Official Publications*. Washington, DC: in preparation.

2165   _____ . *Madagascar and Adjacent Islands: A Guide to Official Publications*. Washington, DC: 1965.

2166   _____ . *Nigeria. A Guide to Official Publications*. Washington, DC: 1966.

2167   _____ . *Official Publications of British East Africa. Part 1, The East Africa High Commission and Other Regional Documents; Part 2, Tanganyika; Part 3, Kenya and Zanzibar; Part 4, Uganda*. Washington, DC: 1960–1963.

2168   _____ . *Official Publications of French Equatorial Africa, French Cameroons and Togo, 1946–1958: A Guide*. Washington, DC: 1959.

2169   _____ . *Official Publications of Sierra Leone and Gambia*. Washington, DC: 1963.

2170   _____ . *Official Publications of Somaliland, 1941–1959: A Guide*. Washington, DC: 1960.

2171   _____ . *Portuguese Africa; A Guide to Official Publications*. Washington, DC: 1967.

2172 _____. *Spanish-Speaking Africa; A Guide to Official Publications*. Washington, DC: 1973.

2173 _____. *Tanzania. Official Publications*. Washington, DC: in preparation.

2174 _____. *Uganda: Subject Guide to Official Publications*. Washington, DC: 1977.

The preceding guidebooks identify and locate the official publications held in the Library of Congress and other major libraries in the United States for various former colonial administrations and independent countries in Africa. No annotations are provided with the listings, but sources of identification are given. The indexes of the guidebooks include names of persons, countries, and subjects.

ASIA

2175 Ohta, Thaddeus Y. *Japanese National Government Publications in the Library of Congress: A Bibliography*. Washington, DC: U.S. Government Printing Office, 1981.

Japanese government publications are available in two principal depository libraries in the United States, namely, the Library of Congress and the University of California Library at Berkeley. This bibliography lists 3,376 titles in the LC collection under four sections: Legislative Branch, Executive Branch, Judicial Branch, and Public Corporations and Research Institutes. Entries are arranged under romanized Japanese names and contain full bibliographic information, including frequency, holding statements, call numbers, and supplementary notes. A listing of full agency names and a title index are also included.

EUROPE

2176 Bond, Maurice F. *Guide to the Records of Parliament*. London: Her Majesty's Stationery Office, 1971.

2177 Ford, Percy, and G. Ford. *A Guide to Parliamentary Papers*. Shannon, Ireland: Irish University Press, 1972.

2178 Olle, James G. *An Introduction to British Government Publications*. London: Aslib, 1973.

2179 Pemberton, John E. *British Official Publications*. Oxford: Pergamon Press, 1973.

2180 Rogers, Frank. *Serial Publications in the British Parliamentary Papers, 1900–1968: A Bibliography*. Chicago: American Library Association, 1971.

The guidebooks cited above offer descriptions and instructions for the use of British official publications.

Several of the guidebooks are devoted to parliamentary papers, including bills, committee reports, command papers, etc.

2181 Maltby, Arthur, and Brian McKenna. *Irish Official Publications: A Guide to Republic of Ireland Papers, with a Breviate of Reports, 1922–1972*. Elmsford, NY: Pergamon Press, 1980.

The bibliography identifies and summarizes some 500 official reports under ten major subject areas, such as agriculture, education, energy resources, health, and transportation. Annual and other serial reports are separately listed. A subject and name index to the listed material is included.

2182 Richard, Stephen. *Directory of British Official Publications. A Guide to Sources*. London: Mansell Publishing Limited, 1981.

2183 Repertoire des Publications Periodiques de l'Administration. Paris: Commission de Coordination de la Documentation Administrative, 1973.

There is no central source for all official publications issued in France and Great Britain. These directories offer entries about publications of official organizations grouped by area and type of organization. Each entry contains information on types of publications issued, subjects covered, and restrictions, if any, on availability of publications.

2184 Richard, Stephen. *British Government Publications; An Index of Chairmen*, Volume 1: 1800–1899. London: Library Association, 1981.

2185 Richard, Stephen. *British Government Publications; An Index to Chairmen and Authors*, Volume 2: 1900–1940. London: Library Association, 1974.

2186 Richard, Stephen. *British Government Publications; An Index of Chairmen*, Volume 3: 1941–1978. London: Library Association, 1981.

Reports known only by name of the chairman or author can be identified in these indexes. Entries are arranged alphabetically by name and provide the number of the command paper or House of Commons paper or other pertinent information.

2187 Pemberton, John E. "European National Official Publications." In *Aslib Proceedings* (London), v. 26, no. 7–8 (July-Aug. 1974): 267–351.

This item is not a separately published guidebook but a bibliographic survey in a periodical that describes the bibliographic control for the official publications of ten European countries. The author lists and describes bibliographies, catalogs, and other reference instruments for the official publications of Belgium, Great Britain, Denmark, France, the Federal Republic of Germany, Ireland, Italy, the Grand Duchy of Luxembourg, the Netherlands, and Northern Ireland.

2188   U.S. Library of Congress. *Spanish Government Publications after July 17, 1936. A Survey.* Washington, DC: 1965–1967.

The guidebook identifies the official publications of Spain available in the Library of Congress and other major libraries in the United States.

2189   Walker, Gregory. *Official Publications of the Soviet Union and Eastern Europe, 1945–1980.* Bronx, NY: Mansell Publishing Ltd., 1982.

Official publications issued during a 35-year period in Albania, Bulgaria, Czechoslovakia, the German Democratic Republic, Hungary, Yugoslavia, Poland, Romania, and the Soviet Union are selectively listed and critically annotated in this guidebook.

LATIN AMERICA

2190   Peraza Sarausa, Fermin. *Bibliografías Sobre Publicaciones Oficiales de la America Latina.* Gainesville, FL: Box 12572 University Station, 1964.

The guidebook identifies and describes special, general, and national bibliographies that list the official publications of Latin American countries.

2191   U.S. Library of Congress. A *Guide to the Official Publications of Other American Republics.* Washington, DC: 1945–1948; New York: Johnson Reprint Corporation, 1964.

2192   Wallach, Kate. A *Union List of Basic Latin American Legal Materials.* South Hackensack, NJ: Fred B. Rothman, 1971.

These reference tools may be used to identify official Latin American publications, notably constitutions, codes, statutes, law collections, official gazettes, etc., available in United States libraries. Entries are arranged by country.

Worldwide Bibliographies

2193   Korman, Richard I. *Checklist of Government Directories, Lists, and Rosters.* Westport, CT: Meckler Publishing, 1982.

Current as well as some retrospective directories listing government offices, key officials, political parties, and other prominent public organizations of 78 nations can be found in this checklist. The entries are arranged by

country and include LC call numbers and occasional annotations.

2194   New York (City). Public Library. Research Libraries. *Bibliographic Guide to Government Publications—Foreign.* Boston: G. K. Hall, 1975– .

Bibliographic control of the official publications issued by governmental agencies in countries other than the United States has been significantly improved with the appearance of this bibliographic series. Each annual volume lists in one alphabetical sequence the official publications of international, national, and provincial governments throughout the world. The listings are based on catalog entries of the Research Libraries of the New York Public Library and the machine-readable (MARC) tapes of the Library of Congress. Entries offer access by personal or corporate author, title, series title, and subject heading, and include full bibliographic information with LC call numbers, but without annotations.

Country Bibliographies

Bibliographic control of government publications is inadequate in many countries of the world. Some countries do not even publish any catalog or national bibliography in which their official publications can be identified. Others list their official publications solely in an annual national bibliography, sometimes without indication that the publication is an official one. A few countries, however, provide adequate, current lists of their official publications. Some of these are listed below in alphabetical sequence by country.

2195   Australia. National Library of Australia. *Australian Government Publications.* Canberra: 1962– .

2196   Canada. Department of Public Printing and Stationery. *Canadian Government Publications: Catalogue.* Ottawa: 1954– .

2197   Finland. Library of Parliament. *Government Publications in Finland.* Helsinki: 1961– .

2198   Great Britain. Her Majesty's Stationery Office. *Catalogue of Government Publications.* London: 1923– .

2199   Great Britain. *Cumulative Index to the Annual Catalogues of HMSO Publications, 1922–1972.* Arlington, VA: Carollton Press, 1977.

2200   Great Britain. *Catalogue of British Official Publications Not Published by HMSO.* Cambridge, England: Chadwyck-Healey, 1983– .

2201   Netherlands. Royal Library. *Bibliografie Van In Nederland Verschenen Officiele En Semi-Officiele Uitgaven*. The Hague: 1929—.

2202   Norway. Universitetsbibliotek. *Bibliografi Over Norges Offentlige Publikasjoner*. Oslo: 1956—.

2203   Switzerland. Swiss National Library. *Bibliographie der Schweizerischen Amtsdruckschriften*. Berne: 1946—.

STATISTICAL SOURCES

The use of statistical data for the evaluation and comparison of governmental policies and political processes in the various regions of the world constitutes an important element of political analysis. The wealth of statistical material offered to the researcher extends primarily to a broad spectrum of societal factors, but the quantifiable elements of election processes and selected national policies, notably in the area of military and other government expenditures, taxation, tourism, etc., are also well covered. Both historical and forecast data are available. For ease of identification the listings for the most important bibliographic and fact retrieval tools are arranged in four subsections, as follows: (1) Bibliographic Tools, (2) Current International Compendia, (3) Retrospective International Compendia, and (4) Current National Compendia.

Bibliographic Tools

2204   Ball, Joyce. *Foreign Statistical Documents*. Stanford, CA: Hoover Institution, 1967.

This guidebook lists for each country of the world the monthly, quarterly, and annual publications that contain general statistics, trade statistics, or agricultural statistics. Listed are mainly publications that use a Western European language either as a first or second language.

2205   Cyriax, George. *World Index of Economic Forecasts*. New York: Facts on File, 1981.

This reference work identifies some 370 organizations that provide economic forecasts, plans, and surveys for over 100 countries. The book is organized in five sections. Sections 2, 3, and 4 offer profiles of macroeconomic forecasters, specialist forecasters, trade cycle and tendency survey organizations. Each profile contains address and contact information, a checklist of forecast components, a brief description of forecast characteristics, and time horizons in addition to the identification of the forecast publications. Section 5 identifies by country the

government organizations responsible for development plans. Indexes by organization, country, and type of forecast (exchange rate, commodity, or other specialization) are found in Section 1 of the book.

2206   Dicks, G. R. *Sources of World Financial and Banking Information*. Westport, CT: Greenwood Press, 1981.

One of the fundamental prerequisites for coherent and successful monetary, foreign exchange, and other economic policies is the existence of detailed financial, fiscal, monetary, and banking statistics. This bibliography identifies international, regional, and country sources of such statistics and related economic reports. Entries for the various publications offer complete bibliographical information, including frequency, language, and content description. Complete address information for the publishing bodies is given in a separate part. Also included are several indexes by subject and country.

2207   Harvey, Joan M. *Statistics Africa*. Detroit: Gale Research Company, 1978.

2208   Harvey, Joan M. *Statistics Europe: Sources for Social, Economic and Market Research*. Detroit: Gale Research Company, 1976.

The sources of socioeconomic and other statistics on Africa and Europe are identified, individually for each country, in the two guidebooks cited above. 1,465 sources for Africa and 1,441 sources for Europe are listed. Listings include not only the major statistical publications of each country but also the central statistical offices and other data collection organizations. Bibliographies of statistical publications are also identified. The guidebook for Europe also includes entries for the statistical sources of the Soviet Union and Turkey.

2209   *Index to International Statistics*. Bethesda, MD: Congressional Information Service, 1983—.

Current access to statistical publications issued by some 75 intergovernmental organizations or their subsidiary bodies is offered by this index. Coverage includes the publications from UN bodies, the OECD, the European Community, the Organization of American States, and other international organizations. The monthly issues of the reference publication describe the statistical contents of each IGO publication, including the level of detail and time coverage provided by the statistical data. This information is indexed by subject and geographical detail. The publisher also issues a companion microfiche collection of the indexed material.

2210   Tokyo. Institute of Developing Economies. *Bibliography of Statistical Materials of Developing Countries*. Tokyo: Maruzen Company, 1969.

Statistical publications published by various government organizations in 100 developing countries in Africa, Asia, and Latin America are listed. Entries are arranged in two parts, one classified by region (Africa, Asia, Middle East, and Latin America), divided by country, and subdivided by up to nine subject categories; the other classified by subject, divided by the four regions, and further subdivided by country.

2211   Rokkan, Stein, and Jean Meyriat. *International Guide to Electoral Statistics*. The Hague: Mouton, 1969.

The guidebook lists and describes the sources of electoral statistics in 14 Western European countries, namely Austria, Belgium, Denmark, France, Germany, Greece, Iceland, Ireland, Italy, Netherlands, Norway, Sweden, Switzerland, and the United Kingdom. Each of the national chapters in the book is prepared by the scholar best acquainted with the electoral statistics of his country. The descriptive part is composed of a brief historical note and a chronologically arranged annotated listing of official and unofficial sources, analyses, and investigations of election data.

Current International Compendia

2212   *Balance of Payments Statistics*. Washington, DC: International Monetary Fund, 1946– .

2213   *BOPS. Balance of Payment Statistics*. Washington, DC: International Monetary Fund, 1965– . (Vendor: Data Resources; Chase Econometrics/Interactive Data)

The balance of payments is a statistical statement for a given period showing (1) transactions in goods, services, and income between a country's economy and the rest of the world, (2) changes in ownership and other changes in that economy's monetary gold, special drawing rights (SDRs), and claims on and liabilities to the rest of the world, and (3) unrequited transfers and counterpart entries that are needed to balance, in the accounting sense, any entries for the foregoing transactions and changes that are not mutually offsetting.

Since 1981 the printed compendium consists of monthly issues and a two-part yearbook containing balance of payment statistics for over 110 countries. Part 1 of the yearbook offers individual country sections. Part 2 provides area and world totals of balance of payments components. The electronic database corresponds to the printed versions and is available by contract with the vendors.

2214   *BI/Data Forecasts*. New York: Business Interna-

tional Corporation, current data only. (Vendor: Dialog — File 129)

2215   *BI/Data Time Series*. New York: Business International Corporation, beginning date varies. (Vendor: Dialog — File 128)

The two computerized compendia, available for online searching with the Dialog system, offer statistical data on the past and future economic performance of up to 131 countries. File 129 contains narrative reports on the political and economic conditions of the country in addition to statistics on national income, private and government consumption, gross national product, capital formation, exports and imports, balance of trade, consumer price index, prime rate, and U.S. dollar exchange rate. The forecast data cover two and four years. File 128 offers up to 317 economic indicators represented in time series. The socioeconomic data are derived from official sources, including the UN, IMF, ILO, and other organizations, as well as from the producer's own international correspondents.

2216   *Deadline Data on World Affairs*. Bridgeport, CT: DMS, Inc., 1956– .

2217   *Deadline Data on World Affairs*. Greenwich, CT: Deadline Data, a Division of DMS, Inc., 1983– . (Vendor: Mead Data Central)

Available in printed and computerized versions, this weekly updated compendium offers statistical country profiles in the following categories:

General data (location, area, boundaries, capital, currency)
Population (total and regional population, major cities, age distribution, population density and growth)
Health care (hospital beds, doctors, mortality, life expectancy)
Culture (ethnic composition, religion, language, education)
Economics (budget, GNP, imports, exports, balance of payments, consumer prices, agricultural, industrial and mining products, energy)
Transportation (roads, vehicles, railroads, ports, aviation)
Communication (radio, television, newspapers, telephones)
Armed forces (army, navy, and air force personnel, equipment inventory, annual military expenditures, military service)
Government (executive, legislative, and judiciary data)
Political parties

The online service offered by Mead Data Central includes only updated files as new information is reported. Over

250 countries, individual states, and territories are covered.

2218   *Europe National Source Data Bank*. Washington, DC: Data Resources, Inc.: 1960–.

2219   *European Economic Indicators*. Washington, DC: ADP Network Services, 1970–.

2220   *European Forecast*. Waltham, MA: Chase Econometrics, 1970–.

The three computerized compendia, available by contract with the producers, offer a variety of macroeconomic, microeconomic, and financial indicators for Belgium, France, Germany, Italy, Netherlands, Spain, the United Kingdom, and other countries. The statistical data refer to industrial activity, wages and prices, labor force and employment, money supply, interest and exchange rates, balance of payments, merchandise trade, etc. and include historical as well as forecast information. Alternate scenarios are frequently compiled for exceptional political events.

2221   *Government Finance Statistics Yearbook*. Washington, DC: International Monetary Fund, 1977–.

2222   *Government Finance Statistics*. Washington, DC: International Monetary Fund, 1977–. (Vendor: Chase Econometrics/Interactive Data)

This compendium, available in printed and electronic versions, provides detailed and comparable statistics on the finances of the central governments in the countries of the world, as well as summary tables for state and local government operations. Detailed statistical tables offer data on central government revenue, expenditure, lending, financing, and debt. In addition to the country tables, data arranged by topic are available in world tables. Accounts and funds utilized by central government units are identified together with the sources of the data. Financial and nonfinancial public enterprises in each country are also identified.

The printed compendium is issued annually. The computerized version, containing more than 21,000 time series for 113 countries, is available by subscription from a vendor.

2223   *Index to International Public Opinion*. Westport, CT: Greenwood Press, 1979–.

A series of annual volumes that contain the highlights of significant surveys conducted by leading opinion research organizations in over 100 countries on controversial international, political, economic, and social issues. The public opinion data, consisting of questions and their response percentages, are grouped by topical category (e.g., economic affairs, government, international relations, military affairs, politics, social problems, etc.) for single-nation surveys and by region for multinational surveys. Each volume in the series also includes a bibliography, arranged by country or region, of the survey reports, a directory of the contributing research organizations, and indexes by topic, country surveyed, and country referenced.

2224   *International Financial Statistics*. Washington, DC: International Monetary Fund, 1948–.

2225   *International Financial Statistics*. Washington, DC: International Monetary Fund, 1948–. (Vendor: ADP Network Services; Chase Econometrics/Interactive Data; Data Resources; others)

This compendium, available in printed and electronic versions, is the standard source for international statistics on all aspects of international and domestic finance. The printed compendium, issued monthly and in annual cumulations, features individual country tables that offer data on a country's exchange rates, international liquidity, money and banking, interest rates, prices, wages, production, employment, government accounts, and international transactions. In addition to the country tables, a number of world tables are also provided.

The electronic database is available from several vendors and contains more than 60,000 time series, with annual data going back to 1948 and monthly data from 1965 to the present.

2226   *International Statistical Yearbook of Large Towns* (*Annuaire de Statistique Internationale des Grande Villes*). The Hague: International Statistical Institute, 1962–.

Statistical data on population, housing and building, public utilities, urban transport, communications, cultural institutions, and special topics are provided for European cities of more than 100,000 inhabitants and cities outside of Europe with more than 750,000 population. The yearbook is issued biennially and constitutes a basic statistical source for the health of urban life in the world.

2227   *LDC Africa/Middle East Data Bank*.

2228   *LDC Asia/Australia Data Bank*.

2229   *LDC Latin America Data Bank*.
Washington, DC: Data Resources, Inc., 1960–.

Available directly from the producer, these three online databases contain national statistics on 32 less-developed countries in Africa, Asia, and Latin America. The statistical data cover national income accounts, prices and wages, foreign exchange, balance of payments, money supply and interest rates, foreign trade, government finances, and industrial production. Chronological coverage varies with each file, with the earliest data going back to 1960.

2230   Organization for Economic Cooperation and Development. Tourism Committee. *Tourism Policy and International Tourism in OECD Member Countries.* Paris: OECD, 1974–.

The annual reference work summarly describes for each of the OECD member countries the current tourism policy objectives and priorities as well as the actions and measures taken in pursuit of these objectives. Statistical annexes offer a variety of data relating to the tourist industry.

2231   *Price Waterhouse Information Guide: Individual Taxes. A Worldwide Summary.* New York: Price Waterhouse, 1975–.

The international comparison of the tax load imposed on the individual citizen or resident is an instructive exercise in political analysis. This handbook, issued biannually, provides a summary of basic information about income and social security tax amounts at various levels of remuneration in 90 countries. No attempt has been made, however, to provide legal rules or interpretations of the national taxation system.

2232   *PTS International Forecasts.* Cleveland: Predicasts, 1971–. (Vendor: Dialog – File 83)

2233   *PTS International Time Series.* Subfile 1, *Worldcasts Composites;* Subfile 2, *Worldcasts Basebook.* Cleveland: Predicasts, 1948–. (Vendor: Dialog – File 84)

Economic growth coupled with a more balanced distribution of employment, production, trade, and consumption among the nations of the world is the scientific prescription for the maintenance of peace and political tranquility in the world. The three computerized compendia, available for online searching with the Dialog system, offer historical as well as forecast data on a variety of societal input factors. File 83 contains abstracts of published forecasts with historical data on general economics, all industries, detailed products and end-use. More than 1,000 international sources are utilized, including annual reports of foreign governments, publications of the UN and other intergovernmental bodies, bank letters, business and trade journals. *Worldcast Composites* contains some 2,500 forecast time series, including historical data, for population, GNP, per capita income, employment, production and usage of major materials and products, etc., for each of the 50 major countries in the world, excluding the United States. *Worldcasts Basebook* contains annual data since 1957 for production, consumption, foreign trade, and national income in all countries of the world. Data originate from UN, OECD, EC, and IMF sources and are updated monthly, quarterly, or irregularly according to availability.

2234   Sivard, Ruth Leger. *World Military and Social Expenditures.* New York: World Policy Institute, 1974–.

2235   U.S. Arms Control and Disarmament Agency. *World Military Expenditures and Arms Transfers.* Washington, DC: U.S. Government Printing Office, 1965–.

In an age of rapidly developing technology and increasing national insecurity, it has seemed natural for many countries to give high priority to defense policies that involve heavy military expenditures. The resulting arms race, currently requiring more than 660 billion dollars annually in military spending, has led to a severe aggravation of debilitating problems encountered in the societal factors area of political systems.

The two annually published compendia cited above provide detailed statistical tables that show by country or region the extent of military expenditures and arms transfers in relation to gross national product (GNP) or other societal factors. Containing military and social figures for 142 countries, the Sivard compendium documents the enormity of unmet human needs for income, employment, health, sanitation, food, and education as a result of the persistent slant toward defense policy objects. The historical growth and current distribution of military spending is well illustrated by numerous graphs, charts, tables, and maps.

The U.S. Arms Control and Disarmament Agency compendium offers four tables that show military expenditures, the value of arms transfers, and the number of arms delivered by country, region, or organization. The statistical data, which include comparisons with GNP, central government expenditure, and population figures, cover ten-year periods. Essays on administration perspectives on U.S. security requirements as well as computational procedures used are also included.

2236   *Statesman's Yearbook. Statistical and Historical Annual of the States of the World.* New York: St. Martin's Press, 1864–.

A variety of statistical data about each country of the world can be found in this annually revised reference work. Specifically included are data about the land area, population, religion, education, agriculture, industry, trade, banking and finance activities, and other societal factors. Bibliographies of additional statistical sources for each country are also included.

2237   United Nations. Department of International Economic and Social Affairs. *Demographic Indicators of Countries: Estimates and Projections as Assessed in 1980.* New York: United Nations, 1982.

Insights into future demographic trends are an essential prerequisite for effective economic, population, and other public policies. This reference book contains population estimates and projections until 2025 for all countries of the world. Data include figures for the total population, by sex, age groups, dependency categories, urban/rural division, and migration. Introductory essays offer an explanation of methods and assumptions applied as well as summaries of the major findings. The United Nations also publishes various individual country studies on population policy.

2238   United Nations, Statistical Office. *Demographic Yearbook.* New York: 1949 — .

Short of nuclear war, population is the gravest issue that the world faces in the coming decades.* Population statistics, along with birth, mortality, nuptuality, divorce, and international migration statistics are presented by this annual compendium for almost 250 geographic entities in the world. A cumulative subject matter index provides a key to all statistical data published in each of the previous volumes.

2239   _____ . *Statistical Yearbook.* New York: 1949 — .

The critical relationship between the size of the population and production, consumption, and international capital flow throughout the world is identifiable with the help of this annual compendium. More than 25 groups of statistical data, collected from the countries of the world, are presented in a subject and country arrangement. Also included are statistics on education, mass communications, wages and prices, manpower, national accounts, etc. There is also a world summary of basic statistical tables. An index by country is included. More recent statistical data are published in the *Monthly Bulletin of Statistics.*

2240   _____ . *World Trade Annual.* New York: Walker and Company, 1964 — .

2241   _____ . *Yearbook of International Trade Statistics.* New York: 1950 — .

The International Trade Statistics Centre in the Statistical Office of the United Nations now collects,

verifies, and standardizes trade data for most countries of the world. Both compendia provide detailed trade data that can be used to determine broad economic trends within a country or to identify world trade in a specific commodity by groups of countries. Data in the first cited compendium are arranged by SITC (Standard International Trade Classification) number and include information about trade provenance or destination, quantity, and value in U.S. dollars. The other compendium provides data about the external trade performance of individual countries in terms of current value, volume and price, commodity, trading partner, trading regions, and the world as a whole. The scope of the data includes historical trends as well as the most recent trade statistics. World trade presently continues as an internationally unbalanced activity in which a majority of the countries has an insufficient share, thus prompting the political demand for a new international economic order.

2242   _____ . *Yearbook of National Accounts Statistics.* New York: 1957 — .

This compendium is the chief reference source for determining the value of human activity on a national basis.* The annual reference work presents for each country of the world statistical data pertaining to expenditure on gross national product, individual origin of gross domestic product, distribution of national income, finance and composition of gross domestic capital formation, composition of private consumption expenditure, general government revenue and expenditure, etc. The form and concepts of the statistical tables are designed to facilitate international comparability.

2243   U.S. Central Intelligence Agency. Office of Economic Research. *International Oil Developments: Statistical Survey.* Washington, DC: CIA, 1976 — .

Economic growth, the target of many governmental policies, continues to depend heavily on the use of petroleum in most countries of the world. This biweekly issued compendium provides statistics on oil and natural gas production, petroleum resources, imports and exports, consumption, and prices for the major countries and regions of the world.

2244   U.S. Domestic and International Business Administration. International Economic Policy and Research. *International Economic Indicators and Competitive Trends.* Washington, DC: U.S. Government Printing Office, to date.

*World Bank President Robert McNamara, in a speech at the Annual IMF/World Bank meeting in Belgrade, *Financial Times,* 3 October 1979, p. 9.

*The term *value* is used here solely in the narrow economic sense of price.

The position of the United States relative to its major international trade competitors is discernible from the statistical tables presented in this quarterly reference work. Statistical data refer to the gross national product, production, investment, exports, imports, and balance of trade.

2245 *World Debt Tables.* Washington, DC: World Bank Publications, 1982—.

The external debts of the developing nations have grown to crisis proportions during recent years as a result of serious policy errors by Third World governments. This compendium offers annually updated data on the external debt of 101 developing countries. For each country, data are shown for the total debt service, outstanding debt, interest payments, principal repayments, disbursements, and commitments.

2246 *World Opinion Update.* Williamstown, MA: Survey Research Consultants International, 1977—.

The success or failure of national policies is often determined by public opinion and popular attitudes expressed on matters of international concern.* This bimonthly compendium presents a summary of public opinion data gathered on a variety of topics by survey research firms, governmental agencies, and social science research institutes in various countries of the world.

2247 *Yearbook of Labor Statistics.* Geneva: International Labor Office, 1931—.

This annual compendium is the primary reference source for the statistical evaluation of the economic, full employment, or labor policies pursued by the various governments of the world. Statistical data are presented for the total economically active population, including data on employment by industry, unemployment, hours of work, wages, consumer prices, occupational injuries, and industrial disputes. The industrial disputes data include the number of disputes, workers involved, and working days lost in general and by major division of economic activity in each country. More recent statistical data can be found in the monthly *International Labour Review.*

Retrospective International Compendia

2248 Banks, Arthur S., and Robert B. Textor. *A Cross-Polity Survey.* Cambridge, MA: M.I.T. Press, 1963.

A computer-produced cross-polity analysis based on 115 independent polities (states) and 57 variables or raw

*Noteworthy examples of public attitudes that contributed to the failure of national policies concern U.S. involvement in the Vietnamese War, or the development of nuclear energy in Austria and other countries.

characteristics, such as areal grouping, population, gross national product, literacy rate, freedom of the press, racial or linguistic homogeneity, ideological orientation, party system, political leadership, legislative-executive structure, etc. Three types of listings are presented, namely, (1) subject listings, (2) polity listings, and (3) predicate listings. All listings offer a dichotomous contrast whose numerical significance is given. The predicate listings consist of pairs of sentences or statements that describe patterns and invite hypotheses concerning process and cause. In addition to the computer printout, a 118-page introduction describes the variables and the methodology used in this cross-national analysis.

2249 Banks, Arthur S. *Cross-Polity Time Series Data.* Cambridge, MA: M.I.T. Press, 1971.

The reference work is a preliminary presentation of longitudinal aggregate data for 115 independent countries. Assembled by the Center for Comparative Political Research at the State University of New York (Binghamton), the data consist of a maximum of 102 separate variables covering periods from 1815 to 1966. Time series data are presented for each country in ten sections with up to 17 variables. Variables refer to area, size and density of population, type of regime, size and changes of cabinet, legislative effectiveness, selection, and election, revenues and expenditures, communication media, exports, imports, education, and conflict phenomena, such as assassinations, general strikes, guerilla warfare, government crises, purges, riots, revolutions, etc.

2250 Kurian, George Thomas. *The New Book of World Rankings.* New York: Facts on File, 1984.

Designed as an international scorecard for the comparison of nations, this reference work presents statistical data that measure national achievement in more than 300 performance areas grouped into 23 subject categories. Specifically included are data on the concentration of political and military power, number of registered voters, size of cabinet, incidence of civil disorder, Communist party membership, index of democratization, deaths from political violence, political executions, assassinations, refugees, foreign aid, men and women under arms, defense expenditures, U.S. military aid, and a host of other economic and societal characteristics of over 190 countries of the world. Apart from the ranking tables and individual country profiles, a bibliography of important reference sources and an index are also provided.

2251 Mackie, Thomas T., and Richard Rose. *The International Almanac of Electoral History.* New York: Facts on File, 1982.

The compendium presents for 24 industrialized countries in the world various electoral data within varying time frames since 1828 or later. Included are the number and percentage of votes cast and party seats won as well as the dates of elections held in Australia, Austria, Belgium, Canada, Denmark, Finland, France, Germany, Greece, Iceland, Ireland, Israel, Italy, Japan, Luxembourg, Netherlands, New Zealand, Norway, Portugal, Spain, Sweden, Switzerland, United Kingdom, and the United States. The sources of the statistical data are identified.

2252   Rummel, Rudolf J. *The Dimensions of Nations.* Beverly Hills, CA: Sage Publications, 1972.

The reference book presents statistical tables with descriptive interpretations of the variations independent countries exhibit in their national characteristics, foreign and dyadic behavior. The variations are shown along major and minor dimensions, and data on the principal indicators of the dimensions are given. Correlations between national characteristics and foreign behavior are also presented. The book includes a bibliography of other publications offering cross-national comparisons, as well as a name and subject index.

2253   Taylor, Charles Lewis, and David A. Jodice. *World Handbook of Political and Social Indicators.* New Haven, CT: Yale University Press, 1983.

This statistical compendium, now in its third edition, offers a comparison of nation-states based on a variety of politically relevant indicators. Issued in two volumes, entitled (1) Cross-National Attributes and Rates of Change and (2) Political Protest and Government Change, the reference work contains measurements and rankings of states in the following areas: (1) the size of

government and the allocation of resources, (2) popular participation and government restraints, (3) wealth, production, and size, (4) inequality and well-being, (5) social mobilization, (6) economic structure, (7) changes within countries, (8) changing patterns of cross-national distribution, (9) political protest, (10) state coercive behavior, (11) governmental change, and national elections. Numerous, separate tables within these areas display the statistical data and country rankings for the individual political and social indicators. Several appendices identify the states for which indicators are available, as well as the source documents for the data. An index is also included. The *World Handbook* is revised each decade, and earlier editions have been published in 1964 and 1972.

Current National Compendia

2254   *Current National Statistical Compendiums.* Westport, CT: Greenwood Publishing Company, 1970–.

An evaluation of governmental policies on a national or international basis is hardly complete without recourse to the national statistical compendia published in the various countries of the world. While library holdings of these national compendia are often fragmentary, the title above refers to a collection, annually updated, of the most recently obtainable statistical compendia of nearly 100 countries throughout the world. All compendia are available on microfiche. A printed checklist and bibliography identifies microfiche code numbers by which the desired compendium can be located in the collection. The compendia themselves contain detailed tables of contents and indexes for locating the desired statistical data.

Chapter 6

Political Theory

INTRODUCTION

The reference literature of political theory is the most undeveloped of all the subfields of political science. There are practically no bibliographies, indexes, abstracts, encyclopedias, or other works of reference devoted exclusively to the information requirements of the field itself. This startling bibliographic situation directly reflects the unresolved debate over the unity, scope, and purpose of political theory. Since works of a theoretical nature appear in all subfields of political science, there is a question whether political theory is a separate field at all. The Library of Congress does not use the term *political theory* as a subject heading, and political writing of a theoretical nature is listed in LC-based subject catalogs under a multitude of broad, general headings. Another unresolved question pertains to variations in the conceptualization of political theory. Doubts have been expressed whether political theory should comprise explanatory, philosophical, moral, or ideological forms of thought.

Differences have also arisen about the aims of political theory, which may variously be historically oriented, descriptive, or prescriptive.

These deep-seated controversies over the theoretical content of political science have so far prevented the appearance of an exclusive, effective, and comprehensive reference system for political theory. In the absence of such a specific reference system, the researcher must have recourse to existing reference material in the individual subfields of political science and law as well as in the social and political sciences in general. Other profitable sources are the reference tools for the disciplines of philosophy and religious science, which offer a significant amount of information on politically oriented thought.

The following sections list and describe a selected number of bibliographies, dictionaries, encyclopedias, and other reference sources that offer a biographical, conceptual, chronological, geographical, descriptive, or analytical approach to individual political thoughts or thought systems.

PHILOSOPHICAL BIBLIOGRAPHIES

Guidebooks

2255   De George, Richard T. *The Philosopher's Guide to Sources, Research Tools, Professional Life, and Related Fields*. Lawrence: Regents Press of Kansas, 1980.

Organized in two main chapters — philosophy and related fields — the guidebook identifies general philosophical reference tools as well as sources for the history of philosophy, specific branches, movements, and regions of philosophy. Also listed are philosophical serials, professional organizations in philosophy, and reference tools in related fields, including political science and other social sciences.

2256   Tice, Terrence N., and Thomas P. Slavens. *Research Guide to Philosophy*. Chicago: American Library Association, 1983.

A characterization and an overview of the main trends and areas of philosophy together with biographical sketches of the principal philosophers can be found in this guidebook. It also identifies key works as well as reference sources. A separate chapter is devoted to social-political philosophy. Author/title and subject indexes are included.

Current Bibliographies

2257   *Bibliography of Philosophy/Bibliographie de la Philosophie*. Paris: Librairie Philosophique J. Vrin, 1954 – .

The bibliography is a book identification tool issued quarterly with annual analytical indexes by author, title and subject, quoted names, and geographical entries by publisher. New philosophical books are listed and abstracted under ten subject categories, including social philosophy, philosophy of politics, philosophy of law, philosophy of values, etc. Coverage is international, with foreign books abstracted in foreign languages. Reprinted books, reeditions, paperbacks, and translations of foreign-language books are also listed but do not receive an abstract.

2258   *Bulletin Signaletique 519: Philosophie*. Paris: Centre National de la Recherche Scientifique, 1947 – .

All categories of philosophical publications, books, periodical articles, dissertations, conference proceedings, and other printed material published throughout the world are made accessible by this quarterly bibliography. The annotated entries are arranged in classified order with separate sections for history of philosophy, history of ideas, philosophy of history, law, religion, economics, logic, etc. Quarterly and anually cumulated indexes to the listed items by author and subject are also provided.

2259   *Philosopher's Index*. Bowling Green, OH: Bowling Green University, 1967 – .

2260   *Retrospective Index to U.S. Publications from 1940*. Bowling Green, OH: Bowling Green University, 1978.

2261   *Philosopher's Index (Database)*. Bowling Green, OH: Bowling Green University, 1940 – . (Vendor: Dialog — File 57)

Philosophical books and articles published in English and other European languages in some 270 periodicals can be identified by author and keyword in context (KWIC) with the help of this index, available in printed and online format. The printed index is issued quarterly and contains brief abstracts in addition to full bibliographic citations for the listed material. The keyword listings include many politically significant words, such as freedom, ideology, power, revolution, rights, etc. A separate book review index and a listing of finished translations or translations in progress are also provided. A separate retrospective index extends coverage back to 1940.

The computerized database, also updated quarterly, offers online display of citations and abstracts for all items published in the printed indexes.

Retrospective Bibliographies

2262   Albert, Ethel M., and Clyde Kluckhohn. A *Selected Bibliography on Values, Ethics, and Esthetics in the Behavioral Sciences and Philosophy, 1920 – 1958*. Glencoe, IL: Free Press, 1959.

The annotated bibliography provides a key to the great quantity, variety, and dispersal of literature published during a period of almost 40 years on values. Listed are books and articles dealing with value inquiry in anthropology, economics, philosophy, political science, psychology and psychiatry, sociology, and other disciplines. A numerical bibliographic guide identifies the various listings according to the following subject categories: (1) definition, classification, and theory for values research, (2) topical studies, (3) area studies, (4) methods of value inquiry, (5) values and science, (6) philosophical values and ethical theories, (7) logico-linguistic analyses, and (8) esthetics and studies of art, humor, literature, and music. An alphabetical author index is included.

2263   Guerry, Herbert. A *Bibliography of Philosophical Bibliographies*. Westport, CT: Greenwood Press, 1977.

More than 2,300 citations, provided by this reference work, offer access to philosophical bibliographies published in English and other languages up to 1976. Bibliographies are identified in two separate listings, namely, (1) by individual philosopher, and (2) by topic. Some entries are annotated.

2264   Matczak, Sebastian A. *Philosophy. A Select, Classified Bibliography of Ethics, Economics, Law, Politics, Sociology.* Louvain: Editions Nauwelaerts, 1970.

The bibliography contains extensive but unannotated listings of the philosophical literature in politics. Entries are subdivided according to general studies, particular periods, specific studies of political ideas or philosophers, particular countries, or special questions, such as authority, colonies, communism, democracy, fascism, internationalism, nationalism, peace and war, state, etc. Philosophical writings in related disciplines — law, economics, and sociology — as well as in ethics are also well represented in this reference work. An author index is included.

2265   *Philosophical Abstracts 1939–1954.* New York: Kraus Reprint Corporation, 1966.

For a period of 16 years prior to the appearance of the *Bibliography of Philosophy*, philosophical publications were indexed and abstracted in this reference set, available now in reprint form. Entries are arranged by countries with a separate author index.

2266   Association for Systems Management. *An Annotated Bibliography for the Systems Professional.* Cleveland: 1970.

2267   Stumpers, F. L. A *Bibliography of Information Theory.* Cambridge, MA: M.I.T. Press, 1953.

2268   U.S. Department of State. *Game Theory and Its Application to the Social Sciences; A Bibliography.* Washington, DC: 1964.

2269   Wasserman, Paul. *Decision-Making, An Annotated Bibliography.* Ithaca, NY: Graduate School of Business and Public Administration, Cornell University, 1958.

————. *Supplement*, 1964.

Modern explanatory theories, such as game theory, decision-making theory, information theory, or systems theory, have produced an enormous literature but only a limited number of bibliographies. The titles listed above may be used to identify a portion of the many books and articles written about these theories.

IDEOLOGICAL AND RELIGIOUS FOUNDATIONS OF POLITICAL SYSTEMS

Introduction

Ideologies are closed political thought and belief systems* that are capable of liberating or redistributing enormous human energies in the pursuit of difficult, seemingly unattainable political goals. In the wake of their initial application, ideologies inevitably cause widespread dislocations in the established political order. Not content to change merely their own immediate environment, ideologies eventually develop strong missionary tendencies, and thereby often subject previously peaceful areas to increasing conflict. None of the major ideologies, has, however, succeeded in gaining world domination, with the result that the present world situation is characterized by a more or less uneasy, conflict-laden coexistence of the various ideologies.

Not suprisingly, there exists an enormous literature stemming from scholarly efforts to investigate and analyze the ideological phenomena in all their aspects. Much of this literature has exposed the fallacies and errors inherent in the various ideologies and religious belief systems. But it is also apparent that ideologies, regardless of their truth content, function as important political steering mechanisms that not only create values and directives but also offer meaning and hope to human beings who would otherwise be unable to live in the horror of an ideological vacuum and the resulting meaninglessness of this world.

Bibliographic control of this literature is satisfactory for some ideologies and religions but deficient for others, notably the Western democratic ideology. Regrettably, there is also no current bibliography devoted exclusively to the retrieval of ongoing documentation about all ideologies. In its absence section B-2 of the *International Bibliography of Political Science* offers annual listings of publications that update and supplement many of the works identified in the following retrospective bibliographies.

Democracy

Although *democracy* is a rather nebulous and ill-defined term, an enormous literature exists on the subject. Unlike the ideologies of nationalism and communism, however, the thought system of democracy has not received proper bibliographic control in the United States and other Western democratic countries. This is perhaps not surprising in view of the fact that it is some-

* A closed thought system is not open to correction, in contrast to the scientific thought systems, which are open to corrections as a result of new findings.

what difficult to look as an objective observer at a system of values that are regarded as self-evident or as the undisputed truth due to cultural habituation. Identification of the literature on democracy must therefore be made from various catalogs, encyclopedias, and general bibliographies under a multitude of headings, such as equality, elections, civil rights, delegation of powers, liberty, representative government, representative federal government, suffrage, separation of powers, and many others. The following scholarly works may also be used because they contain useful bibliographies dealing with important ideological conceptions of democracy.

2270 Heller, Frank A. *International Yearbook of Organizational Democracy*. New York: John Wiley & Sons, 1983 – .

The *Yearbook* is the standard reference source for identifying important theory, practice, and research relating to participative decision making; cooperative organizations; co-ownership, codetermination and self-management groups, and other power-sharing arrangements of organizational or industrial democracy. The reference work is currently issued in four volumes, entitled: Vol. 1 — Organizational Democracy and Political Processes, Vol. 2 — International Perspectives on Organizational Democracy, Vol. 3 — The Organizational Practice of Democracy, and Vol. 4 — Technology and Organizational Choice. Separate sections and articles within these volumes contain country studies, organizational studies, and other evaluations or research findings in this field. A bibliography of additional references and an index are also included.

2271 Lippincott, Benjamin E. *Democracy's Dilemma: The Totalitarian Party in a Free Society*. "Appendix A: A Survey of the Literature," pp. 239–268. New York: Ronald Press, 1965.

The democratic value system faces a fundamental challenge by political parties or movements that advocate the elimination of democracy. The bibliography lists books and articles, published in Great Britain and the United States, that deal directly or indirectly with the totalitarian challenge to democracy.

2272 Livingstone, John C., and Robert G. Thompson. *The Consent of the Governed*. "Bibliography," pp. 561–572. New York: Macmillan, 1966.

2273 Pennock, Roland J. *Democratic Political Theory*. "Bibliography," pp. 527–557. Princeton, NJ: Princeton University Press, 1979.

These books aim to clarify, classify, or evaluate democratic theory, the constitutional principles of democratic government, the democratic behavior of citizens, and the

major issues or operational problems confronting democratic governments. Significant works relating to these topics are identified in the two bibliographies that are part of these works.

2274 Rejai, M. *Democracy. The Contemporary Theories. Further Readings*. "Bibliography," pp. 313–316. New York: Atherton Press, 1967.

A short bibliography providing sources for the historical evolution of democracy, the classical theory, normative-empirical conceptions, ideological conceptions, general, religious, socioeconomic, political, and psychocultural preconditions of democracy.

2275 Wolfe, Alan. *The Limits of Legitimacy. Political Contradictions of Contemporary Capitalism*. "Bibliography," pp. 393–417. New York: Free Press, 1977.

Much recent scholarship has focused on the serious paralysis that has affected many but certainly not all of the Western democracies. This book selects various viewpoints about the inherent predicaments of democracy and describes six solutions currently applied in search of political tranquility. The lengthy bibliography in the book may be used to identify significant publications and unpublished theses about the unresolved contradictions in democracy and their possible elimination, amelioration, or postponement.

Imperialism

Imperialism is presently a discredited ideology, but the concept of central control underlying it is historically well established and still valid. Although a system of central imperative control has many disadvantages, as the historical experience of imperialism well demonstrates, it has proved by its long existence to be a workable solution to the accidents of geography that are responsible for the unequal distribution of raw materials in the world. The spectacular failure of the nationalist successor states in Central and Eastern Europe, Africa, and other parts of the world to maintain their freedom and independence against external and internal competitors in the power struggle, as well as the current economic crisis affecting both developed and undeveloped countries demonstrates the importance of the imperialist idea. Two retrospective bibliographies assemble and categorize the extensive literature about European imperialism during its existence of some 150 years.

2276 Halstead, John F., and Serafino Porcari. *Modern European Imperialism: A Bibliography of Books and Articles, 1815–1972*. Boston: G. K. Hall, 1974.

2277   Ragatz, Lowell Joseph. *The Literature of European Imperialism, 1815–1939*. Washington, DC: Paul Pearlman, 1947.

The Ragatz bibliography contains unannotated entries for works dealing with the British, Danish, German, French, Italian, Dutch, Portuguese, Russian, and Spanish empires and also lists some general works on imperialism and international rivalries. The bibliography by Halstead and Porcari identifies more than 15,000 books and 18,000 articles on this subject.

Marxism, Bolshevism, Communism

Of all the presently existing political thought systems, communism has received the most encompassing bibliographic control by numerous bibliographies. Their listings identify not only the important works about the theoretical aspects of communism but also offer access to publications that deal with the practical application of the communist ideology in the Soviet Union and other countries of the world.

2278   Bochenski, Joseph M. *Guide to Marxist Philosophy: An Introductory Bibliography*. Chicago: Swallow Press, 1972.

The bibliography contains slightly over 200 annotated entries for original and secondary works on the thought of Karl Marx, German classical Marxism, the philosophy of Lenin, Soviet Marxism-Leninism, neo-Marxism, Chinese Marxism, and the New Left. Only English-language publications are included.

2279   Bourgina, Anna M. *Russian Social Democracy: The Menshevik Movement. A Critical Bibliography*. Stanford, CA: Hoover Institution Press, Stanford University, 1969.

Menshevism is the political theory of the more moderate minority in the Russian social democratic party after its Bolshevik majority wing constituted itself as a separate party in 1903. The bibliography offers comprehensive but unannotated listings of books, pamphlets, articles, and other publications about the Menshevik movement. A separate part of the bibliography is devoted to the principal Menshevik periodicals published in Russia and other countries between 1903 and 1965. Most of the items listed in the bibliography are available at the Hoover Institution Library.

2280   Delaney, Robert Finlay. *The Literature of Communism in America: A Selected Reference Guide*. Washington, DC: Catholic University of America Press, 1962.

The annotated bibliography lists books dealing with the theory, philosophy, practice, history, and implications of communism in America. Following a chapter on world Communist literature, separate chapters are devoted to American Communist literature, pro-Communist literature, anti-Communist literature, the history of American Marxism, and biographical and other reference works.

2281   Hsueh, Chun-tu. *The Chinese Communist Movement: An Annotated Bibliography of Selected Materials in the Chinese Collection of the Hoover Institution on War, Revolution, and Peace*. Stanford, CA: Stanford University, 1960, 1962.

Volume 1 of the bibliography lists material dating from 1919 to July 1937 documenting various stages in the development of the Chinese Communist party: the embryonic period (1919–1921), the founding of the Chinese Communist party, Kuomintang, and CCP relations (1923–1927), the period of reorientation (1927–1931), the Kiangsi Soviet (1931–1934), the Long March (1934–1935), and the early Yenan period (1935–1937). Volume 2 lists general works, biographies, and other items pertaining to Mao Tse-tung, material dealing with the Sino-Japanese War (1937–1945), and the postwar years (1945–1949). More than 1,200 items in the Chinese collection of the Hoover Institution are listed.

2282   Lachs, John. *Marxist Philosophy. A Bibliographical Guide*. Chapel Hill: University of North Carolina Press, 1967.

The bibliography lists English, French, and German works about all aspects of dialectical and historical materialism, Marxist thought on captialism, the state, revolution, the nature of man, alienation, freedom, etc. Marxist philosophy in the United States, the Soviet Union, Central and Eastern Europe, and other countries is identified by representative publications. Individual chapters contain introductory headnotes that explain significant aspects of the literature. Also included is a list of periodicals of special relevance for the study of Marxist thought as well as a bibliography of bibliographies.

2283   Lauerhass, Ludwig, Jr. *Communism in Latin America, A Bibliography*. Los Angeles: Center of Latin American Studies, University of California, 1962.

2284   Sable, Martin H. *Communism in Latin America, An International Bibliography: 1900–1945, 1960–1967*. Los Angeles: Center of Latin American Studies, University of California, 1968.

The two bibliographies identify the significant books and periodical articles published during a period of some 70 years on the theory and practice of communism in

Latin America. The Lauerhass bibliography covers the literature between the end of World War II and December 1960. Its entries are arranged by country or region. The Sable bibliography expands bibliographic control for the remaining years since the beginning of this century. It is organized in two sections, namely, (1) books, pamphlets, government publications, conference proceedings, and (2) periodical articles, with subdivisions for each country. Separate author and subject indexes are also provided.

2285   Munton, Alan, and Alan Young. *Seven Writers of the English Left. A Bibliography of Literature and Politics, 1916–1980.* New York: Garland Publishing Company, 1981.

All seven of the English writers whose work is the subject of this bibliography were at one time either close to or full members of the Communist party of Great Britain. Their works have made important practical and theoretical contributions to an understanding of the relationship between literature, politics, and society in the twentieth century. Listed in chronological order are the works of Alick West, Edgell Rickword, Ralph Bates, Ralph Fox, Edward Upward, Rex Warner, and Christopher Caudwell. Many of the entries are annotated. Biographical headnotes about each writer precede the bibliographic listings. A general literature bibliography, author/title, and periodical and newspaper indexes are also included.

2286   Phan Thieu Chau. *Vietnamese Communism. A Research Bibliography.* Westport, CT: Greenwood Press, 1975.

This unannotated bibliography covers most books in Vietnamese, English, and French on the origins, the development, and the contemporary state of Marxist-Leninist communism in Vietnam. Entries are arranged under 12 sections, entitled: (1) Bibliographies and Reference Works; (2) Biographies, Memoirs, and History; (3) Society and Social Conditions; (4) Government and Politics; (5) The Viet Nam Workers' Party; (6) Land Policy and Agriculture; (7) The Nonagricultural Economy; (8) Cultural and Intellectual Life; (9) Military Affairs; (10) Foreign Relations; (11) The South: Internal Affairs; (12) The South: Military and External Affairs. These sections are further subdivided for narrower topics. An introductory, annotated bibliographic guide as well as author and title indexes are also included.

2287   Seidman, Joel. *Communism in the United States.* Ithaca, NY: Cornell University Press, 1969.

7,000 books, articles, and pamphlets published before 1959 on the Communist movement in the United States are identifiable by author and subject with the help of this bibliography. Its annotated entries are arranged alphabetically by author and separately indexed by sub-

ject. The bibliography is limited to the viewpoints and activities of the official Communist party of the United States and does not deal with communism in a wider sense or the communism of dissident groups. Similarly, publications of organizations controlled by or leaning toward the official party line have been for the most part omitted. Only English-language material is listed.

2288   U.S. Library of Congress. Legislative Reference Service. *World Communism: A Selected Annotated Bibliography.* Washington, DC: U.S. Government Printing Office, 1964.

2289   _____ . *World Communism 1964–1969. A Selected Bibliography.* Washington, DC: U.S. Government Printing Office, 1971.

The two bibliographic volumes offer several thousand annotated entries for English-language books, pamphlets, periodical articles, and government publications dealing with Communist doctrine and activities. Apart from the general section, listings are arranged by region and country. Bibliographies, indexes, encyclopedias, and other reference aids are listed separately.

2290   Vigor, P. H. *Books on Communism and the Communist Countries.* London: Ampersand Ltd, 1971.

More than 2,600 English-language books for the study of communism in general, in the USSR, and in other countries are listed in this bibliography. Its annotated entries are arranged under 60 sections, which cover Marxist-Leninist classics, commentaries on the classics, the Soviet system of government, studies of Soviet leaders, studies of Soviet national policies, Communist attitudes toward religion, Soviet intelligence activities, accounts by diplomats and press correspondents, official publications of the United Kingdom and the United States, etc.

2291   Whetten, Lawrence L. *Current Research in Comparative Communism. An Analysis and Bibliographic Guide to the Soviet System.* New York: Praeger, 1976.

The unannotated bibliography may be useful for the identification of more recent publications about the Communist ideology and its practical application in the Soviet Union and the East European countries excluding Albania and Finland. Entries refer to journal articles and books published between January 1965 and December 1975 and are arranged under nine major chapters. These chapters reflect such topics as economic development, social change, collectivization, alienation, centralism, personal expression, public discipline, property relationships in agriculture, etc. An analytical summary of these topics precedes the bibliographic section. No indexes are included.

Nationalism

Nationalism has been a dominant thought in political relations throughout the world at least since the eighteenth century and continues to be a strong cohesive as well as disintegrative force in political order. The nationalist value system favors the selection of political objects on the basis of their utility for a distinct population group, frequently in blatant disregard of the needs of other population groups residing within or outside the political entity. A vast literature has appeared on the causes and manifestations of nationalism, with several retrospective bibliographies offering access to a variety of information.

2292   Buse, Dieter, and J. Doerr. *German Nationalism: A Bibliographic Approach*. New York: Garland Publishing, Inc., 1984.

The reference work offers annotated listings for books, articles, and research studies dealing with German nationalism during the nineteenth and twentieth centuries. It also offers guidance to the major themes, issues, and approaches.

2293   Chan, Gilbert F. *Nationalism in East Asia. An Annotated Bibliography of Selected Works*. New York: Garland Publishing Company, 1981.

East Asian nationalism has been the principal motivating force behind most revolutions, modernizing experiments, and other political activities in East Asian countries. The bibliography contains several overviews of this phenomenon and identifies books and periodicals in English and Asian languages dealing with (1) Chinese nationalism, (2) Communist nationalism in China, (3) nationalism in China in Chinese and Japanese sources, (4) nationalism in Japan, (5) the development of nationalism in prewar Japan, and (6) Korean nationalism. An index is included.

2294   Pinson, Koppel S. *A Bibliographical Introduction to Nationalism*. New York: Columbia University Press, 1935.

2295   Deutsch, Karl Wolfgang. *An Interdisciplinary Bibliography on Nationalism, 1935–1953*. Cambridge, MA: M.I.T. Press, 1956.

2296   Deutsch, Karl Wolfgang, and Richard L. Merritt. *Nationalism and National Development, An Interdisciplinary Bibliography*. Cambridge, MA: M.I.T. Press, 1970.

The three unannotated bibliographies offer multiple access to the scholarly books, periodical articles, and pamphlets published about nationalism during the twentieth century. The growth of the literature on nationalism is reflected in the fact that Pinson's bibliography contains 431 entries, whereas the latest bibliography by Deutsch and Merritt comprises no less than 5,000 items, most of which are published in English or other major European languages.

The Deutsch/Merritt bibliography is organized in 11 sections based on the geographical, economic, linguistic, sociological, psychological, anthropological, cultural, and purely political aspects of nationalism. Separate listings are made for works that focus on a specific geographic area or on imperialism and international integration. The listed entries can also be found with an author index and a computer-produced keyword in context (KWIC) index of titles.

2297   Stokes, Gale. *Nationalism in the Balkans: An Annotated Bibliography*. New York: Garland Publishing, Inc., 1983.

Organized geographically, the bibliography contains approximately 580 annotated entries for post–World War II books and periodical articles dealing with nationalism in Southeastern Europe during the nineteenth and twentieth centuries. Works in all major European languages are cited. An introductory article, entitled "In Defense of Balkan Nationalism," precedes the bibliographic entries.

Religions

The existence and survival of religions during centuries of human history is evidence for the fact that religions fulfill fundamental human needs and serve as an effective source of values for the pursuit of political objects. Religious beliefs in a future world or otherworldly power continue to be responsible for maintaining large population masses in a state of obedience to secular control. Frequently, however, religions also spawn or support opposition to the established political order by withholding divine blessing or other forms of legitimation from it. An enormous literature and a well-developed information retrieval system exist for religious studies. The following reference sources will be useful for identifying information on the political role of religion in addition to the listings provided in Section D-18 of the *International Bibliography of Political Science*.

GUIDEBOOKS

2298   Karpinski, Leszek M. *The Religious Life of Man: Guide to Basic Literature*. Metuchen, NJ: Scarecrow Press, 1978.

Designed to guide the user to reference material as well as important books and periodical articles, this reference work offers annotated listings of religious publications in six separate parts: (1) general material about the religions of mankind, (2) religions of the past, (3) Judaism, Christianity, and Islam, (4) Asian religions (Hinduism, Buddhism, Confucianism, Taoism, etc.), (5) the beliefs of native peoples, (6) the occult, magic, and parapsychology. Suitable subdivisions within the six parts aggregate entries for the fundamental texts, critical works, religious institutions, or specific countries. The various types of reference works (bibliographies, handbooks, dictionaries, encyclopedias, etc.) are listed separately for each religion or major topic. Works dealing with dogma, doctrines, or ethical positions of the various religions are included. A general index of authors, titles, and subjects is also provided.

2299   Kennedy, James R. *Library Research Guide to Religion and Theology.* Ann Arbor, MI: Pierian Press, 1974.

Illustrated instructions for collecting information on religious topics and an unannotated list of basic reference sources in religion are offered by this guidebook. The reference sources are listed under 17 categories: (1) general, (2) Bible, (3) theology, (4) Christian ethics, (5) philosophy of religion, (6) church history, (7) preaching, (8) Christian and religious education, (9) psychology of religion, (10) sociology of religion, (11) world religions (Buddhism, Hinduism, Islam, Judaism), (12) Roman Catholic church, (13) Eastern Orthodox church, (14) denominations, (15) ecumenics, (16) missions, (17) mythology and folklore. Where appropriate, separate listings are made for different types of reference books, such as encyclopedias, indexes, language tools, handbooks, etc.

2300   Kepple, Robert J. *Reference Works for Theological Research. An Annotated Selective Bibliographical Guide.* Washington, DC: University Press of America, 1981.

This guidebook identifies the reference works useful for theological inquiries. The annotated entries are arranged under 39 chapters in two parts, based on the different types of reference works and individual subject areas. The latter include separate listings for works on church/state relationships, Third World churches, Christian education, and ethics. An index listing authors, editors, and titles is also included.

2301   Sandeen, Ernest R. *American Religion and Philosophy. A Guide to Information Sources.* Detroit: Gale Research Company, 1978.

More than 1,600 books and articles dealing with American religions and religious movements are identified in this bibliography. The annotated entries are arranged under 21 chapters that focus on Puritanism, the Catholic church, the formation of denominational patterns, Judaism, black religion, the social gospel, various religious movements, and other religious or philosophical

phenomena. Author, title, and subject indexes are included.

2302   Walsh, Michael J. *Religious Bibliographies in Serial Literature: A Guide.* Westport, CT: Greenwood Press, 1981.

The guidebook lists and describes 178 serialized bibliographic tools that can be of use in identifying religion-oriented information. Many of these bibliographies will cover publications relating to religious beliefs, doctrines, laws, or viewpoints by which current political or social conditions, problems, and issues are evaluated.

2303   Wilson, John F., and Thomas P. Slavens. *Research Guide to Religious Studies.* Chicago: American Library Association, 1982.

Part 1 of the guidebook, titled Introduction to Religious Scholarship, discusses books dealing with the study of religions, history of religions, religious traditions in the West, and religious thoughts and ethics. Part 2 contains annotated listings of reference works that are of a general nature or devoted to particular religions. Author, title, and subject indexes are included.

CURRENT BIBLIOGRAPHIES

2304   *Bulletin Signaletique 527: Sciences Religieuses.* Paris: Centre de Documentation Sciences Humaines, 1947 – .

Issued quarterly, this reference publication offers listings and abstracts of articles selected from some 1,200 French, English, and other-language periodicals in religion, theology, and related fields. Doctoral dissertations and conference proceedings are also included. Entries are arranged according to a classification scheme with divisions for the science of religions and specific religions (Christianity, Judaism, Islam, etc.). Book reviews are also indexed. Apart from the classified listings, there are also separate author and subject indexes in each issue. An annual cumulated index issue is also published.

2305   Catholic Library Association. *The Catholic Periodical and Literature Index.* Haverford, PA: 1930 – .

Bimonthly and biennially cumulated author, title, and subject listings of books and articles published in over 127 Catholic periodicals are offered by this reference work. Papal, conciliar, diocesan, and other official church documents are included in the index coverage.

2306   *Guide to Social Science and Religion in Periodical Literature.* Flint, MI: National Periodical Library, 1965 – .

The quarterly reference publication offers subject access to articles printed in nearly 100 periodicals. Approximately 70 percent of the database are religious periodicals, with the remainder consisting of social science periodicals. The listed entries cover a wide range of religious or theological topics.

2307   *Index to Jewish Periodicals.* Cleveland: 1963– .

Some 40 English-language periodicals published in the United States, Great Britain, and Israel are indexed by author and subject in this semiannual index publication. Its scope includes Jewish history, Judaism, Jewish cultural and intellectual life, Arab-Israeli relations, etc.

2308   *Index to Religious Periodical Literature.* Chicago: American Theological Library Association, 1949–1976.

2309   *Religion Index.* Chicago: American Theological Library Association, 1960– . (Vendor: BRS; Dialog – File 190)

2310   *Religion Index One: Periodicals.* Chicago: American Theological Library Association, 1977– .

2311   *Religion Index Two: Multiauthor Works.* Chicago: American Theological Library Association, 1976– .

Author and subject indexing of books, dissertations, festschriften, and up to 328 periodicals is provided by this index, available in various printed editions as well as in electronic format. The indexed literature frequently contains politically significant information on current issues, but the viewpoints expressed are mainly Protestant and occasionally Catholic or Jewish. The printed index is currently updated annually, whereas the computerized version contains only biannual updates. The latter offers chronological coverage of varying dates with indexing of festschriften since 1960 and periodical indexing since 1975. Both versions of the index also offer author entries for book reviews.

2312   *The Quarterly Index Islamicus.* London: Mansell, 1977– .

Current books, periodical articles, and research papers on Islamic studies can be identified with this index. Entries are alphabetized by author and classified by region, country, or language. Several retrospective supplements provide listings of the Islamic studies literature in all European languages from 1906.

Although the time lag between material being published and appearing in the index is up to one year, the index is a major tool for tracking down writings relating to the political, economic, and social aspects of Islam in the Middle East and other parts of the world.

2313   *Religious and Theological Abstracts.* Myerstown, PA: Religious and Theological Abstracts, Inc., 1958– .

Articles selected from some 130 religious periodicals in the United States and Europe are indexed and abstracted in this quarterly reference publication. Its entries are arranged under five major sections covering biblical, theological, historical, practical, and sociological information. Suitable subheadings are made for religious and secular education, pastoral care, economic, political, legal, and educational institutions, various social processes, church and state affairs, specific religions, etc. Quarterly and annual indexes by subject and author as well as a scripture index are provided.

2314   *Religious Books, 1876–1982.* New York: R. R. Bowker, 1983.

2315   *Religious Books and Serials in Print.* New York: R. R. Bowker, 1978– .

These bibliographic instruments may be used to identify – by subject, title or author – books published throughout the world since 1876 on any aspect of the world's religions, including the religious implications for such politically significant topics as abortion, business ethics, church and state relationships, homosexuality, and others. Subject listings are based on more than 27,000 LC subject headings, including names of persons, organizations, and countries. Entries carry complete LC cataloging information, including call numbers and subject tracings. More than 130,000 books are listed in the retrospective bibliography. Currently available books and serials are listed in the annually revised bibliography cited as the second item above.

RETROSPECTIVE BIBLIOGRAPHIES

2316   Berkowitz, Morris, and J. Edmund Johnson. *Social Scientific Studies of Religion: A Bibliography.* Pittsburgh: University of Pittsburgh Press, 1967.

This unannotated bibliography contains some 6,000 entries for English-language books and articles dealing with religion and its relationship to other social institutions, social behavior, social issues, and social change. Section 4a (pp. 58–73) lists material on religious influences on political behavior and church-state relationships. The book can also be used to identify other bibliographies, dictionaries, and encyclopedias of religion.

2317   Brunkow, Robert de V. *Religion and Society in North America.* Santa Barbara, CA: ABC-Clio, 1983.

This bibliographic reference work is a collection of 4,034 periodical abstracts relating to the religious experience and influence in the United States. The periodical articles were originally published between 1973 and 1980. The entries are arranged under 21 sections that focus on specific subject areas, such as government and politics, business, education, labor, social and economic reform, war and pacifism, socioeconomic groups, religious groups, and similar topics. Since all entries are arranged by author under these sections, separate author and subject indexes provide additional access to the listed material.

2318   Hussain, Asaf. *Islamic Movements in Egypt, Pakistan and Iran*. Bronx, NY: Mansell, 1983.

The three most powerful and politically influential fundamentalist Islamic movements, the Ikhwan al-Muslimun in Egypt, the Jamaat-i-Islami in Pakistan, and the Shiite revolutionary movement in Iran, are the subject of this annotated bibliography listing English-language books and periodical articles. A separate section on each movement provides a brief biographical sketch of the founder, an outline of the ideology, and a summary of the political activities.

2319   Mitros, Joseph F. *Religions. A Select, Classified Bibliography*. New York: Learned Publications, 1973.

All important religions of modern times and antiquity are covered by this bibliographic volume. It is organized in seven parts, entitled (1) Methods of Studying Religions, (2) Reference Books, (3) Non-Christian Religions, (4) Christianity, (5) Patristic Studies, (6) Scriptures, (7) Journals. These parts are divided into chapters and subheadings that provide a classified framework for the listed reference and literature sources relating to individual religions, their history, fundamental texts, and adherents. Introductory headnotes precede the listed material, consisting mainly of English-language books. The titles of the leading religious periodicals offering current information are listed in part 7. An author index is also included.

HANDBOOKS

2320   Zehavi, A. M. *Handbook of the World's Religions*. New York: Franklin Watts, 1973.

Organized in seven chapters, the handbook offers basic information about the organized religions of the world, namely, (1) Christianity, (2) Judaism, (3) Buddhism, (4) Islam, (5) Hinduism, (6) other religions, such as Bahai, Jainism, Shinto, Sikhs, Taoism, Zoroastrianism. A seventh chapter contains a summary on religions. Each chapter provides a general description of the religion and information on major denominations, sects, and orders, foremost personalities, and appropriate religious terms. An index is included.

Socialism

After more than a century of development, socialism has emerged in recent decades as a leading though still contested political ideology in many countries of Western Europe and the Third World. Its fundamental values stand in opposition to Marxist-Leninist communism as well as American-style individualism but affirm the basic tenets of parliamentary democracy. Socialism favors the selection of political objects on the basis of distributive justice, which aims to provide the individual with a remarkable degree of economic security at the expense of a heavy tax burden.

Bibliographic control of the vast literature on socialism is most inadequate, but the following reference works may be used in addition to the current listings offered in Section B-22 of the *International Bibliography of Political Science*.

2321   *Bibliographische Information . . ./Bibliographic Information: The Labour Movement, Marxism, Socialism, Revolutionary and Liberation Movements, Third World*. Zurich: Pinkus Genossenschaft, 1970– .

Books published in English, French, German, and Italian about socialism, Marxism, and related political philosophies and movements can be identified in this monthly bibliography, whose scope transcends the conceptual boundaries of socialism. All entries are arranged alphabetically by author, but a subject index included in each issue helps to identify the appropriate socialist literature.

2322   Braunthal, Julius. *Geschichte der Internationale*. Hannover: J. H. W. Dietz, 1961–1971.

2323   Cole, G. D. H. *A History of Socialist Thought*. New York: St. Martins, 1953–1960.

2324   Dolléans, Edouard, and Michel Crozier. *Mouvements Ouvriers et Socialistes: Chronologie et Bibliographie*. Paris: Éditions Ouvrières, 1950–1959.

The three-volume set by Braunthal is the most up-to-date historiography of the socialist ideology and movement. It offers a detailed bibliography on pages 654–680 of Volume Three. Tables of conferences, congresses, presidents and secretaries of the movement are also presented. For non-German readers the historiography by Cole in five volumes will be the preferred reference choice. The five-volume bibliographic set by Dolléans/Crozier appears to be the standard guide to socialist publications and works about socialism, but appears not to have been updated.

PHILOSOPHICAL AND POLITICAL THOUGHT

Introduction

Apart from the indirect approach bibliographies offer for political thought expressed in books, periodicals, and other publications, many political ideas are more directly identifiable through other categories of reference instruments, namely dictionaries, encyclopedias, and historiographical compendia and summaries. Dictionaries are particularly useful in many instances where political ideas suffer from terminological ambiguity. Dictionaries will either offer a precise definition or reveal a lack of precision, thus exposing a basic weakness of the political idea. The essential details of a political idea together with its public acceptance or rejection may often be found in encyclopedias under an alphabetical arrangement by name of the principal exponent or the specific term by which the political idea has become known. Regrettably, no encyclopedia offers a complete inventory of political ideas or political philosophers. Historiographies provide a summary or panoramic overview of the mass of political thought expressed throughout the ages. The methods for summarizing political ideas are varied, often disputed, and frequently misleading. Many authors prefer a strictly historical or chronological approach, which has led to the myth that political thought has shown progressive improvement resulting in a final, superior form of government. Several summaries link political ideas exclusively with political philosophers, thereby creating the impression that political thought is confined to scholars alone. A majority of summaries begin with Plato or Aristotle and thus ignore the fundamental and permanently valuable ideas expressed by earlier Greek thinkers. The emphasis of Western political thought expressed in most summaries is equally unfortunate. This has led to a widespread and doubly fallacious conclusion that political thought is confined to the Western world, where ideas are superior to those of the non-Western world.

The following titles constitute a selective inventory of dictionaries, encyclopedias, and historiographies that in spite of some imperfections have proven useful for the retrieval of essential information about political thoughts expressed during various periods of time in many parts of the world.

Dictionaries

2325   Bottomore, Tom. A *Dictionary of Marxist Thought*. Cambridge, MA: Harvard University Press, 1983.

This dictionary contains entries for the basic concepts of Marxism and the different individuals and schools of thought whose work has contributed to the body of Marxist ideas. All entries offer detailed definitions, descriptions, or explanations, and present citations for additional information sources. Also included is a separate bibliography for the works of Marx and Engels, and other authors cited in the dictionary.

2326   Cranston, Maurice, and Sanford A. Lakoff. A *Glossary of Political Ideas*. New York: Basic Books, Inc., 1968.

This dictionary, the result of a cooperative effort by British scholars, offers an excellent introduction to the problems of political terminology and thought associated with ubiquitous and overused concepts or doctrines. It contains definitions for some 50 abstract terms or exposes ambiguities where definition is impossible. Entries are included for anarchism, authority, common good, communism, democracy, dictatorship, equality, fascism, federalism, human rights, imperialism, individualism, justice, law, Marxism, nationalism, populism, power, race, and several other terms. Each entry concludes with bibliographic citations for further reading and study.

2327   Runes, Dagobert David. *The Dictionary of Philosophy*. New York: Philosophical Library, 1942.

This is one of the general philosophical dictionaries that may be used for the quick identification of politically significant philosophers or ideas. It contains entries for philosophers, schools of philosophy, and philosophical terms. Brief definitions or explanations are given, and representative publications are cited wherever appropriate.

2328   Scruton, Roger. A *Dictionary of Political Thought*. New York: Harper & Row, 1982.

The dictionary lists in an alphabetical arrangement the principal ideas through which modern political beliefs find expression. Each entry offers a definition of the key term together with a description of the conceptual content. Political events are mentioned only when they cast light on intellectual conceptions. Names contained in the dictionary are those of thinkers rather than those of politicians.

Encyclopedias

2329   *The Encyclopedia of Philosophy*. New York: Macmillan, 1967.

The multivolume set is the only encyclopedia that covers both Western and Eastern philosophy, providing lengthy articles on the history and nature of political philosophy as well as on individual political ideas. More than 900 entries are devoted to individual philosophers, whose life and major thoughts are described. All articles conclude with excellent bibliographies. The index contains entries for names, terms, and concepts.

2330   *Great Books of the Western World*. Volumes 2, 3, *The Great Ideas, A Syntopicon*; Volumes 1, 4–54: *Miscellaneous Authors*. Chicago: Encyclopedia Britannica, 1952.

The reference set offers an inventory of 102 basic ideas contained in 443 works by 74 authors from antiquity to the twentieth century. Each of the fundamental ideas, many of which are of political importance, is described at moderate length and broken up into numerous topics. The syntopicon gives bibliographic citations to those of the 443 works in the set that are pertinent to each idea.

2331   Urmson, J. O. *The Concise Encyclopedia of Western Philosophy and Philosophers*. New York: Hawthorn Books, 1960.

The one-volume encyclopedia contains articles of varying length on philosophical ideas and thinkers of the Western world. No bibliographic references are given in the articles.

2332   Weiner, Philip F. *Dictionary of the History of Ideas*. New York: Charles Scribner's Sons, 1973.

Scholars from various countries contributed articles for this multivolume encyclopedia, which deals with pivotal topics in intellectual history. The articles trace the evolution of an idea in the minds of its leading proponents, pursue an idea chronologically from antiquity to later periods, or present a cross-cultural study of an idea for a given period. Bibliographic references conclude each article. A separate index volume and the analytical table of contents in Volume 1 offer access to all articles concerned with the historical development of political ideas.

Historiographies

The following publications, listed in cohesive order, may be used as works of reference that provide biographical, geographical, regional, chronological, or analytical access to essential information about political thought.

BIOGRAPHICAL ACCESS

2333   Catlin, George E. *The Story of Political Philosophers*. New York: Tudor Publishing Company, 1957.

2334   Ebenstein, William. *Great Political Thinkers: Plato to the Present*. New York: Holt, Rinehart and Winston, 1969.

The exposition of political thought in these books is essentially biographical. The material is arranged by the name of selected political philosophers, whose lives are briefly described and work illustrated by extracts from original sources. Bibliographic listings offer access to additional information material.

GEOGRAPHICAL ACCESS

2335   Anderson, Thornton. *Russian Political Thought, An Introduction*. Ithaca, NY: Cornell University Press, 1967.

2336   Jaworski, Michael. *Soviet Political Thought*. Baltimore: Johns Hopkins Press, 1967.

2337   Beitzinger, A. J. A *History of American Political Thought*. New York: Dodd, Mead and Company, 1972.

2338   Dolbeare, Kenneth M., and Patricia Dolbeare. *American Ideologies: The Competing Political Beliefs of the 1970's*. Chicago: Markham Publishing Company, 1971.

2339   Chen, Paky. A *Brief History of Chinese Political Thought*. Melbourne: Hawthorne Press, 1971.

2340   Feith, Herbert, and Lance Castles. *Indonesian Political Thinking, 1945–1965*. Ithaca, NY: Cornell University Press, 1970.

2341   Varma, Vishwanath Prasad. *Modern Indian Political Thought*. Agra: Lakshmi Narain Agarwal, 1963.

These titles represent a category of reference books that summarizes, surveys, or analyzes the political thought of a particular country.

REGIONAL ACCESS

2342   Bowle, John. *Western Political Thought*. New York: Barnes & Noble, 1961.

2343   McDonald, Lee Cameron. *Western Political Theory from Its Origins to the Present*. New York: Harcourt, Brace and World, 1968.

2344   Jorrin, Miguel, and John D. Martz. *Latin American Political Thought and Ideology*. Chapel Hill: University of North Carolina Press, 1970.

2345   Seidler, G. L. *The Emergence of the Eastern World*. Oxford: Pergamon Press, 1968.

2346   Skurnik, W. A. E. *African Political Thought—Lumumba, Nkrumah, Toure*. Denver: Graduate School of International Studies, University of Denver, 1968.

The cited titles are examples of historiographies that

describe or analyze the political thought of a specific region in the world.

CHRONOLOGICAL ACCESS

2347   Burns, Edward McNall. *Ideas in Conflict: Political Theories of the Contemporary World*. New York: W. W. Norton & Company, 1960.

2348   Gyorgy, Andre, and George D. Blackwood. *Ideologies in World Affairs*. Waltham, MA: Blaisdell Publishing Company, 1967.

2349   Roucek, Joseph S. *Contemporary Political Ideologies*. Paterson, NJ: Littlefield, Adams & Company, 1961.

2350   Sargent, Lyman Tower. *Contemporary Political Ideologies. A Comparative Analysis*. Homewood, IL: Dorsey Press, 1972.

2351   Brecht, Arnold. *Political Theory; The Foundations of Twentieth Century Political Thought*. Princeton, NJ: Princeton University Press, 1959.

2352   Bowle, John. *Politics and Opinion in the Nineteenth Century*. London: Jonathan Cape, 1954.

2353   Nicholson, H. G. *The Age of Reason: The Eighteenth Century*. Garden City, NY: Doubleday, 1961.

2354   Gunn, J. A. W. *Politics and the Public Interest in the Seventeenth Century*. Toronto: University of Toronto Press, 1969.

2355   Allen, J. W. *A History of Political Thought in the Sixteenth Century*. New York: Dial Press, 1928.

2356   Lerner, Ralph, and Muhsin Mahdi. *Medieval Political Philosophy: A Sourcebook*. New York: Free Press, 1963.

The first five titles cited above survey the political ideologies and major ideas in the contemporary world. Specifically covered is the theoretical content of communism, national socialism, Marxism, nationalism, pan-Africanism, socialism, Zionism as well as democracy and conservatism. The remaining five titles summarize the political thoughts expressed during a particular century of the past. Indexes, footnotes, and bibliographies provide a key to information about individual thinkers and their political ideas.

2357   Dunning, William Archibald. *A History of Political Theories*. New York: Macmillan, 1902–1920.

The three-volume set, the first and foremost work in the descriptive, chronological school of political his-

toriographies, describes in a chronological arrangement the principal thoughts of each period from antiquity to the beginning of the twentieth century. Selected bibliographic references, name and subject indexes offer additional access to the desired information.

ANALYTICAL ACCESS

2358   Parkinson, Cyril N. *Evolution of Political Thought*. Boston: Houghton Mifflin, 1959.

2359   Sabine, George H. *History of Political Theory*. New York: Holt, Rinehart and Winston, 1961.

G. H. Sabine made the first comprehensive break with the descriptive method in the historical study of political theory in 1937. Today this is still the standard work for a critical, evaluative, and analytical treatment of the political ideas that have emerged throughout human history. C. N. Parkinson sees only three basic alternatives in political thought, namely, rule by one, rule by a few, and rule by many. Details of the variations occurring within these three categories of political thought are analyzed. Bibliographic references offer access to original sources.

PHILOSOPHERS AND IDEOLOGISTS

Directories

2360   *Directory of American Philosophers*. Bowling Green, OH: Philosophy Documentation Center, Bowling Green State University, 1972– .

The biennially revised directory lists almost 10,000 philosophers and their affiliations with colleges, universities, and other institutions in the United States and Canada. Also included is a list of some 3,000 colleges and universities, arranged by states, with information about the department under which philosophy is taught. The names of faculty members in the philosophy departments are identified together with information about highest degree earned, rank, and area of specialization. The directory also identifies philosophical societies, philosophy journals, and more than 100 publishers of philosophy books.

2361   *International Directory of Philosophy and Philosophers*. Bowling Green, OH: Philosophy Documentation Center, Bowling Green State University, to date.

The irregularly revised directory identifies all major international philosophical associations, societies, institutes, or research centers. Also listed are university departments, research centers, associations, and societies maintaining philosophical activities in each country of the world. Philosophers and philosophical journals are also identified.

2362   Wilcox, Laird M. *Guide to the American Left*. Kansas City, MO: Editorial Research Service, 1984.

2363   _____ . *Guide to the American Right*. Kansas City, MO: Editorial Research Service, 1984.
    The two directories identify organizations that prop-agate political ideas on the fringes of the political spectrum. The first directory lists liberal, social protest, pacifist, socialist, communist, New Left, and other left-wing organizations in the United States and Canada. The second directory lists patriotic, nationalist, anti-Communist, libertarian, conservative, and other right-wing organizations in the United States and other English-speaking countries. Both directories also contain bibliographies for the publications issued by these organizations.

Chapter 7

Public Administration

INTRODUCTION

Among the various academic and professional fields of political inquiry with which it developed, public administration is critically handicapped in one sense, but fortunate in another. Like political science, the academic study of public administration—sometimes called administrative science—suffers from an identity crisis in respect of its scope, rubric, and methods. As a subject of study, public administration means different things to different groups of academicians. Some argue with considerable justification that the subject matter of public administration is totally identical with that of political science, while others believe that it is or should be completely separate. This lack of academic consensus is reflected in the course offerings of American universities and colleges, which may range from a bare minimum to an astounding proliferation of courses. There are courses in public works administration, hospital administration, disaster control administration, fire prevention administration, police administration, correctional institution administration, personnel administration, comparative administration, and many others.

Public administration shares, however, with the discipline of legal science the fortunate distinction of being able to focus on a specific element of the political world, namely, the political process. Just as there is a judicial process for law, there is an administrative process for nonlegal affairs, even though the separation between legal and nonlegal affairs may often be blurred or artificial. The administrative process, nevertheless, encompasses a variety of distinct activities, such as investigating, planning, organizing, staffing, directing, supervising, budgeting, coordinating, reporting, assistance, servicing, and management activities in connection with the wide-ranging affairs of government.

Between the pulls of political reality, academic eclecticism, and occupational specialization, it is difficult to devise a completely satisfactory reference system for public administration information. Nearly everything of what has previously been listed in the other six chapters of this guidebook will be useful—in one way or another—for research inquiries in public administration, although considerable gaps remain. Unlike the legislative and judicial processes, the administrative process is unfortunately, despite its label, much less public and labors—in the United States as well as other countries—under a variety of secrecy regulations.

The reference sources listed on the following pages encompass those retrieval tools that either expressly bear the label administration or management, or otherwise focus specifically on a distinct aspect of the administrative process.

BIBLIOGRAPHIES

Guidebooks

2364   Alexander, Ernest R. *Urban Planning. A Guide to Information Sources.* Detroit: Gale Research Company, 1979.

2365   Drucker, Mark L. *Urban Decision Making. A Guide to Information Sources.* Detroit: Gale Research Company, 1981.

2366   McCaffery, Jerry, and John L. Mikesell. *Urban Finance and Administration. A Guide to Information Sources.* Detroit: Gale Research Company, 1980.

2367   Murphy, Thomas P. *Urban Indicators. A Guide to Information Sources.* Detroit: Gale Research Company, 1980.

2368   Ross, Bernard H. *Urban Management. A Guide to Information Sources.* Detroit: Gale Research Company, 1979.

The five guidebooks list and briefly describe scholarly books and articles dealing with various aspects of urban public administration. Entries follow a classified arrangement that focuses on the following topics:

- Planning: theory, methods, and techniques of governmental and nongovernmental planning; evaluation of planning
- Decision Making: issue analysis; cost, performance, and organizational feasibility criteria; objective setting
- Finance: taxes and other revenues, fiscal management, budgeting
- Urban Indicators: types, problems, and applications of urban indicators
- Management: leadership, personnel administration, decentralization, urban bureaucracy, etc.

All five guidebooks contain indexes by author, title, and subject.

2369   Caiden, Gerald, et al. *American Public Administration: A Bibliographical Guide.* New York: Garland Publishing, Inc., 1983.
    This guidebook is the most recent comprehensive guide to reference works, leading journals, and major textbooks in the field of American public administration. The conveniently classified entries are preceded by an introductory essay that explains the scope of American public administration and how it differs from that in other countries.

2370   Rouse, John E., Jr. *Public Administration in American Society: A Guide to Information Sources.* Detroit: Gale Research Company, 1980.
    The guidebook lists and briefly describes nearly 1,700 books, book chapters, periodical articles, and official publications dealing with various aspects of public administration in the United States. Entries are arranged by author in sections of chapters. Appendices contain descriptions of American public administration associations and their principal acativities. Author, title, and subject indexes are included.
    For a condensed review of bibliographic resources and abstracting services in the literature of public administration, see also the author's article "Boundaries of An Emerging Superdiscipline: A Review of Recent and Older Bibliographic Materials in Public Administration" in *Public Administration Review*, v. 42, no. 4 (July/Aug. 1982): 390–398.

2371   Simpson, Antony E. *Guide to Library Research in Public Administration.* New York: Center for Productive Public Management, John Jay College of Criminal Justice, 1976.
    The guidebook identifies published and unpublished sources of information useful for the study of public administration. Many of the listed items are also heavily used in other political science fields. Separate chapters are devoted to the description of literature guides, indexing and abstracting services, published bibliographies, official document collections, archives and nonconventional archival resources, and major periodical publications. An introductory essay informs the reader about various approaches to effective public administration. A combined author and title index helps to locate material listed in the book.

Library Catalogs

2372   Berkeley. University of California. Library. *Subject Catalog of the Institute of Governmental Studies Library.* Boston: G. K. Hall, 1971.

_____ . *First Supplement.* Boston: G. K. Hall, 1978.
    For more than 50 years the Institute of Governmental Studies has collected material on the principles and practices of government administration. The catalog for this collection contains approximately 813,000 cards for pamphlets, books, government documents, and periodical articles. More than 2,000 subject headings unique to this library are used to provide access to a wide range of official and scholarly information material about all aspects of public administration. City, county, and state publications from all parts of the United States are well represented. The catalog also includes a list of the subject headings used as well as a list of periodical titles analyzed.

Current Bibliographies

2373   *Bulletin Signaletique 528: Science Administrative.* Paris: Centre de Documentation Sciences Humaines, 1974– .

Articles published in some 300 periodicals throughout the world are indexed and abstracted in this quarterly reference publication. Entries are arranged according to a subject classification scheme with separate categories for the history, methods, structure, and control of administration. Each issue also provides access to the listed material by a subject index, geographical index, and author index. Annually cumulated indexes are also published.

2374   International Institute of Administrative Sciences. *International Review of Administrative Sciences.* Brussels: 1928— .

The institute is the only international nongovernmental organization concerned with surveys, studies, projects, and agreements for the improvement of administrative science and practice throughout the world. Each issue of this quarterly publication contains a selective annotated list of books as well as an unannotated list of new books and articles dealing with public administration. Entries are arranged by author without subject indexing. Book annotations are in English or French.

2375   *Management Research.* Dolton, IL: A. Thomas Beales, 1968— .

The monthly bibliography offers annotated subject listings of periodical articles dealing with organization, social responsibilities, personnel policy, manpower planning, personnel testing and selection, motivation and performance, human behavior, human resources development, and similar administrative topics. Also included are a list of new books and editorial notes about periodical publications.

2376   *Personnel Literature.* Washington, DC: U.S. Civil Service Commission Library, 1941— .

2377   *Personnel Management Abstracts.* Ann Arbor, MI: University of Michigan, 1955— .

The central idea of public administration — to realize desired goals by rational human action — is closely linked to problems of personnel management.* The two bibliographies provide access to the substantial literature of interest in personnel administration or management. The first item is a monthly annotated subject list of books, pamphlets, periodical articles, unpublished dissertations, and other information material relating to the principal topics in personnel management. Topics covered include recruitment, evaluation, promotion, fringe benefits, position classification, etc. Biennial cumulations of the listed material are published as the *Personnel Bibliography* series. Each bibliography in the series covers one broad subject.

*Much of modern psychology stresses the irrational component in personnel behavior as a result of emotive, subconscious, or conditioned responses.

The second item cited above lists and abstracts books as well as articles published in 85 scholarly periodicals. The scope of the bibliography includes organizational behavior, compensation, managerial and personnel functions, productivity, creativity, training, labor relations, etc. Entries are arranged for author, title, and subject listings. The complete bibliographical citation and a brief abstract will be found under subject listings. Longer abstracts of books and articles are provided in an additional section.

2378   *Police Science Abstracts.* Amsterdam: Kugler Publications Amsterdam, 1973— .

In all political entities the police are entrusted with one of the most important roles in the administrative process, but this role differs widely according to the generic system characteristics of the political entity.

Published bimonthly, *Police Science Abstracts* offers classified author and subject access to and abstracts of the international literature about all aspects of police work and organization. Entries are arranged under 14 sections, namely: (1) General, (2) Police Organization, (3) Police Personnel, (4) Police Equipment, (5) Finance, Budget, (6) Police Power, (7) Police Operations, (8) Traffic and Traffic Control, (9) Crime Prevention, (10) Crime Control, Criminal Investigation, (11) Police Work in Relation to Special Kinds of Persons, (12) Police Work in Relation to Special Types of Offenses, (13) Forensic Sciences, and (14) Forensic Medicine. Further subdivisions within these sections are made for narrower topics. Separate author and subject indexes are also included.

2379   *Recent Publications on Governmental Problems.* Chicago: Joint Reference Library, 1932— .

Books and articles dealing with the external problems of public administration are listed under appropriate subject headings in this weekly, unannotated bibliography. Headings include accident prevention, budget, city planning, community facilities, environment administration, housing, public safety, public welfare, etc. More than 5,500 items are listed annually. A list of the periodicals indexed is printed in each issue of the bibliography.

2380   *Sage Public Administration Abstracts.* Beverly Hills, CA: Sage Publications, 1974— .

Administration, organizational theory and behavior, comparative administration, local administration, budget, finance and revenue sharing, personnel, unions and collective bargaining, professional education and career development, policy analysis, decision making, social program evaluation, foreign policy making are some of the subject headings under which pertinent books, pamphlets, periodical articles, and government publications are listed in this quarterly bibliography. Apart from full bibliographic information, all entries contain brief abstracts of the publications contents. Periodical articles are selected from about 200 English-language periodicals. Quarterly and annually cumulated indexes by subject and author provide additional access to the listed material.

2381   *Top Management Abstracts*. London: British Institute of Managment, 1971 – .

Management may be defined as action intended to achieve rational cooperation in an administrative system.* Current information designed to help top managers in governmental agencies, business corporations, and other bureaucratic organizations can be identified with the help of this bibliography, published eight times per annum. The bibliography lists and abstracts the contents of some 200 periodicals published throughout the world. A subject index is included with two-year cumulations. Earlier editions of this bibliography were published under the title *Anbar Management Services Abstracts* for the period 1961 – 1970.

2382   Universal Reference System. *Administrative Management: Public and Private Bureaucracy*. Princeton, NJ: Princeton Research Publishing Company, 1969 – .

_____ . *Public Policy and the Management of Science*. Princeton, NJ: Princeton Research Publishing Company, 1969 – .

The books, periodical articles, and other publications listed in the bibliographic volumes of the Universal Reference System are intensively indexed according to the Grazian system of topical and methodological descriptors. The titles cited above refer to two separate volumes in the URS base set, which is kept up to date by combined annual supplements. The first item lists 2,311 publications on public or private administrative management, including material on intergroup relations, budgeting and fiscal planning, procedural and work systems, power and participating in decision making, etc. The second bibliographic volume cited above is devoted to the administration of science, which is viewed as an administrative function of government. It lists 1,258 publications, indexed by 14,600 index entries relating to organization, processses of decision making, planning, budgeting, problem solving, and other aspects of administrative behavior.

Retrospective Bibliographies

2383   *Author Index to Public Administration Series: Bibliography No. P 1 to P 1000 (June 1978 – July 1982)*. Monticello, IL: Vance Bibliographies, 1982.

*Dwight Waldo, *The Study of Public Administration* (New York: Random House, 1955), p. 7.

2384   *Subject Index to Public Administration Series: Bibliography No. P 1 to P 1000 (June 1978 – July 1982)*. Monticello, IL: Vance Bibliographies, 1982.

2385   *Title Index to Public Administration Series: Bibliography No. P 1 to P 1000 (June 1978 – July 1982)*. Monticello, IL: Vance Bibliographies, 1982.

More than 1,000 unannotated bibliographies listing books and periodical articles have been issued since 1978 in this continuing public administration series. Each of the bibliographies is devoted to a single topic in public administration or political science, and over the years a wide range of topics — from acid rain to zero-based budgeting — has been covered. Many of the bibliographies deal with problems, issues, or projects in American politics and policies, but public administration topics in other countries have also been included. The cited indexes offer access to the bibliographies by author, subject, and title.

2386   Bowman, James S., et al. *Professional Ethics: Dissent in Organizations, An Annotated Bibliography and Resource Guide*. New York: Garland Publishing, Inc., 1983.

The difficulties and ethical considerations associated with the expression of professional dissent in governmental and other organizations constitute important root causes of administrative inefficiencies and failures. This bibliography is the first systematic attempt to identify court cases, congressional documents, academic studies, newspaper accounts, and other information sources that trace the manifestation of dissent — often referred to as "whistle-blowing" — in public and private sector organizations during the past 15 years. More than 1,300 entries as well as a directory of professional organizations and fraud hotline numbers are provided.

2387   Buse, Michael J., and Dina von Dewitz. *Bibliography on Political Planning*. Baden-Baden: Nomos, 1974.

Planning is an essential element of public administration activity but is an often poorly understood process of adjusting means to desired political objects. This unannotated bibliography lists almost 1,800 monographs, collective works, articles from English- and foreign-language periodicals, as well as reports and publications from governmental sources. The listed entries deal with the concept, theory, method, technique, problems, legal and other aspects of political planning. Listings follow a classified arrangement with a separate section for bibliographies and handbooks. An author index is included.

2388   Carr, T. R. *Quantitative Research in Public Administration and Policy Analysis: A Methodologically Annotated Bibliography*. Norman: University of Oklahoma Bureau of Government Research, 1977.

The annotated bibliography identifies publications dealing with quantitative methods and research techniques used in the study of public administration.

2389   Cayer, N. Joseph, and Sherry Dickerson. *Labor-Management Relations in the Public Sector. An Annotated Bibliography.* New York: Garland Publishing, Inc., 1983.

The annotated bibliography lists and describes all scholarly articles and books published since 1962 about the labor-management relations of U.S. public employees. The volume follows a topical arrangement and includes two appendices: The first lists periodicals that regularly publish labor-management information in the public sector. The second identifies organizations offering information or other services of interest to scholars and practitioners in this field. Author and subject indexes are included.

2390   Dynes, Patrick S. *Program Evaluation: An Annotated Bibliography.* New York: Garland Publishing, Inc., 1984.

Focusing on such topics as utilization, methodology, political and organizational influences, theory, and management, this bibliography lists books and periodical articles published since 1970 in the area of program evaluation. An introductory survey article and an index are also included.

2391   Felkenes, George T., and Harold K. Becker. *Law Enforcement: A Selected Bibliography.* Metuchen, NJ: Scarecrow Press, 1977.

2392   Fremlin, Ronald H. *Modern Judicial Administration — A Selected and Annotated Bibliography.* Reno, NV: National College of the State Judiciary, 1973.

2393   Hewitt, William H. *A Bibliography of Police Administration, Public Safety and Criminology.* Springfield, IL: Charles C. Thomas, 1967.

2394   Prostano, Emanuel T. *Law Enforcement: A Selective Bibliography.* Littleton, CO: Libraries Unlimited, 1974.

2395   Radzinowicz, Leon, and Roger Hood. *Criminology and the Administration of Justice.* Westport, CT: Greenwood Press, 1976.

One of the eminently political but highly complex functions of public administration is the enforcement of authoritative directives or laws regulating social behavior. Not unexpectedly, law enforcement and the administration of justice is the subject of an enormous multidiscipli-

nary literature stemming from psychological, sociological, or legal research. The bibliographies cited above may be used to identify publications that focus mainly on the administrative aspects of law enforcement and judicial administration. The Hewitt bibliography offers the most extensive listings, with citations to no less than 11,000 books, periodical articles, government reports, and other publications. The listed material is arranged in nine chapters: (1) correctional administration, (2) detective bureau administration and criminal investigation, (3) patrol administration, (4) personnel and training administration, (5) police administration, (6) police technical services administration, (7) traffic, (8) industrial and business security, and (9) miscellaneous subjects.

The more recently published bibliographies offer access to an even wider range of publications dealing with police administration, police functions and practices, criminal procedures, and other administrative aspects of law enforcement.

2396   Great Britain. Foreign and Commonwealth Office. Overseas Development Administration Library. *Public Administration. A Select Bibliography.* London: 1973.

Public administration in developing countries with different political systems has been the subject of many special, national, and general studies. The unannotated bibliography selectively identifies such studies, including those that focuses on economic planning and development, lcoal government and community development, civil service, public finance, executive government administration, and similar aspects. Separately listed are the titles of periodicals and other bibliographies that offer additional information material.

2397   Halasz, D. *Metropolis: A Select Bibliography of Administrative and Other Problems in Metropolitan Areas throughout the World.* The Hague: Nijhoff, 1967.

Due to rapidly rising populations, traffic, and housing requirements, the metropolitan areas of the world present the biggest challenges to a successful public administration activity. The unannotated entries of this bibliography identify books, articles, and other publications on urban administrative problems under a geographical arrangement that excludes the United States and Canada. The listings are subdivided by major subject categories, as follows: (1) administration and organization, (2) finance, (3) culture and education, (4) social welfare, (5) health, (6) housing, (7) planning and urbanism, (8) transport and traffic, (9) social aspects, (10) economy, (11) population, (12) geography.

2398   Hills, William G., et al. *Administration and Management: A Selected and Annotated Bibliography.* Norman: University of Oklahoma Press, 1975.

The bibliography is an attempt to select from a mass of literature the 250 works that appear to be most relevant for public administrators, especially those in human service organizations. The bibliography is arranged in six parts. Part I covers the "Development, Scope and Emphasis" of administration. Part II lists books dealing with the "Organization," its theory, behavior, and development. Part III includes works on the "Administrative Process"—decision making, planning and budgeting, leadership and motivation, communication and control, evaluation. Part IV identifies books on "Personnel"—personnel management, manpower, collective bargaining. Part V is devoted to the "Administrative Environment"—public relations, public policy, intergovernmental relations, values, technology and administration. Part VI, entitled "Comparative Administration," deals with bureaucratic systems in various countries and cultures. All entries include lengthy informative annotations. A short list of pertinent reference works is also provided, as well as a list of journals in public administration.

2399   Huddleston, Mark W. *Comparative Public Administration: An Annotated Bibliography*. New York: Garland Publishing, Inc., 1983.

More than 600 books and periodical articles published in the field of comparative public administration between 1962 and 1982 are listed in this bibliography. The annotated entries are arranged topically in ten chapters that focus on budgeting and personnel management processes, organization theories, developmental policies, and other administrative activities. More than 100 countries or regions are represented in the listings and in a comprehensive index. An author index is also included.

2400   Lovrich, Nicholas P., and Max Neiman. *Public Choice Theory in Public Administration: An Annotated Bibliography*. New York: Garland Publishing, Inc., 1983.

Public choice theory is a method of analyzing individual or collective behavior in administrative situations on the basis of rational choice assumptions. This bibliography identifies and describes books, periodical articles, and dissertations that are either supportive or critical of the public choice analytical perspective. Author and subject indexes are included.

2401   Maurice, Nelson R., and Richard U. Miller. *The Management of Public Enterprise: A Bibliography*. Madison: School of Business, University of Wisconsin, 1975.

The management of government-owned enterprises constitutes one of the most challenging tasks of public administration. In some countries such public enterprises contribute decisively to the overall national economy within a democratic free enterprise system. The Maurice/Miller bibliography provides keyword out of context (KWOC) access to some 3,000 books, periodical articles, newspaper items, government publications, and reports dealing with the history, creation, and management of public enterprises throughout the world. Financial institutions, utilities, transportation and communication enterprises as well as agricultural, mining and manufacturing industries are covered.

2402   Mosher, Frederick C. *Basic Literature of American Public Administration 1787–1950*. New York: Holmes and Meier, 1981.

This bibliographic volume is an anthology of selected articles and book chapters that constitute landmarks in the development of the study of public administration. The material is arranged in chronological sequence under four parts, entitled: (1) The Heritage, (2) Birth and Growth of the Public Management Movement, (3) Maturation of an Orthodox Public Administration, and (4) Expanding Horizons. Each of the included excerpts or reproductions is preceded by introductory headnotes and a biographical summary about the author. Full bibliographic citations are provided about the source publications of the included items.

2403   Seckler-Hudson, Catherine. *Bibliography on Public Adminstration. Annotated*. Washington, DC: American University Press, 1953.

The study of public administration has undergone various phases of development. Much of the earlier administrative literature can be identified in this formerly standard bibliography. Its annotated entries describe guidebooks and other bibliographies, periodicals, government publications, as well as general works pertaining to the study of public administration.

2404   Stogdill, Ralph M. *Leadership Abstracts and Bibliography 1904–1974*. Columbus: Ohio State University Press, 1977.

In the attempt to arrive at a scientifically valid understanding of leadership, the decisive element of the administrative process, scholars have produced a rather massive literature on the various aspects of this baffling subject. The bibliography lists and briefly annotates some 3,000 books and articles written during a period of 70 years. Entries are arranged alphabetically under author names with separate author and subject indexes to the listed material. A scholarly analysis of this literature was separately published under the title *Handbook of Leadership* (New York: Free Press, 1974).

2405   Suljak, Nedjelko D. *Administration in a World of Change*. Davis: Institute of Governmental Affairs, University of California, 1970.

The bibliography presents a well-annotated selection

of books published from 1960 to 1969 on administrative phenomena. Entries are arranged in eight chapters, namely, (1) Behavioralism and Organizational Structure, (2) Utilization of Human Potentiality, (3) Group Involvement — "Linking Pin" and Group Development, (4) Values Change — Interpersonal Competence, (5) Administrative Team Work — Group and Organizational Development, (6) Organization by Decision — Decision Determines Organization Arrangement, (7) Commitment to the Goals of the Organization, and (8) Organization and Contingency Theory. A separate author index is included.

2406   Tompkins, Dorothy Campbell. *Research and Service. A Fifty Year Record.* Berkeley: Bureau of Public Administration, Institute of Governmental Studies, University of California, 1971.

Studies and reports issued by this research center for public administration during a 50-year period are listed in this bibliography. Its entries are unannotated and follow a chronological arrangement. An author and subject index is included.

2407   Whelan, Robert K. *Intergovernmental Relations: An Annotated Bibliography.* New York: Garland Publishing, Inc., 1984.

Some 750 books, dissertations, and periodical articles published since 1960 in the field of intergovernmental relations are listed in this bibliography. The annotated entries are arranged in six categories: (1) fiscal federalism, (2) federal-state relationships, (3) interstate relationships, (4) federal-local relationships, (5) state-local relationships, and (6) interlocal relationships. Names and addresses of professional groups active in this field are separately listed.

CASEBOOKS

2408   Anderson, James E. *Cases in Public Policy Making.* New York: Praeger, 1976.

2409   Blau, Peter Michael. *The Dynamics of Bureaucracy; A Study of Interpersonal Relations in Two Government Agencies.* Chicago: University of Chicago Press, 1963.

2410   Cohen, Harry. *The Demonics of Bureaucracy; Problems of Change in a Government Agency.* Ames: Iowa State University Press, 1965.

2411   Golembiewski, Robert T. *Perspectives on Public Management; Cases and Learning Designs.* Itasca, IL: F. E. Peacock, 1968.

2412   _____ . *Cases in Public Management.* Chicago: Rand McNally, 1980.

2413   Inter-University Case Program. *Governmental Reorganization: Cases and Commentary.* Indianapolis: Bobbs-Merrill, 1967.

2414   Keegan, Warren J. *Case Studies in the Management of Economic Development.* New York: Oxford University Press, 1968.

2415   Lutrin, Carl E. *American Public Administration: Concepts and Cases.* Palo Alto, CA: Mayfield Publishing Company, 1976.

2416   Meyer, C. Kenneth. *Practicing Public Management: A Casebook.* New York: St. Martin's Press, 1983.

2417   Stillman, Richard J. *Public Administration: Concepts and Cases.* Boston: Houghton Mifflin, 1976.

2418   Uveges, Joseph A., Jr. *Cases in Public Administration: Narratives in Administrative Problems.* Rockleigh, NJ: Allyn & Bacon, 1978.

The case study method is frequently used in the field of public administration, permitting a careful, photographic view of administrative problems or episodes. The titles listed above represent a selection of useful casebooks dealing with a variety of problems of bureaucratic organization and management. Additional case studies are listed in the *Index and Summary of Case Studies of the Inter-University Case Program* (Syracuse: IUCP, 1971) and its supplements.

DICTIONARIES

2419   Chandler, Ralph C., and Jack C. Plano. *The Public Administration Dictionary.* New York: John Wiley & Sons, 1982.

The principal concepts, theories, theorists, and institutions of public administration are defined and their significance explained in this dictionary. Entries are arranged in seven chapters, entitled: (1) Fundamentals of Public Administration, (2) Public Policy, (3) Public Management, (4) Bureaucracy and Administrative Organization, (5) Personnel Administration, (6) Financial Administration, (7) Public Law and Administration. A bibliography of important works about public administration and an index are also included.

DIRECTORIES

2420   Davis. University of California. Institute of Governmental Affairs. A Directory of Governmental Public and Urban Research Centers at American Colleges and Universities. Davis: 1968.

2421   *Public Administration Organizations, A Directory of Unofficial Organizations in the Field of Public Administration in the United States and Canada.* Chicago: Public Administration Clearing House, 1932– .

These directories may be used to identify American organizations that impinge upon or affect public administration. The first cited directory lists research organizations that study problems of public administration. Many of these research institutes publish their findings in pamphlets, monographs, or serial publications that are not regularly distributed through the commercial book trade. The second directory lists organizations of public officials or administrators, professional and technical societies, and citizen organizations. Each entry notes the address, membership, activities, and publications for the organization.

DOCUMENT COLLECTIONS

2422   Mosher, Frederick C. *Basic Documents of American Public Administration, 1776–1950.* New York: Holmes and Meier, 1976.

2423   Stillman, Richard J., II. *Basic Documents of American Public Administration Since 1950.* New York: Holmes and Meier, 1983.

The two collections contain the most significant official documents fundamental to the understanding of public administration in the United States. Documents in Mosher's collection are arranged in four parts, entitled: (1) The Foundations, (2) The Management Movement, (3) The Depression and New Deal, and (4) The Postwar Period. Individual documents can also be located with the help of a topical contents list that identifies documents under the following headings: budgets and finance, departments, agencies and offices, general government organization and reorganization, goals and principles, local government, national defense, personnel and civil service, presidency, and protection of citizen rights. Stillman's collection contains more recent documents focusing on public sector enterprises, personnel systems and practices, budgeting and finance, and administrative accountability.

PART III
THE INDEXES

Part III of the guidebook contains four separate indexes:

All numbers in the indexes refer to entry numbers in Part II, *not* page numbers.

Author Index

Adams, J.H., 437
Adams, James Truslow, 622
Aggarwal, J. C., 499
Ago, Roberto, 1535
Agwani, M. S., 1779
Aitchison, J., 324
Albert, Ethel M., 2262
Alderfer, Harold F., 1965
Alexander, Ernest R., 2364
Alexander, Robert J., 2107
Alexander, Yonah, 1725
Ali, Sheikh R., 1197
Allaby, Michael, 540
Allen, J. W., 2355
Alman, Miriam, 2156
Alston, Jon P., 838
Aman, Mohammed M., 224
American Association for State and Local
    History, 627
American Enterprise Institute for Public
    Policy Research, 909
American Geographical Society, 519–520
American Historical Association, 583, 598
American Political Science Association,
    677, 712
American Psychological Association, 779
American Society of International Law,
    1558
American Sociological Association, 854
American Universities Field Staff, 1893
American University (Washington, DC),
    1922
Ammer, Christine, 438
Ammer, Dean S., 438
Amoia, Alba, 1939
Amstutz, Mark R., 1627
Anderson, James E., 2408
Anderson, Thornton, 2335
Andrews, William G., 723
Andriot, John L., 867–869, 1145, 1242
Anglemyer, Mary, 531
Antinoro-Polizzi, Joseph, 824
Argranoff, Robert, 1246
Arkin, William M., 1632
Arnold, W., 782
Aronson, Elliott, 787
Arpan, Jeffrey S., 471
Ashford, Douglas E., 1898
Association for Systems Management, 2266

Association of American Geographers, 548
Aster, Sidney, 1611
Atherton, Alexine L., 1809
Atiyeh, George Nicholas, 2003
Atkins, Thomas V., 56
Attar, Chand, 1598
Aufricht, Hans, 1868
Auld, Douglas A. L., 439
Australia.
    Department of Foreign Affairs, 188
    National Library of Australia, 2195
Azevedo, Ross E., 375

Baatz, Charles Albert, 481
Baatz, Olga K., 481
Back, Harry, 698
Baer, George W., 1810
Bain, Richard C., 1266
Ball, Joyce, 2204
Ball, Nicole, 1661
Ballentine, James A., 1328
Banks, Arthur S., 1923, 2248–2249
Bannock, Graham, 440
Barkun, Michael, 1488
Barnes, Catherine A., 1087
Barone, Michael, 940
Barrett, Edward L., Jr., 1353
Barrett, Jane R., 1602
Bart, Pauline, 798
Barton, Roy, 533
Baudot, Marcel, 1679
Bayitch, S. A., 2077
Bayliss, Gwyn M., 1646
Beal, George M., 320
Beaney, William M., 1354
Beaumont, Jane, 1602
Bebout, Lois, 482
Beck, Carl, 699, 1899
Becker, Harold K., 2391
Becker, Theodore L., 922
Beddie, J. S., 1797
Beede, Benjamin R., 2129
Beers, Henry Putney, 584
Beitzinger, A. J., 2337
Belfield, Robert, 1853
Bell, Alan P., 835
Bell, James Edward, 749
Bemis, Samuel F., 1581
Berenyi, John, 441

Bergquist, Charles W., 1900
Berkeley.
    University of California.
        Library, 2372
Berkowitz, Morris, 2316
Berman, Larry, 1097
Bernsdorf, Wilhelm, 855
Berring, Robert C., 233
Besterman, Theodor, 101
Bibby, John F., 1065
Bidwell, Robin, 628
Bieber, Doris M., 1329
Bienen, Henry, 828
Bilboul, Rober R., 121
Birch, Carol L., 910
Birchfield, Mary Eva, 1869
Birkos, Alexander S., 222, 226, 228
Biswas, A., 499
Bitner, Harry, 1303
Black, Henry Campbell, 1330
Blackey, Robert, 1654, 1663
Blackstock, Paul W., 1633
Blackwood, Goerge D., 2348
Blanchard, Carroll H., 1647
Blanchette, Arthur E., 1758–1759
Blandford, Linda A., 1379
Blau, Peter Michael, 2409
Blaustein, Albert P., 2127–2129
Blaustein, Eric B., 2127
Bloomberg, Marty, 1648
Bloomfield, Valerie, 1901
Blum, Albert A., 1924
Blum, Eleanor, 1272
Boast, Carol, 1375
Bochenski, Joseph M., 2278
Boehm, Eric H., 231
Boehm, Klaus, 1831
Bolden, C. E., 1079
Bollens, John C., 1231
Bond, Maurice F., 2176
Bonjean, Charles M., 830
Booth, David Albin, 1232
Borchardt, D. H., 750
Boston, Guy D., 829
Boston University.
    Libraries, 2151
Bottomore, Tom, 2325
Boulding, Elise, 1639
Bourgina, Anna M., 2279

Taylor, John W. R., 1708
Taylor, Philip A. S., 456
Texas.
   University at Austin.
    Library, 2069
Textor, Robert B., 374, 2248
Theis, Paul A., 1270
Theodorson, Achilles G., 850
Theodorson, George A., 850
Thomae, Hans, 791
Thomas, Daniel H., 582
Thomas, J. B., 505
Thompson, Robert G., 2272
Thornberry, Terence, 842
Tice, Terrence N., 2256
Timberlake, Charles E., 1741
Tingley, Donald F., 592, 1254
Tingley, Elizabeth, 1254
Todd, Trudy A., 1906
Tokyo.
   Institute of Developing Economies,
    2210
Tolchin, Susan, 965
Toman, Jiri, 1529
Tompkins, Dorothy Campbell, 432, 920,
   1086, 2406
Toomey, Alice F., 102
Toscano, Mario, 1724
Tracy, Kathleen, 1099
Trask, David F., 593, 1591
Trask, Roger, 1591
Tregonning, Kennedy G., 2008
Treyz, Joseph H., 96
Triandis, Harry C., 792
Trittschuh, Travis, 1204
Tunney, Christopher, 629

Ujifusa, Grant, 940
Umemura, Michael Takaaki, 1546
UNESCO, 2009
United Nations, 1524
   Dag Hammarskjold Library, 317,
    1622, 1874–1876
   Department of International
    Economic and Social Affairs,
    2237
   Industrial Development
    Organization, 463
   Vienna, 1878
   International Law Commission,
    1505
   Library.
    Geneva, 318
   Office of Legal Affairs, 1553
   Office of Public Information, 1886
   Statistical Office, 2238–2242
United States.
   Arms Control and Disarmament
    Agency, 2235
   Bureau of the Census, 1147–1152,
    1161–1167, 1245
   Central Intelligence Agency, 1941,
    2106
   Office of Economic Research,
    2243

Civil Aeronautics Board, 1422
Consulate.
   Hong Kong, 189
Council of Economic Advisors, 1175
Department of Commerce,
   954–955, 1182
   Bureau of Economic Analysis,
    1176–1178
   Bureau of International
    Commerce, 1691
   Bureau of the Census, 1170
   National Technical Information
    Service, 887–891
Department of Defense, 1743,
   1836–1837
Department of State, 1513,
   1517–1518, 1695–1699, 1738,
   1744–1751, 1753, 1827, 1942,
   2268
   Bureau of Intelligence and
    Research, 1623
   Bureau of Public Affairs,
    1692–1693
   Division of Publications, 1594
   Historical Office, 1595
   Library, 1677
   Office of External Research,
    Bureau of Intelligence and
    Research, 1573
   Office of External Research,
    Foreign Affairs Research
    Documentation Center, 1574
   Secretary of State, 1752
Department of the Army,
   1973–1974, 2010–2018,
   2052–2053, 2089
Domestic and International Business
   Administration.
   International Economic Policy
    and Research, 2244
Federal Communications
   Commission, 1423
Federal Power Commission, 1424
Federal Trade Commission, 1425
Foreign Broadcast Information
   Service, 262
General Accounting Office,
   1066–1067
   Comptroller General, 976
Immigration and Naturalization
   Service, 1426
Internal Revenue Service, 1419
Interstate Commerce Commission,
   1427
Library of Congress, 66, 85, 225,
   556, 907, 2126, 2188, 2191
   African Section, 1975
   Catalog Publication Division, 138
   Congressional Research Service,
    1068
   Exchange and Gift Division, 1213
   General Reference and
    Bibliography Division, 223,
    1102
   General Reference and

   Bibliography Division,
    Bibliography and Reference
    Correspondence Section,
    1100
   Legislative Reference Service,
    1023, 1363, 2288–2289
   Manuscript Division, 1103–1124
   Office of the Federal Register,
    1366
   Orientalia Division, 1988
   Reference Division, 2157–2174
   Special Division, 878
   Subject Cataloging Division, 57
National Historical Publications and
   Records Commission, 574
National Labor Relations Board,
   1428
Office of Management and Budget,
   1127–1131
Office of the Federal Register, 1413
Securities and Exchange
   Commission, 1429
Small Business Administration, 1070
Social Security Administration.
   Office of Research and Statistics,
    1932
Superintendent of Documents, 892,
   895, 900–903, 1028, 1030,
   1033, 1038
Tax Court, 1410–1411
United States Congress, 975, 1006–1013,
   1022, 1027, 1029
   House of Representatives.
    Committee on Foreign Affairs,
    1593
    Committee on Post Office and
    Civil Service, 953
   Senate, 1271
United States National Archives, 557–573
   Audiovisual Archives Division.
    Motion Picture and Sound
    Recording Branch, 1392
United States Supreme Court, 1393–1394,
   1397–1401
Universal Reference System, 415, 676, 821,
   921, 1286, 1326, 1572, 1897, 2382
University of Michigan, 1987
Urmson, J. O., 2331
Uveges, Joseph A., Jr., 2418

Van de Merwe, Caspar, 851
Van Dyke, Vernon, 735
Van Zant, Nancy Patton, 879
Varma, Vishwanath Prasad, 2341
Verba, Sidney, 930
Verdini, Jennifer, 1196
Verna, Mary Ellen, 1277
Veron, Enid L., 1337
Versage, Joseph V., 824
Vesala, Heimo, 2054
Vesenyi, Paul E., 279
Vexler, Robert, 977
Viet, Jean, 852
Vigor, P. H., 2290
Vincent, Jack E., 1678

Title Index

INFORMATION SOURCES OF POLITICAL SCIENCE

Subject Index

SUBJECT INDEX

Countries (OPEC), 1861–1867
Organizational Psychology, 785
Outer space law, 1494

Pacific Islands, 2015
Pakistan, 581, 1907, 1929
Palestine. *See* Middle East
Panama, 1730, 1907
Paperbound books, 39–43, 50
Paperwork requirements, 1070
Parliament, 1832, 1928
Patents and trademark law, 1310
Peace groups, 983
Peace research, 1639–1644
Peacekeeping operations, UN, 1883
Periodicals
    bibliographic directories,
      208, 210, 211–236
    abstracting and indexing services,
      87, 204, 206, 210, 216
    Africa, 222, 223
    Asia, 224, 225
    business and economics,
      378–380, 382
    ethnic, 217
    Europe, 226, 227
    general, 205, 206, 208, 210, 211
    geography, 518
    history, 231, 232
    ideological, 212–215, 218–220
    Latin America, 228–230
    law, 233, 1092
    political science, 234, 666
    psychology, 235, 749, 750, 752
    reprints, 203
    social sciences, 221, 277
    sociology, 236
    guidebooks, 200, 201
    indexes. *See* Typology Index
    union lists, 237–243
Permanent Court of International Justice, 1543
Personnel management, 2376, 2377
Petroleum, 295–298, 522–526, 1072–1075, 1861–1866, 2243
Philosophy, 2255–2265, 2327, 2329–2332, 2360–2361
Pierce, Franklin, 1112
Platforms, 1261–1263
Poland, 1794, 1907, 2040, 2041, 2044, 2049
Policies. *See* Political Reference Theory section
Policy science, 710, 714, 716–718, 722, 747
Political action committees (PACs), 982, 989, 993
Political actors. *See* Political Reference Theory section
Political entities. *See* Political Reference Theory section
Political events. *See* Political Reference Theory section
Political objects. *See* Political Reference Theory section

Political parties, U.S., 990, 1257–1259, 1261–1263, 1266, 1267; worldwide, 1918, 1920, 1921, 1938, 2107–2110, 2112
Political planning, 2387
Political processes. *See* Political Reference Theory section
Political psychology, 786, 1886
Political risk, 1688–1690, 1694
Political science
    bibliographies, 669–686
    book reviews, 687–697
    dictionaries, 698–704
    directories, 705–719
    encyclopedias, 720–722
    guidebooks, 665–668
    handbooks, 723–726
    summaries, 727–746
    yearbooks, 747–748
Political theory, 2255–2363; *see also* Political thought in Political Reference Theory section
Polk, James K., 1110
Polls. *See* Public opinion
Pollution, 522–524, 528, 529
Population, 813–815, 859, 1908
Population statistics, U.S., 1154, 1155, 1166–1170; worldwide, 544, 1921, 2216, 2217, 2236–2238
Poverty, 431, 432, 819, 820, 936
Presidency and presidents, 637, 1094–1144
Procurements, 954, 955
Product safety regulation, 1463
Professional meetings. *See* Meeting and conferences, scholarly
Propaganda, 1278, 1280–1283, 1286, 1660
Protest songs, 1650
Psychology
    bibliographies, 753–762
    book reviews, 763
    dictionaries, 764–777
    directories, 779, 780
    encyclopedias, 781–784
    guidebooks, 749–752
    handbooks, 785–793
    thesauri, 778
    yearbooks, 794–797
Public administration
    bibliographies, 2373–2407
    casebooks, 2408–2418
    catalogs, 2372
    dictionaries, 2419
    directories, 2420, 2421
    document collections, 2422, 2423
    guidebooks, 2364–2371
Public enterprise, 2401
Public issues, 935, 936
Public law. *See* Political Reference Theory section
Public opinion, 1272, 1275–1298, 2223
Publishers of books, 39, 51; microforms, 124; policy, 717

Q1 Systems. *See* Online Databases in

Typology Index

Race relations, 816
Racism, 319, 762
Radicalism, 218, 319, 533
Radio broadcasts, 257, 260–270
Rankings, 2250
Reagan, Ronald, 962, 1095, 1125
Reference sources, general, 1–273
Refugees, 1059, 1645
Religion
    bibliographies, 2304–2319
    guidebooks, 2298–2303
    handbooks, 2320
Reprints, 49, 203
Revolution and revolutionists, 319, 1654, 1663, 1935, 2113, 2115
Rhodesia/Zimbabwe, 1907
RLIN, 64
Romania, 2040, 2042, 2044, 2047–2049
Roosevelt, Franklin D., 1135, 1137, 1140–1142
Roosevelt, Theodore, 1121

Saudi Arabia, 1907, 1929; *see also* Middle East
Scales, 810, 830
Scandinavia, 2050, 2053, 2064
Scientific methods. *See* Political Reference Theory section
SDC (Systems Development Corporation). *See* Online databases in Typology Index
Sea law. *See* Maritime law
SEC corporate filings, 1156–1158
Secretaries of defense, 1739
Secretaries of state, 1736–1738
Securities and Exchange Commission (SEC). *See* SEC filings, Securities law
Securities law, 1421, 1429, 1464, 1470, 1479
Security, income, 915
Security, national, 1628–1638, 1731–1735
Security, social, 1932
Senate, U.S., 1013, 1056; *see also* Congress
Serials, 202, 207, 209, 210, 215, 223, 224, 229, 230, 237–243
Sharp, I. P., Associates. *See* Online databases in Typology Index
Ships, 1636, 1710
Slavic studies, 226, 227, 2037, 2038, 2040–2044, 2047–2049, 2052, 2054, 2065
Social change, 214, 758, 810, 819, 820, 828, 834, 836, 899
Social criticism, 321
Social indicators, 320, 866, 1159, 1182, 2253
Social intervention, 866, 937
Social problems, 810, 819, 820, 866
Social programs, 915, 934, 937, 949
Social sciences
    bibliographies, 283–320
    book reviews, 321–323
    dictionaries, 324–326, 328, 329
    directories, 330–335

409

Typology Index

ABSTRACTS

Administrative law, U.S., 1434, 1435
Africa, 1963
Anthropology, 346
Communication, 1273
Congress, U.S., 1002, 1004, 1005, 1024, 1031, 1036
Criminology, 802, 803
Economics, 386, 392, 393, 394–397, 404, 409, 411, 412, 418, 420, 424
Education, 487, 490–493, 498
Energy, 296, 297, 298, 1072–1074
Environment, 522, 523, 528, 529
Geography, 527
Government research, U.S., 887, 889, 891, 1057
History, 596, 597, 600, 601
Labor documentation, 411, 412
Legal book reviews, 1327
Middle East, 2000
Newspaper and periodical articles, 172, 246
Peace research, 1642
Philosophy, 2257, 2259, 2261, 2265
Political science, 671, 673–675
Psychology, 753, 756, 757
Public administration, 2373, 2377, 2378, 2380, 2381, 2404
Refugees, 1645
Religion, 2304, 2313, 2317
Social sciences, 308
Sociology, 808, 816, 818–820, 823
Statistics, 1154, 1155, 1160, 1167
Televised news, 259
Urban studies, 817, 1229, 1230
Women's studies, 822

BIBLIOGRAPHIES

Africana
    current, 1956–1964
    retrospective, 1965–1975
American politics and government
    official publications, 882–903
    scholarly publications, 909–921
Anthropology
    current, 346–349, 355, 357, 358
    retrospective, 359

Asian studies
    current, 1996–2002
    retrospective, 2003–2019
Bibliographies
    current, 97–100
    retrospective, 101–105
Biographical information, 2098–2102
Black studies, 806, 807
Communism and Communist
    organizations, 1825, 1826, 2278–2291
Comparative government and politics
    current, 1893–1897
    retrospective, 1898–1914
Computerized reference instruments, 5–11
Democracy, 2270–2275
Digests, 87
Directories, 88
Economics
    current, 386–418
    retrospective, 419–435
Education, 486–498
Elections and electoral processes, 919, 1246–1260
Energy, 295–298, 918, 1072–1074
European studies
    current, 2044–2048
    retrospective, 2049–2054
European organizations, 1833–1840
General reference
    books, 28–55
    dissertations, 117–123
    micropublications, 124–127
    newspapers, 131–139
    periodicals, 203–243
    translations, 271–273
Geography
    current, 520–530
    retrospective, 531–539
History
    current, 596–604
    retrospective, 605–611
Imperialism, 2276, 2277
International law
    current, 1485
    retrospective, 1486–1494
Judiciary, U.S., 1078–1086
Latin American studies
    current, 2072–2076
    retrospective, 2077–2090

Local government, U.S., 1228–1239
Marxism, 2278, 2282
Multinational corporations, 1848–1853
Nationalism, 2292–2297
Newspapers, 131–139
Official publications
    Africa, 2156–2174
    Australia, 2195
    Canada, 2196
    Eastern Europe, 2189
    Finland, 2197
    Great Britain, 2176–2180, 2182, 2184–2186, 2198–2200
    Ireland, 2181
    Japan, 2175
    Latin America, 2190–2192
    Netherlands, 2201
    Norway, 2202
    Soviet Union, 2189
    Switzerland, 2203
    United States, 882–903, 1212, 1213, 1228
    worldwide, 2193, 2194
Organization of American States (OAS), 1855–1858
Periodicals, 203–243
Political ideologies, 2270–2297, 2321–2324
Political parties, U.S., 1257–1259
Political science
    current, 669–676
    retrospective, 677–686
Political theory and philosophy
    current, 2257–2261
    retrospective, 2262–2269
Population, 813–815, 1908
Presidency, U.S., 1095–1102
Psychology
    current, 753–757
    retrospective, 758–762
Public administration
    current, 2373–2382
    retrospective, 2383–2407
Public law
    other than U.S., 2121–2126
    U.S., 1306–1326, 1346–1352
Public opinion, 1272–1286
Religions
    current, 2304–2315

413

THESAURI

UNION LISTS

YEARBOOKS